VideoHound's
EPICS

Also available from Visible Ink Press

VideoHound's Horror Show: 999 Hair-Raising, Hellish, and Humorous Movies
Mike Mayo. Foreword by William Lustig. 524 pages. $17.95. ISBN: 1-57859-047-7

VideoHound's Video Premieres: The Only Guide to Video Originals and Limited Releases
Mike Mayo. 431 pages. $17.95. ISBN: 0-7876-0825-4

VideoHound's Soundtracks: Music from the Movies, Broadway, and Television
Didier Deutsch. Foreword by Lukas Kendall. 1024 pages. $24.95. ISBN: 1-57859-025-6

VideoHound's Independent Film Guide
Monica Sullivan. Foreword by Mare Winningham. 558 pages. $17.95. ISBN: 1-57859-018-3

VideoHound's Vampires on Video
J. Gordon Melton. Foreword by Jeanne Keyes Youngson. 335 pages. $17.95. ISBN: 1-57859-002-7

VideoHound's Sci-Fi Experience: Your Quantum Guide to the Video Universe
445 pages. $17.95. ISBN: 0-7876-0615-4

VideoHound's Complete Guide to Cult Flicks and Trash Pics
438 pages. $16.95. ISBN: 0-7876-0616-2

VideoHound's Family Video Guide, 2nd Edition
Martin F. Kohn. Foreword by Brian Henson. 760 pages. $17.95. ISBN: 0-7876-0984-6

Magill's Cinema Annual 1998
716 pages. $39.95. ISBN: 1-57859-056-6

VideoHound's Golden Movie Retriever 1999
1,815 pages. $21.95. ISBN: 1-57859-041-8

VideoHound's World Cinema: The Adventurer's Guide to Movie Watching
Elliott Wilhelm. 1,700 pages. $19.95. ISBN: 1-57895-059-0

VideoHound's
EPICS
Giants
of the
Big Screen

Glenn Hopp

VISIBLE
INK
PRESS

DETROIT • LONDON

VideoHound's® Epics: Giants of the Big Screen

Copyright © 1999 by Visible Ink Press

Published by Visible Ink Press®, a division of Gale Research
27500 Drake Rd.
Farmington Hills, MI 48331-3535

Most Visible Ink books are available at special quantity discounts when purchased in bulk by corporations, organizations, or groups. Customized printings, special imprints, messages, and excerpts can be produced to meet your needs. For more information, contact Special Markets Manager, Gale Research, 835 Penobscot Bldg., 645 Griswold St., Detroit MI 48226.

Art Director: Pamela A.E. Galbreath

Photos: The Kobal Collection

Library of Congress Cataloging-in-Publication Data
Hopp, Glenn, 1954-
Videohound's epics : giants of the big screen / Glenn Hopp.
        p.   cm.
    Includes indexes.
    ISBN 1-57859-074-4 (paper)
        1. Motion pictures—Catalogs.   2. Video recordings—catalogs.
I. Title.
PN1998.H66 1998
016.79143'75—dc21   98-36754
                                                                                 CIP

ISBN 1-57859-074-4
Printed in the United States of America
All rights reserved

10 9 8 7 6 5 4 3 2 1
A Cunning Canine Production®

CONTENTS

Adventure Epics

Biblical Epics

Epic Comedy

285 Horror Epics

299 Musical Epics

325 Epic Romance

365 Silent Epics

389 Epic Tragedy

413 Wartime Epics

463 Western Epics

Introduction

What is an epic? Well, you know one if you see it. Everyone recognizes James Cameron's *Titanic* as an epic (big boat, big budget, big hype, big effects, big stars, big box office), and its success will inevitably draw a backwash of grand-scale films to theaters. Epics generally provide a richer form of entertainment, drawing upon and affirming cultural myths, or in the case of the revisionist epic, bending or destroying the myth. Hollywood, and the movie business in general, has always at its core been built around the epic, from *Intolerance* to *Saving Private Ryan*. The big movie creates a ripple effect, drawing people to the theater for other smaller films, and enriching our perception of movie-making as a whole. *VideoHound's Epics: Giants of the Big Screen* surveys 200 movies aiming at epic stature, covering all genres. These are, for the most part, movies ripe for reacquaintanceship or first-time discovery.

Epic is one of those terms—like *tragedy*, *realism*, and *humanism*—that has both firm and flexible definitions. Any label around long enough to have acquired the sort of richness that comes with centuries of use inevitably develops an annoying slipperiness to make you wonder how much agreement really exists about its meaning. Ask ten people what an epic movie is, and you'll surely get a variety of answers. Some will emphasize a film's running time and contend that no film under three hours should qualify; some will look to cast size and assume that unless a movie boasts a cast of thousands it cannot claim an epic status. Multiple plotlines converging in a sprawling generational saga define the genre for some. Others will gauge an epic by its budget, the bigger the better.

While size often matters, qualitative concerns deserve a place in the discussion as well. To some an epic film is one with larger-than-life dimensions, a mythic, timeless movie. In this sense epic stature is something that a movie with a large cast or a big budget or a lengthy running time can strive for and not necessarily attain, just as a serious story ending in death may or may not acquire the dignity and distinction of tragedy. This approach to the epic may be less exact than those described above, but it is more thoughtful and can provoke some lively and enjoyable discussions. *Titantic* seems to deserve its epic classification by fitting every definition mentioned so far, but what about other films? Is *High Noon*, for example, only a compelling drama about one misunderstood man acting on his beliefs, or does this short, inexpensive-looking film actually achieve mythic proportions with Will Kane's plight becoming suggestive of all principled, reluctant heroes racked by self-doubt and backed into a corner by circumstance? *Rocky* is a small film that plugs into a larger American myth, the lovable loser who gets one more chance for the big time, and does battle with external and internal demons. Other movies may have similar intent, but the storytelling and technical virtuosity required are lacking. To reach the zenith of the myth, the storytelling must be very, very good. Only then does the viewer find that sense of transcendence that only the best art supplies.

The roots of this qualitative approach to the epic probably reach back to the definition of a literary epic: a long narrative poem with a hero who embodies the traits central to a culture. This definition soon became more flexible as it turned into a compliment as well as a simple description. When, for example, the ancient Roman poet Virgil wrote *The Aeneid*, he filled his poem with the same epic machinery he found in *The Iliad* and *The Odyssey*—"an invocation of the muse for inspiration, catalogues, aria-like similes, a descent to the underworld"—by way of showing that his story of the founding of Rome could rival in importance the epics of the Greeks. The term broadened as well, since an epic poem had come to be regarded as a literary badge of honor, something no self-respecting culture should lack. And so the slipperiness of the term results from these various firm or flexible applications, sometimes simple and descriptive ("Renaissance poets began writing pastoral poetry and worked up to the epic"), sometimes laudatory ("That see-saw, thirteen-inning baseball game was truly an epic").

Epic movies cut across genres, another factor that complicates any effort to find a handy definition but one that enriches the growing body of epic films by broadening it. Since film genres are constantly evolving, epic films can appear at any stage of their change. Film historians often mention four stages in the growth of a genre: a primitive phase in which the staples of the genre begin to take shape (Douglas Fairbanks's silent *Robin Hood* is an example in the swashbuckler genre); a classical phase in which the traits of the genre are affirmed and usually shared by the audience (Errol Flynn's *Robin Hood* is an example), a revisionist phase in which the traits of the genre are questioned and sometimes undermined, often with an ironic tone (an example is *Robin and Marian*, in which Sean

Connery and Audrey Hepburn play an older Robin Hood and Maid Marian and grapple with the changes in their lives and their world); and a parodic phase in which the elements of the genre are so well known they may be mocked (Mel Brooks's *Robin Hood: Men in Tights,* for example). Louis Giannetti insightfully discusses, illustrates, and contrasts these stages in his book *Understanding Movies.* The middle phases are probably the more interesting and the more likely to initiate lively discussion among movie buffs since the classical and revisionist phases seem to offer filmmakers greater possibilities for development. It is entertaining and often informative to see how a newer movie rethinks and reimagines material presented effectively in a previous classic, as Laurence Olivier's and Kenneth Branagh's versions of Shakespeare's *Henry V* show.

VideoHound's Epics: Giants of the Big Screen includes discussions in each chapter on a range of films that combine various points of view, attitudes, and subgenres of the epic. The historical chapter, for example, includes some biographical epics (*Gandhi*, *A Man for All Seasons*), period films more suggestive of the traditional epic (*Spartacus*), and films about more contemporary events (*Exodus*, *Nashville*). The adventure chapter also covers a wide range: swashbuckler epics, British colonial films, literary adaptations (*Moby Dick*, *Around the World in Eighty Days*), and a harder-to-classify assortment of others, like *Aguirre, The Wrath of God* and *Yojimbo*.

Shorter chapters also provide diversity. The section on tragedies, for instance, examines classic tragedies like Kenneth Branagh's film of the uncut text of *Hamlet*. It also reviews the modern twist to the most ancient of dramatic forms, describing films in a contemporary setting that bring a tragic sensibility to their subjects, like *Citizen Kane*, *Raging Bull*, and *Nixon*. For those chapters where the rules of the genre greatly inhibit diversity, such as war films and westerns, both classical and revisionist films emerge. Directors such as John Ford are responsible for both types, creating classical westerns (*Stagecoach*) early in his career and returning with a revisionist bent years later (*Cheyenne Autumn*).

One of the favorite topics of the film buff is big films that go bust. *Titanic* was rumored to be sinking under the weight of its $200 million budget long before release, as film seers forecast doom and gloom for its box office prospects. The chapter on failed epics examines movies that reached for classic status but stumbled, including costly, event films that bombed at the box office (*Cleopatra*, *Heaven's Gate*, *Waterworld*), all richly deserved. It also reviews financial failures that deserved a better fate (Erich von Stroheim's *Greed*, Elia Kazan's *America America*, and Billy Wilder's *The Private Life of Sherlock Holmes*).

Deciding on the chapter placement for some films, of course, required educated guesses more than exact science. Should *Reds* and *Doctor Zhivago* be grouped with historical epics or romantic ones? (While love and revolution figure in both, here Beatty's film is put in the history chapter and Lean's in the romantic chapter, an indication of how we interpreted their ultimate emphasis.) Is *1900* more a drama about family or about politics? And wouldn't it be possible to discuss Orson Welles's *The Magnificent Ambersons* as a rich example of any of at least four types of epics: a family drama, an epic tragedy, a romance, or a historical epic? To ask such questions, to explore how each film succeeds or fails as an epic, and to see each in context with others in its chapter is to heighten our enjoyment and knowledge of movies.

The ratings in this book follow the guidelines in the annual *VideoHound's Golden Movie Retriever* with the reminder that we have tried to determine these ratings by placing films on some common ground, so that *Airplane!* would not be evaluated in a context with *Ran* but rather in one for generally comparable comedies.

Having said that, here is the rating scale: four bones describe a film that is a masterful expression of cinematic intent. Three bones and a half represent superior movie fare. Three bones go to a film that is above-average entertainment: a good story, fine acting, and a nice return on your video investment. Two bones and a half is the average movie, in this case usually blessed with a giant budget but less will to live. The epic earning two bones or less should make the viewer beware. No bones (or a "woof" rating) refers to a movie for which watching your neighbor's vacation videos may be less painful. These films may be redeemed by stretches of unintentional amusement.

While *VideoHound Epics* is by no means conclusive on the epic movie, it is a great starting point. At the end of each chapter is a section entitled "They Might Be Giants," where other would-be epics are discussed. More than 200 photos and a full array of indexes also await the reader.

A Note on Sources

A number of sources have been very helpful in gathering facts and trivia and in finding and double-checking information about the films discussed in this book. *Magill's Survey of Cinema*, the twenty-one volume core series that covers thousands of films, and the extensive annuals published by Gale Research which have kept the series up to date, makes a very useful resource. The interesting comments by B. Reeves Eason on filming epic battle scenes (in the entry on *The Charge of the Light Brigade*), the remarks by George Cukor on *Romeo and Juliet*, and Kenneth Branagh's short quote about *Henry V* being a "political debate in an adventure story" come from *Magill's* essays. As does, in part, background information in the entries to a number of films, especially *Around the World in Eighty Days*, *1900*, *Ivanhoe*, *The Seven Samurai*, and the Eisenstein films. *The Motion Picture Guide*, another impressive multi-volume reference work, is also useful for background facts and for double-checking information about a film's casts, credits, budgets, and box office. The same is true for the Internet Movie Database (www.imdb.com), a comprehensive web site that any film lover would enjoy browsing.

Some books are sure bets for reliability, insight, and wit simply because they carry a particular author's name, and the three film books written by Louis Giannetti for Prentice Hall—*Understanding Movies*, *Masters of the American Cinema*, and *Flashback: A Brief History of Film* (co-written with Scott Eyman)—are models of forceful writing and smart, engaging comments. Having re-read and taught from Giannetti's texts for almost ten years, I am happy to acknowledge my grateful debt to their author, whose lucid approach to film has informed me and so many others. The short quote by Orson Welles about his characters being variations of Faust and the brief comment by D. W. Griffth about nineteenth-century fiction in the entry for *Intolerance* are from *Masters of the American Cinema*. (The quote in which Welles refers to Kane as an "empty box" is from Peter Bogdanovich's fascinating *This Is Orson Welles*.)

A handful of biographies stand out among those consulted for their usefulness: Jan Herman's life of William Wyler, *A Talent for Trouble*; Charlton Heston's autobiography *In the Arena*; Joseph McBride's life of Frank Capra titled *The*

Catastrophe of Success; Richard Schickel's *D. W. Griffith*; Donald Spoto's *The Dark Side of Genius: The Life of Alfred Hitchcock*; Larry Swindell's *The Last Hero* (about Gary Cooper); and both Billy Wilder biographies (by Maurice Zolotow and Kevin Lally).

Louis Giannetti's discussions of silent film; Kevin Brownlow's excellent *The Parade's Gone By* and *Napoleon*; *The Film Encyclopedia*, a true epic by the late Ephraim Katz; and David A. Cook's classic *A History of Narrative Film* were all particularly useful for information about silent film and world cinema. *The Parade's Gone By* also includes comments by B. Reeves Eason on editing epic battle scenes as well as a remark by Francis X. Bushman about the cruelty to horses during the filming of the silent *Ben-Hur*; David Cook's history has the short comment by De Mille about turning a page or two from the Bible into a movie (quoted in the entry on *Samson and Delilah*), and the Eisenstein quote about the images in the gods sequence being arranged in "descending intellectual scale" in *October*. The Erich von Stroheim quote about the "poor, mangled, mutilated remains" of *Greed* is from the published version of the script by Lorrimar.

Other informative and useful works include William Bayer's *The Great Movies*; *The Complete Directory to Prime-Time Network TV Shows* by Tim Brooks and Earle Marsh; *Past Imperfect: History According to the Movies*, edited by Mark C. Carnes; *The Chronicle History of the Movies*, edited by Derek Elley; *The Films of Gregory Peck* by John Griggs; Pauline Kael's many titles (especially *For Keeps*, her most recent); *Robert Wise on His Films* by Sergio Leeman; Mick Martin and Marsha Porter's *Video Movie Guide*; *A Pictorial History of Westerns* by Michael Parkinson and Clyde Jeavons; Danny Peary's *Alternate Oscars* and *Guide for the Film Fanatic*; *Filmlover's Companion* edited by David Quinlan; *The Star Trek Encyclopedia*; and *Time Out Film Guide*.

Acknowledgments

The indispensable help of a number of people sped the progress of this book, increased its quality, and deepened its insights. I am very grateful for the expertise of the following contributing editors. **David E. Flanagin**, who teaches film at Howard Payne University, wrote all the film reviews except two in the chapter on futuristic epics. David also contributed entries on selected other films, including all the Spielberg films discussed in the book (except *Jaws*, *Hook*, and *Saving Private Ryan*).

Ken Willingham contributed many of the reviews on history-based films.

Evelyn Romig, who teaches courses in children's and adolescent literature, wrote most of the entries in the chapter on fantasy epics (those on the Disney films and *The Wizard of Oz*), and all but three of the entries in the chapter on musical epics.

Other contributors include **James Blaker**, who wrote on ten of the western epics, and **Deborah Dill**, whose contribution also totaled ten entries.

Also contributing to the book were **Jessica Hall**, **Peggy Stair Morales**, **Melissa Clark**, **Julia Furtaw**, and **Amy Prien**.

I very much appreciate the opportunity from Visible Ink to work on this project, and I thank Martin Connors, who originated the concept, shaped the title list, and lent a hand at the final editing, and others—Julia Furtaw, Elliot Wilhelm, Michelle Banks—who also suggested titles and otherwise facilitated the progress. Pam Galbreath is thanked for her cover and interior design, and Marco Di Vita for peerless typesetting. The photos from the Kobal Collection are most appreciated, as is the graphics work of Robert Duncan, Senior Imaging Specialist. Most of all, I thank Beth Fhaner who, with the assistance of Jim Craddock, edited the book at Visible Ink and whose supervision, expertise, energy, and cordiality helped bring the book to completion. I also thank the English Department, Elizabeth Wallace, and Faculty Development Committee at Howard Payne University for their support and the secretarial help of Jan Sartain and Julie Flanagin.

About the Author

Glenn Hopp is a Professor of English at Howard Payne University in Brownwood, Texas. He holds a Ph.D. in English from the University of Missouri and teaches courses in film, Renaissance literature, Shakespeare, and drama, among others. For a number of years he has contributed essay-reviews of current films to the ongoing *Magill's Cinema Annual*, and he reviews university-press titles for *Publishers Weekly* magazine and books on tape for *AudioFile* magazine. He also contributes to the Magill's Book Reviews, a feature of the Dow Jones/News Retrieval online service.

He has written a number of articles on Renaissance literature for various reference books as well as on topics in modern literature (Anthony Burgess, Joseph Conrad, Graham Greene, Bernard Shaw) and popular culture (radio drama, detective fiction), and he contributed an article on seventeenth-century dramatist John Ford to *Concord in Discord*, a collection of essays edited by Donald K. Anderson, Jr.

ADVENTURE

The Adventures of Robin Hood
Aguirre, The Wrath of God
Around the World in 80 Days
Beau Geste
Braveheart
The Charge of the Light Brigade
Contact
Excaliber
Fitzcarraldo
Gunga Din
Indiana Jones and the Last Crusade
Lawrence of Arabia
The Lives of a Bengal Lancer
The Man Who Would Be King
Moby Dick
Mutiny on the Bounty
Raiders of the Lost Ark
The Right Stuff
The Road Warrior
Rob Roy
Rocky
The Sea Hawk
The Three Musketeers
Yojimbo

The Adventures of Robin Hood

1938 – Michael Curtiz, William Keighley – ♪♪♪♪

When Kevin Costner was publicizing his film version of the Robin Hood legend in 1991, he sometimes jokingly referred to the pointy cap that Errol Flynn wore in this adventure classic from 1938. A realist might sneer at the tights and cap and perhaps the splashy Technicolor (the first three-strip Technicolor film ever shot at Warner Bros.), but the Flynn version remains perhaps the best model for heroic, romanticized adventure films. Interestingly, James Cagney was originally set to play Robin for Warners in 1935, but the project stalled when Cagney left the studio during a contract dispute.

The scriptwriters borrowed some of their premise from Walter Scott's *Ivanhoe* and used Bidwell Park in California for Sherwood Forest. Returning from the Crusades, the King of England, Richard (Ian Hunter), is reported to have been taken prisoner in Austria and held for ransom. His brother John (Claude Rains) plots with Sir Guy of Gisbourne (Basil Rathbone) to tax the Saxons for the King's payment and then keep the money so that John can accede to the throne in Richard's absence. The film's structure is nicely worked out to contrast scenes of Norman oppression with comic interludes of Robin (Flynn) meeting and acquiring his band of men. The heroism is enriched by having Robin bettered in contests both by Little John (Alan Hale) and Friar Tuck (Eugene Pallette). No one laughs at his clumsy falls into ponds more loudly than the charming Robin himself, and this self-deprecation helps to establish his appeal.

The film also draws richly on folklore, as in the sequence when Richard escapes and returns to England disguised as a monk. He insinuates himself in secret among his people, and in Sherwood Forest he meets Robin, who steals his money (to give to the overtaxed poor) and then invites him to dine. In one of the film's most stirring moments, Richard questions Robin about his motives for such thievery and elicits from him the news about the traitorous Prince John: "I'd condemn anything that left the task of holding England for Richard to outlaws like me!" Robin passes the king's test with his honesty. Richard appreciates the revolutionary patriotism that would first maintain a loyalty to the traditions of a people rather than blindly support a particular government or ruler. Richard's Englishness mirrors Robin's own.

Errol Flynn takes aim as the heroic outlaw, Robin Hood.

The Adventures of Robin Hood enjoyably handles both the big set pieces—the archery tournament, the gallows scene, the dinner in Sherwood, the final swordfight—and the smaller details, like the final image of swords raining down on shields to signal the end of hostilities. Writer Rudy Behlmer came upon some fascinating material when he probed the Warner Bros. archives in preparing an introduction to the published version of the screenplay. One of the discoveries is a series of memos from producer Hal B. Wallis, who seems to have studied the film shot by shot in an effort to improve it. Among Wallis' notes are the following instructions for tightening the pace: "Cut quicker to Rathbone . . . Take out the stall before the line . . . After Prince John announces that he is regent of England, make the reaction shots all the same footage . . . You stay too long on the man that falls." Wallis' editorial advice and everything else works perfectly in this great film, including the soundtrack by Erich Wolfgang Korngold and sets by Carl Jules Weyl.

Cast: Errol Flynn (Robin Hood), Olivia de Havilland (Maid Marian), Basil Rathbone (Sir Guy of Gisbourne), Claude Rains (Prince John), Patric Knowles (Will Scarlet), Eugene Pallette (Friar Tuck), Alan Hale (Little John), Melville Cooper (High Sheriff of Nottingham), Una O'Connor (Bess), Ian Hunter (King Richard the Lion-Heart), Herbert Mundin (Much-the-Miller's-Son), Montagu Love (Bishop of the Black Canons), Leonard Willey (Sir Essex), Robert Noble (Sir Ralf), Kenneth Hunter (Sir Mortimer), Holmes Herbert (Archery referee) **Screenwriter:** Norman Reilly Raine, Seton I. Miller **Cinematographer:** Tony Gaudio, Sol Polito **Composer:** Erich Wolfgang Korngold **Producer:** Hal B. Wallis for Warner Bros. **Running Time:** 102 minutes **Format:** VHS, LV **Awards:** Academy Awards, 1938: Editing, Interior Decoration, Original Score; Nominations: Picture. **Budget:** $2M.

Aguirre, the Wrath of God
1972 – Werner Herzog – 𝄞𝄞𝄞𝄞

> **"Men measure riches in gold. But it's more. It's power and fame."**
>
> Aguirre (Klaus Kinski)

German director Werner Herzog has created a mesmerizing experience with *Aguirre: The Wrath of God*. The story begins in Peru in 1560 as a group of Spanish conquistadores descend a peak in the Andes. Gonzalo Pizarro (Alejandro Repulles), the half-brother of the man who conquered the Incas, cannot decide whether the density of the jungle will permit the Spaniards to continue their search for the fabled land of gold, El Dorado. Pizarro appoints Don Pedro de Ursua (Ruy Guerra) to take a party of men and scout the territory. When

Ursua decides that they can go no farther, his second-in-command, Don Lope de Aguirre (Klaus Kinski), stages a mutiny, makes Ursua a captive, and declares himself and his followers free from Spain.

Most of the remainder of this claustrophobic film takes place on the large raft Aguirre and his men build to continue their search for El Dorado. As they drift farther and farther, the impassive jungle surrounds them and darts shot from natives in the thickets begin to reduce their ranks. The cramped conditions, lack of food, growing fevers, and unexpected calamities further strain their nerves and shrink their numbers. Aguirre becomes more maniacal, as well. At one stop along the river, he is giving instructions when he overhears the whispering of two men planning a revolt. One confides to the other that if they abandon Aguirre they will still be able to return safely to their company by retracing the bends in the river. As he numbers them off on his fingers ("eight . . . nine"), one of Aguirre's men beheads him from behind with a machete. The camera

Klaus Kinski stars as conquistador Don Lope de Aguirre.

Did you know?...

The film embroiders on history somewhat: for example, the Monk's journal is a dramatic device created by director Werner Herzog, and Gonzalo Pizarro had been dead for two years when the real Aguirre staged his revolt.

swish pans to the man's severed head in the brush where its dying mouth completes the sentence: "Ten."

Aguirre follows this action with his great speech of madness. In Kinski's slithering gait and lizard-like stare, it becomes the character's defining moment: "I am the great traitor. There can be none greater. Anyone considering desertion will be cut into 198 pieces. Those pieces will be stamped on until what is left can only be used to paint walls. Whoever takes one grain of corn or one drop of water too much will be imprisoned 155 years. If I want the birds to drop dead from the trees, then the birds will drop dead from the trees. I am the Wrath of God. The earth I walk upon sees me and quakes. Who follows me and the river will win untold riches. But whoever deserts . . . ." By now, he doesn't have to finish his sentence.

Herzog gives the film and his hero a dark beauty. The simple, parable-like nature of the plot resonates on a number of mythic levels: as an example of hubris, as a case study of greed, as a comment on the supposedly civilizing impulses of European countries, even as a variation on Joseph Conrad's *Heart of Darkness*. The final shot of a strutting Aguirre, the last survivor of a raft now teeming with tiny chattering monkeys, is an indelible image of the costs of obsession.

Cast: Klaus Kinski (Don Lope de Aguirre), Alejandro Repulles (Gonzalo Pizarro), Cecilia Rivera (Flores), Helena Rojo (Inez), Edward Roland (Okello), Dan Ades (Perucho), Peter Berling (Don Fernando de Guzman), Ruy Guerra (Don Pedro de Ursua), Del Negro (Brother Gaspar de Carvajal), Armando Polanha (Armando), **Screenwriter:** Werner Herzog **Cinematographer:** Thomas Mauch **Composer:** Popol Vuh **Producer:** Werner Herzog for Werner Herzog Filmproduktion **Running Time:** 90 minutes **Format:** VHS **Awards:** National Society of Film Critics Awards, 1977: Cinematography.

Around the World in 80 Days
1956 – Michael Anderson, Kevin McClory, Sidney Smith – 🦴🦴🦴

"An Englishman never jokes about a wager."
Phileas Fogg (David Niven)

Mike Todd was more often referred to as a showman than a producer, and his signature flamboyance is everywhere on display in this, his only film. Reportedly, fundraising was still being carried out while shooting was underway. Todd is said to have paid two Paris cab drivers to stage an accident to distract

Passepartout (Cantinflas) rides high in the rigging while Phileas Fogg (David Niven) takes a more conventional seat in their hot air balloon.

Did you know?...

Todd made and lost large sums on a number of show-business gambles. Two of his better decisions were his investment in Cinerama, which led to an association with the American Optical Company and the eventual creation of Todd-AO, the widescreen process with extremely sharp color definition. *Oklahoma* was the first of many films shot in this new process, *Eighty Days* the second.

the police who were about to arrest the film crew for towing away cars in their way. David Niven plays Phileas Fogg, the hero of Jules Verne's novel, who bets his fellow club members in 1872 England that he can circle the world in eighty days; his travels take on the aspect of a chase when Inspector Fix (Robert Newton, in his last film role) determines to follow Fogg suspecting that he is the intrepid adventurer who recently robbed the Bank of England. (Todd was the first to use the word "cameo" to refer to a small part played by a big star. He was afraid that some of the bigger names would consider their walk-on appearances beneath them, so he came up with a term to elevate the importance of these glorified extras. According to Cedric Hardwicke, Todd was shrewd enough to begin this type of casting with the British stars, whose tradition maintains that an actor does not lose prestige by taking a small part.)

The episodic development of the movie is slapped together like the stickers on a steamer trunk. The plot is really a series of set pieces perhaps best appreciated by some of the statistics generated by the 127-day filming tour of Todd and his crew: a wardrobe of nearly 75,000 costumes, scenes shot in 140 locations in thirteen countries, thirty-three assistant directors, sound stages at three separate studios for interior scenes, thirty-four different species of animals totaling 8,000 animals in all. The many shots of Fogg and his manservant Passepartout (Cantinflas) looking at scenery followed by various shots of wildlife, horizons, sunsets eventually produce a lulling effect.

The hero Fogg is so fastidious and regulated in his life that the character seems more of a running joke than a personality. It is, at least, a good joke that Niven plays to perfection: Fogg continually remains unflappable amid many potential disasters. A highlight occurs after Fogg and Passepartout rescue an Indian princess from a funeral pyre. Shirley MacLaine is enjoyable in this part (although she often spoke of herself as miscast). The formal and respectful Princess Aouda joins the travelers and shares a shipboard conversation with Fogg about their mutual passion for whist. For two such emotionally guarded characters, this makes for a charming courtship scene and an effective contrast to the ongoing series of threats to their journey. But when such a touch of subtlety becomes one of the film's memorable moments, you know that the attempts at spectacle often fail to come off.

Cast: David Niven (Phileas Fogg), Cantinflas (Passepartout), Shirley MacLaine (Princess Aouda), Robert Newton (Mr. Fix), Cedric Hardwicke (Sir Francis Gromarty), Trevor Howard (Fallentin), Charles Boyer (Monsieur Gasse), Joe E. Brown (Stationmaster), Martine Carol (Tourist), John Carradine (Col. Proctor Stamp), Charles Coburn (Clerk), Ronald Colman (Railway Official),

Melville Cooper (Steward), Noel Coward (Hesketh-Baggott), Finlay Currie (Whist Partner), Reginald Denny (Police Chief), Andy Devine (First Mate), Marlene Dietrich (Hostess), Ava Gardner (Spectator), John Gielund (Foster), Hermione Gingold (Sporting Lady), Jose Greco (Dancer), Glynis Johns (Companion), Buster Keaton (Conductor), Evelyn Keyes (Flirt), Beatrice Lillie (Revivalist), Peter Lorre (Japanese Steward), Keye Luke (Cameo), Mike Mazurki (Character), Victor McLaglen (Helmsman), John Mills (Cameo), Robert Morely (Ralph), Edward R. Murrow (Narrator), George Raft (Bouncer), Gilbert Roland (Achmed Abdullah), Cesar Romero (Henchman), Frank Sinatra (Pianist), Red Skelton (Drunk), Philip Van Zandt (Cameo), **Screenwriter:** John Farrow, S.J. Perelman, James Poe **Cinematographer:** Lionel Lindon **Composer:** Victor Young **Producer** Kevin McClory, William Cameron Menzies, Michael Todd **Running Time:** 175 minutes **Format:** VHS, Beta, LV **Awards:** Academy Awards, 1956: Adapted Screenplay, Color Cinematography, Film Editing, Picture, Dramatic/Comedy Score; Nominations: Art Direction, Set Decoration, Costume Design, Director (Michael Anderson), Golden Globe Awards, 1957: Actor—Musical/Comedy (Cantiflas), Film—Drama, National Board of Review Awards 1956: 10 Best Films of the Year, New York Film Critics Awards 1956: Film, Screenplay **Budget:** $6M.

Beau Geste

1939 – William Wellman – 🦴🦴🦴

A desert fort defended by a row of corpses looking down from the parapets makes for one of the most unforgettable opening scenes in adventure films. It is the first of many expert storytelling touches that give this story of three brothers (Gary Cooper, Ray Milland, and Robert Preston) who join the Foreign Legion to avoid acknowledging a family disgrace its offbeat, dramatic appeal. In filmmaking parlance, it is ineffective for a script to be too "on the nose" (too pat, too expected). In this film, screenwriter Robert Carson and director William Wellman manage to give nearly every scene an unexpected edge, a touch that keeps the movie awake.

The dramatic opening of the fort of corpses leads to a flashback fifteen years earlier that shows young Beau Geste (Donald O'Connor) secretly at play hiding in a suit of armor. He overhears his aunt, who needs to pay off her husband's debts, sell the famous Blue Water sapphire to a buyer and receive an imitation to put in its place. Years later, when word comes from the husband to sell the original, Beau is the only brother who knows about the copy. On the night before the sale, the family gathers to take a last look at what they think is the Blue Water when the room suddenly goes dark. After the lights come on, the jewel is gone. Beau disappears the next day, leaving behind a note, and his brothers follow him to the Foreign Legion.

> "I don't know much about mutiny, but I do know it isn't good form to plan them at the top of your voice."
> Beau (Gary Cooper), to the loudmouth Schwartz.

Did you know?...

Many actors who later went on to become familiar names appear in small parts: Donald O'Connor (as Beau at age twelve), Susan Hayward (as the love interest), and Broderick Crawford (as a Legion volunteer).

Foreign Legionnaires and brothers Beau (Gary Cooper), John (Ray Milland), and Digby (Robert Preston) Geste prepare for a fight.

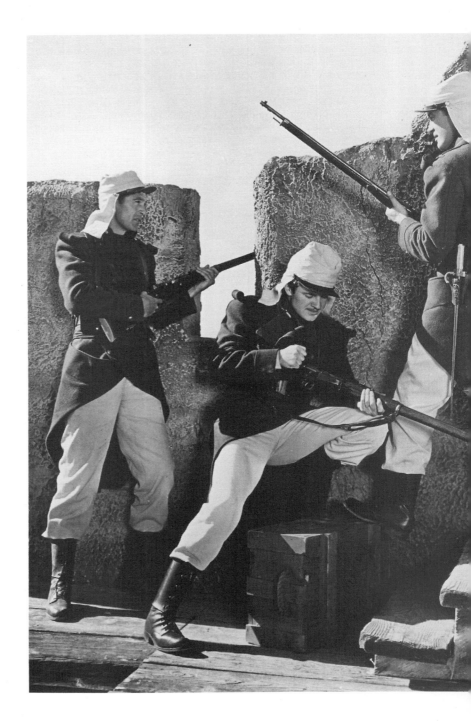

Many fine scenes and images linger in the memory. The introduction of sadistic Sergeant Markoff (Brian Donlevy) as he belittles the new recruits features his gloating signature phrase, "I promise you," a great personalizing touch. The concern the legionnaires show toward their dying comrade Krenke (Barry Macollum) adds depth to the first barracks scene. The impassive reaction shots of the men as Markoff berates a deserter and drives him out into the endless desert visually lays the foundation for the seditious talk by Schwartz (Albert Dekker). The second barracks scene divides the men between those who wish to kill Markoff and those loyal to the Legion flag. A sudden attack by Arabs drags the men out of bed to defend the fort, and they joke between rifle shots about fighting in their long johns.

Most representative of the film's flavor is the eerie "laughing scene," when the garrison is down to just a few men, the corpses of their comrades having been propped by Markoff in the parapets. The sergeant insists that these few men can make enough noise to scare off their attackers ("Seven is going to sound like seventy"). He orders his handful of survivors one by one to start laughing. The rising waves of their maniacal laughter echoing across the desert evinces both the men's fatigue and their hatred of their sergeant. It is yet another "not on the nose" touch that enlivens this smart, dramatic movie.

Cast: Gary Cooper (Michael "Beau" Geste), Ray Milland (John Geste), Robert Preston (Digby Geste), Brian Donlevy (Sergeant Markoff), Susan Hayward (Isobel Rivers), J. Carrol Naish (Rasinoff), Albert Dekker (Schwartz), Broderick Crawford (Hank Miller), James Stephenson (Major Henri de Beaujolais), Charles Barton (Buddy McMonigal), James Burke (Lieutenant Dufour), G.P. Huntley (Augustus Brandon), Harvey Stephens (Lieutenant Martin), Stanley Andrews (Maris), Harry M. Woods (Renoir), Arthur Aylesworth (Renault), Barry Macollum (Krenke), Ronald R. Rondell (Bugler), Heather Thatcher (Lady Brandon), Donald O'Connor (Young Beau Geste), **Screenwriter:** Robert Carson **Cinematographer:** Theodor Sparkuhl, Archie Stout **Composer:** Alfred Newman **Producer:** William Wellman for Paramount **Running Time:** 114 minutes **Format:** VHS **Awards:** Academy Awards, 1939: Nominations: Interior Decoration, Supporting Actor (Brian Donlevy).

Braveheart

1995 – Mel Gibson – 🦴🦴🦴🦴

Set in early fourteenth-century Scotland, *Braveheart* is one of the most powerful movies ever made about resisting oppression and finding freedom, the most precious desire in the heart of man. Sometimes the most unlikely occurrences can begin a chain of events leading to totally unexpected results. Such is the case with *Braveheart*. In this story, the love of a man for a woman leads to the emancipation of Scotland from British rule.

The undertones of the oppression of British rule are evident from the beginning but are downplayed so that the audience gets a look at the amazing character of William Wallace (Mel Gibson). The premise for the movie is the love between William and Murron (Catherine McCormack). Here the story of freedom also begins. William and Murron are married in secret so he will not have to share his wife with an English nobleman in a hideous ritual called "prima nocta," in which, on the first night of a marriage, a nobleman sleeps first with the new wife. They conceal their marriage and some of the English soldiers assault Murron. She is saved by William, but later dies at the hand of a nobleman who executes her to bring William out in her defense. Revenging her death, therefore, becomes the driving force of the rebellion that William Wallace then leads.

As with all epics, this one is filled with large emotions, deception, lies, intrigue, grand conflict, personalities larger than life, great men who are too good, and evil ones who are terribly bad. There is the ongoing deception of the English King Edward I, played convincingly and marvelously by Patrick McGoohan, who is always dreaming and scheming to overcome the rebellion by devious methods and using others to meet his ends in one Machiavellian plot after another. Of major interest is the subplot concerning the betrayal and redemption of Robert the Bruce (Angus McFadyen), the rightful King of Scots. He befriends William and then betrays him in battle. Later repenting his part in the betrayal, Robert redeems himself in the end.

The battle scenes are probably the most memorable aspect of the movie, and some of them are as gory and violent as any ever filmed. Other elements of the film—music, cinematography, the epic scale—are often put to the service of

Did you know?...

The battles at Stirling and Falkirk were filmed in Ireland using 1,700 Irish Army reserve forces.

making these battle scenes more effective, as when the camera shows us the lines of combatants with their faces painted. The action shots are taken so closely that the we feel in the middle of the fray. These bloody scenes used upwards of 1,700 extras, so many that they had to begin getting into makeup, costume, and battle formation at four a.m. to be ready for an eight a.m. shooting schedule.

Scotsman William Wallace (Mel Gibson) leads his soldiers into battle against the English.

Cast: Mel Gibson (William Wallace), Sophie Marceau (Princess Isabelle), Patrick McGoohan (Longshanks—King Edward I), Catherine McCormack (Murron), Angus McFadyen (Robert the Bruce), Brendan Gleeson (Hamish), David O'Hara (Stephen), Ian Bannan (The Leper), James Robinson (Young William), Sean Lawlor (Malcolm Wallace), Sandy Nelson (John Wallace), James Cosmo (Campbell), Sean McGinley (MacClannough), Alan Tall (Elder Stewart), Andrew Weir (Young Hamish), Gerda Stevenson (Mother MacClannough), Mahiri Calvey (Young Murron), **Screenwriter:** Randall Wallace **Cinematographer:** John Toll **Composer:** James Horner **Producer:** Bruce Davey, Mel Gibson, and Alan Ladd, Jr. for Twentieth Century Fox **MPAA Rating:** R **Running Time:** 177 minutes **Format:** VHS, LV **Awards:** Academy Awards, 1995: Cinematography, Director (Mel Gibson), Makeup, Picture; Nominations: Costume Design, Editing, Screenplay, Sound, Original Dramatic/Comedy Score (James Horner), British Academy Awards,

1995: Cinematography; Nominations: Director (Mel Gibson), Score (James Horner), Golden Globe Awards, 1996: Director (Mel Gibson); Nominations: Film—Drama, Screenplay, Score (James Horner), MTV Movie Awards, 1996: Best Action Sequence; Nominations: Film, Male Performance (Mel Gibson), Most Desirable Male (Mel Gibson), Writers Guild of America, 1995: Best Original Screenplay, Broadcast Film Critics Association Awards, 1995: Director (Mel Gibson) **Budget:** $72.6M **Box Office:** $202M (worldwide gross).

The Charge of the Light Brigade

1936 – Michael Curtiz – *ʃʃʃ*

> "The reckless lancers sweep on and on—so that a woman's heart might not be broken! You're not fighting a single legion—you're fighting the entire British army, Surat Khan!"
>
> **Publicity tag line**

Did you know?...

The popularity of the British imperial film led to a sub-genre of empire epics from 1935-1939. They include *The Lives of a Bengal Lancer, Beau Geste, Gunga Din,* and *The Four Feathers.*

Think of directors who are especially associated with epics and you will probably name David Lean, D.W. Griffith, Cecil B. De Mille, and perhaps even Michael Curtiz, that reliable hand at Warner Bros. who directed nine of Errol Flynn's adventure films, including this one. Practically nobody, however, would name B. Reeves Eason, yet Eason directed some of the most famous and effective epic scenes in film history. Eason was primarily a second-unit director who was in charge of filming the chariot race in the silent version of *Ben-Hur*, the tournament scene in Douglas Fairbanks' 1922 film *Robin Hood*, the land rush in *Cimarron*, the burning of Atlanta in *Gone with the Wind*, the battle sequences in *Sergeant York*, and *The Charge of the Light Brigade*'s final cavalry charge. Eason knew how to capture the sweep of an action scene by contrasting closer shots with longer ones and by alternating camera angles.

"You can have a small army of people charging across the screen and it won't matter much to the audience," said Eason. "But if you show details of the action, like guns going off, individual men fighting or a fist hitting someone in the eye, then you will have more feeling of action than if all the extras of Hollywood are running about. That is why real catastrophes often look tame in newsreels. You need detail work and close shots in a movie. Only then does it come to life." Many of the most effective directors in film history have taken his advice.

This practice of assigning the action scenes to second-unit directors while the primary director handles the rest of the picture seems especially odd in a film like *Light Brigade* where the main plot of a love triangle among two brothers (Errol Flynn and Patric Knowles) in the 27th British Lancers and Olivia de Havilland is the most ordinary aspect of the movie. The film was only the second (of

eight) teaming Flynn and de Havilland, and the skills Flynn later developed for light comedy (his self-deprecation and cheerful impudence) are not much on display here. Neither are David Niven's talents put to much use.

Errol Flynn stars as dashing and doomed British officer, Maj. Geoffrey Vickers.

The project came about when Warners wanted a British imperial movie of its own to capitalize on the popularity of Paramount's recent hit *The Lives of a Bengal Lancer*. Warners decided that Tennyson's famous poem about the fatal charge of the light brigade at Balaklava in 1854 during the Crimean War would serve their purpose. The studio then asked its scriptwriters to invent a new reason for the calvary charge to avoid having to dramatize the unheroic military incompetence of the real historical account. What they came up with is the romantic plot with Geoffrey Vickers (Flynn), his brother Perry (Knowles), and the woman they both love, Elsa Campbell (de Havilland).

The first half charts a growing conflict in India between the British forces and Surat Khan (Henry Gordon), an Indian potentate. This former British ally changes his allegiance to Russia. In the sequence that gives Geoffrey Vickers his motive to retaliate, Surat Khan besieges a British garrison at Chukoti, betrays his offer of safe conduct, and orders his forces to kill the British survivors of Chukoti, mostly women and children. Now that Vickers realizes Perry and Elsa do love each other, he forges his superior's signature on an order for the 27th Lancers to attack in the Crimea, a suicidal charge that will nevertheless occupy the Russians and give the British a likely victory at Sebastopol. During the charge, Vickers comes upon his old nemesis Surat Khan among the Russians, and the final scenes allow Vickers the nobility of a sacrifice (he has already sent Perry back to Elsa) and the satisfactions of revenge for the Chukoti massacre.

An interesting if uneven film, *Light Brigade* did have one lasting impact on movie production. During the filming, trip wires were used to bring down the horses, injuring many and resulting in new rules for animal safety during film-making.

Cast: Errol Flynn (Major Geoffrey Vickers), Olivia de Havilland (Elsa Campbell), Patric Knowles (Captain Perry Vickers), Henry Stephenson (Sir Charles Macefield), Nigel Bruce (Sir Benjamin Warrenton), Donald Crisp (Colonel Campbell), David Niven (Capt. James Randall), C. Henry Gordon (Surat Khan), G.P. Huntley (Major Jowett), Robert Barrat (Count Igor Volonoff), Spring Byington (Lady Octavia Warrenton), E.E. Clive (Sir Humphrey Harcourt), J. Carrol Naish (Subahdar-Major Puran Singh), Walter Holbrook (Cornet Barclay), Princess Baigum (Prema's mother), Charles Sedgwick (Cornet Pearson), Scotty Beckett (Prema Singh), George Regas (Wazir), Helen Sanborn (Mrs. Jowett), Holmes Herbert (General O'Neill) **Screenwriter:** Michael Jacoby, Rowland Leigh **Cinematographer:** Sol Polito **Composer:** Max Steiner **Producer:** Samuel Bischoff and Hal B. Wallis for Warner Bros. **Running Time:** 115 minutes **Format:** VHS, LV **Awards:** Academy Awards 1936, Nominations: Sound, Original Score **Budget:** $1.2M.

Contact
1997 – Robert Zemeckis – 🦴🦴🦴

After meeting Ellie Arroway (Jodie Foster) and watching her rush back to her telescope, divinity school dropout Palmer Joss (Matthew McConaughey) leaves her a note: "How can I reach you?" *Contact* is essentially an exploration of that question in its many emotional, spiritual, and astronomical possibilities. Ellie works for SETI (the Search for Extra-Terrestrial Intelligence), and after four years of expensive research, her listening dishes pick up a mysterious sound

from the galaxy Vega, twenty-six light years away. The decoding of the sound leads to the discovery of 63,000 encrypted pages describing what appears to be a transportation device to send someone to Vega. The suspenseful development of the film gains much of its drama by showing the impact such an event would have at the societal, scientific, and personal levels. In one scene, the previously unpopulated listening outpost transforms itself into a makeshift community of

Jodie Fosters stars as Ellie Arroway in *Contact*.

drifters and soul-searchers—crackpot preachers, skinhead Nazis, Elvis impersonators singing "Viva Las Vega"—who have all been drawn to the enormous dishes that have picked up a sliver of meaning from deep space.

Ellie is the best-drawn character and one of the film's real strengths. (McConaughey's character is equally underdrawn). Foster, one of the screen's most intelligent actors, makes Ellie appealing for her relentless intelligence, curiosity, and uncompromising honesty. The film, though sometimes bowing to the pressures of blockbuster appeal, handles with equal honesty the questions of belief and doubt and refuses to stack the deck for either side. *Contact* is never more effective than when the political, scientific, and spiritual implications of the Vega message unfold almost as fast as new developments occur. The fairness with which the screenwriters present their ideas and the way the film encourages the audience to think are quite rare in a Hollywood production. The ambiguity of the ending also merits respect. When her sphere zooms through a "worm-hole" in time (a superior piece of special effects) on its way to whatever awaits on Vega, Ellie sees such beauty that she can only respond, "They should have sent a poet." Based on the Carl Sagan novel and filmed while he was dying of cancer, *Contact* ultimately suggests that a desperate world might find a measure of solace if it brings to the infinitudes of space and doubt a touch of the poet.

Cast: Jodie Foster (Dr. Eleanor "Ellie" Arroway), Matthew McConaughey (Palmer Joss), Tom Skerritt (David Drumlin), James Woods (Michael Kitz), John Hurt (S.R. Hadden), Rob Lowe (Richard Rank), David Morse (Ted Arroway), William Fichtner (Kent Clark), Angela Bassett (Rachel Constantine), Larry King (himself), Leon Harris (himself), Tabitha Soren (herself), Geraldine Ferraro (herself), Bobbie Battista (herself), Robert Novak (himself), Bernard Shaw (himself), Geraldo Rivera (himself), Jay Leno (himself) **Screenwriter:** Carl Sagan, Ann Druyan, Michael Goldenberg **Cinematographer:** Don Burgess **Composer:** Alan Silvestri **Producer:** Steve Starkey and Robert Zemeckis for Warner Bros. **MPAA Rating:** PG **Running Time:** 153 minutes **Format:** VHS, LV, DVD **Budget:** $90M **Box Office:** $101M.

Excalibur

1981 – John Boorman – 🎬🎬🎬

Loosely based on Sir Thomas Malory's *Le Morte d'Arthur*, this version of the Camelot legend tells the story of Arthur from his conception to his death. Director John Boorman's adaptation is a violent, erotic, stylized tale that maintains a sense of reverence for the story's mythic origins. The film depicts many of the major elements of the Arthur legend, but perhaps the attempt to maintain an atmosphere of veneration weakens the character. At times, *Excalibur* seems overly self-aware, populated by characters that seem too obviously based in legend to come across as convincingly real people. Characters from a well-known tale, their story is likewise widely familiar. This adaptation has difficulty getting past the legend and making the story more personal and unique.

The title indicates the emphasis of the story on the supernatural-like power entrusted to a good man and warrior whose arrival was foreseen by mystical prophecy. With the coming of the King (Nigel Terry), and his welcome purity and sense of goodness aided by the magical powers of Merlin (Nicol Williamson), the land is healed and prospers in harmony. Evil appears with the betrayal by his wife (Cherie Lunghi) and friend (Nicholas Clay) and the sinister plottings of his half-sister Morgana (Helen Mirren). With this corruption, Arthur and the land suffer, rejuvenated only by the recovery of the sacred Grail and the return of the sword Excalibur to the King. The filmmakers endow their adaptations with the mystical and the supernatural. Excalibur represents a supernatural force of goodness that may only be wielded by the right and righteous king, one who is intimately connected with the land. When Arthur weakens and becomes ill, the land deteriorates, and the prosperity that came with his arrival is lost. This connection between the King and the land becomes an intriguing, mythical focus of the film.

Excalibur's weaknesses derive from that same mythical tone. Many of the characters—including Arthur himself—do not emerge as fully rendered, believable people. While the production design is both realistic and visually intriguing, at times the characters are more fantastic than realistic. The film is already long at two hours and twenty minutes, but one may wonder if the characters could have been more fully developed had the movie been longer. *Excalibur* is in general an interesting film to watch with a unique though relatively insignificant

> "Good and evil—there never is one without the other."
> Merlin (Nicol Williamson)

Did you know?...

Liam Neeson makes his screen debut playing Gawain.

Nicol Williamson stars as the sorcerer, Merlin.

variation on the legend by emphasizing its violent and erotic aspects, but overall it does not offer much to enjoy emotionally.

Cast: Nigel Terry (King Arthur), Helen Mirren (Morgana), Nicholas Clay (Lancelot), Cherie Lunghi (Guenevere), Paul Geoffrey (Percevel), Nicol Williamson (Merlin), Robert Addie (Mordred), Gabriel Byrne (Uther), Keith Buckley (Uryens), Katrine Boorman (Igrayne), Liam Neeson (Gawain), Niall O'Brien (Cornwall), Patrick Stewart (Leondegrance), Clive Swift (Ector), Ciaran Hinds (Lot), **Screenwriter:** John Boorman, Rospo Pallenberg **Cinematographer:** Alex Thomson **Composer:** Trevor Jones **Producer:** John Boorman for Warner Bros. **MPAA Rating:** R **Running Time:** 140 minutes **Format:** VHS, LV **Awards:** Academy Awards, 1981, Nominations: Cinematography (Alex Thomson).

Fitzcarraldo
1982 – Werner Herzog – 🎭🎭🎭🎭

Those who say that epic tasks have not been undertaken since the mythical days of Achilles and Odysseus should look at this odd and amazing film. Werner Herzog tells the story of a man in 1890s Peru obsessed with building an opera house in the Amazon jungle. The centerpiece of his odyssey up the river and the moment the film lingers over the longest is the attempt to organize hundreds of Indian workers to haul a 320-ton steamship over a hill to reach the next tributary. Herzog reportedly wanted to make the ship bigger and the gradient steeper than those encountered by the real-life character on whom the film is based. (The real Fitzcarraldo simply disassembled the boat and put it back together on the other side.)

Fitzcarraldo resists comparisons with other movies, even perhaps with others by Herzog (this is his only film with a happy ending). One of its most intriguing aspects is the film's seeming refusal to adopt a consistent point of view: is Fitzcarraldo (Klaus Kinski) to be admired for his artistic passions and his valiant task, or is he to be pitied for his blindness to native customs, a flaw all too typical of the colonizers of his day? Most people who have written about the film take one view or the other. But Herzog may be seeking a more ambiguous response, and evidence for both views may be found.

The movie introduces Fitzcarraldo and Molly (Claudia Cardinale) as likable eccentrics who have traveled over two days and a thousand miles to hear the

> "When I build my opera house, I'll see to it you have your own box and a red velvet armchair."
>
> Fitzcarraldo (Klaus Kinski), scratching the ear of his pig as he puts on a record of Caruso.

Did you know?...
"Fitzcarraldo" is the native mispronunciation of Fitzgerald.

Klaus Kinski stars as madman
Fitzcarraldo.

great Caruso. As they rush to catch the performance, they use nothing more than their desperation and their passion for opera to talk their way past the usher (who joins them in the back of the theater for the performance.) The many shots of the steamboat chugging up the Amazon dwarfed by the towering jungle while Fitzcarraldo has Caruso pouring out of the phonograph horn stress the lyricism and passion of his undertaking. *Fitzcarraldo* also includes a stop along the way with two missionaries who measure the Indians' religious progress by the degree their converts separate themselves from the less "civilized" natives up river. Herzog's career has been characterized by a continual respect for otherness, so many viewers will be inclined to see a criticism of the Europeans (though all of the monied characters are presented far worse than Fitzcarraldo). The combination of the quest Fitzcarraldo takes on and the formidable, unspoiled areas he encounters guarantee that most viewers' response will be a complex, ambiguous one. Such an atypical movie could elicit no less.

(Final note: as the letterboxing of widescreen films becomes even more commonplace in newer video formats like DVD, which can hold both versions on one disc, Herzog should be a director whose work will benefit greatly. Some of *Fitzcarraldo*'s most powerful moments derive from the contrast of inching the steamship up the hill and later in watching it swirl briefly out of control as it heads for the Pongo. These images lose much of their vastness when cropped for a pan-and-scan presentation.)

Cast: Klaus Kinski (Fitzcarraldo), Claudia Cardinale (Molly), Jose Lewgoy (Don Aquilino), Miguel Angel Fuentes (Cholo), Paul Hittscher (Orinoco), Huerequeque Enrique Bohorquez (Cook), Grand Otelo (Station Master), Peter Berling (Opera Manager), David Perez Espinosa (Chief of Campa Indians), Milton Nascimento (Usher at Opera House), Rui Polanah (Rubber Baron), Salvador Godinez (Old Missionary), Dieter Milz (Young Missionary), William L. Rose (Notary), **Screenwriter:** Werner Herzog **Cinematographer:** Thomas Mauch **Composer:** Popol Vuh **Producer:** Werner Herzog for Project Filmproduktion **MPAA Rating:** PG **Running Time:** 157 minutes **Format:** VHS **Awards:** Cannes Film Festival, 1982: Best Director (Werner Herzog).

Gunga Din

1939 – George Stevens – 𝄞𝄞𝄞𝄞

This landmark adventure film concerns three Cockney soldiers posted in India who face and overcome a series of threats from a Thugee cult. Sam Jaffe is the brave but lowly waterboy Gunga Din, who yearns to be a soldier. As Cutter, Ballantine, and MacChesney, Cary Grant, Douglas Fairbanks Jr., and Victor McLaglen form a prototypical trio of pals. The film has gone down in history as one of the greatest adventure stories, but the action scenes, while good, would not work without the buddy element. The comradeship of the three manages to inject their sense of fellowship into the moments of danger and give the movie its infectious appeal.

The first appearance of the three friends establishes this tone of action and humor. While a British officer searches for them, they brawl with some locals over the authenticity of a map to an emerald mine. They keep up a shouting match with one another while they smash chairs, slug attackers, and toss people out of windows. The first threat to their solidarity comes from Ballantine's decision to leave the service in six days to marry Joan Fontaine. His two pals concoct a great scheme to discredit his replacement by spiking the punch at Ballantine's betrothal ball with the laxative MacChesney gives his favorite elephant. McLaglen has a hilarious comic routine in which he keeps two superior officers from sampling the punch by pretending to see a fly in it and plunging his hands in the bowl.

Most of the story's richness comes from the way the three friends seem to share their own wavelength so that even insults and abuse are understood as expressions of affection. To these career soldiers, friendship has become a rich form of game playing. (You can tell Howard Hawks, who was originally slated to direct, worked on the project; such indirect expressions of affection—what he called "three-cushion dialogue"—are a staple of his films.) One great example of such communication occurs later when MacChesney wants Ballantine to re-enlist for another tour before granting permission for Ballantine to join him in rescuing Cutter. MacChesney lies, saying that he will later tear up the re-enlistment papers after they return. Ballantine signs but insists that he himself hold the papers. MacChesney looks angry. "Don't you trust me?" he asks. "No," says

Did you know?...

The Rudyard Kipling poem that inspired the film was one of three (with "Bengal Lancer" and "The Charge of the Light Brigade") dealing with British colonialism that were eventually made into movies.

Ballantine, and a big smile breaks out on MacChesney's face. This is just what he wanted to hear: his pal knows him after all.

Besieged British soldiers threaten an Indian guru.

Cast: Cary Grant (Archibald Cutter), Victor McLaglen (MacChesney), Douglas Fairbanks, Jr. (Sergeant Ballantine), Sam Jaffe (Gunga Din), Edward Ciannelli (Guru), Joan Fontaine (Emmy Stebbins), Montagu Love (Colonel), Robert Coote (Higginbotham), Abner Biberman (Chota), Lumsden Hare (Major Mitchell), Charles Bennett (Telegraph Operator), George Du Count (Thug Chiefton), Ann Evers (Girl at Party), Bryant Fryer (Scotch Sergeant), Jamiel Hasson (Thug Chiefton) **Screenwriter:** Fred Guiol, Joel Sayre **Cinematographer:** Joseph H. August **Composer:** Alfred Newman **Producer** Pandro S. Berman for RKO **Running Time:** 117 minutes **Format:** VHS, LV **Awards:** Academy Awards, 1939: Nominations: Black and White Cinematography **Budget:** $1.9M.

Indiana Jones and the Last Crusade

1989 – Steven Spielberg – 🦴🦴🦴🦴

This third film featuring swashbuckling archeologist Indiana Jones (Harrison Ford) restores much of the charm and fun of *Raiders of the Lost Ark* after the series took a dark turn with *Indiana Jones and the Temple of Doom* (1984). Set several years after the events of *Raiders*, the adventure involves a quest for the sacred Holy Grail, simultaneously sought by evil Nazi agents, a traitorous American businessman (Julian Glover), a greedy femme fatale (Alison Doody), and the duo of Indiana Jones and his father Henry (Sean Connery). Like the first Indiana Jones film, *The Last Crusade* revels in almost non-stop adventurous fun, but it also includes more humor and develops Jones' character through the exploration of his relationship with his father.

Director Steven Spielberg and executive producer George Lucas successfully use the same formula of thrilling visual imagery, kinetic suspense, sharp characterizations, and an intriguing, fantastical storyline that made *Raiders* a hit among audiences and critics. Although the plot in many ways mimics that of the first film, in that both include Nazi villains and the search for a mystical religious artifact, *The Last Crusade* avoids simply copying the original by combining the adventure and the epic quest with the story of a father and son reuniting after years of estrangement. The interaction between Indiana and Henry, often taking on the nature of a rivalry, provides some of the most enjoyable and personal moments in the film. The resolution, which completes the quest for the Grail, also completes a sort of quest for renewal between the two Joneses.

Spielberg's skill at creating, filming, and editing exciting action sequences is displayed in full capacity in the many stunt-filled, outrageous chase scenes. Part of the magic of the Indiana Jones series comes from such unbelievable yet thoroughly engaging action scenes—from motorcycle pursuits to aerial attacks—and each one is executed with enough realism to momentarily suspend disbelief. Other filmmakers have attempted to re-create or imitate the success of *Raiders of the Lost Ark*, but Spielberg and Lucas found a way not only to artfully imitate the first movie but to create an equally entertaining and well-made picture. *The Last Crusade* is inspired by and pays homage to its predecessor but is also refreshingly original.

Did you know?...

The opening "Young Indy" sequence explains the origins of Indiana Jones' fear of snakes, first seen in *Raiders of the Lost Ark*, his fedora, and the scar on his chin.

Cast: Harrison Ford (Indiana Jones), Sean Connery (Professor Henry Jones), Denholm Elliott (Marcus Brody), Alison Doody (Dr. Elsa Schneider), John Rhys-Davies (Sallah), Julian Glover (Walter Donovan), River Phoenix (Young Indy), Michael Byrne (Vogel), Kevork Malikyan (Kazim), Robert Eddison (Grail Knight), Richard Young (Fedora), Alexei Sayle (Sulltan), Alex Hyde-White (Young Henry), Paul Maxwell (Panama Hat), Isla Blair (Mrs. Donovan) **Screenwriter:** Jeffrey Boam **Cinematographer:** Douglas Slocombe **Composer:** John Williams **Producer:** Robert Watts for Lucasfilm; released by Paramount **MPAA Rating:** PG-13 **Running Time:** 127 minutes **Format:** VHS, LV **Awards:** Academy Awards, 1989: Sound Effects Editing; Nominations: Original Score (John Williams), Sound; Golden Globes, 1990: Nominations: Supporting Actor (Sean Connery) **Budget:** $39M **Box Office:** $197.2M (domestic gross).

Indiana (Harrison Ford) and his father, Dr. Henry Jones (Sean Connery), find themselves in trouble once again.

Lawrence of Arabia

1962 – David Lean – 🦴🦴🦴🦴

> "Sherif Ali, so long as the Arabs fight tribe against tribe, so long will they be a little people, a silly people— greedy, barbarous, and cruel, as you are."
>
> Lawrence (Peter O'Toole), after Ali kills his guide.

Filmed over an 18-month period in London, Saudi Arabia, Jordan, Spain, and Morocco, David Lean's epic masterpiece about the famous Englishman who united Arab actions in a war for freedom against the Turks is one of the most visually stunning movies ever made. The story of the enigmatic, eccentric T.E. Lawrence (as played by Peter O'Toole and largely based on Lawrence's memoir *The Seven Pillars of Wisdom*) and his incredible quest to become a sort of savior for the Arabs is set against the backdrop of the vast, consuming desert. It is a fascinating tale of an out-of-the-ordinary man who realizes his own greatness, takes it upon himself to become a hero for a land of people to whom he becomes attached, and finally succumbs to his own humanity. The story of a self-appointed prophet, *Lawrence of Arabia* almost reaches the proportions of a biblical epic, a tone that is reinforced by the vast, lonely, ancient setting.

Lean and cinematographer Freddie Young capture beautiful yet hauntingly sprawling vistas of the immense Arabian desert, a place where humans and camels become tiny specks against sandy horizons. The setting, in fact, becomes a sort of character, for it is a mighty and often deadly force that can be challenged only by those with the right fortitude of body and mind. Such a one is Lawrence, whose unique personality and determination raise him to the level of a quasi-religious hero in the eyes of the Arabs. The sequence in which Lawrence goes back to find a lost member of the Arab army, in defiance of the protests of Ali (Omar Sharif), and returns alive—thought impossible by the Arabs—is one of the most effective scenes, dramatizing Lawrence's nature to both the viewer and the Arabs.

Did you know?...

Director David Lean makes a cameo in the film as the motorcyclist who calls out to Lawrence across the Suez Canal.

While the story is a heroic one, it also has its tragic side as Lawrence gets caught up in the importance of his accomplishments and convinces himself that he is not an ordinary human being. Eventually he faces the fact that he is not invincible, first when he is taken by the Turk Bey of Duraa (Jose Ferrer) and beaten, and especially when he realizes that, though he has led the Arabs to take Damascus, the various factions will not unite and live in harmony as he'd hoped. By the end of these events, as Prince Feisal (Alec Guinness) says, everyone is relieved to see him leave. The hero's ascent has run its course, and even T.E. Lawrence is swallowed up by the desert.

The film was fully restored in 1989, restoring cuts and redubbing portions of damaged audio.

British officer T.E. Lawrence (Peter O'Toole) prepares to help his Arab allies by blowing up an enemy train.

Cast: Peter O'Toole (T.E. Lawrence), Alec Guinness (Prince Feisal), Anthony Quinn (Auda abu Tayi), Jack Hawkins (General Allenby), Omar Sharif (Sherif Ali ibn el Kharish), Jose Ferrer (Bey of Deraa), Anthony Quayle (Colonel Harry Brighton), Claude Rains (Mr. Dryden), Arthur Kennedy (Jackson Bentley), John Dimech (Daud), Kenneth Fortescue (Allenby's Aide),

Jack Gwyllim (Club Secretary), I. S. Johar (Gasim), Howard Marion-Crawford (Medical Officer), Hugh Miller (R. A. M. C. Colonel) **Screenwriter:** Robert Bolt, Michael Wilson **Cinematographer:** Freddie Young **Composer:** Maurice Jarre **Producer:** Sam Spiegel for Horizon; released by Columbia Pictures **MPAA Rating:** PG **Running Time:** 216 minutes **Format:** VHS, LV **Awards:** Academy Awards, 1962: Art Direction/Set Decoration—Color, Cinematography—Color (Freddie Young), Director (David Lean), Film Editing, Musical Score (Maurice Jarre), Picture, Sound; Nominations: Actor (Peter O'Toole), Supporting Actor (Omar Sharif), Adapted Screenplay (Robert Bolt); Golden Globe Awards, 1963: Motion Picture—Drama, Director (David Lean), Supporting Actor (Omar Sharif), Cinematography—Color (Freddie Young) **Budget:** $12M **Box Office:** $16.7M (domestic rentals initial release).

The Lives of a Bengal Lancer
1935 – Henry Hathaway – 🐾🐾🐾

"We have ways of making men talk."

the villainous Khan (Douglass Dumbrille)

Balancing the adventure of foiling a native uprising with the drama of a father-son conflict, *The Lives of a Bengal Lancer* is a lesser *Gunga Din*, but is still a pleasing adventure about the British raj. The first plotline supports the authority of British militarism while the second (and more compelling) element undermines it.

In the opening scene, one of the officers of the British forces in northern India is shot by a native sniper. His replacement turns out to be the son of the duty-first colonel (Sir Guy Standing). His two tentmates, McGregor and Forsythe (Gary Cooper and Franchot Tone), eventually befriend him as concern grows among the British that the native chieftain Mohammed Khan (Douglass Dumbrille) plans to unite the surrounding tribes and intercept the forthcoming munitions convoy.

In one of most intriguing scenes, Colonel Stone summons McGregor and Forsythe to his tent, wanting to discuss the welfare of his son. Stone, however, has become so calcified by military tradition that he cannot voice any fatherly concern. He blusters about in the conversation, evading the issue, talking about the quality of various tobaccos and finally questioning Forsythe about his father. The drama of the scene comes entirely from the subtext of the submerged love the colonel cannot express. Back in his own tent, Forsythe is keen enough to tell McGregor that the fault for such estrangement is partly the father's but "partly the system." The natives also see these lapses. They kidnap young Stone

Did you know?...

The novel by Francis Yeats-Brown supplied only the title and the setting. The plot was the invention of the five screenwriters who worked on the project.

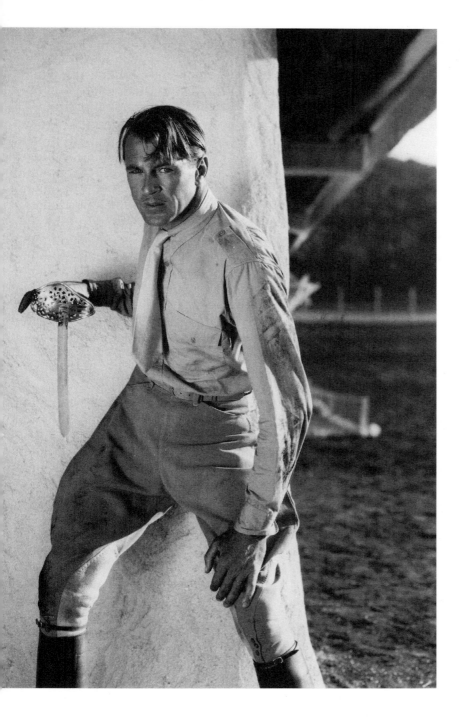

British officer McGregor (Gary Cooper) prepares for battle on the frontier in India.

(Richard Cromwell) in order to coax a rescue mission out in the open. McGregor and Forsythe defy orders, adopt disguises as native peddlers, and attempt to bring back the colonel's son.

Cooper and Tone are enjoyable, but they do not generate anything like the wonderful chemistry that animates the trio of chums in *Gunga Din*. The scenes that show Cooper and Tone becoming friends work well but at a less raucous level than those in the other film. Tone, for example, enjoys irritating Cooper by playing on a snake-charmer's pipe. Unknown to Tone, he is also attracting a cobra that slithers closer and closer. While Tone is frozen in fear and can barely keep playing to prevent the snake's attack, Cooper calmly goes for his gun. The ending of the film also relies on the bond among the comrades-in-arms for much of its force. Captured by the enemy, the friends must endure the torture of burning bamboo under their fingernails. Through their prison bars, they see the powder magazine and begin to design an escape plan. The audience pleasing climax is no surprise, but still effective.

Cast: Gary Cooper (Lieutenant Alan McGregor), Franchot Tone (Lieutenant John Forsythe), Sir Guy Standing (Col. Stone), Richard Cromwell (Lieutenant Donald Stone), C. Aubrey Smith (Major Hamilton), Kathleen Burke (Tania Volkanskaya), Douglass Dumbrille (Mohammed Khan), Monte Blue (Hamzulla Khan), Colin Tapley (Lieutenant Barrett), Akim Tamiroff (Emir of Gopal), J. Carrol Naish (Grand Vizier), Noble Johnson (Ram Singh), Mischa Auer (Afridi), Lumsden Hare (Major General Woodley), James Thomas (Hendricks) **Screenwriter:** Grover Jones, William Slavens McNutt, Waldemar Young, John L. Balderston, Achmed Abdullah **Cinematographer:** Charles Lang **Composer:** Milan Roder **Producer:** Louis D. Lighton for Paramount **Running Time:** 109 minutes **Format:** VHS **Awards:** Academy Awards, 1935, Nominations: Director (Henry Hathaway), Editing, Interior Design, Picture, Screenplay, Sound; National Board of Review Awards 1935: 10 Best Films of the Year.

The Man Who Would Be King
1975 – John Huston – 🦴🦴🦴🦴

> "You call it luck. I call it destiny."
>
> Danny (Sean Connery) to Peachy (Michael Caine)

Director John Huston is as much fascinated by the friendship and camaraderie of his two heroes, Peachy and Danny (Michael Caine and Sean Connery), as he is by their cunning and human frailty. One of the great accomplishments of this adventure epic is the way Huston shares that fascination with the audience. Danny and Peachy are two former sergeants in Victoria's army, circa 1880, still

in India where they had been posted. They meet newspaperman and fellow Mason Rudyard Kipling (Christopher Plummer) and confide in him their plans to cross the nearly impassable stretches to Kafiristan. They intend to use their superior weapons and military training to take over one of the kingdoms and set themselves up as rulers. They even call on Kipling to witness their signed oath.

The easy blend of humor and drama gives the film its warmth. As Peachy and Danny trek across mountains into unchartered areas, a snowy passage collapses, leaving them stranded in the freezing cold. They stoically prepare to die, reminiscing about their adventures and lack of regrets when the echo of their hearty laughter starts an avalanche that creates another passage leading them to safety. It is a perfect piece of plotting, the heroes simultaneously exercising their love of life and friendship and being nearly killed and then saved by these indefatigable traits. Their success in battle with their neophyte tribesmen leads to power, riches, and, of course, temptation. Neither of these blokes is as smart as

Daniel (Sean Connery) declares himself ruler of Kafiristan, with friend Peachy (Michael Caine) as his reluctant adviser.

Did you know?...

Michael Caine's wife Sharika appears as Roxanne. In the wedding scene, Huston coached the nonactress for her closeups by telling her simply to roll her eyes back to suggest fear.

he thinks he is. It is enjoyable to watch them gain power and then to like them all the more for their rascality and growing pride. The dialogue wonderfully captures both the grandiose and ordinary sides of the heroes, as when Danny, acting kingly and full of himself, tells Peachy, "You have our permission to bugger off!"

Huston wanted to film Kipling's short story in 1956 with Humphrey Bogart and Clark Gable, but the death of Bogart delayed the project. He was again returning to the story, this time with Gable and Robert Mitchum, when Gable died. Richard Burton and Marlon Brando (some sources say it was Burton and Peter O'Toole) were then considered for the leads, but Burton's schedule did not give him the necessary time. Paul Newman read and liked Huston's script when it was intended as a vehicle for Newman and Robert Redford, but Newman reportedly suggested casting Caine and Connery in the parts.

Cast: Sean Connery (Daniel Dravot), Michael Caine (Peachy Carnehan), Christopher Plummer (Rudyard Kipling), Saeed Jaffrey (Billy Fish), Doghmi Larbi (Ootah), Jack May (District Commissioner), Karroom Ben Bouih (Kafu-Selim), Mohammad Shamsi (Babu), Albert Moses (Ghulam), Paul Antrim (Mulvaney), Graham Acres (Officer), Shakira Caine (Roxanne) **Screenwriter:** Gladys Hill, John Huston **Cinematographer:** Oswald Morris **Composer:** Maurice Jarre **Producer:** John Foreman for Columbia Pictures **MPAA Rating:** PG **Running Time:** 129 minutes **Format:** VHS, LV, DVD **Awards:** Academy Awards, 1975: Nominations: Adapted Screenplay, Art Direction/Set Decoration, Costume Design, Editing.

Moby Dick

1956 – John Huston –

"To the last I grapple with thee; from hell's heart I stab at thee; for hate's sake I spit my last breath at thee!"

Ahab (Gregory Peck), to the white whale.

Director John Huston's adaptation of Herman Melville's complex classic novel of obsessive revenge has been criticized for its substantial trimming down of Melville's work, but the movie works on a dramatically effective thematic level. Captain Ahab's mad quest to hunt down the white whale that injured him years before is depicted faithfully with an intense performance by Peck. (Peck, however, later spoke of himself as being miscast in the film. He named the director as an ideal choice to play Ahab, and Huston reported that he had at one time thought of his father Walter as a good choice for the part.) The ambiguous yet somehow mystical nature of the whale itself, one of the central issues in the novel, finds its way threaded throughout the film. Consequently, like the novel,

Moby Dick the film becomes not merely a tale of revenge but a tale of an obsessive, against-the-odds, and ultimately foolhardy quest to strike back at the impersonal and uncaring supernatural forces of Nature.

While the epic nature of Ahab's quest drives the story forward and gives the story its dramatic strength, many if not most of the other characterizations lack fully realized personalities. Even Ishmael (Richard Basehart), the narrator, seems only somewhat developed, making it difficult to understand, identify with, or sympathize with him. In the novel, Ishmael is almost as important a character as Ahab, but in this film adaptation he is little more than a narrator, overshadowed by the powerful captain.

An addition to Peck's strong performance and the interesting themes underlying the story, *Moby Dick* includes a number of exciting and suspenseful scenes, particularly those involving the actual hunt of the whale. Huston also does well to incorporate imagery, color, and sound to create an appropriately

It's Captain Ahab (Gregory Peck) vs. the white whale!

Did you know?...

Orson Welles claimed in later interviews that he delivered his sermon as Father Mapple perfectly in one take—fortified by a decanter of spirits that director Huston had left for him in the pulpit.

ominous atmosphere around Ahab and the almost supernatural whale (a 90-foot rubber model that was electronically controlled). Overall, the film has a memorable storyline and is photographed with sufficient artistic skill, but it does not take a great familiarity with Melville's novel to realize that much of the heart of the story has been gutted. Incidentally, the Massachusetts' waterfront portrayed in the movie is actually Youghal, Ireland, while many of the sea-going shots were filmed using the Irish Sea.

Cast: Gregory Peck (Ahab), Richard Basehart (Ishmael), Frederick Ledebur (Queequeg), Leo Genn (Starbuck), Orson Welles (Father Mapple), James Robertson Justice (Captain Boomer), Harry Andrews (Stubb), Bernard Miles (The Manxman), Noel Purcell (Ship's Carpenter), Mervyn Johns (Peleg), Francis De Wolff (Captain Gardiner), Edric Connor (Daggoo), Joseph Tomelty (Peter Coffin), Philip Stainton (Bildad), Seamus Kelly (Flask) **Screenwriter:** Ray Bradbury, John Huston **Cinematographer:** Oswald Morris **Composer:** Philip Stainton **Producer:** Vaughan N. Dean, John Huston for Moulin Productions; released by Warner Bros. **Running Time:** 116 minutes **Format:** VHS **Awards:** National Board of Review Awards, 1956: 10 Best Films of the Year, Director (John Huston); New York Film Critics Awards, 1956: Director (John Huston).

Mutiny on the Bounty
1935 – Frank Lloyd – 🦴🦴🦴🦴

"That's the *Bounty* bound for Tahiti? She isn't very big, is she?"
Byam (Franchot Tone)

"It ain't the size that counts, youngster. It's the salt in the lads that man her."
Old Man on Dock

Some older black and white movies, with their static camera and stylized acting, may be difficult to watch. Others, like *Mutiny on the Bounty*, are true classics. The viewer may have to adjust to this movie since the sound effects and special effects are not what we are accustomed to today. On the other hand, in 1935, a movie had to actually tell a story to hold the viewer's attention, something *Mutiny on the Bounty* does admirably.

Based upon an actual incident in the late eighteenth century, the movie is a study in contrasts. Captain Bligh, vividly portrayed by the distinguished Charles Laughton, is the sadistic, obsessive commander of His Majesty's Ship, *Bounty*. His brutal brand of discipline seems to have no end. He orders flogging for almost any infraction, no matter how minor, even ordering a dead man flogged. A totally despicable character, Bligh is contrasted by Lieutenant Fletcher Christian (Clark Gable), the second in command of the Bounty. His disposition is much more compassionate than the heavy-handed Captain. And the

men, all of them either pressed into the service or prisoners freed to serve on the ship, appreciate Mr. Christian's humanity in dealing with them. This tolerance, of course, creates discord between Christian and Bligh, whose confrontations give the film much of its drama and energy.

The movie's timelessness is also based on history. First, these events changed the way the British Navy operated concerning conduct of officers and seamen toward one another. Second, the simple, easy-to-follow story is a masterful portrayal of antagonist against protagonist. And that simplicity may be one of the biggest drawbacks to today's sophisticated viewer who might demand a little more glitz and razzle dazzle.

Mutiny is based on the first two parts of Charles Nordhoff and James Norman Hall's trilogy, *Mutiny on the Bounty* and *Men Against the Sea*. The Brando remake also included material from the third book, *Pitcairn's Island*.

Fletcher Christian (Clark Gable) discusses life aboard The Bounty with his fellow officers.

Did you know?...

MGM wanted Cary Grant to play the part of Roger Byam, but Paramount would not release him.

Cast: Clark Gable (Fletcher Christian), Charles Laughton (Captain Bligh), Franchot Tone (Roger Byam), Herbert Mundin (Smith), Eddie Quillan (Ellison), Dudley Digges (Baccuus), Donald Crisp (Burkitt), Henry Stephenson (Sir Joseph Banks), Francis Lister (Captain Nelson), Spring Byington (Mrs. Byam), Motiva (Tehanni), Mamo (Maimiti), Byron Russell (Quintal), Percy Warren (Coleman), David Torrence (Lord Hood) **Screenwriter:** Talbot Jennings, Jules Furthman, Carey Wilson **Cinematographer:** Arthur Edeson **Composer:** Herbert Stothart **Producer:** Irving Thalberg for MGM **Running Time:** 132 minutes **Format:** VHS, LV **Awards:** Academy Awards, 1935: Picture; Nominations: Actor (Clark Gable, Franchot Tone, Charles Laughton), Director (Frank Lloyd), Editing, Screenplay, Score; National Board of Review Awards, 1935: 10 Best Films of the Year; New York Film Critics Awards, 1935: Actor (Charles Laughton) **Budget:** $2M.

Raiders of the Lost Ark

1981 – Steven Spielberg – 𝄞𝄞𝄞𝄞

> "You and I are very much alike. Archeology is our religion, yet we have both fallen from the pure faith. Our methods have not differed as much as you pretend. I am but a shadowy reflection of you. It would take only a nudge to make you like me, to push you out of the light."
>
> Belloq (Paul Freeman), to Indiana.

In 1936, adventurous archeologist Indiana Jones sets out on a quest to recover the long-lost Ark of the Covenant before Nazi agents can find the ancient relic and use its mystical power to help Hitler take over the world. Inspired by the adventure serials of the 1940s, executive producer George Lucas and director Steven Spielberg created an endearing swashbuckling character and used a craftily paced style of storytelling that contributed to the film's status as one of the most successful movies of all time (and that led to two blockbuster sequels). The story involves the intrepid Dr. Jones (Harrison Ford) facing peril after peril—from fighting Nazis and evading deadly snakes to rescuing old friends— as he ventures to Egypt to locate the Ark in an ancient lost city, but it is not this continuous excitement alone that makes *Raiders of the Lost Ark* such an enjoyable romp.

Rounded characters, strong performances, clever dialogue, well-placed humor, and fine-tuned pacing (enhanced by John Williams' memorable, rousing music) raise the film above standard adventure movie fare.

Basing his approach on comic books like the "Green Lantern" and the movie serials that originally inspired George Lucas to co-write the story, director Spielberg demonstrates his strengths—particularly his visual talent—at their best in this, his third blockbuster film (after *Jaws* and *Close Encounters of the Third Kind*). Spielberg knows how to create powerful images and is a master of editing action sequences capable of keeping viewers on the edges of their seats.

Many of these sequences, including scenes of Dr. Jones running from a huge boulder, falling into a pit of cobras, and single-handedly taking control of a speeding truck carrying the Ark, are both outrageous and, for the moment, completely believable. Yet with the help of Ford's portrayal of Indiana Jones, *Raiders* also demonstrates Spielberg's ability to fashion memorable, well-developed characters, a quality absent from some of his later films such as *Jurassic Park*.

Indiana Jones (Harrison Ford) prepares to take some precious cargo.

While Indiana Jones by no means lives a normal life, his character comes across as an average, decent person, an Everyman type who simply tries to do his job but repeatedly finds himself in perilous trouble. He also has the added depth of a skeptical yet principled agnostic who has been many places, seen much, and views the world with just a touch of sarcasm. Through the course of the story, he makes something of an intellectual journey as well as a physical one, realizing by the end of the film that the Ark and what it represents are more than just part of a Sunday School story he was taught in his youth.

Tom Selleck was the first choice as Jones and opted out, providing great good fortune for Ford. On the whole, this first installment of the Indiana Jones series may not be much more than very well-crafted entertainment with interesting characters and a few ruminations on the reality of the supernatural, but such entertainment rarely succeeds on as many levels.

Cast: Harrison Ford (Indiana Jones), Karen Allen (Marion Ravenwood), Paul Freeman (Rene Belloq), Ronald Lacey (Toht), John Rhys-Davies (Sallah), Denholm Elliot (Marcus Brody), Alfred Molina (Sapito), Wolf Kahler (Dietrich), Anthony Higgins (Gobler), Vic Tablian (Barranca/ Monkey Man), Don Fellows (Colonel Musgrove), William Hootkins (Major Eaton), Bill Reimbold (Bureaucrat), Fred Sorenson (Jock), Patrick Durkin (Australian Climber) **Screenwriter:** George, Lucas, Philip Kaufman, Lawrence Kasdan **Cinematographer:** Douglas Slocombe **Composer:** John Williams **Producer:** Frank Marshall for Paramount **MPAA Rating:** PG **Running Time:** 115 minutes **Format:** VHS, LV **Awards:** Academy Awards, 1981: Art Direction/Set Decoration, Film Editing, Sound, Visual Effects; Nominations: Cinematography (Douglas Slocombe), Director (Steven Spielberg), Picture, Score (John Williams); People's Choice Awards, 1982: Best Film **Budget:** $20M **Box Office:** $242.37M (domestic gross).

The Right Stuff
1983 – Philip Kaufman – 𝄞𝄞𝄞𝄞

> "Who's the best pilot I ever saw? You're lookin' at him."
>
> Gordon Cooper (Dennis Quaid)

The Right Stuff covers the American space program from October 1947, when Chuck Yeager (Sam Shepard) broke the sound barrier in his X-1 to the flight of the last Mercury astronaut, Gordon Cooper (Dennis Quaid). The spills, the thrills, and the chills are all right there for everyone to see. While Hollywood has made many space movies, only two come to mind that are based on factual events—*Apollo 13* and *The Right Stuff*.

All of the actors who portray astronauts are noteworthy—Charles Frank as Scott Carpenter, Lance Henriksen as Wally Schirra, Scott Paulin as Deke Slay-

ton, Fred Ward as Gus Grissom, Quaid as Gordon Cooper, Ed Harris as John Glenn, and Scott Glenn as Alan Shepard. The casting seems to have been done with equal attention to the actors' physical resemblance to the people they are playing and to their performing skills. Both work to the advantage of the film. The nature of the saga also requires them to handle various scenes with both comic and dramatic elements, which they do quite well. Sometimes they must

The seven Mercury astronauts prepare for a mission.

work as an ensemble and sometimes in isolation, as when John Glenn orbits the earth in *Friendship 7*. In addition, Sam Shepard gives a great performance as Yeager, and Donald Moffat looks and acts like Lyndon Johnson, though the film risks making Johnson into something of a caricature, when he is shown throwing fits and routinely misunderstanding scientists with German accents. The test pilots in the early scenes also believably capture the rowdiness and camaraderie of men in a dangerous situation, sounding at times as if they are stepping off a hay wagon on their way to a barn dance. Into this drawl comes Jack Ridley, one of Yeager's buddies, played nicely by Levon Helm, the drummer for *The Band* (he also played Loretta Lynn's father in *Coal Miner's Daugher*). It's interesting to note that an earlier screenplay by William Goldman omitted Yeager.

The memorable cinematography by Caleb Deschanel can be seen, for example, in the dramatic opening sequence that shows an early attempt to break the sound barrier, a scene that begins with black-and-while film stock and ends in color. The long shot of the astronauts in their gear coming down the corridor toward the camera is inspiring in its simplicity. Bill Conti's award-winning music combines with that of Gustav Holst to produce a memorable score. *The Right Stuff* draws upon the dynamics of danger, heroism, and companionship to produce a fascinating story.

Cast: Sam Shepard (Chuck Yeager), Scott Glenn (Alan Shepard), Ed Harris (John Glenn), Dennis Quaid (Gordon Cooper), Fred Ward (Gus Grissom), Barbara Hershey (Glennis Yeager), Kim Stanley (Pancho Barnes), Veronica Cartwright (Betty Grissom), Pamela Reed (Trudy Cooper), Scott Paulin (Deke Slayton), Charles Frank (Scott Carpenter), Lance Henriksen (Walter Schirra), Donald Moffat (Lyndon Johnson), Levon Helm (Jack Ridley), Mary Jo Deschanel (Annie Glenn), Scott Wilson (Scott Crossfield), Kathy Baker (Louise Shepard), Mickey Crocker (Marge Slayton), Susan Kase (Rene Carpenter), Mittie Smith (Jo Schirra), Royal Dano (Minister), Jeff Goldblum (Recruiter), Harry Shearer (Recruiter), Jane Dornacker (Nurse Murch), Eric Sevareid (Himself), John Dehner (Henry Luce), Chuck Yeager (Fred) **Screenwriter:** Philip Kaufman **Cinematographer:** Caleb Deschanel **Composer:** Bill Conti **Producer:** Robert Chartoff and Irwin Winkler for Warner Bros. **MPAA Rating:** PG **Running Time:** 193 minutes **Format:** VHS, LV **Awards:** Academy Awards, 1983: Editing, Sound, Original Score; Nominations: Art Direction/Set Direction, Cinematography, Picture, Supporting Actor (Sam Shepard) **Box Office:** $21.5M.

The Road Warrior

1981 – George Miller – 𝄢𝄢𝄢

If you're looking for a dialogue-driven movie, *The Road Warrior* is not it. If you want action and base violence, this is definitely the one for you. Set in the post-nuclear world, the film chronicles the adventures of a man who drives the highways in search of fuel for his hopped-up car. And since gasoline is a very scarce commodity, his life is pretty full with just that task. It's a very cold and cruel existence. The roads are prowled by gangs who seek to rule and kill anyone driving something with gas they can steal. Max (Mel Gibson) is sort of a one-man gang, doing the same thing only as an independent agent. He meets a man who has a gyrocopter (Bruce Spence) and is taken to a refinery, perhaps the only one left in existence. The bad guys also want it and Max makes a deal with the refiners. If Max can have all the gas that he can carry, he'll get them a truck so that they can haul their gas past the villains to safety and a better life. Max is finally persuaded to drive the tanker himself.

What makes *The Road Warrior* an epic? It depicts the epic nature of a great struggle. Even in the future, these good guys and the bad guys are differentiated. But in this film, not only is the real conflict man against man, it is also man against nature, since the movie is set in a desert wasteland and survival must be won not only against the villains but also against the harsh reality of the desert.

The Road Warrior emphasizes action to the near-exclusion of all else. This early performance by Gibson showcases him in a totally different light than the character-driven films like *The Year of Living Dangerously*, *Forever Young* and *The Man Without a Face*. *The Road Warrior* is also the second of three movies Gibson made playing this same character. The first one was *Mad Max* (1979), in which he portrays a post-apocalyptic cop out to avenge the death of his wife and kid. The third one is *Mad Max: Beyond Thunderdome* (1985) in which Max becomes a gladiator, is harrassed by Tina Turner, abandoned in the desert, and rescued by feral orphans. Note that director George Miller is not the George Miller of *The Man from Snowy River*, but is the George Miller of *The Witches of Eastwick*.

Cast: Mel Gibson (Max), Bruce Spence (The Gyro Captain), Michael Preston (Poppagallo), Max Phipps (The Toadie), Vernon Wells (Wez), Kjell Nilsson (The Humungus), Emil Minty

"You want to get out of here, you talk to me."
Max (Mel Gibson)

Did you know?...
All of the dialogue in the film would fill approximately twelve to fifteen minutes of screen time.

Max (Mel Gibson) and his dog are temporarily without transportation as they walk a deserted outback highway.

(The Feral Kid), Virginia Hey (Warrior Woman), William Zappa (Zetta), Arkie Whiteley (The Captain's Girl), Steve J. Spears (Mechanic), Syd Heylan (The Curmudgeon), Moire Claux (Big Rebecca), David Downer (Nathan), David Slingsby (Quiet Man), Kristoffer Greaves (Mechanic's Assistant), Max Fairchild (Broken Victim), Tyler Coppin (Defiant Victim), Jimmy Brown (Golden Youth), Tony Deary (Grinning Mohawker) **Screenwriter:** Terry Hayes, George Miller, Brian Hannant **Cinematographer:** Dean Semler **Composer:** Brian May **Producer:** Byron Kennedy for Warner Bros. **MPAA Rating:** R **Running Time:** 94 minutes **Format:** VHS, LV, DVD **Awards:** Los Angeles Film Critics Association Award, 1982: Foreign Film **Budget:** $4M.

Rob Roy

1995 – Michael Caton-Jones –

Revenge is a powerful motivator in this classic tale of good versus evil. Set in the Scottish Highlands in the early 1700s, this is a story about a common man in uncommon circumstances. Due to treachery and murder, McGregor (Liam Neeson) finds that all he once counted as his is now gone except for his family, who have been violated and burned out of their home.

McGregor sets out to restore his good name and right the wrongs done him by Archibald Cunningham, portrayed in an evil but believable way by Tim Roth. In the process, he sees his family lose their home and land, and he hides them high up in the mountains. McGregor then loses a brother, gains a wife pregnant with Cunningham's child (by rape, of course), gets caught, beaten, dragged behind horses, and nearly hanged. Still, he overcomes the odds, and gets the final opportunity to carry out his revenge.

The use of firearms in the movie probably restricts the violence to some relatively bloodless gunplay rather than the shots of heads and arms being liberally lopped off that often occur in period films. Crudeness is not absent, however. The sound of urination competes with that of flatulence, and the rawness of the historical period is suggested by the many crude references to women, sex, and various body parts.

John Hurt does a capable job as Lord Montrose, the snide benefactor of Cunningham. In fact, it is Montrose's desire to harm another nobleman that initially gets McGregor into trouble. Jessica Lange plays the part of Rob Roy's wife with much passion; her versatility and depth capture both her character's devotion to her husband and her spirit of independence. Thanks to Lange's fine work, Mary carries the film in a few places. The Celtic music and breathtaking cinematography are also used quite effectively in creating the period flavor and epic scope of the film.

Cast: Liam Neeson (Rob Roy), Jessica Lange (Mary), John Hurt (Marquis of Montrose), Tim Roth (Cunningham), Eric Stoltz (Alan McDonald), Andrew Keir (Duke of Argyll), Brian Cox (Killearn), Brian McCardie (Alasdair), Gilbert Martin (Guthrie), Vicki Masson (Betty), Gilly Gilchrist (Iain), Jason Flemyng (Gregor), Ewan Stewart (Coll), David Hayman (Sibbald), Brian McArthur (Ranald), David Brooks Palmer (Duncan), Myra McFadyen (Tinker Woman), Karen

> "Women are the heart of honour and we cherish and protect it in them. You must never mistreat a woman or malign a man, nor stand by and see another do so."
>
> Rob Roy (Liam Neeson) to his son.

Did you know?...

The film was shot on location in the Scottish Highlands by cinematographer Karl Walter Lindenlaub (a friend of director Caton-Jones from their days in film school).

Rob Roy MacGregor (Liam Neeson) and wife Mary (Jessica Lange) share a tender moment.

Matheson (Ceilidh Singer), Shirley Henderson (Morag), John Murtagh (Referee), Bill Gardiner (Tavern Lad), Valentine Nwanze (Servant Boy), Richard Bonehill (Guthrie's Opponent) **Screenwriter:** Alan Sharp **Cinematographer:** Karl Walter Lindenlaub, Roger Deakins (uncredited) **Composer:** Carter Burwell **Producer:** Peter Broughan and Richard Jackson for Talisman Productions; released by United Artists **MPAA Rating:** R **Running Time:** 139 minutes **Format:** VHS **Awards:** Academy Awards, 1995: Nominations: Supporting Actor (Tim Roth); British Academy Awards, 1995: Supporting Actor (Tim Roth); Golden Globe Awards, 1996: Nominations: Supporting Actor (Tim Roth) **Budget:** $28M **Box Office:** $31.5M.

Rocky

1976 – John G. Avildsen –

The success and appeal of *Rocky* lies largely in its simple yet moving story of challenging the odds. The story of making *Rocky* is a lot like the movie script. Sylvester Stallone, with bit parts in several movies but no career, wrote the story, his 33rd attempted screenplay and submitted it, stipulating that he play the lead. Producers balked, looking at other, more bankable leads, but Stallone held his ground. Much like the boxer himself, the movie went the distance, coming out of nowhere to win best picture at the Academy Awards.

Rocky Balboa (Stallone) is a poor, well-liked, decent man who boxes for extra money to make ends meet. He gets the opportunity to prove himself when offered the chance to fight the famous world champion Apollo Creed (Carl Weathers). Although no one, especially Creed and his promoters (who conceive of the match as a publicity event), expects Rocky to have even a remote chance of defeating the world champion, Rocky decides to seize the opportunity to prove to himself and to others that he is capable of becoming more than his disadvantaged, humble origins would seem to allow for him.

A simple, honest, hardworking Everyman type who wonders whether he is capable of escaping the lot that life has cast at him, Rocky seizes upon a dream and embarks on a quest to prove his ability to withstand unbeatable odds. Holding his own against Creed all the way to the fight's finish is what matters to him, not winning. In his quest to prepare himself for the grand battle, Rocky finds a trainer and mentor in Mickey (Burgess Meredith), a wise, gruff old man who recognizes that Rocky has the heart of a winner. Along the way, Rocky also finds love with the shy but intelligent Adrian (Talia Shire), a woman he helps out of her reclusive, sheltered life. In return, she helps fill the gaps in his life and becomes an anchor of support for him. The scenes in which Rocky and Adrian draw closer together, such as their first date when Rocky takes Adrian ice skating, provide some of the most interesting and touching moments in the story, for with all their opposite qualities it is clear that the two really do complement each other.

Rocky is in many ways a mythic hero. The love story with Adrian and the mentor-student relationship with Mickey are archetypal staples of the classic

> "It don't really matter if I lose this fight. It don't really matter if this guy opens my head again, 'cause all I wanna do is go the distance. Nobody's ever gone the distance with Creed, and if I can go that distance, see that the bell rings and I'm still standing, I'll know for the first time in my life I'm not just another bum from the neighborhood."
>
> Rocky (Sylvester Stallone) to Adrian (Talia Shire).

A battered Rocky (Sylvester Stallone) with his beloved Adrian (Talia Shire).

Did you know?...

Producers wanted a more bankable name in the lead, and they offered Stallone $150,000 to allow Ryan O'Neal to play the part. When Stallone sold the movie rights, however, he had stipulated that he would play the role.

quest tale, and, in the end, as simple as the story may be, it is ultimately satisfying in that it demonstrates the idea that anybody, regardless of origins, background, or situation, can seize upon a dream and pursue it to its fulfillment.

Cast: Sylvester Stallone (Rocky Balboa), Talia Shire (Adrian), Burt Young (Paulie), Carl Weathers (Apollo Creed), Burgess Meredith (Mickey), Thayer David (Jergens), Joe Spinell (Gazzo), Jimmy Gambina (Mike), Bill Baldwin (Flight Announcer), Aldo Silvani (Cut Man), George Memmoli (Ice Rink Attendant), Jodi Letizia (Marie), Diana Lewis (TV Commentator), George O'Hanlon (TV Commentator), Larry Carroll (TV Interviewer) **Screenwriter:** Sylvester Stallone **Cinematographer:** James Crabe **Composer:** Bill Conti **Producer:** Robert Chartoff and Irwin Winkler for United Artists **MPAA Rating:** PG **Running Time:** 119 minutes **Format:** VHS, LV, DVD **Awards:** Academy Awards, 1976: Director (John G. Avildsen), Film Editing, Picture; Nominations: Actor (Sylvester Stallone), Actress (Talia Shire), Song, Sound, Supporting Actor (Burgess Meredith, Burt Young), Original Screenplay (Sylvester Stallone); Directors Guild of America, 1976: Director (John G. Avildsen); Golden Globe Awards, 1977: Film—Drama; Los Angeles Film Critics Association Awards, 1976: Film; National Board of Review Awards, 1976: 10 Best Films of the Year, Supporting Actress (Talia Shire); New York Film Critics Awards, 1976: Supporting Actress (Talia Shire) **Budget:** $1M **Box Office:** $117M.

The Sea Hawk
1940 – Michael Curtiz – 🦴🦴🦴🦴

Reuniting many of the principals of *The Adventures of Robin Hood*, this attempt to recapture the magic of that classic works almost as well as its predecessor. This time the mythic elements (at least in the first hour) give the film the trappings of a David-and-Goliath-at-sea story. Elizabeth I (Flora Robson) grants tacit approval for Captain Geoffrey Thorpe (Errol Flynn) and other English buccaneers to plunder the ships of the Spanish Armada. The first action sequence depicts Thorpe and his men boarding a Spanish galleass to free English prisoners used as slave oarsmen. After the Spanish and English return to the British royal court, Elizabeth must sympathize in public with the indignant Spaniards demanding restitution while in private she sanctions further piracy with an admirable Machiavellian evasion: "Captain Thorpe, if you undertook such a venture [of piracy] you would do so without the approval of England . . . However, you would take with you the grateful affection of Elizabeth."

For the most part, director Michael Curtiz favors a transparent style. Occasionally he indulges in a flourish, such as the looming shadows Flynn and Henry

"You forget, Don Alvarez, the queen need justify nothing."
Elizabeth (Flora Robson) to Alvarez.

Swashbuckling Geoffrey Thorpe
(Errol Flynn) prepares for another
sword fight.

Did you know?...

Release prints in England
included a closing speech by
Flora Robson as Elizabeth I on
the necessity of preparing a
nation for war. Though she
named the threat of the Spanish
Armada, contemporary audiences
would have heard a warning
about Nazi Germany: "I pledge
you . . . a navy foremost in the
world—not only in our time, but
in generations to come."

Daniell cast on the walls during the climactic rapier fight (a similar effect occurs in Curtiz's *Robin Hood*). Earlier, when Thorpe starts the English revolt aboard a Spanish ship, Curtiz creates a good effect by having one of the Spanish lords glimpse Thorpe's reflection on the surface of his gold goblet.

The Sea Hawk sorely misses the charms of Flynn's leading lady Olivia de Havilland, who sought more ambitious parts after her success in *Gone with the Wind*. As a result, the film has less romance and glamour than *Robin Hood*, but it compensates in part with an emphasis on intrigue and the chess game of national politics. In the middle scenes, after Thorpe has been captured, the Spanish ambassador Don Alvarez (Claude Rains) gloats when he confronts Elizabeth with the results of her scheming. The Queen blusters ("Do you question my word?"), but Alvarez, the master politician, remains calm: "Unfortunately, your grace, my government cannot reconcile your words with the acts of your subjects." *Robin Hood* is the more uplifting and idealistic adventure epic while *The Sea Hawk* is more sly, more knowing about human nature. *Robin Hood* shows us heroes as they should be; *The Sea Hawk* shows us heroes as they are.

Cast: Errol Flynn (Geoffrey Thorpe), Brenda Marshall (Doña Maria), Claude Rains (Don Jose Alvarez de Córdoba), Donald Crisp (Sir John Burleson), Flora Robson (Queen Elizabeth), Alan Hale (Carl Pitt), Henry Daniell (Lord Wolfingham), Una O'Connor (Miss Latham), James Stephenson (Abbott), Gilbert Roland (Captain López), William Lundigan (Danny Logan), Julien Mitchell (Oliver Scott), Montagu Love (King Philip II), Edgar Buchanan (Ben Rollins), Halliwell Hobbes (Astronomer) **Screenwriter:** Howard Koch, Seton I. Miller **Cinematographer:** Sol Polito **Composer:** Erich Wolfgang Korngold **Producer:** Hal B. Wallis for Warner Bros. **Running Time:** 127 minutes VHS, LV **Awards:** Academy Awards, 1940: Interior Decoration, Sound, Score **Budget:** $1.7M.

The Three Musketeers
1974 – Richard Lester – 🦴🦴

Of course, any movie based on a work by Alexandre Dumas should be considered at the very least a potential classic. Possibly an epic. But this version of *The Three Musketeers*, while not lacking in the qualities of an epic—such as its sweeping tale of heroic deeds told with fine production values—loses out in other areas. The story describes the attempts of three daring swashbucklers (Richard Chamberlain, Oliver Reed and Frank Finlay) and a young man who is a swashbuck-

Rochefort (Christopher Lee) escorts Kitty (Nicole Calfan) and Milady (Faye Dunaway).

ler wannabe (Michael York) to save the honor of the Queen of France (Geraldine Chaplin). The Queen is in love, not with the King of France (Jean-Pierre Cassel), but with the Duke of Buckingham (Simon Ward), and is being blackmailed by Cardinal Richelieu (Charlton Heston). A great quest ensues involving daring swordplay—one of the fights takes place in a laundry—and international intrigue.

To be fair, it must be mentioned that *The Three Musketeers* received some very good reviews. One of its strong points is the classic story from which it is drawn. Another is the great cast. Reed, York, and Chamberlain are all very enjoyable to watch, Raquel Welch gives perhaps the best performance of her career, and the film represents one of the few times that Charlton Heston played a villain. (Director Richard Lester first offered Heston the part played by Oliver Reed, but when Heston balked at the long shooting schedule necessary for such a central role, Lester sold him on the idea of playing a villain and coordinated all of Heston's scenes into eight days of work.)

Did you know?...

Parts of the sequel, *The Four Musketeers* were being filmed simultaneously with the same cast. Sources vary as to whether two films were intended at the outset or originally planned as one longer film.

Unfortunately, slapstick and swashbuckling prove funny only for a while. The humor derives in part from the contrast of putting physical comedy into the lavish settings of a big-budget adventure film performed by big-name stars. At times the believability of the story risks getting lost in all the pratfalls. In one scene, a man carrying several trays of eggs manages to dodge a dozen or so wine barrels rolling off a wagon only then to trip over his own feet and land face first in the eggs. In a scene from the sequel, a battle overworks the joke of the musketeers trying to throw back bombs hurled by the enemy before they explode. On the whole, the film is an odd mixture of Dumas meeting the Three Stooges—Larry, Moe, and Charlton.

Cast: Michael York (D'Artagnan), Oliver Reed (Athos), Richard Chamberlain (Aramis), Frank Finlay (Porthos), Faye Dunaway (Milady de Winter), Raquel Welch (Madame Bonancieux), Charlton Heston (Cardinal Richelieu), Geraldine Chaplin (Anna of Austria), Jean-Pierre Cassel (King of France), Joss Ackland (D'Artagnan's Father), Sybil Danning (Eugenie), Christopher Lee (Rochefort), Roy Kinnear (Planchet), Simon Ward (Duke of Buckingham), Spike Milligan (M. Bonancieux) **Screenwriter:** George MacDonald Fraser **Cinematographer:** David Watkin **Composer:** Michel Legrand **Producer:** Alexander Salkind and Ilya Salkind for Twentieth Century Fox **MPAA Rating:** PG **Running Time:** 105 minutes **Format:** VHS **Awards:** Golden Globe Awards, 1975: Actress—Musical/Comedy (Raquel Welch).

> "You will find, young man, that the future looks rosier at the bottom of a glass."
> Athos (Oliver Reed)

Yojimbo

1961 — Akira Kurosawa — 🦴🦴🦴🦴

When a samurai drifter walks into a nineteenth-century village, he sees a dog trotting down the center of the street with a severed human hand in its mouth. In what is often referred to as the most accessible of Japanese films and the basis for the spaghetti western *A Fistful of Dollars*, *Yojimbo* builds on this early image to produce a blackly comic, insightful film. The samurai discovers more about the town when one side of two feuding factions tries to recruit him to orchestrate the defeat of the other. Sanjuro the samurai (Toshiro Mifune) cautiously hears them out, but he and the viewers can soon tell that both sides are equally corrupt. Sanjuro masterfully works both sides against each other and eventually eliminates the two warring factions.

Mifune's star performance provides a focal point for the audience. His skeptical, amused, and cynical looks become the gauge by which the audience

> "Two coffins. No, maybe three."
> Sanjuro (Toshiro Mifune) the samurai, to the coffin-maker after a brief skirmish with gang members.

measures the corruption of one feuding faction (dealing in gambling) and the other (dealing in prostitution). His amusement at the venality of the townspeople increases identification with him. After hearing the sum offered up front by one side, he eavesdrops on a family meeting in which the mother tells her reluctant son that he will save the family the other half of the promised money if he kills Sanjuro as soon as the samurai dispatches their rivals. Sanjuro initially quits at the moment the two gangs confront each other and watches in amusement from a tower as the cowards from both sides alternately approach and retreat in their mock battle. The later scene in which Sanjuro gulls the opposite faction is also impressive: he first reports that all six men guarding a woman they have kid-napped are dead so that the watchman will run off to find the boss; then, he masterfully kills these six guards and directs the woman home to her family. Mifune has all the details right to suggest a man totally confident of his skills: the assured sweep of his arm in sheathing his sword, his ever-present toothpick, and the fury and precision of his sword fighting.

Did you know?...

Director Akira Kurosawa made a sequel with Toshiro Mifune, *Sanjuro.*

When a note of thanks from the woman's family falls into the hands of the gang who kidnapped her, they severely beat Sanjuro. Kurosawa finds the right time to darken the tone of the film from the bemused observations about the costs of social corruption to a story of recovery and a genuine battle for survival between Sanjuro and both factions. *Yojimbo* remains one of Akira Kurosawa's most entertaining, intriguing works.

Cast: Toshiro Mifune (Sanjuro Kuwabatake), Eijiro Tono (Gonji the Sake Seller), Kamatari Fujiwara (Tazaemon), Takasji Shimura (Tokuemon), Seizaburo Kawazu (Seibei), Isuzu Yamada (Orin), Hiroshi Tachikawa (Yoichiro), Kyu Sazanka (Ushitora), Tatsuya Nakadai (Unosuke), Daisuke Kato (Inokichi), Ikio Sawamura (Hansuke), Ko Nishimura (Kuma), Yoshio Tsuchiya (Kohei), Yoko Tsukasa (Nui), Susumu Fujita (Homma) **Screenwriter:** Ryuzo Kikushima, Akira Kurosawa **Cinematographer:** Kazuo Miyagawa **Composer:** Masaru Sato **Producer:** Ryuzo Kikushima, Tomoyuki Tanaka **Running Time:** 110 minutes **Format:** VHS, LV **Awards:** Academy Awards, 1961: Nomination: Costume Design.

They Might Be Giants . . .

Any effort to determine the first screen epic would probably become hopelessly trapped in argument and fun, but as good a case as any can be made for the fourteen-minute 1902 film by Georges Melies, *A Trip to the Moon*, adapted from a novel by Jules Verne. Melies can be considered the first style-conscious filmmaker, though his imagination was always concerned with setting and mise-en-scene in a theatrical rather than a cinematic way. His primitive film of thirty short scenes shows an intrepid group of explorers building their space capsule, entering it, and firing it out of a cannon toward the moon. The scene in which it plops into the eye of the man-in-the-moon has become one of the most famous film stills in history. Once there, the astronomers discover snowstorms, mushrooms, and living creatures (really acrobats from the Folies Bergere, according to film historian David A. Cook). They escape the clutches of the moon creatures and their king and return home as heroes. Home Box Office and Tom Hanks, in a fitting conclusion to *From the Earth to the Moon* (1998), their twelve-chapter mini-series about the history of the American space program, re-enacted the creation of Melies' film as a tribute to the imaginative spirit that led man to the moon.

BIBLICAL

Ben-Hur

1959 – William Wyler – 𝄞𝄞𝄞𝄞

Director William Wyler, who had worked on the 1925 silent production, always joked about the way *Ben-Hur* ruined him with elite film critics. Jan Herman, in his 1995 biography of Wyler, *A Talent for Trouble*, reports that as *Ben-Hur* racked up a sizable pile of awards and money, many French film critics who had praised the subtlety of Wyler's polished character dramas now turned their backs on him for selling out. Though it was a departure for him, Wyler worked hard to make this epic lifelike as well as spectacular, and was helped by a committee of uncredited screenwriters, including Gore Vidal, Christopher Fry, Maxwell Anderson, and S.N. Behrman.

Wyler griped about having to frame his compositions in such wide dimensions for the Cinemascope widescreen format, complaining that the extreme width of the frame took in everything important and unimportant and eventually caused the audience's eye to wander. His reservations notwithstanding, the film has numerous examples of beautifully designed shots that utilize space in dramatic ways. These include the many views of soldiers marching across the horizon, obligatory stuff for spectacle films. Other compositions also stand out. In one, Ben-Hur stands silently in the entrance to the cavernous arena after the chariot race, the camera framing both his meditative foreground figure and the massive Circus Maximus where minutes before he and Messala had competed. In another set in the valley of the lepers, Ben-Hur cringes heartbroken before a boulder to the left of the frame while he listens to Esther (Haya Harareet) speak to his disease-stricken mother (Martha Scott) and sister (Cathy O'Donnell) in the middleground. In another, the emperor crowns him with the laurel while the background is filled with thousands of cheering spectators. The evidence suggests that Wyler solved the problems of the 65mm screen admirably.

Another problem Wyler solved was Charlton Heston's tendency towards inexpressive acting (Cesare Danova had originally been announced as the star and Kirk Douglas had wanted to play the title role, but when offered the part of Messala instead, he turned the gig down). Heston wrote in his diary (again, one of biographer Jan Herman's sources) that Wyler came to him early during filming and told him his performance wasn't good enough. Heston reminded him

Did you know?...

The son of famed stuntman Yakima Canutt doubled for Heston in the chariot race. An accident occurred when his chariot hit some debris and flipped him forward. He managed to catch himself half-in and half-out of the chariot and crawl back in. The shot was left in the picture.

that they had just finished a picture that Wyler was happy with. The director replied that this role was more demanding than the villain he had played in *The Big Country*. With sometimes as many as sixteen takes per shot, Wyler eventually got from his star what he wanted. Heston duly recorded the change in his diary: "Either I've actually improved, which is a happy thought, or Willy's given up, which is contrary to nature." Consequently, unlike his epics with De Mille, Heston's work with Wyler shows a distinctive range of emotions, and his face has never been so expressive. Ben-Hur's amused reactions to the Arab who plays with his horses like pet dogs and his companionable belch after their meal humanize this ancient hero. His pained face on seeing his leprous mother, his realization, as he gives water to Jesus, that this was the one who had earlier tended to him, and his final amazement on seeing his mother and sister miraculously healed are striking moments that speak well for the director's and actor's abilities to portray the intimate aspects of what may be the most famous epic of all.

Ben-Hur (Charlton Heston) tries to win the chariot race.

Cast: Charlton Heston (Judah Ben-Hur), Stephen Boyd (Messala), Jack Hawkins (Quintas Arrius), Haya Harareet (Esther), Hugh Griffith (Shiek Ilderim), Martha Scott (Miriam), Sam Jaffe (Simonides), Cathy O'Donnell (Tizrah), Finlay Currie (Balthasar), Frank Thring (Pontius Pilate), Terence Longdon (Drusus), George Relph (Tiberius), Andre Morell (Sextus), Claude Heater (Jesus), Maxwell Shaw (rower number 43), Noel Sheldon (centurion) **Screenwriter:** Karl Tunberg **Cinematographer:** Robert Surtees **Composer:** Miklos Rozsa **Producer:** Sam Zimbalist for MGM **Running Time:** 212 minutes **Format:** VHS, LV **Awards:** Academy Awards, 1959: Actor (Charlton Heston), Art Direction/Set Decoration, Color Cinematography, Costume Design (Color), Director (William Wyler), Editing, Picture, Sound, Special Effects, Supporting Actor (Hugh Griffith), Original Dramatic/Comedy Score (Miklos Rozsa); Nominations: Adapted Screenplay; British Academy Awards, 1959: Film; Directors Guild of America Awards 1959: Director (William Wyler); Golden Globe Awards, 1960: Director (William Wyler), Film—Drama, Supporting Actor (Stephen Boyd); New York Film Critics Awards, 1959: Film **Budget:** $12-$15M (reportedly the most expensive film to that time) **Box Office:** $70-$76M (worldwide).

The Bible

1966 – John Huston – 🧦🧦

> " . . . .the animals and I struck up a fine relationship."
>
> Director John Huston on his decision to play Noah.

The idea for a film about the Bible was hardly an original one. Various biblical stories have been adapted for both stage and screen, but thankfully John Huston's three-hour account of that all-time best-selling book ends with Genesis, chapter twenty-two.

The movie begins with a very dark yet spectacular rendition of the Creation and creeps along to cover the banishment of Adam and Eve (Michael Parks and Ulla Bergryd) from the Garden of Eden and the story of Cain and Abel (Richard Harris and Franco Nero). Noah's Ark and the story of Abraham and Sarah (George C. Scott and Ava Gardner) receive the most time with briefer segments on the Tower of Babel, Sodom, and Hagar and Ishmael (Zoe Sallis and Luciano Conversi) thrown in for good measure. The film remains reasonably true to the source material, but some artistic license is exercised when Sarah recites a passage from the Song of Solomon (yet to exist) and Abraham, on his way to sacrifice Isaac (Alberto Lucantoni), gives an angry soliloquy that sounds more Shakespearean than biblical.

Did you know?...

The Bible was originally intended to be a fourteen-hour epic covering selections from the Old and New Testaments and including segments directed by directors including Orson Welles and Federico Fellini.

The proportions of *The Bible* are truly epic. Filmed on location in Italy and Africa, the desert scenes are expansive with abundant nomadic extras and plenty of goats. Noah's Ark is titanic and, with a little help from Yahweh, unsinkable.

Eve (Ulla Bergryd) tempts Adam (Michael Parks) with some forbidden fruit.

Although it disrupts the flow of the film with its vague and confusing presence, the tower of Babel is still most impressive as is King Nimrod's stylized eye makeup. However, time has drained much of the shock from the Sodom and Gomorrah sequence. While many of the special effects continue to work, the characters aren't nearly as convincing. John Huston's Noah provides much needed comic relief at times and is delightful to watch, Ava Gardner very touchingly captures the sadness and shame of barrenness, and Peter O'Toole is mysterious and ethereal as the three angels. But the remainder of the cast is alternately cardboard or melodramatic.

Cast: Michael Parks (Adam), Ulla Bergryd (Eve), Richard Harris (Cain), John Huston (Noah), Stephen Boyd (Nimrod), George C. Scott (Abraham), Ava Gardner (Sarah), Peter O'Toole (the Three Angels), Zoe Sallis (Hagar), Gabriele Ferzetti (Lot), Eleonora Rossi-Drago (Lot's wife), Franco Nero (Abel), Pupella Maggio (Noah's wife), Robert Rietty (Abraham's steward), Alberto Lucantoni (Isaac), Luciano Conversi (Ishmael) **Screenwriter:** Christopher Fry **Cinematographer:** Giuseppe Rotunno **Composer:** Toshiro Mayuzumi **Producer:** Dino DeLaurentiis for Twentieth Century Fox **Running Time:** 174 minutes **Format:** VHS **Awards:** Academy Awards, 1966: Nominations: Best Original Score (Toshiro Mayuzumi) **Budget:** $18M **Box Office:** $15M.

The Greatest Story Ever Told

1965 – George Stevens – 🧦🧦

The Greatest Story Ever Told follows the life of Jesus Christ from his birth to his crucifixion and resurrection. Based on Fulton Oursler's book, the film was ten years and several casting changes in the making. Some critics have said the end product wasn't worth the effort, and it may well not have been worth ten years' wait. But it is worth a look, especially around Easter, the film's occasional television air time.

The cast does a consistently fine job portraying familiar characters. Probably the most noteworthy performance is given by Charlton Heston as John the Baptist. He is properly zealous, shouting "repent!" at every available opportunity. Watching him, one might wonder if he will baptize people in the Jordan River or part it and lead them across. Max Von Sydow gives a credible rendition of the Messiah, though at times he seems too much like a monk and too little like a man. Overall, the story suffers for this lack of emphasis on the humanity of Christ. When Jesus goes into the wilderness to be tempted, the film fails to suggest any internal struggle at all.

Consequently, it is the minor matters that linger in the mind, such as some odd-seeming non-biblical changes that were made (Pilate never washing his hands, Judas Iscariot committing suicide by falling into fire rather than by hanging) and cameo performances by well-known celebrities, which were probably impressive at the time of release but that now serve as little more than distractions. The distinctive voices and mannerisms of a few lead the audience to wonder (sometimes aloud): Is that John Wayne? This overly reverent treatment mostly robs the film of the warmth of life, but a few effective moments remain, such as when Jesus looks knowingly into Judas' eyes and tells him to go and do quickly what he must.

Did you know?...

The Greatest Story Ever Told was filmed entirely in the United States. Locations included Arizona, Utah, and Nevada.

Cast: Max von Sydow (Jesus), Charlton Heston (John the Baptist), Sidney Poitier (Simon of Cyrene), Claude Rains (King Herod), Jose Ferrer (Herod Antipas), Telly Savalas (Pontius Pilate), Angela Lansbury (Claudia), Dorothy McGuire (The Virgin Mary), John Wayne (Centurion), Donald Pleasence (The Dark Hermin/Satan), Carroll Baker (Veronica), Van Heflin (Bar Amand), Robert Loggia (Joseph), Shelley Winters (Unnamed Woman), Ed Wynn (Old Aram), Roddy McDowall (Matthew), Pat Boone (Young Man at Tomb), Martin Landau (Caiaphas), Robert Blake (Simon the Zealot), Jamie Farr (Thaddaeus), Joanna Dunham (Mary Magdalene)

Jesus (Max Von Sydow) prays.

Screenwriter: James Lee Barrett, George Stevens **Cinematographer:** Loyal Griggs, William C. Mellor **Composer:** Alfred Newman **Producer:** George Stevens for United Artists **Running Time:** 196 minutes **Format:** VHS, LV **Awards:** Academy Awards, 1965: Nominations: Best Cinematography, Art Direction, Costume Design, Special Visual Effects, Musical Score **Budget:** $20M **Box Office:** $7M.

Quo Vadis?

1951 – Mervyn LeRoy – 🎵🎵🎵🎵

> "Unfortunately, Caesar, as a ruler, you must have subjects to rule. Sheer population is a necessary evil."
>
> Petronius (Leo Genn) to Nero (Peter Ustinov).

Quo Vadis? enjoyably combines romance, religion, and history with big sets and great masses of extras, including Elizabeth Taylor and Sophia Loren. Originally, John Huston planned to direct a version with Gregory Peck and Elizabeth Taylor, but his script never passed muster. The movie was nominated for eight Oscars, but failed to win any.

After three years conquering Britain, Marcus Vinicius (Robert Taylor) returns home to Rome eager to partake in a little pantheistic debauchery. While dining with an old friend and former warrior, his eye catches Lygia (Deborah Kerr), whom he mistakenly assumes is a slave. In reality Lygia, a Christian, is a hostage of Rome and the adopted daughter of the old friend with whom Marcus is dining. Untroubled by such considerations, Marcus arranges with Emperor Nero (Peter Ustinov) to have the guardianship of this hostage transferred to him. That Marcus is a pagan doesn't bother Lygia as much as the fact that he is a soldier who has made killing and conquering weaker people his vocation. Despite her misgivings, they fall in love, but Marcus spurns her suggestion that he convert. The two are not reunited until Nero, in the delusional haze that consumes him for the entire story, decides to burn Rome to make room for the new world capital of Neropolis.

Despite the mildly contrived love story between Marcus and Lygia, this is an engrossing and well-rendered story that dramatizes the persecution of Christians in the years immediately following the crucifixion. The film not only manages to combine its many elements smoothly, but it also remains a noteworthy example of a Hollywood story portraying Christians in a positive yet realistic way, neither impossibly pure nor sweetly saccharin.

Peter Ustinov gives an entertaining, over-the-top performance as the Emperor Nero, giving full vent to the Emperor's wimpy, paranoid, impotent side.

Did you know?...

Quo Vadis? was filmed four times for the big screen: in 1902, 1912, 1925, and 1951 and for Italian TV in 1985.

Robert Taylor is heroic and handsome as Marcus Vinicius, but in a distinctly American fashion, and he seems a little out of place when compared to the classical demeanor of the rest of the cast. Leo Genn also stands out as Petronius. He is wonderfully smooth at the self-protective art of combining truth with flattery in his scenes with Nero. From Nero's approval-hungry style of ruling to the inspirational strength and faith of the Christians as they are led to their slaughter

Christian slave Lygia (Deborah Kerr) resists the advances of her pagan Roman master Marcus (Robert Taylor).

to a few completely unexpected moments of comic relief, *Quo Vadis?* is a spectacle which aims to entertain. And does.

Cast: Robert Taylor (Marcus Vinicius), Deborah Kerr (Lygia), Leo Genn (Petronius), Peter Ustinov (Nero), Patricia Laffan (Poppaea), Finlay Curtis (Peter), Abraham Sofaer (Paul), Marina Berti (Eunice), Buddy Baer (Ursus), Felix Aylmer (Plautius), Nora Swinburne (Pomponia), Ralph Truman (Tigellinus), Norman Wooland (Nerva), Peter Miles (Nazarius), Geoffrey Dunn (Terpnos), Nicholas Hannen (Seneca), D.A. Clarke-Smith (Phaon), Rosalie Crutchley (Acte), John Ruddock (Chilo), Arthur Walge (Croton), Elspeth March (Miriam), **Screenwriter:** S.N. Behrman, Sonya Levien, John Lee Mahin **Cinematographer:** William V. Skall, Robert Surtees **Composer:** Miklos Rozsa **Producer:** Sam Zimbalist for MGM **Running Time:** 171 minutes **Format:** VHS **Awards:** Academy Awards, 1951: Nominations: Best Art Direction/Set Decoration (color), Cinematography, Costume Design, Film Editing, Original Dramatic/Comedy Score, Picture, Supporting Actor (Leo Genn, Peter Ustinov); Golden Globe Awards, 1952: Best Cinematography (color), Supporting Actor (Peter Ustinov) **Budget:** $7M **Box Office:** $10.5M.

The Robe
1953 – Henry Koster – 🦴🦴🦴

> "Worlds are built on force, not charity. Power is all that counts."
> Marcellus (Richard Burton)

The film rendition of the once-popular novel by Lloyd C. Douglas is a classic morality story. It holds the distinction of being the first widescreen film Hollywood produced as a way of addressing the fears raised in the industry by the popularity of television. It is also among the first uses of stereo in a film. In the Cinemascope widescreen video format, these features work together nicely with a separation of audio channels that is unusually distinct and enjoyable. The story, however, is another story.

The Robe first establishes both its epic setting and some important personality traits of Marcellus (Richard Burton), the young Roman tribune whose experiences organize the story. His reunion with Diana (Jean Simmons), a childhood playmate, hints at a life of both drinking and womanizing (her joking attempt to remind him of his childhood promise to marry her brings a genuinely puzzled frown and the question of whether he was drunk at the time). Posted to Jerusalem, Marcellus wins Christ's robe in a dice game. After touching the robe of Jesus, however, Marcellus is bewitched and almost loses his sanity from guilt. He believes that the cure lies in destroying the robe, but nonetheless begins a spiritual journey in which he learns about himself and eventually finds a new faith.

Did you know?...
Laurence Olivier was also considered for the part that eventually went to Richard Burton.

Greek slave Demetrius (Victor Mature) kneels before the crucified Christ.

A representative sample of the film's merits and drawbacks may be found in the short scene when Marcellus questions a stranger in the street during the trial of Jesus. The stranger reports that the prisoner was betrayed by one of his own disciples; he walks off and tells Marcellus his name in parting—Judas Iscariot—as a crash of thunder disturbs the night and a smashing crescendo follows on the soundtrack. The scene makes for effective enough melodrama in its dialogue, but the two sound effects risk ruining the moment through their clumsy excess.

The second half of the film after the crucifixion inevitably loses some interest (though an impressively surreal dream sequence conveys Marcellus' deep guilt over his involvement in the death of Christ). Richard Burton is enjoyable, his youthful energy suggesting the brash foolishness of Marcellus, but his performance often veers into bombast. The movie did, however, make him a star.

Victor Mature is surprisingly effective as Marcellus' slave Demetrius, who leads his master to a change of heart. (This character was used as the basis for the sequel *Demetrius and the Gladiators* in which Mature also appeared.)

Cast: Richard Burton (Marcellus Gallio), Jean Simmons (Diana), Victor Mature (Demetrius), Michael Rennie (Peter), Jay Robinson (Caligula), Dean Jagger (Justus), Torin Thatcher (Senator Gallio), Richard Boone (Pilate), Cameron Mitchell (voice of Christ), Michael Ansara (Judas), Betta St. John (Miriam), Jeff Morrow (Paulus), Ernest Thesiger (Emperor Tiberias), Dawn Addams (Junia), David Leonard (Marcipor) **Screenwriter:** Gina Kaus, Phillip Dunne **Cinematographer:** Leon Shamroy **Composer:** Alfred Newman **Producer:** Frank Ross for Twentieth Century Fox **Running Time:** 135 minutes **Format:** VHS, LV **Awards:** Academy Awards, 1953: Art Direction/Set Decoration (Color), Costume Design (Color); Nominations: Actor (Richard Burton), Color Cinematography, Picture; Golden Globe Awards, 1954: Film—Drama; National Board of Review Awards, 1953: 10 Best Films of the Year, Actress (Jean Simmons) **Budget:** $5M **Box Office:** $17.5M.

Samson and Delilah
1949 – Cecil B. De Mille – 🦴🦴

"Give me any couple of pages from the Bible, and I'll give you a picture," Cecil B. De Mille is famous for claiming. Of course, he didn't promise a *subtle* picture. Take away the widescreen dimensions and the comparatively better special effects in his remake of *The Ten Commandments*, and you end up with

something like De Mille's *Samson and Delilah* with its studio sets and uneasy mix of acting and posturing.

The opening credits claim that the film is based on three chapters from the book *Judges*, but the screenwriters have shaped the material to bring Delilah (Hedy Lamarr) into the narrative sooner by adding a love triangle. Samson loves the Philistine woman Samadar (Angela Lansbury), even though her younger sister Delilah desires Samson for herself. As Samson kills a lion with his bare hands, De Mille cuts to shots of Delilah looking on, aroused by the ferocity of the struggle. She herself all but attacks him after he has slain the lion ("One cat at a time," Samson says, pushing her away). On the night of his wedding to Samadar, he poses a riddle to the many guests, but they coerce Samadar into getting the answer from him. Losing his bride to Ahtur (Henry Wilcoxon), Samson burns down the estate in revenge, which gives Delilah her motive for cooperating with the Philistines to learn the secret of his great strength.

Seductive Delilah (Hedy Lamarr) means to destroy Samson's (Victor Mature) strength.

"If you crush the life out of me, I'd kiss you with my dying breath."

Delilah (Hedy Lamarr), to Samson (Victor Mature).

Did you know?...

Russ Tamblyn, who later as an adult appeared in films (*Peyton Place*, *West Side Story*) and television series (*Twin Peaks*), plays the part of the boy Saul who stands up to the Philistines in an early scene.

The leads do not come off quite as effectively as some of the supporting cast. Mature is better than Lamarr although he only registers the single trait of dignified strength throughout. George Sanders plays the Saran of Gaza with the sole exercise of finesse seen in the movie: the Saran seems to take nothing seriously, and he studiously scrutinizes his ant village as he hears reports of the latest Hebrew uprising. De Mille regular Wilcoxon as Ahtur is the most inexpressive, but George Reeves, who played Superman on 1950s television, has a very good moment as the bleeding messenger who describes Samson's slaying of the Philistines with the jawbone of an ass. If Reeves and Wilcoxon had just switched parts, the film would have had more life.

When Norma Desmond (Gloria Swanson) visits De Mille at Paramount in Billy Wilder's movie *Sunset Boulevard* (1950), she interrupts the filming of *Samson and Delilah*. Surprisingly, De Mille's extras in the scenes from the Wilder picture are costumed more convincingly than in De Mille's own film, where the use of Technicolor led to too much gold lamé. Andrew Lloyd Webber and Christopher Hampton, in their musical version of Wilder's film, also tweaked the image of De Mille when they have a party guest sing: "Behold, my children, / It is I, Cecil B. De Mille. / Meeting me must be quite a thrill, / But there's no need to kneel."

Cast: Hedy Lamarr (Delilah), Victor Mature (Samson), George Sanders (the Saran of Gaza), Angela Lansbury (Samadar), Henry Wilcoxon (Ahtur), Olive Dearing (Miriam), Fay Holden (Hazelelponit), Julia Faye (Hisham), Rusty Tamblyn (Saul), William Farnum (Tubal), Lane Chandler (Taresh), Moroni Olsse (Targil), Francis J. McDonald (streetside storyteller), William Davis (Garmiskar), John Miljan (Lesh Lakish), Arthur Q. Bryan (Philistine merchant), Mike Mazurki (leader of Philistine soldiers), George Reeves (wounded messenger) **Screenwriter:** Jesse L. Lasky Jr., Frederick M. Frank, Harold Lamb, Vladimir Jabotinsky **Cinematographer:** George Barnes **Composer:** Victor Young **Producer:** Cecil B. De Mille for Paramount **Running Time:** 128 minutes **Format:** VHS, LV **Awards:** Academy Awards, 1950: Art Direction/Set Decoration (Color), Costume Design (Color); Nominations: Color Cinematography, Original Dramatic/Comedy Score (Victor Young) **Box Office:** $9M or $11.5M (depending on the source).

The Ten Commandments

1956 – Cecil B. De Mille – 🦴🦴🦴🦴

Upon hearing the word "epic," often the first film to come to mind is Cecil B. De Mille's lavish production of *The Ten Commandments*. So popular that it is reshown on network television every Easter/Passover season, the biblical block-buster includes a bit of every genre: action, romance, philosophical reflection, and disasters (plagues of hail, locusts, blood and death long before disaster epics became a genre). Actually, it was De Mille's second try with the material; he had shot a silent version in 1923.

The story is central to the religious traditions of at least two faiths—Christianity and Judaism. It is also central to the political ideals of freedom as a right and the defiance of tyranny as a duty. Moses (Charlton Heston, in one of his many memorable roles) has every reason to be comfortable; he has been rescued from Hebrew slavery and now is an adopted Prince of Egypt, likely to beat out Yul Brynner's Rameses for the Pharoah's throne. He also is the central love interest of Rameses' intended, Princess Nefretiri, and under the careful pro-tection of his princess mother. But the cries of his tortured people are too much for Moses. He kills an Egyptian overseer and flees Egypt to the desert, only to meet God face to face—and return to lead his people to freedom.

Shot mostly in Egypt, the Exodus itself is one of the grandest sequences ever shot, employing 12,000 Arabs and 15,000 animals. The parting of the Red Sea (done by pouring 300,000 gallons of water into a tank and then reversing the film) was spectacular for 1956, and such effects won the film its only Oscar. The acting may be broad (Edward G. Robinson as a Jewish governor?), the sub-plots a bit simplistic and melodramatic, the scenes often mere tableaux, but the power of the great story and its brilliant, full-color, huge-screen dramatization make it a perennial favorite.

Cast: Charlton Heston (Moses), Yul Brynner (Pharoah Rameses), Anne Baxter (Nefre-tiri), Edward G. Robinson (Dathan), Yvonne de Carlo (Sephora), Debra Paget (Lilia), John Derek (Joshua), Cedric Hardwicke (Sethi), Nina Foch (Bithiah), Martha Scott (Yochabel), Judith Anderson (Memnet), Vincent Price (Baka), John Carradine (Aaron), Eduard Franz (Jethro), Olive Deering (Miriam), Donald Curtis (Mered), Douglas Dumbrille (Jannes), H.B. Warner (Ammi-nadab), Henry Wilcoxon (Pentaur), Fraser Heston (infant Moses), Woody Strode (King of Ethiopia), Mike Connors (herder), Clint Walker (Sardinian captain), Michael Ansara (taskmas-

"Oh, Moses, Moses, you stubborn, splendid, adorable fool!"

Nefretiri (Anne Baxter)

Did you know?...

De Mille cast Charlton Heston as Moses because, bearded, he looked like Michelangelo's famous statue of Moses.

It's Israelite Moses (Charlton Heston) vs. the Egyptian Pharoah (Yul Brynner).

ter), Carl "Alfalfa" Switzer (slave), Robert Vaughan (spearman/Hebrew at Golden Calf), Herb Alpert (drummer) **Screenwriter:** Aeneas MacKenzie, Jesse Lasky Jr., Fredric M. Frank, Jack Gariss **Cinematographer:** Loyal Griggs, John F. Warren, W. Wallace Keley, J. Peverell Marley **Composer:** Elmer Bernstein **Producer:** Cecil B. De Mille for Paramount **Running Time:** 220 minutes **Format:** VHS, LV **Awards:** Academy Awards, 1956: Special Effects; Nominations: Art Direction/Set Decoration (color), Color Cinematography, Costume Design (color), Editing, Picture, Sound **Budget:** $13.5M **Box Office:** $34.2M (initial release); $83M (by 1959).

They Might Be Giants . . .

Lew Grade's two television mini-series *Moses the Lawgiver* (1975) and *Jesus of Nazareth* (1976), both from script adaptations by British novelist Anthony Burgess, stand out as notable epics of the small screen. Though Burt

Lancaster plays the Hebrew patriarch with intelligence and though the six-hour version offers richer character development than the trimmed-down theatrical release of *Moses*, the poor special effects and long running time eventually produce somewhat mixed results. Franco Zefferelli directed *Jesus of Nazareth*, which is often cited as the most sensitive screen treatment of the life of Christ. At 371 minutes and with a cast featuring Robert Powell as Jesus, Laurence Olivier, James Mason, and many other distinguished names, the film is always compelling. Moments such as the parable of the prodigal son are incorporated into the narrative with an eye for dramatic context (that parable is told to heal a rift among disciples). James Farentino is especially good as Simon Peter, and Ennio Morricone's music is also first-rate. (Screenwriter Anthony Burgess later adapted his scripts to other forms: the *Moses* material saw print as a narrative poem in blank verse, and the *Jesus* script turned up later as two novels, *Man of Nazareth* and *The Kingdom of the Wicked*.)

Other biblical epics include *The Silver Chalice* (1954) from the Thomas B. Costain novel, which marked the film debut of Paul Newman (something he has since referred to apologetically), *Barabbas* (1962), in which Anthony Quinn plays the prisoner released to the crowd in exchange for Jesus, Robert Aldrich's Italian production *Sodom and Gomorrah* (1963) with Stewart Granger and Pier Angeli, and *King David* (1985), a more recent scriptural epic, that features Richard Gere in the title role, impressive photography, and a memorable Carl Davis score. Martin Scorsese's *The Last Temptation of Christ* (1988) is notable for its humanizing of the Christ character (Willem Dafoe) and the terrific controversy the movie encountered upon release.

COMEDY

Airplane!

The Court Jester

Dr. Strangelove, or:
How I Learned to Stop Worrying and Love the Bomb

Duck Soup

The Great Race

A Guide for the Married Man

It's a Mad Mad Mad Mad World

Love and Death

Monty Python and the Holy Grail

Pee-Wee's Big Adventure

The Rocky Horror Picture Show

Those Magnificent Men in Their Flying Machines, or How I
Flew to from London to Paris in 25 Hours and 11 Minutes

Young Frankenstein

Airplane!

1980 – Jim Abrahams, David Zucker, Jerry Zucker – ♫♫♫♪

> ### "Surely you can't be serious."
> Stryker (Robert Hays)

> ### "I am serious. And don't call me Shirley."
> Rumack (Leslie Nielsen)

High comedy? Not hardly. If you relish the sophistications of the later Woody Allen, you may not like *Airplane!*. But if you enjoy a good time, like to laugh so hard it brings tears to your eyes, and want a movie so silly it will help you escape the drudgery of everyday life, this might just be your cinematic experience.

Airplane! is about a shell-shocked pilot, Ted Stryker (Robert Hays), who has lost his self-confidence and his girlfriend (Julie Hagerty). She is now a stewardess for an airline and is scheduled to make a flight to Chicago; he boards the flight so that he might have a chance to win her back. Nearly everyone onboard succumbs to food poisoning, including the pilot and co-pilot (Peter Graves and Kareem Abdul-Jabbar), and Stryker has to land the plane against all odds. But this premise is a mere excuse for a barrage of jokes of every kind.

What makes *Airplane!* a comic epic? First, it spoofs the epic pretensions of several films (some of them disaster movies), such as *Airport*, *Jaws*, *Silver Streak*, *From Here to Eternity*, *Knute Rockne, All American*, and *Saturday Night Fever*. Second, it spawned a series of movies that depend on the same ridiculous dialogue and silly but clever sight gags to induce laughter: *Airplane II: The Sequel*, the *Naked Gun* films, *Top Secret*, both *Hot Shots* movies, *Spyhard*, and even *Dumb and Dumber*. That's quite a legacy.

Before *Airplane!*, who knew Leslie Nielsen was all that funny? He mostly played bad guys in cheap westerns, suited-up, young professionals, and sometimes serious authority figures. (His work in *Airplane!* is so good that it makes some of his earlier, over-serious acting—like the parts of the captains in *The Poseidon Adventure* and *Forbidden Planet* now seem funny in retrospect.) *Airplane!* got Nielsen much recognition as a comedic actor, as it did for Robert Stack and Lloyd Bridges, both of whom are superb in the film. It's pretty funny to imagine all of the things McCroskey (Bridges) picked the wrong week to try to stop doing.

Most of the fun comes from the pace, which will probably require multiple viewings in order to catch all of the parodies and gags. Watch for the scene

> ### Did you know?...
> Joseph Biroc, the cinematographer, shot his first movie in 1946, filming part of *It's a Wonderful Life*.

about Stryker's drinking problem and what people do who are trapped into listening to his story. And pay close attention to the closing credits. They're good for a few laughs, too.

Traffic controller Kramer (Robert Stack) gives orders while fellow worker McCroskey (Lloyd Bridges) panics.

Airplane II: The Sequel loses some of the original cast, most of the inspiration, and all of the original directors, but it picks up good performances from Chad Everett, Chuck Connors, Sonny Bono, and William Shatner. It's about the first passenger space shuttle to the moon. Bono is the crazy guy with the bomb on board.

Cast: Robert Hays (Ted Stryker), Julie Hagerty (Elaine Dickinson), Lloyd Bridges (McCroskey), Leslie Nielsen (Doctor Rumack), Peter Graves (Captain Clarence Oveur), Robert Stack (Kramer), Kareem Abdul-Jabbar (Roger Murdock), Lorna Patterson (Randy), Stephen Stucker (Johnny), Frank Ashmore (Victor Basta), Barbara Billingsley (Jive Lady), Rossie Harris (Joey), Ethel Merman (Lieutenant Herwitz) **Screenwriter:** Jim Abrahams, David Zucker, Jerry Zucker **Cinematographer:** Joseph F. Biroc **Composer:** Elmer Bernstein **Producer:** Jon Davidson and Howard W. Koch Jr. for Paramount **MPAA Rating:** PG **Running Time:** 88 minutes **Format:** VHS, LV **Box Office:** $83.4M (gross).

The Court Jester

1956 – Norman Panama, Melvin Frank – 🦴🦴🦴🖤

> "The pellet with the poison's in the chalice from the palace. The vessel with the pestle has the brew that is true."
>
> Griselda (Mildred Natwick) to Hawkins (Danny Kaye)

Not everyone is partial to the antics of Danny Kaye, but the richness of *The Court Jester* combines so many comic devices that it has still earned a wide, appreciative audience. The film gently spoofs swashbuckling, adventure films in the tradition of *The Adventures of Robin Hood* and *The Mark of Zorro*. It has the added merit of featuring Basil Rathbone (at a youthful-looking sixty three when the film was made), who played the villain in both of those classics and who shows great facility for comedy in this one. The complicated plot by Norman Panama and Melvin Frank adds many pleasing touches.

The true king of England is an infant tended to by a Robin Hood-like forest rogue called the Black Fox (Edward Ashley). One of his men, Hawkins (Danny Kaye), seeks to enter the castle of the usurper, King Roderick (Cecil Parker), steal the key to the underground passage, admit the Black Fox's men, and return the rightful king to the throne. Hawkins happens upon the king's new jester Giacomo (John Carradine) on the road, and Hawkins subdues him and adopts his identity as a disguise. Once in the castle, however, he discovers that Giacomo is really an accomplished assassin hired by Ravenhurst (Rathbone) to murder some rival knights. The magic of Griselda (Mildred Natwick) enables Hawkins to change his behavior with the snap of her fingers from that of the bumbling goof he is to that of a polished swordsman who convinces Ravenhurst of his deadly skill.

In addition to the comic slapstick of Kaye in his role as the jester, the film's verbal comedy is consistently enjoyable. In one scene, the lecherous king tries to accost Maid Jean (Glynis Johns), but she quickly concocts a story about the ravages of Breckenridge's Scourge, a highly contagious illness that has all but decimated her family. As the king's lust changes to caution then to repulsion, Jean begins an ardent pursuit of him ("Oh, sire, let us not spoil the magic of this moment by thinking of their swollen, pain-ridden bodies"). The film also manages both to showcase some impressive swordplay and to satirize this staple of adventure epics. In the climactic fight between Hawkins and Ravenhurst, they battle impressively with rapiers. Hawkins at one point nonchalantly quenches his thirst while fending off Ravenhurst's vigorous attack, enraging him further. Other comic reversals include the method for verifying the true king, who must pos-

Did you know?...

Some of the specialty songs were written by Kaye's wife, Sylvia Fine. This film was the second made by a production company the two had created, following *Knock on Wood* (1954).

sess the royal birthmark, the "purple pimpernel." In a great visual touch, Hawkins holds the infant before the assembled masses in the throne room, and dozens of courtiers drop reverently to their knees when he lowers the royal diaper to reveal the birthmark on the baby's bottom.

Would-be court jester Hawkins (Danny Kaye) doesn't seem to be able to make anyone laugh.

Cast: Danny Kaye (Hawkins), Glynis Johns (Maid Jean), Basil Rathbone (Sir Ravenhurst), Angela Lansbury (Princess Gwendolyn), Cecil Parker (King Roderick), Mildred Natwick (Griselda), Robert Middleton (Sir Griswald), Edward Ashley (the Black Fox), John Carradine (Giacomo), Herbert Rudley (Captain of the Guard), Noel Drayton (Fergus), Alan Napier (Sir Brockhurst), Lewis Martin (Sir Finsdale), Patrick Aherne (Sir Pertwee), Richard Kean (Archbishop) **Screenwriter:** Norman Panama, Melvin Frank **Cinematographer:** Ray June **Composer:** Sylvia Fine, Sammy Cahn, Vic Schoen **Producer:** Norman Panama and Melvin Frank for Paramount **Running Time:** 101 minutes **Format:** VHS, LV **Budget:** $4M (reportedly the most expensive comedy at that time).

Dr. Strangelove, or: How I Learned to Stop Worrying and Love the Bomb

1964 – Stanley Kubrick – 🦴🦴🦴🦴

> "I'm not saying we wouldn't get our hair mussed, but I do say no more than 10 to 20 million people killed, tops–depending on the breaks."
>
> General Turgidson (George C. Scott) to President Muffley (Peter Sellers)

Dr. Strangelove is a deliciously black comic look at nuclear annihilation, courtesy of Stanley Kubrick, with Peter Sellers in a three-role tour de force and Sterling Hayden as a mad general. The end of the world comes about not from complicated territorial disputes of geopolitics but from some all-thumbs general out to prove he's virile. General Ripper (Hayden), finally goes crazy in his paranoia and sends U.S. bombers to attack Russia because he is convinced that fluoridation is a Communist plot to taint our "precious bodily fluids." He explains, in one of the most amazing speeches in 1960s cinema, to his second in command that this insight came to him "during the physical act of love. Yes, a profound sense of fatigue and feeling of emptiness followed. Luckily, I was able to interpret these feelings correctly. Loss of essence. I can assure you, it has not recurred, Mandrake. Women sense my power, and they seek the life essence. I do not avoid women, Mandrake, but I do deny them my essence." Another general, played by Scott, outwardly recognizes the dicey situation but underneath wants to trumpet Ripper's attack into an excuse to eliminate Russia.

The film is both howlingly funny and disturbingly scary. The slight but continual undercurrent of fear comes not so much from the plausibility of global destruction as from the film's pitiless point of view that seems to welcome the bomb as the ultimate suicidal joke. Kubrick lets loose characters who all but revel in genocide, and then he sits back and laughs as the final cataclysm gets nearer and nearer. Dr. Strangelove, one of Peter Seller's three roles, is a German scientist with a tendency to give the Nazi salute with his mechanical arm. He joins a War Room dominated by the bluster of Scott's general, who argues for a bombing to prevent future bombings, should anyone survive. The only characters who seem to have any sense, like the President and Mandrake (both played by Sellers) are rendered powerless and laughable by the nightmare spinning out-of-control. One of them tries to reason with the madman Ripper as bullets fly through the SAC office; the other tries to maintain calm in the War Room as

Did you know?...

Peter Sellers was initially cast in four parts, but he could not develop a redneck accent he was happy with, so Kubrick replaced him with Slim Pickens in the role of Major Kong.

fights break out. (The characterization of the President as well-meaning but inef-
fectual appears to be based on Adlai Stevenson, the U.N. ambassador during the
Cuban Missile Crisis, and Dr. Strangelove parodies Werner von Braun, rocket
expert for the Nazis who later defected to the U.S.)

Peter Sellers raises his hands in
his role of Group Capt. Lionel
Mandrake.

Cast: Peter Sellers (Group Captain Lionel Mandrake/President Merken Muffley/Dr.
Strangelove), George C. Scott (General Buck Turgidson), Sterling Hayden (General Jack T. Rip-
per), Peter Bull (Ambassador de Sadesky), Keenan Wynn (Colonel Bat Guano), Slim Pickens
(Major T. J. "King" Kong), James Earl Jones (Lieutenant Lothar Zogg), Tracy Reed (Miss Scott),
Jack Creley (Mr. Staines), Frank Berry (Lieutenant H. R. Dietrich), Glenn Beck (Lieutenant W. D.
Kivel), Shane Rimmer (Captain G. A. Ace Owens), Paul Tamarin (Lieutenant B. Goldberg), Gor-
don Tanner (General Faceman), Robert O'Neill (Admiral Randolph), Roy Stephens (Frank)
Screenwriter: Terry Southern, Peter George, Stanley Kubrick **Cinematographer:** Gilbert Taylor
Composer: Laurie Johnson **Producer:** Stanley Kubrick for Hawk Films; released by Columbia
Running Time: 93 minutes **Format:** VHS, LV, DVD **Awards:** Academy Awards 1964: Nomina-
tions: Actor (Peter Sellers), Adapted Screenplay, Director (Stanley Kubrick), Picture; British
Academy Awards, 1964: Film; New York Film Critics Awards, 1964: Director (Stanley Kubrick)
Box Office: $5M (domestic rentals).

Duck Soup

1933 – Leo McCarey – 𝄢𝄢𝄢𝄢

> "Remember, you're fighting for this woman's honor, which is more than she ever did."
>
> Firefly (Groucho Marx), during the battle scenes.

A government has been mismanaged, if you can imagine such a thing. Mrs. Teasdale (Margaret Dumont), who has already spent half of her late husband's legacy supporting Freedonia, now insists that her choice, Rufus T. Firefly (Groucho Marx), be placed in charge of the country. The comic insolence of the Marxes has never been exercised more freely than in this classic from 1933. Groucho makes his entrance in the massive reception hall sliding down a fire-pole, he plays hopscotch while Mrs. Teasdale delivers her formal speech of welcome, and later he makes the cabinet members wait while he finishes a game of jacks. When one official resigns, saying he is "washing his hands of the whole thing," Groucho tells him to wash his neck too.

Nearly all of the Marx Brothers' most famous films adopt an approach that is, amid the many jokes, selectively satiric: Florida real estate salesmen in *The Coconuts*, country-house mysteries in *Animal Crackers*, academics in *Horse Feathers*, the dignity of high art in *A Night at the Opera*. *Duck Soup* goes the furthest, and the wildness that makes it cherished today may have also made it a popular failure upon its release and led to the Brothers leaving Paramount and moving to MGM. The film savages some of the Marxes' biggest and riskiest targets: government, authority figures, courts, war, patriotism.

Anyone who ever marveled at the inexplicable staying power of incompetent administrators will savor the scene where Groucho recruits a peanut vendor (Chico Marx) off the street as his new Minister of War. Life's occasional surreal moments when the formality of habit and ritual seem to be the only things giving structure to an otherwise absurd situation find great illustration in Chico's pun-filled trial scene.

Freedonia eventually goes to war against Sylvania because Groucho cannot tolerate being called an upstart by Ambassador Trentino (Louis Calhern)—though being called a swine and a worm doesn't bother him. The announcement leads to a musical number in which the massive sound stage fills with extras singing a song ("All God's Chillun Got Guns!") that gives bloodthirsty patriotism the aura of a spiritual. Director Leo McCarey, according to Jean-Pierre Coursodon in *American Directors*, tightened the film by taking out a subplot involving

Did you know?...

Zeppo Marx retired from acting after his work in this film.

a romance between Zeppo and Raquel Torres and by adding the scenes at Mrs. Teasdale's house involving efforts to steal Freedonia's war plans. The anarchy of the film may have made it out of step with its own time when such respected subjects were not to be questioned, but since at least the 1960s, this comedy has been cherished for blowing a raspberry into the dignified corridors of respectability.

The Marx Bros. are up to their usual mayhem in *Duck Soup*.

Cast: Groucho Marx (Rufus T. Firefly), Harpo Marx (Pinky), Chico Marx (Chicolini), Zeppo Marx (Bob Rolland), Margaret Dumont (Mrs. Teasdale), Raquel Torres (Vera Marcal), Louis Calhern (Ambassador Trentino), Edmund Breese (Zander), Leonid Kinskey (Agitator), Charles Middleton (Prosecutor), Verna Hillie (Secretary), George Macquarrie (First Judge), Edgar Kennedy (Lemonade Dealer), Edwin Maxwell (Secretary of War), William Worthington (First Minister of Finance) **Screenwriter:** Bert Kalmar, Nat Perrin, Harry Ruby, Arthur Sheekman **Cinematographer:** Henry Sharp **Composer:** Bert Kalmar, Harry Ruby **Producer:** Herman J. Mankiewicz for Paramount **Running Time:** 70 minutes **Format:** VHS, LV, DVD.

The Great Race

1965 — Blake Edwards — 🎷🎷🎷

"You! I hate you! Your hair is always combed, your suit is always white, your car is always clean!"

Professor Fate (Jack Lemmon) to the Great Leslie (Tony Curtis) on the finish line in Paris.

Dashing daredevil record breaker The Great Leslie Gallant, III (Tony Curtis) enjoys testing the laws of physics with daring and dangerous new stunts. Professor Fate (Jack Lemmon), The Great Leslie's arch nemesis, has a comical and very loud obsession with topping him. Pitting the two against each other in the first-ever New York to Paris car race makes for two and a half hours of laughs. Throw in a perky suffragette and would-be reporter (Natalie Wood) determined to cover the race from start to finish, along with Professor Fate's trusty assistant Max (Peter Falk), and prepare to be thoroughly entertained.

The Great Race employs comedy in all its various forms from slapstick to puns to completely unexpected sight gags. As the Great Leslie effortlessly succeeds at every new stunt he attempts, his foil, Professor Fate, barely survives his botched attempts with a resilience reminiscent of Wile E. Coyote.

The action moves along quickly as the race carries the characters through barroom brawls in the Old West to a floating iceberg. Unfortunately, the pace grinds nearly to a halt as the foursome's iceberg approaches land and a *Prisoner of Zenda* spoof begins. This sizable portion of the film is slower, but it does yield a surprisingly entertaining performance by Lemmon as Prince Hapnik (with the lilting laugh). Once the race recommences, the fun also resumes and continues all the way to the finish line.

The comic caricatures even in the smaller roles, such as Texas Jack played by Larry Storch, are a joy to watch. These comic figures, like the perfect hero Leslie, in gleaming white pitted against the evil villain Fate, in tattered black cape and top hat, work so well because they are easy to recognize and satirize. *The Great Race* is a grand, unsubtle comedy as impressive for its colorful period costumes, automobiles, expansive sets, and destruction of expansive sets as it is for the performances of its players.

Did you know?...

Tony Curtis also worked with Blake Edwards in the writer-director's breakthrough film, *Operation Petticoat*.

Cast: Jack Lemmon (Professor Fate/Prince Hapnik), Tony Curtis (Leslie Gallant, III), Natalie Wood (Maggie DuBois), Peter Falk (Maxamillian Mean), Keenan Wynn (Hezekiah Sturdy), Arthur O'Connell (Henry Goodbody), Vivian Vance (Hester Goodbody), Dorothy Provine (Lily Olay), Larry Storch (Texas Jack), Ross Martin (Rolfe von Stuppe), George Macready (General Kuhster), Marvin Kaplan (Frisbee), Hal Smith (Lord Mayor), Denver Pyle (Sheriff) **Screen-**

writer: Arthur A. Ross **Cinematographer:** Russell Harlan **Composer:** Henry Mancini **Producer:** Martin Jurow for Warner Bros. **Running Time:** 160 minutes **Format:** VHS **Awards:** Academy Awards, 1966: Best Effects, Sound Effects; Nominations: Best Cinematography (Russell Harlan); Film Editing; Song "The Sweetheart Tree"); Sound **Box Office:** $11M (rentals).

The racers take a moment to check out the competition.

A Guide for the Married Man

1967 — Gene Kelly — 🦴🦴🦴

Or should it be called *The Twelve-Year Itch*? Walter Matthau is the happy but bored husband who after twelve years of marriage to beautiful Inger Stevens starts to fancy every woman he passes on the sidewalk as a possible partner for a fling. For tips on how to succeed without getting caught, Matthau turns to his friend Robert Morse, who brims with sage advice. The use of a large cast of Hollywood comedians in cameos to illustrate Morse's series of cautionary tales indicates an attempt after four years to recapture some of the epic scale of *Mad, Mad World*, but the actual effect is more like a long episode of *Love, American Style*. When the two main stars signed on for the project, Morse was cast as the naive one (somewhat similar to the character he played in *How to Succeed in Business Without Really Trying*) and Matthau as the experienced man of the world. It is rumored that Matthau's friend director Billy Wilder suggested that they switch roles and work against type, a change that remains one of the film's clever touches.

All of the comic episodes illustrating Morse's advice are short and snappy. In one of the better interludes, Morse tells Matthau about the mistake of taking his partner to his home for the rendezvous. Terry-Thomas is the friend who learned the hard way: he took his girlfriend, Jayne Mansfield, home for the afternoon, but as they were dressing she couldn't find her bra. Fearful that his wife would later come upon it, Thomas in desperation all but dismantles his house. Weeks later, old and gray before his time, Thomas still hasn't found it, but he knows it's there—somewhere. Jack Benny, who tries to get his lover to break up with him by putting on a cheap act, looks the most uncomfortable of the cameo celebrities. Just a few years later, after the start of the women's movement, this film probably seemed as fossilized as the series of cave drawings that turns up in the opening animation.

Did you know?...

As a cute in-joke, the producer listed all of the celebrities making cameos as "technical advisors."

Cast: Walter Matthau (Paul Manning), Inger Stevens (Ruth Manning), Sue Ane Langdon (Mrs. Johnson), Robert Morse (Ed Stander), Lucille Ball (Technical Advisor), Jack Benny (Technical Advisor), Polly Bergen (Technical Advisor), Joey Bishop (Technical Advisor), Sid Caesar (Technical Advisor), Art Carney (Technical Advisor), Wally Cox (Technical Advisor), Jayne Mansfield (Technical Advisor), Hal March (Technical Advisor), Louise Nye (Technical Advisor), Carl Reiner (Technical Advisor), Ben Blue (Technical Advisor), Phil Silvers (Technical Advisor),

Ann Morgan Guilbert (Technical Advisor), Terry-Thomas (Technical Advisor), Jeffrey Hunter (Technical Advisor), Marty Ingels (Technical Advisor), Sam Jaffe (Technical Advisor) **Screenwriter:** Frank Tarloff **Cinematographer:** Joseph MacDonald **Composer:** John Williams **Producer:** Frank McCarthy for Twentieth Century Fox **Running Time:** 91 minutes **Format:** VHS.

Ruth Manning (Inger Stevens) plays hostess for husband Paul (Walter Matthau) and friend Ed (Robert Morse).

It's a Mad, Mad, Mad, Mad World

1963 – Stanley Kramer – 🦴🦴🦴

Mystery man Smiler Grogan (Jimmy Durante), out of prison and on the run, drives his car off a cliff in California. Four carloads of good Samaritans stop to render aid, and with his dying breaths Grogan tells them of his $350,000 stash from a vague crime committed fifteen years earlier. He speaks in riddles, promising his would-be rescuers that the money is hidden under a giant "W" in the state park in Santa Rosita, California. He drops enough clues to awaken their greed. With that, the race is on.

Mad, Mad represents perhaps the first attempt to make an epic comedy as measured by the size of the cast, the running time of the feature, the overall extravagance, and the ever-present theme of mythic greed (originally, the movie was rumored to be over five hours long). But the comedic range of the film is as confined as its geography and emotions. The slapstick humor sometimes works (the comic plane ride of Mickey Rooney and Buddy Hackett) and sometimes doesn't (the protracted demolition of a gas station by Jonathan Winters). As various attempts to beat the others to the treasure meet with disaster—the film does a good job of leaving all of its characters in cliff-hanging messes right before the intermission—the story manages to foreshadow the ultimate poetic justice these greedy souls will receive. The final, fitting slip on the banana peel and the concluding shots of laughing faces that the film holds on imply an ultimately benevolent view of its all-too-human characters.

As the police captain who has been trying to recover the stolen money for fifteen years, Spencer Tracy makes his next-to-last screen appearance and seems more than a little out of place. Neither his talents nor his years suit him for physical comedy, and the attempts at domestic humor in the running telephone conversation with his wife (Selma Diamond) become rather labored. Often Tracy will simply explain to sidekick William Demarest the whereabouts of the travelers as a way of linking the strands of the plot. (The anniversary edition of the film contains a special feature with Linwood Dunn showing how the optical printer helped to achieve the special effects in the final town square scene.)

Cast: Spencer Tracy (Captain T.G. Culpepper), Milton Berle (J. Russell Finch), Sid Ceasar (Melville Crump), Buddy Hackett (Benjy Benjamin), Ethel Merman (Mrs. Marcus), Mick-

Did you know?...

Ernie Kovacs was originally cast to play Melville Crump, but he died in a car accident before shooting. His real-life wife, Edie Adams, played Monica Crump.

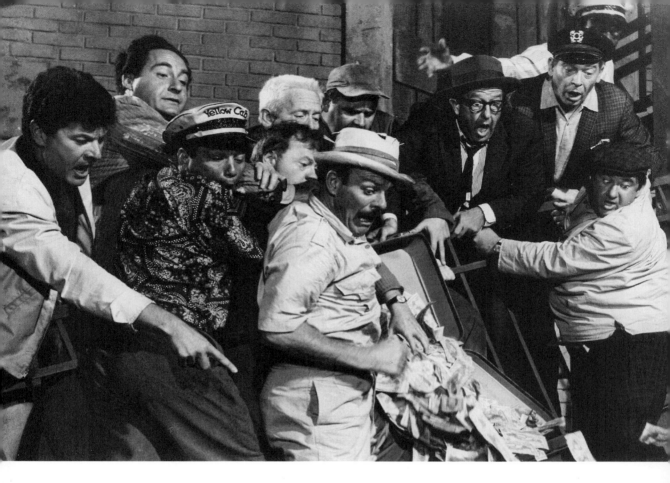

J. Algernon Hawthorne (Terry-Thomas) runs into a spot of trouble.

ey Rooney (Ding Bell), Dick Shawn (Sylvester Marcus), Phil Silvers (Otto Meyer), Terry-Thomas (J. Algernon Hawthorne), Jonathan Winters (Lennie Pike), Edie Adams (Monica Crump), Dorothy Provine (Emmeline Finch), Jim Backus (Tyler Fitzgerald), Peter Falk (Second Cab Driver), Marvin Kaplan (Irwin), Buster Keaton (Jimmy the Crook), Don Knotts (Nervous Man), Carl Reiner (Tower Control), Jimmy Durante (Smiler Grogan), Eddie "Rochester" Anderson (first cab driver), Ben Blue (airplane pilot), Joe E. Brown (union official), Barrie Chase (Sylvester's girlfriend), William Demarest (Aloysius), Selma Diamond (voice of Ginger Culpepper), Andy Devine (Sheriff), Norman Fell (detective), Paul Ford (Colonel Wilberforce), Stan Freberg (Deputy sheriff), Leo Gorcey (third cab driver), Sterling Holloway (fire chief), Edward Everett Horton (Dinckler), Charles Lane (airport manager), Mike Mazurki (Sarge), Charles McGraw (Lieutenant), ZaSu Pitts (switchboard operator), Arnold Stang (Ray), Jesse White (radio-tower operator) **Screenwriter:** Tania Rose, William Rose **Cinematographer:** Ernest Laszlo, Ernest Gold **Producer:** Stanley Kramer for United Artists **MPAA Rating:** G **Running Time:** 188 minutes **Format:** VHS, LV **Awards:** Academy Awards, 1963: Best Sound Effects Editing; Nominations: Best Color Cinematography, Film Editing, Song ("It's a Mad, Mad, Mad, Mad World"), Sound, Original Score **Budget:** $9.4M.

Love and Death

1975 – Woody Allen – 𝄞𝄞𝄞

> "If only God would give me some sign–a burning bush, a parting of the seas, or having my Uncle Sasha pick up a check."
>
> Boris (Woody Allen)

Taking on the melodrama of Russian literature and with sly little send-ups of classic Russian film, *Love and Death* is the last of the joke-first comedies of Woody Allen, a change of interest lamented by some of his fans, appreciated by others. Following its release, Allen acted in Martin Ritt's movie *The Front*, about show-business blacklisting during the Red Scare of the 1950s and then with *Annie Hall*, he began a greater focus on character in his own films, which also grew more personal. (Writer Nancy Pogel speculates that Allen's work in *The Front* may have in part led to this greater artistic seriousness.) *Love and Death* is made up of the recollections of Boris (Allen) on the eve of his execution for trying to assassinate Napoleon (James Tolkan). Boris' memories usually dwell on the themes in the title of the film, and the plot concerns his accidental heroism in battle and his love for Sonia (Diane Keaton).

This plot is mainly an excuse to indulge in jokes of all types. Allen satirizes the philosophy and portentousness of Russian literature, the futility of war, the hunger for meaning in life, the need for love, and even the epic as a film genre. The comedy is so wide-ranging that few will probably be equally taken with all of the humor, but then fewer still will find none of it funny. The silliness of some of the jokes turns up in the closeups of Boris' eccentric family—his uncle who seems unable to stop coughing, his grandparents who simply glare at each other, his father who proudly owns a piece of Russia (a hunk of sod he carries under his coat)—as well as in moments when Sonia and Anna divide up their beloved's letters (and Sonia keeps the vowels).

At the opposite, less silly extreme are the mock philosophic debates between Boris and Sonia, a conversation in Boris' cell that somehow works into the dialogue most of the titles of Dostoevsky's writings, and the references to epic films. On Boris and Sonya's wedding night, Allen alludes playfully in a three-shot sequence to the three stone lions in Sergei Eisenstein's *Potemkin*. One lion slumbers, a second is fully awake, but a third shot of a tired lion replaces that of one roused to ferocity in Eisenstein's film. As the soldiers rush into battle to be slaughtered by the French, Allen intercuts a shot of sheep rushing across a field, an analogy like those in Eisenstein's *Strike*. Both the esoteric

Did you know?...

The score in part comes from the music Sergei Prokofiev wrote for the epics of Sergei Eisenstein.

Boris (Woody Allen) takes a walk
with Death.

and the mainstream humor have their share of hits and misses. Principally filmed in Budapest and Paris, *Love and Death* takes a scattershot, but often effective, approach to its comedy.

Cast: Woody Allen (Boris Petrovich Dimitrovich Greshenko), Diane Keaton (Sonia), Henry Czarniak (Ivan), James Tolkan (Napoleon), Jessica Harper (Natasha), Olga Georges-Picot (Countess Alexandrovna), Georges Adet (Old Nehamkin), Harold Gould (Count Anton), Tony Jay (Vladimir Maximovitch), Alfred Lutter III (young Boris), Edward Ardisson (priest), Feodor Atkine (Mikhail), Yves Barsacq (Rimskey), Lloyd Battista (Don Francisco), Jack Berard (General Lecoq), Eva Bertrand (woman in hygiene lesson), George Birt (doctor), Yves Brainville (Andre), Gerard Buhr (servant), Brian Coburn (Dimitri), Henri Coutet (Minskov), **Screenwriter:** Woody Allen **Cinematographer:** Ghislain Cloquet **Composer:** Sergei Prokofiev **Producer:** Jack Rollins and Charles H. Joffe for United Artists **MPAA Rating:** PG **Running Time:** 85 minutes **Format:** VHS, LV.

Monty Python and the Holy Grail
1974 — Terry Gilliam, Terry Jones — 🦴🦴🦴

> "I didn't know we had a king. I thought we were an autonomous collective."
>
> Peasant (Terry Jones) to King Arthur (Graham Chapman)

The silliness and irreverence of the Monty Python troupe meets the King Arthur legend in this often inspired comedy. The cinematography has a surprisingly impressive look and imparts an earthiness to scenes like the one when the medieval equivalent of a trash collector comes around with a giant pushcart calling for plague victims: "Bring out your dead!" When John Cleese offers him an old man who is just unwanted rather than dead, the problem is solved by conking the victim on the head and tossing him onto the heap of bodies. Some of the verbal comedy takes the form of contemporary attitudes grafted on the Middle Ages. Meeting the king (Graham Chapman), a complaining civil-liberties type is eventually led away as he shouts, "Come and see the violence inherent in the system!"

This violence, not only of the system but also of blood-spurting, *Wild Bunch*-type movies, gets its share of spoofing as well. In one scene Arthur fights a combative knight and severs him down to a torso, limb by gushing limb— even then the knight still taunts Arthur. This film has the distinction of offering up possibly the first flying-cow scene in movies, preceding a comparable moment in *Twister* by a good twenty years (it occurs when some fortified French knights catapult their livestock on Arthur and his men in an effort to repel them). The sketches get a bit more variable in quality as the film progresses and as the

Did you know?...

This film marked the company's second feature after their debut in *And Now for Something Completely Different*, a 1972 film that was unsuccessful, at least in the States.

Director Terry Gilliam.

search for the holy grail becomes the rationale for a series of bits usually introduced by a page from an illuminated manuscript. Fans of Monty Python will savor the film most, but it is clever enough in spots to amuse just about anyone.

Cast: Graham Chapman (King Arthur, minor roles), John Cleese (Sir Lancelot, minor roles), Eric Idle (Sir Robin, minor roles), Terry Gilliam (Old Man from Scene 24, Patsy), Terry Jones (Sir Bedevere, minor roles), Michael Palin (Sir Galahad, minor roles), Connie Booth (The Witch), Carol Cleveland (Zoot and Dingo), Neil Innes (Minstrel, minor role), Bee Duffel (Old Crone), John Young (Dead person, Historian), Rita Davies (Historian's Wife), Avril Stewart (Piglet), Sally Kinghorne (Winston), Mark Zycon (Prisoner) **Screenwriter:** Graham Chapman, John Cleese, Terry Gilliam, Eric Idle, Terry Jones, Michael Palin **Cinematographer:** Terry Bedford **Composer:** DeWolfe, Neil Innes **Producer:** Mark Forstater and John Goldstone for Cinema 5; released by Columbia Pictures **MPAA Rating:** PG **Running Time:** 89 minutes **Format:** VHS, LV.

Pee-Wee's Big Adventure

1985 – Tim Burton – ♪♪♪♪

> "There's things about me you don't know, Dottie. Things you wouldn't understand. Things you couldn't understand. Things you shouldn't understand . . . You don't want to get mixed up with a guy like me. I'm a loner, Dottie. A rebel."
>
> Pee-Wee (Paul Reubens), attempting to explain himself to Dottie (Elizabeth Daily).

With unbelievable antics and his classic annoying laugh, Pee-Wee Herman sets off on his "big adventure" to recover his stolen bike (the one streamlined, red-chromed, glorious perfection that means almost as much to him as his dog Speck). Children and child-hearted adults alike will sympathize with Pee-Wee, the victim of a senseless robbery by the neighborhood bully, who coveted the priceless bike.

In a whirlwind of fantastical events and classic Tim Burton fun, Pee-Wee rides the rails, sets a rodeo record, assists an escaped con, hitches a ride with a ghostly truck driver, barely evades a barroom brawl, disrupts filming on a Warner Bros. set, evacuates a burning pet shop, and lands a bit role in his own movie. As Pee-Wee searches in vain for the one thing that means freedom and independence to any child, his bike, he learns things about himself and about life. In a rare sentimental moment, he confides to his waitress-friend, Simone (Diane Salinger), "They don't tell you that stuff in school. It's just something you have to experience." Despite the fact that this occurs in reference to the Alamo's alleged, non-existent basement, Pee-Wee's journey to find his beloved bike results in more than its simple recovery.

Lighthearted and farcical, Pee-Wee's adventures become a warped wild-goose chase that might become tiring if not for Burton's imaginative style. The montages, like the final chase sequence, show a fondness for sight gags that recalls silent comedy and classic Warner Bros. cartoons. In one example, after Pee-Wee loses his bike, the sidewalks suddenly swarm with bicycled passers-by. He sits on a bench in dejection as odd things peddle in and out of the frame on all sorts of wheeled contraptions. The film also marked the movie debut for Burton, and his imagination enlivens moments such as Pee-Wee's walk down a rainy street at night throwing monster shadows against a wall and the dream sequences (one of a dinosaur, another of ambulance clowns who try to weld the bike in a fun-house hospital set). In a series of nonsensical events and zany settings, Pee-Wee's feature film debut is highly enjoyable if viewed only as a circus charade. Pee-Wee doesn't take himself too seriously; why should we?

Did you know?...
Pee-Wee Herman's birth name is Paul Reubenfeld.

Cast: Paul Reubens (Pee-Wee Herman), Elizabeth Daily (Dottie), Mark Holton (Francis), Diane Salinger (Simone), Judd Omen (Mickey), Irving Hellman (neighbor), Monte Landis (Mario), Damon Martin (Chip), David Glasser (BMX Kid), James Brolin (P.W.), Morgan Fairchild ("Dottie"), Tony Bill (Terry Hawthorne), Phil Hartman (reporter), Twisted Sister (himself), Milton Berle (himself) **Screenwriter:** Phil Hartman, Paul Reubens, Michael Varhol, Victor J. Kemper **Composer:** Danny Elfman **Producer:** Richard Gilbert Abramson and Robert Shapiro for Warner Bros. **MPAA Rating:** PG **Running Time:** 92 minutes **Format:** VHS, LV.

Pee-Wee (Pee-Wee Herman) and his dog Speck.

The Rocky Horror Picture Show

1975 – Jim Sharman – 🎵🎵🎵

"This isn't the Junior Chamber of Commerce, Brad."

Janet (Susan Sarandon)

"I would like, if I may, to take you on a strange journey." These are the first words from the Criminologist (Charles Gray) and narrator. A strange journey, indeed. This rock-music spoof of horror movies begins with two clean cut, straight arrows, Brad Majors (Barry Bostwick) and his betrothed, Janet Weiss (Susan Sarandon), at the wedding of a friend in Denton, the "home of happiness." Later that night while driving in a thunderstorm, they have a blowout and must walk to a mysterious castle to ask to use the phone.

In spite of the voice of Richard Nixon on their car radio (he intones his resignation speech, but the characters ignore it), the movie takes place less in the United States or even in Transylvania than in the never-never land of kinky rock satire. Instead of finding a telephone at the castle, Brad and Janet wind up watching a chorus line of singing butlers and maids in ghoulish makeup. As the couple attempts to leave, Dr. Frank N. Furter (Tim Curry) enters and musically announces himself as the transvestite from Transsexual, Transylvania. The rest of this movie is a tangled, bawdy tale of new experiences for the couple. In two of the more clever scenes, Curry climbs into bed with Janet and Brad at separate times (only the silhouettes are visible behind the bed curtains), and the dialogue plays exactly the same in both scenes. Curry speaks seductively, and first Janet, then Brad responds with shock, innocence, and finally guarded curiosity.

The film's small budget and stage origins show up in the rather lengthy use made of sets like the laboratory (new characters arrive by crashing through the wall rather than director Sharman's opening things up a bit by moving the action elsewhere). Most of the stretches between the songs will hold much less interest in a living-room viewing than at a midnight showing among a raucous audience reciting the dialogue, singing, and throwing bread at the screen. *Rocky's* cult following has given it an epic stature, and most recent cassette editions begin with a featurette about the film's popularity that includes comments by the director, interviews with wildly costumed audience members, and some glimpses of an audience during a showing of the film.

Did you know?...

The film had a sequel called *Shock Treatment* that came out in 1981, but it did not generate the cult following of the original.

Cast: Tim Curry (Dr. Frank N. Furter), Susan Sarandon (Janet Weiss), Barry Bostwick (Brad Majors), Richard O'Brien (Riff Raff), Patricia Quinn (Magenta), Nell Campbell (Columbia),

Jonathan Adams (Dr. Everett Scott), Peter Hinwood (Rocky), Meat Loaf (Eddie), Charles Gray (The Criminologist), Jeremy Newson (Ralph Hapschatt), Hilary Labow (Betty Munroe), Perry Bedden (The Transylvanians), Christopher Biggins (The Transylvanians), Gaye Brown (The Transylvanians), Ishaq Bux (The Transylvanians), Stephen Calcutt (The Transylvanians), Hugh Cecil (The Transylvanians), Imogen Claire (The Transylvanians), Tony Cowan (The Transylvanians), Sadie Corre (The Transylvanians), Fran Fullenwider (The Transylvanians), Lindsay Ingram (The Transylvanians), Peggy Ledger (The Transylvanians), Annabel Leventon (The Transylvanians), Anthony Miller (The Transylvanians), Pamela Obermeyer (The Transylvanians), Tony Then

Dr. Frank N. Furter (Tim Curry) sings "Sweet Transvestite" with some friends.

(The Transylvanians), Kimi Wong (The Transylvanians), Henry Woolf (The Transylvanians), Gina Barrie (The Transylvanians), Rufus Collins (The Transylvanians), Petra Leah (The Transylvanians), Koo Stark (The Transylvanians) **Screenwriter:** Richard O'Brien, Jim Sharman **Cinematographer:** Peter Suschitzky **Composer:** Richard Hartley, Richard O'Brien **Producer:** Michael White for Twentieth Century Fox **MPAA Rating:** R **Running Time:** 105 minutes **Format:** VHS, LV **Box Office:** $44M (rentals).

Those Magnificent Men in Their Flying Machines, or How I Flew from London to Paris in 25 Hours and 11 Minutes

1965 – Ken Annakin – ♪♪♪

> "The trouble with these international affairs is that they attract foreigners."
>
> Lord Rawnsley (Robert Morley), on observing the behavior of some of the contestants.

The first-ever international airplane race from London to Paris is the brainchild of a heroic English pilot, Richard Mays (James Fox), who wants to promote flying and flying machines and who is certain he can win. The financial backers are rounded up, the announcement is made, and contestants from countries all over the world converge on England to test their skill as aviators. After several scenes in which vintage-looking aircraft are maintained and taken for practice flights, the race is finally on. Of course, there is a villain. Sir Percy Ware-Armitage (Terry-Thomas) is determined to win the race himself and sets out to ambush the competition by tinkering with their airplanes before the race begins. Of course, there is a girl. Patricia Rawnsley (Sarah Miles) is the daughter of the race's financial supporter, Lord Rawnsley (Robert Morley), and the love interest of Richard Mays. Richard's toughest competition—not only for the race but also for the love of Patricia—comes from the American contestant, Orvil Newton (Stuart Whitman).

Much of the humor in *Those Magnificent Men in Their Flying Machines* comes from the mildly mocking stereotypes presented through its characters— from the stuffy, stoic Englishman to the American cowboy to the amorous Frenchman. One German cannot seem to manage without his instruction booklet; a woman's fickle interest is found in anyone who will take her up in his air-

plane. The characters are what entertain here. Unfortunately, stereotypical as all these characters are, since no real interest is generated for them as people, the audience does not really care who wins the race.

Performances by familiar comedians such as Red Skelton, playing the Neanderthal Man in a short bit at the beginning, and Benny Hill as Fire Chief Perkins, provide some entertainment. Those who have a special interest in vintage flying machines or one of the film's other actors will probably be entertained as well. But for the rest, *Those Magnificent Men in Their Flying Machines* will move rather slowly and run about an hour too long, even though it is at times a pleasant and well-made film.

Cast: Stuart Whitman (Orvil Newton), Sarah Miles (Patricia Rawnsley), James Fox (Richard Mays), Alberto Sordi (Count Emilio Ponticelli), Robert Morley (Lord Rawnsley), Gert Frobe (Colonel Manfred von Holstein), Jean-Pierre Cassel (Pierre Dubois), Irina Demick (Brigitte/Ingrid/Marlene/Froncioise/Yvette/Betty), Eric Sykes (Courtney), Red Skelton (Neanderthal Man), Terry-Thomas (Sir Percy Ware-Armitage), Benny Hill (Fire Chief Perkins), Yujiro

Dastardly Sir Percival (Terry-Thomas) plots dirty deeds.

Did you know?...

Those Magnificent Men in Their Flying Machines, which itself seems to have been inspired by *The Great Race*, produced a spinoff entitled *Those Daring Young Men in Their Jaunty Jalopies* (also known as *Monte Carlo or Bust*). This comedy is about a automobile race across Europe and was produced by the same group and included many of the same cast members.

Ishihara (Yamamoto), Flora Robson (Mother Superior), Karl Michael Vogler (Captain Rumpel-stoss), Sam Wanamaker (George Gruber), Eric Barker (French Postman), Fred Emney (Colonel), Gordon Jackson (McDougal), John Le Mesurier (French Painter), Zena Marshall (Countess Sophia Ponticelli), James Robertson Justice (Narrator) **Screenwriter:** Ken Annakin, Jack Davies **Cinematographer:** Christopher Challis **Composer:** Ron Goodwin **Producer:** Stan Margulies for Twentieth Century Fox **Running Time:** 138 minutes **Format:** VHS, LV **Awards:** Academy Awards 1965: Nominations: Best Writing, Story and Screenplay **Box Office:** $14M.

Young Frankenstein

1974 – Mel Brooks – 🦴🦴🦴🦴

"Wait! Where're you going? I was going to make espresso."

Harold the Blind Hermit (Gene Hackman) to the Monster (Peter Boyle).

Mel Brooks is the master of some of the finest spoofs of serious movies ever done. *High Anxiety* lampoons *Vertigo* and Hitchcock, *Spaceballs* takes on *Star Wars*, *Blazing Saddles* skewers *Virginia City* and just about every western filmed between 1950 and 1970. Spoofing the original Karloffian *Frankenstein* as well as *The Bride* and other sequels, *Young Frankenstein*, which appeared after *Blazing Saddles*, ranks with it and *The Producers* among Brooks' very best films.

In it, young Dr. Frankenstein (pronounced FRONK-in-steen and played deftly by the very funny Gene Wilder) is teaching medicine in the U.S. when he is informed by Herr Falkstein (Richard Haydn) that he has inherited his grandfather's estate in Transylvania. He leaves to claim his inheritance, not believing his ancestor's conviction that the dead can be reanimated. Once there, he gives in to the physican's temptation to play God, reads in an old journal that dead flesh can be revived, and attempts it. But his random collection of living body parts produces a seven-foot monster (Peter Boyle) with a very weak brain. Brooks worked on the look of the film seemingly as much as on the jokes. Not only did the production get to use the laboratory equipment from the original *Frankenstein* film (the props having been stored, it seems, in a garage), but the black-and-white photography also beautifully captures the sheen of classic movies. This rich photography even contributes to the comic spirit; because the film looks so authentically classic, it becomes funnier to see the outrageous antics that erupt in such a setting. The introduction of the monster to the village and the unexpected dance number in formal attire that follows is just one scene that richly benefits from the carefully crafted photography and the long camera shots. This emphasis on style takes away any bitterness to the comedy and even

Did you know?...

The laserdisc version includes deleted scenes and outtakes, a making-of documentary, and audio commentary by Mel Brooks.

makes the film a tribute of sorts to the classic horror films of the 1930s. Brooks has often acknowledged such to be his intention.

The heavy make-up assists the comically heavy acting. All of the performances are enjoyable, but Gene Hackman, in a scene inspired by a moment from *The Bride of Frankenstein*, makes his very lonely, blind hermit (with boiling soup and ladle at the ready) into one of the movie's most memorable moments.

Frankenstein (Gene Wilder) prepares to give his monster (Peter Boyle) life.

Cast: Gene Wilder (Dr. Frankenstein), Peter Boyle (The Monster), Marty Feldman (Igor), Madeline Kahn (Elizabeth), Cloris Leachman (Frau Bluecher), Teri Garr (Inga), Kenneth Marrs (Inspector Kemp), Richard Haydn (Herr Falkstein), Gene Hackman (Harold the Blind Hermit) **Screenwriter:** Mel Brooks, Gene Wilder **Cinematographer:** Gerald Hirschfeld **Composer:** John Morris **Producer:** Michael Gruskoff **MPAA Rating:** PG **Running Time:** 98 minutes **Format:** VHS, LV **Awards:** Academy Awards, 1974: Nominations: Adapted Screenplay, Sound **Box Office:** $38.8M (rentals).

They Might Be Giants . . .

The epic is a film genre just asking for someone to make fun of it. It takes itself so seriously, often assuming (in the hands of less capable filmmakers) that size and grandness, whether measured by running time or cast members or geographic locations or all of these equals artistic quality. For his first feature-length film, *The Three Ages* (1923), Buster Keaton pricked the balloon of the epic, specifically D.W. Griffith's *Intolerance* by telling three interlocking comic stories of courtship set in the stone age, ancient Rome, and modern times. While the film is not as inspired as Keaton's later work, it still features a number of effective gags, especially one in which Buster rides toward the camera in his beat-up jalopy. In one continuous shot, we see his car get closer, hit a dip in the road, and completely fall to pieces—fenders, wheels, doors, body, everything comes apart before our eyes. Buster is left holding the steering wheel, which he throws on the junkpile of his car in disgust.

Other comic epics also parody the staples of established film genres. Mel Brooks is the master of showing up such established pretensions. *The History of the World, Part One* (1980) may not be as inspired as some of Brooks' better efforts, but it brings a desire to satirize the epic to its series of sketches. The habit that started in the mid-sixties to create epic comedy through the story of some quest (as in *The Great Race* and its imitators) reached a new expression with *The Blues Brothers* (1980), the Dan Ackroyd/John Belushi musical-comedy about efforts to save an orphanage. The epic scale of *Ghostbusters* (1984) and its sequel (1989) comes from comically pitting a trio of intrepid paranormal investigators in this world against the spooks of another and from giving the final showdown proportions both apocalyptic and comic.

CRIME

The Godfather

1972 – Francis Ford Coppola – ♫♫♫♫

> "My father made him an offer he couldn't refuse."
>
> Michael Corleone (Al Pacino)

From the opening scene of a Mafia princess' wedding to the brilliant closing sequence of a baby's christening interlaced with multiple murders, *The Godfather* illuminates the dichotomy of Mafia—and in some ways, American—values. Family, friendship, loyalty, togetherness: all are evident and all are expendable as this story of the Corleone crime family unfolds. Director Francis Ford Coppola provides enough teasing glimpses of actual history, like Frank Sinatra's comeback in a war movie, to captivate a knowledgeable audience.

The juxtaposition of graphic violence with homey moments makes this movie unforgettable: Don Corleone (Marlon Brando) buying an orange before he is gunned down, Michael's (Al Pacino) girlfriend Kay (Diane Keaton) enjoying lasagna as she learns about the grim family business, a brother-in-law sent to execution after a quiet family glass of brandy. Surprisingly, Michael the son, and not the Don, is the central character, and his transformation shapes the Puzo pop novel into a motion picture of depth. Michael returns home as a soldier hero from World War II, following the Don, his father's, dream that he succeed in legitimate ways, perhaps, becoming the first Italian president. But when the Godfather is shot and elder brother Sonny murdered, Michael's courage and determination press him into the family service of murder, exile, and revenge. By the end, the American hero is coolly, rationally commanding a crime empire.

Brando had to audition for the role of Don Corleone, competing with studio candidates such as Lawrence Olivier and George C. Scott. Warren Beatty declined the role of Michael. Director Francis Ford Coppola was third choice as director, behind Arthur Penn and Peter Yates. The end result is one of the greatest movies ever made.

Cast: Marlon Brando (Vito Corleone), Al Pacino (Michael Corleone), James Caan (Sonny Corleone), John Cazale (Fredo Corleone), Robert Duvall (Tom Hagen), Richard Castellano (Clemenza), Sterling Hayden (Captain McClusky), Diane Keaton (Kay Adams), Abe Vigoda (Tessio), John Marley (Jack Woltz), Talia Shire (Connie Corleone Rizzi), Giaani Russo (Carlo Rizzi), Al Martino (Johnny Fontane), Morgana King (Mama Corleone), Lenny Montana (Luca Brasi) **Screenwriter:** Francis Ford Coppola, Mario Puzo **Cinematographer:** Gordon Wills **Composer:** Nino Rota **Producer:** Albert S. Ruddy and Gray Frederickson for Paramount **MPAA Rating:** R **Running Time:** 175 minutes **Format:** VHS, LV **Awards:** Academy Awards, 1972: Actor (Marlon Brando), Adapted Screenplay, Picture; Nominations: Costume Design, Director (Francis

Did you know?...

The baby in the christening scene was Coppola's infant daughter, Sophia, who also appeared in *The Godfather III.*

Ford Coppola), Editing, Sound, Supporting Actor (James Caan, Robert Duvall, Al Pacino); Directors Guild of America Award, 1972: Director (Francis Ford Coppola); Golden Globe Awards, 1973: Actor—Drama (Marlon Brando), Director (Francis Ford Coppola), Film—Drama, Screenplay, Score; National Board of Review Awards, 1972: Ten Best Films of the Year, Supporting Actor (Al Pacino); New York Film Critics Awards, 1972: Supporting Actor (Robert Duvall); National Society of Film Critics Awards, 1972: Actor (Al Pacino); Writers Guild of America Awards, 1972: Adapted Screenplay **Box Office:** $85.7M (initial release).

Don Corleone (Marlon Brando) with his sons Michael (Al Pacino), Sonny (James Caan), and Fredo (John Cazale).

The Godfather, Part II

1974 – Francis Ford Coppola – 🦴🦴🦴🦴

> **"We're bigger than U.S. Steel!"**
> Hyman Roth (Lee Strasberg)

Seldom is a sequel anywhere near as satisfying or well made as the original; this one is both—if it is a sequel at all. In fact, both movies may be regarded as two parts of the same enormous story: the founding, growth, and decline of the Corleone crime family. Not only does *The Godfather, Part II* tie into the original film, but it also tells two distinct but related stories of its own, the life of young Vito Corleone (Robert De Niro) and the middle years of his son Michael (Al Pacino).

Like a double helix, the stories entwine. In 1901, young Vito comes as a child immigrant to the U.S., fleeing violence in Sicily. The hopeful faces passing the Statue of Liberty, the confusion of Ellis Island, the security of a job as a grocery clerk all make the audience see young Vito in a sympathetic light. The sympathy only builds when Vito kills the neighborhood scourge Fanucci (Gastone Moschin). And who can blame a man for accepting a stolen carpet for his beloved wife and babies? But the viewers are caught in a trap of their own (and Francis Ford Coppola's) making, for this is the foundation of a dual life of American success and calculated crime. As compassion grows for young Vito, interlaced scenes of Michael manipulating the mob in Cuba, Michael growing aloof from his wife and children, Michael lying before the Senate investigation of the Mafia turn the audience away from the legacy of the first godfather as we come to despise the second one.

Music, visuals, and stunning recreation of period sets and costumes are captivating. The performances are more nuanced than in *The Godfather* and thus are stronger. It ranks with Robert De Niro's best roles. Particular scenes linger in the memory, like the young Corleone family on the steps of a New York brownstone placidly watching a passing parade—completely unaware that their father has come late from murdering a man. And the final shot of aging Pacino alone, head of a family that no longer resembles one, is the picture of complete alienation.

In *The Godfather Part III* a profoundly lonely Michael still controls the "family business" but seeks forgiveness for the murder of his brother and tries to set his children's futures up securely. But fate takes from him those he loves, through the actions he began decades ago.

> **Did you know?...**
> Coppola edited the first two films in the trilogy into a chronological seven-hour saga called *The Godfather 1902-1959: The Complete Epic*. This work includes footage not used in the theatrical release of the first two films.

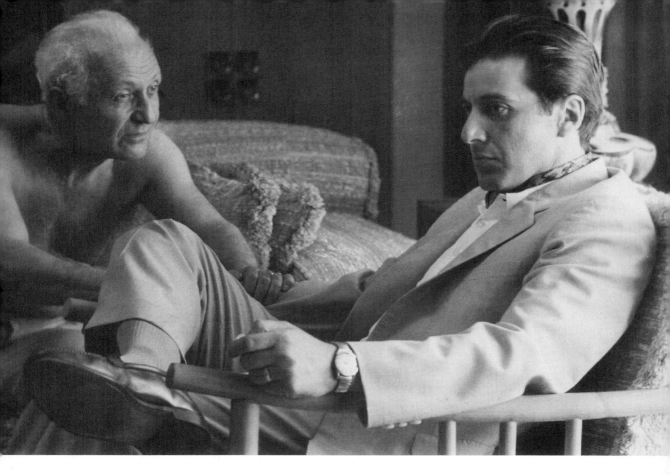

Cast: Al Pacino (Michael Corleone), Robert Duvall (Tom Hagen), Diane Keaton (Kay Corleone), Robert De Niro (Vito Corleone), John Cazales (Fredo Corleone), Talia Shire (Connie Corleone Rizzi), Lee Strasberg (Hyman Roth), Michael V. Gazza (Frank Pentangeli), G. D. Spradlin (Senator Pat Geary), Gastone Moschin (Fanucci), Bruno Kirby (Young Clemenza), Francesca De Sepia (Young Mama Corleone), Dominic Chianese (Johnny Ola), Troy Donahue (Merle Johnson), Oreste Baldini II (Boy Vito Corleone) **Screenwriter:** Francis Ford Coppola, Mario Puzo **Cinematographer:** Gordon Willis **Composer:** Carmine Coppola, Nino Rota **Producer:** Francis Ford Coppola, Gray Frederickson, and Fred Roos for Paramount **MPAA Rating:** R **Running Time:** 200 minutes **Format:** VHS, LV **Awards:** Academy Awards, 1974: Adapted Screenplay, Art Direction/Set Decoration, Director (Francis Ford Coppola), Picture, Supporting Actor (Robert De Niro), Original Dramatic/Comedy Score; Nominations: Actor (Al Pacino), Costume Design, Supporting Actor (Michael Gazzo, Lee Strasberg), Supporting Actress (Talia Shire); Directors Guild of America Awards, 1974: Director (Francis Ford Coppola); National Society of Film Critics Awards, 1974: Director (Francis Ford Coppola); Nominations: Cinematography; Writers Guild of America Awards 1974: Adapted Screenplay **Box Office:** $28.9M.

Michael Corleone (Al Pacino) discusses mob life with Hyman Roth (Lee Strasberg).

Once Upon a Time in America

1984 – Sergio Leone – 🦴🦴🦴

Sometimes a movie can take a collection of characters and follow them over decades in the manner of a long novel. Their lives separate and connect in what first seems to be random ways and later appears part of a pattern—like life itself—so that trivial-seeming details later resonate when put in the context of thirty years. The long (227-minute) version of this movie has that sort of richness.

Director Sergio Leone traces the lives of four boys from a Jewish ghetto beginning in 1921 when they start off as little hoods for hire (their first job is to burn down a newsstand). The second lengthy section dates from 1933 and shows their success in the crime world, running a speakeasy that fronts as a mortuary during the last days of Prohibition. The film concludes in 1968 when betrayals of the past are uncovered, and the two best friends (Robert De Niro and James Woods) see how they became the men they are. This span of years emphasizes the importance of memories and context to the developing story. As young men they all pledge to set aside half of their take in a suitcase that they agree to remove from its public locker only as a group. The whereabouts of the suitcase becomes a structuring device and even provides some transitions from one era to another. The sprawling story features a number of memorable moments. In one of the best, Danny Aiello appears as a cop backing some strikebreakers; he gets his comeuppance when the mob plays hide-and-seek with his newborn son (to the tune of "The Thieving Magpie") in a maternity ward.

Although the full version was shown at film festivals in 1984, Warner Bros. trimmed almost an hour and a half for the version released theatrically in the U.S. They also simplified the structure by making the plot more linear. Both versions have been released on cassette, but the shorter one is much less coherent.

Cast: Robert De Niro (Noodles), James Woods (Max), Elizabeth McGovern (Deborah), Treat Williams (Jimmy O'Donnell), Tuesday Weld (Carol), Burt Young (Joe), Joe Pesci (Frankie Monaldi), Danny Aiello (Police Chief Aiello), William Forsythe (Cockeye), James Hayden (Patsy), Darlanne Fluegel (Eve), Larry Rapp (Fat Moe), Dutch Miller (Van Linden), Robert Harper (Sharkey), Richard Bright (Chicken Joe), Gerard Murphy (Crowning), Amy Ryder (Peggy) **Screenwriter:** Leonardo Benvenuti, Peiero De Bernardi, Enrico Medioli, Franco Arcalli, Franco Ferrini, Sergio Leone, Stuart M. Kaminsky **Cinematographer:** Tonino Delli Colli **Composer:** Ennio Morricone **Producer:** Arnon Milchan for Warner Bros.; distributed by the Ladd Company **MPAA Rating:** R **Running Time:** 227 (139 for the theatrical release) **Format:** VHS, LV **Budget:** $32M.

Gangster Noodles Aaronson
(Robert De Niro) defends his life
and that of his girlfriend, Eve
(Darlanne Fluegel).

Scarface

1983 – Brian De Palma – ♪♪♪

"This country, you gotta make the money first. Then when you get the money, you get the power. Then when you get the power, you get the woman."

Tony's (Al Pacino) ABCs of success in America.

Brian DePalma and screenwriter Oliver Stone remade Howard Hawks' 90-minute gangster classic from 1932 into a large-scale crime drama that charts the rise and fall of Cuban refugee Tony Montana (Al Pacino). Visually and verbally, the film has the appeal of a roadside accident with the wreckage still smoking. You can't quite avert your eyes. The director and writer get a kick from seeing which is the more tawdry side of dealing in cocaine: crassly flaunting the new-found wealth or crassly killing off friends and enemies. The movie spurts blood and flaunts its profanity like a badge of honor. The image of Pacino sitting in a Cadillac convertible with zebra-striped upholstery wearing Elvira's (Michelle Pfeiffer) white bonnet in an effort to make her laugh also illustrates the film's quirky appeal. Just as things start to look hopelessly cartoonish (F. Murray Abraham getting hanged from a hovering helicopter serving as an impromptu gallows), a scene comes along that almost humanizes the characters: Tony visits his mother (Miriam Colon) and sister (Mary Elizabeth Mastrantonio), and his mother's angry rejection of his tainted money actually seems to shame him.

DePalma and Stone allude more directly to Hawks' original film by including the incest-attraction Tony feels for his sister Gina, but until the very end, this remains the only latent element in this explicit film. DePalma also borrows the message from the electric sign ("The World Is Yours") in the original and scrolls it across the side of a blimp that Tony sees in the night sky as he begins his ascent to the top of the drug industry. Predictably, once at the top he finds success hollow. In the great restaurant scene, Stone gives Pacino a soliloquy in which Tony starts addressing a roomful of embarrassed patrons: "You don't have the guts to be what you want to be. You need people like me . . . You're not good. You just know how to hide." The drama of this moment suggests that Stone's interest in Tony is in his potential as a tragic hero. Tony's private office is even designed like a throne room. If it aims for this level, *Scarface* is a revenge tragedy with little insight for the hero—more like a Classics Illustrated *Richard III* than the real thing.

Cast: Al Pacino (Tony Montana), Steven Bauer (Manny Ray), Michelle Pfeiffer (Elvira), Mary Elizabeth Mastrantonio (Gina), Robert Loggia (Frank Lopez), Miriam Colon (Mama Mon-

Did you know?...

The videocassette version adds some clips from the original *Scarface*, the DVD version includes outtakes from the making of DePalma's film.

tana), F. Murray Abraham (Omar), Paul Shenar (Sosa), Harris Yulin (Bernstein), Angel Salazar (Chi Chi), Arnaldo Santana (Ernie), Pepe Serna (Angel), Michael P. Moran (Nick the Pig), Al Israel (Hector the Toad), Richard Belzer (emcee at the Babylon Club) **Screenwriter:** Oliver Stone **Cinematographer:** John A. Alonzo **Composer:** Giorgio Moroder **Producer:** Martin Bregman for Universal **MPAA Rating:** R **Running Time:** 170 minutes **Format:** VHS, LV, DVD.

Miami drug lord Tony (Al Pacino) dances with Elvira (Michelle Pfeiffer).

White Heat

1949 – Raoul Walsh – 🎵🎵🎵

James Cagney was fifty years old when he played Cody Jarrett, one of the first screen psychopaths to seize the public's attention. Earlier misfits, like Humphrey Bogart's Duke Mantee in *The Petrified Forest* and Robert Montgomery in *Night Must Fall*, did not carry those films as Cagney's character does here. The twisted fun of *White Heat* is in the way it takes the audience deeper and deeper inside Cody Jarrett. At the start, when he and his gang rob a train, Jarrett seems like just another hood. But after he kills the conductor for hearing his name and later decides to kill one of his own injured gang members rather than have their escape slowed, Jarrett is defined by his ruthlessness. Cagney modeled his portrayal on real-life psychotic Arthur "Doc" Parker of the infamous Ma Barker Gang.

We soon see that this ruthlessness mixes with a deep mother fixation. Stricken with one of his paralyzing headaches, Cody is taken into the back room of the gang's hideout by his mother (Margaret Wycherly), who rubs his temples and makes sure the gang doesn't see their leader in his moment of weakness. It was reportedly Cagney's idea to climb onto Wycherly's lap, just as he also drew upon youthful memories of visits to a friend's uncle in a hospital for the insane, and all the accompanying sounds of the psych ward. To avoid capture for the murder of the train conductor, Cody decides to confess to a lesser crime and go to prison for a short time. He hears of the death of his mother in the prison mess room, when the whispered word is passed to him down a line of convicts. Cody's berserk scene is one of the movie's great moments. Against a backdrop of long rows of prisoners sitting quietly at their lunch, Jarrett rises with sobs and wails and eventually climbs onto the tabletop, where he staggers out of control and wallows in prison swill until three or four guards can subdue him.

His eventual jailbreak leads to the final insanities. In one scene he ambles alone out of the woods, explaining to Fallon (Edmond O'Brien) that he was just "talking to Ma. I liked it, liked it a lot." The attempt to steal the payroll from an oil refinery brings an army of police with sharpshooters who surround the gang and pick them off one by one. Cody, standing atop an oil rig, is the last survivor. After he is wounded, with flames swirling around him, he screams out his final triumph: "Made it Ma! Top of the world!"

Did you know?...

The central characters are based on Ma Barker and her son Arthur.

Cast: James Cagney (Cody Jarrett), Virginia Mayo (Verna Jarrett), Edmond O'Brien (Hank Fallon/Vic Pardo), Margaret Wycherly (Ma Jarrett), Steve Cochran (Big Ed Somers), John Archer (Phillip Evans), Wally Cassell (Giovanni Valetti), Fred Clark (Daniel Winston), Ford Rainey (Zuckie), Fred Coby (Happy), G. Pat Collins (Herbert), Mickey Knox (Het Kohler), Paul Guilfoyle (Roy Parker), Robert Osterloh (Tommy Ryley), Ian MacDonald (Bo Creel), Ray Montgomery (Ernie Trent), Jim Toney (the breakman), Milton Parsons (the stoolie), Marshall Bradford (the chief of police) **Screenwriter:** Ivan Goff, Ben Roberts **Cinematographer:** Sid Hickox **Composer:** Max Steiner **Producer:** Louis F. Edelman for Warner Bros. **Running Time:** 114 minutes **Format:** VHS, LV **Awards:** Academy Awards 1949: Nominations: Story.

Cody Jarrett (James Cagney) defies the coppers in *White Heat*.

They Might Be Giants . . .

Warner Bros. seemed to hold the rights to the gangster film in the 1930s, in part through the great work of their set designer Anton Grot, who was able to suggest a gritty urban feel in an era of movie escapism. The films that can lay claim to reaching an epic stature probably do so through a defining, indelible performance, such as those of James Cagney in *Public Enemy* (1930), Edward G. Robinson in *Little Caesar* (1930), and perhaps Paul Muni in the original *Scarface: The Shame of a Nation* (1932). Years later, the enormous popularity of *Bonnie and Clyde* (1967) reflected the way its story of anti-establishment outlaws in the 1930s resonated with sympathetic moviegoing audiences in the 1960s. More recently, Martin Scorsese has shown an interest in large-scale gangland films with *GoodFellas* (1990) and *Casino* (1995), both of which span a number of years to chart the various corrupting effects of the mob—the first on the character played by Ray Liotta and the second on the city of Las Vegas itself.

DISASTER

Apollo 13

1995 — Ron Howard — 🦴🦴🦴🦴

> "Are you scared? Well, don't you worry, honey. If they could get a washing machine to fly, my Jimmy could land it."
>
> Jim Lovell's mother (played by the director's mother Jean), to her young granddaughter.

Ron Howard's film about the 1970 Apollo space mission documents the near-tragedy of the mission 200,000 miles above the Earth when two oxygen tanks exploded, and the subsequent successful return of the astronauts. The launch takes place amid the growing indifference of the general public who have become blase over trips to the moon; one of the live telecasts from the capsule isn't even carried by the three networks. This lack of familiarity with the mission may add to the film's drama since most of the audience will know that the astronauts returned safely but might not know how they did so.

One of the impressive things about the script is the way it repeatedly takes complicated matters of math and science and makes them understandable to the audience. The problem of finding sufficient power for the lifeboat of the lunar module becomes more understandable and more compelling as the technicians make analogies to the power it takes to run a vacuum cleaner or work a coffee pot. The cutaways to television anchormen also furnish explanations that keep the strategies clear. The moon mission is aborted about an hour into the story, and the rest of the movie is really a drama of human ingenuity and clear-headedness in the face of physical danger and the tightening constraints of time.

The film therefore celebrates heroism in a somewhat uncommon but enormously refreshing way. What gets the mythic treatment is not the idea of space exploration or the even the glory of human curiosity but rather the work of nerdy guys in white shirts with slide rules who double-check the math and figure out how to take the everyday objects in the module—like socks and duct tape—and transform them into an impromptu survival kit. Howard deglamorizes parts of the hectic scenes when mission control springs into action by having them play out against a backdrop of chalkboards, overhead projectors, cluttered ashtrays, and Dixie-cup-littered counters. Paradoxically, such ordinariness sets off even more this brand of bravery. The movie makes being smart cool. The filmmakers discover genuine heroism and even patriotism in the old-fashioned American resourcefulness of savvy, quick-thinking minds and the poise of a steady hand at the control. In its grace under pressure, *Apollo 13* is a Hemingwayesque space drama.

Did you know?...

The opening party scene on the night of the moon landing never happened. It was Ron Howard's idea as an easy way to introduce the main characters to the audience.

Cast: Tom Hanks (Jim Lovell), Bill Paxton (Fred Haise), Kevin Bacon (Jack Swigert), Gary Sinise (Ken Mattingly), Ed Harris (Gene Kranz), Kathleen Quinlan (Marilyn Lovell), Mary Kate Achellhardt (Barbara Lovell), Emily Ann Lloyd (Susan Lovell), Miko Hughes (Jeffrey Lovell), Jean Speegle Howard (Blanche Lovell), Tracy Reiner (Mary Haise), David Andrews (Pete Conrad), Michele Little (Jane Conrad), Chris Ellis (Deke Slayton), Joe Spano (NASA director), Marc McClure (Glynn Lunney), Clint Howard (EECOM White), Loren Dean (EECOM Arthur), Mark Wheeler (Neil Armstrong), Larry B. Williams (Buzz Aldrin), Rance Howard (Reverend), Roger Corman (Congressman), Jim Lovell (Iwo-Jima Captain) **Screenwriter:** William Broyles Jr., Al Reinert, John Sayles (uncredited) **Cinematographer:** Dean Cundey **Composer:** James Horner **Producer:** Brian Grazer for Universal and Image Entertainment **MPAA Rating:** PG **Running Time:** 140 minutes **Format:** VHS, LV, DVD **Awards:** Academy Awards 1995: Editing, Sound; Nominations: Picture, Adapted Screenplay, Art Direction/Set Decoration, Supporting Actor (Ed Harris), Supporting Actress (Kathleen Quinlan), Original Dramatic/Comedy Score; Directors Guild of America Awards 1995: Director (Ron Howard); Screen Actors Guild Awards 1995: Supporting Actor (Ed Harris); Blockbuster Entertainment Awards 1996: Drama Actor, Theatrical (Tom Hanks); British Academy Awards 1995: Nominations: Cinematography; Golden Globe Awards 1996: Nominations: Film—Drama, Director (Ron Howard), Supporting Actor (Ed Harris), Supporting Actress (Kathleen Quinlan); MTV Movie Awards 1996: Nominations: Film, Male Performance (Tom Hanks); Writers Guild of America Awards 1995: Nominations: Adapted Screenplay **Budget:** $62M **Box Office:** $172M.

Frank W. Haise (Bill Paxton), John L. Swigart (Kevin Bacon), and Jim Lovell (Tom Hanks) are the crew of an ill-fated lunar mission.

The Birds

1963 — Alfred Hitchcock — 🦴🦴🦴🦕

About halfway through *The Birds*, Mrs. Brenner (Jessica Tandy) tries to recover from the grisly sight of discovering a neighbor's corpse with pecked-out eyes. She sits at home propped up in bed and reflects on the death of her husband three years earlier by quietly describing the way he could enter the world of their children and become part of them. "Oh, I wish, I wish, I wish I could be like that," she says desperately. None of the adults are like that deceased father: they are all so isolated, self-absorbed, and withdrawn as to seem by comparison dehumanized. The unexplained bird attacks that occur with increasing severity in the small California town of Bodega Bay, then, are in a way the worst and latest expression of life gone awry for these characters: Mitch Brenner, a lawyer (Rod Taylor) who spends every weekend with his mother; the widowed mother (Tandy) who clings to her son so that she won't be left alone; the discarded girlfriend (Suzanne Pleshette) who stays in the town she doesn't like just to be near Mitch. Another character, Melanie Daniels (Tippi Hedren), is introduced into the mix, a rich, aimless woman who pretends to be a salesgirl in a pet shop and who brings lovebirds to Mitch in Bodega Bay just to continue a flirtation.

The bird attacks shatter the false fronts of routine and conformity. They terrorize a children's birthday party, invade the Brenner house through the chimney, swoop down malevolently as children are taken home from school. Director Alfred Hitchcock coyly leaves their apocalyptic fury unexplained, but the suggestions seem clear enough. If Hitchcock had lived another five years or so, long enough to hear about the deteriorating ozone, the greenhouse effect, antibiotic-resistant bacteria, and AIDS, would he have recognized in his story about the birds of Bodega Bay a foreshadowing of most of our millennial fears?

When screenwriter Evan Hunter published the memoir *Hitch and Me* in 1997 about his experiences working on *The Birds*, he cited his numerous dissatisfactions with some of the characters and with the ending. People who look at the film novelistically like Hunter will probably find the characters unclear since what they say often fails to suggest much depth. But people who look at the film cinematically (those who realize that character in film can be developed visually as well as verbally, an awareness surprisingly few novelists-turned-screenwrit-

Did you know?...

The bird noises are not recordings of actual birds but electronic sounds produced by sound engineers Remi Gossman and Oskar Sala.

Mitch (Rod Taylor) eyes a not-so-fine-feathered friend.

ers share) realize that the deepest scenes in *The Birds* are the moments when words are absent or unimportant, moments when the visuals take over.

These are not always the times when the attacks come. One of the most interesting appears in the scene after the birds have swarmed through the Brenners' chimney. Amid the rubble of the living room, Mitch tries to explain to the sheriff what occurred. His voice is mere background chatter while Melanie observes Mrs. Brenner pacing the room and picking up pieces of broken coffee cups as if she were vainly trying to piece together again their lives. When she straightens the painting of her dead husband, a bird falls from behind the frame, and Mrs. Brenner recoils. The sympathetic reaction shot of Melanie speaks clearly for all those who hunger for substance beneath life's thin veneer.

Cast: Rod Taylor (Mitch Brenner), Tippi Hedren (Melanie Daniels), Jessica Tandy (Lydia Brenner), Suzanne Pleshette (Annie Hayworth), Veronica Cartwright (Cathy Brenner), Doodles Weaver (man at the boat dock), Charles McGraw (Sebastian Sholes), Ruth McDevitt (Mrs. Magruder), Ethel Griffies (Mrs. Bundy), Elizabeth Wilson (waitress in Tides Cafe), Richard Deacon (man in hallway), Morgan Brittany (girl at the school—billed as Suzanne Cupito) **Screenwriter:** Evan Hunter **Cinematographer:** Robert Burks **Composer:** Bernard Herrmann (listed as sound consultant; the film has no music) **Producer:** Alfred Hitchcock (unbilled) for Universal **Running Time:** 120 minutes **Format:** VHS, LV **Box Office:** $11M (shortly after its initial release).

The Hindenburg
1975 – Robert Wise – 🦴🦴

> "Next time let's take the Titanic."
>
> Mrs. Channing (Joanna Moore), to her husband as the dirigible passes through a storm.

A prediction of disaster from an American psychic sets off fear and suspicion as the famous zeppelin starts its transatlantic trip to Lakehurst, New Jersey, in 1937. True to the formula started with *The Poseidon Adventure* and *The Towering Inferno*, this film brings together an odd assortment of passengers who are observed by a Luftwaffe colonel (George C. Scott) and his investigative assistant (Roy Thinnes) to prevent any sabotage. Among the passengers, however, is a member of an anti-Nazi resistance group with a bomb who intends to destroy the ship.

The exposition plods on and on. About forty minutes in, director Robert Wise and his screenwriters create a lengthy conversation between Scott and Thinnes that discusses one by one the other characters on board while we see

The Countess (Anne Bancroft) and Emilio (Meredith Burgess) survive the disaster of *The Hindenburg.*

shots of them moving about the airship. This redundancy of introducing people already presented to the audience not only wastes time but calls attention to the shallowness of the characters. The most interesting parts of the film are those that recreate historical detail and even incorporate newsreel footage, as in a pre-credit sequence and again at the end.

The fatal mistake made by Wise, which James Cameron wisely avoided in his script for *Titanic*, was using the fictional element to compromise the factual one. Cameron gives his fictional love story a separate life from the parallel plot of the sinking ship and thereby allows the facts of the approaching disaster to enrich the fiction. Wise and his screenwriters begin with the "what if" premise that sabotage caused the explosion of the Hindenburg, and that decision manages to dilute both fact and fiction. All of the superficial faithfulness to detail loses much of its impact since the reason for the crash has had its historical grounding weakened by this intrusive speculation. And so Wise missed the

Did you know?...

All of the shots of the airship are of a twenty-seven-foot model matted into various backgrounds with the optical printer by effects artist Al Whitlock.

chance to have what could have been a megahit (though he had already enjoyed the thrill of directing the biggest financial success of the 1960s with *The Sound of Music*). *The Hindenburg* is basically a whodunit set against the backdrop of the promise of spectacle and disaster. Viewers will likely get something other than what they expect.

Cast: George C. Scott (Colonel Franz Ritter), Anne Bancroft (Ursula, the countess), William Atherton (Boerth), Roy Thinnes (Martin Vogel), Gig Young (Edward Douglas), Burgess Meredith (Emilio Pajetta), Charles Durning (Captain Pruss), Richard A. Dysart (Captain Lehman), Robert Clary (Joe Spah), Rene Auberjonois (Major Napier), Peter Donat (Reed Channing), Alan Oppenheimer (Albert Breslau), Katherine Helmond (Mrs. Mildred Breslau), Joanna Moore (Mrs. Channing), Greg Mullavy (Morrison) **Screenwriter:** Nelson Gidding, Richard Levinson, William Link **Cinematographer:** Robert Surtees **Composer:** David Shire **Producer:** Robert Wise for Universal **MPAA Rating:** PG **Running Time:** 126 minutes **Format:** VHS, LV **Awards:** Academy Awards 1975: Sound Effects Editing, Visual Effects; Nominations: Art Direction/Set Decoration, Cinematography, Sound.

The Last Days of Pompeii

1935 — Ernest B. Schoedsack, Merian C. Cooper —

> "Money is all that matters. Well, I can get money. It's easy to get money. All you have to do is kill!"
>
> Marcus (Preston Foster), years after the death of his wife and child, stating his philosophy.

Marcus (Preston Foster) is a gentle giant of a blacksmith whose top priority is his family. After his wife and infant son are run down in the streets of Pompeii by a reckless chariot driver and die as a result of Marcus' inability to pay for a doctor, obtaining wealth becomes his obsession. He turns to fighting in the arena in order to earn more than he could as a mere blacksmith, and it doesn't take long until Marcus is the champion and the most fearsome adversary of all would-be gladiators in Pompeii.

When Marcus kills in gladiatorial combat the father of a young boy, Flavius (John Wood), his buried allegiance to family (and perhaps some guilt about the fate of his own son) inspires him to adopt the boy. But Marcus ages quickly as a result of his dangerous occupation as gladiator, and soon he is defeated. He turns to slave and horse trading and begins to harbor the ambition of becoming the "head of the arena." A soothsayer tells Marcus to take his son to see the "greatest man in Judea," but upon learning that Jesus was born in a stable, Marcus decides that this "greatest man" must be Judea's governor, Pontius Pilate. Flavius does meet Jesus, however, after the boy falls from a horse and is

taken to be healed. Years later, Flavius searches his memory trying to recall the man who touched his life in such a special way. Flavius has now grown into a meek and gentle young man who secretly hides escaped slaves in the hopes of helping them find a place where they can live in freedom. His plans miscarry and he and the slaves are captured and forced to fight the newly conquered Britons. During this fight, Mt. Vesuvius erupts and the city is destroyed.

The filmmakers sacrifice some historical accuracy in order to add the religious element to the film. The life and trials of Jesus are woven into the plot that culminates with the Vesuvius eruption in A.D. 79, more than forty years after the crucifixion of Christ. Flavius was healed by Christ as a boy, but he can't be much older than thirty at the time of the eruption. The sensationalizing publicity for the film described Pompeii as "drunk with wealth and power" and "rotten with pagan pleasures," but little of this sort of decadence is evident in the movie. We are told the story of one man who really isn't all that bad and of his son who

Mt. Vesuvius erupts and it's the end in *The Last Days of Pompeii.*

Did you know?...

Pontius Pilate, written as a major character in *The Last Days of Pompeii,* actually retired from his post as governor of Judea in A.D. 36, more than forty years before Vesuvius destroyed Pompeii in A.D. 79.

is actually good, but aside from the title, there is barely a mention of the fact that a volcano looms over the city. In addition, the action is limited. Some fighting appears in the arena scenes, and some panicking crowds and crumbling buildings create the sense of havoc when the volcano finally erupts. But the film is essentially an hour of dialog and introspection that has little to do with Vesuvius or Pompeii followed by a half hour of special effects (which are fairly good even by today's standards) as the disaster unfolds.

Cast: Preston Foster (Marcus), Alan Hale (Burbix), Basil Rathbone (Pontius Pilate), John Wood (Flavius), Louis Calhern (Prefect), David Holt (Flavius as a boy), Dorothy Wilson (Clodia), Wyrley Birch (Leaster), Gloria Shea (Julia), Frank Conroy (Gaius Tanno), John Davidson (Slave), Murray Kinnell (Judaean peasant), Henry Kolker (Warder), William V. Mong (Creon), Zeffie Tilbury (Wise Woman) **Screenwriter:** Melville Baker, James Ashmore Creelman, Boris Ingster, Ruth Rose **Cinematographer:** Jack Cardiff **Composer:** Max Steiner, Roy Webb **Producer:** Merian C. Cooper for RKO **Running Time:** 96 minutes **Format:** VHS, LV.

A Night to Remember

1958 – Roy Baker – 🦴🦴🦴

> "I'll never be sure of anything ever again."
>
> The second officer, straddling a capsized lifeboat in the water.

Did you know?...

The passenger in the film who returns to her stateroom to get a music box in the shape of a pig is based on a real woman who later bequeathed the music box to author Walter Lord. The prop shown is reported to be the same one the real passenger rescued from the ship.

William MacQuitty was six years old on May 31, 1911, when he watched the launch of the *Titanic* in Belfast. He was also on hand when the ship started its fateful first voyage on April 10, 1912. For years he tried to produce a film about the sinking of the ship, but it was not until Walter Lord's 1955 bestseller that interest was renewed once again. MacQuitty took the book to the Rank Organization and eventually oversaw one of the largest budgets for a British film to that time. MacQuitty's great insight was to view the event as a symbol, like World War I, of the end of the old world of privilege and the myth of invincibility and as the start of the modern world of chaos and uncertainty. In a real sense, the Age of Anxiety began on April 14, 1912.

MacQuitty and director Roy Baker adopt the approach of docudrama. They use composite characters to represent first-, second-, and third-class passengers, but the focus is always on the ship rather than the various human dramas. Minutes before the ship scrapes the iceberg, Baker arranges a series of haunting wordless shots: the nearly-empty grand salon, the second officer bedding down, a second-class passenger slipping into the room of his mistress, a mother tuck-

The Titanic's Capt. Smith (Laurence Naismith) confronts disaster with fellow officer Andrews (Michael Goodliffe).

ing in her young son, and a slow track into a rocking horse in the ship's spacious toy room. When the ship hits the iceberg, the only initial sign in the luxury quarters comes when a champagne glass on a table jiggles ever so slightly. (MacQuitty's technical advisor for the film, one of 64 survivors who met with Walter Lord and the Rank Organization, reported that he was walking on deck at the fateful moment and that the impact did not even cause him to break stride.) The film is filled with fine details like the moment the first-class husband tells his wife (Honor Blackman) to prepare to take their children to the lifeboats and then slips around her neck a glittery necklace. The dignity and controlled passion of the scene suggests the aristocrat's love of wealth but also his perception that his wife will need the income from the jewels to live on during her widowhood.

A number of distinguished names worked on the film behind the cameras. Eric Ambler, the author of a number of respected espionage novels, adapted Lord's book for the screen, and Geoffrey Unsworth, one of Britain's most esteemed cameramen, shot the film. Others also addressed the need for authenticity. Clips from the making of the film show Kenneth More, who played the second officer, conferring with the real-life widow of his character. These filmmakers did not have a hundred million dollars at their disposal, but they produced a dramatic, authentic film with the considerable talent they had.

Cast: Laurence Naismith (Capt. Smith), Kenneth More (Second Officer Charles Herbert Lightoller), Ronald Allen (Mr. Clarke), Robert Ayres (Major Arthur Peuchen), Honor Blackman (Mrs. Lucas), Anthony Bushell (Captain Arthur Rostron), John Cairney (Murphy), Jill Dixon (Mrs. Clarke), Jane Downs (Mrs. Lightoller), James Dyrenforth (Colonel Archibald Gracie), Michael Goodliffe (Thomas Andrews), Kenneth Griffith (John G. Phillips), Harriette Johns (Lady Richard), David McCallum (Harold S. Bride), Alec McCowen (Cottam), Tucker McGuire (Molly Brown), Harold Goldblatt (Benjamin Guggenheim) **Screenwriter:** Eric Ambler **Cinematographer:** Geoffrey Unsworth **Composer:** William Alwyn **Producer:** William MacQuitty **Running Time:** 123 minutes **Format:** VHS, LV, DVD **Award:** Golden Globes Award 1959: Foreign Film; National Board of Review Awards 1958: 5 Best Foreign Films of the Year.

The Poseidon Adventure
1972 – Ronald Neame – 𝄞𝄞𝄞

> "You see, Mr. Scott, in the water I'm a very skinny lady."
> Mrs. Rosen (Shelley Winters), after swimming through a treacherous passage and saving Scott's life.

An oceanic earthquake creates a monster tidal wave that capsizes the cruise liner *Poseidon*, and a New Year's Eve celebration turns into a struggle for survival. The story follows a group of ten passengers searching for safety through the labyrinthine passages of the ship (the *Queen Mary* for the exterior shots). Some may give credit to Alfred Hitchcock for inventing the disaster movie with *The Birds*, but it was really this film that set up most of the staples of the genre such as the ensemble cast of big names and the obstacle-course hazards that make up the plot.

Gene Hackman, as a nonconformist minister, takes control of the group and steers their dwindling number through these dangers. The better scenes use the physical perils to elicit emotions other than the usual fear or anger from the passengers, as when Carol Lynley timidly admits to Red Buttons, the lonely bachelor, that she can't swim. He rises to the challenge of leading her through a twisty underwater corridor and companionway to the next safe haven. This scene also features the best moments for Shelley Winters, who plays a frumpy grandmother. She begs Hackman to let her be the first to navigate the unknown

Did you know?...
Irwin Allen directed a sequel, *Beyond the Poseidon Adventure* (1979), about a group of treasure hunters attempting to loot the capsized ship before it sinks.

corridor and even shows him a medal she won years ago for swimming: "For hours you've all been dragging and pulling me all this way. Now I have a chance to do something I know how to do. Please! May I do this for everybody?" Overall, the movie shows how the formula for disaster films works when the dangers strip away pretenses to reveal the characters' real natures, but other scenes also make clear that danger for danger's sake won't sustain interest for an entire film. Just as the early scenes are set up as a series of snapshots to introduce the principal characters, the later scenes isolate four of the ten as sacrificial lambs. Unfortunately, the wise-guy little brother of Pamela Sue Martin seems to have a charmed life.

Manny (Jack Albertson), Belle (Shelley Winters), and Martin (Red Buttons) struggle as the ship rolls over.

Cast: Gene Hackman (Rev. Frank Scott), Ernest Borgnine (Mike Rogo), Red Buttons (James Martin), Carol Lynley (Nonnie Parry), Roddy McDowall (Acres), Stella Stevens (Linda Rogo), Shelley Winters (Belle Rosen), Jack Albertson (Manny Rosen), Pamela Sue Martin (Susan Shelby), Arthur O'Connell (Chaplain), Eric Shea (Robin Shelby), Fred Sadoff (Linarcos), Bob Hastings (M.C.), Leslie Nielsen (Captain Harrison), Byron Webster (purser) **Screenwriter:**

Wendell Mayes, Stirling Silliphant **Cinematographer:** Harold E. Stine **Composer:** Joel Hirschhorn, Al Kasha, John Williams **Producer:** Irwin Allen **MPAA Rating:** PG **Running Time:** 117 minutes **Format:** VHS, LV **Awards:** Academy Awards 1972: Song ("The Morning After"), Visual Effects; Nominations: Art Direction/Set Decoration, Cinematography, Costume Design, Editing, Sound, Supporting Actress (Shelley Winters), Original Dramatic/Comedy Score; Golden Globe Awards 1972: Supporting Actress (Shelley Winters).

San Francisco

1936 – W.S. Van Dyke – 🎵🎵🎵

> "He's that way, Blackie is. Ashamed of his good deeds as other people are of their sins."
>
> Father Mullen (Spencer Tracy), to Mary.

Somehow scriptwriter Anita Loos brought together the hodgepodge of many story elements and blended them effectively as a backdrop for the 1906 San Francisco earthquake and fire. The film features saloons, opera, boxing, politics, religion, and romance. Clark Gable and Spencer Tracy play boyhood pals, one of whom becomes a priest (Tracy) while the other ends up owning a gambling joint and dance hall on the Barbary Coast. Gable, as Blackie Norton, prides himself on his ability to cater to a different type of "suckers" than those who attend the mission run by Tracy. Jeanette MacDonald plays a minister's daughter whose singing talent gets her a job at the Paradise, the saloon run by Gable, as well as offers to sing at Tracy's mission and at the opera house run by Jack Burley (Jack Holt). Gable and Holt soon becomes rivals not only for MacDonald's services as a singer but also for her love.

The film is a great example of the good, polished (if often artificial) moviemaking of the studio era. It is fun to watch Gable playing a character who enjoys his audacity as much as Blackie does and to see Tracy in the role that made him a star. MacDonald's singing is majestic, and the earthquake and aftershock sequences still look good. But three or four moments break out of this conventional development and really come to life. Two such scenes are the great defining speeches Anita Loos wrote for the two leads. Tracy talks to MacDonald at the mission about the godlessness of San Francisco, his long friendship with Blackie ("nothing in the world, no one in the world is all bad"), and his own decision to enter the priesthood. Tracy voices these lofty feelings with an offhandedness that is completely genuine; you know how deeply he believes what he says because of his simple, self-effacing delivery. Later, Gable expounds to MacDon-

Did you know?...

Jeanette MacDonald pitched the idea to MGM for a film in which she would play an opera singer in love with a rascal of the Barbary Coast against the backdrop of the San Francisco earthquake. She was willing to wait for Clark Gable to be available to appear opposite her.

Father Tim (Spencer Tracy) and gambler Blackie (Clark Gable) in the aftermath of the 1906 earthquake.

ald his own rogue's theology: "What I believe in is not up in the air; it's in here and in here," he says, touching his head and his heart.

But the best example appears in the scene when the opera impresario Burley comes to the Paradise to buy MacDonald's contract. Gable tells him that he can have it for free if she chooses to leave. When they call her in and pose the offer, she asks "Mr. Norton" if he wants to sell her contract. Gable says, "no," and she elects to stay at the Paradise even though Burley keeps bidding higher. Watch for the closeup of MacDonald's face when Gable mentions that he had offered her contract for nothing if she had wanted to go. She rivets her gaze on Gable, understanding this as his expression of affection, and after a pause calls him "Blackie" for the first time. The honesty of that look is as impressive in its own way as all the toppling buildings and smoking rubble in the 20-minute earthquake sequence.

Cast: Clark Gable (Blackie Norton), Jeanette MacDonald (Mary Blake), Spencer Tracy (Father Tim Mullen), Jack Holt (Jack Burley), Jessie Ralph (Mrs. Burley), Ted Healy (Mat),

Shirley Ross (Trixie), Margaret Irving (Della Bailey), Harold Huber (Babe), Edgar Kennedy (Sheriff), Al Shean (Professor), William Ricciardi (Signor Baldini), Kenneth Harlan (Chick), Roger Imhof (Alaska), Charles Judels (Tony), Russell Simpson (Red Kelly), Bert Roach (Freddie Duane), Warren B. Hymer (Hazeltine), Sam Ash (orchestra leader) **Screenwriter:** Anita Loos **Cinematographer:** Oliver T. Marsh **Composer:** Edward Ward **Producer:** John Emerson for MGM, Bernard H. Hyman **Running Time:** 115 minutes **Format:** VHS, LV **Awards:** Academy Awards 1936: Sound; Nominations: Picture, Actor (Spencer Tracy), Director (W.S. Van Dyke), Story **Box Office:** $2.7M (by 1940; the film was MGM's top grosser for 1936).

Titanic
1997 – James Cameron – 🦴🦴🦴🦴

"I'm king of the world!"

James Cameron at the Oscars, quoting from his movie.

The story of the demise of the unsinkable ship of dreams in April 1912 has been told so many times that *Titanic* director James Cameron had to draw audiences in through a solid storyline as well as the obvious disaster. The end result is an epic of gigantic proportions, a combination of spectacular special effects and a love story marred by schmaltzy dialogue. Focusing on Jack and Rose (Leonardo DiCaprio and Kate Winslet), two young lovers with little in common, their story is told in flashback by a 101-year-old survivor (Gloria Stuart). She seeks out a treasure hunter (Bill Paxton) searching for artifacts in the wreckage. His main goal is to find the fabulous Heart of the Ocean diamond, which apparently went down with the ship. Just when he thinks he has it, the safe where it should be turns up empty except for a drawing of a nude woman wearing the necklace. And so begins the story of Rose and Jack. When the *Titanic* hits the iceberg, it is simply a plot development in their relationship, but what a plot development it is.

Did you know?...

A massive 775-foot replica of the original ship built 90% to scale was used; it floated in a huge tank that held 17 million gallons of seawater and was "sunk" with a series of hydraulic lifts that could tilt it up to 90 degrees. A smaller, 44-foot model was also used. No sets in the U.S. were big enough, so Fox built a new studio, Fox Baja, in Mexico.

The final half of the movie is shot almost in real time as the ship takes in water and, ultimately, breaks in half and begins a vertical plunge into the ocean. The effects are overwhelming, but on their own, *Titanic* would simply have been another disaster movie. The reason it gained classic status nearly overnight is due to its human face. Moviegoers identify with the passengers and the dawning realization that not only is the great ship doomed, but so are they. The panic, fear, resignation, strength, arrogance and sheer negligence of the different characters feel real to the audience—they cheer on the good guys and boo the bad guys. At the same time, they're mesmerized by the vision of the tremen-

dously huge sinking ship. Cameron hit on the right mix that audiences were looking for: "We thought there was a hunger for emotion, for character, for drama." Boy, was he right.

Working-class Jack (Leonardo DiCaprio) and well-bred Rose (Kate Winslet) fall in love aboard the *Titanic*.

Cast: Leonardo DiCaprio (Jack Dawson), Kate Winslet (Rose DeWitt Bukater), Billy Zane (Cal Hockley), Kathy Bates (Molly Brown), Frances Fisher (Ruth DeWitt Bukater), Gloria Stuart (Old Rose), Bill Paxton (Brock Lovett), Bernard Hill (Captain Smith), Victor Garber (Thomas

Andrews), Johathan Hyde (Bruce Ismay), David Warner (Spicer Lovejoy), Danny Nucci (Fabrizio), Suzy Amis (Lizzy Calvert) **Screenwriter:** James Cameron **Cinematographer:** Russell Carpenter **Composer:** James Horner **Producer:** James Cameron and Jon Landau for Lightstorm Entertainment; released by Paramount Pictures and Twentieth Century Fox **MPAA Rating:** PG-13 **Running Time:** 194 minutes **Awards:** Academy Awards 1997: Picture, Director (James Cameron), Cinematography, Art Direction, Song ("My Heart Will Go On"), Film Editing, Original Dramatic Score, Visual Effects, Sound, Costume Design; Nominations: Actress (Kate Winslet), Supporting Actress (Gloria Stuart), Makeup; British Academy Awards 1997 Nominations: Film, Director (James Cameron), Music, Cinematography, Production Design, Costumes, Editing, Sound, Special Effects, Make-up/Hair; Broadcast Film Critics Association 1997: Director (James Cameron); Directors Guild of America 1997: Director (James Cameron); Golden Globe Awards 1998: Drama, Director (James Cameron), Original Score, Song ("My Heart Will Go On"); Nominations: Drama—Actress (Kate Winslet), Drama—Actor (Leonardo DiCaprio), Supporting Actress (Gloria Stuart), Screenplay; Los Angeles Film Critics Association 1997: Production Design; Screen Actors Guild Awards 1997: Supporting Actress (Gloria Stuart) **Budget:** $200M **Box Office:** $600M (to date).

The Towering Inferno
1974 – Irwin Allen, John Guillermin – 🦴🦴🦴

> **"You design 'em and I'll build 'em."**
> Jim Duncan (William Holden)

Titanic in a skyscraper? On the night of the gala opening of San Francisco's 138-story The Glass Tower, the world's tallest building, the electrical corner-cutting of the builder's assistant (Richard Chamberlain) leads to a monster fire. The many parallels between this successful film and *Titanic* suggests that a big part of James Cameron's creativity may have been updating a tried and true formula rather than uncovering a new trail: the disaster striking on the debut of a new superstructure, the arrogance of builders wrongly assuming their work is disaster proof, the intermingling of private dramas with the worsening disaster, the effort to save first the women and children, the emphasis on showmanship. Fifty-seven sets were employed, a record for a film shot at the Fox studios. Also like *Titanic*, this expensive production was co-financed by two studios. Twentieth-Century Fox and Warner Bros. each had purchased novels with similar plots and decided to collaborate rather than compete.

Steve McQueen, who is as serious as Jack Webb in *Dragnet* is the biggest disappointment. After the blaze has been put out, he even stops to lecture Paul Newman on the steps of the charred building: "One of these days, you're gonna kill ten thousand in one of these firetraps. And I'm gonna keep eating smoke and

A rescue helicopter tries to save people trapped by fire in the world's tallest skyscraper.

bringing out bodies until somebody asks us how to build them." His performance sticks out as the most boring, but overall the roster of big names works better here than in any other disaster film.

Before the final climax, *Inferno* smartly pauses for some moments of reflection by its many characters stranded on various floors. Not only does this give the audience a breather before the next onslaught of special effects, it also allows the class of the actors to bring off these soap-opera flourishes. William Holden and Paul Newman argue about the ethics of corner cutting while technically staying within the building code. Holden's may be the most enjoyable work in the film, as he first tries to downplay the seriousness of the threat and then directs his anger at his son-in-law who skimped on expenses. He begins to recover his principles toward the end as he decides to let the others be taken to safety first. Fred Astaire has a good scene with Jennifer Jones in which he confesses to his life of conning people. She smiles knowingly. The final action sequences do not disappoint, especially the daring rescue of the people stranded in the scenic elevator by a helicopter outfitted with a grappling hook. Screenwriter Stirling Silliphant combined the endings of the two novels, so that after the tension of the helicopter rescue the movie gears up for the attempt to blow up the water tanks on top of the skyscraper to extinguish the fire. When it's all over, the audience feels like a survivor, too.

Cast: Paul Newman (Doug Roberts), Steve McQueen (Michael O'Hallorhan), William Holden (James Duncan), Faye Dunaway (Susan Franklin), Fred Astaire (Harlee Claiborne), Susan Blakely (Patty Simmons), Richard Chamberlain (Roger Simmons), Jennifer Jones (Lisolette Mueller), O. J. Simpson (Jernigan), Robert Vaughan (Senator Gary Parker), Robert Wagner (Dan Bigelow), Susan Flannery (Lorrie), Sheila Mathews (Paula Ramsay), Norman Burton (Will Giddings), Jack Collins (Mayor Ramsay) **Screenwriter:** Stirling Silliphant **Cinematographer:** Fred Koenekamp, Joseph Biroc **Composer:** John Williams **Producer:** Irwin Allen for Twentieth Century Fox and Warner Bros. **Running Time:** 165 minutes **Format:** VHS, LV **Awards:** Academy Awards 1974: Cinematography, Editing, Song ("We May Never Love Like This Again"); Nominations: Art Direction/Set Decoration, Picture, Sound, Supporting Actor (Fred Astaire), Original Dramatic/Comedy Score; British Academy Awards 1975: Supporting Actor (Fred Astaire); Golden Globe Awards 1975: Supporting Actor (Fred Astaire) **Budget:** $14M.

They Might Be Giants . . .

During the emphasis on disaster films in the 1970s, a few others followed in the wake of *The Poseidon Adventure* and *The Towering Inferno*. *Earthquake*

(1974), adhered to the recipe of using a large cast and contrasting human dramas with a disaster, but the characters (played by Charlton Heston, Lorne Greene, and Ava Gardner, among others) are much less compelling than those in the classic *San Francisco*. *Earthquake* was released in an audio format called Sensurround that supposedly created a tremor or two for the patrons in the theaters. *Meteor* (1979) put together a more impressive cast (Sean Connery, Natalie Wood, Henry Fonda) but disappointed in its special effects.

More recent excursions into the realm of disaster epics have diminished the focus on a large group of characters. *Volcano* (1997), for example, follows the efforts of Tommy Lee Jones and Anne Heche (as a government man and a Cal Tech scientist) in stopping the killer flow of lava from a volcano under Los Angeles. The emphasis of the special effects is as much on the technology of preventing more carnage (they eventually topple a building in the path of the lava) as on the volcano itself. *Dante's Peak* (1997) adopts the same scientists-predicting-and-coping-with-disaster formula. Finally, the career of Jan De Bont seems to be making him one of the current masters of disaster in cinema. De Bont's *Speed* (1994) generates great tension (and made a star out of Sandra Bullock) with the premise of a runaway city bus that must stay above fifty miles per hour or set off a terrorist's bomb; *Twister* (1996) earned its spectacular grosses on the strength of its impressive special effects. The weak premise of *Speed 2: Cruise Control* (1997) made Keanu Reeves look smart for passing on the sequel and Willem Dafoe look dumb for playing yet another psychovillain.

FAILED EPICS

Alexander the Great

America America

Cleopatra

The Conqueror

Dune

Greed

Heaven's Gate

Hook

Ishtar

Lost Horizon

The Postman

The Private Life of Sherlock Holmes

Star!

Waterworld

Alexander the Great

1956 — Robert Rossen — 🦴🦴🦴

> "It is men who endure toil and dare danger that achieve glorious deeds. And it is a lovely thing to live with courage and to die, leaving behind an everlasting renown."
>
> Alexander (Richard Burton)

An epic only in that it covers the life of one of the greatest men in history, *Alexander the Great* grinds away at a glacial pace. The legendary Greek conqueror of the fourth century B.C. apparently had time to kill. Alexander (Richard Burton) is a product of a bizarre upbringing—or to draw a modern-day parallel—a dsyfunctional royal family. His father is Philip, King of Macedonia, portrayed with stoic dignity by Fredric March. Haunted by the fear that his son may prove greater than he, Philip is often gone when Alexander is a child, and the boy is reared by his mother (Claire Bloom), who believes that he is a god.

The original live fast, die young historic icon, Alexander's maturation is marked by vicious fighting in both his family and in Macedonia, a tangle of schemes that leads to a potentially tangled plot. He is taught logic and science by none other than Aristotle (Barry Jones) and receives the best physical training in the known world. His father returns and makes him a regent, but Alexander, spurred by his mother, begins to make bold moves that further threaten his father. Philip, who hates Alexander's mother, sends her away and marries another woman after which Alexander is exiled, and a new heir to the Macedonian throne is born. However, Alexander acquires the skills of a leader and military strategist and returns. He is renewed in his father's favor, but a friend of his murders Philip. After Alexander slays the friend and becomes the new King of Macedonia, he attempts to unite the Greek city states so that he may resume his father's war with Persia. Alexander's greatest trial now becomes his clash with Persia. In a cunning and daring attack, he defeats the Persian King Darius (Harry Andrews) and assumes the Persian throne. In the end, Alexander dies at 33, and his wish is for all of Persia and Greece to live in peace. For all that, the movie is lacking in epic scale, with music and cinematography as unexceptional as the acting. (Some of Robert Krasker's best cinematographic work may be found in *El Cid*).

Alexander is one of Burton's earliest roles, and his ringing voice and confident swagger can't help coming across, as perhaps they are meant to, as somewhat pretentious. The young Burton shouts his way through the film, leaving the impression that playing the greatest, most powerful man in the world, one who is

Did you know?...

Director Robert Rossen's career in films started in the late 1930s. He wrote the gangster film *The Roaring Twenties* (1939); his two biggest successes were *All the King's Men* (1949) and *The Hustler* (1961).

convinced that he is a god, is not that much of a stretch, just a bit of typecasting. Burton's colorfulness is offset by the underplaying of March and Bloom.

Cast: Richard Burton (Alexander), Fredric March (Philip of Macedonia), Claire Bloom (Barsine), Barry Jones (Aristotle), Harry Andrews (Darius), Stanley Baker (Attalus), Niall MacGinnis (Parmenio), Peter Cushing (Memnon), Michael Hordern (Demosthenes), Danielle Darrieux (Olympias), Marisa de Leza (Euridice), Gustavo Rojo (Cleitus), Ruben Rojo (Philotas), Peter Wyngarde (Pausanias), Helmut Dantine (Nectenabus), William Squire (Aeschenes), Frederick Ledebur (Antipater), Virgilio Teixerira (Ptolemy), Teresa del Rio (Roxane) **Screenwriter:** Robert Rossen **Cinematographer:** Robert Krasker **Composer:** Mario Nascimbene **Producer:** Robert Rossen for United Artists **Running Time:** 135 minutes **Format:** VHS, LV.

A pensive Alexander (Richard Burton) prepares to conquer the known world.

America America

1963 – Elia Kazan – 🦴🦴🦴

> "I believe that in America I will be washed clean."
>
> Stavros (Stathis Giallelis), to his betrothed, whom he leaves.

Writer/director Elia Kazan's personal favorite among his films, this movie is probably best described as an acquired taste (or perhaps a taste that is worth acquiring). Beautifully photographed in black and white by Haskell Wexler, the film features some fascinating moments but suffers from a meandering structure.

The plot, set in 1896 and based on the experiences of Kazan's uncle, concerns the struggles of Stavros Topouzoglou (Stathis Giallelis) to escape the deprivations Greeks and Armenians endure at the hands of the Turks. He longs to travel to America and to earn money so the rest of his family can join him. One great segment is the collection of scenes in Constantinople, in which Stavros is betrothed to Thomna (Linda Marsh, who is excellent). Paul Mann, as Stavros' future father-in-law, sits contentedly on his sofa with the women of his house tending to him and in one great speech unfolds what he sees to be their future: "Watch the years go by . . . Pretty soon your eldest will come to you and say, 'Father, I've met a girl, I'd like to get married,' and you'll say . . . what dowry will she bring? . . . You'll get heavier . . . and we'll drink and we'll eat and we'll unbutton the tops of our trousers." Kazan cast nonprofessionals in many of the roles (including the main character), but none of them is as good as Mann and Marsh.

The cinematography in interior scenes uses little pools of light set against a mostly dark background to direct the eye; it is a striking effect. Although animosity was growing between Kazan and Wexler, Kazan recognized the excellence of Wexler's work, especially in the shots done with a hand-held camera. The strong contrast between the deglamorized, almost documentary style and the exhilarating hopes of Stavros and his family for a life in America is always touching. In his autobiography Kazan said that one of the main reasons for filming in Istanbul was to get the shot of the *hamals*, or the human beasts of burden, loading the dockside cargo on the American merchant ship. Though it won some awards, the film lost so much money that Kazan incorrectly feared he would never direct again.

Did you know?...

One of the most stressful relationships during production was that between Kazan and his cinematographer Haskell Wexler. In his autobiography, Kazan explains that he later learned Wexler resented Kazan's naming names in his testimony to the House Un-American Activities Committee in 1952.

Cast: Lou Antonio (Abdul), Katharine Balfour (Sophia Kebabian), Harry Davis (Isaac Topouzoglou), Joanna Frank (Vartuhi), Stathis Giallelis (Stavros Topouzoglou), Estelle Hemsley

(Grandmother), Elena Karam (Vasso Topouzoglou), Salem Ludwig (Odysseus Topouzoglou), Paul Mann (Aleko Sinnikoglou), John Marley (Garabet), Linda Marsh (Thomna Sinnikoglou), Gregory Rozakis (Hohannes Gardashian), Frank Wolff (Vartan Damadian), Robert H. Harris **Screenwriter:** Elia Kazan **Cinematographer:** Haskell Wexler **Composer:** Manos Hadjidakis **Producer:** Elia Kazan for Warner Bros. **Running Time:** 174 minutes **Format:** VHS, LV **Awards:** Academy Awards, 1964: Art Direction/Set Decoration; Nominations: Director (Elia Kazan), Picture, Screenplay; Golden Globe Awards, 1964: Director (Elia Kazan).

Stathis Giallelis stars as struggling Greek immigrant Stavros Topouzoglou.

Cleopatra

1963 – Joseph L. Mankiewicz – 🐟🐟

Two and a half years in the making, the most expensively made movie to date (1963), this is the picture that nearly bankrupted Fox studios while creating international headlines. Unfortunately, the story, either on-screen or off, has no fairy-tale ending. Taylor commanded the unheard-of sum of one million dollars to make the film, and then a grave illness kept her off the set for months and caused a change of location from England to Italy. Once on the set, she scandalized the western world with a torrid affair with her married co-star Richard Burton. The two divorced their spouses, married, later divorced and remarried each other, and divorced again. The story of their star-crossed lives is paralleled on the screen with the legendary fall of the great Roman soldier Marc Antony for the beautiful Egyptian queen Cleopatra.

However, the Burton/Taylor headlines were more gripping than the wooden script. After Taylor fell ill, director Rouben Mamoulian was replaced by Joseph L. Mankiewicz, who rewrote the script and moved the movie to Rome. The sets are spectacular—a true feast for the eye—especially Cleopatra's triumphant entry into Rome with her son by Julius Caesar. Clothed in gold and seated on a massive rolling sphinx, Taylor looks every inch the queen that could rock the foundations of civilization. But when she opens her mouth, she sounds like an elaborate and antique version of Maggie the Cat in Tennessee Williams' *Cat on a Hot Tin Roof*, a slightly neurotic woman driven to the edge by the gutlessness of the men she loves. Surely there was more to the fall of two Caesars than Southern gothic intrigue.

The dialogue is so ponderous that no amount of talent can wring any urgency out of it. Rex Harrison is believable in any role requiring authority, whether it is Henry Higgins, Dr. Dolittle, or Julius Caesar. But his best lines are the short, throwaway kind, usually aphoristic observations or imperious commands. Perhaps Caesar and Cleopatra did spend twenty minutes at a stretch comparing themselves to Alexander, but the audience doesn't need to hear the full discussion to get the idea.

Burton fares most badly, though, with a lavish, poorly edited script. His magnificent voice is a pleasure to listen to, but what a shame his character vacil-

Did you know?...

Taylor's famous salary of one million dollars reportedly came about from the studio taking seriously an amount that she had named as a joke.

lates between pompous boisterousness and extreme self-pity, with no stops in between. Marc Antony was a man so besotted by love that he threw away an empire, but Burton's performance gives few hints of the decline of greatness. Instead, the viewer wonders how the Romans managed to conquer half the world with leadership like this. The movie could have used some leadership, too; a lively, edited version of, say, two and one-half hours might have saved the studio decades of embarrassment.

Richard Burton is Marc Antony to Elizabeth Taylor's seductive *Cleopatra*.

Cast: Elizabeth Taylor (Cleopatra), Richard Burton (Marc Antony), Rex Harrison (Julius Caesar), Pamela Brown (High Priestess), Hume Cronyn (Sosigenes), Andrew Keir (Agrippa), Roddy MacDowell (Octavian), Robert Stephens (Germanicus), George Cole (Flavius), Carroll O'Connor (Casca), Michael Hordern (Cicero), Isabelle Cooley (Charmian), Jean Marsh (Octavia), Gwen Watford (Calpurnia), John Hoyt (Cassius) **Screenwriter:** Sidney Buchman, Ranald MacDougall, Joseph L. Mankiewicz **Cinematographer:** Leon Shamroy **Composer:** Alex North **Producer:** Walter Wanger for Twentieth Century Fox **Running Time:** 243 minutes **Format:** VHS, LV **Awards:** Academy Awards, 1964: Cinematography, Art and Set Decoration, Costume Design, Special Effects; Nominations: Picture, Actor (Rex Harrison), Sound, Score **Budget:** $40-$44M **Box Office:** $26M (rentals).

The Conqueror

1956 – Dick Powell – 🦴

John Wayne, playing twelfth-century cowboy warlord Genghis Khan, rides down with his men from the mountains, waylays a passing caravan, and in one sweeping gesture rips the virginally white dress off Princess Bortai (Susan Hayward). The Duke claims this Tartar woman as his bride, as the first half of the film becomes a primitive marriage manual. Alone with her in his tent, Genghis kisses the princess roughly, and first she resists, then responds. The next day she taunts him as a Mongol and gets under the big guy's skin. Figuring foreplay is the answer, Wayne takes Hayward to the harem of Wang Khan (Thomas Gomez), where they watch dance after seductive dance of the harem girls. "Does not their skill excite your admiration or even envy?" Wayne asks the princess. When he goads her further, saying that she lacks talent, Hayward boldly dances for him with a sword and the audience suspects a phallic connection. For her finish, she hurls the sword at the ogling men just to show them who's boss. Later, when Tartars attack, reclaim the princess, and capture Khan, Princess Bortai evens the war between the nomadic sexes by watching Wayne, whipped and sweating, being used with a yoke of water buffaloes to pull her coach. After letting him suffer for the rest of the day, she frees him under cover of darkness.

Perhaps the biggest disappointment in what is one of the most celebrated bad movies of all time is that only the first half of the film measures up as classic camp. After the Tartar invasion, the focus shifts from the taming of the shrewish princess to the need to retaliate against the enemy. Most of the scenes in the second half are standard fare, the point of view shifting between the two forces and Wayne wondering if his brother (Pedro Armendariz) has remained loyal to him while in the clutches of the enemy. The battle scenes are unspectacular. William Conrad, however, is given a nice death scene when he uses his strength to pry out the bars on a window but then discovers he is too chubby to climb through the opening. As he is stabbed half in and half out of the aperture, he says, in one of the many terrible lines in the film, "My brawn now holds me captive."

The setting for the production was Utah's Escalante Desert, and three of the nearby peaks were renamed Mount Wayne, Mount Hughes, and Mount Powell after the star, the producer, and the director. The nuclear testing a year

Did you know?...

Of the five films former leading man Dick Powell directed, both of his real embarrassments were released in 1956. In addition to *The Conqueror,* Powell attempted an ill-advised musical remake of Frank Capra's *It Happened One Night* starring Powell's wife June Allyson and Jack Lemmon. It was called *You Can't Run Away from It.*

earlier at Yucca (137 miles away), however, seems to have shortened the lives of an uncommonly large number of the cast and crew who were stricken with cancer in later life. Some reports even claim that the film crew transported sixty tons of contaminated soil back to Hollywood for scenes shot on sound stages dressed to look like exteriors. Of the 220 members of the film crew, 91 developed cancer, and 46 had died as of 1981, when Gabe Essoe did a tabulation for his *Book of Movie Lists*. The fatalities include the most famous names in the film: Director Powell died in 1963, John Wayne had three surgeries for cancer before he died in 1979, Susan Hayward died of a brain tumor (her fourth bout with cancer) in 1975, and Pedro Armendariz, told that he had cancer, committed suicide in 1963 following the completion of his scenes in *From Russia, with Love*. Agnes Moorehead seems to have been the first to notice the high death rate for those in the picture: "Everybody in the picture has gotten cancer and died. I should never have taken that part." Moorehead herself died of lung cancer in 1974.

Would you believe John Wayne as a Mongol warrior? And Susan Hayward as a Tartar beauty?

Cast: John Wayne (Temujin), Susan Hayward (Bortai), Pedro Armendariz (Jamuga), Agnes Moorehead (Hunlun), Thomas Gomez (Wang Khan), John Hoyt (Shaman), William Conrad (Kasar), Ted de Corsia (Kumlek), Leslie Bradley (Targutai), Lee Van Cleef (Chepei), Peter Mamakos (Borgurchi), Leo Gordon (Tartar captain), Richard Loo (Captain of the Guard), Sylvia Lewis (Harem dancer) **Screenwriter:** Oscar Millard **Cinematographer:** Joseph LaShelle **Composer:** Victor Young **Producer:** Howard Hughes **Running Time:** 111 minutes **Format:** VHS **Budget:** $6M.

Dune
1984 – David Lynch – 🦴🦴

"I must not fear. Fear is the mind-killer. Fear is the little-death that brings total obliteration. I will face my fear. I will permit it to pass over me and through me."

Paul (Kyle MacLachlan)

Adapted from Frank Herbert's classic science fiction novel, David Lynch's film version of *Dune* suffers from weaknesses common to movies based on long and complex literary works. *Dune* is a vast, sprawling epic that tells the story of young Paul Atreides, a messiah-like hero who represents a new step in the evolution of mankind and who develops a special connection with the desert planet Arakis (also known as Dune). *Dune* presents too many narrative levels and too many elaborate details to render effectively in a feature-length film. Perhaps in realization of this, the filmmakers have either attempted to compensate by filling in missing gaps with awkward voice-overs or ignored the gaps altogether. In addition, while the production design is visually interesting, Lynch has added his own sense of the bizarre to *Dune* in a manner that makes the movie a curiosity with little in the way of coherence.

Set in the distant future long after the planet Earth has been abandoned by humanity and is only a distant memory, *Dune* is the story of powerful, feuding houses with control over entire planets. House Atreides and House Harkonnen seek dominion over the planet Arakis, the source of an addicting spice which has bestowed some humans with psychic abilities. Paul (Kyle MacLachlan) ingests the spice in its pure form and encounters the huge worms of Arakis that produce the spice; he ultimately becomes the hero who puts an end to the conflicts by conquering Arakis itself and House Harkonnen. He also transforms into a sort of superhuman, foreseen by prophecy, and takes the name of Muad'Dib.

The story, as originally written by Herbert, is an intriguing, complex, mythical one with roots in mysticism and religion, touching upon the subjects of

Sting stars as the evil Feyd-Rautha in *Dune*.

Did you know?...

The film was re-edited for a network TV version that is over three hours long and that includes many scenes not included in Lynch's original, including an introductory narration sequence attempting to explain some of the story's background. Lynch had no involvement in the re-editing process and had his name removed from the film out of protest.

drugs and environmentalism. (Arakis represents a planet that has been robbed of life and desecrated by man's greed and industrialism.) However, other than the quasi-religious and mystical aspect of the story, these subjects seem only incidental in the film. Lynch focuses on the mysterious and the strange without offering elaboration or explanation. Several scenes featuring Paul's symbolic and obviously important dreams are simply puzzling and other scenes tend to focus on visually bizarre subjects—such as the twisted, bloody nature of Baron Harkonnen and his House (made by Lynch to be more bizarre but less explained than in the novel).

Lynch cast MacLachlan in a role meant for a boy, but the change is not surprising considering the many additional modifications made in this adaptation. Elements of the narrative, including background information and essential plot elements necessary for understanding the story, are often revealed in bits and pieces of some awkward voice-overs. The viewer is likely to wish Paul would explain a lot more than he does. Those who are familiar with Herbert's novel may follow the storyline without difficulty, but without some knowledge of the story's background may become lost. Visually impressive though frequently strange, the film seems chaotic and incomplete, leaving the viewer with a sense of video interruptus.

Cast: Kyle MacLachlan (Paul Atreides), Francesca Annis (Lady Jessica), Siân Phillips (Reverend Mother Gaius Helen Mohiam), Jüergen Prochnow (Duke Leto Atreides), José Ferrer (Padishah Emperor Shaddam IV), Freddie Jones (Thufir Hawat), Kenneth McMillan (Baron Vladimir Harkonnen), Sean Young (Chani), Richard Jordan (Duncan Idaho), Dean Stockwell (Doctor Wellington Yueh), Patrick Stewart (Gurney Halleck), Max von Sydow (Doctor Kynes), Paul Smith (The Beast Rabban), Sting (Feyd-Rautha), Linda Hunt (Shadout Mapes) **Screenwriter:** David Lynch **Cinematographer:** Freddie Francis **Composer:** Brian Eno (prophecy theme), Toto **Producer:** Dino De Laurentiis and Raffaella De Laurentiis **MPAA Rating:** PG-13 **Running Time:** 137 minutes **Format:** VHS, LV, DVD **Awards:** Academy Awards, 1984: Nominations: Sound **Budget:** $45M **Box Office:** $27.4M.

Greed

1924 – Erich von Stroheim – 🦴🦴🦴🦴

"I consider that I have made only one real picture in my life and nobody ever saw that," director Erich von Stroheim said. "The poor, mangled, mutilated remains were shown as *Greed*." The director of this film earned the nickname "the man you love to hate" for his appearances as screen villains, but the description may also apply to his relations with studio executives. When he was directing *Foolish Wives* at Universal in 1922, von Stroheim shot so much footage (seven hours in a first cut) that twenty-one-year-old studio head Irving Thalberg had to shut down the production. Later, at Metro, von Stroheim started to make *Greed* from Frank Norris' classic naturalistic novel *McTeague* when the same excessiveness resulted in a first cut of forty-two reels (between nine and ten hours). During the twenty-one months or so that it took to shoot and edit the film, the merger had occurred (in April 1924) that changed Metro to Metro-Goldwyn-Mayer, and the artist-supportive Goldwyn front office was now replaced with the budget-minded approach of von Stroheim's old nemesis Thalberg. By now, these two disliked each other personally as well as professionally, and no chance existed of *Greed* ever being released in either the twenty-four reel version that von Stroheim himself cut it to or even the eighteen-reel version that his friend, director Rex Ingram, came up with. Eventually, the version released in 1924 and the one that exists today is a ten-reel version produced by MGM cutters, principally June Mathis.

What is lost is primarily the subplots from Norris' book that contrast the relationship of the main character McTeague (Gibson Gowland) and his wife Trina (ZaSu Pitts) with other couples. Trina has won five thousand dollars in a lottery, but she hoards the money and eventually the ill will created by her excessive frugality poisons the marriage. Meanwhile, one of her rejected suitors, Marcus (Jean Hersholt), harbors resentment about losing Trina to McTeague when he learns of the money.

The picture of marriage that comes across is unrelenting in its squalor and selfishness, and these traits even turn up in the wedding sequence of Trina and McTeague. As the bride and groom stand nervously before the minister surrounded by family and friends, the depth of field shot captures through the win-

> "Say Miss Trina, why can't us two get married? Why not? Dontcher like me well enough?"
> McTeague (Gibson Gowland)

Did you know?...

Director Erich von Stroheim claimed in a letter to his biographer Peter Noble that only twelve people saw *Greed* in its original forty-two-reel uncut version.

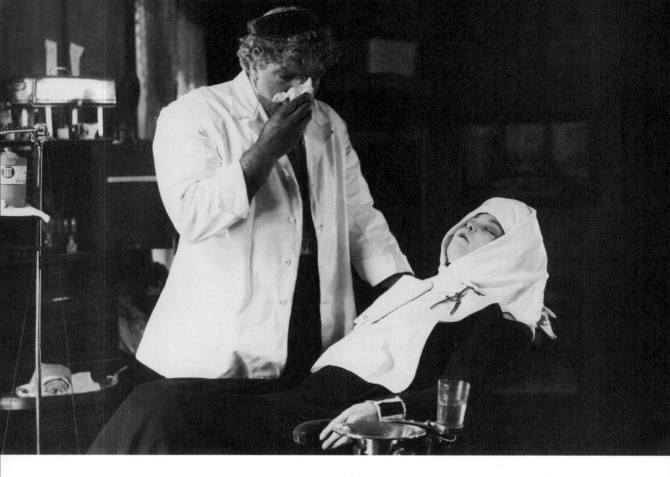

McTeague (Gibson Gowland) and Trina (ZaSu Pitts) in *Greed*.

dow the ominous march of a funeral procession passing in the street. The wedding night richly conveys Trina's fears about her new life. She repeatedly hugs her mother as the family leaves, and then she turns to see McTeague glowering down on her from the top of the staircase. He carries her to bed and the camera gradually pulls back as McTeague slowly draws the curtains shut.

The performances of Pitts and Gowland, the range of feelings their characters eventually display, and the often-praised concluding scenes between McTeague and Marcus in Death Valley give the existing version considerable power, even in its shortened form.

The shooting script for the original version has been published with all the deletions clearly marked (by Lorrimer Publishing, edited by Joel W. Finler). Norris' novel also gives a good sense of what has been omitted from the film, since von Stroheim planned to follow the book with nearly a paragraph-by-paragraph faithfulness.

Cast: Gibson Gowland (McTeague), ZaSu Pitts (Trina), Jean Hersholt (Marcus), Dale Fuller (Marcia Macapa), Joan Standing (Selina), Chester Conklin (Mr. Sieppe), Sylvia Ashton (Mrs. Sieppe), Frank Hayes (Old Grannis), James F. Fulton (sheriff), Jack McDonald (lottery agent), William Barlow (minister), Max Tyron (Mr. Oelberman), Erich von Ritzau (traveling dentist), S.S. Simon (Frena), Austin Jewel (August Sieppe), Hughie Mack (Mr. Heise), Cesare Gravina (Zerkow) **Screenwriter:** Erich von Stroheim, June Mathis **Cinematographer:** William H. Daniels, Ben F. Reynolds, Ernest B. Schoedsack (uncredited) **Producer:** Irving Thalberg, Samuel Goldwyn, and Erich von Stroheim for Metro-Goldwyn **Running Time:** 140 minutes **Format:** VHS, LV.

Heaven's Gate
1980 – Michael Cimino – 🦴🦴

The film that helped sink United Artists and one of the most infamous financial fiascos in movie history, *Heaven's Gate* explores the American Dream in a manner similar to Cimino's lauded *The Deer Hunter* and raises the interesting question: Is it as bad as the critics say? Made for some $40 million, the film was originally budgeted for $11 million. Cimino started slowly, falling five days behind schedule during the first six days of shooting. From there, things went downhill. Cimino eventually assembled 220 hours of footage. As co-star John Hurt aptly describes the movie, "Michael Cimino made this gigantic film without an emotional or intellectual center. He gave himself a brilliant narrative on a plate and then stubbornly refused to serve it."

It begins at a Harvard commencement in 1870 with a class of idealists who graduate and move into the real world to make their marks. Two of them, James Averill (Kris Kristofferson) and Billy Irvine (John Hurt), go west. Both are wealthy by 1890, and they wind up on opposite sides of a hideous undertaking by the cattlemen's association.

Led by Sam Waterson's Frank Canton, the association aims to murder 125 immigrant citizens they consider anarchists, murderers, and thieves. Mostly, the ranchers hate these new citizens for stealing their cattle. Times are hard and the hungry immigrants take branded, free-range cattle to butcher and eat. Averill, the local lawman, opposes this violence toward the immigrants and sets out to stop it, but association employee Nate Champion (Christopher Walken) begins a campaign of violence, killing off the "citizens," as the immigrants are called. Howev-

> "You offset every effort we make to protect our property and that of members of your own class."
> Canton (Sam Waterston)

> "You're not my class, Canton. You never will be. You'd have to die first and be born again."
> Averill (Kris Kristofferson)

Did you know?...
The film's original blistering reviews resulted in United Artists pulling it from circulation.

Federal Marshal James Averill (Kris Kristofferson) takes local madam Ella Watson (Isabelle Huppert) rollerskating.

er, one man cannot kill them fast enough for Canton and the rest of the association, so they recruit a private army and offer them each $5 a day plus expenses and the bonus of $50 for every citizen shot or hanged.

One of the more interesting subplots concerns the local madam, Ella Watson (Isabelle Huppert), and her ongoing love affair with the competing Averill and Champion. Of course, since Ella's name is one of those on the death list, this love plot deeply intertwines with the larger revenge story and ends tragically for all three. Saloon keeper John Bridges (Jeff Bridges) rallies the citizens, and they arm themselves and meet the association's army in the climactic battle of epic proportions. In it, Irvine, a tragic/comic character (who must also be the designated drunk, as he seemingly spends the entire movie in a stupor) is mercifully killed. Being heavily anesthetized by drink, he never feels a thing.

In spite of its poisonous reputation, *Heaven's Gate* is not entirely without merit and can often maintain interest. However, what ultimately undercuts the film is its lack of proportion. For example, Cimino endlessly replays one of David Mansfield's country waltzes past the point of effectiveness, and scenes of meaningful dialogue give way to meaningless moments of inactivity backed by more music. Such an uncertain, plodding development eventually weakens the few sequences with good dialogue. Cimino's unhurried pace bores the viewer, and the overlapping dialogue, often in different languages, confuses the sound-track rather than adds an authentic touch (as seems to have been intended).

The dingy look of the film works against it as well. The film was critically panned (many writers agreeing with Roger Ebert, who called *Heaven's Gate* "one of the ugliest films I have ever seen"). Ebert commented aptly that his response owes not to the film's content but rather to its texture. Framed by camera ace Vilmos Zsigmond, many scenes are shot in brownish tints and soft focus, and it is often difficult to tell what you are seeing. Dirt seemingly circulates in nearly every scene. By the end, the audience is ready for a break and a shower.

Cast: Kris Kristofferson (James Averill), Christopher Walken (Nathan D. Champion), John Hurt (Billy Irvine), Sam Waterston (Frank Canton), Brad Dourif (Mr. Eggleston), Isabelle Huppert (Ella Watson), Joseph Cotten (Reverend Doctor), Jeff Bridges (John H. Bridges), Ronnie Hawkins (Wolcott), Paul Koslo (Mayor), Geoffrey Lewis (Trapper), Richard Masur (Cully), Mickey Rourke (Nick Ray) **Screenwriter:** Michael Cimino **Cinematographer:** Vilmos Zsigmond **Composer:** David Mansfield **Producer:** Joann Carelli for United Artists **MPAA Rating:** R **Running Time:** 220 minutes **Format:** VHS, LV **Awards:** Academy Awards, 1981: Nominations: Art Direction/Set Direction **Budget:** $26M or $44M (depending on the source) **Box Office:** $1.5M.

Hook
1991 – Steven Spielberg – 🦴🦴🦴🦴

Even though critics called *Hook* a failure, audiences of all ages embraced it, and director Steven Spielberg made a profit on his tremendously expensive sequel to the tale of Peter Pan. Featuring the very talented Dustin Hoffman as the Captain, the dignified but spirited Maggie Smith as Granny Wendy, and the irrepressible Robin Williams as Peter, the movie is blessed with star power. The filming and sets are visually fascinating, with a three-dimensional Neverland, epic mock-battles, even undersea *Splash* shots with mermaids. The narrative is Spielberg at his usual high-pace, thrill a minute.

Captain Hook (Dustin Hoffman) clashes with life-long enemy, the now adult Peter Pan (Robin Williams).

"I remember you as being a lot bigger."
Peter (Robin Williams)

"To a ten year-old, I am huge."
Hook (Dustin Hoffman)

So, what's not to like? Very little, unless you misunderstand the basic issues of the movie. *Hook* is not an update, sequel, or retelling of the Peter Pan legend, not even to a new generation of children. You are expected to know the original story going in. *Hook* explores the question: what happens to all of us children, including Peter Pan, when we finally do have to grow up? Is the magic gone forever? Do we sell our souls to make a buck, climb the corporate ladder, and inevitably ignore our own children in the process? It must be a question close to the heart of a hugely successful man like Spielberg. Or is there some way in which we truly never do grow up or grow old? Granny Wendy seems to have the answer, but Peter Banning must learn the hard way, by a trip back to Neverland to find his old nemesis and, incidentally, himself.

Hook includes the classic characteristics of epic: a trip to a faraway place (that is a complete cosmos) and back again, a quest to find or do something heroic, a moral journey, and a discovery of self and purpose. It also involves the great hallmarks of children's literature: the importance of play (the great imaginary supper), the significance of words (is it Home Run or Run Home?), the discovery of our youth through our children (Peter's happy thought that makes him fly is about his fatherhood). One of the great scenes is at the center of *Hook*: when the youngest Lost Boy takes the face of the aging and cynical Peter Banning in his hands, smooths away the wrinkles and cares, finds the boy again in his eyes, and says "Oh, there you are, Peter!" Our kids love this movie automatically; if we watch it with care, it reminds us that there we are, too.

Cast: Dustin Hoffman (Captain Hook), Robin Williams (Peter Banning/Peter Pan), Julia Roberts (Tinkerbell), Maggie Smith (Granny Wendy), Caroline Goodall (Moira Banning), Bob Hoskins (Smee), Amber Scott (Maggie), Charlie Korsmo (Jack), Arthur Malet (Tootles), Dante Basco (Rufio), Jason Fisher (Ace), Thomas Tulak (Too Small), Raushan Hammond (Thud Butt), Laurel Cronin (Liza), Phil Collins (The Inspector) **Screenwriter:** Jim V. Hart, Nick Castle, Malia S. Marno **Cinematographer:** Dean Cundy **Composer:** John Williams **Producer:** Kathleen Kennedy, Frank Marshall, and Gerald R. Molen for Columbia Pictures **Running Time:** 142 minutes **Format:** VHS, LV **Awards:** Academy Awards, 1991: Nominations: Art Direction/ Set Decoration, Costume design, Makeup, Song ("When You're Alone"), Visual Effects **Box Office:** $119M (gross).

Did you know?...
One of the pirates is played by Glenn Close in drag.

Ishtar

1987 – Elaine May – Woof

Notwithstanding the blind camel that steals the movie, *Ishtar* is an epic flop presented as an over-sized $40 million updating of the classic Hope/Crosby road misadventures.

Warren Beatty and Dustin Hoffman play third-rate singer/songwriters who meet and form an act. Singularly terrible, together they really stink, leading to a problem with booking gigs. But their ever-resourceful (and gleefully sleazy) agent, Marty (Jack Weston), finds them work in Ishtar, a mythical North African country. There self-assured urban neurotic (and ladies' man) Chuck (Hoffman) and shy southern boy Lyle (Beatty) become involved in a CIA plot concocted by Jim Harrison (Charles Grodin) to save Ishtar from a Communist takeover. Both Beatty and Hoffman try so hard to seem ordinary and untalented that they never let the audience forget their off-screen celebrity status, and their own role reversal. This is the film's one big joke, inside a joke, and it grows tiresome, though the blind camel does save a scene or two.

As a result, the worst moments are not the intentionally bad segments of Beatty and Hoffman trying to sing and sounding bad (which are wickedly campy) but those times when the movie unintentionally shows how out of touch it truly is with the lives of "ordinary" people. Its idea of a dead-end job is showing fortyish Beatty driving a ice-cream truck and jingling its bell. The dialogue sometimes manages a few amusing moments, as when Hoffman is on the ledge of his building and Beatty comes out to talk him down by saying: "Hey! It takes a lot of nerve to have nothing at your age. Don't you understand that? You know, most guys would be ashamed. But you've got the guts to just say 'the hell with it.' You say that you'd rather have nothing than settle for less. Understand?"

It comes as a sort of worrisome shock when the sound of a gong heralds a change of setting from New York to Ishtar, and we see what appears to be authentic location footage. If ever a movie asked to be shot on a sound stage—even an intentionally hokey 1940s Hollywood sound stage—it is this one.

Elaine May's writing should be one of the film's strengths, but stories about the production reported that script revisions and rewrites and conflicts

went on into the shooting schedule. Even its few defenders acknowledge the gaps and confusions in the story, especially after the espionage plot starts to develop. Overall, a disappointing film.

Bad singing team Lyle (Warren Beatty) and Chuck (Dustin Hoffman) wind up with a gig in Morocco.

Cast: Warren Beatty (Lyle Rogers), Dustin Hoffman (Chuck Clark), Isabelle Adjani (Shirra Assel), Charles Grodin (Jim Harrison), Jack Weston (Marty Freed), Tess Harper (Willa), Carol Kane (Carol), Aharon Ipale (Emir Yousef), Fijad Hageb (Abdul), David Margulies (Mr. Clark), Rose Arrick (Mrs. Clark), Julie Garfield (Dorothy), Christine Rose (Siri Darma), Bob Girolami (Bartender), Abe Kroll (Mr. Thomopoulos), Hanna Kroll (Mrs. Thomopoulos) **Screenwriter:** Elaine May **Cinematographer:** Vittorio Storaro **Composer:** Bajawa **Producer:** Warren Beatty for Columbia **MPAA Rating:** PG-13 **Running Time:** 105 minutes **Format:** VHS, LV **Budget:** $50M **Box Office:** $14M.

Lost Horizon

1937 – Frank Capra – 𝄢𝄢𝄢

Frank Capra's pacifist parable from James Hilton's novel drops a planeload of Westerners fleeing a revolution in China into a snowy Tibetan valley. They trek over mountainous trails to Shangri-La, an idyllic society that lives by a philosophy of moderation. After the dramatic opening scenes, the film settles into a more leisurely pace in which the passengers, Robert Conway (Ronald Colman) in particular, discover the riches of the landscape and its philosophy. All but Conway's brother George (John Howard) replace their worldly concerns with the openheartedness of their new environment. The semi-comic transformations of Edward Everett Horton and Thomas Mitchell are handled well. But the middle section fails to do justice to both Conway's spiritual yearning for the simplicities of utopian life and the ongoing mystery of the detention of this group in Shangri-La against their will. These two concerns lead to some abrupt shifts. One minute George is firing shots at the Tibetan attendants and the next Conway sits in docility at the feet of the High Lama (Sam Jaffe) to hear about the one rule, "be kind." The final twenty minutes return to a more hectic speed than even the first part, as if Capra had glanced at his watch and decided it was time to wrap things up.

Sometimes the misfires of a gifted filmmaker can be as interesting as his greater accomplishments. After Capra's Oscar-sweep in 1934 with *It Happened One Night* and the subsequent success in 1936 of *Mr. Deeds Goes to Town*, he used his cachet to make this curious, meditative film. This choice calls attention to the similarities between the director and the character Conway. Both are serious-minded men who desire more meaning from life but who can't seem to make up their minds how to find it.

Capra's biographer Joseph McBride reports that the initial cut of *Lost Horizon* ran about six hours, that the first previewed version at Santa Barbara's Granada Theatre was about three and a half hours long (and was met with some laughter in the audience), and that with more cuts by Columbia studio head Harry Cohn the length at the official premiere was 132 minutes. McBride discovered Capra's own misgivings about the film by examining the oral history Capra contributed to Columbia University: "Although it's been said that [*Lost Horizon*

Did you know?...

Robert Gitt supervised the American Film Institute's restoration of the film that replaced nearly twenty-two minutes of footage removed in 1942 when the film was re-released under the title *Lost Horizon of Shangri-La*. Capra himself attended the premiere of the restored version on October 18, 1979.

British diplomat Robert Conway (Ronald Colman) treks through the Himalayas.

is] one of my better pictures, I thought that the main part of the film should have been done better somehow. I got lost in the architecture, in Utopia, in the never-never land, and it was only toward the end of the picture that I got back on the track with human beings . . . This is common for one who wants to exploit a theme, and gives the theme too much a part of the story. I wavered several times. I shot several endings before I decided how to end it."

The film was a more respectable failure artistically than financially. The box-office threatened the solvency of Columbia (where profit margins had rarely been very big), strained the director's relationship with Cohn, and all but ended his partnership with screenwriter Robert Riskin, by far his best collaborator. (All failures are relative, of course; compared to Ross Hunter's embarrassing remake in 1973, Capra's original looks pretty good.)

Cast: Ronald Colman (Robert Conway), H.B. Warner (Chang), Edward Everett Horton (Alexander P. Lovett), Thomas Mitchell (Henry Barnard), John Howard (George Conway), Sam Jaffe (High Lama), Jane Wyatt (Sondra), Isabell Jewell (Gloria Stone), Margo (Maria), Chief John Big Tree (Porter), Wyrley Brich (Missionary), Beatrice Blinn (Passenger), Hugh Buckler (Lord Gainsford), John Burton (Wynant), Eli Casey (Porter) **Screenwriter:** Sidney Buchman, Robert Riskin **Cinematographer:** Joseph Walker **Composer:** Dmitri Tiomkin **Producer:** Frank Capra for Columbia **Running Time:** 138 minutes **Format:** VHS, LV **Awards:** Academy Awards, 1937: Film Editing, Interior Decoration; Nominations: Picture, Sound, Supporting Actor (H.B. Warner), Score **Box Office:** Did not break even until the 1942 re-release of this 1937 film.

The Postman
1997 – Kevin Costner – 🦴🦴

> "It takes one postman to make someone else a postman."
> The Postman (Kevin Costner)

> "Sorta like vampires, huh?"
> Ford Lincoln Mercury (Larenz Tate) responds.

The Postman doesn't always deliver, but it often maintains a level of interest in both its uncertain first half and its more unified finale. Set in the parched, post-apocalyptic world of 2013, the film features Kevin Costner as an unnamed character who trudges through the wasteland with his mule Bill. Stopping at small communities, he recites speeches from Shakespeare as best as he can remember them in this world without libraries. A tyrannical, self-proclaimed general named Bethlehem (Will Patton) conscripts Costner for his army, but after a humiliating introduction to these fascist ways, Costner escapes and comes upon an abandoned mail truck. Although he seems to take the cap and the contents of the mailbag initially as a way of further dignifying himself, when he soon makes

his way to a nearby fort to deliver some letters, he begins to see that these scattered gatherings of despairing survivors take heart from the link with distant friends and loved ones that even a primitive mail route provides. He also finds a gift for instilling hope as one of the young men, Ford Lincoln Mercury (Larenz Tate), recruits others to add to the network of routes started by Costner the postman. Eventually, Costner accepts the role of inspiring and leading these people into challenging the domination of Bethlehem and creating a renewed country.

The first hour meanders in an episodic mix that establishes the nature of this setting, dramatizes Costner's drifting and reciting, indulges in the action of kidnap and escape, and finally starts up a love story. The last hour of the film is more assured, as director Costner focuses on events leading to the showdown between the postman and Bethlehem. Though this part is more coherent, many scenes continue past their dramatic peak. As a director, Costner over-relies on closeups and further drains some scenes of their interest.

The Postman (Kevin Costner) checks his route.

Did you know?...

The town of Bridge City was built on the site of Boundary Dam, a massive working powerhouse that supplies half the electricity of Seattle.

Is a mailman really the stuff of which epics are made? The film's inability to make up its mind about how often to acknowledge the built-in humor of the situation gives its first hour or so some off-key moments. You are never quite sure if you are laughing at the things the film wants you to. The characters marvel at the postman's mangled Shakespeare, taking for profundity what could just as well be parody, and later when the postman spots a misspelling in a handbill, the hush of awed reverence among the onlookers creates another bit of comic confusion. The movie seems almost to assume that the lack of basic schooling in this post-millennial world has made some of its characters (including, at times, the postman) not just illiterate but unintelligent. Overlong and under-directed, *The Postman* struggles to effectively address the viewer.

Cast: Kevin Costner (The Postman), Will Patton (Bethlehem), Larenz Tate (Ford Lincoln Mercury), Olivia Williams (Abby), James Russo (Idaho), Daniel von Bargen (Sheriff Briscoe), Tom Petty (Bridge City Mayor), Scott Bairstow (Luke), Giovanni Ribisi (Bandit 20), Roberta Maxwell (Irene March), Joe Santos (Getty), Ron McLarty (Old George), Peggy Lipton (Ellen March), Brian Anthony Wilson (Woody), Todd Allen (Gibbs), Rex Linn (Mercer), Shawn Wayne Hatosy (Billy), Ryan Hurst (Eddie), Charles Esten (Michael), Annie Costner (Ponytail), Mary Stuart Masterson (postman's daughter) **Screenwriter:** Eric Roth, Brian Helgeland **Cinematographer:** Stephen F. Windon **Composer:** James Newton Howard **Producer:** Kevin Costner for Warner Bros. **MPAA Rating:** R **Running Time:** 177 minutes **Format:** VHS, LV, DVD **Budget:** $80M **Box Office:** $17.6M.

The Private Life of Sherlock Holmes
1970 – Billy Wilder – 🦴🦴🦴🦴

> "Some of us are cursed with memories like flypaper."
>
> Holmes (Robert Stephens) to Watson (Colin Blakely).

During the six months it took to shoot this film, the idea of the road show as a way of showcasing movies had fallen into disfavor in Hollywood. In the earlier 1960s, this road-show format had been ideal for epic films: it publicized the movie as an event, included an intermission ("to give your kidneys a break," as Billy Wilder joked to writer Tom Wood), and limited screenings to just two a day with higher ticket prices and reserved seating. The films that began their releases as road shows form a roster of the most successful epics of the decade: *Lawrence of Arabia, My Fair Lady, The Sound of Music, Dr. Zhivago*.

And *The Private Life of Sherlock Holmes* might have been added to that list had it not been for the sudden financial losses incurred by a number of

Holmes (Robert Stephen) and Watson (Colin Blakely) take a stroll with beautiful spy Gabrielle (Genevieve Page).

Did you know?...
Composer Miklos Rozsa may be glimpsed in the ballet scenes conducting the orchestra.

expensive road shows near the end of the decade. *Star!* seems to have flopped the worse, but the box-office disappointments of *Paint Your Wagon* and *Hello, Dolly!*, coupled with indifferent reactions to a preview of Wilder's very personal film about Sherlock Holmes, led to an impasse between Wilder and United Artists. Although the director had the final cut on the Holmes film, the studio refused to release the original 200-minute version that comprised four secret episodes of the detective's life. Wilder reluctantly agreed to their request to shorten the film. Seventy-minutes were cut (two of the four episodes and some flashback sequences). This two-hour version had been the only one available until 1994 when MGM/UA released a laserdisc with two partially restored episodes (one has picture with subtitles instead of sound, and the other has audio but no picture; the discs, however, also include a full screenplay).

The premise for the film is that fifty years after the death of Dr. Watson (Colin Blakely), a strongbox of his secret papers may now be opened in the vault of a London bank. The box contains accounts of the cases of Sherlock Holmes (Robert Stephens) too controversial for publication during the detective's life. Wilder conceived the stories as analogous to the movements in a symphony, each shedding light in a different way behind the facade of coldness and reason that Holmes presents to the world. The greatest loss may be the flashback to Holmes' college days when he wins a lottery sponsored by his rowing team-mates at Oxford. The prize is a night with a prostitute, which Holmes traipses off for reluctantly since he has a crush on a girl he's spotted near the campus; he discovers that the prostitute is really his idealized girlfriend. (Wilder had earlier used nearly the same plot device with the characters played by Jack Lemmon and Shirley MacLaine in *The Apartment*, and it works there too.) Much of the rest of the film seeks to penetrate further the defenses regarding women that Holmes has constructed as a result of this early event. "I wanted to be more daring," said Wilder, "but unfortunately, the son of Conan Doyle was there. I wanted to make Holmes a homosexual. That's why he's on dope."

The film also features some of the finest work by cinematographer Christopher Challis (who had shot Michael Powell's classic *The Red Shoes*), set designer Alexander Trauner, and composer Miklos Rozsa, whose plaintive violin concerto captures beautifully the tone of this elegiac film.

Cast: Robert Stephens (Sherlock Holmes), Colin Blakely (Dr. John Watson), Genevieve Page (Gabrielle Valladon), Christopher Lee (Mycroft Holmes), Tamara Toumanova (Patrova), Clive Revill (Rogozhin), Irene Handl (Mrs. Hudson), Mollie Maureen (Queen Victoria), Stanley

Holloway (First Gravedigger), Catherine Lacey (old lady), Peter Madden (Von Tirpitz), Michael Balfour (Cabbie), George Benson (Inspector Lestrade), James Copeland (Guide), John Garrie (First Carter), Godfrey James (Second Carter), Robert Cawdron (hotel manager), Paul Hansard (monk), Miklos Rozsa (orchestra conductor at the ballet) **Screenwriter:** Billy Wilder, I. A. L. Diamond **Cinematographer:** Christopher Challis **Composer:** Miklos Rozsa **Producer:** Billy Wilder for United Artists **MPAA Rating:** PG-13 **Running Time:** 125 minutes (cut from 200 minutes) **Format:** VHS, LV **Budget:** $10M **Box Office:** $1.5M.

Star!

1968 – Robert Wise – 🎞🎞🎞

The attempt to reteam the producer, director, and star of *The Sound of Music* three years later resulted in probably the biggest box-office flop any of them ever had. *Star!* seems to be a musical film-biography of Gertrude Lawrence, a British stage performer of the 1920s and 1930s. On the surface, the film charts the milestones of Lawrence's life. Starting with a newsreel flashback reminiscent of *Citizen Kane* (*Star!* director Robert Wise had been the editor on *Kane*), the opening scenes trace Lawrence's attempt to find her father (Bruce Forsyth), her early work in music halls, her first marriage, her first big break, and her introduction to Sir Anthony Spencer (Michael Craig) and, through him, to London society. Most of the remainder of the film structures itself around the men she knows, such as her friend Noel Coward (Daniel Massey), and the shows she appears in. The film ends in 1940 with the start of Lawrence's relationship with Richard Aldrich (Richard Crenna) and her preparation for the lead in her stage success *Lady in the Dark*.

The confusion concerning the film and its reception owes partly to this misleading biographical approach. The real Lawrence, as director Wise has admitted, had only a mediocre singing talent (she was known more for her acting and performing personality), and so the choice of casting Andrews in the lead and to stock the film with seventeen lavish musical numbers makes it look as if the filmmakers wanted primarily (and understandably) to capitalize on the popularity of *The Sound of Music* in any way they could. The dramatic element of the film, therefore, is static and episodic, something Wise has also indirectly acknowledged when he says that the aim was not to create a biographical film but simply to capture the flavor of the music-hall era. "It had too many musical

> "In moments of desperation or exhilaration, there's nothing like a nice long lunch; it helps to keep a sense of perspective."
>
> Noel Coward (Daniel Massey) to Gertrude Lawrence (Julie Andrews).

Did you know?...

Noel Coward was the real-life godfather of the actor who played him in this film, Daniel Massey.

Gertrude Lawrence (Julie Andrews) and Noel Coward (Daniel Massey) in a scene from Coward's play "Private Lives."

numbers," said Wise, "we didn't get Gertie Lawrence's character enough on screen. The numbers were great, but there was not enough development of Gertie herself."

The best way to enjoy the film is as a vehicle for Andrews' wonderful performances of the songs by Noel Coward, Buddy DeSylva, Al Jolson, George Gershwin, Cole Porter, and Kurt Weill, among others. At the time of its release, speculation began as to why audiences stayed away, but a shortened, retitled version didn't prevent a loss of ten million dollars. Some theorized that audiences didn't want to see Andrews playing an earthier character than they were accustomed to. Wise himself speculated that the success of the musical biography *Funny Girl* shortly before the release of *Star!* had taken away the audience for his later film. What he should have said was that *Funny Girl* is a much better movie.

Cast: Julie Andrews (Gertrude Lawrence), Richard Crenna (Richard Aldrich), Michael Craig (Sir Anthony Spencer), Daniel Massey (Noel Coward), Robert Reed (Charles Fraser), Bruce Forsyth (Arthur Lawrence), Beryl Reid (Rose), John Collin (Jack Roper), Alan Oppenheimer (Andre Charlot), Richard Karlan (David Holtzman), Lynley Lawrence (Billie Carleton), Garrett Lewis (Jack Buchanan), Elizabeth St. Clair (Jeannie Banks), Jenny Agutter (Pamela), Anthony Eisley (Ben Mitchell), Jock Livingston (Alexander Woollcott), J. Pat O'Malley (Dan), Harvey Jason (Bert), Damian London (Jerry Paul), Richard Angora (Cesare), Matilda Calnan (Dorothy), Lester Matthews (Lord Chamberlain), Bernard Fox (Assistant to Lord Chamberlain), Murray Matheson (bankruptcy judge), Robin Hughes (Hyde Park speaker), Jeanette Landis (Eph), Dinah Ann Rogers (Molly), Barbara Sandland (Mavis), Ellen Plasschaert (Moo), Ann Hubbell (Beryl) **Screenwriter:** William Fairchild **Cinematographer:** Ernest Laszlo **Composer:** Lennie Hayton **Producer:** Saul Chaplin for Twentieth Century Fox **MPAA Rating:** G **Running Time:** 174 minutes **Format:** VHS, LV **Awards:** Academy Awards, 1968: Nominations: Adapted Score, Art Direction/Set Decoration, Cinematography (Ernest Laszlo), Costume Design, Song, Sound, Supporting Actor (Daniel Massey); Golden Globe Awards, 1968: Supporting Actor (Daniel Massey) **Budget:** $14M **Box Office:** $4M.

Waterworld
1995 – Kevin Reynolds – 🦴🦴

Plagued by a troubled shoot, an escalating budget, and creative differences between star and director, *Waterworld* became one of Hollywood's most expensive films—and one of its biggest disappointments in years. Still, were it not for the exaggerated sense of "failure" resulting from the widely reported stories of the production's problems, *Waterworld* would not rank much worse than

Kevin Costner stars as reluctant hero Mariner in *Waterworld*.

"Well, excuse me—did I say anybody could leave before the battle is over?"

Deacon (Dennis Hopper), watching the Mariner, Helen, and Enola escape from the atoll.

many standard adventure films. The story, set in a futuristic world in which the polar ice caps have melted and the Earth is covered in water, has the potential to be original as well as thoughtful. However, shortly after the film begins, the potential quickly falls away as the story turns into an uneven narrative troubled by careless errors of logic, poor—or simply odd—performances by some of its major stars, weak dialogue, and an exaggerated and undeserved sense of self-importance.

The film has some strong points, though they are few. *Waterworld* boasts occasionally impressive imagery, a number of exciting stunts, and a few well-acted, character-driven scenes, mainly between the Mariner (Kevin Costner) and Enola (Tina Majorino). The few sequences involving the development of the friendship between the sea-man and the little girl as they find a common bond (both are considered "freaks") are the most emotionally successful elements of the film and the most serious. Oddly, though, other elements that could have been serious—such as the environmental issues hinted at through the origins and background of this "waterworld"—are overlooked. The tone also seems to fluctuate between the dramatic, the comedic, and the action-oriented, exhibiting little unity of purpose and sending the movie to the boundary of camp, a dangerous place for a $175 million much-delayed production. Director Kevin Reynolds, who also directed Costner in *Robin Hood: Prince of Thieves* and *Fandango*, tries to achieve an epic, important tone, but he strays as well. The narrative frequently fails on that level because it relies far too much on comic relief from the villains, led by the strange, simple-minded, one-liner-spouting Deacon (Dennis Hopper), who seems to be in a different movie, much like Alan Rickman in *Robin Hood*. One can hardly take these villains or their threat seriously, even though they do cause a lot of destruction. Too many characters are played for laughs, and to make matters worse, many of them are not genuinely comic.

Costner's character, a human who has adapted to the world's environment through a mutation resulting in gills and webbed feet, is presented as something of a super-hero, wise about people but often unlikable (such as when he is unnecessarily cruel to Helen and Enola). His abilities and his prowess, however, are not well-explained, and the change in the nature of his relationship with Helen and Enola happens quickly. At times, the story appears almost to idolize the character, as when Enola assures her captors that the Mariner will come after her and that they will be sorry. Her statements about the Mariner are intercut with scenes of Costner's character making his way toward her, effortlessly taking down those in his way. At the end, when the heroes' quest is completed and dry land is found, the Mariner's decision to return to the sea is a somewhat puzzling one, for his evidently special connection to the ocean has not really been developed. Sure, the world has a lot of water, but so what?

Cast: Kevin Costner (Mariner), Jeanne Tripplehorn (Helen), Dennis Hopper (Deacon), Tina Majorino (Enola), R. D. Call (Enforcer), Zakes Mokae (Priam), Gerard Murphy (Nord), Jack Kehler (Banker), Michael Jeter (Old Gregor), Lanny Flaherty (Trader), David Finnegan (Toby), Sean Whalen (Bone), Robert LaSardo (Smitty), Lee Arenberg (Djeng) **Screenwriter:** Peter Rader, David Twohy **Cinematographer:** Dean Semler **Composer:** James Newton Howard **Producer:** Charles Gordon, Kevin Costner and John Davis for Universal **MPAA Rating:** PG-13 **Running Time:** 136 minutes **Format:** VHS, LV, DVD **Awards:** Academy Awards, 1995: Nominations: Sound **Budget:** $175M **Box Office:** $88.25M (domestic gross).

Did you know?...

One of the movie's important sets was a slave colony, but the set sank in a storm, preventing the filmmakers from shooting on it.

They Might Be Giants...

The preceding chapter, as well as a few entries in other chapters, discusses some films that might be called "unjust failures," or "noble failures," or even, to take the phrase that interviewer Leslie Megahey used in his conversation with Orson Welles, "flawed masterpieces." Films like Welles' *The Magnificent Ambersons*, von Stroheim's *Greed*, and Wilder's *The Private Life of Sherlock Holmes* fall into the category of impressive and important movies drastically cut by their studios before their release.

Other flops—whether critical, financial, or both—seem to deserve their status as failures. Ross Hunter's ill-advised 1973 attempt to remake Frank Capra's *Lost Horizon* as a musical prompted film critic Judith Crist to say, "Only Ross Hunter would remake a 1937 movie into a 1932 one." The 1975 film *Hurricane* with Jason Robards and Mia Farrow cost $22 million and took in only four. The 1962 remake of *Mutiny on the Bounty* with Marlon Brando and Trevor Howard lost over ten million. Another embarrassing failure is *Inchon*, the 1982 epic financed by the Unification Church of the Reverend Sung Myung Moon, in which Laurence Olivier plays Douglas MacArthur behind some very heavy make-up. The poisonous industry reaction to the $18 million lost by Blake Edwards' 1970 romantic comedy of spying during World War I, *Darling Lili*, eventually gave him the idea for his black comedy about Hollywood, *S.O. B.* (1981).

FAMILY SAGAS

Babe
The Best Years of Our Lives
Fanny and Alexander
Field of Dreams
The Grapes of Wrath
It's a Wonderful Life
Legends of the Fall
The Magnificent Ambersons
1900
Yankee Doodle Dandy

Babe

1995 – Chris Noonan – 🦴🦴🦴🦴

This charming fantasy about a talking pig who thinks he's a sheepdog, adapted from a children's novel by Dick King-Smith, was something of a surprise hit with audiences and critics and became one of the few films of its kind to be nominated for a Best Picture Oscar. What makes *Babe* such a wonderful movie is that it rises above standard children's film fare. The story is funny yet poignant, with a message about prejudice and about daring to challenge social conformity. The dialogue is clever and witty, the characters (most of whom are animals) are endearing, and the overall tone refuses to condescend or patronize. Consequently, *Babe* is not merely a good family film, but a good film, period, and its appeal reaches adults as well as children.

The world of farm animals in which Babe finds himself in is a microcosm of the human world, with the rivalry between different animals representing the divisions and prejudices so common within humanity. Sheep dogs look down upon sheep, for instance, as inferior, stupid creatures, but Babe learns that the sheep are in fact just as intelligent as any of the animals on the farm. Yet, while such "racism" is targeted for attack, it is shown to be the result of ignorance, and its perpetrators, such as the dogs Fly and Rex, are not depicted as villains.

The innocent yet wise little pig Babe, himself a member of a disenfranchised class, becomes the instrument of peace and the bridge to a tolerant and understanding world. Not only does he overcome the boundaries of prejudice that exist between different animals, but he also challenges social conventions and expectations by learning to herd sheep, a task normally assigned to dogs, thereby saving himself from the fate awaiting most pigs and also demonstrating that through tolerance, understanding, and mutual respect, almost anything can be accomplished. Thus, the little pig who simply wants a nice life and a place in the world becomes a big hero.

Did you know?...
Because the pigs used for the production grew so quickly, it took 48 pigs to play the part of Babe.

Cast: Christine Cavanaugh (voice of Babe), Miriam Margolyes (voice of Fly), Danny Mann (voice of Ferdinand), Hugo Weaving (voice of Rex), Mariam Flynn (voice of Maa), Russi Taylor (voice of Cat), Evelyn Krape (voice of Old Ewe), Michael Edward-Stevens (voice of Horse), Charles Bartlett (voice of Cow), Paul Livingston (voice of Rooster), Roscoe Lee Browne (Narrator), James Cromwell (Farmer Hoggett), Magda Szubanski (Mrs. Hoggett), Zoe Burton (Daughter), Paul Goddard (Son-in-Law) **Screenwriter:** George Miller, Chris Noonan **Cine-**

matographer: Andrew Lesnie **Composer:** Nigel Westlake **Producer:** Bill Miller, George Miller, and Doug Mitchell for Universal **MPAA Rating:** G **Running Time:** 89 minutes **Format:** VHS, LV, DVD **Awards** Academy Awards, 1995: Visual Effects; Nominations: Art Direction/Set Decoration, Director (Chris Noonan), Editing, Picture, Supporting Actor (James Cromwell), Adapted Screenplay (George Miller, Chris Noonan); Golden Globes, 1996: Motion Picture—Comedy/Musical; National Society of Film Critics Awards, 1995: Film; New York Film Critics Circle Awards, 1995: First Film (Chris Noonan) **Box Office:** $66.6M (domestic gross).

Farmer Hoggett (James Cromwell) takes a shine to piglet Babe.

The Best Years of Our Lives

1946 — William Wyler — 🦴🦴🦴🦴

Rarely has simplicity been more eloquent on screen. Opening in the immediate aftermath of the veteran's homecoming, William Wyler's masterpiece of three servicemen returning home after World War II seems dated in only very small ways. Hugo Friedhofer's Oscar-winning score may be a bit over-repeated on the soundtrack, and Robert E. Sherwood's script may overindulge in 1940s good-guy slang ("chum" and "brother"). But what connected the film with its audience in 1946 (and made it the most successful movie since *Gone with the Wind*) also makes it powerful today—the honesty and eloquence of its emotions.

The servicemen represent different parts of American society. Al Stephenson (Fredric March) is a fortyish banker returning to his wife and older children. Homer Parrish (Harold Russell), a middle-class sailor who lost his hands in a fire, wonders about the reception he will get from his fiancee (Cathy O'Donnell). Fred Derry (Dana Andrews) married a woman (Virginia Mayo) while in basic training, and now they discover their incompatibilities. Wyler and Robert E. Sherwood bring out the humanity in seemingly simple things and weave these details into a rich, mosaic plot representative of the feelings of many veterans. For example, Al's simple but moving return to his family echoes Wyler's own after the war: Al sees his wife, Milly (Myrna Loy), at the end of a long hallway, and they eagerly cover the seemingly great distance to embrace.

At the bank, Al approves a loan for a fellow veteran who has no collateral except his skill as a farmer, and later must endure his sniping boss (Ray Collins), who grumbles about "gambling with the depositors' money." At the banquet celebrating Al's return, Milly marks her husband's drinks on the tablecloth with the tines of her fork; she worries that Al will have too many and include in his speech what he really thinks about his boss. Fred's father (Roman Bohnen) comes across his son's distinguished service citation and reads it quietly to his wife. Fred loses his job at a drugstore and wanders through a graveyard of junked airplanes, thinking that he too may now be as useless as these planes he once flew.

Perhaps most representative of the film's emotional realism is Homer. His unresolved feelings for his fiancee, Wilma, and his uncertainty about their future

Did you know?...

Samuel Goldwyn reportedly got the idea for the film from a 1944 *Time* magazine article about returning vets.

together finally lead him to show her his nightly routine of preparing for bed. Taking her upstairs, he wiggles out of the harness that holds his prosthetic hooks onto what is left of his arms and then shoulders his way into his pajama top. He confides that with his hooks on the bed he is as "dependent as a baby." Wilma quietly buttons his pajama top for him, embraces him, and helps him into bed in one of the most unorthodox and intimate love scenes in cinema, and Wyler, in a further desentimentalizing touch, has the actors play it with their backs partly turned to the camera. Screen-amateur Russell, who had lost both arms in the war, was given a special Oscar for bringing "hope and courage to his fellow veterans."

Wyler's technique of staging the action so as to minimize editing and to distract from the performers as little as possible capitalizes on moments like these. (It also put the actors under pressure: Virginia Mayo, in an interview for the 1997 DVD version of the film, was still complaining that Wyler would not cut

Family man and soldier Al Stephenson (Fredric March) tries reasoning with daughter Peggy (Teresa Wright) as wife Milly (Myrna Loy) looks on.

into a long shot with a closeup of her crestfallen reaction on seeing Fred return home; Wyler no doubt trusted Mayo to make her chagrin sufficiently clear to the audience in the long shot.) Many shots and scenes unfold like well-honed, one-act plays. Wyler's films collectively earned 127 Oscar nominations, according to Jan Herman's 1995 biography, a total "not even remotely approached by [Steven] Spielberg's, Billy Wilder's, or John Ford's, their closest competition." *The Best Years of Our Lives* beautifully exemplifies the work of this gifted director.

Cast: Fredric March (Al Stephenson), Myrna Loy (Milly Stephenson), Dana Andrews (Fred Derry), Teresa Wright (Peggy Stephenson), Virginia Mayo (Marie Derry), Cathy O'Donnell (Wilma Cameron), Hoagy Carmichael (Butch Engle), Harold Russell (Homer Parrish), Gladys George (Hortense Derry), Roman Bohnen (Pat Derry), Ray Collins (Mr. Milton), Minna Gombell (Mrs. Parrish), Walter Baldwin (Mr. Parrish), Steve Cochran (Cliff), Dorothy Adams (Mrs. Cameron), Don Beddoe (Mr. Cameron), Marlene Aames (Luella Parrish), Charles Halton (Prew), Ray Teal (Mr. Mollett), Howland Chamberlin (Thorpe), Dean White (Novak), Erskine Sanford (Bullard), Michael Hall (Rob Stephenson) **Screenwriter:** Robert E. Sherwood **Cinematographer:** Gregg Toland **Composer:** Hugo Friedhofer **Producer:** Samuel Goldwyn for the Samuel Goldwyn Company **Running Time:** 170 minutes **Format:** VHS, LV, DVD **Awards:** Academy Awards, 1946: Actor (Fredric March), Director (William Wyler), Editing, Picture, Screenplay, Supporting Actor (Harold Russell), Original Dramatic/Comedy Score, special award to Russell "for bringing hope and courage to fellow veterans"; Nominations: Sound; British Academy Awards, 1947: Film; Golden Globe Awards, 1947: Film—Drama; National Board of Review Awards: Ten Best Films of the Year, Director (William Wyler); New York Film Critics Awards, 1946: Director (William Wyler), Film **Box Office:** $11.3M.

Fanny and Alexander
1983 – Ingmar Bergman – 🦴🦴🦴🦴

Ingmar Bergman's wonderful movie swan song and semi-autobiography opens with the Ekdahl family in 1907 Sweden. The first forty minutes or so show us a family on Christmas, as the wise matriarch (Gunn Wallgren) waits for her three sons, their wives, and children to arrive. The large, lavishly appointed house all but glows with warmth. Many of these events are shown through the eyes of Alexander (Bertil Guve), the ten-year-old son of Oscar Ekdahl (Allan Edwall).

Bergman presents the family's humanity as a force of life-affirming power. Even the visit of Alexander's uncle Gustav (Jarl Kulle) to the room of the young maid Maj (Pernilla August) is tolerated by his wife Alma (Mona Maim), who knows the dalliances of her foolish billy-goat husband will not diminish his love

for her or their sex life. The tone and focus change when shortly after Christmas Alexander's father dies following a rehearsal at the theater the family has worked in for so many generations. Now the focus falls on the life-denying nature of the home Alexander and his sister Fanny (Pernilla Allwin) are taken to when their mother marries a strict Lutheran bishop (Jan Malmsjo). The first meeting between Alexander and the man who will become his stepfather turns into a virtual interrogation of the boy; the Bishop's house is coldly white and austerely furnished. The conflict between Bishop Vergerus and Alexander reaches a head when he beats the boy, and the rest of the Ekdahls must use their wits to rescue the mother and her two children from the Bishop's house.

Bergman fills the film with the sort of family details, both joyful and painful, that remain stored in the recesses of the mind forever, and these privileged moments impart great emotional richness and truth. Most of them concern Alexander: his shaking fear over his father's death; his sneaking out of bed

Young Fanny (Pernilla Allwin) and her brother Alexander (Bertil Guve) find their lives changed forever in Ingmar Bergman's family drama.

Did you know?...

Sven Nykvist, who photographed the film, began his career with Ingmar Bergman in the 1950s and photographed for the director the films *Sawdust and Tinsel, The Virgin Spring, Persona,* and *Cries and Whispers,* among others.

at night to play with his magic lantern; Alexander listening to the soul-rending screams of his mother after his father's death; Alexander's muttered curses as he walks in his father's funeral procession; the cold metal thimble on the finger of the aunt as she holds Alexander down while his stepfather canes him; and the loving servant Maj's ability to decode as a plea for help Alexander's formal post-card about visiting the botanical gardens with his stepfather. Such big and small details imbue the story with the fullness of life. The film blends the non-realistic (ghosts and visions) with the realistic as it celebrates family and imagination and affirms the importance of safe havens like the little worlds of the family and the theater as a shelter from the coldness and uncertainty of the bigger world.

Cast: Gunn Wallgren (Helena Ekdahl), Borje Ahlstedt (Carl Ekdahl), Ewa Froling (Emilie Ekdahl), Christina Schollin (Lydia Ekdahl), Bertil Guve (Alexander Ekdahl), Pernilla Allwin (Fanny Ekdahl), Allan Edwall (Oscar Ekdahl), Jarl Kulle (Gustav-Adolph Ekdahl), Mona Maim (Alma Ekdahl), Jan Malmsjo (Bishop Edvard Vergerus), Kerstin Tidelius (the Bishop's sister), Erland Josephson (Isak Jacobi), Kristian Almgren (Putte), Harriet Andersson (Justina), Pernilla August (Maj), Anna Bergman (Hanna Schwartz), Kabi Laretei (Aunt Anna), Sonya Hedenbratt (Aunt Emma), Svea Holst (Miss Ester), Mats Bergman (Aron), Gunnar Bjornstrand (Filip Landahl), Stina Ekblad (Ismael), Siv Ericks (Alida), Majlis Granlund (Miss Vega), Maria Granlund (Petra), Lena Olin (maid) **Screenwriter:** Ingmar Bergman **Cinematographer:** Sven Nykvist **Composer:** Daniel Bell, Benjamin Britten, Frans Helmerson, Marianne Jacobs **Producer:**Jorn Donner for Svenska Filminstitutet **MPAA Rating:** R **Running Time:** 197 minutes **Format:** VHS, LV **Awards:** Academy Awards, 1983: Art Direction/Set Decoration, Costume Design, Foreign Language Film, Cinematography; Nominations: Director (Ingmar Bergman), Screenplay; Cesar Awards 1984: Foreign Film; Golden Globe Awards 1984: Foreign Film; Los Angeles Film Critics Association Awards 1983: Cinematography, Foreign Film; New York Film Critics Awards 1983: Director (Ingmar Bergman), Foreign Film.

Field of Dreams
1988 – Phil Alden Robinson – ♪♪♪♪

"Are you a ghost?" asks Karen Kinsella (Gaby Hoffmann) of Shoeless Joe Jackson (Ray Liotta). "Do I look like a ghost?" replies Jackson. Karen says, "Ya look real to me." "Well then, I must be real." concludes Shoeless Joe.

As you watch the curious corn farmer Ray (Kevin Costner) plow under his crops, you have to agree with the onlookers—he must be crazy. But then, they never heard the Voice—"If you build it, he will come"—as farmer Ray did. And his conviction to build a baseball field costs him more than he could ever

Dr. Graham (Burt Lancaster) tries to reassure Iowa farmer Ray Kinsella (Kevin Costner).

know. He loses friends, in-laws, and comes close to losing his wife and the farm. But his daughter, who never heard the Voice, never once loses faith in what her Dad is doing. Finally the field is finished, and at first . . . nothing happens. Probably even Ray begins to doubt what he has done. Then, one evening, just about dark, "Daddy, there's a man out on your lawn." Ray goes out, turns on the lights, and discovers to his bewilderment that he has Shoeless Joe Jackson standing in left field as though he just woke up and can't believe where he is. Soon, long-departed ballplayers are loosening up with a little pepper in the cornfield.

Based on W.P. Kinsella's novel *Shoeless Joe*, *Field of Dreams* generally evokes one of two feelings. Some dislike the film because it is too Disneyesque and unrealistic: how could some farmer's wife be so blindly supportive as to smile serenely while her husband destroys part of their living? And why would a sensible farmer plow over his cornfield? Others love this film because they are

Did you know?...

The closing credits include the listing: "Voice . . . Himself."

eager to believe in something unseen and unexperienced, something that transcends today and gives meaning to the drudgery of what we do to exist.

In many ways, this longing to believe makes *Field of Dreams* a love story. In the deeper sense of its family structure, the movie engineers a mythic meeting between father and son. (Ray has unresolved issues with his late dad). This moment of reconciliation, characterized by a tenderness and understanding that surpasses logic, grows beautifully out of the film's non-realistic style and becomes, for those who believe, one of movie history's most memorable moments. Part of the film's great appeal is how it moves the viewer to the brink of longing to right an old wrong, to heal a broken relationship, or simply to be able to talk with someone you love—and can't.

Field of Dreams is also an epic quest that begins with the Voice and continues with Ray destroying his livelihood, alienating many of those around him, and doing strange things like kidnapping authors and chasing down long-dead doctors. It climaxes with Shoeless Joe looking at Ray after playing ball all day and saying, "If you build it, [turning toward the plate] *he* will come." Ray looks at the catcher, puts down his mask, and realizes, "It's my father."

Cast: Kevin Costner (Ray Kinsella), Amy Madigan (Annie Kinsella), Gaby Hoffman (Karen Kinsella), Ray Liotta (Shoeless Joe Jackson), Timothy Busfield (Mark), James Earl Jones (Terence Mann), Burt Lancaster (Dr. Archibald Graham), Frank Whaley (Archie "Moonlight" Graham), Dwier Brown (John Kinsella), Anne Seymour (Chisolm Newspaper Publisher), C. George Biasi (First Man in Bar), Howard Sherf (Second Man in Bar), Joseph R. Ryan (Third Man in Bar) **Screenwriter:** Phil Alden Robinson **Cinematographer:** John Lindley **Composer:** James Horner **Producer:** Charles Gordon and Lawrence Gordon for Carolco; released by Universal **MPAA Rating:** PG **Running Time:** 107 minutes **Format** VHS, LV, DVD **Awards:** Academy Awards, 1989: Nominations: Adapted Screenplay, Picture, Original Score **Box Office:** $64.4M.

The Grapes of Wrath

1940 – John Ford – 🦴🦴🦴🦴

Many big-budget epics organize themselves around a series of set pieces that usually showcase special effects. Based on Steinbeck's novel, this epic of the common man organizes itself around some of the milestones in the life of the Joad family. In the Dust Bowl of Oklahoma during the Depression, countless families are dispossessed by bank foreclosures. Imprisoned for killing a man in self-defense, Tom Joad (Henry Fonda) is paroled when his family is about to begin a journey to California in the hope of finding work. Director John Ford and screenwriter Nunnally Johnson dramatize the milestones that mark the Joad's passage from the life they have known to an uncertain future: the reunion of Tom with his family, the burial of the grandfather on the journey (one of many such graveside scenes that Ford loved), the difficulty of crossing the desert. In one of the most eloquent of these scenes, Ma Joad (Jane Darwell) examines the contents in her box of keepsakes. She has saved the newspaper clipping about Tom's imprisonment. She smiles at the toy dog she has kept from the St. Louis World's Fair, and in a shard from a old mirror we see her reflection holding two earrings to the sides of her face in the darkened cabin as the family loads their dilapidated truck.

What starts as a quest by one family turns into a story of all displaced humanity. The Joads finally get to California, but like their fellow transients they continually come up against authority figures who bully and demean them. These small-time bureaucrats exploit the working masses with take-it-or-leave-it fruit-picking jobs, coldhearted indifference, and starvation wages. The workers are torn between looking out for their own concerns and banding together to help one another. In one transient camp, Tom scares off hungry kids who gather around the Joad's pot of food, but Ma Joad feeds her family first and then offers the rest to the others. Ford and cinematographer Gregg Toland filmed the scenes of the tractors plowing over the Oakies' houses in ways that depersonalize the representatives of officialdom. Toland's shots of the transient camps approximate the authenticity of contemporary photographs by Walker Evans and Dorothea Lange. The clean, democratic government camp the Joads find in the final scenes brightens the tone, but the film still remains focused on the persis-

> "There's somethin' goin' on out there in the West, and I'd like to try and learn what it is."
>
> Casey (John Carradine) on joining the Joad's trip.

Did you know?...

Producer Darryl F. Zanuck oversaw the transformation of John Steinbeck's novel into a film. Zanuck even wrote Ma Joad's final speech.

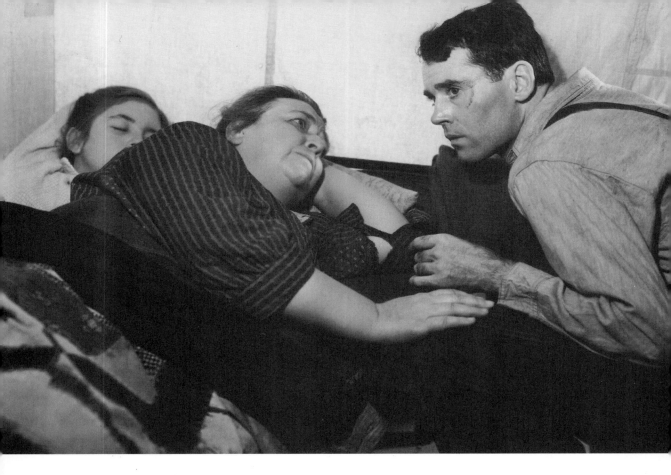

Ma Joad (Jane Darwell) listens to son Tom (Henry Fonda).

tent questions of self-interest versus brotherly love. Ford steeps his film in a genuine love of community. Until people realize that they have more uniting them than dividing them, the film implies, one of the greatest civilizing resources of all will remain untapped.

Cast: Henry Fonda (Tom Joad), Jane Darwell (Ma Joad), John Carradine (Reverend Jim Casy), Charley Grapewin (Grandpa Joad), Dorris Bowdon (Rose of Sharon), Russell Simpson (Pa Joad), O.Z. Whitehead (Al), John Qualen (Muley Graves), Eddie Quillan (Connie), Zeffie Tilbury (Gramma), Irving Bacon (Roy, conductor), Trevor Bardette (Jule), Ward Bond (Police-man), Charles D. Brown (Wilkie), Frank Darien (Uncle John) **Screenwriter:** Nunnally Johnson **Cinematographer:** Gregg Toland **Composer:** Alfred Newman **Producer:** Darryl F. Zanuck for Twentieth Century Fox **Running Time:** 128 minutes **Format:** VHS, LV **Awards:** Academy Awards, 1940: Director (John Ford), Actress (Jane Darwell); Nominations: Actor (Henry Fonda), Editing, Picture, Screenplay, Sound, Score; National Board of Review Awards, 1940: Ten Best Films of the Year; New York Film Critics Awards, 1940: Director (John Ford), Film.

It's a Wonderful Life

1946 — Frank Capra — *♪♪♪♪*

Suicide and Christmas—two staples of Frank Capra's film world—produce an even better mix in this classic than in *Meet John Doe*. How does Capra pay faithful service to both the spirit of Yuletide and fantasy and that of frustration and despair? Much of it comes through his Everyman hero George Bailey (James Stewart). George's deep fear of mediocrity keeps him from seeing that his essential worth lies in the very qualities often mistaken for mediocrity—simple decency, an understanding of fairness, and genuine care for others. Like his guardian angel Clarence (Henry Travers), for whom the first half of the movie is a crash course on who George is, the audience comes to like George Bailey.

He has always wanted to escape his little home town of Bedford Falls, see the world, and accomplish great things. Instead, his frustrations and fear of anonymity mount while he watches his brother (Todd Karns) get the college education he longed for and then receive even more of the spotlight for his wartime heroics. Neither has George excelled in business like Sam Wainwright (Frank Albertson). The sudden death of his father (Samuel S. Hinds) has saddled him to the family's two-bit building and loan, seemingly the community's only alternative to the tightfisted business practices of Mr. Potter (Lionel Barrymore). George has married the girl-next-door, Mary (Donna Reed), rather than Violet (Gloria Grahame), the potential trophy wife. George's forte, in short, lies not so much in doing great things as in preventing bad things: as a boy, he saves the druggist Mr. Gower (H.B. Warner) from a fatal mistake in filling a prescription, and he pulls his little brother out of the icy water of a frozen pond. On his wedding day he and Mary donate their life savings to stave off a run on the family business. But George isn't around to prevent his Uncle Billy (Thomas Mitchell) from losing the building and loan's assets on the eve of the bank examiner's visit. George turns to his nemesis for help, but Potter only gloats that George is worth more dead than alive. A lifetime of unfulfilled ambitions and perceived failures thus sends George out to the snowy bridge to take Potter's hint.

One of Capra's great gifts was finding the heroic in unexpected places. George isn't ordinary, but nobody has any trouble in understanding why he

> **"Look, Daddy, teacher says every time a bell rings an angel gets his wings."**
>
> Zuzu (Karolyn Grimes), as a Christmas ornament chimes.

Did you know?...

The film was remade (in 1977) as a gender-switched TV movie, *It Happened One Christmas*, with Marlo Thomas playing the lead, Wayne Rogers in the Donna Reed role, and Orson Welles as the Scrooge-like villain.

George Bailey (James Stewart) finds the true miracle of Christmas with his family and friends.

thinks he is. The audience comes to adopt the view of Clarence and heaven. We see how all the unspectacular life choices that establish George's heroism have also conspired to rob him of any sense of accomplishment. In the "unborn sequence," as the filmmakers called it, Clarence shows George the corrupted picture of Bedford Falls if he had never lived, but the real miracle comes when George returns home and finds his house clogged with singing friends, family, and neighbors chipping in to cancel George's debt. George Bailey is the ideal hero for all of us who feel unappreciated, unfulfilled, unrecognized.

A box-office disappointment (it lost money), the movie was revived on television, becoming a Christma Eve tradition. The script was based on Philip Von Doren Stern's short story "The Greatest Gift." Originally, the story was purchased by RKO for Cary Grant. Capra always wanted Stewart, who had just returned from the war. Stewart is supported by a strong ensemble, each of the performances ringing true.

Cast: James Stewart (George Bailey), Donna Reed (Mary Bailey), Thomas Mitchell (Uncle Billy), Lionel Barrymore (Potter), Henry Travers (Clarence Oddbody, angel second class), Beulah Bondi (Mrs. Bailey), H. B. Warner (Mr. Gower), Sheldon Leonard (Nick), Gloria Grahame (Violet), Ward Bond (Bert), Frank Faylan (Ernie), Samuel S. Hinds (Mr. Bailey), Frank Albertson (Sam Wainwright), Todd Karns (Harry Bailey), Virginia Patton (Ruth Dakin), Sarah Edwards (Mrs. Hatch, Mary's mother), William Edmunds (Mr. Martini), Argentina Bruneti (Mrs. Martini), Karolyn Grimes (Zuzu), Carol Coombs (Janie), Frank Hagney (Potter's bodyguard), Carl "Alfalfa" Switzer (Freddie), Harry Holman (high school principal), Charles Halton (bank examiner) **Screenwriter:** Frances Goodrich, Albert Hackett, Frank Capra, Jo Swerling **Cinematographer:** Joseph Walker, Joseph Biroc **Composer:** Dmitri Tiomkin **Producer:** Frank Capra for Liberty Films **Running Time:** 129 minutes **Format:** VHS, LV **Awards:** Golden Globe Awards, 1947: Director (Frank Capra); Academy Awards, 1946: Nominations: Picture, Director (Frank Capra), Actor (James Stewart), Editing, Sound **Budget:** $3.7M **Box Office:** $3.3M.

Legends of the Fall
1994 – Edward Zwick – 🦴🦴🦴

Director Edward Zwick's 1989 Civil War film *Glory* was a tragic-heroic exploration of the realities of war and racial oppression, an important movie about a disenfranchised people struggling against the odds to fight for personal freedom. Set during and after World War I, Zwick's *Legends of the Fall*, a story about three brothers who love the same woman, has a grand, important tone but is not quite as significant as it seems to want to be.

Featuring breathtaking cinematography that captures the beauty of natural landscapes and, briefly, the horrors of war, *Legends of the Fall* maintains visual interest. The film has the look of a big western epic, which it strives to be dramatically as well. Sporadic narration by the Native American One Stab (Gordon Tootoosis) attempts to lend a mystical and mythical presence, as when he says of Tristan (Brad Pitt), "Some people hear their own inner voices with great clearness and they live by what they hear. Such people become crazy, but they become legends." However, the character of Tristan and the events in the film do not really merit the description "legendary." Tristan seems merely a troubled man, prone to violent outbursts and bouts of depression arising from his failure to save his brother Samuel (Henry Thomas) from getting killed in the war. His relationship with Susannah (Julia Ormond) also comes across as melodramatic since the two are in love so quickly after supposedly grieving for the lost brother.

"You know, when Samuel died I cursed God. Did I damn everybody around me as well as myself?"
Tristan (Brad Pitt), to his father.

Did you know?...
Though set in Montana, the movie was filmed in British Columbia and Alberta, Canada.

Brothers Samuel (Henry Thomas), Tristan (Brad Pitt), and Alfred (Aidan Quinn) spend a quiet front porch moment together.

Although the legend fails to live up to the implications of its title and the self-important tone it attempts to take, as a drama the film works better. The performances of the actors are more than adequate, the scenery is beautiful, and the melodramatic story is well-paced and sufficiently intriguing. The tension between the brothers Tristan and Alfred, between Tristan and Susannah, and between Ludlow (Anthony Hopkins) and his sons provides an interesting reflection on the ways that a fairly close family can be torn apart and then find healing.

Cast: Brad Pitt (Tristan), Anthony Hopkins (Ludlow), Aidan Quinn (Alfred), Julia Ormond (Susannah), Henry Thomas (Samuel), Karina Lombard (Isabel Two), Gordon Tootoosis (One Stab), Christina Pickles (Isabel), Paul Desmond (Decker), Tantoo Cardinal (Pet), Robert Wisden (John T. O'Banion), John Novak (James O'Banion), Kenneth Welsh (Sheriff Tynert), Bill Dow (Longley), Sam Sarkar (Rodriguez) **Screenwriter:** Susan Shilliday, Bill Wittliff **Cinematographer:** John Toll **Composer:** James Horner **Producer:** Marshall Herskovitz, William D. Wittlif, and Edward Zwick for Bedford Falls; released by Tri-Star **MPAA Rating:** R **Running Time:** 133 minutes **Format:** VHS, LV, DVD **Awards:** Academy Awards, 1994: Cinematography (John Toll); Nominations: Art Direction/Set Decoration, Sound; Golden Globes, 1995, Nominations: Direc-

tor (Edward Zwick), Motion Picture—Drama, Original Score (James Horner), Actor (Brad Pitt)
Box Office: $66.5M (domestic).

The Magnificent Ambersons

1942 – Orson Welles – 𝄢𝄢𝄢𝄢

Somebody should make a movie about the making of *The Magnificent Ambersons*. Tim Robbins could play young Orson Welles, who in 1941 was fresh from the critical success and financial failure of *Citizen Kane* when he chose for his second RKO project Booth Tarkington's 1918 Pulitzer prize-winning novel about an Indianapolis family at the turn of the century and their fall from wealth and prestige. The completed film was previewed twice to caustic and restless audiences, and the studio, fresh from a top management change and still stung over the loss of revenue from *Kane*, ordered changes. Welles was in South America working on the abortive documentary *It's All True* when a wartime embargo on intercontinental flights complicated attempts to involve him in recutting *Ambersons*. Welles' original 131-minute film was trimmed to 88 minutes with some short, transitional scenes and a new ending added. Original editor Robert Wise, who had worked with Welles on *Citizen Kane*, was involved in condensing the final cut. He says it was done thoughtfully. "I feel that all of us tried sincerely to keep the best of Welles' concept and still lick the problems." What remains is probably the best so-called "flawed masterpiece" in cinema history.

Writer, director, and friend of Orson, Peter Bogdanovich dug into the archives at RKO to see what the preview audiences had actually written on their comment cards. He quotes from them in his book *This Is Orson Welles*. Of the 125 cards, Bogdanovich judged 53 to be positive. Of the 72 negative ones, some of the answers to the question "Did you like this picture?" revealed an audience more in the mood for escapist fare: "People like to laff," "I could not understand it," "It is a crime to take people's hard-earned money for such *artistic* trash as Mr. Welles would have us think," "As bad if not worse than *Citizen Kane*."

Welles' focus on the family and their declining fortune makes *Ambersons* one of the first Hollywood films to supplant the traditional hero and heroine with a Chekhov-like ensemble of characters, something more common today in the

"Old times. Not a bit. There aren't any old times. The times are gone. They're not old. They're dead. There aren't any times but new times."

Eugene (Joseph Cotten) to Jack (Ray Collins).

Did you know?...

Tarkington's novel had been filmed previously in 1925 as *Pampered Youth*, a silent film that survives only in fragments. Some of these scenes have been included on the Criterion Collection laserdisc version of Welles' film.

Automobile inventor Eugene Morgan (Joseph Cotten) finds he needs a little help.

films of Robert Altman and Woody Allen, among others. Welles uses the early scenes of the prologue (with his spoken narration) and the last of the great Amberson balls to both introduce characters and convey a flavor of the age of privilege quickly passing away. Every member of the family is defined with regard to others, so that, for example, we see how George's (Tim Holt) spoiled nature ties to Isabel's (Dolores Costello) indulgent mothering and how Fanny's (Agnes Moorehead) introspection and silence grows from her disappointed awareness of Eugene's (Joseph Cotten) love for Isabel. The agitated, overlapping voices in the hallway after the ball wonderfully reflect various states of mind. Welles drew on his experience in radio to create striking sound montages throughout the film (notice the irreverent-sounding emissions from the bathtub faucet when George talks to his uncle).

When asked about the recut film, Welles said "it's all gone," but his emotionalism over the lost material made him too harsh. Its technique is as assured as that in *Citizen Kane*, but the humanity of *The Magnificent Ambersons* is even greater than its more famous predecessor.

Cast: Joseph Cotten (Eugene Morgan), Dolores Costello (Isabel Amberson), Anne Baxter (Lucy Morgan), Tim Holt (George Minafer), Agnes Moorehead (Fanny Minafer), Ray Collins (Jack Amberson), Richard Bennett (Major Amberson), Erskine Sanford (Roger Bronson), J. Louis Johnson (Sam the Butler), Don Dillaway (Wilbur Minafer), Charles Phipps (Uncle John Minafer), Dorothy Vaughn (Mrs. Johnson), Ann O'Neal (Mrs. Foster), Elmer Jerome (townsperson outside Amberson mansion), Maynard Holmes (townsperson outside Amberson mansion), Edwin August (townsperson outside Amberson mansion), Jack Baxley (townsperson outside Amberson mansion), Harry Humphrey (townsperson outside Amberson mansion), Bobby Cooper (George as a boy), Heenan Elliot (laborer terrorized by George), Drew Roddy (Elijah), Gus Schilling (drugstore clerk), James Westerfield (Irish cop), William Blees (young motorist in accident) **Screenwriter:** Orson Welles **Cinematographer:** Stanley Cortez **Composer:** Bernard Herrmann (uncredited) **Producer:** Orson Welles for RKO **Running Time:** 88 minutes **Format:** VHS, LV **Awards:** New York Film Critics Awards 1942: Actress (Agnes Moorehead); Academy Awards 1942: Nominations: Picture, Black and White Cinematography (Stanley Cortez), Interior Decoration, Supporting Actress (Agnes Moorehead).

1900
1976 – Bernardo Bertolucci – 🦴🦴🦴

Bernardo Bertolucci's *1900* falls into the category of sprawling, novel-like epics that exist in versions of various lengths (*Once Upon a Time in America*, featuring the same star and composer, is another). The sympathetic, even affectionate, presentation of the rise of Italian communism, coupled with comments from the director about wanting to create an "explosion" by accepting American corporate funding for such a film, caused a controversy at the time of the release. The movie begins in Emilia-Romagna in 1901 on the day its famous son Guiseppe Verdi dies. It is also the day two sons, Alfredo and Olmo, are born to two families on a single estate, the aristocratic line headed by Alfredo (Burt Lancaster) and the peasant workers headed by Leo Dalco (Sterling Hayden). The film follows these two sons to adulthood as they grow, marry, and come to grips with the rise of fascism and communism.

On the whole, the visual element outpaces the dramatic. A number of set pieces and images stand out for their earthiness or repulsion, two tones which recur and come to mark the passing of years. We see, for example, young Olmo

Did you know?...

Producer Alberto Grimaldi at one point locked director Bertolucci out of the editing room in his effort to try to satisfy Paramount's request that the film be cut by two hours.

Aging Attila (Donald Sutherland) needs some assistance in Bernardo Bertolucci's *1900*.

"I don't want it to look elegant. I want it to look strong. This isn't a shirt. It is a symbol. You're making a flag for the people."

Attila (Donald Sutherland), to the tailor designing his fascist brownshirt.

decorate his hat with a dozen squirming frogs, and the two boys play on the train tracks as the locomotive approaches (a scene echoed at the end). Grandfather Alfredo's naked feet ooze into cow manure before he hangs himself. To bring down the curtain on the film's first half, the fascist Attila (Donald Sutherland), lecturing some onlookers on the foolish open-heartedness of communism, takes a cat ("you care about one cat, you start to think about others"), strings it to a wall with his belt, and then runs at it and smashes it to a pulp with his head. Sutherland's villain is by far the most stereotypical character, an indication of the director's unsubtle polemic. (Bertolucci doesn't disappoint his audience—or cat lovers for that matter—in giving Attila his comeuppance on liberation day in 1945 when he is hunted down by peasants in an open field; Attila's final fate has him staggering about stuck full of pitchforks, a human pincushion.) A compelling collection of scenes rather than a smoothly developing narrative, *1900* is an acquired taste.

Cast: Robert De Niro (Alfredo Berlinghieri), Gerard Depardieu (Olmo Dalco), Dominique Sanda (Ada Fiastri Paulhan), Donald Sutherland (Attila), Francesca Bertini (Sister Desolata), Laura Betti (Regina), Werner Bruhns (Ottavio Berlinghieri), Stefania Casini (Neve), Burt Lancaster (Alfredo Berlinghieri, the grandfather), Sterling Hayden (Leo Dalco), Anna Henkel (Anita), Ellen Schwiers (Amelia), Alida Valli (Signora Pioppo), Romolo Valli (Giovanni), Giacomo Rizzo (Rigoletto), Pippo Campanini (Don Tarcisio), Paolo Pavesi (Alfredo as a Child) **Screenwriter:** Franco Arcalli, Bernardo Bertolucci, Giuseppe Bertolucci **Cinematographer:** Vittorio Storaro **Composer:** Ennio Morricone **Producer:** Alberto Grimaldi **MPAA Rating:** R **Running Time:** 255 minutes (from 320 minutes) **Format:** VHS, LV.

Yankee Doodle Dandy
1942 – Michael Curtiz – 🎵🎵🎵

Yankee Doodle Dandy is the story of the great George M. Cohan, Broadway song and dance legend. The film takes us through his life in a flashback while he speaks to President Roosevelt prior to receiving the Congressional Medal of Honor. As Cohan leaves FDR, he descends a grand White House staircase with a dancing jaunt in his stride, an emblematic image for a film that celebrates the patriotic confidence of America.

The story is just as lively as this hoofer, combining biography, nostalgia, and song and dance. James Cagney does a marvelous job as the fiery but friendly Cohan. His personality and energy carry the entire film, and the audience identifies with his brash self-confidence that covers a kindness and concern for others. A good supporting cast also makes the movie enjoyable and includes Cagney's own sister and Rosemary de Camp (fourteen years younger than Cagney, whose mother she plays).

The filmmakers create a realistic, if Hollywoodesque, environment of the New York theater life. One strength of the movie is that the focus stays squarely on the story of George. What appeals so much is that George Cohan, in his own words, is just an "ordinary guy." The idea that this ordinary guy can use his talent to become a hero and a celebrity is the dream of everyone. The film constantly insists that it is the glory of America that such a dream is possible.

The story is simple: a small-time child actor becomes known in the role of Peck's bad boy, and his career keeps going up. He continues to act with his family of four and eventually adds a wife. He tries his hand at writing and pro-

> "My mother thanks you, my father thanks you, my sister thanks you, and I thank you."
> George (James Cagney)

Did you know?...

Cagney had seen Cohan perform when he was a boy, and modeled his dance steps after that performance. He initially rejected the part, however, as did Fred Astaire.

George M. Cohan (James Cagney) puts on a patriotic display.

ducing shows that ordinary people want to see and becomes a big success. He goes on to write some of the most patriotic American songs, like "Grand Old Flag" and "Over There." This leads to his conference with the President.

Although the story is uplifting, there are times when the movie drags a bit, especially during some of the dance routines that the Cohans stage. If you can look past its datedness, the songs are familiar and the film is inspiring and romanticized. Overall, a great biography through music.

Cast: James Cagney (George M. Cohan), Joan Leslie (Mary Cohan), Walter Huston (Jerry Cohan), Richard Whorf (Sam Harris), Irene Manning (Fay Templeton), George Tobias (Dietz), Chester Clute (Goff), Rosemary de Camp (Nellie Cohan), Jeanne Cagney (Josie Cohan), S.Z. Sakall (Schwab), Eddie Foy Jr. (Eddie Foy), Odette Myrtil (Madame Barthold), George Barbier (Erlanger), Douglas Croft (George M. Cohan at 13), Jack Young (the President) **Screenwriter:** Robert Buckner, Edmund Joseph **Cinematographer:** James Wong Howe **Composer:** George M. Cohan, Heinz Roemheld **Producer:** Hal Wallis for Warner Bros. **Running Time:** 126 minutes **Format:** VHS, LV **Awards:** Academy Awards, 1942: Actor (James Cagney), Sound, Score/Musical;

Nominations: Picture, Supporting Actor (Walter Huston), Director, Original Story, Editing; New York Film Critics Awards 1942: Best Actor (James Cagney) **Box Office:** $4.7M.

They Might Be Giants . . .

During the peak of popularity for the television mini-series during the 1970s, the epic seemed for a while to become more the property of the small screen than the big. Two of the most popular mini-series also dramatized family stories. *Rich Man, Poor Man*, based on Irwin Shaw's novel, aired in 1976, and its popularity led television historians Tim Brooks and Earl Marsh to speculate that "if it had not been overshadowed so quickly by *Roots*, *Rich Man, Poor Man* would probably be ranked today as the biggest dramatic spectacular in the history of television." The entire saga runs for 720 minutes and follows the fortunes of two brothers, Rudy (Peter Strauss) and Tom Jordache (Nick Nolte), through their checkered careers. (A television series followed without Nolte, called *Rich Man, Poor Man—Book II*.) Other stars appearing in the large cast of the original mini-series were Susan Blakely, Edward Asner, Dorothy McGuire, Ray Milland, Kim Darby, Van Johnson, Dorothy Malone, and Andrew Duggan.

The master of all epic mini-series, *Roots*, based on Alex Haley's novel, aired its first installment on January 23, 1977. This generational saga of the descendants of slave Kunta Kinte (LeVar Burton) begins in 1750 in Gambia, West Africa. The story maps the development of this family tree from Africa to a slave plantation in America to 1820s England and back again to America for the Civil War. At the conclusion, the great-grandson of Kunta Kinte hopes for a better future after the end of slavery. Shown on consecutive evenings, *Roots* was truly an event, attracting 100 million viewers for its final episode. Appearing in its large cast are Cicely Tyson, Maya Angelou, O.J. Simpson, Moses Gunn, Edward Asner, Ralph Waite, Louis Gossett, Jr., Vic Morrow, Robert Reed, Chuck Connors, Sandy Duncan, Ben Vereen, and Lloyd Bridges.

FANTASY

Alice in Wonderland

1951 — Clyde Geronimi, Wilfred Jackson, Hamilton Luske — ♪♪♪

> **"I can't explain myself because I'm not myself, you see?"**
> Alice (Kathryn Beaumont), to the Caterpillar.

> **"I don't see."**
> Caterpillar (Richard Haydn) replies.

Lewis Carroll's Victorian classic of the little girl who falls down the Rabbit Hole is one of the most frequently adapted children's stories. It has been made into live-action movies, stage plays, television features, and animated shorts. Walt Disney considered the story as early as 1933, shelving it to make the far more suitable *Snow White* his first animated feature film. So why isn't Alice's fantasy a more effective movie?

Animation seems the perfect vehicle to create talking animals and the radical changes of size that Alice undergoes repeatedly. Colors can be twisted into the fantastic with ease and landscapes metamorphosed as they appear to do in dreams (which, after all, is what Alice is doing). But Disney, like other adaptors, missed two powerful features of the book. First, it is a tale about language. Almost all the jokes are based on word play: Alice being confused for a serpent by a bird who defines her as "something that has a long neck and eats eggs" or the idea that an "unbirthday" is what you have on all days that are not birthdays. Second, unlike Dorothy in *The Wizard of Oz*, Alice has no particular desire to go home, a plot element present in all other movie versions. Alice wants most of all to be a grown-up, and she sees that the topsy-turvy world of grown-up values and hypocrisies is one that is negotiated through words. Alice does not want to leave Wonderland; she wants to succeed there and does when she gets up the courage to tell them all that they are nothing but a pack of cards.

Apart from the digression from the classic story, *Alice* does present an abundance of Disney magic. The movie is fun to watch, especially the whimsical animals that the Disney animators add as little touches. And the music is fun, too—who can resist singing flowers? Plus, who hasn't dealt with a loud, powerful bully like the Queen? We can all cheer when she gets her comeuppance at the end. If the film works as it should, it will still send children to the library for the original classic.

> **Did you know?...**
> Alice actually meets Tweedle Dee and Tweedle Dum in the second volume of her adventures, *Through the Looking Glass.*

Cast: Kathryn Beaumont (voice of Alice), Ed Wynn (voice of the Mad Hatter), Richard Haydn (voice of the Caterpillar), Sterling Holloway (voice of the Chesire Cat), Jerry Colonna (voice of the March Hare), Verna Felton (voice of the Queen of Hearts), Pat O'Malley (voice of the Walrus/Carpenter/Dee/Dum), Bill Thompson (voice of the White Rabbit), Joseph Kearnes

(voice of the Doorknob), Larry Carey (voice of Bill), Heather Angel (voice of Alice's sister), Dink Trout (voice of the King of Hearts), James G. MacDonald (voice of the Dormouse) **Screenwriter:** Winston Hilder, Ted Sears, Bill Peet, Erdman Penner, Joe Rinaldi **Composer:** Mack David, Sammy Fain, Bob Hilliard, Al Hoffman, Ted Sears **Producer:** Walt Disney **Running Time:** 74 minutes **Format:** VHS, LV **Awards:** Academy Awards: 1951: Nominations, Score.

A tiny Alice encounters some remarkable creatures in Wonderland.

Batman

1989 – Tim Burton – 𝄞𝄞𝄞

Unlike the *Superman* films, in which Christopher Reeve's gift for light comedy as mild-mannered Clark Kent turned out to be unexpectedly appealing, the *Batman* films have shuffled around the casting of the hero and made their psycho-villains the biggest draw. This emphasis, of course, is also reflected in Anton Furst's boiler-room production design, which reflects the state of mind of Gotham City. The slate gray, canted structures, billowing steam, and gargoyle turrets have an urban-medieval torture chamber look. "Decent people shouldn't live here," Jack Nicholson's Joker says to Harvey Dent's (Billy Dee Williams) image on TV. "They wouldn't be happy here."

The hero is presented as a man of mystery who is in the process of being deciphered by Vicki Vale (Kim Basinger) and the audience. Which parts of his gothic mansion represent him most accurately—the tasteful art objects or the hall of armor and battle gear? The villain, on the other hand, is a known quantity, and he gets all the good lines. "A lovely beast like that running around," the Joker says on seeing a picture of Vicki Vale, "could put steam in a man's strides." This comedy of anarchy gives the film its weird charm, and the few touches of satire (as in the scene when the Joker's killer cosmetics scare forces two news anchors to go on the air without makeup) seem a little out of place. Director Tim Burton uses music for some dark comedy, letting "Beautiful Dreamer" and "A Summer Place" play ironically under the Joker's scenes with Vicki Vale. (Even the car gets a dramatic entrance. When Batman and Vicki Vale escape from the Joker at the art museum, the first shot of the bullet-shaped Bat-mobile is accompanied by a crescendo on the soundtrack.)

The plot concerns Bruce Wayne's first appearances as Batman, which coincide with the betrayal of Jack Napier (Jack Nicholson) by his fellow hood Carl Grissom (Jack Palance). Napier falls into a vat of chemicals during a shootout with the police and is transformed into the Joker, the chalk-faced, green-haired nemesis of Batman. Many mainstream films confine their darker elements to the villain's part or relegate it to the background. *Batman* brings it center stage and glories in it. The nightmare fantasy of *Batman* puts both hero and villain in the grip of competing obsessions. Batman's discovery of Napier's

Did you know?...

The drawing of the bat-shaped man that the newspaper reporters kiddingly hand Robert Wuhl is the work of Batman creator Bob Kane. His characteristic signature appears in the lower left of the drawing. Kane, however, did not make his planned cameo in the film due to a schedule conflict.

involvement in his own troubled past is the screenwriters' smartest touch. "You're not exactly normal," Vale says to Batman. "It's not a normal world is it?" he replies. In *Batman*, comic books meet grand opera meets film noir.

The three sequels have shifted the focus of the series. In *Batman Returns* Tim Burton increased the number of grotesques among the villains (Danny DeVito as the Penguin), though Christopher Walken's character is the least interesting, and diminished somewhat the role of the hero. Joel Schumacher has directed the two subsequent entries with Val Kilmer and George Clooney, which have in effect turned the hero's part into the guest starring role.

Cast: Michael Keaton (Batman/Bruce Wayne), Jack Nicholson (the Joker/Jack Napier), Kim Basinger (Vicki Vale), Pat Hingle (Commissioner Gordon), Robert Wuhl (Alexander Knox), Michael Gough (Alfred Pennyworth), Billy Dee Williams (Harvey Dent), Jack Palance (Carl Grissom), Jerry Hall (Alicia), Tracey Walter (Bob the Goon), William Hootkins (Lt. Eckhardt), Kate Harper (anchorwoman), Bruce McGuire (anchorman), Richard Durden (TV director), Hugo Blick (young Jack Napier), Charles Roskilly (young Bruce Wayne) **Screenwriter:** Sam Hamm,

The Joker (Jack Nicholson) appears in a commercial for his own toxic brand of toiletries.

Warren Skaaren **Cinematographer:** Roger Pratt **Composer:** Danny Elfman, Prince **Producer:** Peter Guber and Jon Peters for Warner Bros. **MPAA Rating:** PG-13 **Running Time:** 126 minutes **Format:** VHS, LV, DVD **Awards:** Academy Awards, 1989: Art Direction/Set Decoration; People's Choice Awards, 1990: Best Film—Drama **Box Office:** $162M (non-US); $251M (US).

Beauty and the Beast

1946 – Jean Cocteau – 𝄢𝄢𝄢𝄢

> "He is suffering. He is more cruel to himself than to human beings . . . I'll be happy if I can make him forget his ugliness."
>
> Beauty (Josette Day), to her father about the Beast.

Diary of a Film, the book that director Jean Cocteau wrote about the making of *Beauty and the Beast*, describes the string of problems that beset the production, ranging from the difficulty of finding high-grade film stock, reliable equipment, and electrical sources in postwar France to the freak injuries and illnesses that befell the cast and director. More relevant to the look of the finished film is his remark about the visual poetry he sought to create in his version of the familiar fairy tale. Cocteau felt that out-of-focus camera effects failed to achieve the poetic and preferred a sharper use of detail: "In my eyes poetry is precision, numbers. I'm pushing [cinematographer] Alekan in precisely the opposite direction from what fools think is poetic." As a result, this film, Cocteau's second effort as a director, is more grounded in the everyday and less surreal than the style of his first, *The Blood of a Poet*.

The mix of fantasy and realism works brilliantly. Love's power to transform has rarely been expressed with such force. Beauty (Josette Day) rides on the majestic white horse Magnifique to the grounds of the Beast (Jean Marais) to pay the debt owed by her father (Marcel Andre). Rather than take her life, however, the Beast is slowly ennobled by her beauty. He comes to her each evening as she dines and asks her to marry him. Eventually, her father's illness makes her promise the Beast that she will return if he permits her to visit her family once more. The Beast then reveals to Beauty some of the secrets of his magic and entrusts her with the key to Diana's Pavilion, the source of his treasures. He tells her that he will die if she fails to keep her word. Her return is momentarily delayed by the greed of her sisters, who covet her beautiful necklace (which turns to dry sticks when the sisters hold it and then back again to pearls when Beauty takes it). Though the sisters steal the key to Diana's Pavilion, Beauty eventually returns and attempts to restore the dying Beast.

Did you know?...

The Production designer Christian Berard based his sets of Beauty's home on the paintings of Jan Vermeer and the interiors of the Beast's domain on works by Gustave Dore.

Jean Marais stars as the agonized Beast.

Cocteau's imagination thrives on the magical element of the fairy tale. When Beauty enters the main hallway, the candles, held by naked arms that extend from both walls, magically flare to life; sometimes these human sconces release their hovering candelabra to point the visitor to the Beast's quarters. When Beauty prepares to return home, the Beast instructs her in the use of his magic glove, which allows her to appear in her own room by materializing through a wall. In her later scene with her father, when Beauty cries her tears turn to diamonds as they trickle down her cheeks. Such an imaginative presentation gives the film its charming tone and keeps the viewer alert for the next instance of screen magic.

Cast: Jean Marais (Avenant/the Beast/the Prince), Josette Day (Beauty), Marcel Andre (the merchant), Mila Parely (Adelaide), Nane Germon (Felice), Michael Auclair (Ludovic) **Screenwriter:** Jean Cocteau **Cinematographer:** Henri Alekan **Composer:** Georges Auric **Producer:** Andre Paulve **Running Time:** 95 minutes **Format:** VHS, LV, DVD.

E.T. The Extra-Terrestrial
1982 – Steven Spielberg – 🦴🦴🦴🦴

"E.T. phone home."
E.T.

Steven Spielberg's *E.T.*, which for many years was the highest grossing film of all time, tells the story of a 10-year-old boy (Henry Thomas) who befriends an alien accidently left behind on Earth when his ship takes off without him. After meeting the alien, whom he names "E.T.," young Elliot sneaks the extraterrestrial being into his house and develops a close relationship with him as he teaches him about life on Earth. Soon E.T. starts working on a way to contact his people so they can return to retrieve him, but that quest is complicated by government scientists who discover the alien's presence and by E.T. becoming deathly ill. Ultimately Elliot must attempt to rescue the little alien if he is to go "home."

Did you know?...

Perennial favorite M&M's candy was the first choice for a key scene in the film, but M&M/Mars declined a product placement and Reese's Pieces were used instead. After the little candy-coated peanut butter disks were gobbled up by E.T., sales of the candy spiked dramatically.

Though, as always, Spielberg's visual skills are fully on display in this film, the heart of *E.T.*'s success lies in the very personal nature of its story. While it is an epic story of a cosmic traveler trapped far from home trying to find his way back, it is even more an epic story of friendship, loyalty, and family. The most effective scenes in *E.T.* are small-scale and simple, between the alien and

Elliot. E.T. shares the boy's favorite candy, looks at Elliot's toys, dresses up for Halloween to go trick-or-treating with the children, and goes for a magical ride on a bicycle. As might be expected from Spielberg, the film includes its share of fascinating special effects and suspenseful action sequences, but these elements provide only occasional background material in support of a story of two extraordinary friends bonding.

E.T. tells Elliot (Henry Thomas) that he'll always be his friend.

In some respects the movie bears a resemblance to the director's previous "extra-terrestrial" film, *Close Encounters of the Third Kind*, in that both introduce "friendly" aliens and characters who in one way or another find emotional and psychological fulfillment in their contact with them, but *E.T.* is more personal and perhaps more basic in its treatment of human relationships and needs. The film says little that is intellectually profound, yet its success may be best explained in its unique yet simple handling of a universal theme: the need for true friends. Spielberg has sometimes been accused of playing too much to conjured sentimentality, but the sentimentality at the heart of *E.T.* arises from a well-developed, skillfully portrayed relationship between two individuals who need each other. Though *E.T.* is the story of a little alien, it is really a genuine story of the human condition.

Cast: Dee Wallace (Mary), Henry Thomas (Elliot), Peter Coyote (Keys), Robert Mac-Naughton (Michael), Drew Barrymore (Gertie), K. C. Martel (Greg), Sean Frye (Steve), Tom Howell (Tyler), Erika Eleniak (Pretty Girl), David M. O'Dell (Schoolboy), Richard Swingler (Science Teacher), Frank Toth (Policeman), Robert Barton (Ultra Sound Man), Michael Durrell (Van Man), David Berkson (Medic) **Screenwriter:** Melissa Mathison **Cinematographer:** Allen Daviau **Composer:** John Williams **Producer** Steven Spielberg and Kathleen Kennedy **MPAA Rating:** PG **Running Time:** 115 minutes **Format:** VHS, LV **Awards:** Academy Awards, 1982: Visual Effects, Original Score (John Williams); Nominations: Director (Steven Spielberg), Editing, Original Screenplay (Melissa Mathison), Picture, Sound; Los Angeles Film Critics Association Awards, 1982: Director (Steven Spielberg), Film; National Society of Film Critics Awards, 1982: Director (Steven Spielberg); People's Choice Awards, 1983: Film; Writer's Guild of America, 1982: Original Screenplay (Melissa Mathison) **Box Office:** $399.8M (domestic gross).

The Hunchback of Notre Dame

1996 — Gary Trousdale, Kirk Wise — 🦴🦴🦴

> "What do they have against people who are different, anyway?"
>
> Esmeralda (Demi Moore)

Did you know?...

The film represents the last role for 85-year-old Mary Wickes, who died six weeks after voicing the part of gargoyle Laverne.

The Disney version of Victor Hugo's 1831 novel may owe as much to RKO's 1939 film with Charles Laughton and Maureen O'Hara as to its literary source. The early scenes follow the development of the previous one with surprising faithfulness. The contrast between Esmeralda's unselfish prayer in the cathedral and the chorus of those around her chanting their self-centered petitions ("I ask, I ask . . . ") comes across in both versions, and the animators found in it a perfect moment for their most memorable song, "God Help the Outcasts." The final image of the song lights Esmeralda (voice of Demi Moore and Heidi Mollenhauer) in the glow of the richly textured sunlight streaming through the cathedral's massive stained glass window. Musically, visually, and dramatically, it is one of the film's most uplifting moments.

The animation team worked carefully to capture the shifting patterns of light and dark in the cathedral, partly because such a design represented the duality of the central characters. Judge Frollo (Tony Jay) embodies all that is life-denying in unhealthy religion. Sneering, self-assured, harsh, and judgmental, he

displays a self-righteousness that cannot tolerate the passion aroused in him by Esmeralda, and he faults her for his own growing lust. Never has there been a Disney animated villain so psychologically and morally conflicted, nor do the filmmakers shrink from exploring Frollo's divided feelings. In his musical soliloquy "Hellfire," which contrasts Esmeralda's earlier song of Christian humility and compassion, Frollo fondles Esmeralda's scarf and stares into the swirling

Reclusive bell-ringer Quasimodo enjoys looking at Paris from high atop a Notre Dame gargoyle.

flames of his hearth as the image of the gypsy girl taunts him. The lyrics are a chilling combination of self-justification and self-disgust: "It's not my fault / I'm not to blame / It is the gypsy girl, the witch who sent this flame. / It's not my fault / If in God's plan / He made the Devil so much / Stronger than a man." Later during the climax, the filmmakers find the perfect image for Frollo as he is glimpsed approaching young Quasi (Tom Hulce) speaking of duty but concealing a dagger behind his back.

Some feared that the grown-up nature of the conflict might pose a problem for parents having to explain aspects of the film to their children, and some purists complained that the film streamlined too much of the classic novel (and of course dispensed with the tragic ending). The Disney animators, however, deserve praise for their willingness to take on ambitious challenges in a genre that Disney has made its own.

Cast: Tom Hulce (voice of Quasimodo), Tony Jay (voice of Frollo), Demi Moore (speaking voice of Esmeralda), Heidi Mollenahauer (singing voice of Esmeralda), Kevin Kline (voice of Phoebus), Paul Kandel (voice of Clopin), Jason Alexander (voice of Hugo), Charles Kimbrough (voice of Victor), Mary Wickes (voice of Laverne), Jane Withers (additional voice of Laverne), David Ogden Stiers (voice of the Archdeacon) **Screenwriter:** Tab Murphy, Irene Mecchi, Bob Tzudiker, Noni White, Jonathan Roberts **Composer:** Alan Menken **Producer:** Don Hahn for Walt Disney Pictures; released by Buena Vista **MPAA Rating:** G **Running Time:** 86 minutes **Format:** VHS, LV **Awards:** Academy Awards, 1996: Nominations: Original Score (Alan Menken); Golden Globe Awards, 1997: Nominations: Original Score (Alan Menken) **Box Office:** $100M (domestic); $284M (worldwide).

Peter Pan

1953 – Clyde Geronimi, Wilfred Jackson, Hamilton Luske – 🎵🎵🎵

> "Fly? All it takes is faith and trust . . . and a little pixie dust!"
>
> Peter Pan (Bobby Driscoll)

James M. Barrie's story of the boy who refuses to grow up has been told in a variety of forms, from his own exceptionally popular stage play to his novelization, then later to a successful television musical with Mary Martin and Walt Disney's animated version. Barrie loyalists prefer the live stage version, but many children know the story only through the cartoon feature. It contains many of the elements of the original. First is the transformation of the grumpy father, Mr. Darling, into the nefarious Captain Hook. The animated version retains only the same voice, while the stage show uses the same actor for both roles, so the parallel is not so obvious

in the movie. Second is the magic of flight, rendered much more believably through animation, since there are no wires or tracks to limit the actors. The movie also indulges Barrie's sweetly sentimental emphasis on mothers, both Wendy's own understanding mother and Wendy's attempt to nurture the Lost Boys.

Finally, the Disney version has the important ingredient of play. Play is a complex issue in the story. It sometimes makes modern audiences wince in embarrassment when the stereotypical Indians break into the song "What Makes the Red Man Red?" But these are not real Native Americans, any more than Neverland is a real place. Neverland is an elaborate playground, with mermaids and Indians and pirates all rubbing elbows together. Fights never last, no one is really hurt—even the youngest viewer knows that Captain Hook will elude the ravenous crocodile to fight another day. The movie is an extension of the nursery; we must all grow up and leave it, but as even Mr. Darling comes to realize, our memories of that childhood time are always there within us.

Peter Pan and Tinkerbell look around the Darlings' home.

Did you know?...

In all previous stage productions, Peter had been played by a young woman. This is his first appearance as an actual boy.

By the time of the making of *Peter Pan*, Walt Disney had become involved in live-action films and the design of a revolutionary kind of theme park, so this is the first animated feature that has little of Walt's own direction. He still attended story meetings and gave advice on small details like the expression of the crocodile. While many worried about the fate of such a feature without Disney's direct supervision, *Peter Pan* was a much bigger box-office success than the previous movie, *Alice in Wonderland*.

Cast: Bobby Driscoll (voice of Peter Pan), Kathryn Beaumont (voice of Wendy), Hans Conried (voice of Captain Hook and Mr. Darling), Bill Thompson (voice of Smee), Heather Angel (voice of Mrs. Darling), Paul Collins (voice of John), Tommy Luske (voice of Michael), Candy Candido (voice of Indian Chief), Tom Conway (Narrator) **Screenwriter:** Milt Banta, William Cottrell, Winston Hibler, Bill Peet **Composer:** Sammy Cahn, Frank Churchill **Producer:** Walt Disney **Running Time:** 77 minutes **Format:** VHS, LV.

Pinocchio
1940 – Ben Sharpsteen, Hamilton Luske – 🦴🦴🦴🦴

> "A lie keeps growing and growing until it is as clear as the nose on your face."
> Blue Fairy (Evelyn Venable)

Audiences were surprised when Walt Disney did not follow the smashing success of *Snow White* with another romantic fairy tale. But for his second feature-length animated film, Walt didn't want more of the same—he broke ground again by choosing the classic Italian tale by Carlo Collodi of the puppet who wanted to become a real boy. Pinocchio is hardly a lovable hero; he is as wooden-headed in judgment as he is in body. He has every possible advantage—a father who loves him, the care of the Blue Fairy, a friendly cricket as his best friend and mentor. Yet he blows one chance after another, running off to join the puppet show where he is imprisoned by the evil Stromboli and escaping only to buy a ticket to Pleasure Island. Pleasure Island is the thing of every child's nightmares: an amusement park that turns sinister, transforming children into donkeys who will never see their parents again.

However, Pinocchio redeems himself by growing an unselfish heart. He seeks his father Geppetto in the dark belly of the whale Monstro and sacrifices himself to get his father safely to shore. Once again, the Blue Fairy intervenes, and this time the puppet is a real boy. A happy ending combined with one of the greatest American songs, "When You Wish Upon a Star" guarantees a pleased audience.

Did you know?...
Some forest backdrops were used again in *Bambi.*

Pinocchio is befriended by a cricket named Jiminy.

Visually, the film is an eyeful, too. Disney lavished great care on backgrounds like the toy shop and Pleasure Island, on extensive detailing of movement like bubbles and waves beneath the sea, and on wonderfully sinister characters like Stromboli, Honest John, and Monstro. Songs like "An Actor's Life For Me" are so engaging that we are tempted to forget school and our conscience and run off to the theater too. Animation of small gestures makes the film a masterpiece as well: the antics of the goldfish Cleo, Jiminy Cricket warming his backside at Geppetto's hearth, and Pinocchio lying and watching astonished as his nose grows and sprouts flowers and birds' nests. *Pinocchio* showed, and still shows, the world what animation can accomplish as a visual and narrative form.

Cast: Dick Jones (voice of Pinocchio), Christian Rub (voice of Geppetto), Cliff Edwards (voice of Jiminy Cricket), Evelyn Venable (voice of the Blue Fairy), Walter Catlett (voice of Honest John), Mel Blanc (voice of Gideon), Charles Judels (voice of Stromboli and the Coachman), Frankie Darro (voice of Lampwick) **Screenwriter:** Ted Sears, William Cottrell, Webb Smith, Otto Englander **Composer:** Paul J. Smith, Leigh Harline **Producer:** Walt Disney **Running Time:** 88 minutes **Format:** VHS, LV **Awards:** Academy Awards, 1940: Score, Song ("When You Wish Upon a Star").

Snow White and the Seven Dwarfs
1937 – David Hand (supervising director) – 🦴🦴🦴

"Mirror, mirror on the wall, who's the fairest of them all?"
the Queen (Lucille LaVerne)

It is hard for the modern viewer to believe that one of the world's landmark films was called "Disney's Folly" as it was being produced and that most cynics predicted that the costly venture would sink the fledgling studio and all its investors. But the idea was so new, so different—an animated film that was feature-length rather than the standard eight minutes, and one that told a story with detailed, developed, human characters. One skeptic was not sure if viewers' eyes could actually focus on animation for a full hour! However, it was Walt Disney who had the last laugh. Pushing the studio to the brink of bankruptcy, the film cost $1.5 million (Walt had even mortgaged his house and car), but made over $8 million in its first release. Furthermore, it was the financial and creative foundation that the Disney entertainment empire would build upon.

In 1934, Walt called in his animators and acted out for them the old fairy tale story from the Brothers Grimm. The story contained all the elements of a

great movie. There was the lovely young girl abused and threatened by her cruel stepmother. Romantic interest was provided by the handsome Prince Charming, and comic relief by the little dwarfs and their eccentricities. There were complications, the tragedy of the Poisoned Apple, and the happy ending. By the end of his performance, the animators were convinced, and the same would be true of theater audiences as well. In the following months, Disney sent his animators to art school to learn to draw humans more realistically. Film footage was shot of action and dance sequences to use as models for animation. The drawing boards were enlarged to handle the more detailed imagery. In all, 570 artists created 250,000 drawings. A multi-plane camera was developed by partner Ub Iwerks that gave the images more depth and complexity than those in previous cartoons.

The result of such care was resounding success. Audiences worldwide adored Snow White and her sidekicks, and clamored for more feature-length animated films. A new industry was born, as well as new ties to marketing with

The jealous Queen disguises herself as an old peddlar woman in order to give Snow White a poisoned apple.

Did you know?...

Disney hated to show incomplete products to anyone, but the banker insisted on seeing what he was financing. He sat silently through the film, walked to his car, turned and said, "Walt, that picture is going to make you a hatful of money."

Snow White dolls, clothes, and figurines. The Great Depression had reached its darkest days, but a cheerful heroine, songs like "Whistle While You Work" and "Someday My Prince Will Come," and the sure hope of a happier tomorrow made the film a ray of light in the darkest corners of the globe.

Cast: Wicked Queen (voice of Lucille LaVerne), Magic Mirror (voice of Moroni Olsen), Snow White (voice of Adriana Caselotti), Doc (voice of Roy Atwell) **Screenwriter:** Ted Sears, Otto Englander, Earl Hurd, Dorothy Ann Blank, Richard Creedon, Dick Richard, Merrill de Maris, Webb Smith **Composer:** Frank Churchill, Leigh Harline, Paul Smith **Producer** Walt Disney **Running Time:** 82 minutes **Format:** VHS, LV **Awards:** Academy Awards, 1938: Special Award to Walt Disney for his significant screen innovation of feature-length animated film; the award was an Oscar flanked by seven tiny Oscars. Academy Awards, 1938: Nominations: Score. **Budget:** $1.5M **Box Office:** $8M (in its first release).

Superman

1978 – Richard Donner – 🧦🧦🧦

> "I'm here to fight for truth and justice and the American way."
> Superman (Christopher Reeve)

> "You're going to end up fighting every elected official in this country."
> Lois (Margot Kidder), with a laugh.

The seriousness director Richard Donner brought to the legendary comic-book story starts in the precredit sequence. Set in June 1938 (the year Jerry Siegel and Joel Shuster's hero appeared in Action Comics), the introduction shows a parting curtain and a child's voice seriously reading from the pages of a comic about the hope the *Daily Planet* gave people during the Depression. After the credits, the first sound is Marlon Brando's voice sternly announcing: "This is no fantasy." The optimism of the film can be traced to the changing mood in America brought about by the end of Watergate and the election of Jimmy Carter. Both the Man of Steel and the president-elect promised never to lie to the American people. During production, Donner pointed out to interviewers a sign hanging in his office reading "verisimilitude."

The production design by John Berry is one of the film's real strengths. Krypton is realized as a blindingly white, frozen chip of a planet about to destroy itself. When Superman later builds his Fortress of Solitude in the Arctic, this setting visually recalls the buried memories of his origin. The script furthers the seriousness of the production by using the dialogue at times to emphasize (some would say *over*emphasize) the mythic materials. The conversation of Jor-

El (Marlon Brando) and La-Ra (Susannah York) as they ready their infant for his escape from Krypton identifies the elements that will define Superman's life on Earth: "He will look like one of them," the father says. "But he won't *be* one of them," the mother corrects him; "he'll be odd, different." "He'll be fast, virtually invulnerable," says Jor-El. "Isolated, alone," replies La-Ra. This seriousness is one of the film's welcome surprises.

Another strength is some of the comedy in the Metropolis scenes. The romantic comedy among Lois, Clark, and Superman blends more smoothly with the tone of the earlier scenes than the later slapstick of the villains. Of greater appeal than even the special effects is Christopher Reeve as Clark Kent, whose performance suggests rich film associations. His comic timidity and romantic reticence recalls Cary Grant in *Bringing Up Baby*, silent film comic Harold Lloyd, and even perhaps the meekness of Kermit the Frog. The montage of superfeats that introduces the Man of Steel to Metropolis is arranged as a series of chal-

Superman (Christopher Reeve) doing one of the things he does best.

Did you know?...

Forty-nine minutes cut before the theatrical release were restored for a network television broadcast.

lenges (from pulling a kitty from a tree to holding aloft a lightning-damaged Air Force One), as if both hero and film are flexing their special-effects muscles.

As the movie progresses, it loses some of its balance when parody sets in. Ned Beatty and Valerie Perrine's characters epitomize the efforts to hedge the financial gamble of the film by trying to appeal to other tastes. Though it eventually turns into something of a patchwork, the film has real strengths, mostly in the first two-thirds.

The first sequel, in which the three renegade Kryptonians escape from the Phantom Zone and threaten Superman, has greater unity of tone but lacks mythic appeal. The last two sequels are less noteworthy: in the first Robert Vaughan and Richard Pryor team up to design a computer scam, and in the second (for which Christopher Reeve received a story credit) Superman rids the world of nuclear weapons. (In his 1998 autobiography *Still Me*, Reeve wrote, "The less said about *Superman IV* the better.")

Cast: Christopher Reeve (Superman/Clark Kent), Margot Kidder (Lois Lane), Gene Hackman (Lex Luthor), Jackie Cooper (Perry White), Marlon Brando (Jor-El), Susannah York (La-Ra), Valerie Perrine (Miss Teschmacher), Ned Beatty (Otis), Glenn Ford (Jonathan Kent), Phyllis Thaxter (Martha Kent), Marc McClure (Jimmy Olson), Trevor Howard (Kryptonian leader), Sarah Douglas (Ursa), Terence Stamp (General Zod), Jack O'Halloran (Non), Noel Neill (train passenger), Larry Hagman (soldier), Rex Reed (himself) **Screenwriter:** Mario Puzo, David Newman, Leslie Newman, Robert Benton **Cinematographer:** Geoffrey Unsworth **Composer:** John Williams **Producer:** Alexander Salkind and Ilya Salkind for Warner Bros. **MPAA Rating:** PG **Running Time:** 144 minutes **Format:** VHS, LV **Budget:** $55M **Box Office:** $134M.

The Wizard of Oz
1939 – Victor Fleming – 🦴🦴🦴🦴

"Toto, I have a feeling we're not in Kansas anymore."
Dorothy (Judy Garland)

In one of the most beloved children's classics, a little Kansas girl named Dorothy (Judy Garland) is transported to the magical land of Oz when her farmhouse is whirled away by a tornado and lands over the rainbow, far away from friends, family, and mean old Elmira Gulch (Margaret Hamilton). But is Dorothy really away at all? As she and her new friends—a brainless scarecrow, a heartless tin man, and a cowardly lion—set off for the Emerald City and the wonderful wizard to get the things they lack, they discover that they had them all along.

The movie is a true extravaganza. It assembled the largest cast of little people ever to play the Munchkins, who are rescued when Dorothy's house falls on the Wicked Witch of the East. The special effects are delightful and believable, including Glinda the Good Witch's pink transport bubble and the tornado that sweeps Dorothy and her dog Toto to Oz. The Wizard's vast head is spectacular, and generations of children have been terrified by Hamilton's green makeup and flying monkey henchmen. The music is also unforgettable; "Somewhere Over the Rainbow" (which was almost cut from the final film) became Judy Garland's signature song. And a surprising number of Americans can break into the melody of "We're Off to See the Wizard" after decades of not seeing the film! Originally, Wallace Beery was offered the role of The Wizard; Buddy Ebsen was cast as the Scarecrow, swapped roles with Tin Man Ray Bolger and discovered he was allergic to the metallic paint; and even Hamilton was a second choice behind Edna May Oliver. An uncredited King Vidor directed the sepia shots at the beginning and end.

Dorothy (Judy Garland) with her companions, the Cowardly Lion (Bert Lahr), the Tin Man (Jack Haley), and the Scarecrow (Ray Bolger).

Did you know?...

MGM originally wanted Shirley Temple or Deanna Durbin to play the part of Dorothy.

Not that many people can go decades without seeing the film, for it is so popular that it is reshown almost yearly on network television, and a huge theater re-release is planned for its sixtieth anniversary in 1999. But the chemistry of the characters' friendships is so endearing and the hope for that fantasy escape and safe return home so enduring, that this movie will forever be dearly beloved.

Cast: Judy Garland (Dorothy Gale), Frank Morgan (Professor Marvel/Wizard of Oz/Guardian of the Gate/Cabbie), Ray Bolger (Scarecrow/Hunk Andrews), Bert Lahr (Cowardly Lion/Zeke), Jack Haley (Tin Man/Hickory Twicker), Billie Burke (Glinda the Good Witch), Margaret Hamilton (Wicked Witch of the West/Elmira Gulch), Charley Grapewin (Uncle Henry), Clara Blandick (Auntie Em), Billy Bletcher (Mayor/Lollipop Guild), Harry Stanton (Munchkin Coroner), Buster Brody (Winged Monkey), Lorraine Bridges (Ozmite/Lullaby League), Pat Walshe (Nikko), Mitchell Lewis (Captain of the Guard) **Screenwriter:** Noel Langley, Florence Ryerson, Edgar Allan Woolf **Cinematographer:** Harold Rosson **Composer:** Harold Arlen **Producer:** Mervyn LeRoy for MGM **Running Time:** 112 minutes **Format:** VHS, LV **Awards:** Academy Awards, 1939: Musical Score, Song ("Somewhere Over the Rainbow"), special miniature Oscar for Judy Garland; Nominations: Picture, Art Direction **Budget:** $2.7M **Box Office:** $4.5M.

They Might Be Giants . . .

Many children's films, both animated and live-action, fall into the epic category. The viewer might also consider the following animated classics: *Charlotte's Web* (1972), the story of the runt of the litter whose life is saved by a spider who can write; *The Lion, the Witch, and the Wardrobe* (1993), the story of four children's trip to enchanted Narnia with the great lion Aslan; and the seasonal *Muppet's Christmas Carol* (1993), a funny and musical recreation of Dickens' favorite tale of Scrooge and Tiny Tim with a cast of cuddly muppets.

There are also a host of newer generation Disney animated epics: *Beauty and the Beast* (1992), where the lovely and spirited Belle meets and tames the Beast with a kind, hidden heart; *Aladdin* (1993), a high-energy romp through the Arabian nights classic with Robin Williams as the voice of the unforgettable blue genie; *The Lion King* (1994), a coming of age story of Simba the African lion cub; *Pocahontas* (1996), which recreates the American legend of the Indian princess who risked her life to make peace with the white settlers; and *Toy Story* (1996), a new kind of movie altogether, entirely computer animated, with an epic cast of toy characters having adventures in and out of the nursery.

Epic live-action is available in abundance as well. From the beloved story of the classic nanny *Mary Poppins* (1964), which won Julie Andrews an Oscar, to the exotic island adventure *Swiss Family Robinson*, complete with tree house and pet ostrich, to the action-packed Disney retelling of *The Jungle Book* (1994) and the game-become-real tale of *Jumanji* (1995), lots of fantasy adventure and fun await children and the adults who watch with them. Of course, you'll find the occasional film that will test your patience, like Robert Altman's *Popeye*, with Robin Williams in the lead.

FUTURISTIC

Blade Runner
Close Encounters of the Third Kind
The Empire Strikes Back
Planet of the Apes
Return of the Jedi
Star Trek Generations
Star Trek: The Motion Picture
Star Wars
2001: A Space Odyssey

Blade Runner

1982, 1992 (Director's Cut) – Ridley Scott – 🎵🎵🎵

> "The report read 'Routine retirement of a replicant.' That didn't make me feel any better about shooting a woman in the back."
>
> Deckard (Harrison Ford)

Based on a novel by Philip K. Dick entitled *Do Androids Dream of Electric Sheep?*, Ridley Scott's *Blade Runner* offers a strange, bleak vision of the future that is nonetheless depicted with a sort of gloomy beauty. The year is 2019 and the setting is a perpetually dark and dirty Los Angeles. The city seems ruled by the monolithic Tyrell corporation, a manufacturer of artificial life forms that is housed in a monstrous building resembling an ancient pyramid, as if in testament to the life-generating power of this corporate entity. Police officer Rick Deckard (Harrison Ford) is sent to hunt down a group of illegal, murderous androids (called replicants) that have returned to Earth in search of a way to extend their four-year life spans. Along the way, Deckard meets and falls in love with Rachael (Sean Young), a replicant who had human memories implanted in her, making her think she is human and making the discovery of her true nature particularly sad.

Scott fashions a visually stunning film, an eerily exquisite portrait of a predominantly dark, shadow-filled landscape broken only by dull artificial illumination and occasional shafts of light that never come from the vanquished sun. It is a chaotic world that seems to lack any future or any hope. Mankind has reached new levels of technology, but such advancement has not made for a better or more beautiful world. The visual dynamics of the production design and the photographic artistry make watching *Blade Runner* a fascinating, though cheerless, experience.

The plot is rather slim and the full potential of the characters is not thoroughly realized. Rachael's discovery that she is artificial, for instance, is depicted as merely a sad moment for her, and the full emotional impact of such a revelation does not come across. The quest of the replicants for extended life gives them a near-tragic dimension that almost leads to sympathy, but again the extent of such a driving need seems touched upon only lightly, considering the magnitude of its effect on the androids.

What does remain fascinating, though, are the broader implications of the story and how they reflect on more cosmic issues. Mankind as seen in the person of Tyrell (Joe Turkel), who lives above the city in his high temple, has

Did you know?...

In 1992 a director's cut of the film was released, representing Ridley Scott's original vision. The narration by Deckard was removed and the ending, which was more upbeat according to the demands of the studio, was replaced with a more ambiguous one.

Deckard's (Harrison Ford) dinner gets interrupted by cop Gaff (Edward James Olmos).

reached a sort of godlike power, and he treats his creation as a machine to be exploited, ignored, and destroyed at will, all for the sake of "progress" and the almighty dollar. Tyrell and the humanity he represents thus join the renegade replicants as the villains of the story. In his progress and ascension, man has created life but then rejected it and denied it all its needs. Deckard, in his sympathy for Rachael and his ability to love her (and show her how to love), represents the only redemption either man or replicant can hope for.

Cast: Harrison Ford (Rick Deckard), Rutger Hauer (Roy Batty), Sean Young (Rachael), Edward James Olmos (Gaff), M. Emmet Walsh (Bryant), Daryl Hannah (Pris), William Sanderson (J. F. Sebastian), Brion James (Leon), Joe Turkel (Tyrell), Joanna Cassidy (Zhora), James Hong (Chew), Morgan Paull (Holden), Kevin Thompson (Bear), John Edward Allen (Kaiser), Hy Pyke (Taffey Lewis) **Screenwriter:** Hampton Fancher, David Peoples **Cinematographer:** Jordan Cronenweth **Composer:** Vangelis **Producer:** Michael Deeley for Warner Bros. **MPAA Rating:** R **Running Time:** 117 minutes **Format:** VHS, LV, DVD **Awards:** Academy Awards, 1982: Nominations: Art Direction/Set Decoration, Visual Effects.

Close Encounters of the Third Kind

1977 – Steven Spielberg – 𝄞𝄞𝄞𝄞

> **"Ronnie, if I don't do this, that's when I'm going to need a doctor."**
>
> Roy (Richard Dreyfuss), to his wife as he shovels sod through the kitchen window.

Director Steven Spielberg's first blockbuster tale of aliens from another world (the second, of course, was 1982's *E. T.*) takes a familiar science fiction premise in new directions by suggesting that, if extraterrestrial beings do visit, their intentions might not be hostile—an idea generally absent from previous science fiction movies (with the possible exception of Robert Wise's *The Day the Earth Stood Still*). Released the same year as close friend George Lucas's *Star Wars*, *Close Encounters of the Third Kind* tells the story of several people who become psychically aware that Earth is about to have visitors from outer space and who set out on a quest to meet the aliens when they arrive. Principally it is the story of Roy Neary (Richard Dreyfuss), whose obsession with the aliens drives him away from his family but whose special insight and connection to the extraterrestrial visitors ultimately leads to their inviting him inside the ship to join them on a cosmic journey.

Close Encounters is in many ways a story about dreaming. Roy Neary seems to long for something beyond his ordinary life. When he first has a strange experience with an alien presence while sitting in his truck at the railroad tracks, he awakens to the possibility of something special happening to him. Though he loves his family, his noisy children and unsympathetic wife (Teri Garr) soon lose touch with him, and in fact they may be part of the ordinary, unsatisfying life he hopes to transcend. A recurring musical motif heard throughout is a familiar refrain from "When You Wish upon a Star," underscoring the fairy-tale-like nature of the story and emphasizing the theme of following one's dreams. Spielberg, who at times can be fairly accused of favoring visual and emotional flair over strong character development, wisely delays revealing the aliens until the end of the movie, thus sustaining suspense and a sense of wonder throughout the film. Visual effects are used sparingly until the finale, where the appearance of the alien mother ship ushers in an effective climax to the excitement that has been building through the course of the story.

Paul Schrader submitted the first script for the movie, which was discarded by Spielberg. The film was envisioned starring Jack Nicholson in the Neary role. Locations included the Mojave Desert and the 1,200-foot Devil's Tower National Monument in Wyoming. In a nod toward one of his director heroes,

Spielberg cast French filmmaker François Truffaut in a key role as the scientist Lacombe. The laserdisc version includes scenes edited out and interviews with Spielberg, special effects wizard Douglass Trumbull, and composer John Williams, as well as 1,000 production photos. In the "special edition" version released in 1981, Spielberg takes the viewer inside the spaceship with Neary.

Roy Neary (Richard Dreyfuss) becomes obsessed with sculpting a clay mountain in his living room.

Cast: Richard Dreyfuss (Roy Neary), François Truffaut (Claude Lacombe), Teri Garr (Ronnie Neary), Melinda Dillon (Jillian Guiler), Bob Balaban (David Laughlin), J. Patrick McNamara (Project Leader), Warren J. Kemmerling (Wild Bill), Roberts Blossom (Farmer), Philip Dodds (Jean Claude), Cary Guffey (Barry Guiler), Shawn Bishop (Neary Child), Adrienne Campbell (Neary Child), Justin Dreyfuss (Neary Child), Lance Henriksen (Robert), Merrill Connally (Team Leader) **Screenwriter:** Steven Spielberg **Cinematographer:** Vilmos Zsigmond **Composer:** John Williams **Producer:** Clark L. Paylow, Julia Phillips, and Michael Phillips for Columbia **MPAA Rating:** PG **Running Time:** 132 minutes **Format:** VHS, LV **Awards:** Academy Awards 1977: Cinematography (Vilmos Zsigmond), Sound Effects Editing; Nominations: Art Direction/Set Decoration, Director (Steven Spielberg), Film Editing, Sound, Supporting Actress (Melinda Dillon), Original Score (John Williams); National Board of Review Awards 1977: 10 Best Films of the Year **Budget** $21M **Box Office:** $166M (domestic gross).

The Empire Strikes Back

1980, 1997 (Special Edition) — Irvin Kirshner — 🦴🦴🦴🦴

The second installment in the *Star Wars* trilogy has often been praised as the most complex, and thus the best, of the three space fantasies. Whether its greater complexity makes it a better film is debatable, but *The Empire Strikes Back* certainly takes the saga in new directions stylistically and thematically. While, like its predecessor, *Empire* could be described as a delightful, spirited mythical adventure pitting good against evil, it is also a darker—and in some ways—a more philosophical story. *Star Wars* ended victoriously with the destruction of the Galactic Empire's Death Star by the Rebel Alliance, but little victory is to be found in *Empire*. From the beginning, when the Empire discovers the hidden location of the Alliance and forces the Rebels to flee across the galaxy, until the end, when Luke Skywalker (Mark Hamill) loses his hand in a battle with Darth Vader, and Han Solo (Harrison Ford) is captured by a notorious bounty hunter, the film touches more on loss, personal relationships, and self-discovery.

The Empire Strikes Back is a big film, with a big feel to it. The locations are vast and exotic, and the details, from minor props and alien creatures to grand scale otherworldly sets, are exquisite and elaborate. The story itself is huge, in both its cosmic settings and its plotting, tracing the exploits of a few lone individuals fighting incredible odds against a mighty evil Empire led by potentially unbeatable villains. More significantly, though, the story is mythic in its scope, for at its heart lies Luke's quest to learn more about the mystical powers of the Force and to become a Jedi knight. In his epic quest to become a knight, rescue his friends, and defeat his enemies, Luke discovers timeless inner and cosmic truths about himself and his universe and begins to face the reality that within him lies as much potential evil as exists in his fallen father, Darth Vader. Thus, while *Star Wars* was a story of youth and more simple understandings of good and evil, *The Empire Strikes Back* is a story of maturation as Luke gains knowledge and power and is tempted to use that knowledge for evil, which is not as clearly distinguishable as it once was.

In 1997, a special edition of *The Empire Strikes Back* was released in theaters, featuring enhanced special effects and an improved soundtrack. Although

Did you know?...

In the carbon freezing chamber scene, when Leia tells Han, "I love you," Harrison Ford ad-libbed and changed the scripted response to "I know."

the enhancements add to the visual and auditory feast, the heart of the story needed no enhancement and fortunately remains intact.

Han Solo (Harrison Ford) quiets a talkative C-3PO.

Cast: Mark Hamill (Luke Skywalker), Harrison Ford (Han Solo), Carrie Fisher (Princess Leia), Billy Dee Williams (Lando Calrissian), David Prowse (Darth Vader), James Earl Jones (voice of Darth Vader), Anthony Daniels (C-3PO), Kenny Baker (R2-D2), Peter Mayhew (Chewbacca), Frank Oz (voice of Yoda), Alec Guiness (Obi Wan Kenobi), John Hollis (Lobot), Jack Purvis (Chief Ugnaught), Kenneth Colley (Admiral Piett) **Screenwriter:** George Lucas, Leigh Brackett, Lawrence Kasdan **Cinematographer:** Peter Suschitzky **Composer:** John Williams **Producer:** Gary Kurtz for Lucasfilm and Twentieth Century Fox; Rick McCallum (Special Edition) **MPAA Rating:** PG **Running Time:** 124 minutes; 127 minutes (Special Edition) **Format:** VHS, LV **Awards:** Academy Awards 1980: Sound, Visual Effects; Nominations: Art Direction/Set Decoration, Original Score (John Williams); People's Choice Awards 1981: Film **Budget:** $18M **Box Office:** $290.2M (domestic gross).

Planet of the Apes

1968 – Franklin J. Schaffner – 𝄡𝄡𝄡

> "I'm a seeker too. But my dreams aren't like yours. I can't help thinking that somewhere in the universe there has to be something better than man. Has to be."
>
> George Taylor (Charlton Heston)

It is strange to see an astronaut smoking a cigar on a space ship, but that is what happens in the opening scene of *Planet of the Apes*. George Taylor (Charlton Heston) dictates his final entry into an audio time capsule prior to putting himself to sleep for the rest of the journey . . . a journey through time as well as space, since he and his crew are testing a theory about time/space travel that they hope will return them safely to Earth. However, the ship crashes and Taylor and his crew wake up two thousand years later on a planet run by apes. Man now becomes the animal, and the apes, who speak perfect English, control society. It is a fascinating premise (one sure to be loved by animal rights activists), and a great twist comes in at the end.

Although some of Jerry Goldsmith's music may be a bit cliched (he seems to like the anticipatory ominous chords), the passages underscoring Taylor's escape effectively add to the excitement of the chase. The film style is somewhat uneven as well. In the opening crash scene, for example, the camera simply twists and turns over and over to depict the downward fall of the spacecraft, but the action scenes are handled in a suggestive, mysterious way that makes the viewer alert for potential danger. Some breathtaking panoramas also appear. Exteriors were shot at Lake Powell, Utah, and Page, Arizona, while the surprise ending was filmed at Point Dunne, California.

Did you know?...

The first choice for the part eventually played by Maurice Evans was Edward G. Robinson, who could not accept the role due to health problems that would be aggravated by the rigors of working in hot weather and wearing heavy makeup. Robinson did appear in a science-fiction film with Heston in 1973 when he starred in *Soylent Green*, his final film.

Under all the heavy costumes and thick makeup, the acting manages to stand out. Roddy McDowall and Kim Hunter do a wonderful job as Cornelius and Dr. Zira, a very loving simian couple who befriend Taylor. Charlton Heston is . . . well, Heston. His typical arrogance and headstrong nature suit perfectly a representative of an overconfident culture about to find himself in a position of subservience. A non-empathetic actor like Heston makes the humbling Taylor gets more effective ("Imagine me needing someone. Back on Earth I never did. Oh, there were women. Lots of women. Lots of love-making but no love. You see, that was the kind of world we'd made"). Maurice Evans is marvelous as Dr. Zaius, the ape zealot for religion and science who is referred to as both the "Chief Defender of the Faith" and the "Minister of Science." Linda Harrison plays

Astronaut George (Charlton Heston) finds humans aren't superior on the *Planet of the Apes.*

Nova, Taylor's new girlfriend. Since all of the humans on the planet are mute, she may be the best actor in the cast. Her longing looks are very convincing.

Planet of the Apes certainly deserved its nomination for best costume design (no category for best makeup existed, though John Chambers was awarded an honorary Oscar for his work in creating the convincing apes). Not only do the apes appear life-like and believable, but their facial makeup, which achieves several different looks, is unusually expressive. The male hunter and guard monkey seem to have one look (that of a common simian) while the intelligent, scientist monkey, such as Cornelius and Dr. Zira, have a softer, more keen look to them. And then there is the elite monkey like Dr. Zaius, Honorious, and the President of the Assembly. Their features reveal a lighter coloring (a latent prejudice in the film?) and a more regal and distinguished behavior.

Planet of the Apes finds much of its epic quality in reversing how we see the world. By making our closest relative in the animal kingdom the ruler, the screenwriters show humans being caged and tested, prodded, tortured, given over to medical and scientific experiments, and exploited. "Humans see, humans do," an ape remarks. The film does not fail at developing its premise in a thought-provoking way.

The popularity of the film led in quick succession to four sequels. First came *Beneath the Planet of the Apes* (1969), in which a second mission is sent to find the missing crew from the first. In the 39th century, man has still not learned to live in peace. He has the bomb, and Taylor, seeing how the world of the apes and the mutant humans can never co-exist, uses it to destroy the planet. *Escape from the Planet of the Apes* (1970) sends Zira, Cornelius, and Milo (Sal Mineo) back to the twentieth century to escape the nuclear obliteration of their age. Zira is pregnant with the monkey child who will challenge human supremacy on Earth. In *Conquest of the Planet of the Apes* (1972), the apes turn on the humans and defeat them to assume control of the planet. Finally, *Battle for the Planet of the Apes* (1973), set in 2670 after a nuclear devastation, shows the efforts of a group of mutant humans to disrupt and defeat peaceful apes. Two television series followed, the second one an animated cartoon.

Cast: Charlton Heston (George Taylor), Roddy McDowall (Cornelius), Kim Hunter (Dr. Zira), Maurice Evans (Dr. Zaius), James Whitmore (President of the Assembly), James Daly (Honorious), Linda Harrison (Nova), Robert Gunner (Landon), Lou Wagner (Lucius), Woodrow Parfrey (Maximus), Jeff Burton (Dodge), Buck Kartalian (Julius), Norman Burton (Hunt Leader), Wright King (Dr. Galen), Paul Lambert (Minister) **Screenwriter:** Rod Serling, Michael Wilson **Cinematographer:** Leon Shamroy **Composer:** Jerry Goldsmith **Producer:** Mort Abrahams for Apjac and Twentieth Century Fox **MPAA Rating:** G **Running Time:** 112 minutes **Format:** VHS, LV **Awards:** National Board of Review Awards 1968: 10 Best Films of the Year; Academy Awards 1968: Nominations: Costume Design, Original Score.

Return of the Jedi

1983, 1997 (Special Edition) — Richard Marquand — ♪♪♪♪

The third chapter (actually Episode VI) in George Lucas' enormously successful *Star Wars* saga brings the trilogy to a sweeping, grand-scale conclusion with a story that involves heroic rescues, epic battles, the ultimate triumph of good over diabolical evil, and personal redemption. After saving Han Solo (Harrison Ford) from the gangster Jabba the Hutt, Luke Skywalker (Mark Hamill) and his friends embark on a quest with the Rebel Alliance to destroy the Empire's new Death Star space station, unaware that their plans have been foreseen by the evil Emperor Palpatine. *Return of the Jedi* has occasionally been criticized as being simply more of the same, essentially a retreading of territory already explored by its predecessors; however, even though its dazzling special effects and fascinating action sequences clearly resemble and invite comparison to those of the first two films, the movie stands well on its own as it further develops central themes touched on in the previous chapters and also introduces new ones that bring satisfying closure to the epic saga that began with *Star Wars*.

The *Star Wars* saga is very much the saga of the maturation of Luke Skywalker. In the first film, Luke is an overly confident youth eager to become a hero, while in *The Empire Strikes Back* he begins to mature as he learns the complexity of good and evil and must face the realities of pain and loss. In *Return of the Jedi*, Luke has matured and mellowed into a man whose quest becomes not merely conquering an evil Empire but redeeming his fallen father. In the process, he must face his own "dark side" and resist the temptation to repeat his father's mistakes. When he finally succeeds in his quest—not by besting his enemies in a fight but by appealing to the good within his father and refusing to destroy him even when he has the opportunity—Luke becomes even more of a hero than he was in the first film when he destroyed the original Death Star.

"Take your Jedi weapon! Use it. Strike me down with all of your hatred, and your journey towards the dark side will be complete!"
Emperor Palpatine (Ian McDiarmid), to Luke.

Did you know?...
The film was originally titled *Revenge of the Jedi*, but George Lucas decided that revenge was not a motive or emotion appropriate for a Jedi Knight.

Han (Harrison Ford) and Leia (Carrie Fisher) prepare for a fight.

Another interesting aspect of the film is its message concerning the fallibility of technology. In a galaxy full of technological wonders, from human-like robots and androids to faster-than-light spaceships and light sabers, ultimately it is a tribe of intelligent but primitive bear-like creatures (Ewoks) that foils the Emperor's plans and enables the Rebel Alliance to defeat the Empire. Ironically, while the saga is set in a technologically advanced universe that lends the story much of its appeal, the film ultimately suggests that superior technology does not equal superiority.

The character of the Emperor, who bears a striking resemblance to Death, supplies fascinating tension in some of the film's most dramatic scenes. In a role that could have come across as melodramatic or unbelievable, actor Ian McDiarmid provides some of *Return of the Jedi*'s most memorable moments as he gives a delightfully diabolical performance as a man who has been so corrupted by power that he almost seems the very personification of evil.

In 1997, George Lucas released a special edition of the *Star Wars* trilogy, featuring new footage, digitally enhanced special effects, and an improved, remixed soundtrack. As with *The Empire Strikes Back*, there is very little new footage in *Return of the Jedi*, and much of it is not noticeable, but it does feature a new ending, re-scored by John Williams, that is an improvement over the original version.

Cast: Mark Hamill (Luke Skywalker), Harrison Ford (Han Solo), Carrie Fisher (Princess Leia), Billy Dee Williams (Lando Calrissian), David Prowse (Darth Vader), James Earl Jones (voice of Darth Vader), Anthony Daniels (C-3PO), Kenny Baker (R2-D2), Peter Mayhew (Chewbacca), Frank Oz (voice of Yoda), Alec Guiness (Obi-Wan Kenobi), Ian McDiarmid (Emperor Palpatine), Michael Pennington (Moff Jerjerrod), Kenneth Colley (Admiral Piett), Michael Carter (Bib Fortuna) **Screenwriter:** George Lucas, Lawrence Kasdan **Cinematographer:** Alan Hume **Composer:** John Williams, Jerry Hey (Special Edition) **Producer:** Howard Kazanjian for Lucasfilm and Twentieth Century Fox; Rick McCallum (Special Edition) **MPAA Rating:** PG **Running Time:** 134 minutes; 135 minutes (Special Edition) **Format:** VHS, LV **Awards:** Academy Awards 1983: Visual Effects; Nominations: Art Direction/Set Decoration, Sound, Score (John Williams); People's Choice Awards 1984: Film **Budget:** $32.5M **Box Office:** $309.13M (domestic gross).

Star Trek Generations
1994 — David Carson — ♪♪♪

The first big-screen adventure of the crew from television's popular *Star Trek: The Next Generation* serves as both a bridge between the old and the new and at the same time essentially retires the adventures of the original cast, led by William Shatner's Captain James T. Kirk. As an adventure story, *Generations* is more lively, action-oriented, character-oriented, and philosophical than the original cast's first feature outing, *Star Trek: The Motion Picture*. The story is also more complex (and in fact more complex than any of the previous six *Star Trek* films), something that can be seen as a failing in that the plot at times relies on convoluted and fictitious scientific jargon that will sound odd to many audience members unfamiliar with the television series. Spanning two generations (hence the title), the film involves a mysterious space-faring energy ribbon called the Nexus. Inside the Nexus, time and space have no meaning, and one can experience any reality one wishes. In essence, it is a fantasy-world paradise. Dr. Soran (Malcolm McDowell), a scientist who lost his family tragically,

> "What we leave behind is not as important as how we've lived."
> Picard (Patrick Stewart) to Riker (Jonathan Frakes)

Capt. Jean-Luc Picard (Patrick Stewart) accompanies Capt. James T. Kirk (William Shatner) on a horsey excursion.

Did you know?...

The original ending of the film, in which Soran killed Kirk by shooting him in the back, was re-shot after test audiences reacted negatively to the manner of the captain's death.

becomes obsessed with gaining entrance to the Nexus so that he can revive his loved ones and spend eternity with them, and he is willing to destroy millions of innocent lives in order to do so. Captain Picard (Patrick Stewart) sets out to stop him, and ultimately makes a journey into the Nexus himself, where he finds Captain Kirk (William Shatner), long believed dead. Picard enlists the famous captain to help him leave the Nexus and put a stop to Soran's deadly plans.

On a thematic, philosophical level, the film addresses some interesting notions about death, mortality, and the temptation of escaping into fantasy. Kirk and Picard both struggle with their own mortality, and both eventually find personal peace. However, one of the chief weaknesses is that it does not do enough with the historic meeting of the two captains, one an icon of popular culture and the other his very popular successor. Representing the movie within the *Star Trek* universe, a bridge between two generations, it also represents a bridge between two very influential series and staples of popular culture. Unfortunately, Captain Kirk's presence, which is promising in the opening action sequence (set during Kirk's time), seems almost tacked on at the end, and his death, while heroic, is not rendered with as much sadness and honor as one might expect. One of the elements most touted about this film is that it features the death of the famous star captain, yet that death to some extent seems less mournful than the loss of Picard's starship *Enterprise* (one of the most exciting and tragic sequences of the movie). The epic meeting between the two captains and the resolution of their own inner struggles as well as that with Soran simply could have been more developed. As it is, *Star Trek Generations* is a fun, adventurous film that actually might have been better without the ties to the original series.

Generations was followed in 1996 by *Star Trek: First Contact*, featuring only the cast of *The Next Generation*. This second film was better received by both critics and audiences.

Cast: Patrick Stewart (Captain Jean-Luc Picard), Jonathan Frakes (William Riker), Brent Spiner (Data), LeVar Burton (Geordi LaForge), Michael Dorn (Worf), Gates McFadden (Dr. Beverly Crusher), Marina Sirtis (Deanna Troi), Malcolm McDowell (Dr. Tolian Soran), William Shatner (James T. Kirk), James Doohan (Montgomery "Scotty" Scott), Walter Koenig (Pavel Chekov), Alan Ruck (Captain John Harriman), Jacqui Kim (Demora Sulu), Jenette Goldstein (Science Officer), Thomas Kopache (Com Officer) **Screenwriter:** Ronald D. Moore, Brannon Braga **Cinematographer:** John A. Alonzo **Composer:** Dennis McCarthy **Producer:** Rick Berman and Peter Lauritson for Paramount **MPAA Rating:** PG **Running Time:** 123 minutes **Format:** VHS, LV **Budget:** $35M **Box Office:** $75.67M.

Star Trek: The Motion Picture
1979 – Robert Wise – 🦴🦴🦴

Based on the popular original *Star Trek* television series, this first big-screen adventure for the crew of the starship *Enterprise* promises early on to be a huge spectacle of a movie, but unfortunately *Star Trek: The Motion Picture* raises expectations a little too high and then fails to meet them. The story's plot has potential as an epic adventure: A vast, mysterious cloud surrounding a colossal star vessel is heading for Earth, destroying everything in its path, and Admiral James T. Kirk (William Shatner) takes command of the *Enterprise* to intercept the vessel and uncover its secrets. The potential of the story, however, is lost in self-indulgence and a weak, uninspired resolution.

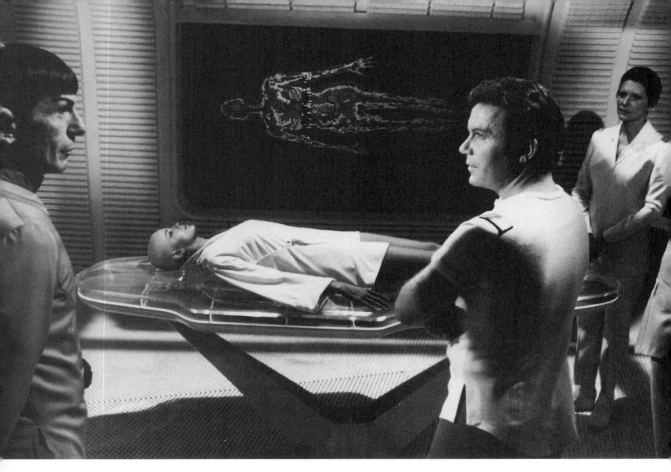

Spock (Leonard Nimoy) and Kirk (William Shatner) check on ship's officer Ilia (Persis Khambatta) in sickbay.

"Each of us, at some time in our lives, turns to someone—a father, a brother, a god—and asks, 'Why am I here? What was I meant to be?'"

Spock (Leonard Nimoy)

Visually, the film includes some intriguing sequences. The vessel inside the cloud (later identified as V'ger) is fascinating for its vastness and elaborate design. However, interesting visual effects like this often become the focus of the film rather than the story. In fact, it often seems that every elaborate special effect becomes a subject of concentration, whether it is the long, silent voyage through the cloud (intercut with shots of the crew staring in amazement) or the introduction of the newly refurbished *Enterprise* (a painstakingly long sequence that seems to want to make sure we get a glimpse of every angle of the ship). The overall effect of this visual self-indulgence, along with the generally somber atmosphere created by the film's pacing and the too-serious performances of the cast, is of a self-important movie trying too hard to be a big, epic picture in order to contrast with its television origins.

One of the interesting aspects of *Star Trek* is that it likes to delve into philosophical, ethical, and occasionally metaphysical questions. *The Motion Picture* promises such an exploration when the V'ger entity reveals that it is searching for its creator. The quest represents a search for a higher level of existence and answers to life's most complex questions. As Mr. Spock (Leonard Nimoy) points out, such a quest is not limited to V'ger. Unfortunately, very few answers are discovered in the story. The conclusion poses an interesting question about man's desire to find and merge with God or some higher intelligence, but the statement is somewhat unsatisfying after all that has come before. *The Motion Picture* was followed by *The Wrath of Khan* (1982), *The Search for Spock* (1984), *The Voyage Home* (1986), *The Final Frontier* (1989), and *The Undiscovered Country* (1991).

Cast: William Shatner (Admiral James T. Kirk), Leonard Nimoy (Mr. Spock), DeForest Kelley (Dr. Leonard "Bones" McCoy), James Doohan (Commander Montgomery "Scotty" Scott), George Takei (Lieutenant Sulu), Majel Barrett (Dr. Chapel), Walter Koenig (Security Officer Chekov), Nichelle Nichols (Lieutenant Uhura), Persis Khambatta (Lieutenant Ilia), Stephen Collins (Captain Willard Decker), Grace Lee Whitney (Janice Rand), Mark Lenard (Klingon Captain), Billy Van Zandt (Alien Boy), Roger Aaron Brown (Epsilon Technician), Gary Faga (Airlock Technician) **Screenwriter:** Harold Livingston **Cinematographer:** Richard H. Kline **Composer:** Jerry Goldsmith **Producer:** Gene Roddenberry for Paramount **MPAA Rating:** G **Running Time:** 132 minutes **Format:** VHS, LV **Awards:** Academy Awards 1979: Nominations: Art Direction/Set Decoration, Score (Jerry Goldsmith); Golden Globe Awards 1980: Nominations: Original Score (Goldsmith) **Budget:** $15M **Box Office:** $82.3M.

Star Wars

Star Wars: A New Hope

1977, 1997 (Special Edition) – George Lucas – 🦴🦴🦴🦴🦴

Writer and co-producer George Lucas directed this amazing space adventure about a farm boy from the planet Tatooine who gets caught up in a great interplanetary war. This was Lucas' second big success after the innovative *American Graffiti.* Using astonishingly realistic special effects that revolutionized the industry, *Star Wars* built on and went way beyond the tradition of science-fiction movies. Fortunately, these marvels are not the only good thing about this film. The story pulls its own weight, and under superb direction from Lucas, story and special effects come together to form an unforgettable adventure. "I researched kid's films," Lucas later remarked, "and how they work and how myths work." Lucas credits mythologist Joseph Campbell with the core inspiration. Borrowing freely from various film genres, Lucas changed the movie business with *Star Wars.*

"I've got a bad feeling about this."
Han Solo (Harrison Ford)

Princess Leia (Carrie Fisher) uses R2-D2 to get a message to the rebel forces.

Did you know?...

Star Wars' interiors were shot at Elstree Studios in England, while exteriors were filmed in Tunisia, Guatemala, and Death Valley.

Rejected by Universal, Lucas took his idea to Fox, which finally gave him the green light. "Nobody thought it was going to be a big hit," Lucas told *Rolling Stone* magazine in 1977. "I kept doing more research and writing scripts. The problem in something like this is you are creating a whole genre that has never been created before." Eventually, *Star Wars* was made for a paltry $8 million, with Lucas receiving approximately $100,000 in up-front salary.

When Luke Skywalker (Mark Hamill) buys a pair of runaway droids, he suddenly becomes involved in a war between the evil Galactic Empire and a resistance known as the Rebel Alliance. The droids are carrying secret plans for a weapon of mass destruction being built by the Empire. They also contain a message for an old hermit named Obi-Wan Kenobi (Alec Guinness), who is one of the last members of a sacred cult called the Jedi. Kenobi will become a leader, teacher, and mentor for young Luke, because Luke is destined to become one of the greatest Jedi knights as he matures. Luke's adventures take him to save Princess Leia (Carrie Fisher), a captive of the Empire and a leader in the Rebel forces. To do this, he teams with renegade smuggler Han Solo (Harrison Ford). With Han's sidekick Chewbacca, a furry and lovable man/beast, they blast into the heart of the Empire, hoping to make it in time and forming a friendship that will keep them together for future adventures.

This film is one of the best-loved classics and box-office smashes because it not only has all the action of a sci-fi thriller, but it also includes themes of love, growing up, and (in a very obvious way) the conflicts between good and evil. The script also supplies a wealth of comedic interludes. It is a fun movie to watch and keeps you on the edge of your seat with its battle scenes and starship races. Hamill, Fisher, and Ford make a great trio filled with energy and chemistry. One rare surprise is the amazing number of creatures and alien scenery that the movie contains. Just watching unimportant action in various spaceports is a treat. Industrial Light and Magic, led by special effects supervisor John Dykstra (who had worked for Douglas Trumbull on *2001: A Space Odyssey*) created the 365 amazing photographic effects, which won an Academy Award. Dykstra built a special optical camera, the Moviola, for the miniature shots. The editing, which was also Oscar-honored, was done by the director's then-wife, Marcia, and Paul Hirsch and Richard Chew. Reportedly it took Marcia Lucas more than eight weeks to cut the battle sequence. The magnificent sound track by John Williams is also enduring and memorable. Overall, *Star Wars* is one of those great moments in entertainment that can be watched again and again by every generation that discovers it.

Cast: Mark Hamill (Luke Skywalker), Harrison Ford (Han Solo), Carrie Fisher (Princess Leia Organa), Peter Cushing (Grand Moff Tarkin), Alec Guinness (Ben Obi-wan Kenobi), Anthony Daniels (C-3PO), Kenny Baker (R2-D2), Peter Mayhew (Chewbacca), David Prowse (Lord Darth Vader), Phil Brown (Uncle Owen Lars), Shelagh Fraser (Aunt Beru Lars), Jack Purvis (Chief Jawa/Praying Mantis (Kitik Keed'kak)/Power Droid EG-6), Alex McCrindle (General Dodonna), Eddie Byrne (Commander Willard), Drewe Henley (Red Leader) **Screenwriter:** George Lucas **Cinematographer** Gilbert Taylor | **Composer:** John Williams **Producer:** Gary Kurtz for Lucasfilm and Twentieth Century Fox **MPAA Rating:** PG **Running Time:** 121 minutes **Format:** VHS, LV **Awards:** Academy Awards, 1978: Art and Set Decoration, Costumes, Effects, Film Editing, Original Score, Sound; Nominations: Director (George Lucas), Picture, Supporting Actor (Alec Guinness), Screenplay; Golden Globe Awards, 1978: Score; Nominations: Director (George Lucas), Picture, Supporting Actor (Alec Guiness); Los Angeles Film Critics Association Awards 1977: 10 Best Films of the Year; National Board of Review Awards 1977: 10 Best Films of the Year; People's Choice Awards 1978: Film **Budget:** $8M. **Box Office:** $461 million (to date).

2001: A Space Odyssey
1968 – Stanley Kubrick – ♪♪♪

> "I honestly think you ought to calm down; take a stress pill and think things over."
>
> HAL (Douglas Rain), to David as he works to disconnect him.

On prehistoric Earth four million years ago, a strange black monolith appears among a group of apes and in some way ushers in the dawn of mankind as the apes reach a higher level of intelligence and learn to use tools to kill for food and to kill each other. In 2001, another mysterious monolith is discovered on the moon, sending a radio signal to Jupiter. The space ship *Discovery* is sent on a mission to Jupiter to unravel the mystery, but ultimately just one crew member survives and reaches Jupiter. He discovers yet another monolith and he finds himself growing old and finally transforming into a space-faring fetus.

Routinely showing up on lists of the greatest films ever made, Stanley Kubrick's widely praised science fiction epic is, more than anything else, a primarily visual work of art that attempts to pose a number of profound questions about the future of humanity. Adapted from Arthur C. Clarke from his story, "The Sentinel," *2001* contains some fascinating imagery and attempts to portray with painstaking realism the experience of traveling and working in space. In his attention to visual and auditory detail (since there is no sound in space, there is literally no sound at all during exterior shots of the ships), and his setting the work to classical music, Kubrick strives to create an important, awe-inspiring, and aesthetically rich masterpiece that challenges its audience to imagine and to consider the unknown and infinite possibilities of existence. The scope is there-

Did you know?...

Special effects supervisor Douglas Trumbull has stated that the total amount of footage shot for the movie would add up to two hundred times the final length of the film.

fore grand, and its subject matter universal and timeless, but unfortunately the film winds up being more of an enigma than a profound statement about humanity and the future, precisely because so many aspects of the story remain unexplained.

Astronauts David Bowman (Keir Dullea) and Frank Poole (Gary Lockwood) aboard the spaceship Orion.

The questions that *2001* raises are never answered: What are the mysterious black monoliths? Why did the HAL 9000 computer apparently malfunction, develop a mean streak, and kill the passengers of the *Discovery*? What exactly is the star-faring fetus, or what does it represent? The puzzling nature of the story is amplified by the lack of character development. Not even Dave (Keir Dullea), the closest thing to a "main" character, who reaches the monolith and transforms into another being, is fully developed. Characters are incidental to the movie, dialogue is kept to a minimum, movement is kept at a slow and deliberate pace, and most of the screen time is devoted to *watching* things. In addition, the visual spectacle often seems to stretch on for longer than necessary—

the landing of a lunar craft seems to take as long as it would in real-time, for example.

As is typical of the director, Kubrick deliberately distances the audience from the story, perhaps in order to maintain the mystery or perhaps to convey the coldness and flatness of his characters or the overwhelming vastness and remoteness of space. The technique of intentionally distancing characters or the story from the audience may work in some of Kubrick's films, but in this film it almost seems at odds with the tone and subject of the themes being addressed. *2001* is a visual treat that attempts to stimulate the mind with its speculations about the progress and evolution of humanity, but the human element seems conspicuously absent.

Cast: Keir Dullea (David Bowman), Gary Lockwood (Frank Poole), William Sylvester (Heywood Floyd), Daniel Richter (Moonwatcher), Leonard Rossiter (Smyslov), Margaret Tysack (Elena), Robert Beatty (Halvorsen), Sean Sullivan (Michaels), Douglas Rain (voice of HAL 9000), Frank Miller (Mission Controller), Ed Bishop (Lunar shuttle captain), Alan Gifford (Poole's Father), Edwina Carroll (Stewardess), Penny Brahms (Stewardess) **Screenwriter:** Stanley Kubrick, Arthur C. Clarke **Cinematographer:** John Alcott, Geoffrey Unsworth **Producer:** Stanley Kubrick for MGM **MPAA Rating:** G **Running Time:** 139 minutes **Format:** VHS, LV **Awards:** Academy Awards 1968: Visual Effects; Nominations: Art Direction/Set Decoration, Director (Stanley Kubrick), Story and Screenplay; National Board of Review Awards 1968: Ten Best Films of the Year **Budget:** $11M **Box Office:** $21M (initial release).

They Might Be Giants . . .

George Pal's production of *The War of the Worlds* (1956), featuring amazing special effects for its day, adapts the classic novel by H. G. Wells, setting it in the mid-twentieth century and turning the epic battle between humans and Martians into an almost religious morality play. The team of Dean Devlin and Roland Emmerich produced the adventurous *Stargate* (1994), a story that offers an explanation for the Egyptian pyramids and that features a villain who is none other than Ra, the ancient sun god. The characters are somewhat comic-book inspired, but the visual effects and the story's premise are intriguing. Devlin and Emmerich also produced the 1996 blockbuster *Independence Day*, an alien invasion film that celebrates the power of a united humanity but also a movie that basically retells every other science fiction movie that came before it. Director Luc Besson's *The Fifth Element* (1997) features a visual smorgasbord of fascinating imagery that includes the ancient past, a quirky, fast-paced future, bizarre aliens, campy villains, and a storyline that is hard to follow but has something to do with an ancient mystery that is the only key to humanity's future survival. The second film to feature the cast of television's *Star Trek: The Next Generation*, Jonathan Frakes' *Star Trek: First Contact* (1996) combines a heroic, epic battle to save mankind's future with an obsessive quest for revenge inspired by *Moby Dick*. In the footsteps of *Star Trek*, the latest science fiction television series to be turned into a film is *Lost in Space* (1998), a visually exciting, darker version of the 60s TV show that tells the story of a family whose mission to establish a colony on another planet is sabotaged and who must struggle to find their way in unknown, dangerous territories of space.

HISTORICAL

Alexander Nevsky

Cleopatra

The Crusades

Empire of the Sun

Exodus

55 Days at Peking

Gandhi

Ivan the Terrible, Part I and II

The Last Emperor

A Man for All Seasons

The Mission

Nashville

Queen Margot

Reds

The Scarlet Empress

Schindler's List

Seven Samurai

Spartacus

Alexander Nevsky

1938 – Sergei Eisenstein, D. Vasilyev – 🎬🎬🎬

Following *October* in 1927, Sergei Eisenstein experienced a frustrating ten-year hiatus during which he completed no films. He was out of favor with Stalin and for a short time he worked at Paramount in Hollywood at the all-too-common trade of writing screenplays that went unproduced. His association with novelist Upton Sinclair, Sinclair's wife, and their Mexican Film Trust almost led to a completed film (*Que Viva Mexico*) on the revolutionary spirit in Mexico until the epic scale Eisenstein sought overwhelmed the small budget Sinclair was willing to support. (Some historians even rank this uncompleted film with the great lost masterpieces *Greed* by von Stroheim and *The Magnificent Ambersons* by Orson Welles. The negative was eventually sold and recut into two films released as *Thunder over Mexico* and *Death Day*.)

Back in Moscow, Eisenstein had his next project, *Bezhin Meadow*, halted during production due to political opposition. It now exists only in fragments, and Eisenstein was forced to grovel a bit with a published apology for the film. Eisenstein was teaching at the State Film Academy in 1938 when he was finally able to complete *Alexander Nevsky*, an epic set in 1242 about Prince Nevsky's and Russia's defeat of the Teutonic invasion.

The subject matter could not have pleased Stalin more: as Russia feared the Nazi threat in 1938, Eisenstein looked to history for a parallel story about a Russian victory over Germany. It was Eisenstein's first sound film, and it uses the music of Sergei Prokofiev to establish a vivid mood. To complete the analogy to contemporary events, the menacing Germans in the film are garbed with flowing capes that feature small crosses on the left shoulder—just an extra stroke or two would complete the swastika. As befits the nature of films made for political propaganda, the popularity and acceptability of this film changed as Russia's views of Germany changed. In 1938, the year of the film's release, *Nevsky* was safe and popular as a warning against German militarism; when the Russo-German nonaggression pact was signed in 1939, it was pulled from release only to be put back in exhibition in 1941 when Germany invaded Russia.

On the whole, *Alexander Nevsky* is more static than Eisenstein's masterpieces of the silent era. Many scenes are strikingly composed, but the move-

ment of the performers, of the camera, and with the cutting seems less invigorating than in his earlier work. At intervals an arresting touch will give the film some life—as when a German warlord stands before a precipice beyond which rages a bonfire and drops infant after infant into the abyss. The grand set piece is the climactic battle on ice at Lake Ilmen, which is truly spectacular. (It was filmed during the summer outside Moscow using artificial snow and ice.)

Nikolai Cherkasov, in the title role, prepares his Russian knights for battle.

Cast: Nikolai Cherkasov (Prince Nevsky), N. Okhlopkov (Vasily Buslai), A. Abrikosov (Gavrilo Olevsich), D. Orlov (Tgnat), V. Novikov (Pavsha), N. Arsky (Domash), V. Ivashova (Olga), A. Danilova (Vasilisa), V. Yershov (Teutonic knight), S. Blinnikov (Tverdilo), I. Lagutin (Anavii), L. Fenin (bishop) **Screenwriter:** P. Pavlenko, Sergei Eisenstein **Cinematographer:** Eduard Tisse **Composer:** Sergei Prokofiev **Producer:** Sergei Eisenstein for Mosfilm **Running Time:** 112 minutes **Format:** VHS **Awards:** National Board of Review Awards, 1939: Five Best Foreign Films of the Year.

Cleopatra

1934 – Cecil B. De Mille – 🦴🦴

Charlton Heston tells a great story in his autobiography about working with Cecil B. De Mille on *The Greatest Show on Earth*. One day De Mille was instructing the assembled cast when he noticed one of the extras in the back whispering to her friend. De Mille imperiously called her down, wondered what she could possibly have to say that was more important than his comments, and made her come before the entire company to repeat her words. The woman silently walked to the front and said clearly, "I was just wondering when that bald sonofabitch was going to call lunch." To his credit, De Mille knew he had been had, suppressed a smile, and let everybody eat.

If only De Mille's epics had more touches of this same self-deprecation and less of the urge to make a Great Movie. The wit in this film, for example, often seems unintentional. Warren William plays Julius Caesar with a barking officiousness reminiscent of De Mille himself. When he comes striding into a gathering of Roman officials, you expect a chair boy with a megaphone to follow. (It may be the most revealing thing about this production that when De Mille visualizes the ruler of the ancient world he depicts him with the demeanor of an old-school movie director.)

But the film has genuine wit as well. When Cleopatra meets Caesar, she comes unfurling out of a Persian rug offered to Caesar as a present. (The writers misfired badly, however, by not making this great touch Colbert's entrance in the film; her few earlier scenes are disappointing.) Cleopatra's seduction of Antony (Henry Wilcoxon) is another highlight. She offers him "clams from the sea—they're catching them now; come and see." Antony looks to see Egyptian slaves working a pulley attached to an enormous net. They swing the net over to Antony, and it opens to reveal five or six maidens clad only in clinging seaweed who squirm decadently at his feet and open clams filled with jewels. De Mille's sly gift for creating scenes of prurience and slipping them past the censor by putting them in biblical or historical contexts was never better displayed than here with its gaping cleavage and near nudity—quite surprising for 1934. Audiences who thronged to De Mille movies could tell themselves it was the respectable subject matter that drew them and then sit back and enjoy the contortions of the handmaidens.

The plot is structured around Cleopatra's two love affairs. The first with Caesar ends with his assassination, after which she learns that he had a greater interest in Egypt's wealth than in its queen. The second with Marc Antony is genuine, but the pressures of world politics eventually make them suspicious of each other. In one scene, a worried Antony sees Egyptian guards carrying away a dead man with the simple explanation, "The Queen is testing poisons." The wooden performances of William and Wilcoxon hurt the film, and Wilcoxon's suicide-death scene is especially bad, with a lot of B-movie ranting. Even worse, he doesn't wound himself deep enough.

Sultry Cleopatra (Claudette Colbert) works her feminine wiles on Marc Antony (Henry Wilcoxon).

Cast: Claudette Colbert (Cleopatra), Warren William (Julius Caesar), Henry Wilcoxon (Marc Antony), Joseph Schildkraut (King Herod), Ian Keith (Octavian), Gertrude Michael (Calpurnia), C. Aubrey Smith (Enobarbus), Irving Pichel (Apollodorus), Arthur Hohl (Brutus), Edwin Maxwell (Casca), Ian MacLaren (Cassius), Eleanor Phelps (Charmion), Leonard Mudie (Pothinos), Grace Durkin (Iras), Ferdinand Gottschalk (Glabrio) **Screenwriter:** Bartlett Cormack, Vincent Lawrence , Waldemar Young **Cinematographer:** Victor Milner **Composer:** Rudolph G.

Kopp **Producer:** Cecil B. De Mille for Paramount **Running Time:** 102 minutes **Format:** VHS, LV
Awards: Academy Awards, 1934: Cinematography; Nominations: Editing, Picture, Sound.

The Crusades
1935 — Cecil B. De Mille — 🦴🦴

> **"There is room in Asia to bury all of you."**
> Saladin (Ian Keith), the Islam ruler, to the assembled kings of Europe.

Usually when a De Mille movie is bad, something still provides compensation—the exaggeration, the spectacle, even the bad taste can amuse. *The Crusades* may be one of the most hollow movies from a director who is all too often known for spectacle at the expense of character, pageantry without drama.

The film centers on King Richard the Lionheart (Henry Wilcoxon), and his crusade to liberate the holy land from Islam invaders. Along the way he marries Berengaria (Loretta Young), the princess of Navarre, or more properly, his sword marries her. Richard is so absorbed with patching an injury to his horse that he sends his minstrel (Alan Hale) to the ceremony with his sword as a token of something approximating good faith. The insulted princess sends back her scarf to Richard, saying that it will be all he will ever see of her, and he uses it for the horse bandage he has been needing. The next day, as Richard and his knights depart, he sees his wife for the first time, and her beauty inspires him to take her on the crusade. Another example of signature De Mille wit comes in a short scene where Richard and Berengaria argue in her bedroom. She climbs on top of the bed and brandishes a sword at him as two of Richard's men rush in to report on some trouble with the infidels. These messengers are caught short by the sight in the room, wondering no doubt about what sort of antics they have interrupted.

> **Did you know?...**
> When he was scouting for an unknown to play Marc Antony in *Cleopatra*, De Mille first saw Henry Wilcoxon in the daily rushes being shown in the Paramount screening room. They became friends and Wilcoxon later appeared in many of the director's films.

Like many of De Mille's films, the characters usually have one overpowering personality trait. Richard is intent on his mission. Berengaria's religious passion (she names her bedposts Matthew, Mark, Luke, and John) comes to include a love for her husband. As he showed in *Cleopatra* and elaborated throughout his career, Wilcoxon doesn't have the personality to carry a whole production, but in the earlier film he had stronger support from his co-stars and a marginally better script. Here he is unable to create any interest for his character. A spotty affair, *Cleopatra* was made again in 1963 with even a deeper level of under-achievement.

As *Halliwell's Film Guide* noted about DeMille's empty extravaganza, "More of the vices than the virtues of its producer are notable in this fustian epic, which is almost but not quite watchable." One of the battle scenes, however, the siege of Acre, does enliven the film for a moment.

Richard the Lionheart (Henry Wilcoxon) must leave wife Berengaria (Loretta Young) for more kingly duties.

Cast: Loretta Young (Princess Berengaria), Henry Wilcoxon (King Richard), Ian Keith (Saladin), C. Aubrey Smith (The Hermit), Katherine De Mille (Princess Alice), Joseph Schildkraut (Conrad, Marquis of Montferrat), Alan Hale (Blondel the minstrel), C. Henry Gordon (King Philip of France), George Barbier (King Sancho of Navarre), Montagu Love (The Blacksmith), Ramsay Hill (Prince John of England), Lumsden Hare (Robert, Earl of Leicester), Maurice Murphy (Alan, Richard's squire), William Farnum (Hugo, Duke of Burgundy), Hobart Bosworth (Frederick of Germany) **Screenwriter:** Harold Lamb, Dudley Nichols, Waldemar Young **Cinematographer:** Victor Miller **Composer:** Rudolph G. Kopp **Producer:** Cecil B. De Mille for Paramount **Running Time:** 127 minutes **Format:** VHS **Awards:** Academy Awards, 1935: Nominations: Cinematography.

Empire of the Sun

1987 – Steven Spielberg – ♫♫♫

Steven Spielberg's tale about a British boy who gets separated from his parents in Shanghai during World War II and winds up in a Japanese prison camp is an exquisitely made film.

Based on the autobiographical novel by J.G. Ballard, it contains a number of powerful dramatic scenes, interesting performances by its cast, and the kind of visual artistry for which Spielberg is known. However, the lengthy story loses its focus and ultimately is not as satisfying dramatically as it is effective visually.

Jim (Christian Bale) is a young boy fascinated by flight. In fact, his interest in airplanes and flying is so strong that he seems unaware of the war erupting around him in Shanghai. As the Japanese invade Shanghai he becomes separated from his parents, one of the film's most moving scenes. Eventually Jim returns to his home to find it taken over by the Japanese, his confusion and painful loss depicted with stirring intensity. However, the film tends to stall when Jim is sent to the prison camp.

Although Jim meets some fascinating characters there, led by the conniving Basie (John Malkovich), and he develops some interesting relationships, the story weakens at the camp. The overall tone the camp scenes strive for is the struggle of survival and the intensity of the suffering that occurs there, but Jim's struggle does not seem as much of a difficulty as the filmmakers want us to believe. His continued fascination with flight and his yearning to escape and find his family are psychologically believable elements of his character, but they do not really drive the story forward. Neither do the difficulties that the boy faces, for he overcomes them without much effort, and his dreaming seems to allay much of the pain of the struggle. Essentially, this largest section of the film drags on with little direction and clarity.

The first major Hollywood opus to be filmed in the People's Republic of China, *Empire of the Sun* is a showcase for the usual spellbinding Spielberg images. The narrative, however, is not quite on par.

Did you know?...

The song heard throughout the movie's score is a lullaby called "Suo Gan." It is sung in Welsh.

Cast: Christian Bale (Jim), John Malkovich (Basie), Miranda Richardson (Mrs. Victor), Nigel Havers (Dr. Rawlins), Joe Pantoliano (Frank Demarest), Leslie Phillips (Maxton), Masato

Ibu (Sgt. Nagata), Emily Richard (Jim's Mother), Rupert Frazer (Jim's Father), Peter Gale (Mr. Victor), Takatoro Kataoka (Kamikaze Boy Pilot), Ben Stiller (Dainty), David Neidorf (Tiptree), Ralph Seymour (Cohen), Robert Stephens (Mr. Lockwood) **Screenwriter:** Tom Stoppard **Cinematographer:** Allen Daviau **Composer:** John Williams **Producer:** Kathleen Kennedy, Frank Marshall, and Steven Spielberg for Amblin; released by Warner Bros. **MPAA Rating:** PG **Running Time:** 154 minutes **Format:** VHS, LV **Awards:** Academy Awards, 1987: Nominations: Art Direction/ Set Decoration, Cinematography (Allen Daviau), Costume Design, Film Editing, Original Score (John Williams), Sound; Golden Globe Awards, 1988: Nominations: Motion Picture—Drama, Original Score (John Williams) **Box Office:** $22.2M (domestic gross).

Young POW Jim Graham (Christian Bale) watches the attack of American P-51's on Soochow Creek Airbase.

Exodus

1960 – Otto Preminger – 🦴🦴

When a terrorist bomb blast damages the King David Hotel about two-thirds through the very lengthy *Exodus*, it wakes up the movie and leads to a somewhat less ponderous final hour. But then almost anything would be better than the heavy-handedness of the pre-intermission hours of Otto Preminger's epic based on Leon Uris' best-selling novel. It's not hard to guess the studio's thinking. A built-in audience probably exists for films that deal with issues torn from headlines on the theory, probably erroneous, that the seriousness of the subject matter—here the creation of the national state of Israel—will also extend to the presentation of that idea on film. Another segment of the audience probably comes when a film is based on a popular novel. Over time, however, as these two audience-appeals diminish, a film will stand or fall on its own merits.

Exodus lacks any sense of drama and pace. The first part of the film depicts the efforts of resistance leader Ari Ben Canaan (Paul Newman) to gain publicity and thereby influence a forthcoming U.N. vote on statehood by collecting a boat-load of Jewish refugees in Cyprus and taking them to Palestine. Once he has bluffed and forged his way into getting them loaded, the British discover his plan and set up a blockade. Ben Canaan and the refugees retaliate by declaring a hunger strike, and for a while the film cuts back and forth from the headquarters of British General Sutherland (Ralph Richardson) to the boat trying to make the inactivity of not eating appear dramatic. Ninety hours without food seemingly leave the passengers no worse in appearance or temperament.

In another plot, an American nurse, Kitty Fremont (Eva Marie Saint), wants to care for and possibly adopt fourteen-year-old Karen (Jill Haworth), one of the exiles. Peter Lawford appears as Major Caldwell, one of Sutherland's subordinates, and his blatant anti-Semitism becomes one of the film's favorite targets in its first hour, skewering his prejudice with the same obviousness with which he reveals it. As Caldwell tells Ben Canaan, for example, who masquerades as a British officer, that he can "tell a Jew by his look," Ben Canaan pretends to have something in his eye and asks Caldwell to inspect it for him, which he does, pouring out more invective.

Jewish freedom fighter Ari Ben Canaan (Paul Newman) impersonates a British officer and fools Maj. Caldwell (Peter Lawford).

The leaden approach Preminger shows here is similar in tone to that of another epic project of his from the 1960s, *The Cardinal*. Preminger and Uris at first attempted to collaborate on adapting the novel to the screen, but had a falling out, and Uris trashed the movie upon its release. Ernest Gold's Oscar-winning score is likely the best thing in the movie.

Cast: Paul Newman (Ari Ben Canaan), Eva Marie Saint (Kitty Fremont), Ralph Richardson (General Sutherland), Peter Lawford (Major Caldwell), Lee J. Cobb (Barak Ben Canaan), Sal Mineo (Dov Landau), John Derek (Taha), Hugh Griffith (Mandria), Gregory Ratoff (Lakavitch), Felix Aylmer (Dr. Lieberman), David Opatoshu (Akiva Ben Canaan), Jill Haworth (Karen), Marius Goring (Von Storch), Alexandra Stewart (Jordana), Michael Wager (David) **Screenwriter:** Dalton Trumbo **Cinematographer:** Sam Leavitt **Composer:** Ernest Gold **Producer:** Otto Preminger **MPAA Rating:** PG **Running Time:** 212 minutes **Format:** VHS, LV **Awards:** Academy Awards, 1960: Score; Nominations: Color Cinematography, Supporting Actor (Sal Mineo); Golden Globe Awards, 1961: Supporting Actor (Sal Mineo) **Budget:** $4M **Box Office:** $8.3M (rentals).

55 Days at Peking
1963 – Nicholas Ray – 🦴🦴

> "I admire Sir Arthur. He always gives me the feeling that God is an Englishman."
>
> Major Lewis (Charlton Heston)

Did you know?...
After suffering a heart attack, Director Nicholas Ray's replacements for the remainder of the film were Guy Green and Andrew Marton.

Some films, like *Casablanca*, illustrate the happy accident of filming just a day or two ahead of the writing of the script and somehow having the hectic process produce a masterpiece. Others, like *55 Days at Peking*, show how risky and self-defeating such last-minute writing and plotting can be.

The film focuses on a British ambassador (David Niven), an American army commander (Charlton Heston), and a Russian duchess (Ava Gardner) in Peking at the time of the Boxer Rebellion in 1900. In his recent autobiography, *In the Arena*, Heston explains that the movie was sold on its concept of foreigners trapped at the flashpoints of political crisis and violence, and the overconfident assumption was that the screenwriters would always be able to come up with a way to connect the presence of the various westerners in Peking to a compelling story. The problems with the film weren't lessened when director Nicolas Ray suffered a heart attack during production. He lived until 1979 but never directed another feature. In his book, Heston suggests that the temperamental behavior of Ava Gardner, who walked off the set for hours in anger after an extra snapped a picture of her, created costly delays and may have played a

part in Ray's collapse: "Ava was shaken by Nick's collapse; I think she even accepted some responsibility for it. Actually, I'm not persuaded she should have. Directing a picture is the toughest job in film; Harry Truman's advice applies here: If you can't stand the heat, get out of the kitchen. I felt sorry for Nick, but I'm afraid Bill Blowitz [Heston's publicist] had been right. Nick was a loser." Typically gracious, Heston modestly went on to *The Ten Commandments*.

The interactions of the characters never jell into a credible drama, and the film becomes yet another epic with impressive large-scale scenes but a neglected personal element. An early scene at a ball where some of the Boxers have been invited by the Chinese government produces the best moments of drama apart from the action scenes. On the other hand, a love affair between Heston's and Gardner's characters never catches fire. The material about the Boxers themselves and the tacit encouragement they get from the dowager empress (Flora Robson) is presented effectively, but this political drama of the govern-

Marine Major Matt Lewis (Charlton Heston) eyeballs a German Baron (Kurt Kasznar) while his lover Natalie (Ava Gardner), the Baron's wife, looks on.

ment's attempt to expel foreigners from Peking really supplies only the fringe of the movie.

Cast: Charlton Heston (Major Matt Lewis), David Niven (Sir Arthur Robertson), Ava Gardner (Baroness Natalie Ivanoff), Flora Robson (Dowager Empress Tzu-Hsi), Robert Helpmann (Prince Tuan), Leo Genn (General Jung-Lu), Paul Lukas (Dr. Steinfeldt), John Ireland (Sergeant Harry), Harry Andrews (Father de Bearn), Elizabeth Sellars (Lady Sarah Robertson), Massimo Serato (Garibaldi), Geoffrey Bayldon (Smythe), Carlos Casaravilla (Japanese Minister), Michael Chow (Chiang), Felix Dafauce (Dutch Minister) **Screenwriter:** Bernard Gordon, Phillip Yordan **Cinematographer:** Jack Hildyard **Composer:** Dimitri Tiomkin, Paul Francis Webster **Producer:** Samuel Bronston **Running Time:** 150 minutes **Format:** VHS, LV **Awards:** Academy Awards 1963: Nominations: Song ("So Little Time"), Score.

Gandhi
1982 – Richard Attenborough – 𝄢𝄢𝄢𝄢

"An eye for an eye only ends up making the whole world blind."

Gandhi (Ben Kingsley)

In some ways, it is surprising that Western audiences, especially American ones, embraced this biography of Gandhi as enthusiastically as they did. After all, this enigmatic, complex man stood firmly opposed to many twentieth-century Western beliefs. Mohandas Gandhi believed in returning to a simple, non-industrial village life instead of relying on the promise of technology. His idea of "satyagraha," the refusal to obey unjust laws with the willingness to accept the penalty for that refusal, runs counter to the American ideal of fighting for your standards and aggressive opposition to tyranny (though it did influence Martin Luther King Jr. and the Civil Rights movement). And yet, the power of one man's will and his sacrifices for the cause of right have never been more engaging and admirably displayed than in this film about "the small man in the loincloth" who brought down the British Raj and freed India.

Scope is one of the film's great strengths—we ride with the camera across the vastness of the Indian subcontinent with glimpses of its three hundred million people. Poverty and beauty, familiarity and strangeness meet in almost every frame. And director Richard Attenborough's choice of Ben Kingsley to play Gandhi was inspired. Famous as a stage actor but unknown to movie audiences, Kingsley looks with luminous searching brown eyes into the souls of those on-screen and off. He also ages more convincingly than the other actors—it is easy to feel the frailty and pain of his continual imprisonment and

Did you know?...

"Mahatma" is not a name; it means "great soul." Gandhi's first name was Mohandas.

Journalist Walker (Martin Sheen) interviews Mahatma Gandhi (Ben Kingsley).

hunger strikes simply through his posture and gait. The story, as Attenborough claims in the introduction, is meant to be true to the "spirit" rather than all the facts of the Mahatma's life, and many incidents are omitted or exaggerated to carry the principal message of the movie.

Still, watching the British Empire finally crack beneath the vision of a single man curiously echoes our own history. Gandhi was called "bapu," the father of his country, spiritually and politically. His courage and complexity remain even after his assassination and deification. Maybe that is one source of the power of *Gandhi*: it is in some ways a reflection of our own great American stand for freedom re-enacted half a world away.

Cast: Ben Kingsley (Mahatma Gandhi), Candice Bergen (Margaret Bourke-White), Edward Fox (General Dyer), John Gielgud (Lord Irwin), Trevor Howard (Judge Broomsfield), John Mills (Lord Clemsford), Saeed Jaffrey (Sardar Patel), Martin Sheen (Walker), Ian Charleson (Charlie Andrews), Alyque Padamsee (Jinnah), Roshan Seth (Nehru), Geraldine James (Mirabehn), Rohini Hattangadi (Kasturbai Gandhi), Amrish Puri (Kahn), Peter Harlowe (Lord

Mountbatten) **Screenwriter:** John Briley **Cinematographer:** Ronnie Taylor, Billy Williams **Composer:** George Fenton, Ravi Shankar **Producer:** Richard Attenborough, Rani Dube, and Suresh Jindal for Goldcrest/Indo-British/International Film Investors. National Film Development Corporation of India; released by Columbia Pictures **Running Time:** 188 minutes **Format:** VHS, LV **Awards:** Academy Awards, 1982: Actor (Ben Kingsley), Art Direction/Set Decoration, Cinematography, Costume Design, Director (Richard Attenborough), Film Editing, Picture, Screenplay, Sound; Nominations: Makeup, Score; British Academy Awards, 1982: Actor (Ben Kingsley), Director (Richard Attenborough), Film, Supporting Actress (Rohini Hattangadi); Golden Globe Awards, 1983: Actor (Ben Kingsley), Director (Richard Attenborough), Foreign Film, Screenplay, New Star (Ben Kingsley); Directors Guild of America Awards, 1982: Outstanding Achievement to Richard Attenborough; Los Angeles Film Critics Association Awards, 1982: Actor (Ben Kingsley); New York Film Critics Awards, 1982: Actor (Ben Kingsley), Film **Box Office:** $24.9M (rentals).

Ivan the Terrible, Part I and II

1944, 1946 – Sergei Eisenstein – 🎬🎬🎬

> "As many coins as are unclaimed after the battle, count that many men fallen."
>
> Ivan (Nikolai Cherkasov), watching his men drop a coin in a bowl as they march off to fight.

Did you know?...

Director Sergei Eisenstein spent two full years studying the subject before beginning the film.

A film pageant, the two parts of *Ivan the Terrible* are stunning in their visual beauty, static in their development. To accept the film on its own terms, one must modify some traditional expectations since director Sergei Eisenstein subordinates seemingly everything to the pictorial design. The actors—star Nikolai Cherkasov complained about some of the strange postures into which he had to contort himself—are at times little more than moving props adorning the sets, some of them cavernous, some of them cramped. The script itself was a series of sketches drawn by Eisenstein and apparently influenced by the paintings of El Greco, about whose work Eisenstein had been writing. The director's great visual sense responded to the shape of even little things like the ruffled collars of the courtiers, the curved pikes of the soldiers, the distorted shadows cast by sleeves that drag the ground. The expressiveness of faces and especially eyes also seized Eisenstein's attention. When, for example, Ivan's aunt (Serafima Birman) plots the death of Anastasia (Ludmilla Tselikovskaya), she wears a black habit and cowl that frames a face in which her two eyes burn maliciously (reportedly, the actor was again regarded as a prop-like adornment since Eisenstein had the natural shape of Birman's eyelids changed with makeup to produce the desired glare). Eisenstein was pushing cinema toward a grand opulence, a kind of visual opera.

The story concerns the sixteenth-century czar who united all the Russias and whose coronation on January 16, 1547, begins the film. Ivan's attempt to

Ivan (Nikolai Cherkasov) broods.

unify his country is opposed by the Boyars, a group of aristocrats represented primarily by his aunt and the archbishop of Novgorod (Alexander Mgebrov). Outside the kingdom, Ivan faces threats from King Sigismond of Poland. In *Part I*, Ivan begins to doubt the rightness of his mission after the murder of his beloved Anastasia. After retreating to the provinces, he sees a seemingly unending line of his subjects stretching across the landscape to petition his return to Moscow. In *Part II*, the plotters turn to Ivan himself, and he must use his wits to keep Vladimir (Pavel Kadochnikov) off the throne. The second part landed Eisenstein in trouble with Stalin and the Communist Party for the perceived unflattering and ambiguous picture of Ivan and some of his inner circle. Though the second part of the film was banned upon its completion, Eisenstein gained permission to plan a final part (to be called *The Battles of Ivan*) of what was meant to be a trilogy, but he died of a heart attack at age 50 before the project could be completed.

Cast: Nikolai Cherkasov (Czar Ivan IV), Serafima Birman (the czar's aunt), Ludmila Tselikovskaya (Anastasia), Pavel Kadochnikov (Vladimir Staritsky), Mikhail Nazvanov (Prince Andrei), Mikhail Zharov (Malyuta Skuratov), Andrei Abrikosov (Boyar Fyodor Kolichev), Alexander Mgebrov (Pimen, archbishop of Novgorod), Maxim Mikhailov (the archdeacon), Vsevolod Pudovkin (Nikola), Amvrosi Buchma (Alexei Basmanov), Ada Voitski (Yelena Glinskaya), Erik Ryriev (Ivan as a child) **Screenwriter:** Sergei Eisenstein **Cinematographer:** Andrei Moskvin, Eduard Tisse **Composer:** Sergei Prokofiev **Producer:** Sergei Eisenstein for Mosfilm Studio **Running Time:** 99 minutes (Part I); 85 minutes (Part II) **Format:** VHS.

The Last Emperor

1987 – Bernardo Bertolucci – 🎬🎬🎬

> "You did not believe I could be emperor again, but I am."
>
> Pu Yi (John Lone), to Wan Jung (Joan Chen).

> "You are blind."
>
> Wan Jung

Did you know?...

Bertolucci received special permission to actually film inside the Forbidden City.

Bernardo Bertolucci's generally acclaimed biography of Pu Yi, who went from being an Emperor to an ordinary citizen of China, boasts some spectacular cinematography, costume design, and location filming inside the Forbidden City. Throughout the story, from the moment the boy Pu Yi (John Lone) assumes the throne, to his imprisonment and re-education by the Communist government, momentous and revolutionary events take place, but Pu Yi plays no active role in any of it.

As Emperor and as a man, Pu Yi seems to have no effect on anyone or anything around him. He does not make things happen—things happen to him. As a youth he is spoiled and treated with the reverence of a god, at least inside the Forbidden City, but at the same time he has no real power and is prevented from learning anything really useful. He is a puppet for other people, and even when he attempts to regain some of the Emperor's power and spearhead some type of reform, he finds that he is still a pawn, and his hopes are largely ignored. Ultimately, his life becomes useful as an ordinary citizen in the Communist republic, learning to be a simple gardener.

Unfortunately, although *The Last Emperor* is a visually impressive film, this record of Pu Yi's life at times seems to lack dramatic depth. This may be due in part to the passive nature of his character, but it is difficult to see into the man and understand his needs and motivations, an obscurity of character that also tends to make the major themes of the story murky.

Occasionally, some of the acting is stilted, particularly in scenes portraying the emperor's early life. Narration is awkwardly inserted quite some time after the story begins—in one way an understandable attempt to explain events but perhaps also a signal of the difficulty the filmmakers had in streamlining the span of years the film covers into a coherent pattern. Essentially, *The Last Emperor* offers wonderful visual compositions but lacks the coherence and dramatic involvement that would have made it both a great film and a great story. Thousands of extras are used in the grandest manner, giving the film a lyrical strength that often transcends its faults.

Chinese emperor Pu Yi (John Lone) does his royal duty, meeting and greeting.

Cast: John Lone (Pu Yi), Joan Chen (Wan Jung), Peter O'Toole (Reginald Johnston), Ruocheng Ying (The Governor), Victor Wong (Chen Pao Shen), Dennis Dun (Big Li), Ryuichi Sakamoto (Amakasu), Maggie Han (Eastern Jewel), Ric Young (Interrogator), Vivian Wu (Wen Hsiu), Cary-Hiroyuki Tagawa (Chang), Jade Go (Ar Mo), Fumihiko Ikeda (Yoshioka), Richard Vuu (Pu Yi–3 years), Tao Wu (Pu Yi–15 years) **Screenwriter:** Bernardo Bertolucci, Mark Peploe, Enzo Ungari **Cinematographer:** Vittorio Storaro **Composer:** David Byrne, Ryuichi Sakamoto,

Cong Su **Producer:** Jeremy Thomas for Yanko Films, Tao Films, Recorded Picture Company, Screenframe, AAA Soprofilm; released by Columbia Pictures **MPAA Rating:** PG-13 **Running Time:** 160 minutes **Format:** VHS, LV **Awards:** Academy Awards, 1987: Art Direction/Set Decoration, Cinematography (Vittorio Storaro), Costume Design, Director (Bernardo Bertolucci), Film Editing, Original Score (David Byrne, Ryuichi Sakamoto, Cong Su), Picture, Sound, Adapted Screenplay (Bernardo Bertolucci, Mark Peploe, Enzo Ungari); Directors Guild of America, 1988: Outstanding Directorial Achievement (Bernardo Bertolucci); Golden Globes, 1988: Director (Bernardo Bertolucci), Score (David Byrne, Ryuichi Sakamoto, Cong Su), Screenplay (Bernardo Bertolucci, Mark Peploe, Enzo Ungari); Nominations: Actor (John Lone); Los Angeles Film Critics Association Awards, 1987: Cinematography (Vittorio Storaro), Music (David Byrne, Ryuichi Sakamoto, Cong Su) **Box Office:** $43.98M (domestic gross).

A Man For All Seasons

1966 – Fred Zinnemann – 𓂀𓂀𓂀𓂀

> "Oh, Richard. It profits a man nothing to give his soul for the whole world. But for *Wales?*"
>
> Sir Thomas More (Paul Scofield), examining Richard Rich's chain of office for attorney general of Wales after Rich has given false testimony to convict More.

Did you know?...

Vanessa Redgrave appears uncredited in the non-speaking part of Anne Boleyn.

Robert Bolt's celebrated play about Sir Thomas More and his clash with Henry VIII finds the right director in Fred Zinnemann, who specialized in films of conscience. More (Paul Scofield) sees the king's (Robert Shaw) desire to divorce Catherine of Aragon and marry Anne Boleyn in moral terms. The film sanitizes the Renaissance and its hero (as More biographer Richard Marius points out in *Past Imperfect: History According to the Movies*); other than a brief outburst to his future son-in-law (Corin Redgrave), nothing suggests that this More, like the real one, would have persecuted his version of heretics as rigorously as Henry did his. But Bolt and Zinnemann are more concerned with making a film about a hero—a saint—than with accuracy of personality. And they succeed. The film finds a real grandeur in the presentation of its hero.

Scofield had played the part on stage in both London and New York, and his understated acting, precise schoolmasterly diction, and soft voice nicely offset the growing drama of the political conflict. Scofield seems remote in the part (until the final fury at the close of the trial), but the view of More that Bolt presents in his screenplay is so heroic that this approach seems best. The audience sees More as his family does, a larger-than-life, truly uncommon man set apart by his spirituality. His humanness comes from his understandable willingness to avoid the confrontation with Henry by using the evasion of silence and in his knowledge of the way the world sets traps to ensnare the good man. More's great gift is his ability to see the eternal in the everyday; he wants to nurse his

soul through the obstacle course of life without having the crafty world of the royal court fleece him of it.

A wonderful scene toward the end features Meg (Susannah York) coming to her father in the tower and attempting to use her education and training to reason him into accepting the Act of Succession. In reply More relies on his own forensic skills to out-argue her, but York and Scofield brilliantly communicate their mutual love. The daughter of Thomas More knows to use the language of logic if she is to have any success; the father takes pride in his daughter's ability to make such points persuasively in an age when educated women were rare. It is one of the great insights of Robert Bolt's script that this is the way such a father and daughter would show their love for one another—through a debate, even in a dungeon.

Cast: Paul Scofield (Sir Thomas More), Wendy Hiller (Alice More), Leo McKern (Thomas Cromwell), Robert Shaw (King Henry VIII), Orson Welles (Cardinal Wolsey), Susannah York (Margaret More), Nigel Davenport (The Duke of Norfolk), John Hurt (Richard Rich),

Accused of treason, Sir Thomas More (Paul Scofield), states his case before King Henry VIII (Robert Shaw).

Corin Redgrave (William Roper), Colin Blakely (Matthew), Cyril Luckham (Archbishop Cranmer), Jack Gwyllim (Chied Justice), Thomas Heathcote (Boatman), Yootha Joyce (Averil Machin), Anthony Nicholls (King's Representative) **Screenwriter:** Robert Bolt **Cinematographer:** Ted Moore **Composer:** Georges Delerue **Producer:** Fred Zinnemann for Columbia Pictures **MPAA Rating:** G **Running Time:** 120 minutes **Format:** VHS, LV **Awards:** Academy Awards, 1966: Actor (Paul Scofield), Adapted Screenplay, Color Cinematography, Costume Design (Color), Director (Fred Zinnemann); Nominations: Supporting Actor (Robert Shaw), Supporting Actress (Wendy Hiller); British Academy Awards, 1967: Actor (Paul Scofield), Film, Screenplay; Golden Globe Awards, 1967: Actor—Drama (Paul Scofield), Director (Fred Zinnemann), Film—Drama, Screenplay; National Board of Review Awards 1966: 10 Best Films of the Year, Actor (Paul Scofield), Director (Fred Zinnemann), Supporting Actor (Robert Shaw); New York Film Critics Awards, 1966: Actor (Paul Scofield), Director (Fred Zinnemann), Film, Screenplay **Box Office:** $12.8M (rentals).

The Mission
1986 – Roland Joffe – 🦴🦴🦴

> "No. If you're right, you'll have God's blessing. If you're wrong, my blessing won't mean anything. If might is right, then love has no place in the world. It may be so, it may be so. But I don't have the strength to live in a world like that, Roderigo. I can't bless you."
>
> Father Gabriel (Jeremy Irons), to Mendoza (Robert De Niro), denying him a blessing.

Robert Bolt's distinguished career as a writer took in some of the screen's most impressive epics: *Lawrence of Arabia*, *Doctor Zhivago*, *A Man for All Seasons*, and *Ryan's Daughter*. Bolt's script for *The Mission* falls below the level set by his better screen work. The film, set in eighteenth-century South America, concerns the church and the slave trade and their mutual interests in the South American Indians for the souls and dollars they represent. A Jesuit, Father Gabriel (Jeremy Irons), starts a mission and eventually converts Mendoza (Robert De Niro), a slave trader who has killed his brother (Aidan Quinn) in a fit of rage. After an arduous penance, Mendoza decides to become a Jesuit and work at the mission himself. Politics complicates the conflict when the church is shown to side with expediency and to cede the mission to slave-owning Portugal rather than free Spain. Mendoza and Gabriel differ on the response to the church's order to close the mission: Mendoza sides with the faction of Indians who decides to fight over their lost mission home, Gabriel chooses the path of prayer and passive resistance. Both prove a poor defense against the guns and cannon of the troops.

The montages prove to be among the most memorable aspects of the film. Backed by Ennio Morricone's stirring music, these sequences visualize Mendoza's path to the priesthood, the visit to the mission by the church elder,

and the start of the climactic battle. Bolt's script contents itself to regard its characters from the outside, a choice that results in a rather impersonal film on a passionate subject. For instance, more screen time is devoted to Mendoza's penance than to his jail-cell conversion. The penance, in which he attempts to lug a weight up a muddy cliff, makes for better spectacle, but the conversion, had it been explored, would have unlocked deeper recesses of his character. The mixture of resolution and self-loathing visualized in the penance scene succeeds at revealing much about Mendoza, but his conversion is genuine and just as much a key to his later actions as this heroic struggle up the cliff. All in all, *The Mission* is a film easier to respect in its impressive parts than to feel enthusiasm for its whole.

Cast: Robert De Niro (Mendoza), Jeremy Irons (Gabriel), Ray McAnally (Altamirano), Aidan Quinn (Felipe), Ronald Pickup (Hontar), Cherie Lunghi (Carlotta), Chuck Low (Cabeza), Liam Neeson (Fielding), Bercelio Moya (Indian Boy), Sigifredo Ismare (Witch Doctor), Asuncion Ontiveros (Indian Chief), Alejandro Moya (Chief's Lieutenant), Daniel Berrigan (Sebastian), Rolf

Jesuit priest Gabriel (Jeremy Irons) offers forgiveness to slave trader Mendoza (Robert De Niro).

Did you know?...

The story is based on the 1750 Treaty of Madrid, in which Spain ceded part of South America to Portugal.

Gray (Young Jesuit), Alvaro Guerrero (Jesuit), **Screenwriter:** Robert Bolt **Cinematographer:** Chris Menges **Composer:** Ennio Morricone **Producer:** Fernando Ghia and David Puttnam for Warner Bros. **MPAA Rating:** PG **Running Time:** 126 minutes **Format:** VHS, LV **Awards:** Academy Awards, 1986: Cinematography; Nominations: Art Direction/Set Decoration, Costume Design, Director (Roland Joffe), Editing, Picture, Score; Cannes Film Festival, 1986: Film; Golden Globe Awards, 1986: Screenplay, Score; Los Angeles Film Critics Association Awards, 1986: Cinematography **Budget:** $22M **Box Office:** $17.2M (gross).

Nashville
1975 – Robert Altman – ♫♫♫♫

> "I know it sounds arrogant, but I'm on my way to Nashville to become a country singer. Or a star."
> Albuquerque (Barbara Harris)

Influencing both movies and television with its multiple plot lines, improvisation and hand-held cameras, *Nashville* is more than a moldy museum piece. Director Robert Altman departs from some of the assumptions of mainstream movies. He diminishes plot and focuses on the interesting recesses locked away in his characters. The people in his films—like the people in life—seem to come up with more sides to their personalities. As we get to know them, these sides often seem at once funny and sad. Altman's rich ambiguity and his rejection of the pat and simple also de-emphasize the importance of a completed, polished script and stresses the advantages of spontaneity and improvisation. *Nashville* beautifully illustrates all of these traits.

The film observes the tragicomic interactions of twenty-four people over five days in Nashville, actions that are all linked directly or indirectly to country music, a political campaign, and the bicentennial celebration. Reportedly, Altman left writer Joan Tewkesbury to solely decide the general arcs of what these interactions would be while he only stipulated that the film would end in a killing. The actors were encouraged to improvise some of their dialogue, and some scenes were shot with multiple, concealed cameras so that the performers would not know when they were being filmed and were forced to remain in character so as not to spoil the shot. Those who played country-western singers were allowed to collaborate on or even to write some of the songs they performed. One of them, Keith Carradine, won an Oscar for his music.

The results of such an approach to filmmaking, of course, will make some viewers fidget because the movie refuses to release its meaning in the more

> Did you know?...
> Elliot Gould and Julie Christie appear in cameo roles.

Barbara Jean (Ronee Blakley) sings her heart out in *Nashville*.

straightforward ways that other films do. (One of the characters, for example, is a reporter for the BBC, but she is simply offered as one more interesting person out of the flux of humanity rather than the observer and interpreter of events that most directors would have turned her into.)

For those whose curiosity is kindled by such an approach, the rewards are many. One of them is the continual state of surprise that *Nashville* maintains. It has the edginess and unpredictability of life itself. Because Altman simply follows where situations and characters lead, moments of originality and richness spring from the least likely places. In one of these, Lady Pearl (Barbara Baxley) slips into a long reverie about the slain Kennedy brothers. Her angry, tearful comments are mawkish but genuine, wildly idolatrous yet suggestive of a real hunger to serve her country. Should we laugh at her, pity her, or admire her willingness to get involved? (All three, Altman might say.) In another example, Altman shows the Sunday morning before the big rally in a montage of characters singing hymns at different churches, some more dignified in their worship, some more emotional, and one veering toward the Pentecostal. Again, no implied commentary guides the audience response as the shots cut back and forth from congregation to congregation; the film is content simply to capture such moments in their fullness and offer them up as samples of American religion. Altman, who has often compared making films to playing jazz, pours out rich human music in *Nashville*.

Cast: David Arkin (Norman), Barbara Baxley (Lady Pearl), Ned Beatty (Delbert Reese), Karen Black (Connie White), Ronee Blakley (Barbara Jean), Timothy Brown (Tommy Brown), Keith Carradine (Tom Frank), Geraldine Chaplin (Opal), Robert Doqui (Wade), Shelley Duvall (L.A. Joan), Allen Garfield (Barnett), Henry Gibson (Haven Hamilton), Scott Glenn (Pfc. Glenn Kelly), Jeff Goldblum (Tricycle Man), Barbara Harris (Albuquerque), David Hayward (Kenny Fraiser), Michael Murphy (John Triplett), Allan Nichols (Bill), Dave Peel (Bud Hamilton), Christina Raines (Mary), Bert Ramsen (Star), Lily Tomlin (Linnea Reese), Gwen Welles (Sueleen), Keenan Wynn (Mr. Green) **Screenwriter:** Joan Tewkesbury **Cinematographer:** Paul Lohmann **Composer:** Richard Baskin, Karen Black, Ronee Blakley, Keith Carradine **Producer:** Robert Altman for Paramount **MPAA Rating:** R **Running Time:** 159 minutes **Format:** VHS, LV **Awards:** Academy Awards, 1975: Song ("I'm Easy"); Nominations: Director (Robert Altman), Picture, Supporting Actress (Ronee Blakley, Lily Tomlin); Golden Globe Awards, 1976: Song ("I'm Easy"); National Board of Review Awards, 1975: 10 Best Films of the Year, Director (Robert Altman), Supporting Actress (Ronee Blakley); New York Film Critics Awards, 1975: Director (Robert Altman), Film, Supporting Actress (Lily Tomlin); National Society of Film Critics Awards, 1975: Director (Robert Altman), Film, Supporting Actor (Henry Gibson), Supporting Actress (Lily Tomlin).

Queen Margot

1994 – Patrice Chereau –

In this age of restored- and director's-cut editions of films, the assumption seems to be that the more footage that can be put back in a film the better. *Queen Margot* is a film that found more appreciative audiences, however, when some judicious pruning cut its running time from 167 to 144 minutes. The film debuted at the Cannes Film Festival in 1994 to some mixed reviews and, shortly thereafter, disappointing box-office receipts. The American distributor, Miramax, wanted the producers to re-edit the film before releasing it in the U.S., and the 190 cuts and twenty-three minutes that came out resulted in a version that, surprisingly, was praised by director/co-screenwriter Patrice Chereau, producer Claude Berri, and star Isabelle Adjani. Favorable reviews followed. Jean-Hugues Anglade's Charles is at turns pathetic and sympathetic, and Daniel Auteuil and Adjani are supremely convincing.

The film is based on the 1845 novel by Alexandre Dumas and takes as its centerpiece the St. Bartholomew's Day Massacre on August 23, 1572, when thousands of protestant Huguenots who had travelled to Paris for the arranged wedding of Margot (Adjani) to Henri of Navarre (Auteuil) were killed by soldiers of the Catholic French throne. Given the labyrinthine plotting of Dumas and the intricacies of French history, the scenes leading up to the massacre will pose a challenge for most audiences (one reviewer joked that sorting out the characters required an encyclopedia). A character fascinating in her villainy is Catherine of Medici (Virna Lisi), the mother of Margot and King Charles IX (Anglade), who wants to wrest control of her son away from his advisor, the Protestant Coligny (Jean-Claude Brialy). The assassination attempt on Coligny (ordered by Catherine but disguised as an Protestant act) grieves Charles so much that he authorizes the massacre of the Protestants as a measure of retaliation.

The scenes after the massacre are the most memorable. The ruthlessness of the French royal family eventually drives Margot to side with Henri and the Protestants. She also falls in love with La Mole (Vincent Perez), one of the survivors of the slaughter. The personal and political elements mostly center on the intrigue at the French court and La Mole's efforts in Holland to raise troops for a return to France to fight the Catholics. The film's strength is its ability to convinc-

> "You can be proud! Proud to rule over a country of dead bodies. Paris is a cemetery!"
>
> Margot (Isabelle Adjani), to the king after the slaughter of the Protestants.

Did you know?...

Barbet Schroeder, the director of *Reversal of Fortune* and *Single White Female*, appears in the small part of the advisor.

Isabelle Adjani stars as regal French *Queen Margot.*

ingly personalize the villainy of Catherine and the passion of Margot. The diabolic scheming of Catherine is vividly dramatized in her foiled attempt to poison Henri by coating the pages of a book on falconry with a slow-acting poison. Charles, however, comes upon the book and thumbs his way through it, licking his finger to separate the corners and unknowingly poisoning himself page by page.

The muted but rich colors, impressive sets, and fine performances add to the appeal of this handsomely mounted historical film, rich with occasional blood-letting.

Cast: Isabelle Adjani (Margot), Daniel Auteuil (Henri of Navarre), Jean-Hugues Anglade (Charles IX), Vincent Perez (La Mole), Virna Lisi (Catherine of Medici), Dominique Blanc (Henriette of Nevers), Pascal Greggory (Anjou), Claudio Amendola (Coconnas), Miguel Bose (Guise), Asia Argento (Charlotte of Sauve), Julien Rassam (Alencon), Thomas Kretschmann (Nancay), Jean-Claude Brialy (Coligny), Jean-Phillipe Ecoffey (Conde), Albano Guaetta (Orthon) **Screenwriter:** Daniele Thompson, Patrice Chereau **Cinematographer:** Philippe Rousselot **Composer:** Goran Bregovic **Producer:** Claude Berri for Renn Productions, France 2 Cinema/D.A. Films (Paris), -NEF Filmproduktion GmbH,/Degeto pour Ard,/Wing (Munich), -R.C.S. Films and Television (Rome), with the participation of the Centre National de la Cinematographie and Canal Plus; released by Miramax Films **MPAA Rating:** R **Running Time:** 144 minutes **Format:** VHS, LV **Awards:** Academy Awards, 1994: Nominations: Costume Design; British Academy Awards, 1995: Nominations: Foreign Film; Cannes Film Festival, 1994: Special Jury Prize, Actress (Virna Lisi); Cesar Awards, 1995: Actress (Isabelle Adjani), Cinematography, Costume Design, Supporting Actor (Jean-Hugues Anglade), Supporting Actress (Virna Lisi); Nominations: Foreign Film; Golden Globe Awards, 1995: Nominations: Foreign Film **Box Office:** $2M (U.S. gross).

Reds

1981 – Warren Beatty – 🦴🦴🦴🦴

An intelligent and historical saga, *Reds* features Warren Beatty at the height of his Hollywood power. Beatty co-wrote with Trevor Griffiths (with an uncredited assist from Robert Towne and Elaine May), directed, and produced, as well as starred. *Reds* traces the lives of radical writers John Reed (Beatty) and Louise Bryant (Diane Keaton) from their meeting in Portland, Oregon, in 1915 to Reed's death in 1920. It combines their love story with the bohemianism of Greenwich Village, the creativity of the Provincetown Playhouse, the excitement of the 1917 Bolshevik Revolution, and the politics of Reed's later efforts to win formal recognition for American Communist activities. The film

> "Look at me. I'm like a wife. I'm like a boring, clinging, miserable little wife. Who'd want to come home to me?"
> Louise (Diane Keaton)

Journalists John Reed (Warren Beatty) and Louise Bryant (Diane Keaton) take a personal look at the Bolshevik Revolution.

makes a great point of its historical accuracy, partly through the effective use of thirty-two "witnesses" who recall the Reeds and the political climate of the early century. It would be wrong to regard these comments as coming from friends of the Reeds since the witnesses' remarks are often presented for irony or simply for the flavor of the era (Georgie Jessel sings patriotic songs), but for the most part this innovative device works well. The film also gains authenticity by including historical characters into its narrative like Eugene O'Neill (Jack Nicholson) and Emma Goldman (Maureen Stapleton).

Beatty plays John Reed as someone who reveals his passions in torrents of words. The script smartly uses his verbal nature as a tool for revealing character and developing the love plot. When he first meets Louise Bryant, she asks him one question about politics, and he talks the night away. Reed seems charmingly unaware of his tendency to babble. He gives the impression of someone who comes up with ideas faster than he can clothe them in words:

there always seems to be more opinions backlogged waiting to come out. In one of the best moments from the St. Petersburg scenes, Reed is spilling out a hurried summary of his day when Louise quietly comes up next to him, patiently waits for these verbal waters to recede, and then simply says, "Thank you for bringing me here." In the context of the film and their relationship, it is a deep expression of love, as are his moments when he checks his urge to chatter and listens to Louise's frustrations or anger about her lack of recognition as a writer. Reed's character coalesces for a brief stretch in the second half of the film when he appears to regard himself more as a writer than a politician.

The film really hits its stride, however, about halfway in when Reed and Louise cover the events leading to the October Revolution. The montage sequences beautifully link the romantic plot with the political one as we hear them on the soundtrack speedily reading excerpts from their reportage about Lenin and Trotsky while we see them in St. Petersburg attending meetings, scurrying through the snow, speaking at rallies. Their politics fuel their love, and their love increases a commitment to politics. Now they offer and accept criticisms of each other's writing constructively. The movie declines from this peak briefly when the American Communist movement splits and Reed is selected to return to Russia to seek formal recognition of his faction. After this lapse, however, the movie rouses itself to a memorable finish when Reed challenges a party boss (Jerzy Kosinski) over changing a word ("class war" to "holy war") in the translation of his speech and struggles with failing health while Louise travels to be with him.

Cast: Warren Beatty (John Reed), Diane Keaton (Louise Bryant), Edward Herrmann (Max Eastman), Jerzy Kosinski (Grigory Zinoviev), Jack Nicholson (Eugene O'Neill), Paul Sorvino (Louis Fraina), Maureen Stapleton (Emma Goldman), Nicolas Coster (Paul Trullinger), Gene Hackman (Pete Van Wherry), George Plimpton (Horace Wingham), William Daniels (Julius Gerber), M. Emmet Walsh (Speaker—Liberal Club), Ian Wolfe (Mr. Partlow), Bessie Love (Mrs. Partlow), MacIntyre Dixon (Carl Walters), Pat Starr (Helen Walters), Eleanor D. Wilson (Mrs. Reed), Max Wright (Floyd Dell), Roger Baldwin ("witness"), Henry Miller ("witness"), Adela Rogers St. Johns ("witness"), Dora Russell ("witness"), Scott Nearing ("witness"), Tess Davis ("witness"), Heaton Vorse ("witness"), Hamilton Fish ("witness"), Isaac Don Levine ("witness"), Rebecca West ("witness"), Will Durant ("witness"), Will Weinstone ("witness"), Oleg Kerensky ("witness"), Emmanuel Herbert ("witness"), Arne Swabeck ("witness") , Adele Nathan ("witness"), George Seldes ("witness"), Kenneth Chamberlain ("witness"), Blanche Hays Fagen ("witness"), Galina Von Meck ("witness"), Art Shields ("witness"), Andrew Dasburg ("witness"), Hugo Gellert ("witness"), Dorothy Frooks, ("witness"), George Jessel ("witness"), Jacob Bailin ("witness"), John Ballato ("witness"), Lucita Williams ("witness"), Bernadine Szold-Fritz ("witness"), Jessica Smith ("witness"), Harry Carlisle ("witness"), Arthur Mayer ("witness") **Screenwriter:** Warren Beatty, Trevor Griffiths **Cinematographer:** Vittorio Storaro **Composer:** Stephen Sondheim **Producer:** Warren Beatty for Paramount **MPAA Rating:** PG **Run-**

Did you know?...

Preparing for the Baku conference scene with a number of extras, director Beatty explained the background for them by citing John Reed's commitment to the working man and his struggle for better conditions and higher pay. The extras learned well. Before the scene was completed, they struck for higher pay and got it.

ning Time: 195 minutes **Format:** VHS, LV **Awards:** Academy Awards, 1981: Cinematography, Director (Warren Beatty), Supporting Actress (Maureen Stapleton); Nominations: Actor (Warren Beatty), Actress (Diane Keaton), Art Direction/Set Decoration, Costume Design, Editing, Screenplay, Picture, Sound, Supporting Actor (Jack Nicholson); British Academy Awards, 1982: Supporting Actor (Jack Nicholson), Supporting Actress (Maureen Stapleton); Directors Guild of America Awards, 1981: Director (Warren Beatty); Golden Globe Awards, 1982: Director (Warren Beatty); Los Angeles Film Critics Association Awards, 1981: Cinematography, Director (Warren Beatty), Supporting Actress (Maureen Stapleton); National Board of Review Awards, 1981: Director (Warren Beatty), Supporting Actor (Jack Nicholson); New York Film Critics Awards, 1981: Supporting Actress (Maureen Stapleton); Writers Guild of America, 1981: Screenplay **Budget:** reports vary from $34-45M **Box Office:** $45M.

The Scarlet Empress

1934 – Josef von Sternberg – 𝄢𝄢𝄢

> "You wouldn't think that once I had skin like velvet. Empress, bah! I haven't even the power to iron out a single wrinkle."
>
> The old Empress (Louise Dresser), to her mirror.

Did you know?...

The working title for the film was *Her Regiment of Lovers*, but the censor requested a change.

In his autobiography *Fun in a Chinese Laundry*, director Josef von Sternberg refers to *The Scarlet Empress* as "a relentless excursion in style." If anything, that assessment understates the baroque qualities of this film supposedly based, as the opening titles claim, on the diaries of Catherine the Great. (For the record, historian Carolly Erickson finds only a few surface details—like Peter's toy soldiers—that correspond faithfully to the habits of the characters.) Sternberg is less concerned with accuracy than in putting together a highly ornate, cynical film that appeals to the mind rather than the heart.

The film follows the arranged marriage of Catherine (Marlene Dietrich) to the half-wit Peter (Sam Jaffe) and her eventual accession to the throne of eighteenth-century Russia. When she arrives at the palace, she is a naive girl who spends the first forty minutes or so staring wide-eyed at the splendors around her and at the handsome Count Alexei (John Lodge), her preferred choice to Peter. Though the film was made in 1934, Sternberg seems almost to envision it as a silent film with atmospheric music and little dialogue. He uses explanatory title cards to summarize the various stages in Catherine's maturation (which is basically her fall into the sexual politics and cynicism of the court).

The episodic nature of these scenes impedes identification, as do the magnificent sets and props, which literally dwarf the characters. The sets teem with sculpted gargoyles in the background, on the staircase, and around the throne. The throne itself is in the shape of what seems to be a fifteen-by-twenty-

Marlene Dietrich stars as Russian empress Catherine the Great.

foot eagle with wings fully spread. During the establishing shot for this piece of palace architecture, it takes a while to notice that someone, the elderly Elizabeth (Louise Dresser), is actually sitting on this throne. The old empress gives the film much of its unexpected comedy; she cracks wise like a hard-boiled dame in a 1930s melodrama. When she is told that the French and Austrian ambassadors and their wives await, she waves her hand dismissively: "Send 'em home and tell 'em to come for breakfast. I never did like these diplomatic functions. They lead to nothing." After complaining about her age and wrinkles, she tells Catherine to leave her bedroom by the secret stairs to avoid running into Alexei, her lover, a little tidbit that shatters Catherine's romantic view of the count.

The movie never gets dull, thanks to its many unexpected touches. Peter, grinning like a monkey, tries to spy on Catherine by boring a hole through the bedroom wall with a drill the size of a javelin (on the other side, the drill bit comes spinning out of the eye of a gargoyle). Alexei is caught passing a love note to Catherine by the old empress, who scolds the two of them like a school-marm and then needs an attendant to read the note for her. In the conclusion that depicts the assassination of Peter, dozens of soldiers storm the palace and ride up the grand staircase on horseback, a truly impressive effect. It is tempting to dismiss a film that is so overwhelmed by all these oddities, but *The Scarlet Empress* never intends to create sympathy for any of these characters. It is content simply to laugh at them for all their decadent excesses and to have the viewer join in.

Cast: Marlene Dietrich (Catherine II), John Lodge (Count Alexei), Sam Jaffe (Grand Duke Peter), Louise Dresser (Empress Elizabeth), C. Aubrey Smith (Prince August), Jay C. Flippen (Hamilton Garth), Gavin Gordon (Gregory Orloff), Olive Tell (Princess Johanna), Ruthelma Stevens (Coutness Elizabeth), Davison Clark (Archimandrite Simeon/Tevedovsy), Erville Alderson (Chancelor Bestuchef), Phillip Sleeman (Count Lestoq), Marie Wells (Marie), Han Heinrich von Twardowski (Ivan Shuvolov), Gerald Fielding (Lt. Dimitri) **Screenwriter:** Paul Osborn, Borden Deal **Cinematographer:** Bert Glennon **Composer:** Josef von Sternberg **Producer:** Adolph Zukor for Paramount **Running Time:** 110 minutes **Format:** VHS.

Schindler's List
1993 — Steven Spielberg — 🦴🦴🦴🦴

> "Stern, if this factory ever produces a shell that can actually be fired, I'll be very unhappy."
> Schindler (Liam Neeson), to Stern (Ben Kingsley)

Hailed as one of the best pictures of the year and winner of multiple Oscars, Spielberg's heart-wrenching adaptation of the book by Thomas Keneally is also one of the successful director's best films, a powerful drama with a depth of artistry on every level that serves the tragic subject matter well. Other films about the Holocaust have done an excellent, effective job in depicting the horror of the Nazi attempt at genocide, but *Schindler's List* stands on its own as a rich blending of visual film art with a stirring, often disturbing tale of suffering and loss, evil at its worst, and unexpected heroism. Based on the true story of Oskar Schindler, the film tells of a man (Liam Neeson) who pursues wealth and prominence, employing hundreds of Jews in his enamel-ware factory because their labor costs him virtually nothing—until, moved by the horrors committed by the Nazis, his quest finally turns from making money to saving lives.

Spielberg's use of black-and-white photography casts a grim, cold shadow over the horrible events and heightens the realism of it all. The one use of

color outside of the bracketing opening shot and ending sequence is of a little girl's red coat that becomes a visual symbol of the innocent humanity falling victim to the merciless, malicious evil of the Nazis. Also, since the actual photographs and footage we've all seen from the era are in black and white, the absence of color tends to give the film a documentary look, as if all those grim photographs have come to life. The evocativeness and potential artistry of black-and-white also allows Spielberg to create hauntingly composed scenes with meaningful shadows and shafts of light that would not be possible in color.

Although the film stirs the emotions through its graphic depiction of the violence and brutality of the Holocaust, one of the most significant elements of the film is the moral development of Oskar Schindler. Initially, Schindler is not likable and far from a hero. He is a greedy man, a womanizer, and a self-serving schemer. Though Schindler initially uses Jewish workers to increse profits, the humanity somewhere within him is deeply moved as he comes face to face with the harsh

German industrialist Oskar Schindler (Liam Neeson) and Jewish accountant Itzhak Stern (Ben Kingsley) assemble a list to protect Jewish workers.

Did you know?...

German authorities would not allow Spielberg to film inside Auschwitz, so the director had a set built on the outside of the gates of the actual site.

reality of their treatment. This confrontation with darkness prompts him to take action. In the end, he ultimately sacrifices all his earnings to save his factory workers, and the final scene in which he mourns not having saved more lives is one of the most touching and humanly personal moments of the film. Schindler's heroism and humanity have finally emerged, making this flawed man an unlikely hero.

Cast: Liam Neeson (Oskar Schindler), Ben Kingsley (Itzhak Stern), Ralph Fiennes (Amon Goeth), Caroline Goodall (Emilie Schindler), Jonathan Sagalle (Poldek Pfefferberg), Embeth Davidtz (Helen Hirsch), Malgoscha Gebel (Victoria Klonowska), Shmulik Levy (Wilek Chilowicz), Mark Ivanir (Marcel Goldberg), Beatrice Macola (Ingrid), Andrzej Seweryn (Julian Scherner), Friedrich von Thun (Rolf Czurda), Krysztof Luft (Herman Toffel), Harry Nehring (Leo John), Norbert Weisser (Albert Hujar) **Screenwriter:** Steven Zaillian **Cinematographer:** Janusz Kaminski **Composer:** John Williams **Producer:** Branko Lustig, Gerald R. Molen, and Steven Spielberg for Ambin; released by Universal **MPAA Rating:** R **Running Time:** 197 minutes **Format:** VHS, LV **Awards:** Academy Awards, 1993: Art Direction/Set Decoration, Cinematography (Janusz Kaminski), Director (Steven Spielberg), Film Editing, Original Score (John Williams), Picture, Adapted Screenplay (Steven Zaillian); Nominations: Actor (Liam Neeson), Costume Design, Makeup, Sound, Supporting Actor (Ralph Fiennes); Directors Guild of America Awards, 1993: Director (Steven Spielberg); Golden Globe Awards, 1994: Director (Steven Spielberg), Film—Drama, Screenplay (Steven Zaillian); Nominations: Actor—Drama (Liam Neeson), Supporting Actor (Ralph Fiennes), Original Score (John Williams); Los Angeles Film Critics Association Awards, 1993: Cinematography (Janusz Kaminski), Film; National Board of Review Awards, 1993: Film; New York Film Critics Awards 1993: Cinematography (Janusz Kaminski), Film, Supporting Actor (Ralph Fiennes); National Society of Film Critics Awards, 1993: Cinematography (Janusz Kaminski), Director (Steven Spielberg), Film, Supporting Actor (Ralph Fiennes); Writers Guild of America, 1993: Adapted Screenplay (Steven Zaillian) **Budget:** $25M **Box Office:** $96.1M (domestic gross).

Seven Samurai
1954 – Akira Kurosawa – 𝄢𝄢𝄢𝄢

> "Find hungry samurai! Even bears come out of the forests when they're hungry."
>
> The village patriarch (Kuninori Kodo)

Seven Samurai is another masterpiece by Japanese director Akira Kurosawa. It tells of a small farming community in sixteenth-century Japan beset with marauding bandits. Kurosawa's inspired by the American western, especially the films of John Ford, and the *Seven Samurai* itself inspired the classic western *The Magnificent Seven*. The elders of the group visit the village patriarch (Kuninori Kodo), who instructs them to hire samurai warriors to defend their village. The film takes this simple situation and develops it to evoke an incredible array of emotions.

The farmers first find Kambei (Takashi Shimura), a warrior in a nearby village who outsmarts a bandit holding a child hostage. Although the farmers have nothing to offer Kambei except food in return for his services, his sense of honor and compassion is sufficiently intrigued by their plight. He agrees to recruit some additional swords to help oppose the bandits. Kurosawa uses this sequence to particularize the samurai who join the group and also to elicit some of the suppressed emotions of the village. He seems to miss nothing in dramatizing the humanity of the situation: the village is dependent on the skill of the samurai, but they hide or disguise their daughters in fear that these roughened warriors will rape the women. The farmers know they must obey the instructions of Kambei in setting up their defenses, but those living in the outlying huts are reluctant to evacuate their homes and possessions and join the safety of the community. Some fearful farmers jeopardize the plan of defense by seeming to break ranks; others swell a bit with overconfidence in the company of the samurai. Kambei masterfully handles all these threats to the solidarity of the village.

The samurai display their valor in Akira Kurosawa's epic drama.

Did you know?...

Filming took over a year due to the difficulty in raising funds and obtaining horses.

Comedy leavens the mix of emotions with the antics of Toshiro Mifune's character, a youth named Kikuchiyo who insists that he too join the group.

Kurosawa paces the film (at least in the longest, 204-minute version) so as to instill a greater sense of drama and inevitability in the moments preceding the final attack. The comic interludes, the captured spying party from the bandits, and even a growing romance prepare for the climactic assault. This battle scene plays out in a driving rainstorm with the bandits thundering through the village on horseback. The flurry of arrows, flash of swords, torrential rain, and deepening mud add to the realism and horror of the climax.

Cast: Takashi Shimura (Kambei), Toshiro Mifune (Kikuchiyo), Ko Kimura (Katsushiro), Yoshio Inaba (Gorobei), Seiji Miyaguchi (Kyuzo), Minoru Chiaki (Heihachi), Daisuke Kato (Shichiroji), Kamatari Fujiwara (Manzo), Keiko Tsushima (Shino), Kuninori Kodo (Gisaku), Yoshio Tsuchiya (Rikichi), Bokuzen Hidari (Yohei), Yoshio Kosugi (Mosuke), Keiji Sakakida (Gosaku), Jiro Kumagai (Gisaku's son), Haruko Toyama (Gisaku's daughter-in-law), Fumiko Homma (peasant woman), Ichiro Chiba (priest) **Screenwriter:** Shinobu Hashimoto, Hideo Oguni, Akira Kurosawa **Cinematographer:** Asakazu Nakai **Composer:** Fumio Hayasaka **Producer:** Shojuro Motoki for Toho **Running Time:** 204 minutes **Format:** VHS, LV, DVD **Awards:** Venice Film Festival, 1954: Silver Prize; Academy Awards, 1954: Nominations: Art Direction/Set Decoration (B&W), Costume Design (B&W).

Spartacus
1960 – Stanley Kubrick – ♫♫♫♥

Although *Spartacus* is probably Stanley Kubrick's least personal film, you can still recognize in this story of a slave-led rebellion in ancient Rome the director's continual interest in the idea of dehumanization. Kubrick inherited the directorial chores from Anthony Mann, who had a difference of opinion with star and executive producer Kirk Douglas, and never had full control of the script. The film was publicized as a thinking-person's epic that explored the clash of slavery and freedom, but Dalton Trumbo's script really makes it more of an epic for liberals. The opening narration sounds almost like a tract from the Thracian chapter of the ACLU: "Spartacus lived out his youth and his young manhood dreaming the death of slavery, 2,000 years before it finally would die."

In spite of Kubrick's consistently negative remarks about the film (resentful over his lack of control), *Spartacus* is full of wonderful moments both large

and small. Peter Ustinov's Oscar-winning performance as the cherubically grubby Batiatus enriches every scene he is in. Ustinov seems to be enjoying a private joke throughout the movie, and he rewrote some of the dialogue in his scenes with the equally impish Charles Laughton to enhance both their parts. The extreme long shots in the prologue to the final battle scene, showing the Roman legions marching into place (8,000 Spanish soldiers worked as extras), fill the Super Technirama-70 screen majestically. This and other moments, such as the long perspectives showing the crucifixions of 6,000 captured slaves on the Appian Way, the gladiator fight between Spartacus (Kirk Douglas) and Daraba (Woody Strode), and the expansive shots in the Senate meetings, make rich use of the widescreen dimensions.

A number of scenes are effectively designed to contrast foreground and background elements. When Spartacus and Daraba fight for the amusement of Crassus (Laurence Olivier) and his guests, the combatants grunt and bleed in

Spartacus (Kirk Douglas) leads a slave rebellion against Rome.

the background while in the foreground, the aristocrats giggle and gossip, practically ignoring the life-and-death struggle below. Later, when Crassus shows Antoninus (Tony Curtis, who never quite drops his Bronx accent) the splendors of Rome, he gestures expansively beyond a portico, where a legion of troops sprawls impressively across the screen.

The 1991 reissue, supervised by Robert A. Harris and James C. Katz, generated a new 65mm preservation negative and restored Alex North's original overture and five minutes of footage that didn't pass the censor in 1960. For this flirtatious "oysters and snails" scene between Olivier and Curtis, Olivier's widow Joan Plowright selected Anthony Hopkins to dub her husband's voice on the deteriorated soundtrack. Tony Curtis read his own lines, and his voice was then "lightened" electronically to approximate the timbre of a younger man.

Cast: Kirk Douglas (Spartacus), Laurence Olivier (Marcus Licinius Crassus), Jean Simmons (Varinia), Tony Curtis (Antoninus), Charles Laughton (Lentulus Gracchus), Peter Ustinov (Lentulus Batiatus), John Gavin (Julius Caesar), Nina Foch (Helena Glabrus), John Ireland (Crixus), Herbert Lom (Tigranes), John Dall (Glabrus), Charles McGraw (Marcellus), Joanna Barnes (Claudia Marius), Harold Stone (David), Woody Strode (Daraba), Peter Brocco (Ramon) **Screenwriter:** Dalton Trumbo **Cinematographer:** Russell Metty, Clifford Stine **Composer:** Alex North **Producer:** Kirk Douglas and Edward Lewis for Bryna Productions; released by Universal **MPAA Rating:** PG-13 (restored 1991 version) **Running Time:** 184 minutes **Format:** VHS, LV, DVD **Awards:** Academy Awards, 1960: Art Direction/Set Decoration, Color Cinematography, Costume Design, Supporting Actor (Peter Ustinov); Nominations: Film Editing, Score; Golden Globe Awards 1961: Film—Drama **Budget:** $12M **Box Office:** $14M (rentals).

They Might Be Giants . . .

Some historical epics, like *Gandhi*, adopt a biographical approach. In another attempt to bring an epic dimension to the story of a life, Richard Attenborough directed *Chaplin* (1992), but the film's 144 minutes rush through the events of the great comedian's life all too quickly. If too many three-hour films would benefit from cutting an hour or so, *Chaplin* may be one of the rare cases when an extra hour of development would have capitalized more satisfyingly on the great performance by Robert Downey Jr. (who even altered his posture to approximate the gait of the Little Tramp), and the excellent period detail. Spike Lee's *Malcolm X* (1992) minimizes the director's usual flamboyance of style to settle instead for a controlled but compelling portrait of its hero, personified memorably by Denzel Washington. Far less effective is *El Cid* (1961), the account of the eleventh-century leader who liberated Spain, and *Cromwell* (1970) with Richard Harris in the title role, a film that focuses on the clash with Charles I (though the battle scenes are superior). The two parts of *Peter the First* (1937, 1938), directed by Vladimir Petrov, maps out the life of the czar in scenes more visually than dramatically impressive.

Another biographical effort makes an interesting note for the curious: the unfinished attempt in 1937 to film Robert Graves' novel *I, Claudius* reportedly resulted in some of Charles Laughton's finest moments before the camera. The fascinating story of this aborted project is told in the documentary *The Epic That Never Was* (currently included with the videocassettes for the BBC mini-series of Graves' novels with Derek Jacobi).

Other mini-series have also focused primarily on history. One of the longest—at twenty-four hours—was *Centennial*, based on the novel by James A. Michener. It aired in 1978 and dramatized the changes occurring in one location, a piece of land in what became Colorado, from 1795 to the present. The series featured, among others, Robert Conrad, Richard Chamberlain, Raymond Burr, Sally Kellerman, Chad Everett, Mark Harmon, Timothy Dalton, Richard Crenna, Brian Keith, Lynn Redgrave, and Andy Griffith. One of the best mini-series, *Holocaust* (1978), won eight Emmys and featured excellent work by Meryl Streep, James Woods, Fritz Weaver, Michael Moriarty, David Warner, and Ian Holm, among others. The nine-hour epic traces the impact of the war years on two very different families—one victims, the other, benefactors—and has often been touted as one of television's finest moments.

Other epics based on history would include two giant film versions of Tolstoy's *War and Peace*, one at 208 minutes from Hollywood (1956) with Audrey Hepburn and Henry Fonda directed by King Vidor, the other at 373 minutes from the Soviet Union (1968). Both are easier to respect than to enthuse over, though the Russian version was five-plus years in the making at a rumored $100 million cost and a meticulous attention to the source. *The Fall of the Roman Empire* (1964), an expensive epic from Anthony Mann, with Alec Guinness and James Mason, succeeds at spectacle and action more than at personalizing the drama. *The Agony and the Ecstasy* (1965) features two memorable performances from Rex Harrison and Charlton Heston in a drama based on Irving Stone's historical novel about the clash between Michelangelo and the Pope. Toshiro Mifune and Akira Kurosawa reunited in 1965 for *Red Beard*, the story of a nineteenth-century doctor whose social aspirations conflict with his posting at a clinic for the poor (Mifune plays Niide, the clinic supervisor). *The War Lord* (1965) in a sense reverses one of the emphases of *Braveheart*, by having its hero (Charlton Heston) invoke the law of "prima nocta" to claim the first night with a peasant's bride (Rosemary Forsyth), the woman to whom he declares his love.

Finally, the only Indian filmmaker to earn international acclaim, Satyajit Ray, adapted the novel *Aparajito* into a trilogy of films (*Pather Panchali*, *Aparajito*, and *The World of Apu*) from 1954 to 1959 that follows in neorealistic fashion (Ray had marveled over Vittorio De Sica's *The Bicycle Thief*) the coming-of-age of one boy.

HORROR

Alien
Aliens
Jaws
Jurassic Park
King Kong

Alien

1979 – Ridley Scott – 🦴🦴🦴🦴

> "You still don't know what you're dealing with, do you? Perfect organism. Its structural perfection is matched only by its hostility . . . I admire its purity, a survivor, unclouded by conscience, remorse, or delusions of morality."
>
> Ash (Ian Holm), on the alien.

This science fiction/horror classic that inspired three sequels works on visual, dramatic, and emotional levels as a suspenseful, skillfully constructed variation on the conventional "one man against unbeatable odds" storyline, though in this case, it's a woman. After the crew of the *Nostromo* responds to a distress signal and discovers a wrecked space craft, their crew is invaded by a seemingly undefeatable alien creature that hunts everyone down until only Ellen Ripley (Sigourney Weaver) is left alive. Ripley and the deadly alien face off in a battle of wits and brute strength, a series of sequences that stand out as some of the most intense and suspenseful scenes ever filmed.

Director Ridley Scott achieves a dark and lonely mood and sustains a suspenseful pace and a visual artistry that is rare in this class of "monster movies." Many films of the genre simply seem content with attempting to frighten the audience, often suffering from shallow or stock characterizations, contrived emotions, hackneyed or simplistic plots, and reliance on gore rather than on genuine suspense to instill fear. While the basic "monster versus man" plot of *Alien* offers relatively nothing new, the story is enriched by the unveiling of the mysteries surrounding the alien creature and by the complications created by the traitorous android Ash (Ian Holm). And, although the film has its share of blood and guts (and is creative in its violence), the filmmakers understand that gore in itself does not generate true fear and horror. More often than not, an atmosphere of terror is generated through the mysterious, powerful, unstoppable nature of the alien and through calculated suspense. The creature does not appear on screen for long, and its attacks on the human victims are brief. The real terror is in waiting to see what the creature will do next, or wondering when it will suddenly appear. Although scenes of the alien pursuing humans are intensely paced, some of the most effective scenes are those between the chases and attacks, when crew members search for the creature, try to determine a way to kill it, or fearfully wait for it to show its ugly face. Setting the story on a space ship with few ways to escape, thus isolating Ripley and the others, also creates a feeling of claustrophobia and loneliness that adds to the intensity of the conflict.

Did you know?...

The laserdisc version features a separate section of scenes not included in the theatrical release.

Parker (Yaphet Kotto), Ripley (Sigourney Weaver), and Ash (Ian Holm) play hunt the alien.

One of the most fascinating aspects of the film is the production design. Both the interior of the wrecked alien vessel where the eggs are found and the deadly creature itself are strange, disturbing, and hauntingly intricate. The characterization of Ripley, along with those of other crew members, is also a strong point. As a woman placed in a seemingly unbeatable life-threatening situation, Ripley exhibits an intelligence and inner strength that enable her to adapt to a situation beyond her experience and heroically overcome incredible odds. What makes her an endearing character is that she is not a stock hero but, a reluctant hero brought out by unusual circumstances.

Cast: Tom Skerritt (Dallas), Sigourney Weaver (Ripley), Veronica Cartwright (Lambert), Harry Dean Stanton (Brett), John Hurt (Kane), Ian Holm (Ash), Yaphet Kotto (Parker), Bolaji Badejo (Alien), Helen Horton (voice of Mother) **Screenwriter:** Dan O'Bannon **Cinematographer:** Derek Vanlint **Composer:** Jerry Goldsmith **Producer:** Gordon Carroll, David Giler, and Walter Hill for Twentieth Century Fox **MPAA Rating:** R **Running Time:** 117 minutes **Format:** VHS, LV **Awards:** Academy Awards, 1979: Visual Effects; Nominations: Art Direction/Set Decoration **Budget:** $11M **Box Office:** $60.2M (domestic gross).

Aliens
1986 — James Cameron — 🦴🦴🦴🦴

> "You're going out there to destroy them, right? Not to study, not to bring back, but to wipe them out?"
> Ripley (Sigourney Weaver) to Burke (Paul Reiser).

Whereas Ridley Scott's original *Alien* was a moderately paced, dark, almost melancholy film deriving much of its mood from the isolation and entrapment of its characters, James Cameron's *Aliens* propels its story forward, retaining a certain dark atmosphere but taking the tale in a new direction by emphasizing action and by turning the cat-and-mouse hunt of the first movie into a full-scale war. *Aliens* picks up fifty-seven years after the end of the previous film, as Ellen Ripley (Sigourney Weaver) wakes from a cryogenic freeze and discovers that a human colony has been established on the planet where she and the crew of the *Nostromo* discovered the vicious alien predators almost six decades before. However, communication with the colony has been cut off, so Ripley accompanies a team of marines to find out what has happened. They soon realize, of course, that the colony has been destroyed by the aliens, and before long the team is trapped on the base with the creatures. The intensity of action that follows as Ripley and the band of soldiers battle the aliens does not

Ripley (Sigourney Weaver) tries to protect Newt (Carrie Henn) from *Aliens*.

Did you know?...

Jenette Goldstein, who plays Vasquez, auditioned for and got the part initially thinking that the film was about illegal immigrants. The filmmakers refer to this mixup in the film when Hudson says of Vasquez, "She thought they said 'illegal aliens' and signed up," an in-joke referring to Goldstein's misunderstanding.

let up until the end of the movie, and neither does Cameron's skill at creating memorable images—many of them dark and dreadful—and at manipulating the emotions of the audience. For sheer excitement and terror, the last fifty minutes of this film can hardly be matched.

As in *Alien*, Ripley becomes an almost mythical hero who finds herself in a seemingly unbeatable situation but manages to use her wits and considerable physical prowess to rise above the occasion. After her horrible experience on board the *Nostromo* years before, Ripley has no desire to go back to the planet where the aliens were found. Initially, she simply goes along for the ride, to offer advice to the military team since she is the only one with knowledge of the aliens, but eventually she must take charge and help lead the fight. Ripley also becomes a mother figure as she protects and nurtures Newt (Carrie Henn), the young girl the team finds alive on the colony. Cameron effectively utilizes the scenes between the two of them to create another level of human interest and suspense. In fact, motherhood becomes one of the major themes threaded throughout the story, not only in Ripley's relationship to Newt but also in the unveiling of the queen alien, a previously unknown creature that sends her brood out to kill and to find hosts for the alien embryos. Ultimately the film becomes the story of two maternal beings battling to survive and to protect their "children." Thus *Aliens* merges two of the most basic forces that have driven the course of humanity throughout history: motherhood and war.

The scenes in which the alien creatures attack and pursue the doomed humans are unrelenting in their effort to keep the audience on edge. The barrage of suspense, violence, and kinetic energy as the humans, the aliens, and the camera itself move and confront one another is at times almost exhausting, but the film achieves what its makers set out to do—unsettle, scare, and thrill the viewer. Fortunately, the fast-paced action is complemented by interesting characters (particularly those of Ripley and Newt) that in some respects are better defined than those of *Alien*. Perhaps the only unfortunate thing about the success of this action thriller is that it sets up a pattern that the next two movies in the series attempted to imitate but failed to do so with originality. One can only tell the story of decimating the cast in so many ways. With *Aliens*, Cameron found a good way to do so.

Cast: Sigourney Weaver (Ellen Ripley), Carrie Henn (Rebecca "Newt" Jorden), Michael Biehn (Corporal Dwayne Hicks), Paul Reiser (Carter Burke), Lance Henriksen (Bishop), William Hope (Lieutenant Gorman), Jenette Goldstein (Private Vasquez), Bill Paxton (Private Hudson),

Al Matthews (Sergeant Apone), Mark Rolston (Private Drake), Ricco Ross (Private Frost), Colette Hiller (Corporal Ferro), Daniel Kash (Private Spunkmeyer), Cynthia Scott (Corporal Dietrich), Tip Tipping (Private Crowe) **Screenwriter:** James Cameron, David Giler, Walter Hill **Cinematographer:** Adrian Biddle **Composer:** James Horner **Producer:** Gale Anne Hurd for Twentieth Century Fox **MPAA Rating:** R **Running Time:** 137 minutes **Format:** VHS, LV **Awards:** Academy Awards, 1986: Sound Effects Editing, Visual Effects; Nominations: Actress (Sigourney Weaver), Art Direction/Set Decoration, Film Editing, Original Score (James Horner), Sound; Golden Globe Awards 1987, Nominations: Actress—Drama (Sigourney Weaver) **Budget:** $18.5M **Box Office:** $81.8M (domestic gross).

Jaws

1975 – Steven Spielberg – 🦴🦴🦴🦴

Peter Benchley's best-selling novel was the basis for *Jaws*, the movie that put Steven Spielberg in the big leagues and generated the all-time biggest box office. While the audience waits for their first good look at the killer shark that has "staked a claim" in the beach waters off a New England resort island, the film succeeds in creating life-like characters in a real setting. The treat of *Jaws* is that it delivers more than just the chills of a horror film. *Jaws* the family drama (as opposed to *Jaws*, the man-eating shark movie) is concerned with police chief Brody (Roy Scheider), his fear of the water, and his hope that moving his wife and two boys to the island from New York will better their lives ("In Amity, one man can make a difference"). After the mother (Lee Fierro) of the Kintner boy (Jeffrey Voorhees) accuses Brody of causing her son's death, Spielberg and the scriptwriters include a moment at the dinner table when Brody's younger son lovingly mimics his dad's movements, when Brody finally notices what the audience has seen, he hugs his son, a great example of how movies can develop character wordlessly. The overlapping dialogue that fills most of the first half of the film adds energy to every scene. Its real sound gives a flavor of the hustle-bustle of the tourist season and pinpoints the anger generated by the different vested interests. It is no surprise that one of the film's Oscars was for achievement in sound. *Jaws'* commerce vs. safety plot, involving the mayor and the question of when to close the beaches, is also great fun in the clash of personalities, though it is less subtle than the story about Brody. By the time the heroes take to sea and the shark appears, with his own theme song, courtesy of Spielberg stalwart John Williams, an impressive drama has already been established on a number of levels.

"You're gonna need a bigger boat."

Brody (Roy Scheider), to Quinn (Robert Shaw) after first seeing the shark.

Did you know?...

Both scriptwriters have small parts in the film: Benchley appears as a TV reporter on the beach, and Gottlieb plays the newspaper publisher.

Shark! Everybody out of the water!

Verna Fields' Oscar-winning editing may rival the special effects in their impact. The first beach scene creates intense emotions simply through the expert joining of images. Brody sits on the crowded beach anxiously watching the swimmers and fearing a shark attack. The ordinariness of the beach sounds increases the sense of danger. We see shots of Brody scanning the waters mixed with various shots of beach activity, and amid all the holiday festivities we can always sense Brody's nervous feelings. (Many of the cuts unobtrusively occur as a person passes by the camera and blots out the view.) A girl squeals in fun as her boyfriend raises her on his shoulders in the water, and the reaction shot of Brody's intense face rising into the frame mirrors the audience's own panic. A vivid moment, Hitchcockian in its intensity and tease, which Spielberg milks for its full dramatic value. When the attack finally comes, Spielberg employs the same zoom-in, track-back effect that Hitchcock used to suggest James Stewart's disorientation in *Vertigo*. The power of the editing to create emotions entirely through visual means has rarely been illustrated as well.

Filmed at Martha's Vineyard, *Jaws* used three hydraulic sharks. Originally, Sterling Hayden was to play Quint and both Jeff Bridges and Timothy Bottoms were considered for Hooper. Three lesser sequels were released, none directed by Spielberg.

Cast: Roy Scheider (Martin Brody), Robert Shaw (Quint), Richard Dreyfuss (Matt Hooper), Lorraine Gary (Ellen Brody), Murray Hamilton (Mayor Larry Vaughan), Jeffrey Kramer (Hendricks), Jonathan Filley (Cassidy), Chris Rebello (Michael Brody), Jay Mello (Sean Brody), Lee Fierro (Mrs. Kintner), Jeffrey Voorhees (Alex Kintner), Craig Kingsbury (Ben Gardner), Susan Backlinie (Chrissie Watkins), Peter Benchley (reporter on the beach), Carl Gottlieb (newspaper publisher) **Screenwriter:** Peter Benchley, Carl Gottlieb **Cinematographer:** Bill Butler **Composer:** John Williams **Producer:** David Brown and Richard D. Zanuck for Universal **MPAA Rating:** PG **Running Time:** 124 minutes **Format:** VHS, LV **Awards:** Academy Awards 1975: Editing, Sound, Original Score (John Williams); Nominations: Picture; Golden Globes 1975: Score (John Williams); People's Choice Awards 1976: Film **Budget:** $12M **Box Office:** $260M.

Jurassic Park
1993 – Steven Spielberg – 🦴🦴🦴

Michael Crichton's blockbuster novel was the basis for this tale of genetically resurrected dinosaurs that quickly became one of history's highest grossing films. Billionaire John Hammond (Richard Attenborough) has found a way to extract dinosaur DNA preserved in amber and uses it to create living dinosaurs. Hammond intends for the prehistoric animals to be the center of the world's most exciting and unique theme park, located on a remote island, but nature defies his plan when the dinosaurs get loose and create havoc and carnage on the island. *Jurassic Park* represents a landmark in filmmaking, not because of its story or its characterizations, but because of its technological display of unprecedented developments in computer-generated visual effects. Like most Spielberg films, the movie is exceptionally well-made on a visual level, both in terms of imagery and editing, but what the story lacks is character development. For all intents, the stars of *Jurassic Park* are the dinosaurs, which demonstrates both the movie's greatest strength and its greatest weakness.

The plot of the film involves a group of scientists brought to Hammond's island to evaluate the park's feasibility. Unfortunately, while they are there, a disgruntled employee of Hammond's, in an attempt to smuggle out dinosaur

"Your scientists were so preoccupied with whether or not they could, they didn't stop to think if they should."

Scientist/mathematician Ian Malcolm (Jeff Goldblum), discussing the genetic engineering of dinosaurs.

A T-Rex stares down at paleontologist Alan Grant (Sam Neill) and Lex (Ariana Richards).

Did you know?...

Though uncredited in the film, Spielberg's friend and fellow filmmaker George Lucas helped supervise the editing so that Spielberg could work on his next project, the Academy Award-winning *Schindler's List.*

embryos to sell to a competitor, shuts down all security measures in the park, allowing the dinosaurs to break free and roam around the island. The rest of the story consists of the main characters running from and narrowly escaping being eaten by the big lizards, a terrifying encounter with a T-rex.

While a few interesting questions are raised about responsibility in scientific research and the arrogance of mankind, character development in the story is slim. John Hammond realizes his arrogance has put those dearest to him at risk, and scientist Dr. Allen Grant (Sam Neill) learns to tolerate children as he gets to know Hammond's grandchildren, but for the most part the human characters in *Jurassic Park* serve as dinosaur appetizers or predictable "types." Maybe all that time acting before a blank blue screen took a certain toll.

The most effective elements of *Jurassic Park* involve the creatures themselves. The tyrannosaurus rex and velociraptors are certainly some of the most stunningly realistic creatures ever developed for the screen, and much of the fascination of the movie lies in watching these believable, frightening creatures move. Spielberg's talent for creating intensity and suspense provides the film with some of its most memorable moments, as when Hammond's grandchildren see a vibration in a glass of water resulting from the footstep of an as-of-yet unseen tyrannosaurus, or when the children are trapped in a kitchen with two highly intelligent velociraptors. In some ways, the superb visual effects and these kinds of suspenseful sequences compensate for the lack of story and character development, but little would remain if these elements were absent.

Cast: Sam Neill (Allen Grant), Laura Dern (Ellie Satler), Jeff Goldblum (Ian Malcolm), Richard Attenborough (John Hammond), Bob Peck (Robert Muldoon), Martin Ferrero (Donald Gennaro), B.D. Wong (Dr. Henry Wu), Joseph Mazzello (Tim Murphy), Ariana Richards (Lex Murphy), Samuel L. Jackson (Ray Arnold), Wayne Knight (Dennis Nedry), Jerry Molen (Dr. Gerry Harding), Miguel Sandoval (Rostagno), Cameron Thor (Lewis Dodsgon), Christopher John Fields (Volunteer #1) **Screenwriter:** Michael Crichton, David Koepp **Cinematographer:** Dean Cundey **Composer:** John Williams **Producer:** Kathleen Kennedy and Gerald R. Molen for Universal **MPAA Rating:** PG-13 **Running Time:** 127 minutes **Format:** VHS, LV **Awards:** Academy Awards, 1993: Sound, Sound Effects Editing, Visual Effects; MTV Movie Awards, 1994: Nominations: Film, Villain, Action Sequence **Budget:** $63M **Box Office:** $356.78M (domestic gross).

King Kong

1933 – Merian C. Cooper, Ernest B. Schoedsack – 🐾🐾🐾🐾

"It wasn't the airplanes. It was Beauty killed the Beast."

Carl Denham (Robert Armstrong), the last line of the film.

A filmmaker, Carl Denham, takes a crew to a remote island where his leading lady is abducted by natives. The inhabitants offer the actress to their god, Kong, who, we discover, is a giant ape. The big ape falls for Ann (Fay Wray), but then he's captured. He's taken to New York City and exhibited, is maltreated, and escapes. Eventually he climbs the Empire State Building with his beloved Ann in hand, pursued by the authorities.

In spite of the opening quote from what is called an "old Arabian proverb" and all the speechifying by Denham (Robert Armstrong), *King Kong*'s mythic qualities come as much from the clash of nature and civilization as from the old beauty-and-beast element. Anyone who hates setting the alarm clock and who has thought about dropping out of the rat race can't help but suppress a little cheer for Kong as he smashes a commuter train and rampages around the urban jungle. The movie beautifully sets up the audience for the first appearance of the monster by slowly releasing the information about the purpose of filmmaker Denham's voyage to Skull Mountain. He discovers a girl (Wray) at a soup kitchen (the only evidence of the Depression in the movie) to star in his new adventure film; they are far out at sea before Denham produces the old map to the unchartered island.

No one would have predicted from Bruce Cabot's wooden performance that he would have such a long career in movies. The dated dialogue and acting simply point out all the more how much the movie depends on its special effects, created by Willis O'Brien. The rear projection and the use of the optical printer had not attempted such depth of field effects until this film. These were realized through painted-glass backgrounds at different distances from the camera, an effect Walt Disney would later use in *Snow White*.

King Kong set many standards for movie spectacles: the teasing, delayed appearance of the monster (a rule Steven Spielberg follows in *Jaws*); the effects-driven vehicle with minimal attention given to character, acting, and dialogue; the plot as a series of memorable set pieces (as in the sacrifice scene with Fay Wray, Kong fighting the tyrannosaurus, the escape from Kong's lair, the destruction of the native village); the marketing of the film as an event (this one

Did you know?...

When RKO re-released the film in 1938, the Hays Office, which hadn't been in effect in 1933, demanded that some of the more graphic scenes be removed. A full restoration was not done until 1969.

was billed on its initial release as "the eighth wonder of the world"); and the re-release of the film to new audiences. Most of all, as a movie spectacle, *King Kong* came to be regarded as something that audiences had never seen before.

Atop the Empire State Building, Kong does battle with some pesky airplanes.

Cast: Fay Wray (Ann Darrow), Robert Armstrong (Carl Denham), Bruce Cabot (Jack Driscoll), Frank Reicher (Captain Englehorn), Sam Hardy (Weston), Noble Johnson (native chief), Steve Clemente (Witch King), James Flavin (second mate), Vera Lewis (woman at the theater) **Cinematographer:** Edward Linden, J.O. Taylor, Vernon L. Walker **Composer:** Max Steiner **Producer:** Merian C. Cooper, Ernest B. Schoedsack, and David O. Selznick for RKO **Running Time:** 105 minutes **Format:** VHS, LV.

They Might Be Giants . . .

The original *Frankenstein* (1931), though it runs for only seventy-one minutes, can lay claim to attaining a mythic stature in its Faustian scientist who hungers to create life. Original prints deleted the line Colin Clive deliriously and blasphemously babbles after the creature first moves, "Now I know what it feels like to be God!" James Whale also directed the first sequel, *The Bride of Frankenstein* (1935); the epic dimension in *Son of Frankenstein* (1939) largely comes from the spectacular, medieval sets by James Otterson. In one scene Wolf Frankenstein (Basil Rathbone) and his family sit at dinner in a spacious hall under two spires capped with gargoyles that extend out over their table, a sinister and effective way of foreshadowing the dark doings still to come. Universal eventually started putting multiple monsters in their 1940s horror films, but not much else in these later films can claim distinction. *Frankenstein Meets the Wolf Man* (1943) takes a while to gets its action going, and *House of Frankenstein*, in spite of a title that promises something resembling an ancient Greek curse, is a disappointment. The sense of parody that eventually sets in when a genre has already peaked may be found in the enjoyable mixture of comedy and horror in *Abbott and Costello Meet Frankenstein* (1948).

The increasing emphasis on special effects that has marked so many movie genres since *Star Wars* has revealed itself in monster epics mostly through more gore. John Carpenter's 1982 remake of Howard Hawks' 1951 science-fiction thriller *The Thing* rejects the subtleties of the original in favor of a series of truly frightening set pieces in which the members of an Antarctic crew try to determine how many of their number have been possessed by the chameleon-like alien. A movement to get away from cinematic traditions of horror and return to literary source material may be seen in both *Bram Stoker's Dracula* (1992) and *Mary Shelley's Frankenstein* (1994). The first, directed by Francis Ford Coppola, is a much stronger film with a number of indelible images. *Godzilla*, the marketing blockbuster of the summer of 1998 with a reported budget of $120 million, organizes itself into a series of set pieces that eventually includes the need to kill off his/her babies.

MUSICAL

Camelot
Carousel
Evita
The King and I
Oklahoma!
Oliver!
Paint Your Wagon
The Sound of Music
South Pacific
West Side Story

Camelot

1967 – Joshua Logan – ♫♫

The story of King Arthur exerts a powerful hold over the minds of almost any generation. This film version of the Broadway musical is a retrospective: on the eve of his last battle, Arthur reflects about meeting Guinevere and establishing the new British culture of Camelot. All the elements are there—musings about Merlin and pulling the sword from the stone, the establishment of the Round Table with its motto of "Might For Right," the sinister threat of the bastard son Mordred, the love triangle involving Lancelot and the Queen, and the emblematic sword Excalibur. In addition to the timeless strength of the story, the movie is visually beautiful. Splendid costumes and sets make the Middle Ages look quite opulent, and colors and costumes dazzle the eye. Specific scenes linger in the memory, like the wedding scene lit only by candles and the luminous faces of the happy couple or the fabulous bird-like robes and headgear of the regal pair. All the pomp and pageantry of chivalry are there on the screen.

So, why is this film one of the great box-office disasters? First, it is a musical and the story must be conveyed by song. None of the principal actors have a memorable voice, though all are serviceable. Guinevere is too whimsical, Arthur too quirky, Lancelot too operatic. They find their dominant mood, and vary little during the entire three hours. Furthermore, the three hours is the larger problem. Never has a film cried out for editing more than this one. Interludes drag by endlessly, whether they are Arthur explaining the concepts of law or the lovers musing on their futures. When the viewer watches banished knights trudge away, he wants to shout "Pick up the pace!" both to the knights and the director who thought this scene was needed.

Camelot does have some strengths that poor editing and singing cannot diminish. First is the essential humanity of the characters. These people are like us. Arthur finds it a little daunting suddenly to be king; Guinevere and Lancelot want to do the right thing but their attraction is just too strong; even Mordred's hatred mirrors our own dark sides. And the pain of adultery is almost palpable: three people who all love each other are caught in a situation that makes them all suffer dreadfully while hurting their loved ones as well. And the ending has such hope—hope that, in spite of our capacity to foul things up, great ideas do

survive and flourish, and the future will be the better because we strive to make the great ideas come true.

King Arthur (Richard Harris) takes Guinevere (Vanessa Redgrave) as his Queen.

Songs: "I Wonder What the King is Doing Tonight," "The Simple Joys of Maidenhood," "Camelot," "C'est Moi," "Guinevere," "The Lusty Month of May," "Follow Me," "How To Handle a Woman," "Then You May Take Me to the Fair," "If Ever I Would Leave You," "I Loved You Once in Silence," and "What Do the Simple Folk Do?"

Cast: Richard Harris (King Arthur), David Hemmings (Mordred), Lionel Jeffries (Pellinore), Franco Nero (Lancelot), Vanessa Redgrave (Queen Guinevere), **Screenwriter:** Alan Jay Lerner **Cinematographer:** Richard H. Kline **Composer:** Ken Darby, Frederick Loewe, Alfred Newman **Producer:** Jack Warner for Warner Bros. **Running Time:** 177 minutes **Format:** VHS, LV **Awards:** Academy Awards, 1968: Adapted Score, Art direction, Costumes, Music Direction; Nominations: Cinematography, Sound; Golden Globe Awards: Actor—Musical/Comedy (Richard Harris), Song ("If Ever I Would Leave You"), Score.

Carousel

1956 – Henry King – ♫♫♫

The musicals of Rodgers and Hammerstein proved ideal for widescreen treatment, and in the mid-1950s the new emphasis on spectacle in Hollywood (an effort to win audiences away from television) led to a succession of screen versions of their stage hits. One advantage of this is that in the movie theater, the extra-wide dimensions of the screen capture beautifully the plains of Oklahoma, or Bali Hai in the South Pacific, or the Austrian alps over which the Von Trapps climb.

You don't have to be a video purist, however, to recognize that those long, rectangular CinemaScope 55 images look sloppily composed on the squarish television screen. Those who complain about letterboxing because it blacks out the top and bottom of the TV picture should try to appreciate (or even to recognize) the visual design of *Carousel* by looking through the keyhole of this panned-and-scanned version. Hardly five minutes pass without a scene in which you're aware of important action and characters taking place off the sides of the TV image. Shirley Jones sings "If I Loved You" staring into empty space since Gordon MacRae is chopped off on the video tape. Even worse, dance numbers lose their sense of depth and perspective. In the song "June Is Bustin' Out All Over" and in Agnes De Mille's celebrated ballet, only two or three dancing couples and an assortment of arms and legs coming in and out of the television frame replace balanced lines of dancers in careful symmetry in the original wide shots. *Oklahoma!* and *The Sound of Music* have already been issued in widescreen versions, and *Carousel* will look like a new film when it is, too.

Other weaknesses owe to the material and the filmmakers. Billy Bigelow (Gordon MacRae) is one of two heel-heroes in the long career of Richard Rodgers (along with *Pal Joey*), but Billy lacks Joey's rich personality. The clambake and ballet scenes in *Carousel* are done on soundstages, and they fit awkwardly with the location footage shot in Maine. The scenes that take place in heaven have not had their theatricality reimagined in screen terms. In the opening, Billy, a former carnival barker, sits on a ladder among cardboard-spangled stars hanging from a ceiling when he asks about his loved ones back on earth. He hears from a character named Starkeeper (Gene Lockhart) about his wife Julie (Shirley Jones) and their daughter, who is about to graduate from high

Carnival barker Billy (Gordon MacRae) charms innocent mill girl Julie (Shirley Jones).

school. The film presents in flashback Billy and Julie's courtship, marriage, and Billy's early death. Billy wins the chance to go back for one day and speak anonymously to his daughter. The score features some of Rodgers and Hammerstein's most memorable songs ("You'll Never Walk Alone," "Soliloquy"), but the presentation on video necessarily plays a big part in the film's reception.

Songs: "If I Loved You," "Soliloquy," "You'll Never Walk Alone," "What's the Use of Wond'rin?" "When I Marry Mr. Snow," "When the Children Are Asleep," "A Real Nice Clambake," "Carousel Ballet," "Carousel Waltz," "Blow High, Blow Low," "June Is Bustin' Out All Over," "Stonecutters Cut It on Stone," "There's Nothin' So Bad for a Woman," and "You're a Queer One, Julie Jordan."

Cast: Gordon MacRae (Billy Bigelow), Shirley Jones (Julie Jordan), Cameron Mitchell (Jigger Craigin), Barbara Ruick (Carrie Pipperidge), Claramae Turner (Cousin Nettie), Robert Rounseville (Mr. Enoch Snow), Gene Lockhart (Starkeeper/Dr. Selden), Audrey Christie (Mrs. Mullin), Susan Luckey (Louise Bigelow), William LeMassena (heavenly friend), John Dehner (Mr. Bascombe), Jacques D'Amboise (Louise's dancing partner), Richard Deacon (policeman), Tor Johnson (strong man), Sylvia Stanton (contortionist) **Screenwriter:** Phoebe Ephron, Henry Ephron, Benjamin Glazer **Cinematographer:** Charles G. Clarke **Composer:** Richard Rodgers **Producer:** Henry Ephron for Twentieth Century Fox **Running Time:** 128 minutes **Format:** VHS, LV **Box Office:** The film lost $2M on its initial release.

Evita
1996 – Alan Parker – ♫♫♫♪

> "You let down your people, Evita. You were supposed to have been immortal."
> Che (Antonio Banderas)

Few people outside politics knew much about the life and death of Eva Peron until she burst onto the world's musical stages in the early 1980's in Andrew Lloyd Webber's hit musical *Evita*. But hers is a life so melodramatic, so filled with "Rainbow Highs" and degrading lows that, if she had not lived, some writer would have had to invent her. On one level, Eva's story (as she sings) is quite usual: young bastard child seeks new future in the big city of Buenos Aires, finds powerful men friends to sleep with her and promote her, marries a military man/politician who rises to the top and takes her with him, and dies tragically of cancer when she is 33.

On another level, however, is a more complex story of Eva Peron. Who was she, really? The saint whose foundation built hundreds of schools, hospitals,

and housing developments for the poor of her country? The swindler who used millions of dollars of volunteer contributions to dress and bejewel herself and her cronies? The simple woman who understood the needs of her people and helped translate them to her powerful husband? The manipulator who tried to grab as much personal power as she could? The movie does a fine job of presenting the complex personality of Eva. The viewer both loves and hates her, sympathizes and condemns her. And the exquisite location shooting and detail enliven the film.

Antonio Banderas, who can sing as well as act, presents a much stronger Che than in the stage version of the musical. This character is not the legendary guerilla (who didn't figure in Argentine history, anyway); he is the outside observer—waiter, journalist, citizen, patriot—hoping for the best from Evita and her regime, but smart and cynical enough to see the fraud behind the surface. Finally, he speaks (or sings) for all of us; when we dare to hope for too much from frail human leaders, we will be disappointed, and "It's our funeral, too."

Madonna stars as Argentina's controversial first lady, Eva Peron.

Did you know?...

The movie used 40,000 extras in period dress on 320 different sets involving 24,000 props.

Songs: "A Cinema in Buenos Aires," "Requiem for Evita," "Oh What a Circus," "On This Night of a Thousand Stars," "Eva and Magadi," "Eva Beware of the City," "Buenos Aires," "Another Suitcase in Another Hall," "Goodnight and Thank You," "The Lady's Got Potential," "Charity Concert," "The Art of the Possible," "I'd Be Surprisingly Good For You," "Hello and Goodbye," "Peron's Latest Flame," "A New Argentina," "On the Balcony of the Casa Rosada," "Don't Cry For Me Argentina," "High Flying, Adored," "Rainbow High," "Rainbow Tour," "The Actress Hasn't Learned the Lines," "And the Money Kept Rolling In," "Partido Feminista," "She is a Diamond," "Santa Evita," "Waltz for Eva and Che," "Your Little Body's Slowly Breaking Down," "You Must Love Me" and "Lament."

Cast: Madonna (Eva Peron), Antonio Banderas (Che), Jonathan Pryce (Juan Peron), Jimmy Nail (Augustin Magaldi), Victoria Sus (Dona Juana), Julian Littman (Brother Juan), Olga Menediz (Blanca), Laura Pallas (Elisea), Julia Worsley (Erminda), Maria Lujan Hidalgo (Young Eva), Andrea Corr (Peron's Young Mistress), Gabriel Kraisman (Cinema Manager), Alan Parker (Tormented Film Director), Eva Vari (Senora Magaldi), Luis Boccia (Senor Jabon) **Screenwriter:** Andrew Lloyd Webber, Tim Rice, Alan Parker, Oliver Stone **Cinematographer:** Darius Khondji **Composer:** Andrew Lloyd Webber **Producer:** Alan Parker, Robert Stigwood, and Andrew Vajna for Cinergi and Dirty Hands Productions; released by Hollywood Pictures **Running Time:** 134 minutes **Format:** VHS, LV **Awards:** Academy Awards, 1997: Music, Song ("You Must Love Me"); Nominations: Art Direction/Set Decoration, Cinematography, Editing, Sound; Golden Globe Awards, 1997: Actress—Musical/Comedy (Madonna), Film—Comedy/Musical, Song ("You Must Love Me"); Nominations: Actor—Musical/Comedy (Antonio Banderas); Director (Alan Parker); British Academy Awards, 1996: Adapted Screenplay; MTV Movie Awards, 1997: Nominations: Female Performance (Madonna), Song ("Don't Cry for Me, Argentina") **Box Office:** $23M.

The King and I
1956 – Walter Lang – ♫♫♫♫

> ### "Etcetera! Etcetera! Etcetera!"
> The King (Yul Brynner), using his new command of English.

The classic film rendition of the Rodgers and Hammerstein Broadway hit is based on both a book by Margaret Landon and a movie *Anna and the King of Siam*. The story follows a widowed Victorian English woman (Deborah Kerr) who goes to Thailand in the 1860s to become governess to the many children of the King of Siam (Yul Brynner). While Mrs. Anna loves the children, she clashes immediately with the strong-willed king—who is entranced by both the ways of the West and a woman strong enough to stand up to him.

Mrs. Anna (Deborah Kerr) shows the King (Yul Brynner) the way the English dance.

Did you know?...

Brynner played (live and on film) more than 4,000 performances of the King of Siam.

Choreographed by Jerome Robbins, the film is deliberately stagey, but the staginess is part of the charm: stair steps of identically dressed royal children presented in parade to Mrs. Anna and the King, a familiar yet foreign ballet of *Uncle Tom's Cabin*, and the spectacular sweep of hoop skirts in a land of bare feet. There is such energy in the film; Yul Brynner's "A Puzzlement" number is a delight. When Anna and the King finally meet physically in "Shall We Dance," the result is one of the finest dance scenes in a Hollywood musical. Some Broadway conventions, however, like the tragic subplot of Tuptim (Rita Moreno, singing voice assisted by Leona Gordon) and LunTha (Carlos Rivas, singing voice by Reuben Fuentes), translate rather woodenly to the screen. The King's death of a broken heart as the Crown Prince assumes the new role stretches the viewer's credulity, but the emotional impact is still strong. Brynner became a legend with the role, and the screen offers ample evidence of his dynamic charisma.

This film represents one of the first dubbing jobs for singer Marni Nixon, who had been a former messenger at MGM. Here Nixon's singing replaces the voice of Deborah Kerr on all of her high notes (according to John Eastman in his book *Retakes*) and for the entire song "Hello, Young Lovers." Nixon went on to sing the film parts of Maria in *West Side Story* and, most famously, Audrey Hepburn in *My Fair Lady*. Robert Wise gave Nixon her few seconds of on-screen time when he cast her as one of the singing nuns in *The Sound of Music*.

Songs: "Shall We Dance," "Getting To Know You," "Hello, Young Lovers," "We Kiss in a Shadow," "I Whistle a Happy Tune," "March of the Siamese Children," "I Have Dreamed" "A Puzzlement," "Something Wonderful," "The Small House of Uncle Thomas," and "Song of the King."

Cast: Deborah Kerr (Anna Leonowens), Yul Brynner (King Mongkut of Siam), Rita Moreno (Tuptim), Martin Benson (Kralahome), Terry Saunders (Lady Thiang), Rex Thompson (Louis Leonowens), Carlos Rivas (Lun Tha), Patrick Adiarte (Prince Chulalongkorn), Alan Mowbray (British Ambassador), Geoffrey Toone (Ramsey), Charles Irvin (Captain Orton), Robert Baras (Keeper of the Dogs), Marion Jim (Simon Legree), Michicko Iseri (Angel in Ballet), William Yip (High Priest) **Screenwriter:** Margaret Landon, Ernest Lehman **Cinematographer:** Leon Shamroy **Composer:** Richard Rogers, Ken Darby, Alfred Newman **Producer:** Charles Brackett for Twentieth Century Fox **Running Time:** 133 minutes **Format:** VHS, LV **Awards:** Academy Awards 1957: Actor (Yul Brynner), Art Direction/Set Decoration (Color), Costume Design (Color), Sound, Scoring of a Musical; Nominations: Actress (Deborah Kerr), Color Cinematography, Director (Walter Lang), Picture; Golden Globe Awards 1957: Actress—Musical/Comedy (Deborah Kerr), Film—Musical/Comedy **Box Office:** $8.5M.

Oklahoma!

1955 – Fred Zinnemann – ♫♫♫♪

Maybe the most popular of all Richard Rodgers and Oscar Hammerstein's musicals, *Oklahoma!* is the classic American story of family and community. The 1943 opening of the play launched the collaboration of the duo, who based their work on *Green Grow the Lilacs*, an earlier play by Lynn Riggs. Laurey (Shirley Jones), the farm girl and Curly (Gordon McRae), the cowboy, fall in love, spar playfully with one another, misunderstand each other, quarrel, then reconcile and marry to start a new family on the Oklahoma frontier at the turn of the century. They are threatened by sinister farmhand Jud (Rod Steiger), who covets Jones. In the meantime, a community is being forged as well. One of the major scenes is the "raising" of a schoolhouse, with the chorus singing about the territory becoming a state, and the differences between former enemies dissipating as the "farmer and the cowman will be friends." Unity, loyalty, and hope are the great values of the music and the action. Humor also plays a major role, especially in the comic subplot of the love triangle of Ado Annie (Gloria Grahame), Will (Gene Nelson), and Ali Hakim (Eddie Albert).

The Todd-A-O high resolution color filming, used for the first time in this film, is perfect for crisp landscapes and sparkling white farmhouses (though the film was released in a Cinemascope version a year later). The "surrey with the fringe on top" springs from imagination to real life as the camera pans beneath the wheels to ducks scattering along a country road. Shirley Jones' Laurey is the picture of blonde, wholesome youth and energy—domestic yet spirited, vulnerable yet confident in the future ahead of her as a prairie wife. Curly the cowboy doesn't have to woo her much with words (or songs); they are so visibly right for each other. Paul Newman and James Dean had tested for the role of Curly, and Joanne Woodward auditioned for Laurey. Rod Steiger's Jud Fry is a menace; he is virile but coarse, ignorant yet cunning. He is the loner, and the frontier community has no place for loners. The only way Jud can be a part of the group is not through giving money for the school—even his money seems tainted—but through starring at his own funeral, parodied in the bizarre but funny number "Poor Jud is Daid."

Oklahoma! is as much American myth as it is American musical theater. The songs mirror our hopes ("People Will Say We're in Love") and our flaws ("I

> "Sure, I wanted to marry her when I saw the moonlight gleaming on the barrel of her father's shotgun."
> Ali Hakim (Eddie Albert) on marriage.

Did you know?...
The film was actually shot on location in Arizona.

Laurey (Shirley Jones) listens to Curly (Gordon MacRae) sing "Oh, what a Beautiful Mornin.'"

Cain't Say No") and our boundless energy (the show-stopping signature song "Oklahoma!"); the dance numbers, choreographed by Agnes de Mille, trace our experience, our dreams, and our nightmares. Statehood and weddings: both are ceremonies of hope for the future, and that hope shines through this film version of a beloved musical classic.

Songs: "Oh, What a Beautiful Mornin'," "Surrey with the Fringe on Top," "I Cain't Say No," "Many a New Day," "People Will Say We're in Love," "Poor Jud is Daid," "All 'Er Nuthin'," "Everything's Up to Date in Kansas City," "The Farmer and the Cowman," and "Out of My Dreams."

Cast: Gordon MacRae (Curly), Gloria Grahame (Ado Annie Carnes), Gene Nelson (Will Parker), Charlotte Greenwood (Aunt Eller), Shirley Jones (Laurey Williams), Eddie Albert (Ali Hakim), James Whitmore (Carnes), Rod Steiger (Jud Fry), Barbara Lawrence (Gertie), Jay C. Flippen (Skidmore), Roy Barcroft (Marshal), James Mitchell (Dream Curly), Bambi Linn (Dream Laurey), Jennie Workman (Dancer), Virginia Bosler (Dancer) **Screenwriter:** Sonya Levien, William Ludwig **Cinematographer:** Floyd Crosby, Robert Surtees **Composer:** Robert Russell Bennett, Jay Blackton, Adolph Deutsch, Richard Rodgers **Producer:** Arthur Hornblow Jr. **Running Time:** 145 minutes **Format:** VHS, LV **Awards:** Academy Awards 1955: Sound, Score of a Musical; Color Cinematography, Editing **Box Office:** $7M.

Oliver!
1968 – Carol Reed – 🦴🦴🦴🦴

Most people have heard of Charles Dickens and his famous fictional orphan Oliver Twist, but few realize that the 26-year-old writer was one of the first men to explore the link between poverty, ignorance, and crime. Victorians looked upon criminals (children or adult) as morally depraved and innately bad, and more than forty crimes were punishable by death during that century. Enter Dickens, and his picture of a young boy, delicate and naturally kind, starved and beaten and sold by a system that denies his essential humanity in London of 1830. This same boy finds the first kindness and care of his life in a den of thieves. They are cynical, of course, hoping to transform him into a pickpocket, but Oliver is torn between following the impulses of right and being loyal to the gang. Add a touch of passion, several kidnappings, a housebreaking, and a gory murder, and you have the plot of *Oliver Twist*.

"Please, sir, can I have some more?"
Oliver (Mark Lester)

"MORE?!"
Beadle Bumble (Harry Secombe)

Young Oliver (Mark Lester) with Fagin's pickpocketing boys.

What is remarkable about this musical is that it keeps the basic attitude of the novel. Yes, there are songs and dance numbers aplenty, many laced with rueful humor. Nancy (Shani Wallis) sings a comic ballad about being judged harshly by those who "don't have to sin to eat." There is color and motion and choreography—but what a difference between the dark chaos of the pubs and alleys, and the light order and symmetry of the world of the rich. No wonder Oliver (Mark Lester) wants to buy and keep "this beautiful morning" when he supposes himself safe with kind Mr. Brownlow (Joseph O'Conor).

Repeating the role he first perfected on stage, Ron Moody as Fagin walks away with the picture, and renders the gang leader/fence so well that his portrayal supplants any imaginary one when the reader returns to the novel. He has that perfect blend of high spirits and self-interest, sneaky cruelty and sly humor—he sings his own motto when he reviews his situation and realizes "I'm a bad un and a bad un I will stay." Even the horribly sinister Bill Sikes (Oliver

Did you know?...

Oliver Reed was the nephew of the film's director Carol Reed.

Reed) makes one stop and wonder what childhood formed him thus. And Dickens himself realized that the prostitute Nancy was the character best drawn from life: belonging to the streets from infancy, longing to escape, and yet bound by cords of emotion and loyalty to her dark world and its people. Musical and drama blend seamlessly here to create Hollywood storytelling at its best and truest to the spirit of the original. At least eight other versions of the tale have been filmed, including Disney's animated *Oliver and Company*, with the characters depicted as cats and dogs.

Songs: "Food, Glorious Food," "Oliver," "You've Got to Pick a Pocket or Two," "I'd Do Anything," "Be Back Soon," "As Long As He Needs Me," "Boys for Sale," "Consider Yourself," "It's a Fine Life," "Oom Pah Pah," "Reviewing the Situation," "Where is Love?" and "Who Will Buy?"

Cast: Ron Moody (Fagin), Shani Wallis (Nancy), Oliver Reed (Bill Sikes), Harry Secombe (Mr. Bumble), Mark Lester (Oliver), Jack Wild (Artful Dodger), Hugh Griffith (Magistrate), Sheila White (Bet), Peggy Mount (Mrs. Bumble), Joseph O'Conor (Mr. Brownlow), Wensley Pithey (Dr. Grimwig), Hylda Baker (Mrs. Sowerberry), Kenneth Cranham (Noah Claypole), Leonard Rossiter (Mr. Sowerberry), Fred Emney (Workhouse Chairman) **Screenwriter:** Lionel Bart, Vernon Harris **Cinematographer:** Oswald Morris **Composer:** Lionel Bart, Johnny Green **Producer:** Donald Albery and John Woolf for Columbia **Running Time:** 153 minutes **Format:** VHS, LV **Awards:** Academy Awards, 1969: Adapted Score, Art Direction/Set Decoration, Director (Carol Reed), Picture, Sound, Score, Special Oscar to Onna White for choreography; Nominations: Actor (Ron Moody), Adapted Screenplay, Cinematography, Costume Design, Editing, Supporting Actor (Jack Wild); Golden Globe Awards, 1969: Actor—Musical/Comedy (Ron Moody), Film—Musical/Comedy; National Board of Review Awards, 1968: 10 Best Films of the Year **Budget:** $10M.

Paint Your Wagon
1969 – Joshua Logan – 🎵🎵🎵

"Where am I going? I don't know! . . . But who gives a damn! We're on our way!" Few can resist those infectious opening lines of this infectiously energetic musical set during the 1849 gold rush in California. The sentiments are our own; most Americans still have a shred of the pioneering spirit about them somewhere—thus our love affair with sport utility vehicles. The opening number is also matched by the beauty of the opening shot, a still life of a wagon train in sepia that turns colored and then into panoramic live action. The rest of the

> "Pardner, there's a shifty side to you I'm just beginning to appreciate."
> Ben (Lee Marvin)

Prospecting team Ben (Lee Marvin) and Pardner (Clint Eastwood).

action is just as quick and comic. Extra-crusty Ben Rumson (Lee Marvin), who is the epitome of the mountain man, teams up with the obvious tenderfoot Pardner, played with remarkable success by the (more clean-cut) Clint Eastwood. This Eastwood character is a long way from "make my day" Dirty Harry; he even sings numbers with titles like "I Talk to the Trees."

The plot is funny, though preposterous. Two mining partners in gold-rush California agree to share the Mormon wife (Jean Seberg, with Anita Gordon's singing voice) that one of them has bought. She is agreeable, because she loves them each in his own way. In No Name City, whose very existence began with the importation of prostitutes from San Francisco, such arrangements are socially and morally quite all right. That is, until a farming party with conventional values arrives in camp. The viewer's sympathy in the movie, regardless of what he feels in real life, is clearly with the trio. After all, as Ben so engagingly sings, who wants to join forces with those who "civilize left and civilize right/Till nothing is left, till nothing is right?" And young farmer Horton (Tom Ligon), with a natural bent for dissipation, is a delightful protégé for Ben after the general disappointment of Pardner's basic decency.

The movie is not without its rough spots, mostly caused by the conversion of stage play into film. Written by Alan Jay Lerner, the script is based on an adaptation by Paddy Chayevsky of Lerner's book for the 1951 Broadway musical. Lerner tossed out half the songs he had written with composer Frederick Loewe for the play, adding five new ones with music by Andre Previn. The natural landscape (filmed in Oregon) dwarfs the less rousing musical numbers, the action drags between crises, and the final comic scene of No Name City's collapse goes on far too long. Location shooting and musicals may be combinable; add slapstick to the mix and it just does not work. But the melodies, hilarious ones like "Hand Me Down That Can o' Beans" and haunting ones like "They Call the Wind Maria" make the overall experience worthwhile and memorable.

Songs: "I Talk to the Trees," "I Still See Elisa," "I'm On My Way," "Hand Me Down That Can o' Beans," "Whoop-Ti-Ay," "They Call the Wind Maria," "There's a Coach Comin' In," "Wandrin' Star," "Best Things," "The First Thing You Know," "Gold Fever," "The Gospel of No Name City," and "A Million Miles Away Behind the Door."

Cast: Lee Marvin (Ben Rumson), Clint Eastwood (Pardner Sylvester Newel), Jean Seberg (Elizabeth), Harve Presnell (Rotten Luck Willy), Ray Walston (Mad Jack Duncan), Tom Ligon (Horton Fenty), Alan Dexter (Parson), Alan Baxter (Mr. Fenty), Paula Trueman (Mrs. Fenty), Robert Easton (Atwell), Terry Jenkins (Joe Mooney), William O'Connell (Horace Tabor), Sue Casey (Sarah Woodling), John Mitchum (Jacob Woodling), Karl Bruck (Schermerhorn) **Screenwriter:** Paddy Chayefsky, Alan Lerner, Frederick Loewe **Cinematographer:** William A. Fraker **Composer:** Frederick Loewe, Andre Previn, Nelson Riddle **Producer:** Alan Jay Lerner and Tom Shaw for Paramount **Running Time:** 164 minutes **Format:** VHS, LV **Awards:** Academy Awards 1969: Nominations: Scoring of a Musical.

The Sound of Music

1965 – Robert Wise – ♫♫♫♩

Initially given a cool critical reception, *The Sound of Music* became the box office king of its time. Few movies have generated such extreme comments, both positive and negative, as this musical about the novice governess who marries a widowed father of seven children while the Nazi threat looms in Austria in the late 1930s. How do you solve a problem like *The Sound of Music*? Is its sweetness as refreshing as its defenders say or as saccharin as its detractors insist? It is wrong to see the movie as a cinematic ink blot test that brings to the surface either the rosy-tinted or jaundiced attitudes of its viewer. The truth is that both elements—the idealized and the self-deprecating—appear throughout the film in effective and interesting ways.

Based on a true story, the film seems to be alternately swelling with sweetness and then deflating itself back to reality, a cinematic breathing exercise that works amazingly well. No sooner do the seven Von Trapp children march in wearing matching outfits and crisply responding to a series of whistles from their father (Christopher Plummer) than their new governess Fraulein Maria (Julie Andrews in a mature role following *Mary Poppins*) skewers the Captain by asking what whistle she should use to summon him. As the children later fall in for another song, Elsa the Baroness (Eleanor Parker) asks Max (Richard Haydn) under her breath why he didn't tip her off to bring her harmonica.

Chatting with Nazi officials, Max returns a Nazi salute with an indifferent scratch of the head. The opening scene contains a nun critical of Maria. And so it goes, alternating from sugary sentiment to a slightly darker version of the family's predicament. More subtly, a moment like the majestic "Climb Every Mountain" is staged in the dark, burnished glow of the Mother Abbess' quarters, a visual design that nicely contrasts with the soaring lyrics.

The credit for treading this tightrope belongs as much to screenwriter Ernest Lehman, who had worked on the script for over six months, as to Robert Wise, who was brought in to direct as a replacement for William Wyler. Adapting the Rodgers and Hammerstein musical, which starred Mary Martin, Lehman rearranged a few songs, making "My Favorite Things" a song Maria sings to the children rather than to the Mother Abbess, as on stage. Wise and Lehman want-

Governess Maria (Julie Andrews) entertains the Von Trapp children on a mountaintop.

ed the part of the Captain rounded and humanized from the martinet in the stage musical. The casting of intense Plummer (Wise worked hard to talk the classically trained Canadian actor into accepting the part) was a conscious effort to strengthen a weak element of the story materials. The vastness and beauty of the Salzburg exteriors may keep the sugary aspects in check as well. Some would be surprised, and others wouldn't, to learn that Lehman, who adapted this script with its singing nuns and sweet children, also wrote Hitchcock's sly and cynical *North by Northwest*. Though different themes, both scripts are polished, professional jobs. Even for the many who put up their defenses, this movie has a way of coming in under the radar. As Lehman himself said, "I'm sorry, I can't help it, but every time I see *The Sound of Music*, I cry a little, sigh a little. It makes life seem to have such beautiful possibilities."

Songs: "I Have Confidence in Me," "Something Good," "The Sound of Music," "Preludium," "Morning Hymn," "Alleluia," "How Do You Solve a Problem Like Maria?" "Sixteen Going on Seventeen," "My Favorite Things," "Climb Every Mountain," "Edelweiss," "Do-Re-Mi," "The Lonely Goatherd," and "So Long, Farewell."

Cast: Julie Andrews (Maria), Christopher Plummer (Captain von Trapp), Eleanor Parker (the Baroness), Richard Haydn (Max Detweiler), Peggy Wood (Mother Abbess), Charmian Carr (Liesl), Heather Menzies (Louisa), Nicholas Hammond (Friedrich), Duane Chase (Kurt), Angela Cartwright (Brigitta), Debbie Turner (Marta), Kym Karath (Gretl), Daniel Truhite (Rolfe), Norma Varden (Frau Schmidt), Gil Stuart (Franz), Marni Nixon (Sister Sophia) **Screenwriter:** Ernest Lehman **Cinematographer:** Ted McCord **Composer:** Richard Rodgers **Producer:** Robert Wise and Saul Chaplin for Twentieth Century Fox **Running Time:** 174 minutes **Format:** VHS, LV **Awards:** Academy Awards 1965: Adapted Score, Director (Robert Wise), Film Editing, Picture, Sound; Nominations: Actress (Julie Andrews); Art Direction/Set Decoration (Color), Color Cinematography, Costume Design (Color), Supporting Actress (Peggy Wood); Directors Guild of America Award 1965: Director (Robert Wise); Golden Globe Awards 1966: Actress—Musical/Comedy (Julie Andrews), Film—Musical/Comedy; National Board of Review Awards 1965: 10 Best Films of the Year **Budget:** $8M **Box Office:** $160M.

South Pacific
1958 – Joshua Logan – 🎬🎬

> "Is it true that all the planters on these islands—are they really running away from something?"
>
> Nellie (Mitzi Gaynor)

> "Who is not running away from something? There are fugitives everywhere."
>
> Emile (Rossano Brazzi)

One of Rodgers and Hammerstein's biggest Broadway hits, *South Pacific* has a score filled with American classics: "There is Nothing Like a Dame," "I'm Gonna Wash That Man Right Out of My Hair," and "Some Enchanted Evening." Based on James Michener's first best-seller, *Tales of the South Pacific*, the play has the surefire plot of wartime romance, exotic travel, and heroic sacrifice for one's country. But the energy and timing that fuel a Broadway hit are largely missing in the movie. The major production numbers are melodic and powerful, but between numbers, the story slows the pace too much. And cinematographer Leon Shamroy made what most contemporary audiences consider to be a huge mistake. Figuring that the island scenery and natural lighting would be too harsh for two full hours (heck, people save for a lifetime to spend two weeks in such lighting!), Shamroy shot major songs through colored filters, so that "Bali Hai" is blue and "Some Enchanted Evening" renders everything gold. This technique is far more distracting than the harshest natural light, and the viewer comes to dread the approach of the next wash of color.

A classic tale of wartime, the story follows people far from home in the midst of a different culture, forced to like or reject the foreignness of it all. Nellie Forbush (Mitzi Gaynor) loves French planter DeBeque (Rossano Brazzi) only to be horrified that he has children from his dead native wife. Meanwhile, Lt. Joe Cable (John Kerr) falls headlong in love with island girl Liat (France Nuyen), whose mother Bloody Mary (Juanita Hall) realizes the potential of marriage with an American officer. The endings are predictable: Nellie learns to love the half-caste children and embraces a new life, but Cable is unable to leave Philadelphia racism behind and marry Liat. However, he dies heroically in battle against the Japanese, presented as utterly foreign and detestable—making the question of tolerance a pretty limited one for this movie.

The true color location scenes are breathtaking, but most of the major songs are rather lifelessly staged; a native boar tooth dance (which the credits imply is authentic) looks like a Hollywood choreographer's idea of native rituals.

Navy nurse Nellie Forbush (Mitzi Gaynor) wants everyone to know that "I'm in Love with a Wonderful Guy."

Did you know?...

Director Joshua Logan also hated the scenes with color filters. He was told that he could delete them, but then producer Buddy Adler decided that it would be too costly.

The best songs are the comic ones, where the lyrics keep the viewer's focus rather than the visuals, like "Honey Bun," "Bloody Mary is the Girl I Love," and "There is Nothing Like a Dame." All in all, some Broadway hits are best left on Broadway.

Songs: "My Girl Back Home," "Dites-Moi," "Bali Hai," "Happy Talk," "A Cock-Eyed Optimist," "Soliloquies," "Some Enchanted Evening," "Bloody Mary," "I'm Gonna Wash That Man Right Out of My Hair," "Honey Bun," "There is Nothing Like a Dame," "I'm in Love with a Wonderful Guy," "This Nearly Was Mine," "Younger Than Springtime," and "You've Got to Be Carefully Taught."

Cast: Rossano Brazzi (Emile de Beque), Mitzi Gaynor (Ensign Nellie Forbush, USN), John Kerr (Lt. Joseph Cable, USMC), Ray Walston (Luther Billis), Juanita Hall (Bloody Mary), France Nuyen (Liat), Russ Brown (Capt. George Brackett, USN), Floyd Simmons (Com. Bill Harbison, USN), Tom Laughlin (Lt. Buzz Adams), Ken Clark (Stewpot), Candace Lee (Ngana), Warren Hsieh (Jerome), Doug McClure (Pilot), Buck Cless (Pilot) **Screenwriter:** Oscar Hammerstein, Joshua Logan, Paul Osborn **Cinematographer:** Leon Shamroy **Composer:** Richard Rodgers, Ken Darby, Alfred Newman **Producer:** Buddy Adler **Running Time:** 151 minutes **Format:** VHS, LV **Awards:** Academy Awards 1958: Sound; Nominations: Cinematography, Scoring of a Musical **Budget:** $6M **Box Office:** $16.5M.

West Side Story
1961 – Robert Wise, Jerome Robbins – ♪♪♪♪

This energetic musical inspired by *Romeo and Juliet* places the familiar story in 1950s New York among rival street gangs, the Jets (composed of Anglos) and the Sharks (composed of Puerto Ricans). Exteriors were shot at the current site of the Lincoln Center Performing Arts complex. Based on the stage play written by Arthur Laurents and directed by Jerome Robbins and retaining the brilliant Leonard Bernstein/Stephen Sondheim score, *West Side Story* tells of the ill-fated love between Tony (Richard Beymer), former member of the Jets, and Maria (Natalie Wood), sister to the leader of the Sharks, Bernardo (George Chakiris). After falling in love at first sight while at a dance, Tony and Maria find themselves in the midst of increasing conflict between the two gangs as the lovers defy the loyalties and biases of their respective backgrounds. Ultimately, immature gang mentality, violence, and prejudice run their course and result in tragedy for the two.

On one level, *West Side Story* is intriguing for the way it utilizes and re-interprets the plot of Shakespeare's play to comment on street gang life in the mid-twentieth century. The real magic of the film, however, lies in its ability to transport the audience into the surrealistic world of its unfolding drama. With enjoyable songs that capture the mood of the moment, thrilling choreographed movements that turn fights into dances and dances into silent conversations, and striking images that result from both the production design and the kinetic ener-gy of the camera, *West Side Story* creates a fascinating backdrop for the tale of the "star-crossed" lovers. Even the love between Tony and Maria, which is at once magical, intense, and fervently devoted, manages to remain believable. Wood and Beymer had their singing voices dubbed by Marni Nixon and Jim Bryant, respectively, while Rita Moreno was vocally bolstered by Betty Wand.

Throughout the film, though especially during the musical numbers, directors Robert Wise and Jerome Robbins choreograph and edit smoothly

Maria (Natalie Wood) meets with love Tony (Richard Beymer) on the fire escape.

paced sequences, each of which seems to tell a little story. The night of the rumble, for instance, includes a sequence prior to the actual confrontation that pieces together, in the form of continuing verses in the same song, parallel events from different characters' perspectives as they all prepare for the night; the flow of images, movement, and sound in this sequence is so harmonious and vibrant that the sequence could be described as a dance itself. The final scene brings the drama to an end with a somber sequence, also artistically choreographed, that closes the curtain on Tony's and Maria's struggle to love each other against all opposition, but it also offers a glimmer of hope that the tragedy may help lead to peace.

Songs: "Prologue," "Jet Song," "Something's Coming," "Dance at the Gym," "Maria," "America," "Tonight," "One Hand, One Heart," "Gee, Officer Krupke," "A Boy Like That," "I Feel Pretty," "Quintet," and "Somewhere."

Cast: Natalie Wood (Maria), Richard Beymer (Tony), Russ Tamblyn (Riff), Rita Moreno (Anita), George Chakiris (Bernardo), Simon Oakland (Lieutenant Schrank), Ned Glass (Doc), William Bramley (Officer Krupke), Tucker Smith (Ice), Tony Mordente (Action), David Winters (A-Rab), Eliot Field (Baby John), Bert Michaels (Snowboy), David Bean (Tiger), Robert Banas (Joyboy), John Astin (Glad Hand) **Screenwriter:** Arthur Laurents, Ernest Lehman **Cinematographer:** Daniel L. Fapp **Composer:** Leonard Bernstein **Producer:** Robert Wise and Saul Chapin for Twentieth Century Fox **Running Time:** 151 minutes **Format:** VHS, LV **Awards:** Academy Awards 1961: Art Direction/Set Decoration, Color Cinematography, Costume Design (Color), Director (Robert Wise, Jerome Robbins), Editing, Picture, Sound, Supporting Actor (George Chakiris), Supporting Actress (Rita Moreno), Scoring of a Musical; Nominations: Adapted Screenplay (Arthur Laurents, Ernest Lehman); Directors Guild of America Awards, 1961: Director (Robert Wise), Director (Jerome Robbins); Golden Globe Awards, 1962: Film—Musical/Comedy, Supporting Actor (George Chakiris), Supporting Actress (Rita Moreno); New York Film Critics Awards 1961: Film **Box Office:** $19M.

They Might Be Giants . . .

When Al Jolson started talking to the audience in *The Jazz Singer* (1927)—"Wait a minute, wait a minute! You ain't heard nothin' yet"—he assured that musical's place in cinema history, although it was the musicals throughout the long career of Busby Berkeley that brought a showman's love of epic theatricalism to the screen. Berkeley's fondness for overhead shots, rigidly geometrical patterns, and latent sexuality (in one water number, a swimmer navigates through a line of girls that slowly parts like the teeth of an opening zipper) gives a sense of kaleidoscopic fun to classics like *42nd Street* (1933), the proto-typical backstage musical, and *Gold Diggers of 1933*. The RKO musicals of Fred Astaire and Ginger Rogers, especially *Top Hat* (1935) and *Swing Time* (1936), are more cinematic than theatrical, and thanks to the talents of the stars and the films' many gifted composers (George and Ira Gershwin, Irving Berlin, Jerome Kern) their classics continue to live on. (These two films also sport two of the nicest "meet cutes" of romantic comedy. The first culminates in Astaire's sand dance in a hotel room, the second in the song and dance "Pick Yourself Up.")

Later musicals that could claim at least partial epic status include *Meet Me In St. Louis* (1944), where the family's love for their midwestern city on the eve of the 1903 World's Fair is rendered in mythic terms. Arthur Freed, who pro-duced this film for MGM, also set the musical free from the sound stage with *On the Town* (1949), in which the location scenes, the dances by Jerome Robbins, and the athleticism of Gene Kelly, give the film great life. *An American in Paris* (1951) and *Singin' in the Rain* (1952), two other Freed MGM musicals with Kelly, also show great imagination and visual flair. The widescreen musicals from 1955-1967 that coincided with the road-show exhibition format relied often on length and scale to achieve spectacle; their decline around 1968 has been followed by other isolated successes like *Grease* (1978), probably the most successful musical of the 1970s.

ROMANCE

Casablanca

Cyrano de Bergerac

Doctor Zhivago

The English Patient

Far and Away

Far From the Madding Crowd

Farewell My Concubine

From Here to Eternity

Gone With The Wind

The Greatest Show on Earth

The Horse Whisperer

Ivanhoe

The Last of the Mohicans

Out of Africa

Ryan's Daughter

The Story of Adele H.

The Wind and the Lion

Casablanca

1942 – Michael Curtiz – 🦴🦴🦴🦴

The sense of place that most epics seek to achieve is accomplished in this studio-bound film less through creating a realistic sense of Casablanca than by exploring the international states of mind that characterize Rick's place. The opening narration tells us that the refugee trail of monied and desperate exiles leads to Casablanca, where they wait and wait for exit visas to Lisbon, but the development of the movie points out how Rick's Cafe Americain seems to be the emotional gathering place for the many heroes, villains, and hopefuls who populate the city. When Ugarte (Peter Lorre) arrives early in the film with the two letters of transit that Rick reluctantly hides in Sam's (Dooley Wilson) piano, and when Rick's former love Ilsa (Ingrid Bergman) appears with her resistance-leader husband (Paul Henreid), events fall into place that will sharpen the conflict and eventually transform Rick from an uninvolved cynic to a man heeding once more the call of ideals.

It is a surprise to learn that some of the screenplay was written hurriedly during shooting including the ending. The script uses Rick's cafe to connect the concerns of the many characters with Rick so that as we learn more about their outward struggles, we find out more about Rick's inner struggle. He exudes cool disdain, especially when tearing up the credentials of angry Germans. (He restricts the German banker from his gambling room and later tears a marker another German leaves at the bar.) The mosaic plotting scatters these seemingly unimportant details so carefully that we are continually pleased to see as things develop how it all fits so seamlessly.

One of the great feats of the writing is its finesse in showing Rick's cynical shell and allowing at the same time the audience to surmise that on the inside he is, as Renault (Claude Rains) says, a "rank sentimentalist." When the womanizing Renault says of him, "He is the kind of man that if I were a woman . . . I should be in love with Rick," it somehow sounds perfectly natural. The vignettes between Rick and Yvonne (he sends her home because she is tipsy and because she has fallen in love with him) and Rick and Annina, the young Bulgarian bride (he crooks the roulette wheel in her husband's favor to keep her out of Renault's clutches), foreshadow the final great scene at the foggy airport when he nobly

Did you know?...

Composer Max Steiner told director Curtiz that the 1931 song "As Time Goes By" would weaken the film. His suggestion was to replace it with a Steiner song, but since Ingrid Bergman had already had her hair cut for her upcoming part in *For Whom the Bell Tolls* the necessary scenes could not be reshot.

sends away another woman. Rick is so compelling that the film may ultimately be less about love and recovering wartime ideals than about holding on to integrity. Everybody respects Rick because they know that nothing will make him sell out.

Casablanca is based on a play by Murray Burnett and Joan Alison that was never produced. Before Bogart and Bergman signed on, George Raft had

Ilsa (Ingrid Bergman) and Rick (Humphrey Bogart) enjoy a moment together in Paris before their troubled reunion in *Casablanca*.

declined the role of Rick, and Ronald Reagan and Ann Sheridan were considered for the starring roles. Michael Curtiz was the fourth director to be offered the helm, proving once again that the Hollywood merry-go-round was not an absolute block to inspired moviemaking.

Cast: Humphrey Bogart (Richard Blaine), Ingrid Bergman (Ilsa Lund), Paul Henreid (Victor Laszlo), Claude Rains (Captain Louis Renault), Sydney Greenstreet (Ferrari), Peter Lorre (Ugarte), S.Z. Sakall (Carl the waiter), Conrad Veidt (Major Strasser), Dooley Wilson (Sam), Marcel Dalio (croupier), Madeleine Le Beau (Yvonne), Annina (Joy Page), John Qualen (Berger), Leonid Kinskey (Sascha), Dan Seymour (Abdul) **Screenwriter:** Julius J. Epstein, Philip G. Epstein, Howard Koch **Cinematographer:** Arthur Edeson **Composer:** Max Steiner **Producer:** Hal B. Wallis for Warner Bros. **Running Time:** 102 minutes **Format:** VHS, LV **Awards:** Academy Awards, 1943: Director (Michael Curtiz), Picture, Screenplay; Nominations: Actor (Humphrey Bogart), Black and White Cinematography, Editing, Supporting Actor (Claude Rains), Original Dramatic/Comedy Score; National Board of Review Awards, 1945: 10 Best Films of the Year **Budget:** $950,000 **Box Office:** $3.7M.

Cyrano de Bergerac
1990 – Jean-Paul Rappeneau – 🦴🦴🦴🦴

> "What would you have me do? Seek out a powerful protector, pursue a potent patron? Cling like a leeching vine to a tree? *Crawl* my way up? Fawn, whine for all that sticky candy called success? No, thank you."
>
> Cyrano (Gerard Depardieu)

Edmond Rostand's 1898 play about the famous hero that translator Anthony Burgess described in an apt phrase as "big-nosed, big-voiced, big-souled" was labeled by its author an heroic comedy. One of the most expensive French productions ever made, this film version is the first really to capture the heroic side of the story, and it makes the 1950 version produced by Stanley Kramer seem cramped and stagey. The built-in comedy of the role and its tendency toward buffoonery come across in a modernization like *Roxanne*, Fred Schepisi's and Steve Martin's film, just as the cleverness of Rostand's mistaken-identity plot becomes the centerpiece of *The Truth about Cats and Dogs*. Rappeneau's *Cyrano* takes the romanticism of Rostand's play and localizes it in an earthy but exuberant, seventeenth-century Parisian world where a street simpleton steals one of Roxane's letters and runs off grinningly and where battle scenes from the Siege at Arras feature 2,000 extras and hundreds of swords, pikes, muskets, and cannons. It is a lush, soaring production.

Through all the fire and smoke of battle, Cyrano's expansive soul remains unsullied, and Depardieu is more memorable than even the period sets and the

beautiful photography. His excellent performance somehow always makes clear that his bear-like form and swaggering demeanor mask the timidity and vulnerability of unrequited love. Rostand's play and this production also explore the connection between verbal facility and refinement of emotions. Does a rare gift for expression lead to a better understanding of ideas and emotions, or do even the less articulate grasp just as fully the complex stirrings of emotion they can't explain? Christian (Vincent Perez), the man for whom Cyrano ghosts the love letters to Roxane (Anne Brochet), certainly thinks that somewhere inside him is the dignity of thought and feeling that Cyrano so effortlessly voices. But his attempts to sunder himself from his spokesman lead to bumbling efforts at declaring his love. Roxane tires of his desperate "I love you's."

One of the play's infectious qualities is the way it imparts a smoothness and simplicity to eloquence, making something that is quite rare seem everyday. The English subtitles by Anthony Burgess capture the intricate rhymes of the

Cyrano (Gerard Depardieu) enthralls the crowd with both his wit and his rapier.

Did you know?...

A real-life Cyrano de Bergerac lived from 1619 to 1655 and wrote about voyages to the moon, the sort of fantasy Rostand's dramatic character draws upon to delay DeGuiche from foiling the wedding of Roxane and Christian.

French dialogue. Those of us verbally addled like Christian can for a moment identify with Cyrano and feel a little of what it's like to pour out the poetry of our affection into these verbal rhapsodies. Rostand, of course, like most poets, sides with his hero, and though he gives Christian a brave soldier's death, it is Cyrano who possesses both the verbal and spiritual refinement of a peerless soul.

Cast: Gerard Depardieu (Cyrano de Bergerac), Anne Brochet (Roxane), Vincent Perez (Christian de Neuvillette), Jacques Weber (Count DeGuiche), Roland Bertin (Ragueneau), Phillippe Morier-Genoud (Le Bret), Josiane Stoleru (Roxane's handmaid), Anatole Delalande (the child), Ludivine Sagnier (the little sister), Alain Rimoux (the father), Phillippe Volter (Viscount of Valvert), Jean-Marie Winling (Ligiere), Louis Lavarre (Le Facheux), Gabriel Monnet (Montfleury), Francois Marie (Bellerose), Pierre Triboulet (Jodelet), Jacques Pater (Le Tirelaine), Lucien Pascal (Academy Member), Catherine Ferran (Lise Ragueneau), Madeleine Marion (Mother Superior), Claudine Gabay (Naughty Sister) **Screenwriter:** Jean-Claude Carriere, Jean-Paul Rappeneau, Anthony Burgess **Cinematographer:** Pierre Lhomme **Composer:** Jean-Claude Petit **Producer:** Rene Cleitman and Michel Seydoux for Hachette Premiere, Camera One, Films A2, D. D. Prods., and UGC; released by Orion Pictures **MPAA Rating:** PG **Running Time:** 138 minutes **Format:** VHS, LV **Awards:** Academy Awards, 1990: Costume Design; Nominations: Actor (Gerard Depardieu), Art Direction/Set Decoration, Foreign Language Film, Makeup; Cannes Film Festival, 1990: Actor (Gerard Depardieu); Cesar Awards, 1991: Actor (Gerard Depardieu), Art Direction/Set Decoration, Cinematography, Costume Design, Director (Jean-Paul Rappeneau), Film, Sound, Supporting Actor (Jacques Weber), Score; Golden Globe Awards, 1991: Foreign Film **Budget:** $20M.

Doctor Zhivago
1965 – David Lean – 🦴🦴🦴

Doctor Zhivago is a romantic, war-time epic that captures the emotions of the people caught up in the Russian Revolution. The story of Yuri Zhivago (Omar Sharif) is told in a flashback by his half-brother Yevgraf (Alec Guinness), and most of the movie occurs during winter amid many beautifully photographed locations backed with memorable music. A newly married physician, Zhivago meets and falls in love with Lara (Julie Christie) while they nurse the soldiers returning from the front. Returning to Moscow he reunites with his wife Tonya (Geraldine Chaplin), until much later circumstances take him back to Lara. Zhivago is a man trapped between the passion of his life represented by Lara and the love he has for his wife, between poetry and the growing disapproval of his writing by the state.

These feelings of confinement, passivity, and reflection are portrayed in part by the many montages of Zhivago looking through windows at various times in his life. He looks out of a window at the beginning of the movie after going to live with his adoptive parents while a storm rages outside; he does so again while on the train during the great exodus from Moscow as he passes scorched villages. The sense of contemplation and separation reoccurs in various scenes. While with Tonya he thinks about Lara in the cottage and when again on a train at the end of the movie he sees Lara walking on the street and tries desperately to get her attention. Such meditative moments, coupled with Sharif's soulful screen presence and David Lean's gift for intercutting the shots of Zhivago with revealing details, give the film a contemplative, literary quality. Lean and screenwriter Robert Bolt also achieve this effect in a curious scene when Zhivago meets his half-brother. During their talk, Guinness describes his words to his brother for the audience in a voice-over narration ("I then told him . . . .") while Sharif speaks his lines directly to Guinness during the scene.

Dr. Zhivago (Omar Sharif), his wife Tonya (Geraldine Chaplin), and their child huddle for warmth by the train.

These touches enrich the film's emotions while the magnificent settings contrast the personal elements effectively. One of Lean's greatest accomplishments is the winter scenes. He turns Russia into a harsh but beautiful winter wonderland. In one scene where Zhivago and Lara seek refuge in an abandoned cottage, they find that snow and ice have already invaded, leaving everything covered. But with the beauty of the snow and ice also comes the reality of the freezing population. The poor must take the boards from fences in order to heat their homes. The audience can see the plight of the Russians when they are cramped in the close quarters of the train and they look out onto the vast, desolate land. *Doctor Zhivago* is a heart-wrenching epic that explores love and loss.

Cast: Omar Sharif (Yuri Zhivago), Geraldine Chaplin (Tonya), Julie Christie (Lara), Tom Courtenay (Pasha/Strelnikov), Alec Guinness (Gen. Yevgraf), Siobhan McKenna (Anna), Ralph Richardson (Alexander Gromeko), Rod Steiger (Komarovsky), Rita Tushingham (The Girl), Jeffrey Rockland (Sasha), Tarek Sharif (Yuri as a boy), Bernard Kay (Bolshevik), Klaus Kinski (Kostoyed), Gerard Tichy (Liberius), Noel Willman (Razin) **Screenwriter:** Robert Bolt **Cinematographer:** Freddie Young **Composer:** Maurice Jarre **Producer:** Carlo Ponti and David Lean for MGM **MPAA Rating:** PG-13 **Running Time:** 197 minutes **Format:** VHS, LV, DVD **Awards:** Academy Awards, 1965: Art Direction-Set Direction, Cinematography, Costume Design, Score, Adapted Screenplay (Robert Bolt); Nominations: Director (David Lean), Editing, Picture, Sound, Supporting Actor (Tom Courtenay); Golden Globe Awards, 1965: Picture—Drama, Actor—Drama (Omar Sharif), Director (David Lean), Original Score (Maurice Jarre), Screenplay (Robert Bolt); Golden Globe Awards, 1965: Actor (Omar Sharif), Director (David Lean), Film—Drama, Screenplay (Robert Bolt), Score (Maurice Jarre); National Board of Review Awards, 1965: 10 Best Films of the Year, Actress (Julie Christie) **Budget:** $15M **Box Office:** $60M.

The English Patient
1996 – Anthony Minghella – 🧦🧦🧦🧦

The English Patient is a romantic epic that explores love, loss, and healing. Based on the novel by Michael Ondaatje and filmed in Italy and Tunisia, the film pieces together the life of a dying man with no memory of his past. The movie covers a span of eight years of Count Laszlo Almasy's (Ralph Fiennes) life through a series of flashbacks. Director Anthony Minghella's complex use of flashbacks is very well done, with some of them lengthy and some lasting only seconds. One of these scenes occurs when Hana (Juliette Binoche) reads to Almasy from Herodotus, and Almasy remembers Katherine (Kristin Scott

Thomas) reciting the same passages. The voices of Katherine and Hana alternate as Almasy begins to remember some of his past.

The use of flashbacks aids in connecting the past and the present by drawing parallels between the characters. The opening scene of the movie shows a primitive painting of a figure which then blends into the sand dunes of a desert. We then see a plane shot out of the sky with Almasy and Katherine aboard, the event that begins the story. Almasy is severely injured in the crash and is eventually left in a monastery with a nurse named Hana, who believes she is cursed because everyone she has loved has died. The two develop a loving friendship. A Canadian spy, Caravaggio (Willem Dafoe), also stays at the monastery. He believes he knows who the "English patient" is and he wants revenge.

One of the themes concerns the healing of these three characters who have emotional as well as physical scars. At the end of the movie, Hana is ready to reenter life, Almasy is ready to leave life, and Caravaggio can release his hatred

Mysterious Count Almasy (Ralph Fiennes) dances with his married lover, Katherine (Kristin Scott Thomas).

and longing for revenge. Another theme that *The English Patient* explores is love. When Almasy and Katherine meet for the first time Katherine says, "I wanted to meet the man who could write such a long paper with such few adjectives." Almasy answers, "A thing is a thing no matter what you put in front of it." Katherine's reply: "Love. Romantic love. Platonic love. Filial love. Quite different things surely." The movie goes on to explore different types of love—the forbidden love between Almasy and Katherine, the love between nurse and patient, the tender love between Hana and Kip (Naveen Andrews), and love of country.

Cast: Ralph Fiennes (Count Laszlo Almasy), Juliette Binoche (Hana), Willem Dafoe (David Caravaggio), Kristin Scott Thomas (Katharine Clifton), Naveen Andrews (Kip), Colin Firth (Geoffrey Clifton), Julian Wadham (Madox), Jüergen Prochnow (Major Muller, German Officer), Kevin Whately (Sergeant Hardy), Clive Merrison (Fenelon-Barnes), Nino Castelnuovo (D'Agostino), Hichem Rostom (Fouad) **Screenwriter:** Anthony Minghella **Cinematographer:** John Seale **Composer:** Gabriel Yared **Producer:** Saul Zaentz **MPAA Rating:** R **Running Time:** 160 minutes **Format:** VHS, LV **Awards:** Academy Awards, 1996: Picture, Director (Anthony Minghella), Supporting Actress (Juliette Binoche), Art Direction, Costume Design, Sound, Film Editing, Original Dramatic Score (Gabriel Yared), Cinematography (John Seale); Nominations: Actor (Ralph Fiennes), Actress (Kristin Scott Thomas), Adapted Screenplay (Anthony Minghella), Sound Effects Editing; Directors Guild of America, 1996: Director (Anthony Minghella); Golden Globe Awards, 1997: Film-Drama, Original Score (Gabriel Yared); Nominations: Actress-Drama (Kristin Scott Thomas), Actor-Drama (Ralph Fiennes), Supporting Actress (Juliette Binoche), Director (Anthony Minghella), Screenplay (Anthony Minghella); Los Angeles Film Critics Association, 1996: Cinematography (John Seale); National Board of Review, 1996: Supporting Actress (Juliette Binoche), Supporting Actress (Kristin Scott Thomas); Screen Actors Guild, 1996: Nominations: Actor (Ralph Fiennes), Actress (Kristin Scott Thomas), Supporting Actress (Juliette Binoche), Cast; Writers Guild of America, 1996: Nominations: Adapted Screenplay (Anthony Minghella) **Budget:** $27M **Box Office:** $78M (domestic gross).

Far and Away
1992 – Ron Howard – 🎞🎞🎞

Ron Howard may be one of the most imaginative and inspiring filmmakers of our time. When he is coupled with one of the great masters of movie music, John Williams, the result is a movie that not only looks like an epic, but sounds like one too.

This is a story about a most unlikely romance between Joseph Donnelly (Tom Cruise) and Shannon Christie (Nicole Kidman). Joseph, the son of an Irish

Irish immigrants Shannon (Nicole Kidman) and Joseph (Tom Cruise) find romance together in America.

tenant farmer, leaves home after the death of his father and the subsequent burning of his home by the agents of his landlord. The purpose of his first quest is to murder the landlord, Daniel Christie (Robert Prosky), a loveable old gentleman who has no real idea of the business dealings in which he is involved.

This murder plot fails, and Joseph is captured and held prisoner in the landlord's home until he can fight a duel with the overseer of the landlord's business, the same man who burned Joseph's home. Christie's daughter Shannon comes to his room and tells him of her plan to flee to America. He escapes the duel in the morning fog with Shannon. Once in America, the couple is forced to take menial jobs while back in Ireland, Christie's tenants revolt and burn his home. He and his wife (Barbara Babcock) also decide to immigrate to America.

Occasionally meandering the film dramatizes a quest that covers two continents, and therein lies its epic quality. Filmed on location in Ireland and Montana, it is a sweeping tale of love and desire, not only the passion Joseph has for

"There's nothing I like more than the glow of murder in a young man's eyes."

An old man, giving Joseph a rifle to take revenge on the landlord.

Shannon but also the desire they both have to own land. Joseph knows well what his dying father told him—that a man without land is worthless. Shannon desires to be a modern and independent woman, and she sees America as the answer to both of these ambitions. In Ireland her father is the lord of the manor, but in America Shannon herself becomes the driving force behind the Christie family. The characters reunite in Oklahoma for the spectacular land rush (excitingly photographed by Mikael Salomon), illustrating beautifully how the quests of Joseph and Shannon not only cover vast distances but also make them equally at home with poor Irish tenant farmers and in the landscapes of the American West. The transition from one to the other is spectacular and moving. Opie makes great movies.

Cast: Tom Cruise (Joseph Donnelly), Nicole Kidman (Shannon Christie), Thomas Gibson (Steven), Robert Prosky (Daniel Christie), Barbara Babcock (Nora Christie), Cyril Cusack (Danty Duff), Eileen Pollack (Molly Kay), Colm Meaney (Kelly), Douglas Gillison (Dermody), Michelle Johnson (Grace), Wayne Grace (Bourke), Niall Toibin (Joe), Barry McGovern (McGuire), Gary Lee Davis (Gordon), Jared Harris (Paddy), Steve O'Donnell (Colm), Wesley Murphy (Landlord), Jimmy Keogh (Priest), Clint Howard (Flynn), Rance Howard (Tomlin) **Screenwriter:** Bob Dolman, Ron Howard **Cinematographer:** Mikael Salomon **Composer:** John Williams **Producer:** Brian Grazer, Ron Howard **MPAA Rating:** PG-13 **Running Time:** 134 minutes **Format:** VHS, LV, DVD **Box Office:** $58.9M (domestic gross).

Far From the Madding Crowd
1967 – John Schlesinger – 🦴🦴🦴

> **"I love you more than common."**
> Gabriel (Alan Bates) to Bathsheba.

Far From the Madding Crowd is an ambitious but slack romantic epic that chronicles the life of a beautiful young woman, her relationships with the three men who love her and how their love changes her life. The movie is based on Thomas Hardy's classic 19th century novel. A poor farmer, Gabriel Oak (Alan Bates), is smitten early on by the beautiful Bathsheba Everdene (Julie Christie) and proposes marriage only to be refused because in Bathsheba's mind he is not good enough for her. He remains steadfastly by her, working on the farm she inherits from an uncle and becoming one of her most trusted employees, after he loses his own farm. A prosperous farmer down the lane, William Boldwood (Peter Finch), also falls desperately in love with Bathsheba. He too proposes marriage, but he too is refused because Bathsheba doesn't love him. It is the

A caddish Sgt. Troy (Terence Stamp) bedazzles the beautiful Bathsheba Everdene (Julie Christie).

Did you know?...
Filmed on location in Dorset and Wiltshire, England.

handsome young soldier, Sergeant Troy (Terence Stamp), who captivates Bathsheba's heart but with disastrous results.

Julie Christie is excellent as the young woman who is so enamored with the idea of love that she never sees the real thing standing before her. Soulful Alan Bates is likewise wonderful as the loyal friend who denies himself happiness for a woman who won't marry him. The strengthening bond between these two characters is a major element in the plot, but it isn't satisfactorily developed. Boldwood loves Bathsheba obsessively, and Sergeant Troy, who is described as a bad sort of man, loves Bathsheba for what she can do for him. A few subtle scenes shed a little light into the characters, but not enough for the audience to connect with them. The film is breathtakingly filmed and skillfully acted and the characters are often interesting. But their motivation for acting as they do is not always clear, nor is it always realistic. Perhaps it is simply that, after nearly three hours of a bittersweet love story, we still do not know these people well enough to be concerned about what happens to them.

Far From the Madding Crowd presents three very different types of love in the three men who love Bathsheba. It is more of a beautifully photographed and interesting film with a story that will keep an audience's attention rather than a gripping, emotional drama.

Cast: Julie Christie (Bathsheba Everdene), Peter Finch (William Boldwood), Alan Bates (Gabriel Oak), Terence Stamp (Sergeant Troy), Fiona Walker (Liddy), Prunella Ransome (Fanny Robin), Alison Leggatt (Mrs. Hurst), Paul Dawkins (Henry Fray), Julian Somers (Jan Coggan), John Barratt (Joseph Poorgrass), Freddie Jones (Cainy Ball), Andrew Robertson (Andrew Randle), Brian Rawlinson (Matthew Moon), Vincent Harding (Mark Clarke), Victor Stone (Billy Smallbury) **Screenwriter:** Frederic Raphael **Cinematographer:** Nicolas Roeg **Composer:** Richard Rodney Bennett **Producer:** Joseph Janni for MGM **MPAA Rating:** PG **Running Time:** 168 minutes **Format:** VHS, LV **Awards:** Academy Awards, 1967: Nominations: Score; National Board of Review Awards, 1967: 10 Best Films of the Year, Actor (Peter Finch).

Farewell My Concubine
1993 – Chen Kaige – 𝄞𝄞𝄞𝄞

Perhaps everyone at some point has believed that he or she was delivered into this world for some particular purpose. Fate. Fortune. Destiny. Whatever it is called, it is a major theme in *Farewell My Concubine*. For some of the film's characters, the acceptance of fate is as natural as breathing; for others it is a lifelong struggle, but for all it is the force that drives their lives and the history of their country.

Farewell My Concubine spans fifty years of Chinese history from a time when feudalism still held the country in its weakening grip through occupation by the Japanese and the subsequent rise of Communist power to the Cultural Revolution. On its way, the film tells the tragic story of two young boys, abandoned to the Peking Opera, who form a friendship that is lifelong and ultimately ill-fated. Although all the other boys in the Peking Opera endure the same abusive and unrelenting training, Douzi (Leslie Cheung) and Shitou (Zhang Fengyi) are special. They are destined to play the parts of the Concubine and the King in a traditional and beloved opera, and they become pampered celebrities. From the time they are small children, their lives and emerging personalities are controlled by external forces. The opera itself is one of those forces as their lives parallel those of the characters they play, thus rendering them unable effectively to handle the unscripted conflicts that arise in the offstage world. But fate is not a thing to be trifled with. A scene that proves the point is one in which Douzi and Shitou find an abandoned infant. Although their wise old guardian tells them to leave the child, they take the baby home, and that child grows to be an active force in the destruction of their beloved opera and their lives.

The romance in *Farewell My Concubine* takes the form of a triangle. The delineation between the genders is confused early for Douzi (who has changed his name to Cheng Dieye) when he is groomed to play the female role of the concubine. Unable to completely separate himself from the character he plays, he falls in love with his childhood companion and stage brother (now known as Duan Xiaolou) and makes no effort to mask his hostility when Xiaolou marries the prostitute Juxian (Gong Li). While there is no question about Dieye's love for Xiaolou and jealousy of Juxian, the relationship between Xiaolou and Juxian

"Leave him to his fate!"

The guardian, to Douzi and Shitou when they find the abandoned infant.

Did you know?...

Farewell My Concubine was banned twice by the Chinese government due to its portrayal of homosexuality as well as for the strife and suffering depicted during the Cultural Revolution.

Juxian (Gong Li) expects trouble in *Farewell, My Concubine.*

is less clear. It is hard to tell if they marry for love, or for convenience, or some combination of the two. But no matter what their reasons for getting married, the marriage becomes one of love and faithfulness, and Juxian manages to accept and support both men despite Dieye's open animosity toward her.

Evocative and poetic, *Farewell My Concubine* raises profound questions and then leaves them hanging, unanswered—as life itself all too often does. The film presents heroes who are tossed, powerlessly from tragedy to tragedy in a cruel world, their suffering relieved only briefly by instances of beauty and love born of the very cruelty that seems fated to destroy them.

Cast: Leslie Cheung (Cheng Dieye/Douzi), Zhang Fengyi (Duan Xiaolou/Shitou), Gong Li (Juxian), Lu Qi (Master Guan), Ying Da (Manager), Ge You (Master Yuan), Li Dan (Laizi), David Wu (Red guard), Jiang Wenli (Douzi's mother), Tong Di (Zhang), Li Chun (young Xiao Si), Lei Han (Xiao Si), Ma Mingwei (Douzi as a child), Fei Yang (Shitou as a child) **Screenwriter:** Lillian Lee, Lu Wei **Cinematographer:** Gu Changwei **Composer:** Zhao Jiping **Producer:** Hsu Feng for Tomson Films, Artificial Eye, China Film, and Beijing Film; released by Miramax **MPAA Rating:** R

Running Time: 157 minutes **Format:** VHS, LV **Awards:** Academy Awards, 1994: Nominations: Best Cinematography, Foreign Language Film; Cannes Film Festival, 1993: Golden Palm; Golden Globe Awards, 1994: Best Foreign Language Film; New York Film Critics Circle Awards, 1993: Best Supporting Actress (Gong Li) **Box Office:** $5.2M (domestic gross).

From Here to Eternity

1953 — Fred Zinnemann — 🎵🎵🎵🎵

What other film better illustrates brilliant casting than this one, based on James Jones' blockbuster novel, tracing the interactions of assorted people at Pearl Harbor during the six months preceding the Japanese attack? Frank Sinatra's career revived when he convinced studio-head Harry Cohn that he could play the nonsinging part of Angelo Maggio, taking scale salary. After he won an Oscar for his work, this film was thought of as his official comeback vehicle. Sinatra is engaging and convincing, but the performers cast against type are less animated, more subtle and just as powerful: Deborah Kerr (rather than Joan Crawford, who quit the film when she saw her wardrobe) plays the lonely captain's wife. Her beautifully delivered speech to Sergeant Warden (Burt Lancaster) about the night she went into labor while her husband was off romancing a hat check girl distills her bitter, hungry character just as accurately as the memorable beach scene. Beautiful Donna Reed, as the classy prostitute who loves Prewitt (Montgomery Clift), has a scene in which she initially rejects him because she longs for a life back home in Oregon that is proper ("because when you're proper, you're safe"). There is not an indifferent performance in the movie: Ernest Borgnine as Fatso Judson, the loudmouth, knife-carrying bully; Lancaster as the sergeant who prides himself on not being an officer; and Philip Ober as his captain insulated by his rank from the costs of his own weakness and stupidity. Ober's weasely, B-movie acting is perfect for this officer whose stripes are the only distinguishing thing about him.

But most amazing of all is Montgomery Clift, whose every expression tells of his absolute honesty. His performance as Prewitt is one of the wonders of his career. Clift can evoke an emotional response from the audience with a passing observation (such as his pride on being picked to play "Taps" at Arlington Ceme-

> "He was always a hardhead, sir. But he was a good soldier. He loved the army more than any soldier I ever knew."
>
> Sergeant Warden's (Burt Lancaster) epitaph for Prewitt.

Did you know?...

The army, still angry over James Jones' harsh picture of the military in his famous novel, refused permission for the film crew to use Schofield Barracks until changes were made to soften the plot. Though the resulting portrayal is hardly flattering to the army, Jones angrily denounced the agreement between Columbia and the military.

Unhappy military wife Karen Holmes (Deborah Kerr) finds some beach time for lover Sgt. Milton Warden (Burt Lancaster).

tery on Armistice Day before FDR) or with an emotional scene (his many reactions to watching the death of Maggio).

Usually director Fred Zinnemann lets the camera record the good work by the actors, but when the subject requires a more style-centered approach, he delivers. The editing and camera placement during the morning attack contain some unforgettable images: the ground shot of a running soldier overtaken by the parallel lines of airplane gunfire, the sky shot of a plane sweeping the barracks as men scatter below like ants, Lancaster on the roof facing the onslaught, teeth gritted, guns blazing.

Cast: Burt Lancaster (Milton Warden), Montgomery Clift (Robert E. Lee Prewitt), Deborah Kerr (Karen Holmes), Donna Reed (Lorene), Frank Sinatra (Angelo Maggio), Philip Ober (Captain Dana Holmes), Mickey Shaughnessy (Sergeant Leva), Harry Bellaver (Mazzioli), Ernest Borgnine (Sergeant Fatso Judson), George Reeves (Malin Stark), John Dennis (Sergeant Ike Galovitch), Merle Travis (Sal Anderson), Tim Ryan (Sergeant Pete Karelsen), Claude Akins (Dhom), Jack Warden (Buckley) **Screenwriter:** Daniel Taradash **Cinematographer:** Floyd Crosby, Burnett Guffey **Composer:** George Duning **Producer:** Buddy Adler for Columbia **Running Time:** 118 minutes **Format:** VHS, LV **Awards:** Academy Awards, 1953: Picture, Director (Fred Zinnemann), Screenplay (Daniel Taradash), Sound, Black-and-White Cinematography, Editing, Supporting Actor (Frank Sinatra), Supporting Actress (Donna Reed); Nominations: Actor (Montgomery Clift), Actor (Burt Lancaster), Actress (Deborah Kerr), Costume Design, Original Dramatic/Comedy Score; Directors Guild of America Awards, 1953: Director (Fred Zinnemann); Golden Globe Awards, 1954: Supporting Actor (Frank Sinatra); Nominations: Director (Fred Zinnemann); National Board of Review Awards, 1953: 10 Best Films of the Year; New York Film Critics Awards, 1953: Film, Actor (Burt Lancaster), Director (Fred Zinnemann).

Gone With The Wind

1939 – Victor Fleming – 🦴🦴🦴🦴

Based on the runaway best-selling novel by Margaret Mitchell, this story follows Southern belle Scarlett O'Hara (Vivien Leigh) as she braves the years during and after the Civil War. Armed with nothing but beauty and self-confidence, Scarlett goes through many tribulations as she moves from one husband to the next, flees from the Yankees, and saves her home plantation, Tara, from the carpetbaggers. She pursues the intellectual Ashley Wilkes (Leslie Howard) and spurns Rhett Butler (Clark Gable), the man who loves and understands her, until a series of tragedies open her eyes to her folly. But by then, Rhett "doesn't give a damn."

This most famous of all Hollywood classic movies has everything: Civil War action for the men, abiding romance for the women, authentic and decorative sets and costumes (the laundry bill alone for the hoop skirts was $10,000), and some history lessons thrown in. After a world-wide search, British Vivien Leigh was selected as the perfect Scarlett O'Hara, and readers nationwide had demanded Clark Gable for the role of Rhett Butler. They fit the parts so well that it is impossible to imagine others in those roles, as clips of old screen tests make evident. But the principals are brilliantly supported with figures like Hattie McDaniel as protective and canny Mammy and Olivia de Havilland as Melanie, quiet reservoir of strength and compassion.

The most expensive film that had been made, *Gone With The Wind* is still the platinum yardstick by which film success is measured. For years, it held the record as the biggest grossing movie of all time (and does still with inflation fac-

> "No, I'm not going to kiss you, although you need it. You need kissing and often and by someone who knows how."
>
> Rhett (Clark Gable) to Scarlett

Did you know?...

Sidney Howard's screenwriting Oscar came posthumously, for he had been killed in a farm accident shortly before the awards ceremony.

Rhett (Clark Gable) and Scarlett (Vivien Leigh) share a passionate moment.

tored in). The movie ran in 1940 wartime London for 232 weeks, with its message that individual survival is possible even if the civilization around you crumbles. Generations of Americans have gained their knowledge of our country's bloodiest war not from history texts but from the images in this film, especially the wounded and dying at Atlanta's train depot. Far from romanticizing war, *Gone With The Wind* spends half of its four-hour run chronicling the hideous poverty, greed, and despair that are war's aftermath. For African-Americans and for women, the movie was also a landmark. Blacks were still cast in servant roles, but the stereotypes were enriched and individuated; no one would confuse Mammy's rock-solid practicality with Prissy's empty-headed laziness. And Scarlett, for all her hoop skirts and flirtatious ways, is a complex picture of a woman—energetic but limited, admirable and maddening, self-confident and self-deceived.

Cast: Clark Gable (Rhett Butler), Vivien Leigh (Scarlett O'Hara), Olivia de Havilland (Melanie Hamilton), Evelyn Keyes (Sue Ellen O'Hara), Ann Rutherford (Carreen O'Hara), Thomas Mitchell (Gerald O'Hara), Barbara O'Neil (Ellen O'Hara), Hattie McDaniel (Mammy), Leslie Howard (Ashley Wilkes), Oscar Polk (Pork), Butterfly McQueen (Prissy), Everett Brown (Big Sam), Carroll Nye (Frank Kennedy), Ona Munson (Belle Watling), Laura Hope Crews (Aunt Pittypat), Rand Brooks (Charles Hamilton) **Screenwriter:** Sidney Howard **Cinematographer:** Ernest Haller, Ray Rennatron **Composer:** Max Steiner **Producer:** David O. Selznick for Selznick International; released by MGM **Running Time:** 222 minutes **Format:** VHS, LV **Awards:** Academy Awards, 1939: Picture, Director, Actress (Vivien Leigh), Art Direction, Cinematography, Director, Supporting Actress (Hattie McDaniel), Screenplay, Film Editing; Nominations: Actor (Clark Gable), Effects, Score, Sound recording, Supporting Actress (Olivia de Havilland) **Budget:** $3.9M **Box Office:** $31M (initial release).

The Greatest Show on Earth
1952 – Cecil B. De Mille – 🦴🦴🦴

One of the interesting things about the success of *Titanic* is the showmanship connected with the film, the way this megahit has created excitement about moviegoing itself that previous box-office champs like *Jurassic Park* did not. Cecil B. De Mille's famous film about a circus flaunts its showmanship too, and did it so well that it convinced Oscar-voters to give it Best Picture, despite its cinematic limitations.

Charlton Heston plays Brad, the circus boss who puts the welfare of his show above all else, including his own love life. To help guarantee a long run and safeguard everyone's jobs, Brad has hired the Great Sebastian (Cornel Wilde), a big-name aerialist. This rankles Holly (Betty Hutton), who must relinquish her center ring spot to make way for the new headliner. Holly and Sebastian begin a dangerous competition working without a net to see who can outperform the other. Other subplots involve Angel (Gloria Grahame), the elephant girl,

> "I was a fool to believe you. You'd sell out your own grandmother for a main act."
> Holly (Betty Hutton) to Brad

Aerialists Sebastian (Cornel Wilde) and Holly (Betty Hutton) share a romantic moment under the big top.

Did you know?...

Bob Hope and Bing Crosby appear briefly in cameos. They can be spotted in the crowd munching popcorn in sync as the camera pans across a row of spectators.

who also loves Brad but must endure the possessive jealousies of Klaus (Lyle Bettger), a trainer. Jimmy Stewart plays Buttons the Clown, who never removes his makeup and whose past remains a mystery. De Mille works real circus acts into the flow as well as a few songs. In one, Stewart sings while bouncing with Betty Hutton and real clown Emmett Kelly on a trampoline.

The climax of the film makes no attempt to hide its melodrama. The circus train derails in a wreck that leaves acres of smashed cars, loose animals, and smoking debris. Brad is seriously injured and pinned under heavy wreckage. The series of rapid plot twists that follow could only come from a director who grew up savoring the melodramas of the late-nineteenth century stage. These breaking events involve an elephant, an FBI agent (De Mille regular Henry Wilcoxon), the secret identity of one of the circus workers, an unexpected sacrifice, and, above all, the continual conviction that the show must go on. The script is stuffed with cliches, and the acting is heavy on the ham (especially Heston, who screams at the financial backers that little kids need the circus too!). When De Mille worked with contemporary characters, they sometimes behaved as if they should wear togas and sandals and carry swords. Overall, the movie carries itself along, like the circus, on its showmanship.

Cast: Charlton Heston (Brad), Betty Hutton (Holly), Cornel Wilde (The Great Sebastian), Dorothy Lamour (Phyllis), Gloria Grahame (Angel), James Stewart (Buttons the Clown), Henry Wilcoxon (Gregory), Lyle Bettger (Klaus), Lawrence Tierney (Mr. Henderson), Emmett Kelly (Himself), John Ringling North (Himself), Bob Carson (Ringmaster), Lillian Albertson (Buttons' Mother), William Boyd (Hopalong Cassidy), Bing Crosby (Circus Spectator), Bob Hope (Circus Spectator), Alberto Zoppe (Trick Rider) **Screenwriter:** Frank Cavett, Fredric M. Frank, Barre Lyndon, Theodore St. John **Cinematographer:** George Barnes, J. Peverell Marley **Composer:** Victor Young **Producer:** Cecil B. De Mille for Paramount **Running Time:** 153 minutes **Format:** VHS, LV **Awards:** Academy Awards, 1952: Picture, Story (Frank Cavett, Fredric M. Frank, and Theodore St. John), Nominations: Costume Design, Director (Cecil B. De Mille), Editing; Golden Globe Awards, 1953: Director (Cecil B. De Mille), Film—Drama.

The Horse Whisperer
1998 – Robert Redford – 𓃒𓃒𓃒

Based on Nicholas Evans' best-selling novel, *The Horse Whisperer* unfolds through most of its near-three-hour length a bit uncertainly, like a young cowhand tiptoeing atop a fence beam. On the one side is the ripeness of the corral, on the other the soft safety of tall grasses. Ultimately, Robert Redford's film maintains its footing fairly well, though a few moments arise when it totters uneasily. Kristin Scott Thomas plays Annie MacLean, a woman driven in her roles as mother and as magazine editor but not, it seems, as wife. After her fourteen-year-old daughter Grace (Scarlett Johansson) suffers a severe injury and the loss of a leg resulting from a riding fall, Annie searches for ways to help with the healing. She reads about a type of holistic vet called a horse whisperer (someone who can "see into the creature's soul and soothe the wounds they find there"), packs up her daughter and her injured horse (but not her husband) and drives them to Montana, where she hopes Tom Booker (Robert Redford) will be able to calm and train the horse.

The epic dimensions of the story begin in Montana, where the hyperactive New Yorker Annie at once appreciates the beauty of the country but not the wise

> "The more I try and fix things, the more everything falls apart."
> Annie (Kristin Scott Thomas)

> "Maybe you should let them fall."
> Booker (Robert Redford)

Cowboy Tom (Robert Redford) lets nature take its course with city-bred Annie (Kristen Scott Thomas).

serenity of its attitudes. The remainder of the film traces her movement from an appreciation of the first to that of the second, which includes a somewhat chaste love affair with Booker. The shots of the Montana terrain, the burnished sunsets, and the endless horizons are exhilarating, and the soundtrack of the film seems to have been given equal consideration (not unusual in the films Redford has directed). The movie is especially good at using sound to suggest character, as in the near-wordless sequence when Annie drives Grace and her horse Pilgrim west. A montage of high-speed truck noises along with the jostle and whinny of the horse in the trailer, one of the most tense moments in the film, immediately recalls the accident that so traumatized Pilgrim and Grace and transmits the horse's fear to the audience. Similarly, the filmmakers use the disruptive beep of Annie's cell phone during Booker's session with Pilgrim to suggest Annie's dislocation in this new landscape. The strains from Dvorak's cello concerto also bring out the more personal side of Booker by recalling his musician wife.

These moments when the film rejects a stereotypical view of character help it maintain a surefooted balance. Just when the songs around the campfire and the western wisdom threaten to become a bit too mawkish, *The Horse Whisperer* puts some flesh on the waxworks of its characters. Booker confides to Annie about his own unrest in loving and marrying a woman from Chicago who could not adapt to the isolation of the West. Later, he soothes Grace by relating a story about a paralyzing injury to a ranch hand and Booker's inability to understand or communicate his array of feelings. Best of all is the way the film handles the character of the husband (Sam Neill), who arrives at the ranch in the final third of the movie. He senses the love between Booker and his wife and unexpectedly delivers a simple but humanizing speech to her. One way or another, *The Horse Whisperer* personifies its characters and delivers its points.

Cast: Robert Redford (Tom Booker), Kristin Scott Thomas (Annie MacLean), Sam Neill (Robert MacLean), Scarlett Johansson (Grace MacLean), Dianne Wiest (Diane Booker), Chris Cooper (Frank Booker), Cherry Jones (Liz Hammond), Catherine Bosworth (Judith), Don Edwards (Smokey), Ty Hillman (Joe Booker), Austin Schwartz (Twin #1), Dustin Schwartz (Twin #2), Jeanette Nolan (Ellen Booker), Steve Frye (Hank), Jessalyn Gilsig (Lucy) **Screenwriter:** Eric Roth, Richard LaGravenese **Cinematographer:** Robert Richardson **Composer:** Thomas Newman **Producer:** Patrick Markey and Robert Redford for Wildwood Productions; released by Touchstone **MPAA Rating:** PG-13 **Running Time:** 168 minutes.

Ivanhoe
1952 – Richard Thorpe – 🦴🦴🦴

"The man with the perfect profile," as Robert Taylor was once known, suits well this story of Saxon and Norman strife during the exile of King Richard the Lionheart (Norman Wooland). Richard languishes as the prisoner of Leopold of Austria. Taylor's Ivanhoe travels, sometimes in disguise, to help restore Richard to his throne even if it comes by ransom. The overall approach is so reverential that the few touches of wit seem almost inadvertent. Ivanhoe returns to his father (Finlay Currie) and the Lady Rowena (Joan Fontaine) but conceals himself under his tunic at dinner since two Normans also share their table. When Rowena elicits from one of the Normans, Sir Brian De Bois-Guilbert (George Sanders), the reluctant admission that he was once bettered in a duel by Ivanhoe, the film cuts, first, to the father for his guarded reaction, and, then,

Brave Saxon knight Ivanhoe (Robert Taylor) vows to protect the beautiful Rebecca (Elizabeth Taylor) from the lustful Normans.

"We shall need no pledge on paper, you and I. Let Richard promise justice to each man, whether he be Saxon or Norman or Jew. For justice belongs to all men, or it belongs to none."

Isaac (Felix Aylmer), to Ivanhoe, as he agrees to help ransom Richard.

to the family pooch, who also turns his head to look at the partially hidden face of Ivanhoe. If the film offered up more lighter moments like that, its solemnity would be easier to take.

As it is, action and pageantry are the strong suits. The sense of drama also intensifies in the second half when Rebecca (Elizabeth Taylor), the daughter of the Jew who ransoms Richard, is captured by the Normans and accused of witchcraft. For a while the film's interest unexpectedly falls on the villain Sir Brian and his conflicted feelings. His unrequited love for Rebecca matches hers for Ivanhoe. The dilemma concerning Rebecca brings Sir Brian's humanity to the surface, and he becomes the film's most complicated character, the only one to bring out some of the contradictions in the chivalric code (as writer Blake Lucas has pointed out in *Magill's Survey of Cinema*). Sir Brian desires to spare Rebecca from the charges of witchcraft. He even offers to default to Ivanhoe in their final duel and endure the resulting disgrace if only she will return his feelings. Although famed composer Miklos Rozsa turned in one of his best scores, the final fight plays without any background music, an odd choice that highlights the clank of chain and mail in an attempt to capture the savagery of the duel.

According to her biographer Donald Spoto, Elizabeth Taylor's entire part had to be dubbed by her when the film company returned to Hollywood from England. Her love life was in disarray (divorced, she was realizing that she could not endure the solitude between relationships), and her line readings were unemotional and garbled. After two weeks of shooting, producer Pandro Berman told director Thorpe to continue filming with the intention of having her redo the lines later. Spoto reports that Taylor tended to dismiss the film despite its popularity as "a big medieval western."

Cast: Robert Taylor (Ivanhoe), Elizabeth Taylor (Rebecca), Joan Fontaine (Lady Rowena), Emlyn Williams (Wamba), George Sanders (Sir Brian De Bois-Guilbert), Robert Douglas (Sir Hugh De Bracy), Finlay Currie (Cedric), Felix Aylmer (Isaac), Francis De Wolff (Font De Boeuf), Norman Wooland (King Richard the Lionheart), Basil Sydney (Waldemar Fitzurse), Harold Warrender (Locksley), Patrick Holt (Philip De Malvoisin), Roderick Lovell (Ralph De Vipont), Sebastian Cabot (Clerk of Copmanhurst) **Screenwriter:** Noel Langley **Cinematographer:** Freddie Young **Composer:** Miklos Rozsa **Producer:** Pandro S. Berman for MGM **Running Time:** 107 minutes **Format:** VHS **Awards:** Academy Awards, 1952: Nominations: Color Cinematography, Picture, Original Dramatic/Comedy Score **Box Office:** $6M.

Did you know?...
The film was photographed by Freddie Young, who later shot David Lean's *Lawrence of Arabia*.

The Last of the Mohicans

1992 – Michael Mann – 🐾🐾🐾

The Last of the Mohicans is an epic adventure with passion and romance set in 1757 in the frontier west of the Hudson River. From the opening scene of three men running gracefully through a forest in pursuit of a deer to the beautiful music of Randy Edelman (*Beethoven, Come See the Paradise*) and Trevor Jones (*Excalibur, The Dark Crystal*), the audience is captivated by the sleek Hawkeye (Daniel Day-Lewis). Based on the novel by James Fenimore Cooper and the screenplay by Philip Dunne (for the 1936 version) and shot in the magnificent scenery of North Carolina, the story of Chingachgook (Russell Means) and his two sons—Uncas (Eric Schweig) and Hawkeye is brought to life by screenwriter/director Michael Mann so well that we don't really care if it is true history or not.

Set in 1751 as the French and English clash in North America, the beginning of the movie alternates between Hawkeye and Cora Munro (Madeleine Stowe), the woman with whom he will fall in love and the daughter of the British commanding officer. The first time we see Cora, she sits with Major Duncan Heyward (Steven Waddington) and tries to think of a nice way to refuse his proposal. Duncan wants her to rely on his and her father's judgment about marriage, but Cora has a mind of her own and she is too adventurous and daring for the dull Duncan. We see her courage when she takes a gun from a dead soldier, puts it in her skirt, speaks sedition to her father, and asks him to free Hawkeye.

When Hawkeye and Cora initially meet, he and his family have just saved the lives of Cora, her sister Alice (Jodhi May), and Duncan. Soon after, their romance begins, although it gets off to a rough start when Cora accuses Hawkeye of being indifferent because he refuses to bury the bodies of settlers attacked by a war party.

Sometimes the style-conscious approach becomes a little too obvious. For example, the camera focuses on Magua's (Wes Studi) tomahawk when he is about to kill a British soldier and start an attack. In the scene where the two generals are discussing surrender, their country's flags fill the background. Both of these scenes would be effective without these obvious touches. But many of the moments are very well done. The scene in which Colonel Munro surrenders

Did you know?...

Michael Mann ordered a reconstruction of Fort William Henry (the colonial outpost at the center of the action) based on the archival plans of an actual eighteenth-century building. A twenty-acre area of forest was cleared, and 188 carpenters built the fort.

Frontiersman Hawkeye (Daniel Day-Lewis) and English officer's daughter, Cora Munro (Madeleine Stowe), fall in love.

arouses sympathy for the soldiers on the losing side. Munro says, "Death and honor are thought to be the same, but today I have learned they are not," as the camera pans over the soldiers awaiting his decision. The French agree to free the English if they will return to their homes and not fight again. The French, however, do not keep their promise, and the low angle of the camera shows the sinister Magua looking down on the homeward-bound Englishmen from the darkness of the trees before attacking. His looming presence above in the gloom suggests that his hatred has made him powerful and merciless.

The letterbox format allows us to see the expanse of the beautiful scenery as well as the destruction and damage of war. Despite the graphic violence, *The Last of the Mohicans* is a stunning epic well worth watching.

Cast: Daniel Day-Lewis (Hawkeye; Nathaniel Poe), Madeleine Stowe (Cora Munro), Russell Means (Chingachgook), Eric Schweig (Uncas), Jodhi May (Alice Munro), Wes Studi (Magua), Steven Waddington (Major Duncan Heyward), Maurice Roeves (Colonel Edmund Munro), Patrice Chereau (General Montcalm), Edward Blatchford (Jack Winthrop), Terry Kinney (John Cameron), Tracey Ellis (Alexandra Cameron), Justin M. Rice (James Cameron), Pete Postlethwaite (Captain Beams), Colm Meaney (Major Ambrose) **Screenwriter:** Michael Mann, Christopher Crowe **Cinematographer:** Dante Spinotti **Composer:** Randy Edelman, Trevor Jones **Producer:** Michael Mann and Hunt Lowry for Morgan Creek; released by Warner Bros. **MPAA Rating:** R **Running Time:** 110 minutes **Format:** VHS, LV **Awards:** Academy Awards 1993: Best Sound; Golden Globe Awards 1993: Nominations: Best Original Score **Budget:** $40M **Box Office:** $72.455M (domestic gross).

Out of Africa
1985 – Sydney Pollack – 🧦🧦🧦🧦

> "There are some things worth having, but they come at a price. And I want to be one of them."
>
> Karen (Meryl Streep) to Denys.

With beautiful cinematography, a grand musical score, and acting that cleverly portrays the complex Danish writer Karen Blixen (Meryl Streep) and British hunter Denys Finch Hatton (Robert Redford), Sydney Pollack's award-winning film *Out of Africa* exquisitely captures the spirit of Africa, its natives, and the foreigners that attempt to call it home. Taking the story of Danish writer Karen Blixen's, who wrote under the pen name Isak Dinesen, stay in early twentieth-century East Africa, Kurt Luedtke creates a screenplay based on her novel *Out of Africa* and Judith Thurman's *Isak Dinesen: the Life of a Storyteller*. The film begins with a marriage of convenience to Baron Bror Blixen (Klaus Maria Bran-

Karen Blixen (Meryl Streep) enjoys the assistance of adventurer Denys Finch Hatton (Robert Redford) while on safari.

dauer), and Karen finds herself in Kenya single-handedly running a coffee farm. Although the marriage and farm are both failed ventures, her life is strengthened by the free-spirited safari hunter Denys Finch Hatton. Streep and Redford portray the multi-faceted characters Karen and Denys. We applaud Karen's independent spirit and determination but are made uneasy by her superficial, possessive, and controlling side. She works alongside the natives on her farm, takes a bullwhip to an attacking lion, leads a convoy of supplies through the treacherous bush country, yet insists on fine dining surrounded by her Limoges crystal, her china, and her appropriately prepared meals. At times Karen connects well with the natives, as shown in her ability to convince them of medical and educational needs. But she also insensitively insists that the house servant, Farah (Mallick Bowens), wear cumbersome white gloves. Symbolically, she later removes them from Farah after her attempts at taming her African farm have failed. Equally complex and contradictory is Denys, the skilled hunter who feels that a gramophone and Mozart are as necessary on safari as rifles.

Did you know?...

Director Sydney Pollack was refused permission to film on the coffee plantation in Kenya that had been owned by Isak Dinesen.

On a grand scale, *Out of Africa* explores the issues of boundaries and ownership not only of a country, but of individuals as well. As the independent characters of Karen and Denys draw together, their personal boundaries begin to blur. Two scenes in particular capture this gently developing relationship. On safari Denys washes Karen's badly tangled hair and does so while quoting lines of poetry. Perhaps the greatest gift Denys gives Karen is a flight above East Africa. While zooming over the untamed land, wildebeest, and flocks of flamingoes, Karen receives a "glimpse of the world through God's eye—the way it was intended."

Cast: Meryl Streep (Karen Blixen-Finecke), Robert Redford (Denys Finch Hatton), Klaus Maria Brandauer (Baron Bror Blixen-Finecke), Michael Kitchen (Berkeley), Mallick Bowens (Farah), Joseph Thaika (Kamante), Michael Gough (Delamere), Suzanna Hamilton (Felicity), Rachel Kempson (Lady Belfield), Graham Corwden (Lord Belfield), Leslie Phillips (Sir Joseph), Shane Rimmer (Belknap), Mike Bugara (Juma), Job Seda (Kanuthia), Mohammed Umar (Ismail) **Screenwriter:** Kurt Leudtke **Cinematographer:** David Watkin **Composer:** John Barry **Producer:** Sydney Pollack for Mirage Productions; released by Universal **MPAA Rating:** PG **Running Time:** 161 minutes **Format:** VHS, LV **Awards:** Academy Awards, 1985: Screenplay, Art Direction/Set Decoration, Cinematography, Director (Sydney Pollack), Picture, Sounds, Score; Nominations: Actress (Meryl Streep), Costume Design, Editing, Supporting Actor (Klaus Maria Brandauer); British Academy Awards, 1986: Adapted screenplay; Golden Globe Awards, 1986: Film—Drama, Supporting Actor (Klaus Maria Brandauer), Score (John Barry); Los Angeles Film Critics Association Awards, 1985: Actress (Meryl Streep), Cinematography; New York Film Critics Awards, 1985: Cinematography, Supporting Actor (Klaus Maria Brandauer) **Budget:** $31M **Box Office:** $87M (domestic gross).

Ryan's Daughter

1970 – David Lean – 🦴🦴🦴

Filmed along the coast of Ireland's Dingle Peninsula, *Ryan's Daughter* is the story of a young girl's struggles with love and politics in the midst of the 1916 western Irish uprising against the British. Rosy Ryan (Sarah Miles), married to schoolteacher Charles Shaughnessy (Robert Mitchum), has a torrid love affair with Doryan (Christopher Jones), a British military hero, leading the entire town to believe that she is an informant. This is another film in a series of respected works by director David Lean, a list that includes classics like *The Bridge on the River Kwai* (1957), *Lawrence of Arabia* (1962), and *Dr. Zhivago* (1965). This continued critical and popular acclaim, however, may have led to a

touch of "epic-itis," the feverish assumption that a sufficient number of beautifully rendered shots of natural scenery can make any story impressive. Not quite up to Lean's impeccable standard, *Ryan's Daughter* is weakened by its empty grandness and artistic pretentiousness.

The lengthy film includes several long combination nature/love scenes which slow the story and detract from the excitement of the Irish rebellion and the lovers' roles in it. In one long and pointless scene, the couple makes love in the woods with only the music of their heavy breathing to accompany shots of trees and creatures of the forest. This scene and others like it clearly strive for lyricism and rapture but risk seeming a near-gratuitous exploration of the new freedom in films in 1970.

The film's strengths lie more in its treatment of the effects of war on the human spirit and the struggle between Irish and British. In one scene, a corporal commends Major Doryan for his bravery on the front lines. While the corporal

Irish Rosy (Sarah Miles) betrays her family when she falls in love with British officer Randolph (Christopher Jones).

speaks, the camera focuses on the Major and the sounds of battle echo in the background. We see that this shell-shocked Major is struggling to stay calm as the very real memories of combat threaten again to overwhelm him, the echoing sound effect bringing the drama of wartime heroics and their cost skillfully into the scene. In the larger plot, the west Irish hatred of the British even extends to their willingness to cooperate with the Germans. Plans have been arranged for a German boat in the area to drop boxes of arms and ammunition overboard so that the villagers may gather them up and fight the English stationed among them. The local dislike of Rosy and the knowledge of her English lover, however, directs suspicion her way as a secret informant once the English have been tipped off about the rebellion. The melodrama of the film's stories of love and politics can't help seeming inflated when stretched to epic scale.

Cast: Robert Mitchum (Charles Shaughnessy), Trevor Howard (Father Collins), Christopher Jones (Randolph Doryan), John Mills (Michael), Leo McKern (Tom Ryan), Sarah Miles (Rosy Ryan), Barry Foster (Tim O'Leary), Marie Kean (Mrs. McCardle), Archie O'Sullivan (McCardle), Evin Crowley (Moureen), Douglas Sheldon (Driver), Gerald Sim (Captain), Barry Jackson (Corporal), Des Keogh (Lanky Private) **Screenwriter:** Robert Bolt **Cinematographer:** Freddie Young **Composer:** Maurice Jarre **Producer:** Anthony Havelock-Allan for Faraway Productions; released by MGM **MPAA Rating:** PG **Running Time:** 194 minutes **Format:** VHS, LV **Awards:** Academy Awards, 1970: Cinematography, Supporting Actor (John Mills); Nominations: Actress (Sarah Miles), Sound; Golden Globe Awards, 1971: Supporting Actor (John Mills); National Board of Review Awards, 1970: 10 Best Films of the Year.

The Story of Adele H.
1975 – Francois Truffaut – ♫♫♡

The Story of Adele H. is the sad but true tale of Adele Hugo, the second daughter of French writer and political activist Victor Hugo. Overshadowed all her life by her famous father and her family's favorite sister who drowned, Adele (Isabelle Adjani) uses a ream of paper a week to write her fragmented diary as she follows the object of her obsessive and unrequited love, Lieutenant Albert Pinson (Bruce Robinson) and his regiment from station to station. The Lieutenant and Adele met in Guernsey where her family was living and he was stationed. The two had a romantic relationship and the Lieutenant left Guernsey with Adele believing that he had promised to marry her. Whether he proposed

or not is never clear. What is clear, however, is that Adele believes many things that have no basis in reality.

Adele literally stalks the object of her obsession, following him to Halifax, Nova Scotia, and refusing to leave as long as he is there. He spurns her repeatedly, but this does not deter her. Believing that she can win him over, she spies on him, prays to his enshrined photograph, tells people they are married and even pretends to be pregnant with his child. Odd as this behavior is, it would seem that Lieutenant Pinson's very presence in Halifax is what keeps Adele from losing all touch with reality. As soon as she believes him to be gone, with no idea where he is, her mental state rapidly deteriorates. She wanders the streets disheveled and destitute like a mad woman.

The Story of Adele H. is not an easy film to watch. The characters are rendered beautifully and the story is told well, but the portrayal of a woman unable to control her words, actions, even her thoughts is almost too realistic

Lt. Pinson (Bruce Robinson) is surprised his French lover, Adele (Isabelle Adjani), has followed him to Canada.

and brutal to be comfortable. Adele is neither harmless nor evil, as obsessive, mentally unstable lovers are typically depicted in films. Even more unsettling than Adjani's performance is the fact that the events in this film really happened to the daughter of Victor Hugo. The obsessional nature of the plot produces a film that is curious in its premise but slow and uninvolving in its execution.

Cast: Isabelle Adjani (Adele Hugo), Bruce Robinson (Lt. Pinson), Sylvia Marriott (Mrs. Saunders), Reubin Dorey (Mr. Saunders), Joseph Blatchley (The Bookseller), Ivry Gitlis (Hypnotist), Carl Hathwell (Lt. Pinson's Batman), Francois Truffaut (Officer), M. White (Colonel White), Raymons Falla (Judge Johnstone), Roger Martin (Doctor Murdock), Madame Louise (Madame Baa), Jean-Pierre Leursse (Black penpusher), Louise Bourdet (Victor Hugo's servant), Ralph Williams (Canadian), Edward J. Jackson (O'Brien) **Screenwriter:** Jan Dawson, Jean Gruault, Francis Vernor Guille, Suzanne Schiffman, Francois Truffaut **Cinematographer:** Nestor Almendros **Composer:** Maurice Jaubert **Producer:** Marcel Berbert and Claude Miller for Films du Carrosse/Artistes Associes **Running Time:** 96 minutes **Format:** VHS, LV **Awards:** Academy Awards, 1975: Nominations: Actress (Isabelle Adjani); National Board of Review Awards, 1975: Best Foreign Films of the Year, Actress (Isabelle Adjani); New York Film Critics Awards, 1975: Actress (Isabelle Adjani), Screenplay; National Society of Film Critics Awards, 1975: Actress (Isabelle Adjani).

> "My work requires solitude. Think of my name and who my father is. I would never give up the name of Hugo."
>
> Adele (Isabelle Adjani), talking to Mrs. Saunders as she packs her belongings to leave the boarding house.

Did you know?...

The film represented director Francois Truffaut's return to filmmaking after a two-year hiatus.

The Wind and the Lion
1975 – John Milius – 🦴🦴🦴

> "You are like the wind who doesn't know its place."
>
> Letter from the Raisuli (Sean Connery) to President Roosevelt

Director John Milius opens this tale of desert adventure with Arabian horses pounding through the surf, sabers glistening, and robes flying. *The Wind and The Lion* tells of the early twentieth-century struggle between Teddy Roosevelt (Brian Keith) and the Ruffian chief Raisuli (Sean Connery). Set in the Moroccan desert and the city of Tangier, this epic is loosely based on Raisuli's kidnaping of an American citizen, Mrs. Pedecaris (Candice Bergen), and her two children in exchange for much sought after land. Americans, Germans, Russians, and French have peacefully invaded the Moroccan desert, making for a political powderkeg in the area. Roosevelt's sending of United States Marines to rescue Mrs. Pedecaris makes the situation more volatile, but in this election year Roosevelt publicly demands respect for Americans and their property: "Pedecaris alive or Raisuli dead!" Ironically, with the help of the Marines, Mrs. Pedecaris and children end up helping Raisuli escape from the Germans and the Bashaw (Vladek Shaybal). And it is easy to see why Mrs. Pedecaris resolves to rescue her previ-

ous captor. The film includes tender scenes throughout the harsh desert that reveal a growing respect and fascination between Pedecaris and the Raisuli.

Rebellious Arab chieftain Raisuli (Sean Connery) kidnaps American Eden (Candice Bergen) to prove a point.

An excellent job of casting the roles of President Roosevelt and the Raisuli helps the audience see the bullishness and barbarism of these two leaders, while at the same time invoking feelings of sympathy and endearment for these two boys playing King of the Mountain. Brian Keith and Sean Connery bring together both boyish innocence and didactic insolence. We cringe when Raisuli beheads a man for stealing water and smile when he challenges Mrs. Pedecaris to a game of chess. Even the children's fear of this Barbary pirate transforms to admiration as they begin to wear turbans and robes and look with fascination on his strong arm of desert law. Likewise, Roosevelt shows childlike charm when asking what kind of rifle the Raisuli owns, but he reveals imperialistic greed when contemplating the territory his Marines could gain while rescuing Mrs. Pedecaris.

Did you know?...

Composer Jerry Goldsmith has been one of the most prolific writers of music for the screen with sixteen Academy Award nominations and one win (for *The Omen*).

Although very well executed, the concluding battle scene is at times confusing—Arabs fight along side the German forces while the Raisuli's band aids the U.S. Marines. Who are the good guys? Which saber-swinging Arab are we to root for? In a larger sense the movie calls into question who the real barbarians are—those quick to slash Arabs or the leaders competitively dispatching armed forces into territories not their own?

Cast: Sean Connery (Mulay el-Raisuli), Candice Bergen (Eden Pedecaris), Brian Keith (Theodore Roosevelt), John Huston (John Hay), Geoffrey Lewis (Gummere), Steve Kanaly (Captain Jerome), Vladek Sheybal (The Bashaw), Nadim Sawalha (Sherif of Wazan), Roy Jenson (Admiral Chadwick), Deborah Baxter (Alice Roosevelt), Jack Cooley (Quentin Roosevelt), Chris Aller (Kermit Roosevelt), Simon Harrison (William Pedecaris), Polly Gottesmann (Jennifer Pedecaris), Antoine St. John (Von Roerkel) **Screenwriter:** John Milius **Cinematographer:** Billy Williams **Composer:** Jerry Goldsmith **Producer:** Herb Jaffe and Phil Rawlins for Columbia; released by MGM **Running Time:** 119 minutes **Format:** VHS, LV **Awards:** Academy Awards, 1975: Nominations: Sound, Score.

They Might Be Giants . . .

In addition to those epics with a strong romantic element (like *Reds*) included in other chapters, additional epics that emphasize romance would include *The Thorn Birds*, the 1983 mini-series from the novel by Colleen McCullough featuring one of the last performances by Barbara Stanwyck and one of the first by Rachel Ward. The 486-minute series is a dynastic story set in the Australian outback, Rome, and Greece with Richard Chamberlain as a priest who falls in love with Ward. The series also features Jean Simmons, Ken Howard, Mare Winningham, Richard Kiley, Piper Laurie, Bryan Brown, and Christopher Plummer. Another familiar romantic epic, Tolstoy's novel *Anna Karenina*, has been filmed as least ten times with silent versions in 1914 (a Russian film), 1915, and 1918 (a Hungarian film). *Love* (1927), a silent film with Greta Garbo and John Gilbert, puts this story of a woman's love affair with a military man in a modern setting but is much less effective than the MGM sound remake from 1935, which returns to the time of the novel and again stars Garbo, Fredric March (as Vronsky), and Basil Rathbone. A 1948 version with Vivian Leigh and Ralph Richardson, another Russian version in 1967, a BBC mini-series (with Nicola Pagett and Eric Porter) in 1977, a made-for-television adaptation in 1985 with a surprisingly good cast (Jacqueline Bisset, Christopher Reeve, Paul Schofield, Anna Massey), and a 1997 version (with Sophie Marceau and Sean Bean) complete the roster, we think, of this durable romantic classic.

SILENT

The Battleship Potemkin

1925 — Sergei Eisenstein — 🦴🦴🦴🦴

"Comrades! The ship is in our hands!"

Cry of the mutinous sailors.

The central committee of the Communist government decided in 1925 to commemorate the twentieth anniversary of the unsuccessful 1905 revolution against the Czar by sponsoring a series of films. Sergei Eisenstein and his collaborator Nina Agadzhanova-Shutko planned an epic that would encompass dozens of locations from Moscow to Siberia. All that changed when poor weather forced the film crew to the seaport of Odessa, where Eisenstein began elaborating on the visual potential of the flights of steps leading to the harbor. He decided to abandon his more elaborate plans and focus instead on the sailors' mutiny aboard the battleship *Potemkin*, their return to port, the ensuing rebellion of the masses inspired by the example of the crew, and the bloody massacre of the people by the Czar's troops.

At first it seems that the film has no hero, but then the infectious spirit of revolt makes clear that Eisenstein saw the oppressed masses as the true heroes of his drama. Politically he was right, but cinematically he may be wrong. The genuine power of the film derives from the masterful technique, and perhaps the true hero is the celebrated displays of editing; at least that is what lifts the heart. The shots fly by in Eisenstein's montage sequences at an average of one every two seconds; in the film as a whole the average shot lasts about four seconds, a much faster pace for films then and probably even now. Eisenstein's theory was to assemble brief, individual shots that would assume greater emotional meaning and impact as a sequence (just as individual words mean more when arranged in a sentence). And he was right. A snappily cut-together trailer can make audiences eager to see a film that is really a dud, the flash cutting in a music video can make a mediocre song sound better, and of course many people buy soft drinks based in part on the rapid-fire editing of an appealing cola commercial.

The propaganda of montage, in other words, can inspire the emotions, and Eisenstein used it masterfully. The flurry of shots of the Czar's troops shooting the masses on the Odessa steps juxtapose the helpless faces of the people, long lines of jackbooted cossacks, the smoke of rifle fire, sprawling bodies, menacing shadows, a slain mother, and her baby carriage helplessly rolling down the steps amid the chaos. Other great montages get overlooked due to the fame of the steps

Did you know?...

The train station scene in *The Untouchables* alludes to the Odessa Steps sequence.

An old woman (Repnikova) discovers the child she tried to protect has been killed by the Cossacks.

sequence, but they are moving as well. When the battleship takes to the sea in anticipation of the Czar's flotilla, Eisenstein cuts back and forth rapidly from shots of the engine's grinding pistons and spinning cam shafts to those of the water churned up off the hull. You can almost feel the ship pick up speed, and even a conservative Republican would find it hard not to root for the rebellious sailors as they go off to level their guns at more representatives of the evil Czar. Such is the power of montage. The film may be silent in that it has no words on the sound-track, but the power of the editing gives *Potemkin* a voice that is loud and clear.

Cast: Alexander Antonov (Vakulinchuk), Vladimir Barsky (Comdr. Golikov), Grigori Alexandrov (Senior Officer Gilyarovsky), Mikhail Gomorov (Sailor Matyushenko), Levchenko (Boatswain), Repnikova (woman on the steps), Marusov (officer), I. Bobrov (recruit), A. Fait (recruit), Sergei Eisenstein (priest), Alexander Lyovshin (petty officer), Beatrice Vitoldi (mother with baby carriage), Konstantin Feldman (student), Protopopov (old man), Korobei (legless vet-eran), Yulia Eisenstein (woman bringing food to mutineers), Zerenin (student) **Screenwriter:** Sergei Eisenstein **Cinematographer:** Edouard Tisse, V. Popov **Composer:** Eric Allaman, Edmund Meisel **Producer:** Jacob Bliokh **Running Time:** 71 minutes **Format:** VHS, LV.

Ben-Hur: A Tale of the Christ

1926 – Fred Niblo – 🦴🦴🦴

When the famous 1959 remake of *Ben-Hur* was passing through the many hands that worked on the script, someone (perhaps director William Wyler) had the sense to call in British playwright Christopher Fry to work during the shooting and to doctor the dialogue so that contemporary-sounding lines ("Did you like your dinner?") took on a more classic sound ("Was the food to your liking?"). Charlton Heston credits Fry with ridding the script of what Heston called the "MGM medieval" sound. The problem with films set in ancient times, however, is that even with such adjustments the mere presence of sound—ambient sound effects as well as the dialogue—can still impede the illusion of antiquity.

This earlier film version of Lew Wallace's novel benefits greatly from the larger-than-life quality of silent dramas. The stylized nature of silent films, resembling in some ways the grand emotions of opera, allows a story set in the ancient world to gain in verisimilitude. A simple scene like the one where Judah Ben-Hur (Ramon Navarro) catches a pigeon and gives it to Esther (May McAvoy) assumes great tenderness by acquiring the nature of a tableau in its silent presentation. The acting of Roman Navarro is also effectively understated as Ben-Hur, the Jew separated from his family, who must toil as a galley slave on a Roman trireme before impressing his captors with his bravery. When the ship is attacked by pirates, Ben-Hur saves the life of Arrius, the commander of the ship and even prevents him from ending his disgrace in "the Roman way" by committing suicide. Francis X. Bushman as Messala, the Roman commander and rival of Ben-Hur, indulges in the declamatory gestures associated with earlier styles of acting. His moments are the most dated. After Arrius adopts Ben-Hur, Messala and his former childhood friend meet again as opponents in the famous chariot race. It is a measure of this film's power that in the remake the opening sequence of the chariot race echoes shot by shot the development of that scene in the original.

The sea battle with the pirates and the chariot race are the great set pieces, and they still look impressive today. The later scenes arrange a number of memorable smaller moments: Esther finding Ben-Hur's family in the valley of the lepers, the healings on the way to Calvary. The lavish production was one of

Did you know?...

The man who directed the famous remake, William Wyler, was one of sixty assistant directors working on October 3, 1925, when the chariot race in the silent version was shot.

the big gambles of the silent era. MGM sent a crew for months to Italy while some of the parts were still being cast. Thousands of extras were hired for the maritime scenes, and rumors have persisted ever since that at least three of them drowned when one of the ships caught fire too quickly and the crew had to jump overboard wearing heavy costumes. The two-strip Technicolor sequences (in the restored version with the stereo score performed by the London Philharmonic) for the scenes depicting events from the gospels are beautiful. Their rarity truly enlivens this compelling and often powerful film.

Ben-Hur (Ramon Navarro) faces his old nemesis, charioteer Messala (Francis X. Bushman).

Cast: Ramon Novarro (Ben-Hur), Francis X. Bushman (Messala), May McAvoy (Esther), Betty Bronson (Mary), Claire McDowell (Princess of Hur), Kathleen Key (Tirzah), Carmel Myers (Iras), Nigel De Brulier (Simonides), Mitchell Lewis (Sheik Ilderim), Leo White (Sanballat), Frank Currier (Quintus Arrius), Charles Belcher (Balthazar), Dale Fuller (Amrah), Winter Hall (Joseph), Myrna Loy (spectator in crowd) **Screenwriter:** June Mathis, Bess Meredyth, Carey Wilson **Cinematographer:** Clyde De Vinna, Rene Guissart, Percy Hilburn, Karl Struss **Composer:** Carl Davis (restored version) **Producer:** Charles B. Dillangham, Abraham L. Erlanger, and Florenz Ziegfeld, Jr., for MGM **Running Time:** 148 minutes **Format:** VHS, LV **Box Office:** $9M.

The Big Parade

1925 – King Vidor – 🦴🦴🦴🦴

Those who have never seen a silent movie might choose well to make *The Big Parade* their first. Those who have seen many will savor this masterpiece. King Vidor's film about John Apperson (John Gilbert) and his various adventures after enlisting in World War I holds up amazingly well. We think that the silent cinema is more primitive or at least more stylized and artificial than polished, modern films, but the surprising range of emotions in this movie and the sureness and subtlety of its blend of humor and drama make it a model of moviemaking for any era. The rhythm of the editing (something director King Vidor always did well), the placement of the camera, and the (mostly) natural acting all seem refreshingly modern. It is hard to imagine a contemporary audience not responding with pleasant surprise to *The Big Parade*, especially with the addition of Carl Davis' recent orchestral score.

The film constantly surprises the viewer, especially in the first ninety minutes. After John has enlisted and arrives in France, the expected battle scene to acquaint the troops with the brutality of war fails to appear; instead, the doughboys, after a long day's hike, receive a command to shovel a pile of manure. The subsequent scenes capitalize on the humanity of the new friends Jim, Bull (Tom O'Brien), and Slim (Karl Dane) in unfamiliar surroundings doing mundane chores of washing clothes in a stream and rigging a makeshift shower. Jim acquires a French girlfriend (Renee Adoree) and teaches her to chew gum. As in sound films, the words (in the title cards) sometimes enrich the visuals by contrasting them. After the three friends are first buzzed by a German airplane, they take cover in a ditch. Slim asks Bull for a cigarette and they nervously joke about their plight. The looks on their faces, however, register their true feelings of uncertainty and dread. Ultimately, the film is better than *All Quiet on the Western Front* because it is less tied to its anti-war message. Whereas *All Quiet* intends to win converts to its message about the inhumanity of war and seems preachy at times, Vidor's film strives to capture the wartime experience in all its fullness and seems real. This 74-year-old film is as fresh, honest, and smoothly made as anything at the local multiplex.

Did you know?...

Cedric Gibbons, the art director for *The Big Parade* and one of the industry's most respected production designers, is also credited with designing the Oscar statuette.

Cast: John Gilbert (James Apperson), Renee Adoree (Melisande), Tom O'Brien (Bull), Karl Dane (Slim), Robert Ober (Harry), Hobart Bosworth (Mr. Apperson), Claire McDowell (Mrs.

Apperson), Claire Adams (Justyn Reed), Rosita Marstini (Melisande's mother) **Screenwriter:** Harry Behn, King Vidor (uncredited) **Cinematographer:** John Arnold **Composer:** William Axt, David Mendoza **Producer:** Irving Thalberg for MGM **Running Time:** 141 minutes **Format:** VHS, LV **Budget:** $382,000 **Box Office:** $3.485M (reportedly, the top-grossing silent film).

American soldier James Apperson (John Gilbert) charms a French miss, Melisande (Renee Adoree).

The Birth of a Nation

1915 – D.W. Griffith – 𝅘𝅥𝅘𝅥𝅘𝅥𝅘𝅥

"The dawn of a new art!"

Publicity tag line

In *Speed*, as Sandra Bullock and Keanu Reeves wheel a bus at high speed through the streets of Los Angeles, there is a cutaway to a woman pushing a baby carriage toward a street corner. The film then returns to Bullock and Reeves racing along. A few seconds later, another shot appears of the woman on the corner, easing her baby carriage onto the street and starting across. Movie audiences, of course, understand that the woman crossing the street is a few blocks ahead of the runaway bus and that in the editing of this scene director Jan de Bont is establishing a visual relationship of dramatic anticipation between the woman and the bus. Such classical cutting is just one of the legacies of D.W. Griffith. The assassination of Abraham Lincoln in *The Birth of a Nation* shows the same expert orchestration of suspense. Griffith arranges shots of different durations of Lincoln in the presidential box, of the Stoneman family in the audience, of John Wilkes Booth, of Lincoln's inattentive guard. He even uses the reflected light of a mirror to direct the audience's eye. The strategy is not simply to tell what happened on that fateful night but to make the visual climax of the scene coincide with the dramatic climax, a strategy that movies have been using ever since, thanks to Griffith.

The movie's blatant and unapologetic racism marks it as more of a representative of an earlier world than the logic of its cinematic style. The story follows the fortunes of two families, the northern Stonemans and the southern Camerons, through the Civil War and into Reconstruction. The second half of the film depicts the rise of the Ku Klux Klan, which is presented in a favorable light (the film was used as a recruiting tool for the KKK; riots in some northern cities accompanied the release of the film). Griffith meticulously worked on the historical details, conferring with veterans of the war and examining the photographs of Matthew Brady. The scene at Ford's Theater, like the previous one set at Appomattox, is preceded by a title card that announces its accuracy.

The film is equally effective, however, at capturing personal moments. Film scholar Louis Giannetti identifies one of Griffith's "most astonishing gifts [as] his ability to make intimate epics." The return of Henry Walthall after the war and his reunion with his sister (Mae Marsh) is often cited as one of Griffith's

Did you know?...

Raoul Walsh, who later became a director (*High Sierra*, *White Heat*) of some note, played John Wilkes Booth.

most understated moments of poetry: as the tired soldier walks up to the front door two feminine arms emerge from the house to welcome him home in a loving embrace. Griffith has been credited with creating or perfecting nearly all the elements of film grammar. He seemed always ahead of his time in his technique, always behind his time in his attitudes.

A Confederate soldier loads a cannon in a scene from *Birth of a Nation*.

Cast: Lillian Gish (Elsie Stoneman), Mae Marsh (Flora Cameron), Henry B. Walthall (Ben Cameron), Miriam Cooper (Margaret Cameron), Mary Alden (Lydia Brown), Ralph Lewis (Austin Stoneman), George Siegmann (Silas Lynch), Robert Harron (Ted Stonemann), Wallace Reid (Jeff), Joseph Henabery (Abraham Lincoln), Elmer Clifton (Phil Stoneman), Josephine Crowell (Mrs. Cameron), Spottiswoode Aitken (Dr. Cameron), George Andre Beranger (Wade Cameron), Maxfield Stanley (Duke Cameron), Jennie Lee (Cindy), Donald Crisp (Gen. Ulysses S. Grant), Howard Gaye (Gen. Robert E. Lee), Sam De Grasse (Sen. Charles Sumner), Raoul Walsh (John Wilkes Booth) **Screenwriter:** D.W. Griffith, Frank E. Woods, Jr. **Cinematographer:** Billy Bitzer **Composer:** Joseph Carl Breil **Producer:** D.W. Griffith **Running Time:** 174 minutes **Format:** VHS, LV **Budget:** Reports vary from $90,000 to $300,000 **Box Office:** Reports vary from $5 to $18 to $50M.

The Four Horsemen of the Apocalypse

1921 – Rex Ingram – 𝄞𝄞𝄞

> "Peace has come—but the Four Horsemen will still ravage humanity—stirring unrest in the world—until all hatred is dead and only love reigns in the heart of mankind."
>
> Final title card.

If *The Big Parade* is a silent film that showcases that art form especially well, *The Four Horsemen of the Apocalypse*, coming four years earlier, features the static compositions that many contemporary viewers might expect when they think of silent film. The movie is noteworthy for making a star out of Rudolph Valentino, whose performance makes the film worth watching. He is controlled and natural throughout (unlike, for example, the exaggerated gestures of Francis X. Bushman in the silent version of *Ben-Hur*). Director Rex Ingram designs richly textured sets, especially in the first half, and often elects to bring his actors in and out of the frame rather than rely too much on closeups. By following the geography of the set rather than the frame, Ingram dissipates the emotion from some scenes. His technique slows the pace of the film markedly, but it also creates a painterly effect that often gives the film an effective stylization.

The film is based on a best-selling novel by Vincente Blasco Ibanez, and the extended development of the early scenes of the Desnoyers family in Argentina likely owes to screenwriter June Mathis' desire to be faithful to a book that many in the audience would have known. When the patriarch (Pomeroy Cannon) of the Desnoyers family dies, the estate is divided between the French and German sides of his clan. Grandson Julio (Rudolph Valentino) moves to France to become an artist. At a tango palace Julio meets Marguerite (Alice Terry), the wife of a French politician (John Sainpolis). Julio and Marguerite begin an affair. The husband discovers Marguerite's unfaithfulness and plans to divorce her and challenge Julio to a duel when the assassination of the archduke and the tensions of the war intervene. The lovers try to atone for their behavior—Marguerite becomes a nurse, and Julio eventually enlists even though his Argentine nationality exempts him from service—but the war throws them together at Lourdes, where she attends to her blinded husband. The final battle scenes bring about a climax between Julio and his cousin Captain von Hartrott (Stuart Holmes), a representative of the German side of the Desnoyers family.

The sizable budget is visible in sets such as the Desnoyers castle and adjoining village, which were built by the film company near Griffith Park. The publicity for the film claimed that over 12,500 people took part in the produc-

Did you know?...

Alice Terry, who plays Marguerite Laurier, married director Rex Ingram in November 1921. She continued to appear in Ingram's films throughout the 1920s.

tion, that 125,000 tons of masonry were used for the sets, and that fourteen cameras recorded the battle scenes.

Rudolph Valentino stars as the tango-loving Julio.

Cast: Rudolph Valentino (Julio Desnoyers), Alice Terry (Marguerite Lurier), Pomeroy Cannon (Madariaga), Josef Swickard (Marcelo Desnoyers), Alan Hale (Karl von Hartrott), Nigel De Brulier (Tchernoff), John Sainpolis (Laurier), Stuart Holmes (Captain von Hartrott), Brinsley Shaw (Celedonio), Bridgetta Clark (Dona Luisa), Mabel Van Buren (Elena), Bowditch Turner (Argensola), Mark Fenton (Senator Lacour), Virginia Warwick (Chichi), Derek Ghent (Rene Lacour), Wallace Beery (Lt.-Col. von Richthoffen), Minnehaha (the old nurse), Jean Hersholt (Professor von Hartrott), Henry Klaus (Henrich von Hartrott), Jacques D'Auray (Captain d'Aubrey) **Screenwriter:** June Mathis **Cinematographer:** John F. Seitz **Composer:** Carl Davis (restored 1993 version) **Producer:** Rex Ingram for Metro **Running Time:** 110 minutes **Format:** VHS **Budget:** $800,000.

Intolerance

1916 – D.W. Griffith – ♫♫♫♪

Like Hollywood itself, there's not much good or bad you can say about this epic of epics that isn't true. Following the controversy surrounding charges of racism in *The Birth of a Nation*, D.W. Griffith combined the urge to reply to his critics with the showman's desire to top himself. The result was *Intolerance*, which connects four separate stories from different time periods into a continuous narrative. Griffith usually credited the novels of Charles Dickens as his influence in coming up with his celebrated crosscutting between separate actions ("Novelists think nothing of leaving one set of characters in the midst of affairs and going back to deal with earlier events in which another set of characters is involved"). In *Intolerance* Griffith links his stories conceptually and dramatically rather than chronologically. Each receives an exposition: a contemporary love story, the story of Christ, the conflict between Catholic and Huguenot in 1575 France, and the fall of ancient Babylon. Early transitions among the stories are signaled by a shot of the turning pages of a book and the image of a woman rocking a cradle (an idea Griffith adapted from a Walt Whitman poem). Later, as the plots developed, he assumed greater audience familiarity and dispensed with some of the transitions. All four stories concern themes of injustice or intolerance. Three of the four conclude with ride-to-the-rescue finales in which Griffith alternates shots of different durations and from different distances (usually shorter and closer as the climaxes near) in order to protract the suspense.

What Griffith gained in structure and pace, however, he lost in emotional intensity. As Richard Schickel observes in his biography of Griffith, "The trouble with *Intolerance* at the popular level is that it kept interrupting one narrative with another, spoiling the identificatory impulse just as it started to build." The contemporary story, about a boy falsely accused of murder and his sweetheart's attempt to secure the governor's reprieve before his execution, is thought by many to be the most compelling. The Christ story gets the sketchiest retelling, little more than three scenes (a miracle, a teaching, and the crucifixion). The sets for the Babylonian story were spectacular, and Griffith added a footnote to a title card detailing their dimensions. Surviving photographs show him directing these sequences from the basket of a hot-air balloon. He mounted the camera

Did you know?...

In the United States, two of the four interlocking stories were released separately under the titles *The Mother and the Law* and *The Fall of Babylon.*

on a makeshift elevator built on a flatbed train car, thereby creating the first crane shot.

Belshazzar's Babylon before its biblical destruction.

Cast: Lillian Gish (the woman who rocks the cradle), Mae Marsh (the dear one), Fred Tucker (her father), Robert Harron (the boy), Sam De Grasse (Arthur Jenkins), Vera Lewis (Mary T. Jenkins), Miriam Cooper (the friendless one), Ralph Lewis (the governor), Lloyd Ingraham (the judge), Tod Browning (owner of the racing car), William Brown (the warden), Howard Gaye (the Christ), Lillian Langdon (Mary, the Mother), Olga Grey (Mary Magdalene), Erich von Stroheim (Pharisee), Frank Bennett (Charles IX), Josephine Crowell (Catherine de Medici), Constance Talmadge (Marguerite de Valois), W.E. Lawrence (Henry of Navarre), Alfred Paget (Belshazzar), Seena Owen (Attarea), Carl Stockdale (King Nabonidus) **Screenwriter:** D.W. Griffith **Cinematographer:** Billy Bitzer, Karl Brown **Composer:** Joseph Carl Breil **Running Time:** 175 minutes **Format:** VHS, LV **Budget:** $2.5M.

Napoleon

1927 — Able Gance — 🦴🦴🦴🦴

Probably the worst luck that befell *Napoleon* was to have had its premiere six months before the debut of *The Jazz Singer*, the film that started the industry transition to sound. Gance's twenty-eight reel (or about six hour) silent epic covering the life of Napoleon from his boyhood to the Italian campaign was shown in its original form in only eight European cities. Its cinematic innovations as much as its length quickly made it one of the near-forgotten giants of the silent era. Gance's astonishing work anticipated numerous cinematic developments. The lighter French cameras of his day inspired him to create moving camera shots of exhilarating speed. In the scene that opens the film, a snowball fight between young Napoleon (Wladmir Roudenko) and a dozen or so of his friends versus sixty other classmates, Gance suggests the viewpoint of one of the boys by putting the camera in a sled and sliding it toward the snow fortress of the opposition. A blizzard of snowballs come flying at and away from the camera. In later scenes, he strapped the camera on the back of a horse to suggest the kinetics of riding. Most famously, he engineered three, parabola-like harnesses to swoop like a pendulum over the actors playing the scene of the frenzied Paris Convention on the eve of the revolution (although the finished film only uses the more dramatic shots from the highest of the three harnesses). These shots he intercut with scenes of the older Napoleon (Albert Dieudonne) tossing at sea in a skiff to connect metaphorically the storm at sea with the emotional storm of the revolution.

Gance also loved superimposing shots over each other, as when pictures of the fury of the Convention, captured by the dizzying swinging camera, are superimposed over shots of a guillotine with the blade about the fall. His most striking innovation was an effect he called Polyvision. Gance said that the first appearance of this effect in the film occurs during the pillow fight scene when young Napoleon retaliates against his classmates for setting free his pet eagle. As the fight begins, the frame suddenly divides into four images in each corner of the screen; then it divides into twelve images, each one different from the others and each changing in staccato fashion as feathers from the pillows fly. The most famous instance of Polyvision, however, occurs when Gance widens the screen to three times its regular size to project three 35mm images from three

projectors side by side. A truly spectacular effect, these triptychs in effect used Cinerama in a more complex way than filmmakers would thirty years later. Gance sometimes created one panoramic vista with his three-camera shots, but often he would have the center projector show a closeup of Napoleon while the two side projectors rapidly alternated shots of the Italian campaign, thereby creating a contrapuntal effect. He also tinted the film stock at times and used Polyvision to turn the screen into the tricolor French flag, one of the film's bravura moments.

Certainly few if any other films bring an epic approach to the cinematic technique as well as to the subject matter, and so it is no surprise that for many years the uniqueness of *Napoleon* placed it in obscurity as the age of silent movies passed away. Future film historian Kevin Brownlow, however, when still a young student, saw some segments of the film and began hunting more in shops that sold 16mm films for home and school exhibition. Brownlow spent twenty

Albert Dieudonne stars in the title role.

years laboring at the job of restoring Gance's nearly lost epic to very close to its original twenty-eight reels (two earlier scenes using Polyvision seem to be the only footage that has eluded Brownlow). The culmination of Brownlow's work was an outdoor showing of the restored *Napoleon* with the synchronized three-projector Polyvision finale in September 1979 at the Telluride Film Festival in Colorado. Gance, at age 89, watched appreciatively from his hotel window.

The next two years saw more interest in touring the film. A British showing of the film followed with a new score by Carl Davis, and Francis Ford Coppola helped support a series of American performances of a slightly shortened version before an audience of 6,000 at Radio City Music Hall with new music by Coppola's father, Carmine. Brownlow writes about the reconstruction and this January 1981 debut at Radio City Music Hall in his book *Napoleon: Able Gance's Classic Film*. Gance had become more frail over the two years between the Colorado and New York showings, and he did not attend the 1981 premiere. But the audience's reaction was so wildly enthusiastic that Brownlow placed a call to Gance from the theater. The phone receiver was dragged on stage to the length of the cord as the audience cheered madly. "It was like telephoning heaven," Brownlow writes, "and waking Beethoven to hear what we mortals thought of his work." Able Gance died eighteen days later at age 91.

Cast: Albert Dieudonne (Napoleon Bonaparte), Wladmir Roudenko (young Napoleon), Gina Manes (Josephine de Beauhamais), Nicolas Loline (Tristan Fleuri), Annabella (Violine Fleuri), Serge Freddykarll (Marcellin Fleuri), Emond Van Daele (Robespierre), Alexandre Koubitzky (Danton), Antonin Artaud (Marat), Abel Gance (Saint-Just), Max Maxudian (Barras), Philippe Heriat (Salicetti), Acho Chakatouny (Pozzo di Borgo), Eugenie Buffet (Laetizia Bonaparte), Yvette Dieudonne (Elisa Bonaparte), Georges Lampin (Joseph Bonaparte), Sylvio Cavicchia (Lucien Bonaparte), Simone Genevois (Pauline Bonaparte), Louis Dance (Louis XVI), Suzanne Bianchetti (Marie-Antoinette), Pierre Batcheff (Gen. Lazare Hoche), Philippe Rolla (Massena), Alexandre Bernard (Dugommier), W. Percy Day (Admiral Hood), Genica Missirio (Capt. Joachim Mjrat), Robert de Ansorena (Capt. Desaix), Harry Krimer (Rouget de l'Ilse), Marguerite Gance (Charlotte Corday), Roger Blum (Talma), Jean Henry (Sgt. Andoche Junot), Maryse Damia (La Marseillaise), Henri Baudin (Santo-Ricci), Georges Henin (Eugene de Beauharnais), Henry Krauss (Moustache) **Screenwriter:** Abel Gance **Cinematographer:** Jules Kruger, Leonce-Henry Burel **Composer:** Arthur Honegger (original version), Carl Davis (British restored version), Carmine Coppola (American restored version) **Producer:** Abel Gance for Societe generale de Films **Running Time:** 235 minutes (American restored version) **Format:** VHS, LV.

October

1927 – Sergei Eisenstein, Grigori Alexandrov – 🎬🎬🎬

"Formalist excess!"—one of the first and most important reviews of this film was that delivered by the inner ring of the Communist Party. Director Sergei Eisenstein was accused of caring more about film technique than about his film subject of the ten days that shook the world in October 1917, the Bolshevik Revolution. One famous example from Eisenstein's earlier classic, *Potemkin*, foreshadows his later emphasis on abstract ideas in *October*. As the battleship levels its guns on the cossacks, three shots of stone lions are intercut into the narrative, one of a lion sleeping, another of one stirring awake, and then a third ready to roar. The sculptured lions are not part of the setting or the dramatic development involving the ship and the cossacks. Eisenstein introduces the montage of the lions solely as a symbol of the awakened revolutionary spirit. Such an abstract idea injected in this limited way into one of the film's climactic sequences works well. It is as if the stones themselves roar in anger at the cossacks.

In *October*, however, this technique is put to a much greater use, and it cannot help seeming heavy-handed and obtrusive. In the scene when General Kerensky (Nikolai Popov) of the provisional government stands before double doors, the film cuts repeatedly between closeups of Kerensky's polished boots, cocky stance, and glove—and closeups of a peacock. When the doors fan open to admit Kerensky, the film cuts to the peacock's tailfeathers, which also open out widely. Later, the militia of this provisional government is ridiculed when a shot of the real soldiers is followed by one of a row of tin soldiers and then by one of a row of empty wine glasses. This last analogy provides a more subtle touch, suggesting the ornate and essentially decorative function of Kerensky's proud military, but audiences were understandably confused by such rapid, abstract parallels. Eisenstein's ties to the Stalinist regime began to unravel over the unfavorable reception of this film.

October exists in a variety of lengths. One of the director's proudest flourishes is the gods sequence, which was cut from American prints. In it, Eisenstein attempts to discredit the idea of God by arranging, in "descending intellectual scale" as the director put it, images from a statue of Christ to garish pagan idol. The first cut of the film ran just under four hours, but when Leon Trotsky

Did you know?...

In the scene of the storming of the Winter Palace, 11,000 extras were used. Reportedly, the power consumption of the film crew caused a blackout for the rest of the city.

Vasili Nikandrov stars as Russian leader Lenin in *October*.

was exiled for planning demonstrations against the Party, Eisenstein had to eliminate Trotsky from the film narrative. This job required five months of recutting and reduced the film to under two hours. The experimental nature of the film has resulted in some impressive moments, but the overall effect is of a brilliant technical exercise rather than a film with a life of its own.

Cast: Layaschenko (Minister), Boris Livanov (Minister), Vasili Nikandrov (Lenin), Nikolai Popov (Kerensky), Edouard Tisse (German soldier) **Screenwriter:** Grigori Alexandrov, Sergei Eisenstein **Cinematographer:** Vladimir Nilsen, Vladimir Popov, Edouard Tisse **Composer:** Edmund Meisel, Dimitri Shostakovich (reissue) **Running Time:** 104 minutes **Format:** VHS, LV.

Orphans of the Storm
1921 – D.W. Griffith – ♪♪♪

In *Intolerance*, D.W. Griffiths' lofty ambitions to intercut stories from four historical periods defeated his attempts to balance spectacle with a compelling personal element. But with *Orphans of the Storm* he returned to the form of the intimate epic that he created in *The Birth of a Nation*. Set against the background of pre-revolution France, the film follows the fortunes of two girls who grow up as sisters. One is a foundling discovered on the steps of Notre Dame and brought home by the father of the other, Henriette (Lillian Gish). A plague leaves the parents dead and young Louise (Dorothy Gish) blind. The two girls travel to Paris in the hope of finding a doctor to restore Louise's sight, but they are separated when Henriette is abducted by a dissolute nobleman (Morgan Wallace). In the other plot, Louise's blindness is exploited by a cruel peasant family who torture her until she agrees to beg for them. After many complications that encumber some of the chances for character development, the two sisters finally reunite just as the revolution starts. The final third of the movie shows the peasants to be as cruel as the aristocracy and concludes with an exciting sequence of Danton's (Monte Blue) ride to the rescue of Henriette on the guillotine.

Griffith's eye for detail is keenly alert. He establishes the gulf between rich and poor by contrasting shots of aristocratic women whose ornate hats barely fit inside their carriage windows with those of starving peasants begging for bread. The bacchanal where Henriette is abducted includes women bathing in fountains

"**Among all these nobleman, isn't there one man of honor?**"
Henriette (Lillian Gish), at the fete where she is attacked.

Did you know?...
The film marked the last time Griffith worked with Lillian Gish.

The Gish sisters star as adoptive sisters Henriette (Lillian Gish) and Louise (Dorothy Gish).

of wine and a fop who drinks champagne from a glass held between the feet of a woman perched on a balcony. As usual, Griffith's title cards vary between the preachy and the dramatic. One of the most effective appears after a grisly scene in which the nobleman's coach drives over a peasant child. (There is no cutaway to the faces of onlookers to spare the audience.) The commoners surround the Marquis de Praille, waving their fists, and he calmly scatters a few coins in their direction and the title card reads: "Dead? Sorry—this is for the mother. Are the horses hurt?"—*"An historical incident."*

Working with less sprawling material likely led to the coherent structure, greater suspense, and more affecting human element in *Orphans* (though its scenes of spectacle fall below the level of the majestic *Intolerance*). Griffith also tinkers a bit with frame size. In two of the shots of the people storming the Bastille, he masks the image with a rectangular iris, creating a letterbox frame perfectly matching the swarm of people. It is a widescreen effect anticipating both Able Gance's Polyvision in *Napoleon* and Hollywood's widescreen aspect ratios in the 1950s.

Cast: Lillian Gish (Henriette), Dorothy Gish (Louise), Joseph Schildkraut (Chevalier de Vaudrey), Frank Losee (Count de Linieres), Katherine Emmett (Countess de Linieres), Morgan Wallace (Marquis de Praille), Lucille La Verne (Mother Frochard), Sheldon Lewis (Jacques Frochard), Monte Blue (Danton), Creighton Hale (Picard), Leslie King (Jacques-Forget-Not), Sidney Herbert (Robespierre), Lee Kohlmar (King Louis XVI), Kate Bruce (Sister Genevieve), Louis Wolfheim (Executioner), Herbert Sutch (Meat Carver at the Fete) **Screenwriter:** D.W. Griffith (as Gaston de Tolignac) **Cinematographer:** Billy Bitzer, Hendrik Sartov **Composer:** William F. Peters **Producer:** D.W. Griffith **Format:** VHS, LV **Budget:** $950,000 **Box Office:** Griffith's biographer Richard Schickel reports that the film lost $112,854.

The Thief of Bagdad
1924 – Raoul Walsh – 🦴🦴🦴

An enjoyable taste of *The Thief of Bagdad* occurs in the scene when the princess (Julanne Johnston) watches from a balcony with two waiting women as her would-be suitors ride through the palace gate. Unknown to the men, a prophecy has forecast that her future husband will be the one who first touches the rose tree in the courtyard. The audience knows that the dashing thief of Bagdad (Douglas Fairbanks, Sr.) will be the first to touch the rose bush, but they, along with the princess, must suffer some doubt when the pompous Mongol

> **"Happiness must be earned."**
> Opening and closing title.

The Caliph (Brandon Hurst) confronts the Thief (Douglas Fairbanks).

Did you know?...
The 1940 British remake produced by Alexander Korda, one of the early uses of Technicolor, is also a highly regarded film with a rousing musical score by Miklos Rozsa.

prince (So-Jin) walks purposefully toward the bush. Then a bee frightens both the Mongol and the thief's horse, which flips the thief on his back into the roses. As he removes thorns, the princess smiles contentedly and walks off, her arms around her waiting women. The movie's continual playfulness often undercuts the dignity of the hero and serves to keep the audience off balance. Such irreverence and sense of play strengthens the early scenes. After winning the hand of the princess, the thief must prove his worth, undertake the Journey of the Seven Moons, and return to Bagdad with the desired treasure.

Fairbanks' athleticism competes with the sets of William Cameron Menzies to see who is the more spectacular. Probably it was a friendly competition since the two had worked together on Fairbanks' 1922 star vehicle *Robin Hood*, for which Menzies had constructed a full-scale Norman castle. Even in the 1920s moviemakers felt the urge to top themselves, and hardly a scene goes by in *The Thief of Bagdad* where the size and exotic design of the sets do not create a surreal, fantasy world.

The film has probably kept its admirers over the years thanks to director Raoul Walsh's striking use of space. Walsh creates long shots of considerable power by placing his actors carefully in Menzies' towering sets and then shooting them from a distance. The gate to Bagdad stands as high as twelve men, and it parts outward in four directions when it opens. Before the Mongols attack Bagdad, two tiny-seeming watchmen stand on the palace balconies waving signal torches. The thief rides across endless stretches of desert to return to liberate Bagdad from the Mongols. Many of the special effects, such as in the scenes when the thief battles the dragon, the giant bat, and the undersea spider, have aged a bit, but others still hold up well and contribute to the fantasy—as in the scenes with the flying carpet and the thief's cloak of invisibility, which changes him into a transparent whirlwind. To prepare for the expected big finish of the thief and the princess flying off on the magic carpet while all Bagdad cheers, the filmmakers add a touch reminiscent of the wit of the rose-bush scene. The thief wraps his cloak of invisibility around himself and the princess, and it just about covers them. The onlookers in the palace watch in astonishment as two pairs of feet tiptoe up the staircase and settle on the flying carpet.

Cast: Douglas Fairbanks (the thief of Bagdad), Snitz Edwards (the evil associate), Charles Belcher (the holy man), Julanne Johnston (the princess), Anna May Wong (the Mongol slave), Winter-Blossom (the slave of the lute), Etta Lee (slave of the sand board), Brandon Hurst (the caliph), Noble Johnson (the Indian prince), So-Jin (the Mongol prince), Tote Du Crow (the soothsayer), Mathilde Comont (the Persian prince), Charles Stevens (his awaker),

Sam Baker (the sworder), K. Nambu (counselor to the Mongol prince), Sadakichi Hartmann (Mongol court magician) **Screenwriter:** Lotta Woods, Douglas Fairbanks (billed as Elton Thomas) **Cinematographer:** Arthur Edeson **Producer:** Douglas Fairbanks **Running Time:** 153 minutes **Format:** VHS, LV, DVD **Budget:** $1-2M.

They Might Be Giants . . .

A nine-reel silent film from Italy, *Quo Vadis?* (1912), directed by Enrico Guazzoni, is credited by many with establishing the conventions of the spectacle film with its cast of thousands, memorable set pieces (a chariot race, the burning of Rome, lions in the Coliseum), and massive sets. Another influential early silent epic was Piero Fosco's *Cabria* (1914), which boasted even more magnificent sets and location shooting. Film historian David Cook credits *Cabria* with an influential use of traveling shots that reframe action and with atmospheric lighting (the so-called "Rembrandt lighting"). The first American epic was D.W. Griffith's *Judith of Bethulia* (1913), which combines, as Griffith would later do in *Intolerance*, four concurrently developing story lines. As silent film moved into the 1920s, noteworthy films appeared like King Vidor's *The Crowd* (1928), which brings out the universal by looking intently at the life of one office worker. Other significant films include Victor Seastrom's *The Wind* (1928), in which Lillian Gish plays a woman struggling in the harsh American frontier, Josef von Sternberg's *The Last Command*, about a Russian general after the revolution who tries to hold on to his dignity as he looks for work in Hollywood, and *Wings* (1927), a World War I story with epic aerial scenes directed by William Wellman, who had been himself a member of the Lafayette Flying Corps.

TRAGEDY

Antony and Cleopatra

Citizen Kane

Hamlet

Julius Caesar

Long Day's Journey into Night

Nixon

Patton

Raging Bull

Ran

Romeo and Juliet

Antony and Cleopatra

1973 – Charlton Heston – 🧦🧦

If *Henry V* is Shakespeare's attempt at a stage epic (assisted greatly by his poetry that addresses and rouses the audience's imagination), *Antony and Cleopatra* may well be his mock epic. The play certainly enjoys deflating the noble image of Marc Antony, who is torn between the Roman ideal of duty and the love-lust he feels for the pleasure-loving Cleopatra. His tragedy becomes his inability to reconcile these two sides of his divided self. The first shot of Charlton Heston in this film—that he also adapted and directed—captures this conflict well (both Lawrence Olivier and Orson Welles were sought for the lead). Antony is pictured lounging and napping while Cleopatra (Hildegard Neil) applies some lip-liner to his mouth. Later, when Enobarbus (Eric Porter) describes Cleopatra on her barge ("Age cannot whither her nor custom stale her infinite variety"), Heston inserts a few cutaways to Antony, who seems unable to keep his mind on Octavia (Carmen Sevilla), his betrothed. Heston is much better than Hildegard Neil as Cleopatra. The chief drawback is her inability to suggest the captivating, mercurial quality of the queen or even to convey a personality that would make plausible Antony's obsession with her.

The battle scenes at sea disappoint as well. The usual approach in the film superimposes the face of one of the participants over a shot of a ship or two while martial music thunders on the soundtrack, as if the filmmakers are trying to disguise a budget that won't support many action sequences. Most of the other scenes overuse rather tight closeups, which makes the compositions on a non-letterboxed version seem careless and unbalanced. One of the best effects comes in the quiet moment when Eros (Garrick Hagon), Antony's aptly named slave, rows his master at night across a lake, and Antony compares himself to a cloud that the wind continually reshapes. The flicker of the torchlight on Antony's meditative face calls attention to his tragic insight about the variability of human nature and his own inability to be the sort of man he feels he ought to be.

Cast: Charlton Heston (Marc Antony), Hildegard Neil (Cleopatra), Eric Porter (Enobarbus), John Castle (Octavius), Fernando Rey (Lepidus), Carmen Sevilla (Octavia), Freddie Jones (Pompey), Monica Peterson (Iras), Aldo Sambrell (Ventidius), John Hallam (Thidias), Jane Lapotaire (Charmian), Fernando Bilbao (Menecrates), Luis Barboo (Varius), Warren Clarke (Scarus), Roger Delgado (Soothsayer), Garrick Hagon (Eros) **Screenwriter:** Charlton Heston

Did you know?...

Heston tried unsuccessfully to interest Orson Welles in the project, as he had been able to do previously with *Touch of Evil,* which Welles wrote, directed and starred in with Heston and Janet Leigh.

Upon hearing of Cleopatra's death, Antony (Charlton Heston) asks Eros (Garrick Hagan) to kill him.

(from Shakespeare) **Cinematographer:** Rafael Pacheco **Composer:** John Scott **Producer:** Peter Snell for Izaro and Folio Films; released by Transac and the Rank Organization **MPAA Rating:** PG **Running Time:** 150 minutes **Format:** VHS.

Citizen Kane
1941 – Orson Welles – 🦴🦴🦴🦴

> "Mr. Kane was somebody who got everything he wanted, and then lost it. Maybe Rosebud was something he couldn't get or something he lost."
>
> Thompson (William Alland) the reporter.

Did you know?...

Welles claimed that the title of the film was the idea of RKO studio head George Schaefer. None of the writers or actors could think of a suitable title for months, though Welles said he never forgot one awful suggestion by a secretary: *A Sea of Upturned Faces.*

Orson Welles' first film explored the life of press baron Charles Foster Kane (Welles) in the effort to solve the riddle of his dying word "rosebud." The movie has been so often called the greatest film ever made and the world's most honored film that we forget how much of its mythic power derives from Welles' deep tragic sensibility. "All of the characters I've played," he has said, "are various forms of Faust: all have bartered their souls and lost." Hard to find a better epitaph for Kane. In spite of the bravura cinematic style and the fascinatingly fair (buying up the world's artifacts and then leaving them unopened) and unfair (the harsh treatment of Kane's second wife) parallels to the life of William Randolph Hearst, this view of Kane as tragic hero may be the richest approach to the film and the one that also gives it an epic scale. Lending power to that essential grand drama of the American dream bought and lost is the dynamic editing by Robert Wise and an uncredited Mark Robson, and Greg Toland's astonishing and still influential cinematography. Toland uses a deep focus within the frame to give perspective on the character and his surroundings, and deploys light and shadow to exploit the dramatic urgency. Welles intersects strands of nonlinear narrative to create a rich dynamic whole. The overall level of sophistication and innovation is astonishing; even more so when you consider that Welles was 26 when the movie opened.

An old rule of thumb about tragedy maintains that "tragedy happens when you lose what means most to you." Kane's tragedy, as Leland (Joseph Cotten) points out ("Charlie wanted everyone to love him, but he wanted love on his own terms"), is the lost sense of being loved and Kane's increasingly desperate attempt to reclaim it. The trip to view the objects from his mother's estate on the night he meets Susan Alexander (Dorothy Comingore) is one attempt. The career in politics and buying up the world's art are others. Kane's awareness of this loss of love gives his character much of his complexity. He has to live with

A young Charles Foster Kane (Orson Welles) looks happy on his wedding day, but his happiness won't last.

himself knowing what he is turning into. When his best friend is about to walk out of his life, he tells Leland, "Here's to love on our own terms, Jedidiah; those are the only terms anyone knows anything about," but of course he sounds like someone voicing a fact he wishes weren't so. The scene in the big hall when Kane campaigns for governor is probably the only one that can claim the vastness of size that we often associate with epics, but the real mythic scale lies in what this scene represents: a man who so badly wants the sense of security and love of his childhood that he seeks it in the votes of the faceless thousands before him. The use of space in the scenes at Xanadu—the cavernous fireplace, a living room the size of a gymnasium—all visually suggest what Welles has said about Kane: "a man who turned out to be an empty box."

Cast: Orson Welles (Charles Foster Kane), Joseph Cotten (Jedediah Leland), Dorothy Comingore (Susan Alexander), Everett Sloan (Mr. Bernstein), Ray Collins (Boss Jim Gettys), Paul Stewart (Raymond), Ruth Warrick (Emily Norton), Erskine Sanford (Mr. Carter), Agnes Moorehead (Kane's mother), Harry Shannon (Kane's father), George Coulouris (Walter Parks

Thatcher), William Alland (Thompson), Fortunio Bonanova (Matiste), Gus Schilling (waiter), Katherine Trosper (reporter), Philip Van Zandt (Rawlston), Buddy Swan (young Kane), Thomas A. Curran (Teddy Roosevelt), Alan Ladd (reporter with the pipe) **Screenwriter:** Orson Welles, Herman J. Mankiewicz **Cinematographer:** Gregg Toland **Composer:** Bernard Herrmann **Producer:** Orson Welles for RKO and the Mercury Theater **Running Time:** 119 minutes **Format:** VHS, LV **Awards:** Academy Awards 1941: Original Screenplay; Nominations: Actor (Orson Welles), Black and White Cinematography (Gregg Toland), Director (Orson Welles), Editing, Interior Decoration, Picture, Sound, Original Dramatic/Comedy Score (Bernard Herrmann).

Hamlet

1996 – Kenneth Branagh – 🦴🦴🦴🦴

> "Here is a man faced with the prospect of murder or his own death. He faces both as absolute realities, and it is the most quiet and terrifying dread he has ever known."
>
> Kenneth Branagh, in directions from the screenplay about Hamlet's "To be or not to be" soliloquy.

Did you know?...
Julie Christie, who plays Gertrude, appears in her first Shakespearean role.

Shakespeare's tragedy of the Danish prince (Kenneth Branagh) who is visited by his father's ghost (Brian Blessed) and learns that his uncle (Derek Jacobi) killed him is performed with an uncut text—all 3,906 lines of it. In contrast, Franco Zeffirelli's 1990 version with Mel Gibson retained only 37% of the original text. It's not just the full text that gives the play an epic scope. Branagh also filmed the interiors on the largest sound stage at Shepperton Studios in England, and he makes great use of these large spaces in the opening scene at court and in the final sword fight between Hamlet and Laertes (Michael Maloney). The mirrored doors lining the sides of the expansive foyer create the illusion of even greater spaces.

Such spectacle balances the moments when the film uses the labyrinthine corridors behind these doors to dramatize the dissembling so pervasive to the play. Behind one of them is the padded room where Ophelia (Kate Winslet) is confined after going mad from grief at the death of her father. The scene before the intermission (featuring the speech "How all occasions do inform against me") is the film's greatest attempt to impart the physicality of an epic scope to the materials. As Hamlet explains how the sight of the Norwegian army marching off to fight for a worthless patch of ground spurs him on to take revenge, the camera pulls back to reveal an enormous stretch of soldiers behind Hamlet filling the wide dimensions of the 70mm screen accompanied by Patrick Doyle's rousing music. (The process photography looks a bit fuzzy in spots in what is obviously a matte shot.)

Branagh's acting may risk overdoing some speeches, and his direction sometimes uses spinning camera moves in fussy, disorienting ways. His chief

Queen Gertrude (Julie Christie) tries to reason with her maddening son (Kenneth Branagh).

contribution may be the overall concept of the play, which stresses the gap between Hamlet's encounter with proof of a life beyond this one and the selfish absorption in worldly pleasures indulged in by king and court. The major performances are subtle and effective, especially Derek Jacobi, whose rich voice registers the blank verse most sharply. His nuanced work presents Claudius as a personality pieced together from a gallery of momentary disguises: politician, king, murderer, lover, drinker, schemer. Under them all sweats the worried sinner who wants to repent of his murder but who loves too much the fruits of his sins.

Cast: Kenneth Branagh (Hamlet), Derek Jacobi (Claudius), Richard Briers (Polonius), Julie Christie (Gertrude), Kate Winslet (Ophelia), Michael Maloney (Laertes), Nicholas Farrell (Horatio), Brian Blessed (Ghost), Timothy Spall (Rosencrantz), Reece Dinsdale (Guildenstern), Billy Crystal (First Gravedigger), Simon Russel Beale (Second Gravedigger), Robin Williams (Osric), Gerard Depardieu (Reynaldo), Jack Lemmon (Marcellus), Charlton Heston (Player King), Rosemary Harris (Player Queen), Ian McElhinney (Bernardo), Ray Fearon (Francisco), Rufus Sewell (Fortinbras), Richard Attenborough (English Ambassador), John Gielgud (Priam), John Mills (Old Norway), Judi Dench (Hecuba), Ken Dodd (Yorick), Melanie Ramsay (Prostitute) **Screenwriter:** Kenneth Branagh (from Shakespeare) **Cinematographer:** Alex Thomson **Composer:** Patrick Doyle **Producer:** David Barron for Castle Rock Entertainment and Fishmonger Films; released by Columbia and Sony **MPAA Rating:** PG-13 **Running Time:** 242 minutes **Format:** VHS, LV **Awards:** Academy Awards 1996: Nominations: Adapted Screenplay (Kenneth Branagh), Art Direction, Costume Design, Original Dramatic Score (Patrick Doyle) **Box Office:** $582,904.

Julius Caesar

1953 – Joseph L. Mankiewicz – 𓂀𓂀𓂀

"Cowards die many times before their death; the valiant never taste of death but once."

Caesar (Louis Calhern) to Calpurnia.

Did you know?...

John Houseman had worked with Orson Welles on the famous Federal Theater Project production of the play in the 1930s. That contemporary version drew explicit parallels between the power politics of the play and the rise of fascism in Europe.

Shakespeare's tragedy of the assassination of Julius Caesar and its aftermath is famous for its refusal to take sides among the conspirators. This objectivity in the play may be one of the saving graces for this film since the movie combines so many different acting styles. The variety among the players and the overall quality of their work ultimately serves the production well by suggesting the many-sided nature of men's ambitions and the complexities that necessarily result from such a drastic, irrevocable act.

Director Joseph L. Mankiewicz attempts to capture a sense of spectacle in the brief early scene when Caesar (Louis Calhern) enters Rome and later in the extended pair of speeches by Brutus (James Mason) and Antony (Marlon Brando) following the killing. These are played before a large, boisterous crowd. The contrast between the reactions of the crowd and the speeches works wonderfully to show the fickleness of the doltish masses. First, Brutus' self-justifying, idealistic words gain rousing support; minutes later, Antony—his voice cracking with emotion—delivers the masterpiece of irony and manipulation that turns the people against the men they had just extolled. The final image after the funeral oration places the now-rioting masses in the background as Antony turns to re-enter the senate chamber in the foreground. Once his back has turned on the citizens, the flicker of a smile plays on his lips. Visually, emotionally, and dramatically, this scene is the highlight of the film.

All of Brando's best moments come immediately after the assassination, from the time he arrives to view the body and coldly greets the conspirators. Alone after they go to address the populace, Brando brings out Antony's anguish and anger ("let slip the dogs of war"), and his entry carrying the body of Caesar

makes for a stunning moment. The earlier scenes of conspiratorial plotting and the later battle scenes are staged by Mankiewicz to emphasize strategy and humanity rather than spectacle, but the quality of the acting maintains interest throughout. John Gielgud is excellent as the dissembling Cassius; Mason captures the thoughtful sensitivity and idealism of Brutus, a part often said to be Shakespeare's early version of Hamlet.

Marc Antony (Marlon Brando) tells his fellow Romans he has not come to praise a fallen Caesar.

Cast: Louis Calhern (Julius Caesar), Marlon Brando (Marc Antony), James Mason (Brutus), Edmond O'Brien (Casca), John Gielgud (Cassius), George Macready (Marulius), Richard Hale (soothsayer), Alan Napier (Cicero), Greer Garson (Calpurnia), Deborah Kerr (Portia), Ian Wolfe (Ligarius), Douglass Dumbrille (Lepidus), Michael Ansara (Pindarus), William Cottrell (Cinna), Ned Glass (cobbler) **Screenwriter:** Joseph L. Mankiewicz (from Shakespeare) **Cinematographer:** Joseph Ruttenberg **Composer:** Miklos Rozsa **Producer:** John Houseman for MGM **Running Time:** 120 minutes **Format:** VHS, LV **Awards** Academy Awards 1953: Art Direction/Set Decoration (B&W); Nominations: Actor (Marlon Brando), Black and White Cinematography (Joseph Ruttenberg), Picture, Original Dramatic/Comedy Score (Miklos Rozsa); British Academy Awards 1953: Actor (Marlon Brando), Actor (John Gielgud); National Board of Review Awards 1953: 10 Best Films of the Year; Actor (James Mason) **Budget:** $2M.

Long Day's Journey into Night

1962 – Sidney Lumet – 𝄞𝄞𝄞𝄞

> "The dead part of me hopes you won't get well. Maybe he's even glad the game has got Mama again! He wants company, he doesn't want to be the only corpse around the house!"
>
> Jamie (Jason Robards, Jr.) to his brother Edmund.

It is sometimes said that in tragedy something of value dies (usually a physical something) and something of value gets born (usually an intangible something). This work by America's greatest playwright focuses on the difficulty of that birth process. On July 22, 1941, Eugene O'Neill presented his wife Carlotta with the manuscript of this play for their twelfth wedding anniversary. It had the longest gestation of any of his plays and is a work of seeming simplicity but filled with emotional and structural complexity. From 8:30 in the morning until midnight on a day in August 1912, at their Connecticut summer home, the four Tyrones talk about themselves and their past. The complexity partly comes from O'Neill's subtlety in assigning each character alternating voices of anger and apology, the two feelings that fight for dominance over this long, fog-shrouded day. He has also skillfully arranged the many conversational duets, trios, and quartets into something of a spoken opera. These seemingly random exchanges start and end in ways that eventually expose the souls of each family member.

The overall pattern is one of attack and forgive. The power of the play, captured well in this film, comes from O'Neill's ultimately benevolent attitude toward these characters based on himself, his brother, and their parents. The characters all reach moments toward the end when they are able to do that most difficult thing of looking at themselves with honesty. The actor father (Ralph Richardson), for example, has been haunted his whole life by his decision to tour in one popular role rather than to develop himself in less lucrative but more artistically challenging parts. He admits to Edmund (Dean Stockwell) for the first time that he was ruined by the "promise of an easy fortune." Suffering from tuberculosis, Edmund, the younger son (the character based on the author), is inspired by his father's confession and describes his own transcendent joy when he was at sea and laments his small poetic gift for expressing these pent-up feelings: "Stammering is the native eloquence of us fog people." Later, older brother Jamie (Jason Robards, Jr., repeating his stage role), in a scene of remarkable candor and self-scrutiny, reveals the motives for his alcoholism and the depth of his self-disgust when he admits how the part of him "that's been

Did you know?...

No screenwriter was listed for the film since no rewriting and very few cuts were made in O'Neill's play. When Katharine Hepburn asked director Sidney Lumet who was doing the script, he replied, "O'Neill." She then agreed to appear.

dead so long" never wanted Edmund to succeed "and make me look worse by comparison." And the mother Mary (Katharine Hepburn), who became addicted to morphine years before when treated by an incompetent doctor Tyrone, Sr. called in to save money, voices her longing for a fuller sense of family and her deep hunger for spiritual redemption.

Unhappy Mary Tyrone (Katharine Hepburn) turns away from her equally unhappy family.

O'Neill takes a tolerant attitude toward the life lies and illusions his characters require to cope with their difficult existences. He seems to feel that deep down people still need to see the truth about themselves and that, given the chance, they will choose to embrace it in all its pain. The richness of that honesty and the mutual acceptance it implies is the something of value that gets born in *Long Day's Journey*. Perhaps O'Neill realized this when he inscribed his dedication of the script to his wife with thanks for enabling him to "face my dead and write this play—write it with deep pity and understanding and forgiveness for all the four haunted Tyrones."

Cast: Katharine Hepburn (Mary Tyrone), Ralph Richardson (James Tyrone, Sr.), Jason Robards, Jr. (Jamie Tyrone), Dean Stockwell (Edmund Tyrone), Jeanne Barr (Cathleen) **Screenwriter:** Eugene O'Neill (based on his play) **Cinematographer:** Boris Kaufman **Composer:** Andre Previn **Producer:** Jack J. Dreyfus, Jr., Ely Landau, and Joseph E. Levine for Embassy **Running Time:** 174 minutes **Format:** VHS, LV **Awards:** Cannes Film Festival 1962: Actress (Katharine Hepburn); National Board of Review Awards 1962: 10 Best Films of the Year, Supporting Actor (Jason Robards, Jr.); Academy Awards 1962: Nominations: Actress (Katharine Hepburn) **Budget:** $435,000.

Nixon

1995 – Oliver Stone – 🎵🎵🎵

> "What would I find out that I haven't known for years? What makes it so sad is that you couldn't confide in any of us. You had to make a record ... for the whole world ... They're not yours. They *are* you. You should burn them."
>
> Pat (Joan Allen), to Nixon about what is on the secret tapes.

Did you know?...

Both Nixon daughters denounced the film on its release.

The considerable obstacle to appreciating this film results from the choice to place in a tragic framework such relatively recent events. Shakespeare wrote tragedies about historical kings—Richard II, Richard III—who had ruled over a hundred years earlier, and the ancient Greeks based their tragedies on myth and legend. Oliver Stone's attempt to bring tragedy out of modern politics met with resistance and box-office failure since appreciating Stone's view required some objectivity about Richard Nixon, perhaps the most polarizing political figure of our age.

The great power of Stone's film comes from the human picture of Nixon (Anthony Hopkins) that he presents. Even the most passionate Nixon hater watching the film for a cinematic bashing session can come away from it with perhaps his first awareness of Nixon as a real person. For Stone to have put all the character's flaws to the service of humanizing one of the great dissemblers and hiders of our public life is both amazing and smart. The most powerful scenes in the film all derive their impact from the glimpses they afford behind the plastic Nixon smile and the robotic persona. He travels in the pre-dawn hours to the Lincoln Memorial to meet the student protesters of Vietnam, but his attempts to make small-talk about college sports miscarry ludicrously. One woman (Joanna Going) senses that the president is helplessly in the grip of the system or "the beast." The power-hungry Nixon comes away stung by this intuition that he himself has hardly grasped over a lifetime in politics. Later, he is aghast at reading his own profanities when shown the verbal transcripts of his secret audio recordings in the Oval Office. He cannot reconcile the mental pic-

ture of himself as a Quaker and as the child of devout Hannah Nixon (Mary Steenburgen) with the torrent of filth that he reads. Pat (Joan Allen, in a striking performance) comes to him in the final days and articulates the tragic irony of his life—that he could put on tape (and be undone by) the feelings inside of him but could not confide them to any of his own family. The final insight, authenticated by journalist Tom Wicker, comes when he stands on the eve of his resignation before a painting of JFK: "When they look at you, they see what they want to be; when they look at me, they see what they are."

As much could be said about Stone's impressive technique as about his point of view. The film's style has a kaleidoscopic feel to it with images flying by at different angles, from different time periods of the story, and in different film stocks, even including some use of film negatives. The abrupt, brief shift from positive to negative images (as in the second or two of Nixon sitting at his desk as an all-white mass against the dark surroundings of the office) suggests, in

President Nixon (Anthony Hopkins) dances with wife Pat (Joan Allen) during his 1968 inauguration.

critic Owen Gleiberman's great phrase, an "X-ray of the soul." The opening quotation from Matthew 12:26 ("What shall it profit a man if he shall gain the whole world and lose his own soul?") also invites such an approach. *Nixon* succeeds at providing the X-ray of the soul that all tragedy strives for.

Cast: Anthony Hopkins (Richard Nixon), Joan Allen (Pat Nixon), James Woods (H.R. Haldeman), J.T. Walsh (John Ehrlichman), Paul Sorvino (Henry Kissinger), Powers Boothe (Alexander Haig), David Hyde Pierce (John Dean), E.G. Marshall (John Mitchell), Madeline Kahn (Martha Mitchell), David Paymer (Ron Ziegler), Saul Rubineck (Herb Kline), Kevin Dunn (Chuck Colson), Tony Plana (Manolo Sanchez), Bob Hoskins (J. Edgar Hoover), Brian Bedford (Clyde Tolson), Fyvush Finkel (Murray Chotiner), Tony Lo Bianco (Johnny Roselli), John Diehl (G. Gordon Liddy), Ed Harris (Howard Hunt), Larry Hagman (Jack Jones), Robert Beltran (Frank Sturgis), James Karen (Bill Rogers), Richard Fancy (Mel Laird), Annabeth Gish (Julie Nixon), Marley Shelton (Tricia Nixon), Tom Bower (Frank Nixon), Mary Steenburgen (Hannan Nixon), Sean Stone (Donald Nixon), Joshua Preston (Arthur Nixon), Corey Carrier (Richard Nixon, age 12), David Barry Gray (Richard Nixon, age 19), Tony Goldwyn (Harold Nixon), Dan Hedaya (Trini Cardoza), Sam Waterston (Richard Helms), George Plimpton (Fred Buzhardt), Edward Herrmann (Nelson Rockefeller), Joanna Going (young woman at Lincoln Memorial), Donna Dixon (Maureen Dean), Mary Rudolph (Rosemary Woods), Bob Marshall (Spiro Agnew) **Screenwriter:** Stephen J. Rivele, Christopher Wilkinson, Oliver Stone **Cinematographer:** Robert Richardson **Composer:** John Williams **Producer:** Clayton Townsend and Oliver Stone for Hollywood Pictures; released by Cinergi and Illusion Entertainment **MPAA Rating:** R **Running Time:** 192 minutes **Format:** VHS, LV **Awards:** Los Angeles Film Critics Association Awards 1995: Supporting Actress (Joan Allen), National Society of Film Critics Awards 1995: Supporting Actress (Joan Allen), Academy Awards 1995: Nominations: Actor (Anthony Hopkins), Screenplay, Supporting Actress (Joan Allen), Original Dramatic/Comedy Score (John Williams); British Academy Awards 1995: Nominations: Supporting Actress (Joan Allen); Golden Globe Awards 1996: Nominations: Actor—Drama (Anthony Hopkins); Screen Actors Guild Awards 1995: Nominations: Actor (Anthony Hopkins), Actress (Joan Allen) **Budget:** $50M **Box Office:** $13M.

Patton

1970 – Franklin J. Schaffner – 🎵🎵🎵🎵

> "I do this job because I've been trained to do it. You do it because you love it!"
>
> General Omar Bradley (Karl Malden)

Great men are bred throughout history. Some of them are born to greatness. Some of them reach for greatness. But very few of them actually believe that they have been great all through history. George S. Patton embodied a type of historical hubris, honestly believing that he had fought on nearly every famous battlefield since the dawn of time. It would be difficult to see any other actor than Scott in this role. He plays the part of Patton so well you actually think you are seeing "Old Blood and Guts" himself. In one scene, Patton stands in the middle

Formidable WWII leader, General George Patton (George C. Scott), sizes up the situation.

Did you know?...

On the night he won the Oscar for *Patton*, George C. Scott spent the evening at home, watching a hockey game. He turned down the award.

of the road during a German air raid, shaking his fist and firing his pistol at oncoming planes. Opposite the very animated Scott, Karl Malden portrays General Omar Bradley in a convincing, quiet, and humble way. Malden's portrayal emphasizes decency and lowliness and contrasts Patton so effectively as to leave nearly no difference but rank between Bradley and the lowliest private in his army.

The movie gives an historically accurate account of Patton as his own worst enemy. For every great thing he does, he seems to follow-up with disruptive behavior (through his unchecked mouth or, in one case, the back of his hand) that significantly hinders him. Patton truly is a tragic character. On the one hand, he is a brilliant strategist and commander. On the other, as Bradley tells him, he never knows when to back down. Like all tragic heroes, he begins to self-destruct. With the end of the war comes the end of the general.

Patton contains, in particular, two great battle scenes. The first one is in the desert of North Africa as Patton has his first great armor battle against the Germans. The second is in the Ardennes during the Battle of the Bulge. The cinematography is superb. And the movie is made to fit the big screen, or at least a letter-box format. The wide angles of the battle scenes are spectacular.

Based on Ladislas Farago's book *Patton: Ordeal and Triumph* and General Omar Bradley's autobiography, *Patton* received seven Oscars. Scott, who won and rejected the best actor award, citing performance shortcomings, was the fifth choice for the role, following Burt Lancaster, Rod Steiger, Lee Marvin, and Robert Mitchum. Scott did a small-screen encore as the General in 1986, starring in television's *The Last Days of Patton*.

Cast: George C. Scott (Gen. George S. Patton), Karl Malden (Gen. Omar N. Bradley), Michael Bates (Field Marshal Sir Bernard Law Montgomery), Edward Binns (Major General Walter Bedell Smith), Stephen Young (Captain Chester B. Hansen), Lawrence Dobkin (Colonel Gaston Bell), John Doucette (Major General Lucian K. Truscott), James Edwards (Sergeant William G. Meeks), Frank Latimore (Lieutenant Colonel Henry Davenport), Richard Munch (Colonel General Alfred Jodl), Morgan Paull (Captain Richard N. Jensen), Siegfried Rauch (Captain Oskar Steiger), Paul Stevens (Lieutenant Colonel Charles R. Codman), Michael Strong (Brigadier General Hobart Carver), Karl Michael Vogler (Field Marshal Erwin Rommel), Tim Considine (Slapped Soldier) **Screenwriter:** Francis Ford Coppola, Edmund H. North **Cinematographer:** Fred J. Koenekamp **Composer:** Jerry Goldsmith **Producer:** Frank McCarthy for Twentieth Century Fox **MPAA Rating:** PG **Running Time:** 171 minutes **Format:** VHS, LV **Awards:** Academy Awards 1970: Actor (George C. Scott), Art Direction/Set Direction, Director (Franklin J. Schaffner), Film Editing, Picture, Sound, Story and Screenplay; Nominations: Cinematography (Fred J. Koenekamp), Original Score (Jerry Goldsmith); Director's Guild of America Awards 1970: Director (Franklin J. Schaffner); Golden Globe Awards 1971: Actor—Drama (George C. Scott); National Board of Review Awards 1970: 10 Best Films of the Year, Actor (George C. Scott); New York Film Critics Award 1970: Actor (George C. Scott); Writer's Guild of America 1970: Original Screenplay.

Raging Bull

1980 – Martin Scorsese – 🦴🦴🦴🦴

What supplied this film with much of its punch when it first appeared was its language. Martin Scorsese and Robert De Niro had talked about making a prizefighting film based on middleweight Jake La Motta's autobiography since the early 1970s. The original script by Mardik Martin and the rewrite by Paul Schrader employed a more grammatical, literary dialogue. Scorsese and De Niro revised the script again and made the language more colloquial, fragmented, and, above all, profane. In addition, the lines in the film are often delivered in jumbled, overlapping, indistinct ways. The violence of Jake La Motta (De Niro) is shown to erupt in a flurry of verbal attacks as likely as in a volley of punches. When Steven Spielberg saw *Raging Bull*, as he explains in the short film *Martin Scorsese Directs*, the spontaneous-seeming speech gave him a sense of embarrassment and a feeling of eavesdropping "on real situations with real people whose dignity and privacy I should respect." Since 1980, however, explicit profanity has become such a staple of mainstream films that it may be hard to watch *Raging Bull* with the same voyeuristic feelings that Spielberg had of observing privileged moments. Of course, the parallels to the Mike Tyson story add an extra jolt.

Although the verbal rhythms may not stand out as distinctively as they did in 1980, the shock of observing the behavior of La Motta still remains. He seems to be at peace only in the ring; elsewhere, the ease with which he turns an everyday situation into an occasion for rage is chilling. Waiting for dinner, he berates his first wife for taking too long with his steak and then overturns the table in fury. Later, he lets a simple kiss of greeting from his second wife (Cathy Moriarty) to his brother (Joe Pesci) fuel his suspicions that she has betrayed him. His self-destructive nature alienates his brother and motivates his wife to divorce him. When he is arrested for selling liquor to a minor at his nightclub, he tries to pawn his middleweight championship belt to make bail, but like so much of his life he botches even that by prying out the jewels from the belt rather than recognizing the belt's greater worth as a unique, intact trophy.

Jake's tragedy may lie somewhere in his brutish, animal-like nature that carries him to the top of his profession while tearing apart his private life. Scors-

> ## "I've done a lot of bad things, Joey. Maybe it's coming back to me."
>
> Jake (Robert De Niro), to Joey in the dressing room after losing to Sugar Ray Robinson.

Did you know?...

Robert De Niro gained over fifty pounds for the scenes of Jake in retirement at his nightclub.

Fight manager Joey (Joe Pesci) whispers to his brother, boxer Jake LaMotta (Robert De Niro).

ese has said that he intends the ending of the film (after Jake's release from prison) to show a man who has finally reached a sense of peace. Many viewers disagree and find in Jake's cryptic dressing-room recitation of Marlon Brando's speech from *On the Waterfront* yet another low point in his continuing downward slide.

Cast: Robert De Niro (Jake La Motta), Cathy Moriarty (Vickie La Motta), Joe Pesci (Joey La Motta), Frank Vincent (Salvy), Nicholas Colasanto (Tommy Como), Theresa Saldana (Lenore), Frank Adonis (Patsy), Mario Gallo (Mario), Frank Topham (Toppy), Lori Anne Flax (Irma), Joseph Bono (Guido), James V. Christy (Dr. Pinto), Bill Mazer (reporter), Bill Hanrahan (Eddie Egan), Rita Bennett (Emma), Mike Miles (sparring partner), Kevin Mahon (Tony Janiro), Johnny Barnes (Sugar Ray Robinson), Ed Gregory (Billy Fox), Louis Raftis, (Marcel Cerdan), Johnny Turner (Laurent Dauthuille), Charles Scorsese (man with Tommy Como), Martin Scorsese (Barbizon stagehand) **Screenwriter:** Mardik Martin, Paul Schrader **Cinematographer:** Michael Chapman **Composer:** Robbie Robertson **Producer:** Robert Chartoff and Irwin Winkler for United Artists **MPAA Rating:** R **Running Time:** 129 minutes **Format:** VHS, LV, DVD **Awards:** Academy Awards 1980: Editing, Actor (Robert De Niro); Nominations: Cinematography (Michael Chapman), Director (Martin Scorsese), Picture, Sound, Supporting Actor (Joe Pesci),

Supporting Actress (Cathy Moriarty); Golden Globe Awards 1981: Actor—Drama (Robert De Niro); Los Angeles Film Critics Association Awards 1980: Actor (Robert De Niro), Film; National Board of Review Awards 1980: Actor (Robert De Niro), Supporting Actor (Joe Pesci); New York Film Critics Awards 1980: Actor (Robert De Niro), Supporting Actor (Joe Pesci); National Society of Film Critics Awards 1980: Cinematography (Michael Chapman), Director (Martin Scorsese), Supporting Actor (Joe Pesci) **Budget:** $14M.

Ran

1985 – Akira Kurosawa – 🦴🦴🦴🦴

To list the many obstacles preventing most viewers from watching renowned Japanese director Akira Kurosawa's *Ran* is to confirm how small a mainstream audience the film will usually enjoy. First, it is based on *King Lear*, not Shakespeare's most accessible play. Next, Kurosawa sets his adaptation in 16th-century Japan as the aging warlord Hidetora (Tatsuya Nakadai) chooses to divide his kingdom among his sons and then must endure the civil strife and rejection of himself that follows once he has ceded his power. In addition, Kurosawa's cinematic style over the years has moved away from a greater reliance on editing to the recurrent use of longer takes that position and observe many characters in a single shot with an unmoving camera, a style that will often seem visually static rather than layered and rich. Finally, it is nearly three hours long.

To list the many benefits that may be enjoyed from watching the film in spite of these obstacles is to confirm what a remarkable, profound film it truly is and what pleasures await those who make the effort. First, the film, like Shakespeare's play, explores some of life's most elemental truths: the blinding effects of pride, the ferocity of hate, the loyalty of those who follow their leaders regardless of cost, the painful humility that must acknowledge hurts inflicted on loved ones, the ultimate pitilessness of life. Kurosawa made the film at age 75, and when it appeared for years that the necessary money would not be forthcoming, he filled his time by producing paintings and sketches of shots from the film that he already had in his mind. It is in many ways an aging artist's summation of his life's work.

The epic battle scenes rival in their scale and richness those in any other movie. The first of these occurs as Hidetora resides in an abandoned castle with his thirty remaining samurai, and the armies of his two disloyal sons surround

"One arrow is easily broken, but not three together."
Hidetora (Tatsuya Nakadai), teaching his three sons the lesson of unity.

Did you know?...
The title is the Japanese character for fury, madness, chaos.

Tatsuya Nakadai stars as powerful 16th-century warlord, Lord Hidetora.

him. The battle scene plays in a different style from the previous scenes, unfolding as a series of brief shots with no sound other than the haunting music of Toru Takemitsu. The effect is to heighten the detachment of the audience and perhaps even to suggest the way Hidetora must have observed the event as his kingdom begins its slide into chaos. He sees the battle as a series of chilling tableaux of bloodied warriors shot full of arrows sprawled over battlements, a blur of passing horses, flickers of rifle fire, drifting smoke, and carnage. Some of the extreme long shots exert considerable power, like the memorable image of Hidetora staggering down the steps of the burning castle while the opposing armies (one dressed in bright red, the other in yellow) flank him the courtyard below. The film richly rewards those who undertake the effort to enter its world. Its small audience will be an enthusiastic one.

Cast: Tatsuya Nakadai (Lord Hidetora), Akira Terao (Tarotakatora), Jinpachi Nezu (Jiromasatora), Daisuke Ryu (Saburonaotora), Mieko Harada (Lady Kaede), Yoshiko Miyazaki (Lady Sue), Kazuo Kato (Ikoma), Masayuki Yui (Tango), Peter (Kyoami), Hitoshi Ueki (Fujimaki),

Hisashi Ikawa (Kurogane), Takeshi Nomura (Tsurumaru), Jun Tazaki (Ayabe), Norio Matsui (Ogura), Kenji Kodama (Shirane), Toshiya Ito (Naganuma), Takeshi Kato (Hatakeyama) **Screenwriter:** Akira Kurosawa, Hidwo Oguni, Masato Ide **Cinematographer:** Takao Saito, Masaharu Ueda, Asakazu Nakai **Composer:** Toru Takemitsu **Producer:** Masato Hara and Serge Silberman for Herald-Ace and Nippon-Herald; distributed by Greenwich Films **MPAA Rating:** R **Running Time:** 160 minutes **Format:** VHS, LV **Awards:** Academy Awards 1985: Costume Design; Nominations: Art Direction/Set Decoration, Cinematography, Director (Akira Kurosawa); British Academy Awards 1985: Foreign Film; Los Angeles Film Critics Awards 1985: Cinematography, Film; National Board of Review Awards 1985: Director (Akira Kurosawa); New York Film Critics Awards 1985: Foreign Film; National Society of Film Critics Awards 1985: Cinematography, Film **Box Office:** $11M (the most expensive movie ever made in Japan).

Romeo and Juliet
1968 – Franco Zeffirelli – 🎵🎵🎵

The two leads were only 15 (Olivia Hussey) and 17 (Leonard Whiting) when filming began, and though the demands of the Shakespearean verse sometimes overmatch them (especially Whiting), young audiences in the late 1960s responded to this story of young love from the early 1590s. Much of Zeffirelli's attention wisely goes toward "ventilating" the play, as it used to be called, opening up scenes with lavish production values and an epic scope. Fight scenes that might take a minute or two in a stage production receive full-scale choreography in the film. Sometimes Zeffirelli revels in the new freedom in films by injecting some Renaissance earthiness, as in the quick shots of Michael York's sword thrust into an opponent's eye, Mercutio's exploratory sniff under the nurse's dress, and the glimpse of Romeo's bare bottom in the morning-after scene (this last was both celebrated and slightly notorious at the time of the film's release). The richness of style offsets in many ways the acting limitations of the leads and the extensive cuts in the text (Zeffirelli omitted over half of the play). Consequently, what most people will remember is not the poetry that remains in the film but some of Zeffirelli's images, many of them shot from very high vantage points: the clash between Montagues and Capulets in the opening, the bodies of Mercutio and Tybalt strewn at the feet of the Prince (Robert Stephens), Romeo standing in the half-light reflecting on his new love.

George Cukor, who directed the 1936 MGM version of the play with Leslie Howard and Norma Shearer, commented on the differences between the two

"She doth teach the torches to burn bright."
Romeo (Leonard Whiting), on seeing Juliet.

Did you know?...
Laurence Olivier, unbilled at his own request, speaks the prologue.

Juliet (Olivia Hussey) prepares to take her life as Romeo (Leonard Whiting) lays dead beside her.

films with some insightful remarks about both. He conceded that Zeffirelli infused the later version with more energy and even a sense of tragic desperation. Cukor sounded as if he envied the young audiences the newer film pulled into theaters, and he admitted that Howard and Shearer were not "really passionate actors," going even so far as to call them "too stodgy." On the other hand, Cukor maintained that his version was more faithful to the poetry and that if he were to remake the film he would "get the garlic and the Mediterranean into it."

Cast: Leonard Whiting (Romeo), Olivia Hussey (Juliet), Michael York (Tybalt), Pat Heywood (the Nurse), John McEnery (Mercutio), Milo O'Shea (Friar Laurence), Roberto Bisacco (Paris), Paul Hardwick (Lord Capulet), Natasha Parry (Lady Capulet), Bruce Robinson (Benvolio), Antonio Pierfederici (Lord Montague), Esmeralda Ruspoli (Lady Montague), Robert Stephens (Prince of Verona), Laurence Olivier (prologue narrator), Dyson Lovell (Sampson), Richard Warwick (Gregory) **Screenwriter:** Franco Brusati, Maestro D'Amico, Franco Zeffirelli **Cinematographer:** Pasqualino De Santis **Composer:** Nino Rota **Producer:** John Brabourne and Anthony Havelock-Allan for Verona; distributed by Paramount **MPAA Rating:** PG **Running Time:** 138 minutes **Format:** VHS, LV **Awards:** Academy Awards 1968: Cinematography, Costume Design; Nominations: Director (Franco Zeffirelli), Picture; Golden Globe Awards 1969: Foreign Film; National Board of Review Awards 1968: 10 Best Films of the Year, Director (Franco Zeffirelli).

They Might Be Giants . . .

Orson Welles sometimes said that every character he played in his own films was a variation of Faust, that they had all bartered their souls and lost. Although his *Othello*, for example, was filmed over four years with uncertain financial backing, Welles still managed to invest some of the scenes with an epic scope. The opening shots of Iago, played by Michael MacLiammoir, being hoisted in a basket as a funeral cortege carries off Othello's body, attain a grandeur that Olivier's stagebound 1965 version of the play does not. Neither for that matter does Welles' own *Macbeth* (1948), shot for very little money at Republic, one of Hollywood's poverty-row studios. Welles' fascination with Shakespeare's Falstaff led to *Chimes at Midnight* in 1967, an excellent film that assembles materials from four plays about the fat knight. Welles invests the film with a rich nostalgia and sense of tragedy for the end of the chivalric age, and his affectionate reading of Falstaff as one of the few truly good figures in dramatic literature provides for an invariably fresh approach. The battle scenes, announcing the start of the hard modern world, add a dark, epic touch. It was Welles' personal favorite: "If I had to get into heaven on the basis of one picture," he told British interviewer Leslie Megahey, "that's the one I'd offer up."

WARTIME

All Quiet on the Western Front

1930 — Lewis Milestone — 🦴🦴🦴🦴

> "We live in the trenches out there. We fight. We try not to be killed, but sometimes we are. That's all."
>
> Paul Baumer (Lew Ayres)

At the start of World War I, a German professor makes a zealous plea on behalf of the fatherland, and ten of his students enlist. The film follows them through their initial training into battle and charts how the brutality of the war first disillusions, then kills them all. Director Lewis Milestone offsets scenes of battle with those showing conversations among the recruits that fill the intervening lulls. Both types of scenes are consistently effective. We see the butchery of machine guns mowing down lines of advancing soldiers, rat-infested trenches, bayonet fighting, and hand-to-hand combat. The battlefield scenes, utilizing innovative crane shots for imposing panoramas and shot on a ranch in California, were filmed with silent equipment, and the sound effects were added later. As a result, the soundtrack in these moments is sometimes muffled and slightly out of sync with the images.

The stylized acting does not weaken the impact of scenes like the one in which Lew Ayres talks to the corpse of the French soldier he has just killed in a trench struggle. "If you jumped in here again, I wouldn't do it," he says. He finds in the pocket of the dead man a photograph of his wife and daughter folded in his pay book, and starting to sob, he implores the staring eyes to forgive him. The connecting scenes between the battles further humanize the film. In one, the camera follows the boots of a hospitalized soldier with an amputated leg to their new owner, who brags that he could now march to the front; one or two bomb blasts later, he too lies dead. In another, Ayres obtains a furlough and returns to his home town where his realistic awareness of war clashes with the pampering of his mother and the false idealism of the local burgomaster discussing the war in a pub like a sports fan rehashing a big game. Surprisingly, the realism of the soldiers' night with a trio of French women is not compromised either. The women clearly want the bread and sausage the men bring but are perfectly willing to let them stay the night. The morning-after scene between Ayres and one of the girls is discreetly suggested by the shadow of the bedpost on the wall and the sounds of their conversation.

In creating this first masterful anti-war movie, Milestone adapted Erich Maria Remarque's famous novel. His final brilliant shot superimposes over an

Did you know?...

The final butterfly scene was suggested by Karl Freund, one of the most admired cameramen of his day. Freund, who had recently come to America, assisted Arthur Edeson but did not receive a screen credit.

endless field of crosses the image of a line of troops marching off to war and one by one looking innocently back at the audience. This closing shot works on many levels: as a tribute to the soldiers' heroism, a glimpse of their lost innocence, and an epitaph to their ultimate sacrifice.

German soldiers Muller (Russell Gleason) and Paul Baumer (Lew Ayres) share a quiet moment before another battle begins.

Cast: Louis Wolheim (Kat), Lew Ayres (Paul), John Wray (Himmelstoss), Arnold Lucy (Kantorek), Ben Alexander (Kemmerick), Scott Kolk (Leer), Owen Davis, Jr. (Peter), Walte Browne Rogers (Behn), William Bakewell (Albert), Russell Gleason (Mueller), Richard Alexander (Westhus), Harold Goodwon (Detering), Slim Summerville (Tjaden), Pat Collins (Bartinok), Beryl Mercer (Paul's Mother), Edmund Breese (Herr Meyer) **Screenwriter:** Lewis Milestone, Maxwell Anderson, Del Andrews, George Abbott **Cinematographer:** Arthur Edeson **Composer:** David Broekman **Producer:** Carl Laemmle, Jr. for Universal **Running Time:** 130 minutes **Format:** VHS, LV **Awards:** Academy Awards, 1930: Director (Lewis Milestone), Picture; Nominations: Cinematography (Arthur Edeson), Writing; National Board of Review Awards, 1930: 10 Best Films of the Year **Budget:** $1.2M.

Apocalypse Now

1979 – Francis Ford Coppola – 🎬🎬🎬

"I love the smell of napalm in the morning. It smells like . . . victory."

Kilgore (Robert Duvall)

Apocalypse Now is too much of a mythic and surreal journey into the heart of darkness of all war to be the definitive film on the war in Vietnam. However, it does tell a very powerful story. The plot centers on Capt. Willard (Martin Sheen), who has been hand-picked by the upper brass (G.D. Spradlin) to assassinate Col. Walter Kurtz (Marlon Brando), a commander gone mad and the leader of a group of soldiers and natives in Cambodia. Ordered to "terminate" Col. Kurtz's command with "extreme prejudice," he heads upriver to Cambodia to do just that. Along the way he meets an extraordinary collection of people and witnesses an equally extraordinary series of events.

He is piloted along by Chief Phillips (Albert Hall), an experienced skipper of a small patrol boat manned by Clean, Chef, and Lance (Laurence Fishburne, Frederic Forrest, and Sam Bottoms). One of the most colorful characters he meets is Col. "Wild Bill" Kilgore (Robert Duvall), commander of the 1st Air Cavalry and surfing enthusiast. The main problem with his hobby is that the best beaches belong to "Charlie." Kilgore, however, is undeterred, sweeping in, taking a beach, sending out his men to surf while the carnage is mopped up.

Apocalypse Now is marvelously and memorably filmed: the aerial shots of Willard travelling to meet the boat, the beautiful sunsets, the impressive pyrotechnics on the beach, the action scene of Kilgore's choppers taking the village with missiles flying and Wagner thundering on the soundtrack. Moreover, the scene of the battle when the bridge is shot up shows the incredible power of the ordinance. The lighting during the night scenes is also of note, especially when the boat lands at the bridge. In this scene the Americans are fighting the Viet Cong for the bridge while Lance is tripping on acid. The combination of almost strobe-like light and the music of the era produces a very surreal experience.

The film loses much of its realism at this point and becomes more of an illusion, sometimes a dream, sometimes a nightmare. The nightmare exists mostly in the film's inclination to depict very graphic violence. The final sequence with Kurtz is mysterious, dark, and moody with human heads littering the ground and Willard confronting a type of more primitive evil. The hallucinogenic quality of the film gives it a strong sense of doom. Coppola's own comment about the

Did you know?...

The film is based in part on Joseph Conrad's novel *Heart of Darkness.*

film at the Cannes Film Festival probably identifies most clearly the reason many hail it as a masterpiece and others are more guarded in their praise: "It's more of an experience than a movie. At the beginning there's a story. Along the river the story becomes less important and the experience more important."

Col. Kurtz (Marlon Brando) discusses his philosophy with Capt. Willard (Martin Sheen).

Cast: Marlon Brando (Col. Walter E. Kurtz), Robert Duvall (Lt. Col. Bill Kilgore), Martin Sheen (Capt. Benjamin Willard), Frederic Forrest (Chef), Albert Hall (Chief Phillips), Sam Bottoms (Lance Johnson), Laurence Fishburne (Mr. Clean), Dennis Hopper (Freelance Photographer), G.D. Spradlin (General), Harrison Ford (Col. Lucas), Jerry Zeismer (Civilian) **Screenwriter:** Francis Ford Coppola, John Milius **Cinematographer:** Vittorio Storaro **Composer:** Carmine Coppola **Producer:** Francis Ford Coppola for Zoetrope **MPAA Rating:** R **Running Time:** 155 minutes **Format:** VHS, LV **Awards:** Academy Awards, 1979: Cinematography, Sound; Nominations: Adapted Screenplay, Art Direction/Set Direction, Director (Francis Ford Coppola), Film Editing, Picture, Supporting Actor (Robert Duvall); British Academy Awards, 1979: Director (Francis Ford Coppola), Supporting Actor (Robert Duvall); Cannes Film Festival, 1979: Film; Golden Globe Awards, 1980: Director (Francis Ford Coppola), Supporting Actor (Robert Duvall), Score; National Board of Review Awards, 1979: 10 Best films of the Year; National Society of Film Critics Awards, 1979: Supporting Actor (Frederic Forrest) **Budget:** $31.5M **Box Office:** $37.9M.

Battle of Britain

1963 — Guy Hamilton — 🩴🩴

The publicity bragged about rounding up over a hundred vintage aircraft for the film, and the aerial sequences are very impressive. The problem seems to be that the producers forgot to round up some personalities for the characters. The film depicts one of the key moments of the war for England, their greatly outnumbered aerial defense against the Luftwaffe in June 1940, but the unduly solemn approach to the subject robs the film of any humanity.

A number of scenes occur in war rooms of various sorts, usually with Trevor Howard looking down bulldoggishly from a mezzanine as secretaries and messengers post information on maps and shift replicas of gun emplacements on strategy boards. Laurence Olivier, playing Sir Hugh Dowding, usually sits behind his desk commenting on the oversized odds against England. One of the best moments occurs in a tracking shot, when Kenneth More walks across a compound with Susannah York as a bomb blast in the background suddenly takes out a sizable hunk of the airfield and fills half of the frame with red and black flames. The attempts to create a personal drama fail badly, consisting mostly of Christopher Plummer constantly complaining about the war to his wife (York), a section officer.

For a while, the film shifts between action scenes of some impact and those detailing the planning of the defense. The stodginess of the ground scenes, however, eventually detracts from the thrill of the air sequences, as they come to resemble something of a highlight reel. In time, the audience can recognize a pattern to the aerial combat, one that picks out a representative gunner or pilot as the planes engage the enemy and then sacrifices him to a bloody death. *Battle of Britain* is strictly for the most enthusiastic war-film aficionado.

Did you know?...

British director Guy Hamilton, who began his career as an assistant to Carol Reed, also directed a number of the James Bond films: *Goldfinger, Diamonds Are Forever, Live and Let Die,* and *The Man with the Golden Gun.*

Cast: Harry Andrews (Senior Civil Servant), Michael Caine (Squadron Leader Canfield), Trevor Howard (Air Vice Marshal Keith Park), Curt Jurgens (Baron von Richter), Ian McShane (Sgt. Pilot Andy), Kenneth More (Group Captain Baker), Laurence Olivier (Air Chief Marshal Sir Hugh Dowding), Nigel Patrick (Group Captain Hope), Christopher Plummer (Squadron Leader Harvey), Michael Redgrave (Air Vice Marshal Evill), Ralph Richardson (Sir David), Robert Shaw (Squadron Leader), Patrick Wymark (Air Vice Marshal Trafford Leigh-Mallory), Susannah York (Section Officer Maggie Harvey) **Screenwriter:** Wilfred Greatorex, James Kenneway **Cinematographer:** Freddie Young **Composer:** Malcolm Arnold, Ron Goodwin, William Walton **Pro-**

ducer: Benjamin Fisz and Harry Saltzmann for United Artists **MPAA Rating:** G **Running Time:** 133 minutes **Format:** VHS, LV **Budget:** $12M **Box Office:** $2M.

Air Vice Marshal Evill (Michael Redgrave) discusses strategy with Air Chief Marshal Dowding (Laurence Olivier).

The Bridge on the River Kwai

1959 – David Lean – 𝄞𝄞𝄞𝄢

During a television special on the American Film Institute's selection of the 100 Best Movies, Steven Spielberg commented on David Lean's prison camp masterpiece. Spielberg marveled at the plot construction and development—how the film simultaneously propels a number of parallel stories and masterfully brings them all to a thrilling climax. Memorable for its whistling "Colonel Bogey's March" and innumerable classic scenes, *The Bridge on the River Kwai* is still somewhat flawed by a certain implausibility of the main character.

Kwai is set in a Japanese POW camp in Burma during World War II. At the outset, we watch Colonel Nicholson (Alec Guinness) engage heroically in a battle of wills with the camp commander Saito (Sessue Hayakawa). After he endures the solitary confinement of "the oven," Nicholson is taken to Saito's private quarters. The early scenes between these two foes are among the film's best and certainly qualify it for inclusion among those few spectacle films that can be accurately described as "intimate epics." Saito needs men to complete a bridge, and he admits that if he fails it will cost him his life. The bridge will extend the railroad from Bangkok to Rangoon and on to India. Nicholson decides to supervise the construction of the bridge with the labor of his men even though such an act will aid the enemy. He does so seemingly out of British pride and the urge to respond to captivity with a constructive, challenging enterprise that will endure—and show his captors just what British pride can accomplish. He visibly swells with pride, for example, when another officer tells him that the wood in the indigenous trees could produce a bridge that would last six hundred years.

The heroic battle of wills between the Commander and the Colonel is gradually superceded by a moving commentary on the absurdity and futility of war, allegorically demonstrated by the rise and fall of the bridge. This combination of moods has always struck some as an awkward mix. The only American POW, "Commander" Shears (William Holden) is less concerned about duty and more focused on survival. Lean replaces the Colonel's conflict with Saito by moving Shears (who is actually a private) into an adversarial role, contrasting the pragmatic American with the class-conscious and duty-bound British officer. The film hammers together each successive scene and plot point as surely as the men extend and complete their bridge. The

Did you know?...

The author credited for the screenplay, Pierre Boulle, wrote the novel on which the film is based and spoke no English. His name was used on the script as a front for the actual authors, Carl Foreman and Michael Wilson, who were blacklisted for their political views.

climax is powerful, but Nicholson's final actions aren't perhaps fully believable, however consistent Guinness has been with the character.

British guerilla officer Maj. Warden (Jack Hawkins) and American soldier Shears (William Holden) team up to defeat the Japanese in Burma.

Cast: William Holden (Shears), Alec Guinness (Colonel Nicholson), Jack Hawkins (Major Warden), Sessue Hayakawa (Colonel Saito), James Donald (Major Clipton), Geoffrey Horne (Lieutenant Joyce), Andre Morell (Colonel Green), Peter Williams (Major Reeves), John Boxer (Major Hughes), Percy Herbert (Grogan), M.R.B. Chakrabandhu (Yai), Kannikar Dowklee (Siamese girl), Harold Goodwin (Baker), Keiichiro Katsumoto (Lieutenant Muira), Henry Okawa (Captain Kanematsu) **Screenwriter:** Carl Foreman, Michael Wilson **Cinematographer:** Jack Hilyard **Composer:** Malcom Arnold **Producer:** Sam Spiegel for Horizon Pictures; released by Columbia **MPAA Rating:** PG **Running Time:** 161 minutes **Format:** VHS, LV **Awards:** Academy Awards, 1957: Actor (Alec Guinness), Screenplay, Cinematography, Director (David Lean), Editing, Picture, Score; Nominations: Supporting Actor (Hayakawa); British Academy Awards, 1957: Actor (Alec Guinness), Film, Screenplay; Directors Guild of America Awards 1957: Director (David Lean); Golden Globe Awards, 1958: Actor—Drama (Alec Guinness), Director (David Lean), Film—Drama; National Board of Review Awards, 1957: 10 Best Films of the Year, Actor (Alec Guinness), Director (David Lean), Supporting Actor (Sessue Hayakawa); New York Film Critics Awards, 1957: Actor (Alec Guinness), Director (David Lean), Film **Budget:** $3M **Box Office:** $15M.

A Bridge Too Far

1977 – Richard Attenborough – 🎖🎖🎖

A bit too big, in some ways *A Bridge Too Far* is a magnificent war movie about the defeat of the Allied forces at Arnheim in World War II. The troops attempt a daring invasion of the German factories in the Ruhr to inhibit Germany's ability to produce armaments. The problems with the film are those that can easily weaken historical or wartime epics: a large cast of famous faces playing characters involved in intersecting plots at various strategic locations can eventually create a plodding or confusing effect. As the Allies' advance targets three bridges, the preparations and assault take the viewer from one command post to another with a dizzying sense of disorientation at times, robbing the movie of some dramatic coherence. Based on Cornelus Ryan's epic novel, the film integrates newsreel footage of battles with staged conflicts, sometimes with less than effective results.

The film is anchored by the famous stars who turn in effective performances. Anthony Hopkins plays a brash leader of troops at the Arnheim bridge. Sean Connery, Ryan O'Neal, and Gene Hackman are strong in their parts as commanders of various outfits involved in the assault. Maybe the most interesting performance of all comes from Robert Redford as Major Cook. During a river crossing through a barrage of fire, he provides the best look into the heart of a soldier as he leads his men, paddles the boat with the butt of his rifle, and repeats "Hail Marys." It is a fine portrayal of a sense of duty overcoming a sense of fear.

The sound effects realistically create the sense of war in a number of ways. The filmmakers obtain fine results by including authentic-seeming details: during the shelling the clanking of the brass casings being ejected from the cannons combines with the continual blasts of the explosions. The magnificent experience of the parachute drop is intensified by a rich sound montage of the rustle of the cords coming out of the door on the C-47s and banging against the side of the plane. Such attention to the finer points of sound matches in its immediacy the shot in which the audience sees the plane from the viewpoint of the man going out the door and into his fall. Though its epic dimensions lead to some wobbly plotting, *A Bridge Too Far* offers some pleasant, smaller moments.

Did you know?...

Ryan O'Neal was about 36 years old when *A Bridge Too Far* was filmed. While that may seem young for an actor playing a general, in 1944 Brigadier General James Gavin (the part O'Neal plays) would have turned 37. O'Neal's youth may have been a factor in his casting.

Cast: Dirk Bogarde (Lieut. Gen. Frederich "Boy" Browning), Paul Maxwell (Major General Maxwell Taylor), Sean Connery (Major General Urquhart), Ryan O'Neal (Brigadier General Gavin), Gene Hackman (Maj. General Stanislaw Sosabowski), Walter Kohut (Field Marshal Model), Peter Faber (Captain Harry Bestebreutje), Hartman Becker (German Sentry), Frank Grimes (Major Fuller), Donald Pickering (RAF Briefing Officer), Edward Fox (Lieutenant General Horrocks), Michael Caine (Lieut. Col. Joe Vandeleur), Michael Byrne (Lieut. Col. Giles Vandeleur), Anthony Hopkins (Lieut. Col. John Frost), James Caan (Staff Sgt. Dohun), Maximilian Schell (Lieut. Gen. Brittich), Liv Ulmann (Kate Ter Horst), Elliot Gould (Col. Stout), Denholm Elliott (RAF Meteorological Officer), Laurence Olivier (Dr. Spaander), Robert Redford (Maj. Julian Cook), John Ratzenburger (US Lieutenant), Siem Vroom (Underground Leader), Marlies Van Alcmaer (Underground Leader's Wife), Eric Van't Wout (Underground Leader's Son), Wolfgang Preiss (Field Marshal Von Rundstedt), Hans von Borsody (General Blumentritt), Josephine Peeper (Cafe Waitress) **Screenwriter:** William Goldman **Cinematographer:** Geoffrey Unsworth, Harry Waxman, Robin Browne **Composer:** John Addison **Producer:** Joseph E. Levine and John Palmer for United Artists **MPAA Rating:** PG **Running Time:** 176 minutes **Format:** VHS, LV **Awards:** British Academy Awards, 1977: Supporting Actor (Edward Fox); National Film Critics Awards, 1977: Supporting Actor (Edward Fox) **Budget:** $24M **Box Office:** $20M.

General "Jumping Jim" Gavin (Ryan O'Neal) parachutes into Holland.

The Bridges at Toko-Ri

1954 — Mark Robson — 🦴🦴🦴🦴

This film does not falsify any aspect of its simple story. Harry Brubaker (William Holden), a navy pilot during the Korean War, has to ditch his plane in icy waters but is rescued by a helicopter crew (Mickey Rooney, Earl Holliman). Later, Brubaker gets a short furlough with his wife (Grace Kelly) and daughters during which he explains his imminent mission of taking out enemy bridges spanning a valley between two mountains in North Korea. On this mission, he is shot down and killed. 37-year-old William Holden agreed to appear in the film on the condition that Brubaker die in the movie as he had in James Michener's short novel.

This final scene is brutal in its coldness. The pilot who had a few days ago been relaxing in a Japanese bathhouse is now trapped in a muddy trench as enemy soldiers close in. After his rifle jams, he scurries around like a bug until he is finally shot. The scenes leading up to this moment use editing and silence very effectively to achieve suspense and deepen character. We watch Brubaker's tense reactions during the briefing session as he views footage of the approach to the bridges with flak blasting all around. We watch him unable to sleep, unable to write a letter to his wife. To strengthen his resolve, he goes out to the edge of the naval carrier where the spray hits him in the face; director Mark Robson makes good use of space in these long shots of one lonely man on the vast carrier deck.

The dialogue is equally simple and clipped and perfectly suits Holden's laconic voice, as when he unemotionally describes his rescue in the opening scene for his fatherly admiral (Fredric March): "You're out there all by yourself. You know you can't last very long. You're scared and you're freezing. You curse and you pray. Suddenly, you see that mixmaster whirling at you out of nowhere. You look up, and there's Forney in the green hat. You relax 'cause you know you got it knocked." Fredric March is excellent as the admiral who has lost two sons to war, and Holden's scenes with Grace Kelly are equally strong. In one of the best, a Japanese family enters the bathhouse Brubaker thought he had reserved, coming through a door he thought he had locked. They begin to disrobe as he tries to stop them and as his wife gasps in embarrassment. Soon he is laughing

and the children are exchanging friendly greetings. The film also benefits from being shot on an actual naval carrier, and the aerial scenes are first rate.

Such consistent realism ultimately creates an ambivalent view of war. Although the film is often cited as an antiwar film, an opening title describes the movie as a "tribute" to the navy; the superb aerial photography of Charles G. Clarke is a testament to the action film at the core. Certainly the bravery of the pilots is never questioned, but indirectly the decision to send them on near-suicidal missions—and even the war effort itself—gets scrutinized rather severely. The criticism comes in the honesty with which the film presents the uncertainty many have about such wars of containment. Admiral Tarrant recites half-heartedly the domino theory about stopping Communist aggression, but his real emotions still grieve over his two lost sons and his wife who has been ruined by grief. Brubaker's final insight, as dozens of enemy soldiers move in to kill him, is that you fight the war you're in whether right or wrong, but no one doubts for a

William Holden stars as bomber pilot Lt. Harry Brubaker.

moment that he would rather be a living husband than a dead hero. The film closes with the admiral's baffled question as he watches more planes take off, "Where do such men come from?" Brubaker's fellow pilot Lee (Charles McGraw) tries to convince the admiral that the mission was a success, that they knocked out the bridges, that they suffered only three fatalities, but the human costs of war and blind devotion to duty are what stay in the mind.

Cast: William Holden (Lieutenant Harry Brubaker), Grace Kelly (Nancy Brubaker), Fredric March (Rear-Admiral George Tarrant), Mickey Rooney (Mike Forney), Robert Strauss (Beer Barrel), Charles McGraw (Commander Wayne Lee), Keiko Awaji (Kimiko), Earl Holliman (Nestor Gamidge), Richard Shannon (Lieutenant Olds), Willis Bouchey (Captain Evans), Nadine Ashdown (Cathy Brubaker), Marshall V. Beebe (Pilot), Cheryl Lynn Callaway (Susie Brubaker), Gene Hardy (Chief Petty Officer), James Hyland (Officer of the Day) **Screenwriter:** Valentine Davies **Cinematographer:** Loyal Griggs **Composer:** Lyn Murray **Producer:** William Perlberg and George Seaton for Paramount **Running Time:** 102 minutes **Format:** VHS, LV **Awards:** Academy Awards, 1955: Special Effects; Nominations: Editing.

Das Boot
1981 – Wolfgang Petersen – 🦴🦴🦴🦴

> "What are they doing still on board? Why haven't they been rescued?"
>
> Submarine captain (Jurgen Prochnow) when he sees sailors jumping off a burning enemy ship.

The ultimate claustrophobic epic, *Das Boot* recounts the experiences of a German submarine crew during World War II. It is based on a book by Lothar-Gunther Buchheim, a journalist who wrote about his experiences on a real U-Boat and who serves as the prototype for the character Werner (Herbert Gronemeyer) in the film. Director Wolfgang Petersen wrote two screenplays when he was given the assignment to adapt Buchheim's book into a movie, one for a theatrical release and another for a mini-series that eventually aired on German television. We see the crew members at a nightclub before they ship out and meet their taciturn captain (Juergen Prochnow), who clearly has been aged by his previous experiences at war and who at thirty has already earned the nickname, "the old man." The film shows how the young, unshaven crew also ages over the course of their experiences, and the overall development alternates between crises at sea and personalizing snapshots of the seamen, mostly viewed through the eyes of Werner.

Das Boot was the most expensive German film ever produced, and much of the meticulous and costly preparation went to ensure its authenticity and real-

ism. With blueprints from the Chicago Museum of Science and Industry, Rolf Zehetbauer and his production design team actually built two full-scale submarines, one to use for exterior shots (such as those of the sub leaving its berth) and one rigged to a sound-stage harness for interior scenes. To simulate the shudders produced by depth charges, the harness twisted the sub at various angles while inside the boat the actors and Jost Vacano, the director of photography, tried to capture the scenes of fear and disorientation. Although the second sub was equipped with removable sides, all the interiors were shot inside the boat with a hand-held camera and a gyroscope mount. Consequently, *Das Boot* is one film in which its look—living and working in cramped and crowded spaces—in the moments of lull between action scenes genuinely contributes to the character development. The personal moments of one sailor showing the photo of his girlfriend as well as the need to blast music through the sub and sing seem perfectly natural for men coping with war in such circumstances.

It's cramped quarters and tense moments for German submariners.

Did you know?...

Viewers comparing the dubbed and subtitled versions of the film will notice distinct differences between the explicitness of the language. The dubbed version is far milder, the subtitled version more raw.

Cast: Juergen Prochnow (Captain), Herbert Gronemeyer (Correspondent Werner), Klaus Wennemann (Chief Engineer), Hubertus Bengsch (1st Lieutenant), Martin Semmelrogge (2nd Lieutenant), Bernd Tauber (Chief Quartermaster), Erwin Leder (Johann), Martin May (Ullman), Heinz Hoenig (Hinrich), Uwe Ochsenknecht (Chief Bosun), Claude-Oliver Rudolph (Ario), Jan Fedder (Pilgrim), Ralph Richter (Frenssen), Joachim Bernhard (Preacher), Oliver Stritzel (Schwalle) **Screenwriter:** Wolfgang Petersen, Dean Riesner **Cinematographer:** Jost Vacano **Composer:** Klaus Doldinger **Producer:** Gunter Rohrbach for Columbia **MPAA Rating:** R **Running Time:** 210 minutes **Format:** VHS, LV, DVD **Awards:** Academy Awards, 1982: Nominations: Adapted Screenplay, Cinematography, Director (Wolfgang Petersen), Editing, Sound **Budget:** $15M.

The Deer Hunter

1978 – Michael Cimino – 🦴🦴🦴🦲

> "You have to think about one shot. One shot is what it's all about. The deer has to be taken with one shot."
>
> Michael (Robert De Niro) to Nick on deer hunting.

Did you know?...

John Cazale, who also appeared in *The Godfather* and *Dog Day Afternoon*, died of bone cancer shortly after filming completed, a condition that nearly made the production company cancel the film the day before shooting was to start due to insurance complications.

Few who have seen this film talk about it indifferently. To some, the sprawling story of three men from a steel mill town in Pennsylvania who enlist for service in Vietnam cries out for some cuts and the shaping hand of a good editor; to others, the intensity of the Vietnam scenes is so unsettling as to rob the film of any entertainment value. Even the film's most enthusiastic defenders still acknowledge a few flaws.

Director Michael Cimino dwells on the early scenes of the workers, their unwinding in a bar, the wedding of Steve and Angela (John Savage and Rutanya Alda), and the friends' deer hunting as a contrast to the later horrors that the men encounter in Vietnam. To show the eventual impact of the war, the film must first establish the norms for these characters, and the actors convey the richness of the camaraderie the men feel in their many memorable performances. Since some of the characters, especially Michael (Robert De Niro), are introspective, nonverbal people, their personalities come across more through tone of voice, movement (the joyous dancing and pool playing after work), and facial expressiveness than through the content of their words. A particularly poignant moment occurs with Nick, who is traumatized after his ordeal as a prisoner of the Viet Cong. His crying scene at the hospital in Saigon is gripping and emblematic of the film's strengths, as a moment on screen that we are not quite sure we have ever seen before. Walken's sobs come as a series of violent heaves and retches between shuddering bouts of quiet. His body seems as if it is attempting to rid itself of all the harrowing memories of the war sob by painful

American soldiers Michael (Robert De Niro) and Steven (John Savage) try to survive as POWs in Vietnam.

sob, like a stomach trying to expel its contents. The visceral nature of the material is so intense that much of the characters' behavior (like the argument between John Cazale and De Niro over borrowing hunting boots) seems to lie at the instinctive level.

The impact of the film is also determined by the motif of Russian roulette, which turns up again and again in the plot. Perhaps the film may be accused of manipulation, of taking the sufficiently intense experience of war itself and magnifying it with what is admittedly not an experience representative of many soldiers. But Cimino has often said that he was not attempting to make an anti-war film but one that showed the effects of stress on relationships. It is on another deer hunt after the war that Michael, who now knows what it is like to be the hunted, spares a deer in the cross hairs of his rifle. Cimino's richly textured film then traces how Michael begins to heal from his experiences at war and how Nick does not.

Cast: Robert De Niro (Michael), John Cazale (Stan), John Savage (Steven), Christopher Walken (Nick), Meryl Streep (Linda), George Dzundza (John), Chuck Aspegren (Axel), Shirley Stoler (Steve's mother), Rutanya Alda (Angela), Pierre Segui (Julien), Mady Kaplan (Axel's girl), Amy Wright (bridesmaid), Richard Kuss (Linda's father), Victoria Karnafel (sad-looking girl), Jack Scardino (cold old man), Joe Strand (bingo caller), Po Pao Pee (Chinese referee) **Screenwriter:** Michael Cimino, Deric Washburn **Cinematographer:** Vilmos Zsigmond **Composer:** Stanley Myers **Producer:** Barry Spikings, Michael Deeley, Michael Cimino, and John Peverall for Universal **MPAA Rating:** R **Running Time:** 183 minutes **Format:** VHS, LV, DVD **Awards:** Academy Awards, 1978: Picture, Director (Michael Cimino), Editing, Sound, Supporting Actor (Christopher Walken); Nominations: Actor (Robert De Niro), Cinematography (Vilmos Zsigmond), Original Screenplay, Supporting Actress (Meryl Streep); Directors Guild of America Awards, 1978: Director (Michael Cimino); Golden Globe Awards, 1979: Director (Michael Cimino); Los Angeles Film Critics Association Awards, 1978: Director (Michael Cimino); New York Film Critics Awards, 1978: Film, Supporting Actor (Christopher Walken); National Society of Film Critics Awards, 1978: Supporting Actress (Meryl Streep).

Gallipoli

1981 – Peter Weir – 🦴🦴🦴

This Australian film about the World War I massacre of Australian troops at Gallipoli in Turkey makes a telling point about the futility and butchery of war. The film begins with a training session for Archy (Mark Lee), a gifted runner who plans to compete in an upcoming event. After narrowly defeating Frank Dunne (Mel Gibson) at this contest, Archy becomes friends with Frank. These runners seem to differ only in their views about the war, which Archy, like most of his mates, longs to experience and Frank clearly can do without. Though underage, Archy not only enlists in the Lighthorsemen under an alias but talks Frank into joining him. They train in Cairo, bond with fellow soldiers, laugh at the pre-fur-lough hygiene lecture, and are eventually shipped off with the others to Turkey.

Gibson is the more effective of the two leads, but Lee's character is the tougher to personalize. Archy has been conceived and written as an illustration of the typical patriotic boy of the early century who dreams of success in the military and naively believes that the war will be over in a matter of months. Lee's success at playing Archy may partly come across in his general rather than specific traits: his fresh-faced quality, the love he has for the uncle who helps him train and who wants him to break the record for the 100-yard dash, his confident certainty about the rightness of his beliefs. As Archy and Frank trek across the outback to get to a recruiting station, they meet up with a drifter (Harold Baigent) who has been away from cities for so long he has not even heard about the war. Archy fills him in on the conflict, but the drifter still cannot understand why European aggression should affect life in Australia. After Archy supplies the simplistic, rote response that they are enlisting to stop Germany from taking over Australia, the old man looks across the lifeless flats and says, "Well, they're welcome to it." This comment and Gibson's horsey laugh of agreement reflect the film's point of view. It's representative of both the intensity and perhaps even the lack of subtlety with which the film delivers its point.

The final scenes, when the troops are entrenched to charge the Turkish gun emplacements, are the most harrowing. Otherwise inconsequential events like an error in timing, a miscommunication between officers, and the desire to save face lead to the order for the Australians to charge after the

> "The thing I can't stand about you, mate, is that you're always so bloody cheerful."
>
> Frank (Mel Gibson) to Archy.

Did you know?...

Gallipoli was part of a renaissance of popularity for Australian films at the time of its release. Other popular and critically praised Australian films from this period include *Picnic at Hanging Rock, Breaker Morant,* and *My Brilliant Career.*

Frank (Mel Gibson) and Archy (Mark Lee) join the ANZAC forces in WWI to battle the Turks.

Turks have returned to their guns rather than while they are occupied by artillery shelling. Wave after wave of Australian troops are mowed down by machine gun fire within feet of having gone over the top. Gibson, the company runner, sprints to deliver the message to halt before another surge of troops is sacrificed. According to the strictures of their national pride, these men prepare for what is certain to be their deaths, leaving valuables such as rings and lockets in the trenches and hastily composing letters to loved ones that will contain their last words.

Cast: Mark Lee (Archy), Mel Gibson (Frank Dunne), Bill Kerr (Uncle Jack), Harold Baigent (Camel Driver), Harold Hopkins (Les McCann), Charles Yunupingu (Zac), Heath Harris (Stockman), Ronny Graham (Wallace Hamilton), Gerda Nicolson (Rose Hamilton), Robert Grubb (Billy), Tim McKenzie (Barney), David Argue (Snowy), Brian Anderson (Railway Foreman) **Screenwriter:** Peter Weir, David Williamson **Cinematographer:** Russell Boyd **Composer:** Brian May **Producer:** Robert Stigwood and Patricia Lovell; released by Paramount **MPAA Rating:** PG **Running Time:** 110 minutes **Format:** VHS, LV **Awards:** Australian Film Institute, 1981: Actor (Mel Gibson), Film.

Gettysburg
1993 — Ronald F. Maxwell — 🦴🦴🦴🦴

Depicting the battle that involved 150,000 soldiers on both sides and left a third of them dead or wounded, *Gettysburg* is one of the finest epic war films. The pivotal 1863 battle of the American Civil War is wonderfully documented and dramatically presented in true-to-life scenes that range from one-on-one conversational exchanges to panoramic scenes of unforgettable heroic proportions. With more than 100 speaking parts, the movie is based on Michael Shaara's Pulitzer prize-winning novel, *The Killer Angels*.

While the characters are open to the charge of being stereotypical caricatures, *Gettysburg* effectively presents the era as a simpler time, when the ideas of virtue and chivalry were very real. War, though brutal, was still fought in terms of what was considered to be gentlemanly conduct. That accuracy of attitude is one of the most refreshing things about *Gettysburg*. It is simply a movie about a battle and the people caught up in it. The movie covers the four days from June 30 to July 3, 1863. The obligatory wartime scenes of soldiers swearing violently and indulging in sex during furloughs are entirely absent. *Gettysburg* chooses historical faithfulness over the gratuitous elements of many genre films, and it proves that history can be interesting.

Jeff Daniels plays the philosophical and sensitive Union Col. Lawrence Chamberlain, a commander who leads by compassion and necessity. Martin Sheen portrays Gen. Robert E. Lee and does it more convincingly than one

"To be a good soldier you must love the army. To be a good commander you must be able to order the death of the thing you love."
General Lee (Martin Sheen)

Did you know?...

Over 13,000 Civil War reenactors came to participate in the making of *Gettysburg*, all paying their own way and providing their own uniforms and armaments.

Hand-to-hand combat between the Yankees and the Confederates at the battle of Little Round Top.

might expect from his impassivity. (Lee was known at West Point as the Marble Man, a quality that is certainly brought to the forefront in Sheen's stoic interpretation.) Richard Jordan, in his last role before dying from a brain tumor, also gives a wonderfully compassionate performance as Confederate General Lewis Armistead.

The visual element in *Gettysburg* is breathtaking, as the cameras shoot from extremely wide distances for the large battle scenes, such as the assault at Cemetery Ridge made by Pickett's (a dynamic Stephen Lang) brigade on the third day of the battle. The evocative use of light and subtle colors gives at times a mournful, contemplative mood to the film. In addition, a hauntingly beautiful musical theme permeates *Gettysburg*. Overall, the music along with the lighting creates a powerful picture.

The movie's sense of humanity and drama is always touching. In one scene, Col. Chamberlain, knowing that his men are about out of ammunition and that the Confederates are moving up Little Round Top for their fifth assault, orders a charge down the hill with the command, "Bayonets!"—a blood-curdling order in its implications to both his men and anyone else with a knowledge of military tactics. However, this charge succeeds at repelling the Confederates and saving the Union's left flank. In real life (though not in the movie) Chamberlain was awarded the Congressional Medal of Honor.

Cast: Tom Berenger (Lt. Gen. James Longstreet), Martin Sheen (Gen. Robert E. Lee), Stephen Lang (Maj. Gen. George E. Pickett), Richard Jordan (Brig Gen. Lewis A. Armistead), Andrew Prine (Brig. Gen. Richard B. Garnett), Cooper Huckabee (Henry T. Harrison), Patrick Gorman (Brig. Gen. John Bell Hood), Bo Brinkman (Maj. Walter H. Taylor), James Lancaster (Lt. Col. Arthur Freemantle), William Morgan Sheppard (Maj. Gen. Isaac R. Trimble), Kieran Mulroney (Maj. Gen. Moxley Sorrel), James Patrick Stewart (Col. E. Porter Alexander), Tim Ruddy (Maj. Charles Marshall), Royce D. Applegate (Brig. Gen. James L. Kemper), Ivan Kane (Capt. Thomas J. Goree), Warren Burton (Maj. Gen. Henry Heth), MacIntyre Dixon (Maj. Gen. Jubal A. Early), Joseph Fuqua (Maj. Gen. J.E.B. Stuart), Tim Scott (Lt. Gen. Richard S. Ewell), George Lazenby (Brig. Gen. J. Johnson Pettigrew), Jeff Daniels (Col. Joshua Lawrence Chamberlain), Sam Elliott (Brig. Gen. John Buford), C. Thomas Howell (Lt. Thomas D. Chamberlain), Kevin Conway (Sgt. "Buster" Kilrain), Brian Mallon (Maj. Gen. Winfield Scott Hancock), Buck Taylor (Col. Willliam Gamble), John Diehl (Pvt. Bucklin), Josh Mauer (Col. James C. Rice), John Rothman (Maj. Gen. John F. Reynolds), Richard Anderson (Maj. Gen. George G. Meade), Bill Campbell (Lt. Pitzer), David Carpenter (Col. Thomas C. Devin), Maxwell Caulfield (Col. Strong Vincent), Donal Logue (Capt. Ellis Spear), Dwier Brown (Capt. Brewer), Herb Mitchell (Sgt. Andrew J. Tozier) **Screenwriter:** Ronald F. Maxwell **Cinematographer:** Kees Van Oostrum **Composer:** Randy Edelman **Producer:** Moctesuna Esparza and Robert Katz for Mayfair/Turner **MPAA Rating:** PG **Running Time:** 254 minutes **Format:** VHS **Budget:** $25M **Box Office:** $10M.

Glory
1989 – Edward Zwick – 🦴🦴🦴🦴

Inspiring stories usually prove to be easier to find than to commit to film with critical and commercial success. While *Glory* starts out a little slow, the drama and human interactions that take place once a company of black soldiers comes together eventually prove compelling. Based on the 54th Massachusetts, the first black volunteer infantry regiment in the Civil War, *Glory* takes the viewer into the life of not just any soldier but a black soldier during a war fought to free his race from slavery. It was a hard enough time for a black man, but it was a terrible time for a black soldier. The film follows the 54th Massachusetts from its inception to its fateful assault on Fort Wagner in July 1863.

> "Ain't nobody gonna win. It's gonna go on and on."
>
> Trip (Denzel Washinhgton) to Shaw about the war.

The 54th Regiment of Massachusetts Volunteer Infantry storms a Confederate fort.

The film benefits from some fine actors who portray engaging characters. The sensitive, but firm Colonel Shaw is played by Matthew Broderick in his best performance. The kid from *WarGames* and *Ferris Bueller's Day Off* is now mature and believable commanding a regiment of black volunteers. Cary Elwes portrays Cabot Forbes, Shaw's childhood friend who becomes his second-in-command. Denzel Washington brings to life Trip, a trouble-making runaway slave whose bitterness is often masked by indifference. For his efforts he was awarded the best supporting actor Oscar and became a star. Morgan Freeman gives a powerful performance as Sergeant Major John Rawlins. His character may be the most philosophical member of the 54th. He begins the war as a gravedigger, and in one memorable scene with Trip, he puts the entire war in perspective for him and everyone else within earshot when he confronts Trip over his hatred of whites.

Fine ensemble acting is not the only thing *Glory* has going for it. James Horner has written a hauntingly beautiful score that helps magnify the wonderful camera work of Freddie Francis. Together, they create some impressive moments, highlighted by the suicidal attack on a confederate hilltop stronghold. The lighting of the night scene of the assault on Fort Wagner is also impressive, intensified by the pyrotechnics that simulate exploding shells in front of the Union forces in the assault.

Cast: Matthew Broderick (Colonel Robert G. Shaw), Denzel Washington (Trip), Cary Elwes (Cabot Forbes), Morgan Freeman (John Rawlins), Jihmi Kennedy (Sharts), Andre Braugher (Lieutenant Thomas Searles), John Finn (Sergeant Mulcahy), Donovan Leitch (Morse), John David Cullum (Russell), Alan North (Governor Andrew), Bob Gunton (General Harter), Cliff De Young (Colonel Montgomery), Christian Baskous (Pierce), Ronreaco Lee (Mute Drummer Boy), Jay O. Sanders (General Strong), Richard Riehle (Quartermaster) **Screenwriter:** Kevin Jarre **Cinematographer:** Freddie Francis **Composer:** James Horner **Producer:** Freddie Fields for Columbia Pictures **MPAA Rating:** R **Running Time:** 122 minutes **Format:** VHS, LV **Awards:** Academy Awards, 1989: Cinematography, Sound, Supporting Actor (Denzel Washington); Nominations: Art Direction/Set Direction, Film Editing; Golden Globe Awards, 1990: Supporting Actor (Denzel Washington) **Box Office:** $26.8M.

Did you know?...

Raymond St. Jacques appears uncredited as Frederick Douglass. St. Jacques, who made his film debut in *Black Like Me* and acted in numerous television shows, died shortly after the completion of the film.

The Great Escape
1963 – John Sturges – 𝄞𝄞𝄞𝄞

The Germans have put all the rotten POW eggs in the basket of one camp, but unknowingly they have also assembled a team of artists with every necessary skill to engineer an ingenious mass escape. Director John Sturges and some of the cast from *The Magnificent Seven* (Steve McQueen, James Coburn, Charles Bronson) reteamed to make this film based on a real World War II escape. The film's great appeal lies in the cast and camaraderie. Watching them work their magic: making uniforms out of blankets, systematically disposing of dirt in the compound, and communicating via a series of taps enables the audience to identify with them as they bond with one another. Richard Attenborough and James Donald are the Brits who mastermind the operation, Charles Bronson the claustrophobic tunnel man, James Garner the con-man scrounger, Donald Pleasence the forger. The heroism revealed in their physical daring is matched by another type of valor that shows up in the uncompromising attachments that form among the men, best seen in Garner's willingness to risk his own escape so as not to leave behind his nearly-blind friend Pleasence. The sympathy creat-

"It is the sworn duty of all officers to try to escape."
Group Captain Ramsey (James Donald) to Von Luger.

Did you know?...

Screenwriter James Clavell later wrote the best-selling novel *Shogun.* Clavell himself had been an inmate in a Japanese POW camp during World War II.

Three American soldiers in a
German POW camp remember
the patriots of The Revolutionary
War.

ed for all the men in the first two-thirds of the film is so strong that the suspense over their final fates becomes almost unbearable.

Steve Rubin's recent documentary about the film, *Return to the Great Escape*, interviewed many of the principals and verified behind-the-scenes information about what seems to have been a charmed production. The script, after having passed through the hands of eleven writers, still needed work, and changes were being made as filming progressed. Then, Steve McQueen saw a rough cut of six weeks' filming and decided that James Garner's character was better written than his and that Garner was stealing the film. Infuriating Sturges and puzzling professionals like Pleasence who had never encountered such displays of temperament, McQueen walked off the production. As Garner tells it, he and James Coburn rounded up McQueen and talked out the difficulties with him. "Steve wanted to be the hero, but he didn't want to do anything heroic" Garner says today with some amusement. He and Coburn then retold the plot of what is really an ensemble piece to McQueen, emphasizing the bravery of his character and making it seem as if the success of the escape all hinged on him. McQueen returned to this project, but he later turned down the role he was offered in *A Bridge Too Far* when he saw that it too was an ensemble project rather than a star vehicle for him.

Cast: Steve McQueen (Capt. Virgil Hilts, "The Cooler King"), James Garner (Hendley, "The Scrounger"), Richard Attenborough (Bartlett, "Big X"), James Donald (Ramsey, "The SBO"), Charles Bronson (Danny Velinski, "Tunnel King"), Donald Pleasence (Colin Blythe, "The Forger"), James Coburn (Sedgwick, "Manufacturer"), Hannes Messemer (Von Luger, "The Kommandant"), David McCallum (Ashley-Pitt, "Dispersal"), Gordon Jackson (MacDonald, "Intelligence"), John Leyton (Willie, "Tunnel King"), Angus Lennie (Ives, "The Mole"), Nigel Stock (Cavendish, "The Surveyor"), Robert Graf (Werner, "The Ferret"), Judson Taylor (Goff) **Screenwriter:** James Clavell, W.R. Burnett **Cinematographer:** Daniel L. Fapp **Composer:** Elmer Bernstein **Producer:** John Sturges for the Mirisch Company; released by United Artists **MPAA Rating:** PG **Running Time:** 169 minutes **Format:** VHS, LV, DVD **Awards:** Academy Awards, 1963: Nominations: Editing; National Board of Review Awards, 1963: 10 Best Films of the Year **Budget:** $4M.

The Guns of Navarone
1961 – J. Lee Thompson – 🦴🦴🦴🦴

This first in the line of sabotage-suspense war movies rather than battle pictures takes place in the Mediterranean Sea in the later years of World War II. Captain Mallory (Gregory Peck) believes that he is going on leave until he is pressed into leading a group of soldiers and guerillas to sabotage a German artillery base on the island fortress of Navarone. To blow up the big guns, the men must first scale a 400-foot cliff and then, if they have survived, sneak undetected into the enemy base and plant explosives. Each man has a particular specialty that qualifies him for this mission—all are renegades. As the movie follows each day of the mission, they encounter storms at sea, German patrols, broken bones, and betrayals from within. Still, they persist in fighting against time to stop the guns that will be used against their fellow troops.

A solid cast makes this film a pleasure to watch. Peck is perfect as the hard, quiet Mallory who hates the assignment but embraces his duty as leader. Anthony Quinn is grand as his Greek buddy who has sworn to kill Mallory after

> "Someone's got to take responsibility if the job's going to get done. Do you think that's easy?"
> Mallory (Gregory Peck)

Did you know?...
Writer Carl Foreman had been blacklisted in the U.S. and moved to England during the 1950s.

Disguised Allied officers Mallory (Gregory Peck) and Miller (David Niven) gain entrance to a German gun base.

the war because of an accident he caused. David Niven is a bit old for Corporal Miller, but catches perfectly the sardonic, resentful attitude of one who hates the mission and the war itself.

The ensemble makes the action feel real, but setting is the other key ingredient to the film's power. Stark Greek islands, ruins that could hide whole regiments undetected, quaint villages of people seeking to celebrate life and to forget the war, German fortifications that look as permanent as the earth itself—all are used to build suspense and further the story as well as provide the backdrop for the movie. Dimitri Tiomkin's award-winning score also combines pathos and suspense with Greek harmonies for authenticity and effect.

The Guns of Navarone has an against-all-odds plot that may seem a bit stale today, but the audience of 1961 had rarely seen anything like it. Part of the credit surely owes to Alistair MacLean, the author of this novel and many other adventure tales that applied the trickery of mystery plotting to the action of a war story. Non-stop conflict and one subplot that played directly into the next left no time for popcorn or a smoke (yes, you could smoke at the movies in 1961). You sat at the edge of your seat, left a little breathless from the exertion, wanted to see the movie again to catch the parts you had missed—and a genre was born.

Cast: Gregory Peck (Captain Keith Mallory), Anthony Quinn (Andrea Stavros), David Niven (Corporal Miller), Stanley Baker (CPO Brown), Anthony Quayle (Major Franklin), James Darren (Spyros Pappadimos), Irene Papas (Maria Pappadimos), Gia Scala (Anna), James R. Jushke (Narrator), Richard Harris (Barnsby), Bryan Forbes (Cohn), Allan Cuthbertson (Baker), Albert Lieven (The Commandant), George Mikell (Sessler), Michael Trubshawe (Weaver) **Screenwriter:** Carl Foreman **Cinematographer:** Oswald Morris **Composer:** Dimitri Tiomkin **Producer:** Carl Foreman for Open Road Productions; released by Columbia Pictures **Running Time:** 156 minutes **Format:** VHS, LV **Awards:** Academy Awards, 1961: Special Effects; Nominations: Director (J. Lee Thompson), Editing, Original Dramatic/Comedy Score, Picture, Sound, Screenplay (adaptation); Golden Globe Awards, 1961: Best Picture—Drama, Score **Budget:** $3M.

Henry V

1944 – Laurence Olivier – 𝄞𝄞𝄞𝄞

Shakespeare begins his play with a chorus lamenting that the "wooden O" of the stage cannot hold the "vasty fields of France," and Olivier starts his film with an extended sequence set on May 1, 1600, at the Globe theater as we watch the opening of this play in the way its original audience might have. They eagerly involve themselves with what they see on stage. These noisy spectators munching on oranges moan at the report of the King's (Laurence Olivier) prior banishment of Falstaff (George Roby), the pub companion of his youth, and laugh at the tedious recitation of Salic law that Henry uses as a pretext for his incursion into France. After the Dauphin (Max Adrian) makes a present to Henry of tennis balls (a joke about his sportive youth and unfitness for the throne) and Henry rouses himself in anger at France, the epic nature of the conflict bursts its bounds. The framing device of watching a performance at the Globe gives way to the spectacle of the siege at Harfleur and the battle at Agincourt.

Olivier's approach stresses the inspirational, patriotic aspects of the play. It lifted the hearts of wartime audiences and still thrills today with outdoor scenes that are bright, colorful, and clean. When long shots capture far off castles, they have an Oz-like look to them, as if they have been taken from some

"He babbled of green fields."

Mistress Quickly (Freda Jackson), reporting the death of Sir John Falstaff.

Did you know?...

Laurence Olivier had wanted his wife Vivian Leigh for the part of Katharine, but producer David O. Selznick, who had her under contract, refused permission for her to appear in such a small part.

England's Henry V (Laurence Olivier) listens to a French envoy.

medieval illuminated manuscript. Olivier's performance is suitably regal. We first see him backstage during the Globe scenes, giving a little cough before he strides on stage to the cheers of the audience. He is fiery in his anger at the French and inspiring in the famous pre-battle speeches. He stages the St. Crispin's Day speech as a horizontal tracking shot that starts as a conversational rebuke to Westmoreland for wanting more men to offset their five-to-one underdog plight and builds to a great verbal and visual crescendo. The film was the best screen version of Shakespeare to that time and is still excellent today.

Cast: Laurence Olivier (King Henry V), Robert Newton (Ancient Pistol), Leslie Banks (Chorus), Renee Asherson (Princess Katharine), Esmond Knight (Fluellen), Leo Genn (Constable of France), Ralph Truman (Mountjoy), Harcourt Williams (King Charles VI of France), Ivy St. Helier (Alice), Ernest Thesiger (Duke of Berri), Max Adrian (The Dauphin), Valentine Dyall (Duke of Burgundy), Russell Thorndike (Duke of Bourbon), Felix Aylmer (Archbishop of Canterbury), Roy Emerton (Lieutenant Bardolph), Robert Helpmann (Bishop of Ely), Niall MacGinnis (MacMorris), John Laurie (Jamy), Michael Shepley (Gower), Freda Jackson (Mistress Quickly), Frederick Cooper (Nym), George Roby (Falstaff) **Screenwriter:** Alan Dent, Reginald Beck, Laurence

Olivier **Cinematographer:** Robert Krasker **Composer:** William Walton **Producer:** Laurence Olivier for Two Cities; released by the Rank Organization **Running Time:** 137 minutes **Format:** VHS **Awards:** National Board of Review Awards, 1946: 10 Best Films of the Year; New York Film Critics Awards, 1946: Actor (Laurence Olivier); Academy Awards, 1946: Nominations: Actor (Laurence Olivier), Interior Decoration, Picture, Score.

Henry V

1989 – Kenneth Branagh – 🦴🦴🦴🦴

Kenneth Branagh's version of Shakespeare's history play, previously filmed by Laurence Olivier, emphasizes ambiguity, complexity, and realism. It suggests that the best way to remake a classic film is to start with an equally strong but different concept and follow it imaginatively. To Branagh, Shakespeare's play is a "political debate inside an adventure story," and his screen treatment opens in darkness as two churchmen (Charles Kay, Alec McCowen) convince the king of a complicated legal pretext to justify an invasion of France. They flank Henry and whisper conspiratorially into each ear. The muted production design uses browns and burgundy to darken the sets; nocturnal scenes abound: in one, at the siege at Harfleur, Henry is framed by the archway to the town and backlit by bursting flames from the battle as his horse rears up and he waves his sword.

The film uses a few flashbacks to mark the changes brought about in Henry by the responsibilities of kingship. During the death of Sir John Falstaff (Robbie Coltrane), we see glimpses of the famous tavern scene from *Henry IV, Part One*, which show Henry as Prince Hal and Falstaff and his cronies sporting at the inn. The hanging of Bardolph (Richard Briers) for looting a French church is one of the best examples of Henry's grim responsibilities as king. After a brief flashback reminds us of the old fun at the tavern, Henry authorizes the death of his erstwhile companion. As Bardolph rises high, legs kicking, hoisted from the branches of a tree, Henry watches and chokes back tears. (The play has the death occur offstage; Laurence Olivier omitted the material altogether.)

The spectacle of the final battle at Agincourt stresses mud, blood, and the human costs of war. (When the king is later handed a report that states only twenty-nine English have died in the fighting, it can only seem like an error.) The

> "We few, we happy few, we band of brothers; for he today that sheds his blood with me shall be my brother."
>
> Henry (Kenneth Branagh), on the eve of battle.

Did you know?...

Kenneth Branagh was twenty-eight when he made the film, one year older than the historical Henry at the battle of Agincourt.

English King Henry (Kenneth Branagh) woos French Princess Katharine (Emma Thompson).

crowning glory to this scene is the long tracking shot Branagh devised as a conclusion. Henry orders a *Te Deum* to be sung honoring the dead, and one soldier begins as Patrick Doyle's music comes up on the soundtrack. Henry carries a body slung over his shoulder past all the carnage and drifting smoke of the previous battle as the camera follows him, showing us the grim victors and the final reckonings of the battle. The film features a roster of British stage veterans, and among the many distinguished performers Ian Holm, Robert Stephens, Derek Jacobi, Brian Blessed, and Judi Dench stand out.

Cast: Kenneth Branagh (Henry V), Derek Jacobi (Chorus), Simon Shepherd (Gloucester), James Larkin (Bedford), Brian Blessed (Exeter), Robert Stephens (Pistol), Ian Holm (Fluellen), James Simmons (York), Charles Kay (Archbishop of Canterbury), Alec McCowen (Bishop of Ely), Fabian Cartwright (Cambridge), Stephen Simms (Scroop), Emma Thompson (Princess Katharine), Paul Scofield (King Charles VI of France), Michael Maloney (Dauphin), Richard Easton (constable), Judi Dench (Mistress Quickly), Geraldine McEwan (Alice), Richard Innocent (Burgundy), Richard Briers (Bardolph), Geoffrey Hutchins (Nym), Jay Villiers (Grey), Edward Jewesbury (Erpingham), Christopher Ravenscroft (Mountjoy), Daniel Webb (Gower), Jimmy Yuill (Jamy), Robbie Coltrane

(Falstaff), Christian Bale (boy) **Screenwriter:** Kenneth Branagh **Cinematographer;** Kenneth MacMillan **Composer:** Patrick Doyle **Producer:** Bruce Sharman for Renaissance Films and the BBC; released by the Samuel Goldwyn Company **MPAA Rating:** PG-13 **Running Time:** 137 minutes **Format:** VHS, LV **Awards:** Academy Awards, 1989: Costume Design; Nominations: Actor (Kenneth Branagh), Director (Kenneth Branagh); British Academy Awards, 1989: Director (Kenneth Branagh); National Board of Review Awards, 1989: Director (Kenneth Branagh).

The Lighthorsemen

1987 — Simon Wincer — 𝄞𝄞𝄞

When most people think of soldiers and horses, they think of the cavalry. But in spite of its title *The Lighthorsemen* is not about the cavalry. It is about the Australian Mounted Infantry and their fighting in Palestine during World War I against the Germans and Turks. Particularly, it is about one Lighthorseman, Dave Mitchell (Peter Phelps), and his inability to shoot at enemy soldiers. New to the outfit, Dave replaces a brave soldier who died in a military hospital after being shot during a skirmish with Turkish cavalry. Dave is placed with three veterans and forms a friendship with them. He begins to see that he will never be able to shoot an enemy soldier, and he asks for reassignment to the medical corps as a stretcher bearer. Already in love with a nurse from the hospital (Sigrid Thornton), he works to develop this relationship. When the unit is ordered to lead the assault on Beersheba, he is in the medical unit that goes in with the troops.

This powerful climax is the big highlight of a film that weaves a number of smaller plots together to create the basic conflict over the water wells of Beersheba. Without those wells the British and Australian armies are doomed. The soldiers cut every supply line and haul only what water they can carry for a two-day trek to Beersheba to take the town and capture the wells. There is no turning back. Once committed, they must either win or die. The first wave of the assault comes down to sending in either the British Cavalry or the Australian Lighthorsemen. The British commander opts to send in the Aussies, and they fool the defending German and Turkish artillery by not stopping to dismount and by rushing directly at the lines in a thundering charge.

The movie has a wonderful look to it. There are majestic scenes of desert landscapes and evening shots with sunsets over the Mediterranean. But perhaps

> "We are fighting in a desert—warfare in its purest form with one simple rule; men and horses must drink. And each time Gaza is attacked we hold out for one or two days at the most, and the British are defeated by the desert."
>
> General Von Kressenstein (Ralph Cotterill)

Did you know?...

In a sense this Australian film provides a companion piece to *Gallipoli*, which also concerns Lighthorsemen fighting in World War I.

Australian soldiers in WWI prepare to fire on the Turkish enemy.

the best work of cinematography comes in the climactic charge of the Lighthorsemen, an enormous scene reminiscent of Pickett's charge in *Gettysburg*. The script also accomplishes the difficult task of clearly keeping the viewer informed about the logistics of the soldiers and pertinent background information leading to this moment without either seeming obvious or sacrificing any of the building suspense. *The Lighthorsemen* effectively dramatizes the race between the Germans to blow up the wells and the British to save them.

Cast: Peter Phelps (Dave Mitchell), Sigrid Thornton (Anne), Nick Waters (Lighthorse Sergeant), John Larking (Station Master), John Heywood (Dave's Dad), Di O'Connor (Dave's Mum), Shane Briant (Reichert), Ralph Cotterill (Von Kressenstein), Bill Kerr (Chauvel), Grant Piro (Charlie), Tony Bonner (Bourchier), Serge Lazareff (Rankin), Gary Sweet (Frank), John Walton (Tas), Tim McKenzie (Chiller), Jon Blake (Scotty) **Screenwriter:** Ian Jones **Cinematographer:** Dean Semler **Composer:** Mario Millo **Producer:** Simon Wincer and Ian Jones for Medusa; released by RKO **MPAA Rating:** PG **Running Time:** 131 minutes **Format:** VHS.

The Longest Day

1962 – Ken Annakin, Andrew Marton, Gerd Oswald, Bernhard Wicki – 🦴🦴🦴

The Longest Day is one of the last war epics to be filmed in black and white. It covers the D-Day invasion of Normandy of June 6, 1944, in a sporadic, almost documentary way. As the movie begins, both the German and Allied forces are watching the weather. The Germans are content with the rain since the Allies have never staged an invasion in anything less than perfect weather. But the Allies are contemplating doing just that. History plays out in a diverse set of vignettes that moves back and forth between the German high command and their forces, and the Allied (mostly American, of course) commanders preparing their armies and invading Europe.

The collage-like collection of subplots gives the film a disjointed feel. Perhaps this is the inevitable result of the many hands that contributed to the project. Four directors worked on the film: the British exteriors were directed by Ken Annakin, Andrew Marton directed the American exteriors, Gerd Oswald was in charge of the parachute-drop sequence, and the German scenes were directed by Bernhard Wicki. Add to this five screenwriters, among them James Jones, the author of *From Here to Eternity* and Cornelius Ryan, the author of the book

"The thing that's always worried me about being one of the few is the way we keep on getting fewer."

Campbell (Richard Burton)

Coming ashore on D-Day, June 6, 1944.

on which the film is based, and four more cinematographers and you begin to feel that this film crew not only dramatizes the action of an army but also resembles one.

Any film so heavily populated behind the cameras would also of course feature a long roster of stars in front of the cameras and *The Longest Day* is no slouch in that department. Part of the attraction of the film seems to be the idea that no small part should be played by an anonymous actor. The advantage of this approach is that the studio can promote the film on the strength of its many famous names; the drawback is that none of the famous faces is on screen long enough to develop a sense of character. The viewer is expected to accept each character predrawn by the personality of its star.

Though the film suffers from having too many good actors in roles that are usually too flat, some of these star personalities work well to bring to life a particular character. Sean Connery, for example, is believable as an sensitive private hitting the beach, and Eddie Albert and Robert Mitchum both do good jobs in their roles. Perhaps one of the best-developed characters in the film is Major Pluskat, portrayed by the lesser known Hans Christian Blech. He may be remembered for his role as Robert Shaw's aide in *The Battle of the Bulge*. In this film he is the one who finally informs the German high command of the impending and imminent invasion. Richard Burton and John Wayne offer no surprises. Burton's acting is overdone, and Wayne, in a scene with Robert Ryan, throws his coat across his chest into a chair with the same cocky, disgusted flair he would give to tossing away a cigarette in a western.

The battle scenes are intricate and exciting, occasionally running for several minutes without an edit. Three hours is not too long for a movie about D-Day, but the fragmentation of this storyline eventually stalls the movie. More coherence and some fully drawn characters would have created more dramatic success.

Cast: John Wayne (Lt. Col. Benjamin Vandervoort), Robert Mitchum (Brig. Gen. Norman Cota), Henry Fonda (Brig. Gen. Theodore Roosevelt, Jr.), Richard Burton (Flight Officer David Campbell), Eddie Albert (Colonel Tom Newton), Paul Anka (U.S. Ranger), Hans Christian Blech (Major Pluskat), Bourvil (Mayor of Colleville), Wolfgang Buttner (Major General Doctor Hans Speidel), Red Buttons (Pvt. John Steele), Sean Connery (Private Flanagan), Irina Demick (Janine Boitard), Fred Durr (Major of the Rangers), Fabian (U.S. Ranger), Mel Ferrer (Maj. Gen. Robert Haines), Steve Forrest (Captain Harding), Jeffrey Hunter (Sgt. John Fuller), Curt Jurgens (Maj. Gen. Gunther Blumentritt), Peter Lawford (Lord Lovat), Roddy McDowall (Pvt. Morris), Sal Mineo (Pvt. Martini), Robert Ryan (Brig. Gen. James Gavin), Tommy Sands (U.S. Ranger), George Segal (1st commando up the cliff), Rod Steiger (Destroyer Captain), Robert Wagner (U.S. Ranger), Stuart Whitman (Lt. Sheen) **Screenwriter:** Romain Gary, James Jones, David Pursall, Cornelius Ryan, Jack Seddon **Cinematographer:** Jean Bourgoin, Pierre Levent, Henri Persin, Walter Wottitz **Composer:** Paul Anka, Maurice Jarre **Producer:** Darryl F. Zanuck and Elmo Williams for Twentieth Century Fox **Running Time:** 180 minutes **Format:** VHS, LV **Awards:** Academy Awards, 1962: Cinematography (Black and White), Special Effects; Nominations: Art Direction/ Set Decoration, Editing, Picture; National Board of Review Awards, 1962: 10 Best Films of the Year **Budget:** $10M **Box Office:** $17M.

Paths of Glory

1957 – Stanley Kubrick – 𓂃𓂃𓂃𓂃

Some anti-wars films, like *All Quiet on the Western Front*, are defined by a mood of futility, some, like *Dr. Strangelove*, by one of absurdity. This one, directed and co-written by Stanley Kubrick, runs on anger. The rage is directed at the inhumanity of the people behind the war, especially two generals, who are portrayed by two great actors. Not since he played an abortionist for William Wyler in *Detective Story* (and clashed again with Kirk Douglas's character) has George Macready been given a role as villainous as Mireau, the World War I French general who orders artillery to fire on his own men because they do not charge the Ant Hill, an impregnable enemy fortification. Adolphe Menjou plays General Broulard as a satanic little pixie. He is more crafty than Mireau, and the film delights in peeling back his layers and exposing the horrors inside. (The final one comes when he sabotages Mireau in the name of patriotism.) Kirk Douglas plays Colonel Dax, the loyal soldier who faithfully tries to lead his men on what appears to be a suicide mission to take the Ant Hill. He returns across No Man's Land to his trench when he sees that part of his battalion did not charge. Mireau, who has seen it too, calls up the artillery fire to force the men to attack. After the ruinous, botched effort, three men are chosen by lot, tried for cowardice, convicted, and executed.

Kubrick marshals all his cinematic resources to contrast the generals and the soldiers. Mireau and Broulard have set their headquarters in a splendidly appointed chateau. When Mireau rejects Broulard's first suggestion that they attack the Ant Hill, Broulard saunters around the spacious room, Mireau and the camera following him. It is really a little dance of seduction that Broulard carries out as he coyly dangles a promotion for Mireau if he will change his mind. In contrast, Dax and the soldiers live in mud-encrusted dugouts in a trench. When Mireau makes a visit, the camera tracks backward in a long unbroken shot. The general stops to chat with the men ("Hello, soldier, ready to kill more Germans?") as bombs explode outside the trench and debris rains down on them.

The generals, of course, come off as caricatures, as villains will in a film fueled by anger, but the film also richly succeeds at humanizing the soldiers. In the whispering scene before the attack on the Ant Hill, for example, two infantrymen ponder whether death itself or the pain associated with death instills the greater

Col. Dax (Kirk Douglas) states his case.

fear. Execution eve exposes the condemned men's most naked feelings: anger at the priest bringing comfort, envy for a cockroach able to live through tomorrow, amazement over the loss of all carnal desires before the specter of death.

The understated final scene makes for a benedictory close to Kubrick's first masterpiece.

Cast: Kirk Douglas (Colonel Dax), Ralph Meeker (Corporal Paris), Adolphe Menjou (General Broulard), George Macready (General Mireau), Wayne Morris (Lieutenant Roget), Richard Anderson (Major Saint-Auban), Joseph Turkel (Private Arnaud), Timothy Carey (Private Ferol), Susanne Christian (German girl), Jerry Hausner (cafe owner), Peter Capell (Colonel Judge), Emile Meyer (priest), Fred Bell (shell-shock victim) **Screenwriter:** Stanley Kubrick, Calder Willingham, Jim Thompson **Cinematographer:** George Krause **Composer:** Gerald Fried **Producer:** James B. Harris for Bryna Productions; released by United Artists **Running Time:** 87 minutes **Format:** VHS, LV **Budget:** $935,000.

Platoon
1986 – Oliver Stone – 🦴🦴🦴🦴

> "I think now looking back, we did not fight the enemy, we fought ourselves and the enemy was in us."
> Chris (Charlie Sheen), from the closing narration.

Directed by Vietnam veteran Oliver Stone, *Platoon* uses the intensity of the Vietnam War to present a modern morality play about the battle for the soul of a young enlistee, Chris Taylor (Charlie Sheen, in the performance of his career). As Chris and his platoon arrive near the Cambodian border in 1967, they leave the womb-like mouth of the transport plane and are welcomed by the sight of a litter of body bags ready to be flown out. The starkness of the imagery characterizes the entire film. Life and death, innocence and experience, good and evil are reflected in the often graphic realism of the film's style, and one of the defining traits of the film (praised by some, faulted by some) is the way the many horrors of war never appear without a sense of their larger spiritual dimensions.

We hear Chris' voice-over narration as he composes letters home to his grandmother—just about the only organizing trait in the film. Like writer-director Oliver Stone, Chris has dropped out of college after two years to enlist; he now finds his background at odds with his platoon-mates, most of whom were drafted. Stone conveys the disorientation of battle with many hand-held, kinetic camera shots. The numerous closeups also deny the audience a chance to accustom themselves during jungle scenes, creating a sense of dislocation.

Did you know?...
Filming took place in the Philippines over fifty-four days.

The key scene in the first half of the film occurs when the platoon enters a farming village suspected of using its system of underground tunnels to hide enemy soldiers. After finding one of their own tied and killed, Sergeant Barnes (Tom Berenger) begins threatening the villagers. He kills one woman and holds a pistol to the head of a little girl when Sergeant Elias (Willem Dafoe) stops him and the two begin to fight. Barnes is portrayed as the evil, animalistic one for whom survival has become the only good, even at the expense of innocent civilians; Elias is the humane soldier who respects the sanctity of life and resists the war's efforts to brutalize him. The platoon eventually splits in support of their two sergeants. Chris initially reveres Barnes, as his profane threats upon first entering the Vietnam village show, but he soon sides with Elias and stops his fellow soldiers from raping a village woman. The remainder of the film pits Barnes against Elias with Chris becoming less and less an innocent observer.

Grunts Chris (Charlie Sheen) and King (Keith David) bond in Vietnam.

The real power of the village scene and the battle sequences, as writer Danny Peary has observed, lies in the way they suggest that such My Lai brutality was the norm rather than the exception in Vietnam. It is a chilling thought. This intensity renders the usual inner resources of the soldiers in war films— bravery, patriotism, a sense of discipline or order—nearly meaningless in what becomes a desperate fight to survive. The barbarity of that struggle creates the ruthlessness of the Barneses of the war, but the desire not to be engulfed by such barbarity also creates the Eliases of the war. Between them is Chris, waiting to see what the war will make of him.

Cast: Tom Berenger (Sgt. Barnes), Willem Dafoe (Sgt. Elias), Charlie Sheen (Chris Taylor), Keith David (King), Forrest Whitaker (Big Harold), Francesco Quinn (Rhah), Kevin Dillon (Bunny), John C. McGinley (Sgt. O'Neill), Reggie Johnson (Junior), Mark Moses (Lt. Wolfe), Corey Glover (Francis), Johnny Depp (Lerner), Chris Pedersen (Crawford), Bob Orwig (Gardner), Corkey Ford (Manny), David Neidorf (Tex), Dale Dye (Harris) **Screenwriter:** Oliver Stone **Cinematographer:** Robert Richardson **Composer:** Georges Delerue **Producer:** Arnold Kopelson for Orion Pictures **MPAA Rating:** R **Running Time:** 120 minutes **Format:** VHS, LV, DVD **Awards:** Academy Awards, 1986: Director (Oliver Stone), Editor, Picture, Sound; Nominations: Cinematography, Screenplay, Supporting Actor (Tom Berenger, Willem Dafoe); British Academy Awards, 1987: Director (Oliver Stone); Directors Guild of America Awards, 1986: Director (Oliver Stone); Golden Globe Awards, 1987: Director (Oliver Stone), Film/Drama, Supporting Actor (Tom Berenger); Independent Spirit Awards, 1987: Cinematography, Director (Oliver Stone), Film, Screenplay; National Board of Review Awards, 1986: 10 Best Films of the Year **Budget:** $6M.

Saving Private Ryan
1998 – Steven Spielberg – 🦴🦴🦴🦴

Much has been made of the opening 25 minutes, as Steven Spielberg, cinematographer Janusz Kaminski, sound designer Gary Rydstrom, editor Michael Kahn, special effects supervisor Neil Carbould and stunt coordinator Simon Crane recreate the horrific D-Day assault on Omaha Beach, utilizing the Irish coastline of County Wexford and 850 extras from the Irish Army, many of them *Braveheart* veterans. The extras were organized into platoons, each with their own leader. Retired Marine Corps Captain Dale Dye was the chief consultant on the film (he also has a bit part as one of the War Department colonels). Before each shot of the beach invasion, Dye gave specific instructions to the platoon leaders, who then passed the information onto their men. Dye also

addressed the actors via a loudspeaker system high on the cliffs. "It was extra-ordinary," he says. "It was like being a battalion commander in combat and watching your troops maneuver while the cameras are rolling." Additional realism was achieved by having several amputees fitted with artificial limbs that were then blown off during the battle scene. The visuals take their inspiration from the famous photographs shot by Robert Capa. "There was terror in each frame," Spielberg notes. "Each frame was blurry, shaky and messed up, chaotic. They're frightening to look at, horrifically kinetic, and each photograph told the story of what it was like to be in combat. I thought, 'Well, if I could do something like that at 24 frames a second, that would be interesting.'"

The carnage is graphically, coldly presented, shorn of the usual Hollywood glamorization of battle. It's the sort of grim, terror-filled chaotic nightmare never talked about by survivors, their psychic wounds too great. As the men attempt to reach the beach from their amphibious landing craft, they are caught

Captain Miller (Tom Hanks) and Privates Reiben (Edward Burns) and Ryan (Matt Damon) wait for battle.

in a withering cross-fire from the invisible German artillery positioned above them. Many soldiers never make it off the landing craft, and the foam runs red with the blood of dead soldiers bobbing in the surf with thousands of dead fish. Camera and digital sound capture bullets ripping and mortar rounds exploding into flesh and organs, maiming and killing at high speed, as the beach is quickly littered with the dead and dying. Shells clank off the iron hedgehogs erected by the Germans to deter an amphibious assault. Hand-held cameras capture the annihilation from the point of view of the terrified U.S. soldiers as they press forward and are mowed down. We first meet Captain John Miller (Tom Hanks) and his Ranger squad as they are about to debark from the landing craft, as the camera focuses on his compulsively trembling hand. Somehow he and his men reach the bluff and destroy a German pillbox, opening an exit off the beach, and we are on are way to the heart of a war story masterfully told.

Screenwriters Robert Rodat and an uncredited Frank Darabont, utilizing sources such as *Citizen Soldiers* by Stephen Ambrose and the recollections of D-Day participants, capture the soldiers' intense physical and moral struggle to survive. War imposes continual ethical choices upon the men, between doing their duty as it is continually redefined (and may likely result in death) and survival. The men are confronted with choice at every juncture, deciding between self preservation and the necessity of a greater duty. Philosophically, the limited choices keep the story simple on an intellectual level, but deeply felt emotionally. Capt. Miller is the moral center of the movie, as Hanks brings to his portrayal a sense of solitude, private anguish, and decency, and a low-key but powerful devotion to duty. As a citizen soldier, Hanks gives Miller a sense of an ordinary man forced to become an extraordinary leader under the most pressing of circumstances. "Tom has the most memorable forgettable face in film history," says Spielberg. "Tom could be any of us at any time."

Upon surviving the beach invasion, Miller and his squad, a stereotypical ethnic hodgepodge, are assigned to retrieve paratrooper Private James Ryan (Matt Damon) from somewhere within the Normandy countryside, which is ripe with Nazi troops. Private Ryan does not know that three of his brothers have been recently killed in action, and the Army wants to send the lone surviving brother home to his mother. So Miller and his crew are given the luckless task of first finding Ryan and then getting him out alive. The squad includes Sergeant Horvath (Tom Sizemore with a performance that anchors the film), the no-nonsense right-hand man who shares a tight bond with the Captain. And there's cynical Brooklyn boy Private Reiben (director/actor Edward Burns); Private Mellish (Adam Goldberg), who proudly flaunts his Star of David before German prisoners; Private Caparzo (Vin Diesel), the extroverted Italian; Private Jackson (Barry Pepper), the southern sharp-shooter who says a prayer and fires away with astonishing accuracy; and medic Wade (Giovanni Ribisi), who feels the utter frustration of an overwhelmed healer. The group takes on a translator, Corporal Upham (Jeremy Davies of *Spanking the Monkey*), an intellectual pen-pusher who has never seen action. Why, the men ask, should we risk our lives to save one man? "This Private Ryan better be worth it," grumbles one of the men.

As the men move inland, they encounter terrified civilians and U.S. paratroopers in disarray, as well as the occasional run-in with a German unit. When Private Ryan is finally found, he doesn't want to be rescued. He refuses to desert his depleted platoon, which has been ordered to defend a bridge in the bombed out village of Ramelle. Unable to persuade Ryan to leave, Miller and his squad decide to join forces with Ryan's platoon and await the inevitable German company. The final fire fight in the village, which was built by set designer Tom Sanders in a former plane-making facility 20 miles outside London, is equal to the Omaha invasion in its drama, quick cuts, jumpy cameras, and overall intensity. The battle is brilliantly choreographed and claustrophic in its confined spaces, as German tanks thunder through the town center and the outnumbered Americans resort to guerilla tactics to stop the superiorly armed Nazis.

Spielberg's triumph is using the conventions of the war movie in a fresh, vital way that evades a cliche look and creates a close-hand experience for the viewer. Both a tribute to the men who fought and a warning about the unforgiving nature of battle, *Saving Private Ryan* may just be the best war movie ever made.

Cast: Tom Hanks (Capt. John Miller), Edward Burns (Pvt. Reiben), Tom Sizemore (Sgt. Horvath), Jeremy Davies (Cpl. Upham), Vin Diesel (Pvt. Caparzo), Adam Goldberg (Pvt. Mellish), Barry Pepper (Pvt. Jackson), Giovanni Ribisi (Medic Wade), Matt Damon (Pvt. James Ryan), Dennis Farina (Lt. Col. Anderson), Ted Danson (Capt. Hamill), Harve Presnell (Gen. George Marshall), Paul Giamatti (Sergeant Hill), Joerg Stadler (Steamboat Willie), Max Martini (Corporal Henderson) **Screenwriter:** Robert Rodat **Cinematographer:** Janusz Kaminski **Composer:** John Williams **Producer:** Steven Spielberg, Ian Bryce, Mark Gordon, Gary Levinsohn **MPAA Rating:** R **Running Time:** 169 minutes **Budget:** $65M **Box Office:** $126M (to date).

Tora! Tora! Tora!

1970 – Richard Fleischer, Kinji Fukasaku, Toshio Masuda – 🗾🗾🗾

> "To awaken a sleeping giant and fill him with terrible resolve is sowing the seed for certain disaster."
>
> Yamamoto (Tatsuya Mahashi)

Sometimes history-based films are faulted for using fictional characters as composites for real-life people or for conflating separate events for the purposes of coherence or dramatic effect. *Tora! Tora! Tora!* avoids any such fictionalizing of its historical materials, but the resulting film shows that dramatic license is not always misplaced. The first hour of this joint production of American and Japanese film crews jumps from various meeting rooms, carrier decks, and private conversations in Hawaii, Washington, and Japan to create the background of the Japanese attack on Pearl Harbor. As the attack nears, these scenes grow shorter, tension mounts, and the viewer is grateful. The actual historical background involving the event, however, takes in so many elements, going back at least to Japan's invasion of China in 1937 and its effect on American-Japanese relations, that historians like Akira Iriye have mildly faulted the film for taking a far too limited view of its pre-intermission events. The film presents American and Japanese diplomats meeting for negotiation, though these scenes lack any specific points of contention, such as the Japanese pact with Germany in 1940. Condensing the sprawl of history creates a formidable challenge, but some streamlining and dramatic license would have given greater coherence and sweep to the film's historic point of view.

Though the first hour or so lumbers a bit, after the intermission the movie proceeds more effectively. The filmmakers add some welcome personalizing touches. On their flight to Hawaii, for example, the Japanese pilots glimpse the rising sun out of their cockpit window and share a moment of celebration. Another scene shows Japanese pilots shouting out their guesses of ships' names from flash cards their superior holds up; one of them misidentifies his own flagship as the U.S. Oklahoma to the razzing of his friends. Another scene shows a hunt-and-peck Japanese typist slowly tapping out the crucial fourteenth part of a message Japanese diplomats are to deliver to Washington before the attack. (Although the film also shows that the U.S., with their decoding device called Magic, had intercepted the message and failed to act decisively through bureaucratic ineptitude). In one of the few humorous touches in the film, a student pilot taking a lesson on Sunday, December 7, suddenly finds himself amid

Did you know?...

Famed Japanese director Akira Kurosawa was fired from the Japanese sequences when his work on the film proceeded too slowly.

the swarm of the Japanese attack squadron. Such moments prepare for the Oscar-winning visual effects that conclude a film whose appeal is probably more educational than dramatic.

Japanese Naval officers plan their strategy for a surprise attack on Pearl Harbor.

Cast: Martin Balsam (Admiral Husband E. Kimmel), So Yamamura (Admiral Isoroku), Joseph Cotten (Secretary of State Henry L. Stimson), Tatsuya Mahashi (Commander Genda Yamamoto), E.G. Marshall (Lt. Colonel Bratton), James Whitmore (Admiral William F. Halsey), Takahiro Tamura (Lt. Commander Mitsuo Fuchida), Eijiro Tono (Admiral Chuichi Nagumo), Jason Robards (Gen. Walter C. Short), Wesley Addy (Lt. Commander Alwin D. Kramer), Shoga Shimada (Ambassador Nomura), Frank Aletter (Lt. Commander Thomas), Koreya Senda (Prince Konoye), Leon Ames (Frank Knox), Junya Usami (Admiral Yoshida), George Macready (Cordell Hull) **Screenwriter:** Larry Forrester, Ryuzo Kikushima, Hideo Oguni **Cinematographer;** Osamu Furuya, Sinsaku Himeda, Masamichi Satoh, Charles F. Wheeler **Composer:** Jerry Goldsmith **Producer:** Elmos Williams for Twentieth Century Fox **Running Time:** 144 minutes **Format:** VHS, LV **Awards:** Academy Awards, 1970: Visual Effects; Nominations: Art Direction/Set Decoration, Cinematography, Editing, Sound; National Board of Review Awards 1970: 10 Best Films of the Year **Budget:** $25M **Box Office:** $14M.

The Victors

1963 – Carl Foreman – 🦴🦴🦴

The only film directed by writer-producer Carl Foreman, *The Victors* follows the adventures and loves of a group of American foot soldiers who travel from town to town in Europe near the end of World War II. Foreman, who had written such classics as *High Noon*, *The Bridge on the River Kwai*, and *The Guns of Navarone*, intended this as his greatest screen achievement. That may have been his mistake. Almost all of the weaknesses derive from the overly solemn preoccupation with art and the conscious aim to create a masterpiece. Foreman intercuts the dramas of the soldiers with clips of newsreel footage documenting the era complete with an iron-voiced narrator.

The strength of the film is in some of the smaller moments of the soldiers entering each town and interacting with the locals. In one scene in a cafe, George Hamilton watches the celebration of his fellow GIs degenerate into a race riot; his matter-of-fact acceptance of this shocks the Italian barmaid: "Why you fight? You all the same people. Why you fight?" In another, a private (Peter Fonda) who has looked after a stray dog climbs into the back of a troop truck heading to a new town. Unable to take his pet, he watches in anguish as his fellow soldiers bet on who is a good enough marksman to shoot the dog running after the truck. Fonda, though he wants to speak up, can't allow himself to seem soft and sentimental in front of his comrades. Most of the episodes convey a similarly dark tone as the film eventually acquires the feel of a cinematic short-story collection.

One near-wordless scene illustrates both the film's merits and its heavy-handedness. At Christmas in Belgium, GIs are chosen by lot to witness the execution of a deserter. As the MPs lead out the prisoner, Foreman effectively alternates closeups of the faces of the Americans with stark, long shots of the deserter and the firing squad against the bleak, snowy landscape. He makes his point about the inhumanity and irony of the event by playing Frank Sinatra on the soundtrack singing "Have Yourself a Merry Little Christmas." But as so often in the film, Foreman can't leave well enough alone: after the fatal shots, Sinatra's voice is replaced by some rousing hallelujahs from a choir, and a scene intense enough to have spoken for itself has lost its subtlety.

A tired WWII infantry squad takes a break.

Cast: George Hamilton (Trower), George Peppard (Chase), Eli Wallach (Craig), Rosanna Schiaffino (Maria), James Mitchum (Grogen), Jeanne Moreau (French woman), Romy Schneider (Regine), Michael Callan (Eldridge), Peter Fonda (Weaver), Melina Mercouri (Magda), Elke Sommer (Helga), Albert Finney (Russian soldier), Mervyn Johns (Dennis), Senta Berger (Trudi) **Screenwriter:** Carl Foreman **Cinematographer:** Christopher Challis, Austin Dempster **Composer:** Sol Kaplan **Producer:** Carl Foreman for Open Road Productions; released by Columbia Pictures **Running Time:** 175 minutes.

They Might Be Giants...

Other wartime epics have turned up on both the big and the small screen. On television, the source is often sprawling novels. Herman Wouk's *The Winds of War*, which follows the Henry family through the events leading to World War

II, mixes historical characters in cameo-type appearances with fictional ones, and it requires the reader to accept that this one family knew quite a few luminaries in the corridors of power. The 1983 mini-series based on the book runs to 900 minutes and stars Robert Mitchum, Ali McGraw, Ralph Bellamy, Polly Bergen, Jan-Michael Vincent, John Houseman, and Peter Graves. Wouk's fictional sequel, *War and Remembrance*, continues the story after Pearl Harbor and also generated a television sequel (and then a sequel to the sequel called *War and Remembrance: the Final Chapter*) with many of the same cast members. Novelist John Jakes is, if anything, more accustomed to soap-opera historical fiction than Herman Wouk. His three novels about the Civil War, beginning with *North and South*, produced two mini-series in 1985 and 1986, both running over 500 minutes. With Patrick Swayze and James Read as the two friends on opposing sides tested by the war, the series and its sequel also featured Lesley-Anne Down, Parker Stevenson, Lloyd Bridges (as Jefferson Davis), Olivia de Havilland, Hal Holbrook (as Lincoln), and Anthony Zerbe (as Ulysses S. Grant). The third installment did not follow until 1994 and was much less popular.

From the big screen, other wartime epics include Otto Preminger's *In Harm's Way* (1965), which concerns the American navy in the aftermath of Pearl Harbor. The film is one of many war epics that collect a gallery of famous names (like Henry Fonda) in some of the smaller parts as perhaps compensation for a long running time, the use of miniatures in the special effects, and black-and-white film stock. Robert Wise directed *The Sand Pebbles* (1965) with Steve McQueen and Candice Bergen. Though set in China in 1926, this story of the crew of an American gunboat and their growing respect for the Chinese was apparently meant as an ironic comment on the Vietnam War.

WESTERN

The Alamo
The Big Country
Butch Cassidy and the Sundance Kid
Cheyenne Autumn
Cimarron
Dances With Wolves
Giant
High Noon
How the West Was Won
Little Big Man
The Long Riders
The Magnificent Seven
Once Upon a Time in the West
The Plainsman
Red River
The Searchers
Shane
Shenandoah
Stagecoach
Unforgiven
The Wild Bunch

The Alamo

1960 – John Wayne –

The Alamo has some things going for it. The cinematography often creates an effective sense of scale in its panoramic angles. The lighting and color add to the ambiance, especially during the evening and dusk scenes. The score nicely blends the martial-sounding strains of Mexican music with that of American popular melodies. All this combines pleasingly at times to create a distinctive mood for the film.

But these merits do not offset some drawbacks, both big and small. For one thing, the story, as presented, is not exactly correct. In the film Crockett (John Wayne) is said to have been born in Kentucky. (He was born in Tennessee.) Houston (Richard Boone) tells Travis (Laurence Harvey) to hold the Mexican army "right here on the Rio Grande." (The Alamo is not on the Rio Grande, a river that lies over a hundred miles to the south.) The river adjacent to The Alamo is the San Antonio River, but in the movie no river runs anywhere near the fort. Another problem is topography. The real Alamo is not on a plain in a desert. San Antonio is on the southern edge of the Balcones Escarpment and just north of Austin Chalk Cliffs, two rather prominent geological features. While these features are not the Swiss Alps, neither are they the Sahara Desert. Also, since San Antonio is the second oldest city in North America, by 1836 it would certainly have been much larger than the several adobe buildings depicted in the movie. Perhaps John Wayne got a really good deal on land near Bracketville, Texas, where the exteriors were shot.

Worse than the nagging historical and geographic inaccuracies is the overblown acting. Though perhaps limited in range like most personality stars, John Wayne in his better work (*The Quiet Man*, *Red River*, *The Searchers*) is still enormously effective and compelling. Here, however, Wayne comes off as stiff and strutting, his moments of humor not nearly as funny as he perceives them to be. The drunk that Richard Widmark tries to play is totally unconvincing, with a performance that includes every stereotype imaginable. In Texas public schools, all seventh graders have to take Texas history and read the letter Colonel William Travis wrote asking for reinforcements, wherein they learn that he was quite proper. However, Laurence Harvey's disappointing portrayal of Travis seems very unrealistic. In the film Travis never draws the line in the sand

Did you know?...

Watch for stuntmen falling onto mattresses as they fall over the walls of the fort. Also, there is a beautiful shot of a Bracketville school bus in one of the wide-angle scenes of the Alamo.

with his sword as he did in history. The overdone acting serves to create caricatures of the actual people. In light of the memory of the brave men who fought
and died at the Alamo, it is a real pity. *The Alamo* reveals little of the historical
accuracy and integrity of better battle films such as *Glory* and *Gettysburg*. It is
almost as though Wayne tried too hard with too little to recreate one of the most
unselfish, heroic moments in American history.

Bowie (Richard Widmark) and
Crockett (John Wayne) get set for
trouble at *The Alamo*.

Cast: John Wayne (Colonel Davy Crockett), Richard Widmark (Jim Bowie), Laurence Harvey (Col. William Travis), Frankie Avalon (Smitty), Patrick Wayne (Captain James Butler Bonham), Linda Cristal (Flaca), Joan O'Brien (Mrs. Dickinson), Chill Wills (Beekeeper), Joseph Calleia (Juan Seguin), Ken Curtis (Captain Almeron Dickinson), Carlos Arruza (Lieutenant Reyes), Jester Hairston (Jethro), Veda Ann Borg (Blind Nell Robertson), John Dierkes (Jocko Robertson), Denver Pyle (Thimblerig, the Gambler), Richard Boone (Gen. Sam Houston) **Screenwriter:** James Edward Grant **Cinematographer:** William H. Clothier **Composer:** Dimitri Tiomkin **Producer:** John Wayne for Batjac Productions; released by United Artists **Running Time:** 167 minutes **Format:** VHS, LV **Awards:** Academy Awards, 1960: Sound; Nominations: Cinematography (Color), Editing, Picture, Song ("The Green Leaves of Summer"), Supporting Actor (Chill Wills), Score; Golden Globe Awards, 1961: Score **Budget:** $12M **Box Office:** $2M.

The Big Country

1958 – William Wyler – ♫♫♡

"What you don't understand is that the nearest law is at the county seat 200 miles away. You can't call a policeman here. You have to be your own law."

Major Terrill (Charles Bickford) to Jim McKay.

Did you know?...

The author of the novel on which the film is based is Donald Hamilton, who also writes the Matt Helm series of espionage novels.

The tensions of the Cold War may stand behind this western of two feuding families, based on a novel by Donald Hamilton. James McKay (Gregory Peck) is an ex-sea captain who travels west to San Rafael to meet up with his betrothed, Patricia Terrill (Carroll Baker), heiress to the immense Terrill ranch. Out of his environment, McKay is a stranger to the machismo that manifests itself in almost every encounter he has with the inhabitants of this vast and formidable land. Even his wife-to-be comes to feel that his pacifist, tenderfoot nature ill-equips him to confront the challenges facing a real man in the West. Yet the film shows how the former sea captain, familiar with expanses of ocean, eventually finds his bearings in the vastness and bleakness of the open range.

From the outset, McKay is continually threatened, not only by the land but by the people of the land. McKay discovers a feud (ironically, over water rather than land rights) between the Terrills and the owners of the neighboring ranch, the Hannasseys. McKay attempts to mediate between the two families by devising a plan to end the fighting and implement a compromise. With the exception of the local schoolteacher, Julie (Jean Simmons), everyone takes his non-aggression for cowardice. McKay continually shrouds his courage with secrecy in the face of danger. He refuses, for example, to fight Steve Leech (Charlton Heston), the foreman on the Terrill ranch, when Leech belittles McKay's bravery in front of Patricia; that night, however, McKay challenges Leech to a fight that becomes one of the film's highlights. Only later, as a last resort to save Julie,

with whom he has fallen in love, does he reluctantly take an aggressive position against the Hannasseys.

Gregory Peck stars as James McKay with Charlton Heston as business and romantic rival Steve Leech.

Throughout the film the performances are never less than interesting, especially that by Burl Ives, the only Oscar-winner from the cast. As Rufus Hannassey, head of the clan, Ives accurately displays a fierceness deftly offset by a sense of misguided justice. It is Hannassey's character flaw of devotion, pride, and loyalty for the undeserving Buck (Chuck Connors) that leads to the eventual demise of father, son, and foe alike. Through this character, the filmmakers show the futility of the blind patriotism of their day. In addition, Wyler works the symbol of the wagon wheel into his visual compositions in different, interesting ways: when, for example, Chuck Connors runs and cowers behind one, it is as if he is hiding behind the skirt tails of the west. But performance, story, and technique are all inevitably dwarfed by the panorama of the cinematography of the big country.

Cast: Gregory Peck (James McKay), Jean Simmons (Julie Maragon), Carroll Baker (Patricia Terrill), Charlton Heston (Steve Leech), Burl Ives (Rufus Hannassey), Charles Bickford (Major Henry Terrill), Alfonso Bedoya (Ramon), Chuck Connors (Buck Hannassey), Buff Brady (Dude Hannassey), Jim Burk (Cracker Hannassey), Dorothy Adams (Hannassey Woman) **Screenwriter:** James R. Webb, Sy Bartlett, Robert Wyler **Cinematographer:** Franx Planer **Composer:** Jerome Moross **Producer:** William Wyler and Gregory Peck for United Artists **Running Time:** 168 minutes **Format:** VHS **Awards:** Academy Awards, 1958: Supporting Actor (Burl Ives); Nomination: Score; Golden Globe Awards, 1958: Supporting Actor (Burl Ives); British Academy Awards, 1958: Film **Budget:** $4.1M.

Butch Cassidy and the Sundance Kid

1969 – George Roy Hill – 🦴🦴🦴▽

> **"You just keep thinkin', Butch. That's what you're good at."**
>
> Sundance (Robert Redford)

Did you know?...
Robert Redford suggested that he and Paul Newman, who was originally cast as the Sundance Kid, switch roles.

What's not to like about this enormously appealing film? Not much, but there may be a few reasons to quibble a bit with its rank as number fifty on the American Film Institute's list of the 100 Best Movies. The general approach of presenting two outlaws as antiheroes, the anti-establishment tone, and the infusion of comedy all seem to derive from *Bonnie and Clyde*, which had come out two years earlier. But that film produces a better blend of those elements than *Butch Cassidy*, where the comedy is used more as a crutch to get an easy laugh and sometimes to evade rather than to reveal character.

The plot concerns the two legendary outlaws (Paul Newman, Robert Redford) who rob trains until one rail tycoon tires of being their favorite victim and hires a superposse to track them. The boys flee with Etta Place (Katharine Ross), an ex-schoolteacher, to Bolivia, where they try to go straight but are eventually gunned down. Initially, the comedy effectively breaks the tension and adds to some dramatic scenes, like Butch's showdown with the giant Harvey Logan (Ted Cassidy) and the two train robberies. Eventually, however, the reliance on humor, usually a self-deprecating line at the end of a tense scene, becomes a way of evading a closer look at the personalities of the two leads.

One of the most unjustly overlooked scenes occurs when Etta suggests to Butch and Sundance some legitimate occupations they might try, and they reject ranching and farming because of the harshness of the labor and their inexperience with the work. The honesty of their comments lends weight to defining the shared characteristic of arrested adolescence that they express in their rob-

Outlaws Butch (Paul Newman) and Sundance (Robert Redford) ponder their destinies.

beries, as well as how they sense the need to adopt a safer, if less exciting, way of life. An extra moment or two like this one would have added to the film's emotional range.

The final shootout begins at an outdoor cafe as Butch and Sundance sit to eat. After the first bullet flies by, Butch takes cover and quips, "That's the last time I bring my business to this place." A funny line, but the circumstance might justify a deeper response. According to John Eastman, even William Goldman, the author of the Oscar-winning screenplay, thought his script had a "case of the cutes." These are offered up as minor objections. The film appeals mainly on the strength of the performances and the chemistry of the leads rather than on its ideas. The banter is always appealing, even if there may be too much of it.

Cast: Paul Newman (Butch Cassidy), Robert Redford (The Sundance Kid), Katharine Ross (Etta Place), Strother Martin (Percy Garris), Henry Jones (Bike Salesman), Jeff Corey (Sheriff Bledsoe), George Furth (Woodcock), Cloris Leechman (Agnes), Ted Cassidy (Harvey

Logan), Kenneth Mars (Marshal), Donnelly Rhodes (Macon), Jody Gilbert (Large Woman), Timothy Scott (News Carver), Don Keefer (Fireman), Charles Dierkop (Flat Nose Curry), Francisco Cordova (Bank Manager), Sam Elliot (card player) **Screenwriter:** William Goldman **Cinematographer:** Conrad L. Hall **Composer:** Burt Bacharach **Producer:** John Foreman for Twentieth-Century Fox **MPAA Rating:** PG **Running Time:** 110 minutes **Format:** VHS, LV **Awards:** Academy Awards, 1969: Cinematography, Song ("Raindrops Keep Falling on My Head"), Story and Screenplay, Score; Nominations: Director (George Roy Hill), Picture, Sound; British Academy Awards, 1970: Actor (Robert Redford), Actress (Katharine Ross), Director (George Roy Hill), Film, Screenplay; Golden Globe Awards, 1970: Score; Writers Guild of America, 1969: Adapted Screenplay **Budget:** $6.2M **Box Office:** $60M.

Cheyenne Autumn
1964 – John Ford – 🦴🦴🦴

> "It takes a blue coat to make a white soldier, but a Cheyenne is a soldier from the first slap on his butt . . . war is his life . . . he's fierce, he's smart, and he's meaner than sin."
>
> Capt. Archer (Richard Widmark), to schoolteacher Deborah Wright.

Throughout his career the venerable John Ford often examined the effects of civilization coming to the American frontier. The famous comment by Frederick Jackson Turner that "the frontier is the outer edge of the wave—the meeting point between savagery and civilization" receives one of its best cinematic expressions in a Ford film like *My Darling Clementine*. Other Ford movies offered a classically glamorized and mythological version of the Old West. *Cheyenne Autumn*, however, is unique for Ford in that he attempts to show how the advancement of civilization has victimized the American Native. Prior Ford films—*Stagecoach* is an example—had typically portrayed the American Indian in a very prejudiced and stereotypical light. White travelers or settlers are usually shown as peaceful and decent, only wanting to raise their families and make a new start. Rarely does Ford depict any wrong with driving off the American Indian from their homelands. In this true story from the Mari Sandoz novel of the same name, *Cheyenne Autumn* is Ford's most sympathetic gesture, a kind of cinematic apology to the Native American.

Set in September, 1878, the story depicts a desperate but proud group of 300 Cheyennes attempting a treacherous 1500 mile migration from a desolate Oklahoma reservation to their homelands in Wyoming. For once Ford uses his normally heroic American Cavalry as the villains, inflicting callous and cruel mistreatment upon the Indians.

Star cameos turn up frequently in this epic, along with hundreds of Navajo extras. The scenery, typical of Ford, is magnificent. The story is at times

Did you know?...

This was John Ford's ninth film shot in Monument Valley and his last western.

Richard Widmark stars as reluctant Indian fighter, Captain Thomas Archer.

moving and generally well acted. Overall, however, it lacks the boldness and grit one would expect of a John Ford endeavor. In a sincere effort to make amends for his previous cinematic attitudes toward the American Indian, Ford gives his tale the grandeur of an epic. Possibly a more intimate and less panoramic approach would have proved more effective for the more personal point he sought to make. What sympathy Ford does achieve may well be negated by the incongruous comedy relief of James Stewart as Wyatt Earp in an irrelevant Dodge City interlude. This small subplot seems rudely out of place considering Ford's very somber theme.

Cast: Richard Widmark (Capt. Thomas Archer), Carroll Baker (Deborah Wright), Karl Malden (Capt. Oscar Wessles), Delores del Rio (Spanish Woman), Sal Mineo (Red Shirt), Edward G. Robinson (Carl Schultz), James Stewart (Wyatt Earp), Ricardo Montalban (Little Wolf), Gilbert Roland (Dull Knife), Arthur Kennedy (Doc Holliday), Patrick Wayne (2nd Lt. Scott), Victor Jory (Tall Tree), John Carradine (Maj. Jeff Blair), Mike Mazurki (1st Sgt. Stanislaus Wichowsky), John Qualen (Svensen), George O'Brien (Maj. Braden) **Screenwriter:** James R. Webb **Cinematographer:** William H. Clothier **Composer:** Alex North **Producer:** Bernard Smith for Warner Brothers **Running Time:** 156 minutes **Awards:** Academy Awards, 1964: Nomination: Color Cinematography.

Cimarron
1931 – Wesley Ruggles – 🦴🦴

"'The Oklahoma Wigwam prints all the news all the time, knowing no law except the law of God and the government of these United States.' Say that's a pretty good slogan!"
Yancey (Richard Dix) to Sabra.

This maudlin, melodramatic film is of interest more for historical than for dramatic reasons. It represents an early effort in the sound era to make a convincing epic. Based on Edna Ferber's novel, the film begins with its best moment, a sweeping recreation of the 1899 Oklahoma land rush. Yancey Cravat (Richard Dix) takes his wife Sabra (Irene Dunne) from Kansas to the new territory, and we see the civilizing changes of the next forty years. The first half is more coherent than the second. The film toys with a number of possibilities in developing itself—becoming a movie about civilizing the West, a family drama about Yancey and Sabra, and a town-taming saga with Yancey improbably playing the roles of crusading newspaper editor, roughneck lawman (he shoots it out with Billy the Kid), frontier lawyer, part-time preacher, and eventually would-be governor.

One of the problems is with the adaptation. The sprawling Ferber novel seems to have overwhelmed the screenwriters, and their effort to span the forty

Yancey Cravat (Richard Dix) and wife, Sabra (Irene Dunne), enjoy some time together.

Did you know?...

Irene Dunne campaigned for her part by sending photographs of herself made up from youth to old age to prove to producer William LeBaron that she would be convincing in a role requiring her character to age forty years.

years of the book results in an episodic gallery of scenes. Transitions are accomplished by the tired device of citizens standing before a newspaper bulletin board discussing the news of the day. The last hour leaves the biggest gaps in the story, and events take place ridiculously fast. Yancey returns from five years of adventure seeking, hugs his family, and within minutes decides to the defend the town's scarlet woman Dixie Lee (Estelle Taylor) against charges of immorality. The acting dates the film as much as the scratchy print and the long master shots of the early sound era. Irene Dunne is somewhat subtler than Richard Dix, and she ages into a rather convincing, frumpy middle-aged woman. Dix declaims in the worst manner, and when he rises to address the jury in the trial scene, his determination shows he's getting ready for some of his biggest ranting. *Cimarron* probably ranks with *Wings* and *The Greatest Show on Earth* as the worst movies ever to win a Best Picture Oscar.

Cast: Richard Dix (Yancey Cravat), Irene Dunne (Sabra Cravat), Estelle Taylor (Dixie Lee), Nance O'Neil (Felice Venable), William Collier Jr (The Kid), Roscoe Ates (Jess Rickey), George E. Stone (Sol Levy), Stanley Fields (Lon Yountis), Robert McWade (Louie Heffner), Edna May Oliver (Mrs. Tracy Wyatt), Nancy Dover (Donna Cravat), Eugene Jackson (Isaiah), Frank Beal (Louis Venable), Tyrone Brereton (Dabney Venable), Dolores Brown (Ruby Big Elk) **Screenwriter:** Howard Estabrook **Cinematographer:** Edward Cronjager **Composer:** Max Steiner **Producer:** William LeBaron for RKO **Running Time:** 131 minutes **Format:** VHS **Awards:** Academy Awards, 1931: Adapted Screenplay, Interior Decoration, Picture; Nominations: Actor (Richard Dix), Actress (Irene Dunne), Cinematography, Director (Wesley Ruggles); National Board of Review Awards, 1931: 10 Best Films of the Year **Box Office:** $2M.

Dances With Wolves
1990 – Kevin Costner – 𝄞𝄞𝄞𝄞

The modern western has become more sensitive to the charge of injustice to the American Native (or perhaps more sensitive to political correctness). Unlike previous sensationalized and exploitative predecessors such as *A Man Called Horse* and its two less-accomplished sequels, *Dances With Wolves* is much more sensitive and effective.

"I felt that economically, it was too big a risk to make a movie about Indians and not treat them right," Costner told *Rolling Stone* in 1990. "I thought a movie like that would get creamed. That's not a highbrow approach. It's just eas-

Lt. Dunbar (Kevin Costner) contemplates the frontier in *Dances with Wolves.*

"I was just thinking that of all the trails in this life, there is one that matters most. It is the trail of a true human being. I think you are on this trail, and it is good to see."
Kicking Bird (Graham Greene) to Dunbar

ier to go with the truth." If the film fails a bit in its complexity of character and theme, it compensates with plenty of sincerity and panoramic splendor, including a buffalo hunt scene featuring 3500 thundering beasts. Taking on the burdensome task of such a grand project as both producer and director certainly says much for Kevin Costner's talent and confidence. He had been greatly criticized and even mocked during the production of *Dances With Wolves*, with some in the media calling it an extravagant folly, a charge that resurfaced with *Waterworld*. (Pauline Kael said in her review of the film that the Indians should have named Costner's character Plays with Camera.) The public, however, found the film intriguing and made it a major box-office success.

The film begins in a Union field hospital with the wounded Lt. John Dunbar (Kevin Costner) refusing to have his foot amputated. Depressed and disillusioned, Dunbar attempts suicide by riding between enemy lines while each side is determined to attack. Remarkably, he survives a hail of enemy bullets. Considered a hero and given his choice of duty assignments, he chooses the frontier. Assigned to a desolate one-man post, he eventually encounters a wolf whom he calls Two Socks and a tribe of Sioux Indians. With both the wolf and the Sioux, Dunbar experiences a gradual building of trust that eventually changes him. Dunbar eventually gives up his old identity and becomes one of the Sioux, winning the Indian name Dances With Wolves. Life with the Sioux leads him to discover his true self.

The film's strengths and weaknesses are pretty much two sides of the same coin. The sensitivity to the portrayal of the Sioux uncovers truths about both societies depicted, yet it also may lead to some reverse stereotyping by emphasizing everything positive about the American Indian and portraying the U.S. Cavalry as little more than narrow-minded brutes. The liberalism of the film, however, does establish some strong ironies. The urge to depict the generally peaceful Sioux as harmonious with nature serves as a reminder that it was indeed the white man who had become the uncivilized predator.

Cast: Kevin Costner (Lt. John W. Dunbar), Mary McDonnell (Stands with a Fist), Graham Greene (Kicking Bird), Rodney Grant (Wind in his Hair), Floyd "Red Crow" Westerman (Chief Ten Bears), Tantoo Cardinal (Black Shawl), Robert Pastorelli (Timmons), Charles Rocket (Lt. Elgin), Maury Chaykin (Maj. Fambrough), Jimmy Herman (Stone Calf), Nathan Lee Chasing His Horse (Smile a Lot), Wes Studi (Toughest Pawnee) **Screenwriter:** Michael Blake **Composer:** John Barry **Producer:** Kevin Costner and Jim Wilson for Tig Productions **MPAA Rating:** PG-13 **Running Time:** 181 minutes **Format:** VHS, LV **Awards:** Academy Awards, 1990: Picture, Director (Kevin Costner), Editing, Score, Sound, Adapted screenplay, Cinematography; Nominations: Supporting Actress (Mary McDonnell), Costume Design, Actor (Kevin Costner), Supporting

Actor (Graham Greene), Art Direction; Berlin International Film Festival: Silver Bear for outstanding achievement (Kevin Costner); British Academy Awards, 1990: Nominations: Actor (Kevin Costner), Director (Kevin Costner), Adapted Screenplay, Picture; Golden Globe Awards, 1990: Best Film—Drama, Screenplay; Nominations: Actor (Kevin Costner), Supporting Actress (Mary McDonnell), Score, Director (Kevin Costner); National Board of Review of Motion Pictures: 10 Best Films; New York Film Critics Circle Award, 1990, Nominations: Best First-Time Director (Kevin Costner) **Box Office:** $184M (domestic gross), $424.2M (worldwide).

Giant

1956 – George Stevens – 🦴🦴🦴🦴

The adjective "sprawling" is overused but fits exactly the feel of George Stevens' movie of a Texas cattle family. From the grand opening music to the sweeping panorama of barren West Texas cattle land that runs to the horizon, *Giant* lives up to its name. The center of the movie is the ranch Reata, half a million acres with its nearest neighbor fifty miles away. The huge Gothic mansion in the center of this desolate land is indicative of wealth still unable to tame or soften harsh nature. The people are also big and harsh. Bick Benedict (Rock Hudson) and his sister Luz (Carroll Baker) are brave, honest, narrow, stubborn, and take their wealth and whiteness for granted.

Enter the civilizing influence of Maryland-bred Leslie (Elizabeth Taylor), Bick's beautiful wife. As the years go by, even the sets show the force of her quiet, capable hand. Dark colors are lightened in the mansion, paintings replace cow heads on the walls, and a lawn and pool shut out part of the desert. Even the hired hand Jett Rink, the role that helped to make James Dean a legend, responds to Leslie's kindness and compassion. In fact, all of his success when he strikes big oil cannot fill his yearning for her love.

In addition to sweeping vistas, a cast of dozens of memorable characters populate the story: the children who are determined to make their own lives, the kindly old uncle who smooths troubled waters, the simple neighbors who have struck oil and make a "million a month"—dollars, that is. And the feel of Texas is here, too, from the scorching heat to the smell of barbequed calves' head to the squalor of poor villages and the grandeur of oil and cattle money. Stevens also tackled a number of issues that were uncommon for the 1950s, like the indepen-

> "You should have shot that fellow Jett a long time ago. Now he's too rich to kill."
> Uncle Bawley (Chill Wills) to Bick.

Did you know?...

James Dean was killed in a car crash three days after the studio-imposed ban on driving his sports car ended; some of Dean's closing narration was inaudible, and Nick Adams looped the lines for Dean's character in the supper scene.

Refined Leslie Benedict (Elizabeth Taylor) pleads with roughneck Jett Rink (James Dean).

dent woman and the cancer of racial bigotry. In fact, watching Bick Benedict grow as he finds himself saddled with a thinking wife, rebellious children, and a "muchacho" grandson is one of the lasting satisfactions of an epic that promises that we can hold on to good traditions while changing the bad ones.

Cast: Elizabeth Taylor (Leslie Lynnton Benedict), Rock Hudson (Jordan "Bick" Benedict), James Dean (Jett Rink), Carroll Baker (Luz Benedict the younger), Mercedes McCambridge (Luz Benedict the elder), Chill Wills (Uncle Bawley), Jane Withers (Vashti Smythe), Robert Nichols (Pinky Smythe), Dennis Hopper (Jordan Benedict III), Fran Bennett (Judy Benedict), Elsa Cardenas (Juana Benedict), Carolyn Craig (Lacey Lynnton), Judith Evelyn (Mrs. Horace Lynnton), Paul Fix (Dr. Horace Lynnton), Sal Mineo (Angel Obregon), Earl Holliman (Bob Dace), Alexander Scourby (Old Polo), Rod Taylor (Sir David Karfrey), Sheb Wooley (Gabe Target), Nick Adams (voice of Jett Rink in narration) **Screenwriter:** Fred Guiol, Ivan Moffat **Cinematographer:** William C. Mellor **Composer:** Dimitri Tiomkin **Producer:** George Stevens and Henry Ginsberg for Warner Bros. **Running Time:** 201 minutes **Format:** VHS, LV **Awards:** Academy Awards, 1957: Director (George Stevens); Nominations: Picture, Actor (James Dean), Actor (Rock Hudson), Supporting Actress (Mercedes McCambridge), Screenplay, Art/Set Direction, Score, Film Editing, Costume design; Directors Guild of America Awards, 1956: Director (George Stevens) **Box Office:** reportedly, the film made $12M.

High Noon

1952 — Fred Zinnemann — 𝄞𝄞𝄞𝄞

The 1950s brought a new aspect to the western. Previously, many westerns consisted of simplistic tales and glamorous characters in outdoor settings. Critical respectability emerged with the increase of psychological intensity of both character and plot. No longer the mere confrontation of good guys and bad guys, westerns now began to reveal greater moral ambiguities. No better example of this can been seen than *High Noon*.

Will Kane (Gary Cooper) is the marshal who had years before cleaned up the small town of Hadleyville, New Mexico, much to the gratitude and respect of its citizens. However, on his last day of the job, his wedding day, the aging lawman is confronted by Frank Miller (Ian MacDonald), a killer Will sent to prison. Miller, now released by the courts up north, has vowed to kill the man responsible for his conviction. The townspeople, including his new bride, Amy (Grace Kelly), encourage Will to run. Within this morality play, Will is driven by his conscience to face his evil tormentors alone. He will not abandon his duty or the town though its people have abandoned him. *High Noon* rejects scenic color for the stark black-and-whites of this claustrophobic town. Hadleyville is shown to be as isolated and bleak as most of its inhabitants

High Noon premiered at the time of the Communist witch hunts of the McCarthy era. Writer and co-producer Carl Foreman used the script as an allegory for his own views. By making Hadleyville an analogy for Hollywood, Foreman equated the townspeople's psychological confusion, ambivalent loyalties, and love of safety and conformity with the complacent attitudes that permitted the blacklisting and betrayal of his own day. (Foreman was later blacklisted himself and needed a front for his work on *The Bridge on the River Kwai*.)

This is in many way an editor's film, on which the talents of Elmo Williams helped assure its classic status. After an unsuccessful preview, a subplot involving the new marshal trying to get to Hadleyville and being delayed was dropped entirely (including all the scenes with actor James Brown). Now the film—with some additional tightening—concentrated its story as if it were actually happening minute by minute in real time. Another stoke of editing genius was to eliminate much of the footage of the inexperienced Grace Kelly while still retaining

> "They're making me run. I've never run from anybody before."
>
> Will (Gary Cooper) commenting on the MacDonalds.

Did you know?...

To increase the tension, numerous shots of clocks were cut into the film. Each one shows progressively larger clockfaces and slower pendulums.

Lawman Will Kane (Gary Cooper) and his Quaker bride, Amy (Grace Kelly), must decide what to do next.

her unique screen presence. The introduction of the narrative ballad of the theme song sung by Tex Ritter also adds much to the tension and emotion.

Shot in only twenty-eight days, *High Noon* marked the return of Gary Cooper from a string of mediocre films undeserving of his talents. Though notably older and weathered and ill with a bleeding ulcer and an injured hip, Cooper was able to draw on these very factors to aid his portrayal of the anguished and time-worn Will Kane and earn his second Academy Award for Best Actor.

Cast: Gary Cooper (Will Kane), Grace Kelly (Amy Fowler Kane), Lloyd Bridges (Harvey Pell), Lon Chaney, Jr. (Martin Howe), Thomas Mitchell (Jonas Henderson), Otto Kruger (Judge Percy Mettrick), Katy Jurado (Helen Ramirez), Lee Van Cleef (Jack Colby), Henry Morgan (William Fuller), Ian MacDonald (Frank Miller), Sheb Wooley (Ben Miller), Robert Wilke (James Pierce), William Phillips (Barber), Harry Shannon (Cooper), Eve McVeagh (Mildred Fuller) **Screenwriter:** Carl Foreman **Cinematographer:** Floyd Crosby **Composer:** Dimitri Tiomkin **Producer:** Stanley Kramer **Running Time:** 85 minutes **Format:** VHS, LV **Awards:** Academy Awards, 1952: Actor (Gary Cooper), Editing, Song, Score; Nominations: Director (Fred Zinnemann), Picture, Screenplay; Golden Globe Awards, 1953: Actor-Drama (Gary Cooper), Supporting Actress (Katy Jurado), Score; National Board of Review Awards, 1952: 10 Best Films of the Year; New York Film Critics Awards, 1952: Director (Fred Zinnemann), Film **Budget:** $730,000 **Box Office:** $3.4M.

How the West Was Won
1963 – Henry Hathaway, George Marshall, John Ford – 🌵🌵🌵

This is the episodic story of the panoramic exploits of three generations of the pioneering Prescot family. Beginning on their trek west during the 1830's and continuing through the taming of the West, the storyline is simple but impressive in its grandeur of landscape and exciting action sequences. The film's efforts to incorporate a background of historical events (such as the California Gold Rush and the Civil War) into the adventures, exploits, and tragedies of this pioneer family, however, prove somewhat ponderous. It is the appearance of the numerous stars and character actors and the familiar voice of Spencer Tracy providing the linking narration that hold the attention of the audience.

Audiences at some theaters for the original release of the film also had the attraction of the ambitious Cinerama filming process. This method used three interlocked cameras to photograph the film and then projected the prints

> "Eve, You make me feel like a man standing on a narrow ledge coming face to face with a grizzly bear . . . . There just ain't no ignoring the situation."
>
> Linus Rawlings (James Stewart)

James Stewart portrays
mountain man Linus Rawlings.

Did you know?...

Richard Thorpe was also a
director on the film, albeit an
uncredited one. He supervised
the transitional sequences on
history.

in specially built theaters on a wrap-around tryptic screen with three synchronized projectors. (The French filmmaker Abel Gance had pioneered pretty much the same thing in the late 1920s, calling it Polyvision, with his epic *Napoleon*, and the Cinerama process had been in existence for ten years showcased in various nonfiction works like *This is Cinerama* attempting to compete with the threat of television.) Though it lasted longer than 3-D, Cinerama was in danger of being dismissed as something of a novelty when the epic story materials of *How the West Was Won* (and later *The Greatest Story Ever Told*) permitted it briefly to come into its own. The epic materials of the western allowed the audience to participate in overwhelming battle scenes, a raft ride in treacherous waters, train wrecks, and horse chases. Unfortunately, much of this spectacle is now diminished with its transition to the small screen. Since the film was never shot in a single-lens version, one can easily detect the dividing lines of the three joined images in a pan-and-scan format. In a letterbox format, the film requires such severe masking of the television screen that this alternative is also problematic.

In addition, the use of three different directors makes for somewhat sporadic quality in *How the West Was Won*. Henry Hathaway provides a naive but enthralling saga of the lives of the Prescott family in three episodes titled "The Rivers," "The Plains," and "The Outlaws." George Marshall directs one episode called "The Railroad," and John Ford handles the Civil War episode. All three men have done better work on other projects, and Ford, the best known of the three directors, has sometimes been singled out for turning in the weakest of the five episodes. Perhaps all three chafed under the constraint of not being in charge of the whole production.

Cast: Gergory Peck (Cleve Van Valen), Henry Fonda (Jethro Stuart), James Stewart (Linus Rawlings), Debbie Reynolds (Lilith Prescott), Carroll Baker (Eve Prescott), Lee J. Cobb (Marshal Lou Ramsey), Walter Brennan (Col. Hawkins), Karl Malden (Zebulon Prescott), Richard Widmark (Mike King), Robert Preston (Roger Morgan), George Peppard (Zeb Rawlings), Carolyn Jones (Julie Rawlings), Thelma Ritter (Agathe Clegg), Eli Wallach (Charlie Gant), Agnes Moorehead (Rebecca Prescott), Russ Tamblyn (Confederate soldier), Raymond Massey (Abraham Lincoln), Thelma Ritter (Agatha Clegg), Walter Brennan (Colonel Hawkins), Andy Devine (Corporal Peterson), John Wayne (Gen. Sherman), Harry Morgan (General Ulysses S. Grant), Spencer Tracy (narrator) **Screenwriter:** James R. Webb **Cinematographer:** Harold E. Wellman, William H. Daniels, Charles B. Lang, Jr., Milton Krasner, Joseph La Shelle **Composer:** Alfred Newman, Ken Darby **Producer:** Bernard Smith for MGM **Running Time:** 155 minutes **Format:** VHS, LV, DVD **Awards:** Academy Awards, 1962: Editing, Sound, Story and Screenplay; Nominations: Art Direction/Set Direction (color), Color Cinematography, Costume Design (color), Picture, Original Score; National Board of Review Awards, 1962: 10 Best Films of the Year **Box Office:** $12.2M.

Little Big Man

1970 – Arthur Penn – 🦴🦴🦴🦴

The revisionist urge especially prevalent in the 1970s of questioning the received truths and myths handed down from the past has rarely been exercised more fully than in *Little Big Man*. Just as the romanticized version of the Custer's last stand in *They Died with Their Boots On* casts Errol Flynn as an inspiring George Armstrong Custer, this legend-smashing mock epic by Arthur Penn portrays the calvary general as a stupid, strutting peacock too self-assured to act on the sensible advice not to enter the Indian-packed valley of the Little Big Horn.

The film is based on Thomas Burger's grand tale of deglamorized heroes. It is all set within the framework of the fanciful yarns recounted mostly in flashback by the 121-year-old Jack Crabb, played in a tour-de-force performance by Dustin Hoffman. Crabb professes to have been nearly everything—an Indian, a gunfighter, a Buffalo hunter, a scout, a shop owner, a hermit, and a drunk. He maintains that he was friends with Wild Bill Hickock (Jeff Corey) and that he was the sole white survivor of Custer's Last Stand.

Fact and fancy simultaneously intertwine in Crabb's tales, but it is Penn's poignant depiction of the cruel, systematic extermination of the American Indian that generates deep emotions of truth and guilt. Beautifully and sensitively depicted are the Cheyenne who call themselves "The Human Beings." *Little Big Man* was stunningly shot on actual locations and shows perhaps the deepest sympathy and understanding for the plight of the American Indian in any film to that time. Dan George was seventy-one when he played Old Lodge Skins, the Cheyenne chief. He adopts the young Jack Crabb after the massacre of Jack's family by an opposing tribe. The authenticity that George brings to the part could only have been achieved through the knowledge of and empathy toward actual American Indian traditions. He deservedly snagged an Academy Award nomination for Best Supporting Actor.

Did you know?...

Dustin Hoffman's old-age makeup was achieved through the talents of artist Dick Smith, who also performed similar special effects of makeup on Marlon Brando in *The Godfather* and Linda Blair in *The Exorcist.*

Cast: Dustin Hoffman (Jack Crabb), Chief Dan George (Old Lodge Skins), Faye Dunaway (Mrs. Pendrake), Martin Balsam (Allardyce T. Merriweather), Jeff Corey (Wild Bill Hickock), Richard Mulligan (Gen. George A. Custer), William Hickey (Historian), Kelly Jean Peters (Olga), Carol Androsky (Caroline), Robert Little Star (Little Horse), Steve Shemayne (Burns Red in the Sun), Thayer David (Rev. Silas Pendrake) **Screenwriter:** Calder Willingham **Cinematographer:** Harry Stradling **Composer:** John Hammond **Producer:** Stuart Miller for National General **MPAA**

Rating: PG **Running Time:** 135 minutes **Format:** VHS, LV **Awards:** New York Film Critics Circle Awards, 1970: Supporting Actor (Chief Dan George); National Society of Film Critics Awards, 1970: Supporting Actor (Chief Dan George); Academy Awards, 1970: Nominations: Supporting Actor (Chief Dan George) **Box Office:** $15M (domestic rentals).

Lusty Mrs. Pendrake (Faye Dunaway) helps Jack (Dustin Hoffman) wash off the prairie dust.

The Long Riders

1980 – Walter Hill – 🧦🧦🧦

"All the world likes an outlaw. For some damn reason they remember 'em."

Jesse James (Publicity tag line)

A cult favorite, *The Long Riders* is a stylistic shoot 'em up, telling the story of the infamous James/Younger gang and starring the Carradine brothers, the Quaids, the Keaches, and the Guest siblings. The film opens with the robbery of a small bank in which Ed Miller (Dennis Quaid) needlessly kills a bystander and is forced out of the gang by Jesse James (James Keach); it culminates with the aftermath of the fabled Northfield, Minnesota, bank robbery in which the Pinkertons outfox the gang and capture most of them. That robbery attempt becomes one of the great cinematic shoot outs, as both the visual and audio components shift into slow motion, permitting ample opportunity to inspect the bullet fest. This technique is somewhat reminiscent of the slow-motion death scenes in *The Wild Bunch* and countless films influenced by Sam Peckinpah. The James/Younger gang is ambushed in Northfield by the waiting Pinkerton man, Mr. Rixley (James Whitmore, Jr.), who anticipates that they will strike there next. *The Long Riders* spends much of its first part demystifying the gang members, presenting them as real people with real feelings. After the opening robbery, Jesse expels Ed from the gang for his sloppiness in the killing and leaves him behind on the river bank almost as if Jesse believes his profession to be an honorable one with an unwritten code. Most of the members of the gang have love interests, and the viewer watches as they make believable attempts to create worthwhile lives apart from robbing banks, trains, and stagecoaches. At one point on the train to Northfield, Jesse appears to be reading a Bible. And later he is shown with his children to be a loving and caring father. Such an emphasis creates an odd, almost surrealistic, contradiction of personalities in each one of the outlaws. On the one hand most of them are tender, loving people; on the other, they are all robbers who will steal without remorse and will have to kill to save their own lives.

Did you know?...

There is one scene where Clell Miller (Randy Quaid) goes up to the band and tells the singer to stop his song and sing one to Dixie. The fellow on the guitar is none other than Ry Cooder, the composer of the original music for the film.

Cast: James Keach (Jesse James), Stacy Keach (Frank James), David Carradine (Cole Younger), Keith Carradine (Jim Younger), Robert Carradine (Bob Younger), Randy Quaid (Clell Miller), Dennis Quaid (Ed Miller), Christopher Guest (Charlie Ford), Nicholas Guest (Bob Ford), Pamela Reed (Belle Starr), Shelby Leverington (Annie Ralston), Kevin Brophy (John Younger), James Remar (Sam Starr), James Whitmore, Jr. (Mr. Rixley), West Buchanan (McCorkindale), John Bottoms (Mortician) **Screenwriter:** Bill Bryden, James Keach, Stacy Keach, Steven Smith

Cinematographer: Ric Waite **Composer:** Ry Cooder **Producer:** Tim Zinnemann for Huka Productions; released by United Artists **MPAA Rating:** R **Running Time:** 95 minutes **Format:** VHS, LV.

The James/Younger gang are shown in a rare peaceful moment for *The Long Riders.*

The Magnificent Seven

1960 – John Sturges – 🎵🎵🎵

The most compelling aspect of John Sturges' translation of Akira Kurosawa's *Seven Samurai* onto the more familiar terrain of the American West is its rich sense of the end of an age. Seven gunslingers band together to help a Mexican village resist the despoiling raids by the bandit Calvera (Eli Wallach), but these men are haunted by the rootlessness brought on by their own violent ways. They also sense, as do the samurai in Kurosawa's original film, the oncoming change to a more modern society where men like themselves will be obsolete. This awareness deepens the characters and gives the film much of its edge. As some children gather around one of the gunman, the stoic O'Reilly (Charles Bronson), one of the boys mentions that the gunmen are braver than his father. O'Reilly immediately grabs the boy and spanks him: "You think I'm brave because I carry a gun; well, your fathers are much braver because they carry responsibility."

The first part of the movie follows its source very closely. Sturges and his screenwriters devote more time to creating a formidable villain when they have Calvera sit with the villagers in his initial incursion and mock their church as well as their village. The scenes that show Chris (Yul Brynner) recruiting the six guns usually stamp each of the men in a memorable way (Bronson's character is even discovered chopping wood, like his prototype in the original). As many critics have said, a good deal of the fun comes from watching actors whose work here helped to launch their careers. James Coburn, for example, is memorable as a fighter whose speed and prowess with a knife excels most men's with a gun; Robert Vaughn plays an outlaw on the run whose outcast status has made him a victim of his own growing fears of capture. He awakens from a nightmare and cringes as the surprised villagers console him. Horst Buchholz appears in the part of the would-be gunfighter (the equivalent of the role played by Toshiro Mifune in the original), and he adds some touches of comedy and romance. The love scene here, however, is completely conventionalized—soft words backed by violin music—as compared to the stunning counterpart in the original when a village girl and a samurai, convinced that tomorrow they will die in the attack of the bandits, meet in mingled love and lust by the campfire that suggests their

desperate passions. The last section of Sturges' film may be the weakest, but what precedes it is impressive and enjoyable. A number of sequels followed, none after the first with the original cast: *Return of the Seven* (1966), *Guns of the Magnificent Seven* (1969), and *The Magnificent Seven Ride!* (1972). A television series also debuted in 1998.

Seven tough hombres ride to the rescue of a besieged Mexican town.

Cast: Yul Brynner (Chris Adams), Eli Wallach (Calvera), Steve McQueen (Vin), Charles Bronson (Bernardo O'Reilly), Robert Vaughn (Lee), Horst Buchholz (Chico), Brad Dexter (Harry Luck), James Coburn (Britt), Jorge Martinez de Hoyos (Hilario), Vladimir Sokolov (Old Man), Whit Bissell (undertaker), Val Avery (Henry), Rosenda Monteros (Petra), Rico Alariz (Sotero), Pepe Hern (villager), Natividad Vacio (villager) **Screenwriter:** William Roberts **Cinematographer:** Charles Lang **Composer:** Elmer Bernstein **Producer:** Walter Mirisch and John Sturges for the Mirisch Company; released by United Artists **Running Time:** 128 minutes **Format:** VHS, LV **Awards:** Academy Awards, 1960: Nominations: Score.

Once Upon a Time in the West
1969 – Sergio Leone – 🦴🦴🦴

The final gunfight in this intricately plotted story concludes with the survivor fitting a harmonica into the mouth of the man he has just shot. The victim's dying breaths are then transformed into eerie music as they wheeze out across the prairie in a dissonant death rattle. This scene, like all of the film, shows director Sergio Leone's emphasis on an ornate, embellished style, something that has won him a number of enthusiasts but probably also cost him the support of mainstream audiences (this film, like his subsequent, final one *Once Upon a Time in America*, failed at the box-office in versions of various lengths). The style easily lends itself to parody, and television commercials and comedy shows have drawn upon the staples of Leone's approach: a reliance on long, tight closeups of faces with darting eyes in lengthy wordless sequences backed by the haunting music of Ennio Morricone, usually with whistling or a solo soprano accompaniment.

Such a style slows the pace, and Leone's interest in mood and atmosphere also withholds a good bit of plot information until late in the film, a decision that might induce some restlessness among viewers. It isn't until past the half-way point that we begin to see connections among the mysterious arrivals of a number of strangers at a water town on the new railway line. These characters include Jill (Claudia Cardinale), a woman from New Orleans who only months ago married Brett McBain (Frank Wolff), one of the settlers in town; a drifter (Charles Bronson), who arrives in the opening scene and shoots it out with the men waiting for him; and a gunslinger (Henry Fonda), who with his men kills McBain and others and leaves their bodies stretched out on the long picnic tables they had set to welcome the new bride. After Jill takes up residence in town, Cheyenne (Jason Robards), another mysterious gunman, arrives. It develops that McBain had had the foresight to buy up land where the railroad would travel and now the rail baron (Gabriele Ferzetti) wants to move his train through town less expensively—or so it seems until the final showdown, which introduces still more backstory to the complex plot. To Leone's detractors, the stress on style at the expense of pace is fussy and distracting; his defenders recognize a mythic, archetypal element that such a style accentuates. This film and *The Good, the Bad, and the Ugly* represent the director's best work in the genre.

Did you know?...

Director Sergio Leone's first western was *A Fistful of Dollars*. Looking for an American actor whose services he could obtain for little money, Leone spotted young Clint Eastwood in an episode of *Rawhide* and decided to cast him in the first film of what became a trilogy (with *For a Few Dollars More* and *The Good, the Bad, and the Ugly*).

Cast: Claudia Cardinale (Jill McBain), Henry Fonda (Frank), Jason Robards (Cheyenne), Charles Bronson ("Harmonica"), Gabriele Ferzetti (Morton), Paolo Stoppa (Sam), Woody Strode (Stony), Jack Elam (Knuckles), Keenan Wynn (Sheriff), Frank Wolff (Brett McBain), Lionel Stander (Barman), Marilu Carteny (Maureen), Claudio Mancini (Harmonica's Brother), Enzo Santaniello (Timmy McBain) **Screenwriter:** Dario Argento, Bernardo Bertolucci, Sergio Donati, Mickey Knox, Sergio Leone **Cinematographer:** Tonino Delli Colli **Composer:** Ennio Morricone **Producer:** Bino Cicogna and Fulvio Morsella for Rafran Productions; released by Paramount **MPAA Rating:** PG **Running Time:** 165 minutes **Format:** VHS, LV.

The Harmonica Man (Charles Bronson) gets the drop on Frank (Henry Fonda).

The Plainsman

1937 – Cecil B. De Mille – 🐾🐾🐾

The popularity of the western in the 1930s led to more quantity than quality in films. John Wayne's career is a good example: cast in an important role in Raoul Walsh's *The Big Trail* in 1930, Wayne still failed to become a star (the film failed too) and spent the rest of the decade in B-westerns and serials until 1939 when he finally reached a level of success playing the Ringo Kid in *Stagecoach*. Prestige, big-budget westerns were less common than the sort of quickie fare that Wayne toiled in. *The Plainsman* remains one of the few large-scale westerns of significance from the decade.

This was The West according to Cecil B. De Mille, and it became one of the high points of his career as a producer of screen extravaganzas. The film is an extremely romanticized fantasy that connects the lives of Wild Bill Hickock (Gary Cooper), Calamity Jane (Jean Arthur), Buffalo Bill Cody (James Ellison), General Custer (John Miljan), and even Abraham Lincoln (Frank McGlynn). The opening scene is a good sample of the film's lack of finesse: it shows Lincoln meeting with his cabinet as they address the problem of the frontier and the need to keep guns out of the hands of the Indians. Seemingly near a solution, they are interrupted by Mary Todd (Leila McIntyre), who reminds her husband about their plans for the evening. Lincoln leaves saying, "Gentlemen, I promised to take Mrs. Lincoln to Ford's Theater tonight. We will continue this tomorrow. For the frontier must be made safe!" Historically, it may have been totally inaccurate, but audiences seem to suspend their disbelief, especially after Gary Cooper enters the action. Jean Arthur as Calamity Jane may have seemed questionable casting, though the idea to reteam her and Cooper was probably an attempt to capitalize on the popularity of their appearance in Frank Capra's *Mr. Deeds Goes to Town* in 1936.

De Mille's epic westerns are noted as flamboyant costume dramas, with what now seems like very corny dialogue. *The Plainsman* is no different. Though stylish enough, the extensive use of rear-projection during action scenes makes it appear somewhat less authentic. The film carries itself on the strength of its stars: Cooper's appeal as the fatalistic Hickock attempting to prevent the evil Charles Bickford from selling guns to the Indians and Arthur's zesty

Gary Cooper stars as western legend Wild Bill Hickock.

unrequited love for the taciturn Hickock. (Jean Arthur's tomboy performance may have even influenced Doris Day in the later film *Calamity Jane*.)

Cast: Gary Cooper (Wild Bill Hickock), Jean Arthur (Calamity Jane), James Ellison (Buffalo Bill Cody), Charles Bickford (John Lattimer), Paul Harvey (Chief Yellowhand), Helen Burgess (Louise Cody), Porter Hall (Jack McCall), Fuzzy Knight (Dave), Frank McGlynn, Sr. (Abraham Lincoln), Leila McIntyre (Mary Todd Lincoln), John Miljan (Gen. George Armstrong Custer), Charles Stevens (Injun Charlie), George "Gabby" Hayes (Breezy), Charles Herzinger (William H. Seward), Victor Varconi (Painted Horse) **Screenwriter:** Waldemar Young, Lynn Riggs, Jeannie Macpherson, Harold Lamb **Cinematographer:** Victor Milner, George Robinson **Composer:** George Antheil **Producer:** Cecil B. De Mille for Paramount **Running Time:** 113 minutes **Format:** VHS, LV.

Red River
1948 – Howard Hawks – 🦴🦴🦴🦴

A success at thirty-two thanks to *Stagecoach*, John Wayne by all accounts was beginning to wonder if at age forty-one he might be headed from leading roles to character parts when Howard Hawks cast him in *Red River* as Tom Dunstan. It was one of the first times that Wayne played a character older than he was at the time of the film and certainly the first time he had played such a part in such a prominent film. Both the star and the movie were a success, and Wayne would consistently show up on the top ten stars list for the next twenty years.

Red River has been often been called the best western of the of the 1940s. Wayne's portrayal of the heroic but ruthless leader of the first cattle drive on the Chisholm Trail was felt by many to be deserving of an Academy Award. The story concerns rancher Dunstan who, after spending many years building up his cattle ranch, is determined to keep financially afloat after the Civil War. This can only be done by undertaking a massive cattle drive to Missouri. He is accompanied on this treacherous journey with his good friend and sometime conscience Groot (Walter Brennan) and his surrogate son Matthew Garth (Montgomery Clift, in his debut role). As the drive progresses, so does Wayne's obsession and tyranny. This is by far one of Wayne's most unsympathetic and intriguing roles. He drives himself and his men to the brink of exhaustion, and we see him mentally deteriorate to the point of paranoia. Clift leads a successfull rebellion to take the drive

Did you know?...
The film marked the last appearance on screen for movie veteran Harry Carey, Sr.

on a shorter route through Abilene in hopes of using the rumored railhead there. Wayne vows to kill him if they should ever meet again.

It is this final showdown in Abilene that is paradoxically the strongest and weakest point of the film. The fight scene between Wayne and Clift had to be most keenly and precisely choreographed considering the disparity in the sizes of the actors. It is Wayne's sudden self-recognition of his love and respect for Clift that may be somewhat untrue to character. After a maudlin intervention by Tess (Joanne Dru), the film ends leaving the audience to deal with Wayne's incredulous and too pat character transformation. The ending (changed from the original script) and its attempt to force a reconciliation between father and son, weakens but does not ruin an otherwise excellent movie.

Cast: John Wayne (Tom Dunstan), Montgomery Clift (Matthew Garth), Walter Brennan (Nadine Groot), Joanne Dru (Tess Millay), John Ireland (Cherry Valance), Noah Beery, Jr. (Muster McGee), Paul Fix (Teeler Yacey), Harry Carey, Jr. (Dan Latimer), Chief Yowlachie (Quo),

Matthew Garth (Montgomery Clift) eyes his adoptive father, ruthless cattleman Tom Dunson (John Wayne).

Ivan Parry (Bunk Kenneally), Harry Carey, Sr. (Mr. Millville), Hal Taliaferio (Old Leather), Tom Tyler (Quittler), Dan White (Laredo), Hank Worden (Simms), Collen Grey (Fen) **Screenwriter:** Borden Chase, Charles Schnee **Cinematographer:** Russell Harian **Composer:** Dimitri Tiomkin **Producer:** Howard Hawks for United Artists **Running Time:** 133 minutes **Format:** VHS, LV **Awards:** Academy Awards, 1948: Nominations: Editing, Story **Budget:** $3.5M **Box Office:** $4.5M.

The Searchers
1956 – John Ford – 𝄞𝄞𝄞𝄞

> "If they're human men at all they gotta stop."
> Martin (Jeffrey Hunter)

> "No, a human rides a horse till it dies. Then he goes on afoot. Comanch' comes along, gets that horse up, rides him twenty more miles, then eats him."
> Ethan (John Wayne)

Did you know?...

John Wayne was so intrigued with the character of Ethan Edwards that he named his third son John Ethan.

Director John Ford once said in describing himself, "My name's John Ford. I make westerns." Ford may have simplified his own legend, but if so, the legend, not unlike his favorite scenery, is monumental. By this decade Ford's attitude toward the western was changing. He was becoming more introspective and melancholy. These feelings culminated in one of the finest westerns to date. Today *The Searchers* is considered one of Ford's greatest achievements and probably the best western if not one of the most influential films ever made. It is not a typical sprawling western extravaganza. Though filmed in the majestic settings of Monument Valley, it is, thanks to its psychology, something of a confined epic. Contemporary critics have justifiably noted *The Searchers* as not just a film of a fine adventure story but also a mythic story of obsession.

The story tells of Ethan Edwards (John Wayne), an ex-Confederate war hero, a loner, and an outsider. Three years after the Civil War, he returns to a family who attempts to accept him. They realize that he is the eternal wanderer, closer in spirit to his adversaries the Indians than to the ways of civilization. John Wayne infuses his role with psychological intensity and haunting depth of feeling, making the character quite unlike any other Ford protagonist. After his family is slaughtered by Comanches, Ethan goes on a five-year search fed by passionate revenge to find his young niece Debbie (Natalie Wood), who has been taken captive. Ethan reluctantly allows his adopted nephew Martin (Jeffery Hunter) to accompany him. Knowing that Debbie has been adopted by the Comanches and has probably been made a squaw, Ethan becomes obsessed with racial hatred and vengeance. He would rather see his niece dead than allow her to live as an Indian. Martin stays with the search for

fear of what may happen if Debbie is found. Ethan's own savagery rivals that of the Indians he hates.

When Ethan's quest ends, we see a tragic, sensitive side of this hero. Yet as the final scenes reveal, this does not mean that Ethan has resolved his duality. He does not enter the house that embodied the warmth of his family and

Ethan (John Wayne) rescues Comanche-held niece, Debbie (Natalie Wood), with cowpoke Martin (Jeffrey Hunter) alongside.

chooses to turn his back on the civilization that has alienated him and to return to the freedom of wilderness.

Cast: John Wayne (Ethan Edwards), Jeffery Hunter (Martin Pawley), Vera Miles (Laurie Jorgensen), Natalie Wood (Debbie Edwards), Ward Bond (Capt. Rev. Samuel Clayton), John Qualen (Lars Jorgensen), Harry Carey, Jr. (Brad Jorgensen), Olive Carey (Mrs. Jorgensen), Antonio Moreno (Emililo Figueroa), Henry Brandon (Chief Scar), Hank Wordon (Mose Harper), Walter Coy(Aaron Edwards), Lana Wood (Debbie as a Child), Dorthy Jordan (Martha Edwards), Patrick Wayne (Lieutenant Greenhill) **Screenwriter:** Winton Hoch, Frank S. Nugent **Composer:** Max Steiner **Producer:** Merian C. Cooper for C.V. Whitney Pictures **Running Time:** 119 minutes **Format:** VHS, LV, DVD **Box Office:** $4.9M.

Shane
1953 — George Stevens — 🦴🦴🦴🦴

> "A gun is a tool, Mary, no better or worse than any other tool ... an ax, a shovel, or anything. A gun is as good or as bad as the man using it."
>
> Shane (Alan Ladd), about Marian's dislike of firearms.

With the 1950s came the two most influential westerns of their time—*High Noon* and *Shane*. Though *High Noon* was the more intense and introspective of the two, it was *Shane* that won more widespread acclaim and was the number three moneymaker of 1953. Its format and style have won it the reputation for being the one of the best examples of the Hollywood western. It has been a lesson for many directors and imitated by the best. Some critics even maintain that film's only fault is that it is too obviously perfect—the cinematography too beautiful, the characters too pat, and the presentation of good and evil too delineated. (Adrian Turner's comment in *Hollywood: 60 Great Years* states this view well: "the film is a stacked deck devoid of the jittery intensity of the [Anthony] Mann films or the spontaneity of a Hawks.")

Filming in the Grand Tetons, director Stevens contrasts the vast Wyoming wilderness with the small town and homesteads of the story. The conflict between civilization and brutish nature, peace and violence, is represented by the homesteaders and the ranchers. The premise of the mysterious stranger with a past riding in to save the farmers from the ruthless cattle ranchers is classic western material. Shane (Alan Ladd) is a retired gunfighter who would like to rid himself of the ghosts of his past and settle down with a home and family of his own. He becomes the friend of Joe Starrett (Van Heflin), maintains a suppressed love for Starrett's wife Marian (Jean Arthur), and becomes the idol of

Did you know?...
The film marks Jean Arthur's last appearance on screen, ending a thirty-year career.

Shane (Alan Ladd) reassures
young Joey (Brandon de Wilde).

Starrett's son Joey (Brandon de Wilde). Shane evokes considerable empathy, but it is Joey who embodies the enthusiasm of every boy of the 1950s who ever dreamed of being or at least knowing a "gunslinger."

Every deliberately magnificent scene of this story directs the audience toward the final showdown between Shane and the ranchers. Shane realizes that it is only his knowledge and skill as a gunfighter that can save the farmers from having to give up their lands. The home and family he has acquired in this newly found civilization can only be saved by killing the menacing ranchers and relying on the part of his past that he would like to forget. In doing so, he protects the farmers but also loses the type of life for which he truly yearns. Joey's closing comment echoes the sentiments of the entire audience: "Shane, Come back!"

Cast: Alan Ladd (Shane), Van Heflin (Joe Starrett), Jean Arthur (Marian Starrett), Brandon de Wilde (Joey Starrett), Jack Palance (Jack Wilson), Ben Johnson (Chris Callaway), Elijah Cook, Jr. (Torrey), Edgar Buchanan (Fred Lewis), Emile G. Miles (Rufe Ryker), John Dierkes

(Morgan Ryker), Ellen Corby (Mrs. Torrey), Helen Brown (Mrs. Lewis), Martin Mason (Ed Howells), Nancy Kulp (Mrs. Howells), Paul McVey (Grafton) **Screenwriter:** Jack Sher, A.B. Guthrie, Jr. **Cinematographer:** Loyal Griggs **Composer:** Victor Young **Producer:** George Stevens for Paramount **Running Time:** 117 minutes **Format:** VHS, LV **Awards:** Academy Awards, 1953: Color Cinematography; Nominations: Director (George Stevens), Picture, Screenplay, Supporting Actor (Brandon de Wilde, Jack Palance); National Board of Review Awards, 1953: 10 Best Films of the Year, Director (George Stevens) **Box Office:** $8M.

Shenandoah

1965 – Andrew V. McLaglen – 🎵🎵🎵

> "These are my sons, and they don't belong to the state. We never asked anything of the state and never expected anything."
>
> Charlie Anderson (James Stewart)

This underrated film features a great star performance by James Stewart as a crusty Virginia patriarch with six sons and a daughter in the waning days of the Civil War. Widower Charlie Anderson (Stewart) tries to keep his family out of the hostilities that close in on his farm. He does not own slaves, has never asked for any government help, and sees no reason to take sides in the conflict. The anti-establishment attitudes are probably more representative of 1965 than 1865, but the film continually maintains interest with its intelligence and surprising touches of realism. In one example, Anderson gives a fatherly talk to his prospective son-in-law (Doug McClure) about the unpredictability of women's emotions; as soon as this business begins to seem like nothing more than unsubtle comedy forced in to let Stewart be charmingly cantankerous, the film cuts to Ann (Katharine Ross), the sister-in-law, advising Jennie (Rosemary Forsyth), the young bride-to-be, about how to recognize the recurrent moodiness of men and their need to be alone. In another example, Anderson uses the evening meal as a way of sounding the views of his sons on slavery and the war. He solicits their true feelings, uses inductive questions to prod them to speak up, and encourages them to think for themselves rather than adopt his views as hand-me-downs. In its free flow of ideas, the dinner table of this Virginia family almost takes on the feel of a platonic academy.

Most of the film concerns the family's attempt to find the youngest child, a sixteen-year-old boy (Philip Alford) taken prisoner by Union soldiers, when they spot him wearing a Confederate cap. The filmmakers seem to know that Stewart is their main strength. Two of the best scenes during this search center on his confrontations with officials who impede the family's efforts, and another

Did you know?...
The film marked the screen debut of Katharine Ross.

Wealthy Virginia farmer Charlie Anderson (James Stewart) poses with his children in the days before the Civil War.

strong moment occurs at their night campfire as he fairly lets the family decide whether to return home. The final moments of this return are bitter but honest, and the film concludes with an understated graveside scene (no patented Stewart drawling) in which Anderson reveals his fears and grief once again to his dead wife.

Cast: James Stewart (Charlie Anderson), Doug McClure (Sam), Glenn Corbett (Jacob Anderson), Patrick Wayne (James Anderson), Rosemary Forsyth (Jennie Anderson), Philip Alford (Boy Anderson), Katharine Ross (Ann Anderson), Charles Robinson (Nathan Anderson), James McMullan (John Anderson), Tim McIntire (Henry Anderson), Eugene Jackson Jr. (Gabriel), Paul Fix (Dr. Witherspoon), Denver Pyle (Pastor Bjoerling), George Kennedy (Colonel Fairchild), James Best (Carter) **Screenwriter:** James Lee Barrett **Cinematographer:** William H. Clothier **Composer:** Frank Skinner **Producer:** Robert Arthur for Universal **Running Time:** 105 minutes **Format:** VHS, LV **Awards:** Academy Awards, 1965: Nominations: Sound. **Box Office:** $7.8M (domestic rentals).

Stagecoach

1939 – John Ford – ♫♫♫♫

"We're the victims of a foul disease called social prejudice, my child. These fair ladies of the Law and Order League are scouring out the dregs of the town. Come on. Be a proud, glorified dreg like me."

Doc Boone (Thomas Mitchell), to Dallas the prostitute as they both prepare to leave Tonto.

Director John Ford loved praising *Stagecoach* for not having a single respectable person among its characters. This theme of social ostracism serves as a linchpin to unite the film and seemed to interest the director even more than the many staples of the genre that this pioneering movie (Ford's first sound western) helped to establish. The nine people who gather to take the stagecoach from Tonto to Lordsburg feature among them a prostitute named Dallas (Claire Trevor), who is literally escorted to the stagecoach by the vinegar-faced ladies of the Law and Order League, and a drunken doctor (Thomas Mitchell, in an Oscar-winning performance), who barely has time to grab his shingle as he is told to clear out. These two, along with the Ringo Kid (John Wayne), an escaped prisoner out to revenge himself on the killers of his family in Lordsburg, give the film its rich heart and soul. (And also its irreverence: as the stage pulls out of Tonto, Ford shows the gasping faces of the Law and Order League as the doctor salutes them off-screen with an obscene gesture.)

Some of the other characters appear primarily for comic relief. Andy Devine plays Buck, the stagecoach driver with a safety-first policy about riding into Apache territory. Donald Meek plays a whiskey salesman who naturally attracts the doctor's friendship and concern. The remainder of the cast represents various degrees of unhealthy civilization. Curly (George Bancroft), the marshal, rides along with Buck to do his duty and make sure the Ringo Kid is returned to prison. A genteel cardsharp (John Carradine) looks out for Mrs. Mallory (Louise Platt), the pregnant wife traveling to meet her calvary-officer husband. The longest tirade of complaints comes from Gatewood (Berton Churchill), the banker who has embezzled payroll funds and hugs his fat satchel lovingly. Ford balances scenes of action with stops along the way to emphasize the character drama. In Dry Fork, Ringo chides Curly about snubbing Dallas in taking the vote to ride into Apache country. As the other travelers discreetly move away from Dallas at the lunch table, Ringo befriends her, and these two outcasts form an attraction.

The sweeping Monument Valley vistas that Ford used for the first time in this film are the more powerful by being connected to the story thematically.

Did you know?...

Famed stunt man Yakima Canutt performed both daring stunts (one as an Indian, one as Ringo) that required him to leap onto the running horses pulling the stagecoach.

They epitomize the real frontier spirit of honor and integrity that Curly comes to respect in the Ringo Kid rather than the tainted standards of corrupted civilization represented by Gatewood and the ladies of the Law and Order League. *Stagecoach* happily stands social convention on its ear. It is an anarchic western, and the most fitting summation of its spirit comes from Ford's mouthpiece, the doctor, who in the final shot of the film watches the Ringo Kid and Dallas ride off toward the border and says, "That's saved them from the blessings of civilization."

(The negative had so deteriorated that for many years it looked as if the film might never be seen again in pristine shape. A clean set of release prints, however, were struck around 1970 from a private copy of the film owned by John Wayne. Since then the film has been restored. Newer cassettes and the DVD version feature this restored print, which captures the rich textures of the nighttime shots in Bert Glennon's Oscar-winning cinematography.)

Shady lady Dallas (Claire Trevor) shares a meal with The Ringo Kid (John Wayne).

Cast: John Wayne (the Ringo Kid), Claire Trevor (Dallas), Andy Devine (Buck), John Carradine (Hatfield), Thomas Mitchell (Doc Boone), Louise Platt (Lucy Mallory), George Bancroft (Curly), Donald Meek (Mr. Peacock), Berton Churchill (Mr. Gatewood), Tim Holt (Lieutenant Blanchard), Tom Tyler (Luke Plummer), Yakima Canutt (Calvary Scout), Duke Lee (sheriff of Lordsburg), Louis Mason (sheriff of Tonto), Bryant Washburn (calvary captain) **Screenwriter:** Dudley Nichols **Cinematographer:** Bert Glennon **Composer:** Gerard Carbonara, Richard Hageman, W. Franke Harling, John Leipold, Leo Shuken, Walter Wanger **Running Time:** 96 minutes **Format:** DVD **Awards** Academy Awards, 1939: Supporting Actor (Thomas Mitchell), Score; Nominations: Black and White Cinematography (Bert Glennon), Director (John Ford), Editing, Interior Decoration, Picture; National Board of Review Awards, 1939: 10 Best Films of the Year; New York Film Critics Awards, 1939: Director (John Ford), Picture **Budget:** $531,000 **Box Office:** $1M.

Unforgiven

1992 – Clint Eastwood – 🦴🦴🦴🦴

> "It's a hell of a thing, killing a man. You take away all he's got and all he's ever gonna have."
>
> Will (Clint Eastwood)

Did you know?...

The final title after the end credits reads "Dedicated to Sergio and Don," a reference to Sergio Leone, the director who cast Eastwood in his first screen westerns, and Don Siegel, the man who directed him in *Dirty Harry*.

"You ain't ugly like me," Will Munny (Clint Eastwood) says gently to Delilah (Anna Thomson), a prostitute whose face is covered with stitches from a slashing by a customer, "it's just that we both got scars." In *Unforgiven*, physical scars aplenty are present, but it's the emotional and spiritual scars that disturb the deepest. The prostitutes of Big Whisky have come up with $1,000 dollars to pay anyone who takes revenge on the two men who cut Delilah. The Schofield Kid (Jaimz Woolvett) has heard stories about the bloodthirstiness of Will Munny as a gunslinger; the Kid finds Will on his pig farm in Kansas and asks him to be his partner in revenging Delilah. Will first tells the Kid that his dead wife has reformed him from his violent ways, but the need to provide for his two young children eventually leads him to ask his friend Ned (Morgan Freeman) to accompany him to Big Whisky. Meanwhile, the sheriff Little Bill (Gene Hackman) has thrashed to near unconscious anyone who tries to accept the women's offer, and English Bob (Richard Harris), the famous gun who comes to town with his biographer (Saul Rubinek) in tow, is brutally beaten and jailed.

Few if any mainstream popular films have the sense of moral doom that pervades *Unforgiven*. The only character who seemingly is not described by the title is the deceased wife. Furthermore, the film bristles with disturbing ironies: Will wants to be a good man and honor the memory of his wife, but as an inept farmer and a remote father, Will is really only good at killing. The sense of purg-

Little Bill (Gene Hackman) and
Will Munny (Clint Eastwood) try
a little conversation.

ing and release that comes to him when he again practices this skill deepens and complicates a man whose soul troubles him but who has nevertheless again found his calling. We see other characters—especially the sadistic sheriff—who are just as cruel and bloody but who are completely untroubled by the moral or spiritual implications of their acts. The film parts company with most westerns by taking a staple of the genre that is usually accepted unthinkingly and showing the emotional and spiritual price attached to killing, which in *Unforgiven* is something that chips away resolutely at one's soul.

The rich gloom of the film can be measured partly in Will's friend Ned. When he has one of Delilah's attackers at his mercy, Ned finds that he can't pull the trigger. He next tries to absolve himself of bounty hunting and return home, but some townsmen find him and turn him over to Little Bill, who whips him to death. Part of the power of the film lies in the pitilessness of its cause-effect: Ned's attempt to obey his conscience leads only to his death, which prompts

Will to return to town to confront Little Bill and his deputies. This gives Will a wholeness and certainty he has lacked, but it cannot assuage the ache in his soul. Christianity teaches that all people are redeemable, but religion seldom dwells on what this dark, meditative, and profound motion picture finds most fascinating: the enormous difficulty of becoming one of the forgiven.

Cast: Clint Eastwood (William Munny), Morgan Freeman (Ned Logan), Gene Hackman (Little Bill Doggett), Richard Harris (English Bob), Jaimz Woolvett (the "Schofield Kid"), Saul Rubinek (W.W. Beauchamp), Frances Fisher (Strawberry Alice), Anna Thomson (Delilah Fitzgerald), David Mucci (Quick Mike), Rob Campbell (Davey Bunting), Anthony James (Skinny Dubois), Tara Dawn Frederick (Little Sue), Beverley Elliott (Silky), Lisa Repo-Martell (Faith), Josie Smith (Crow Creek Kate) **Screenwriter:** David Webb Peoples **Cinematographer:** Jack N. Green **Composer:** Lennie Niehaus **Producer:** Clint Eastwood for Warner Bros **MPAA Rating:** R **Running Time:** 130 minutes **Format:** VHS, LV, DVD **Awards:** Academy Award, 1992: Director (Clint Eastwood), Editing, Picture, Supporting Actor (Gene Hackman); Nominations: Actor (Clint Eastwood), Art Direction/Set Decoration, Cinematography, Original Screenplay, Sound; British Academy Awards, 1992: Director (Clint Eastwood), Film, Supporting Actor (Gene Hackman); Directors Guild of America Awards, 1992: Director (Clint Eastman); Golden Globe Awards, 1993: Director (Clint Eastwood), Supporting Actor (Gene Hackman); Los Angeles Film Critics Association Awards, 1992: Actor (Clint Eastwood), Director (Clint Eastwood), Film, Screenplay, Supporting Actor (Gene Hackman); New York Film Critics Awards, 1992: Director (Clint Eastwood), Film, Screenplay, Supporting Actor (Gene Hackman) **Box Office:** $101M (domestic gross).

The Wild Bunch
1969 — Sam Peckinpah — 🦴🦴🦴🦴

> "When you side with a man you stay with him, and if you can't do that you're like some animal. You're finished."
>
> Pike (William Holden) to Tector.

When this film appeared, it was notorious for its use of slow-motion violence that emphasized the grace and beauty of something audiences had been conditioned to regard as ugly. Since its release, however, this shock has receded as the mainstream of films has largely adopted Sam Peckinpah's use of slow-motion. *The Wild Bunch* today seems noteworthy for what might have been its most important trait all along—the sense of tarnished honor and heroism the bunch adheres to in a world becoming hopelessly corrupted.

The film is set in 1913 Texas and Mexico, when people sense the end of the age of frontier expansion and the old west. In one scene the bunch marvels over seeing a car, and they speculate on the stories they have heard about airplanes. These bandits are being hunted down by Deke Thornton (Robert Ryan), a former friend of Pike (William Holden), the leader of the bunch. Thornton's

interests are self-serving: he has been promised that he will not be returned to jail if he brings in the wild bunch alive or dead. After a failed attempt to rob a bank in the opening scene, the bunch travels to Mexico where they accept an offer from the warlord Mapache (Emilio Fernandez) to steal arms from a U.S. army supply train.

Tector (Ben Johnson), Lyle (Warren Oates), Pike (William Holden), and Dutch (Ernest Borgnine) survey their territory.

Pike's character serves as the center of the film. He defends the oldest gang member, Sykes (Edmond O'Brien), for no other reason than loyalty when Tector (Ben Johnson) turns on him. Late in the film, when Mapache has captured another member, Angel (Jaime Sanchez), for stealing a crate of weapons for his village, Pike is repulsed by the punishments Mapache inflicts on Angel. Though he has been paid by Mapache for delivering the weapons, Pike and three other gang members go back to Mapache and offer to barter their money for the return of Angel. The final bloodbath starts as a last stand and instinctive response to Mapache's returning Angel with his throat slit.

Did you know?...

Lee Marvin was the first choice to play Pike, but he elected to appear in *Paint Your Wagon*.

The film repeatedly contrasts the rugged honor of the bunch with the inhuman greed of the bounty hunters. After the bloody shootout in the opening bank robbery, two bounty hunters, Coffer and T.C. (Strother Martin and L.Q. Jones), pick their way among the corpses littering the street and argue over who shot whom. The mercenary nature of these human vultures even sickens Thornton, who hates that the circumstances of his parole make him associate with the likes of them. Peckinpah continually humanizes Pike and the bunch, as in the scene when they ride out of Angel's village. This town has recently been attacked by Mapache, but they now welcome the bunch as their friends, and when they leave, the villagers line the road to wish them well. Peckinpah cuts the scene together to emphasize Pike's concern for the town. We see closeups of him, followed by shots of the smiling villagers, followed by his kind reactions. He embodies the rogue individualism and independent spirit quickly dying out as the modern age replaces the Old West.

Cast: William Holden (Pike Bishop), Ernest Borgnine (Dutch Engstrom), Robert Ryan (Deke Thornton), Edmond O'Brien (Sykes), Warren Oates (Lyle Gorch), Jaime Sanchez (Angel), Ben Johnson (Tector Gorch), Emilio Fernandez (Mapache), Strother Martin (Coffer), L.Q. Jones (T.C.), Albert Dekker (Pat Harrigan), Bo Hopkins (Crazy Lee), Dub Taylor (Mayor Wainscoat), Paul Harper (Ross), Jorge Russek (Lieutenant Zamorra) **Screenwriter:** Walon Green, Sam Peckinpah **Cinematographer:** Lucien Ballard **Composer:** Jerry Fielding **Producer:** Phil Feldman for Seven Arts; released by Warner Bros. **MPAA Rating:** R **Running Time:** 145 minutes **Format:** VHS, LV, DVD **Awards:** Academy Awards, 1969: Nominations: Screenplay, Score; National Society of Film Critics Awards, 1969: Cinematography. **Budget:** $6M.

They Might Be Giants . . .

Film historian Louis Giannetti has called the western the most popular epic genre in the United States. Raoul Walsh's *The Big Trail* (1930) is probably most noted as the film that announced the potential of John Wayne as a star. This should not overlook the initial use of 70mm to produce a spectacle that displays magnificent and vast scenery while relaying the saga of a wagon train on its treacherous journey west. Nothing this big will be seen for the rest of the decade of the 1930s. King Vidor's *Duel in the Sun* (1946) was an ambitious venture by producer David O. Selznick to outglamorize *Gone with the Wind* (1939). Not quite realizing that goal, the film nonetheless features some fine cinematography that holds more interest than the storyline of brothers (Gregory Peck and Joseph Cotten) competing for the family empire. The film proved a blockbuster and one of the highest-grossing westerns of all time. John Ford took advantage of the popularity and talent of John Wayne by directing Wayne in a calvary trilogy—*Fort Apache* (1948), *She Wore a Yellow Ribbon* (1949), and *Rio Grande* (1950). Each film has Ford's signature of absorbing post-Civil War stories that question what the soldier is told about his duty versus what he knows is right. Of course, the films are all set within the stunning and remote background of Monument Valley.

Two of the most recent western epics have been produced and released in such close proximity that comparisons have to be made, especially since the storylines are almost identical. George Pan Cosmatos' *Tombstone* (1993) and Lawrence Kasdan's *Wyatt Earp* (1994) both used the well-worn myth of Wyatt Earp, Doc Holliday, and the shootout at the O.K. Corral. The 1993 production uses the violence of the Old West to emphasize the response of character, while its 1994 counterpart skimps on action and over-emphasizes character. Most critics agreed that *Tombstone* wins out when it comes to adhering to the genre and providing sheer entertainment.

Cast Index

A

Aames, Marlene
The Best Years of Our Lives

Abdul-Jabbar, Kareem
Airplane!

Abraham, F. Murray
Scarface

Abrikosov, Andrei
Alexander Nevsky
Ivan the Terrible, Part I and II

Achellhardt, Mary Kate
White Heat

Ackland, Joss
The Three Musketeers

Acres, Graham
The Man Who Would Be King

Adams, Claire
The Big Parade

Adams, Dorothy
The Best Years of Our Lives
The Big Country

Adams, Edie
It's a Mad Mad Mad Mad World

Adams, Jonathan
The Rocky Horror Picture Show

Adams, Nick
Giant

Addams, Dawn
The Robe

Addie, Robert
Excalibur

Addy, Wesley
Tora! Tora! Tora!

Ades, Dan
Aguirre, the Wrath of God

Adet, Georges
Love and Death

Adiarte, Patrick
The King and I

Adjani, Isabelle
Ishtar
Queen Margot
The Story of Adele H.

Adonis, Frank
Raging Bull

Adoree, Renee
The Big Parade

Adrian, Max
Henry V

Agutter, Jenny
Star!

Aherne, Patrick
The Court Jester

Ahlstedt, Borje
Fanny and Alexander

Aiello, Danny
Once Upon a Time in America

Aitken, Spottiswoode
The Birth of a Nation

Akins, Claude
From Here to Eternity

Alariz, Rico
The Magnificent Seven

Albert, Eddie
The King and I
The Longest Day

Albertson, Frank
It's a Wonderful Life

Albertson, Jack
The Poseidon Adventure

Albertson, Lillian
The Greatest Show on Earth

Alda, Rutanya
The Deer Hunter

Alden, Mary
The Birth of a Nation

Alderson, Erville
The Scarlet Empress

Aletter, Frank
Tora! Tora! Tora!

Alexander, Jason
The Hunchback of Notre Dame

Alexandrov, Grigori
The Battleship Potemkin

Alford, Philip
Shenandoah

Alland, William
Citizen Kane

Allen, Joan
Nixon

Allen, John Edward
Blade Runner

Allen, Karen
Raiders of the Lost Ark

Allen, Ronald
A Night to Remember

Allen, Todd
The Postman

Allen, Woody
Love and Death

Aller, Chris
The Wind and the Lion

Allwin, Pernilla
Fanny and Alexander

Almgren, Kristian
Fanny and Alexander

Amendola, Claudio
Queen Margot

Ames, Leon
Tora! Tora! Tora!

Amis, Suzy
Titanic

Anderson, Brian
Gallipoli

Anderson, Eddie "Rochester"
It's a Mad Mad Mad Mad World

Anderson, Judith
The Ten Commandments

Anderson, Richard
Paths of Glory

Andersson, Harriet
Fanny and Alexander

Andre, Marcel
Beauty and the Beast

Andrews, Dana
The Best Years of Our Lives

Andrews, David
White Heat

Andrews, Harry
Alexander the Great

The "Cast Index" provides a complete listing of cast members cited within the reviews. The actors' names are alphabetical by last name, and the films they appeared in are listed chronologically, from most recent to the oldest (please note that only the films reviewed in this book are cited).

Battle of Britain
55 Days at Peking
Moby Dick

Andrews, Julie
The Sound of Music
Star!

Andrews, Naveen
The English Patient

Andrews, Stanley
Beau Geste

Androsky, Carol
Little Big Man

Angel, Heather
Peter Pan

Anglade, Jean-Hugues
Queen Margot

Angora, Richard
Star!

Anka, Paul
The Longest Day

Annabella
Napoleon

Annis, Francesca
Dune

Ansara, Michael
Julius Caesar
The Robe
The Ten Commandments

Antonio, Lou
America America

Antonov, Alexander
The Battleship Potemkin

Antrim, Paul
The Man Who Would Be King

Arcalli, Franco
Once Upon a Time in America

Archer, John
White Heat

Ardisson, Edward
Love and Death

Arenberg, Lee
Waterworld

Argento, Asia
Queen Margot

Argue, David
Gallipoli

Arkin, David
Nashville

Armendariz, Pedro
The Conqueror

Armstrong, Robert
King Kong

Arrick, Rose
Ishtar

Arruza, Carlos
The Alamo

Arsky, N.
Alexander Nevsky

Artaud, Antonin
Napoleon

Arthur, Jean
Once Upon a Time in the West
Red River

Ash, Sam
The Poseidon Adventure

Ashdown, Nadine
The Bridges at Toko-Ri

Asherson, Renee
Henry V

Ashley, Edward
The Court Jester

Ashmore, Frank
Airplane!

Ashton, Sylvia
Greed

Aspegren, Chuck
The Deer Hunter

Astaire, Fred
The Towering Inferno

Astin, John
West Side Story

Ates, Roscoe
Cimarron

Atherton, William
The Hindenburg

Atkine, Feodor
Love and Death

Attenborough, Richard
The Great Escape
Hamlet
Jurassic Park

Auberjonois, Rene
The Hindenburg

Auclair, Michael
Beauty and the Beast

Auer, Mischa
The Lives of a Bengal Lancer

August, Edwin
The Magnificent Ambersons

August, Pernilla
Fanny and Alexander

Auteuil, Daniel
Queen Margot

Avalon, Frankie
The Alamo

Avery, Val
The Magnificent Seven

Awaji, Keiko
The Bridges at Toko-Ri

Aylesworth, Arthur
Beau Geste

Aylmer, Felix
Exodus
Henry V
Ivanhoe
Quo Vadis?

Ayres, Robert
A Night to Remember

B

Babcock, Barbara
Far and Away

Backlinie, Susan
Jaws

Backus, Jim
It's a Mad Mad Mad Mad World

Bacon, Irving
The Grapes of Wrath

Badejo, Bolaji
Alien

Baer, Buddy
Quo Vadis?

Baigent, Harold
Gallipoli

Baigum, Princess
The Charge of the Light Brigade

Bailin, Jacob
Reds

Bairstow, Scott
The Postman

Baker, Carroll
The Big Country
Cheyenne Autumn
Giant
The Greatest Story Ever Told

Baker, Hylda
Oliver!

Baker, Kathy
The Right Stuff

Baker, Kenny
The Empire Strikes Back
Return of the Jedi
Star Wars

Baker, Sam
The Thief of Bagdad

Baker, Stanley
Alexander the Great
The Guns of Navarone

Balaban, Bob
Close Encounters of the Third
    Kind

Baldini II, Oreste
The Godfather, Part II

Bloom, Claire
Alexander the Great

Blossom, Roberts
Close Encounters of the Third
    Kind

Blue, Ben
A Guide for the Married Man
It's a Mad Mad Mad Mad World

Blue, Monte
The Lives of a Bengal Lancer
Orphans of the Storm

Blum, Roger
Napoleon

Bobrov, I.
The Battleship Potemkin

Boccia, Luis
Evita

Bogarde, Dirk
A Bridge Too Far

Bohnen, Roman
The Best Years of Our Lives

**Bohorquez, Huerequeque
    Enrique**
Fitzcarraldo

Bolger, Ray
The Wizard of Oz

Bonanova, Fortunio
Citizen Kane

Bond, Ward
The Grapes of Wrath
It's a Wonderful Life
Red River

Bondi, Beulah
It's a Wonderful Life

Bonehill, Richard
Rob Roy

Bonner, Tony
The Lighthorsemen

Bono, Joseph
Raging Bull

Boone, Pat
The Greatest Story Ever Told

Boone, Richard
The Robe

Boorman, Katrine
Excalibur

Booth, Connie
Monty Python and the Holy Grail

Boothe, Powers
Nixon

Borg, Veda Ann
The Alamo

Borgnine, Ernest
From Here to Eternity
The Poseidon Adventure

The Wild Bunch

Bose, Miguel
Queen Margot

Bosler, Virginia
The King and I

Bostwick, Barry
The Rocky Horror Picture Show

Bosworth, Catherine
The Horse Whisperer

Bosworth, Hobart
The Big Parade
The Crusades

Bottoms, John
The Long Riders

Bottoms, Sam
Apocalypse Now

Bouchey, Willis
The Bridges at Toko-Ri

Bouih, Karroom Ben
The Man Who Would Be King

Bourdet, Louise
The Story of Adele H.

Bourvil
The Longest Day

Bowdon, Dorris
The Grapes of Wrath

Bowens, Mallick
Out of Africa

Bower, Tom
Nixon

Boxer, John
The Bridge on the River Kwai

Boyd, Stephen
The Bible

Boyd, William
The Greatest Show on Earth

Boyer, Charles
Around the World in 80 Days

Boyle, Peter
Young Frankenstein

Bradford, Marshall
White Heat

Bradley, Leslie
The Conqueror

Brady, Buff
The Big Country

Brady, P.J.
Far and Away

Brahms, Penny
2001: A Space Odyssey

Brainville, Yves
Love and Death

Bramley, William
West Side Story

Branagh, Kenneth
Hamlet
Henry V

Brandauer, Klaus Maria
Out of Africa

Brando, Marlon
Apocalypse Now
The Godfather
Julius Caesar
Superman

Brandon, Henry
Red River

Braugher, Andre
Glory

Brazzi, Rossano
South Pacific

Breese, Edmund
Duck Soup

Brennan, Walter
High Noon
Red River

Brereton, Tyrone
Cimarron

Brialy, Jean-Claude
Queen Margot

Briant, Shane
The Lighthorsemen

Brich, Wyrley
Lost Horizon

Bridges, Jeff
Heaven's Gate

Bridges, Lloyd
Airplane!
High Noon

Bridges, Lorraine
The Wizard of Oz

Briers, Richard
Hamlet
Henry V

Bright, Richard
Once Upon a Time in America

Brittany, Morgan
The Birds

Brocco, Peter
Spartacus

Brochet, Anne
Cyrano de Bergerac

Broderick, Matthew
Glory

Brody, Buster
The Wizard of Oz

Brolin, James
Pee-Wee's Big Adventure

Bronson, Charles
The Great Escape

The Magnificent Seven
Once Upon a Time in the West

Brooks, Rand
Gone With The Wind

Brophy, Kevin
The Long Riders

Brown, Charles D.
The Grapes of Wrath

Brown, Dolores
Cimarron

Brown, Dwier
Field of Dreams

Brown, Everett
Gone With The Wind

Brown, Gaye
The Rocky Horror Picture Show

Brown, Helen
Red River

Brown, Jimmy
The Road Warrior

Brown, Joe E.
Around the World in 80 Days
It's a Mad Mad Mad Mad World

Brown, Pamela
Cleopatra

Brown, Phil
Star Wars

Brown, Roger Aaron
Star Trek: The Motion Picture

Brown, Russ
South Pacific

Brown, Timothy
Nashville

Brown, William
Intolerance

Browne, Roscoe Lee
Babe

Browning, Tod
Intolerance

Bruce, Kate
Orphans of the Storm

Bruce, Nigel
The Charge of the Light Brigade

Bruck, Karl
Paint Your Wagon

Bruhns, Werner
1900

Bruneti, Argentina
It's a Wonderful Life

Bryan, Arthur Q.
Samson and Delilah

Brynner, Yul
The King and I
The Magnificent Seven
The Ten Commandments

Buchanan, Edgar
The Sea Hawk

Buchanan, West
The Long Riders

Buchholz, Horst
The Magnificent Seven

Buchma, Amvrosi
Ivan the Terrible, Part I and II

Buckler, Hugh
Lost Horizon

Buckley, Keith
Excalibur

Buffet, Eugenie
Napoleon

Bugara, Mike
Out of Africa

Buhr, Gerard
Love and Death

Bull, Peter
Dr. Strangelove, or: How I
    Learned to Stop Worrying
    and Love the Bomb

Burgess, Helen
Once Upon a Time in the West

Burk, Jim
The Big Country

Burke, Billie
The Wizard of Oz

Burke, James
Beau Geste

Burke, Kathleen
The Lives of a Bengal Lancer

Burns, Edward
Saving Private Ryan

Burton, Jeff
Planet of the Apes

Burton, John
Lost Horizon

Burton, LeVar
Star Trek Generations

Burton, Norman
Planet of the Apes
The Towering Inferno

Burton, Richard
Alexander the Great
Cleopatra
The Longest Day
The Robe

Burton, Zoe
Babe

Busfield, Timothy
Field of Dreams

Bushell, Anthony
A Night to Remember

Buttner, Wolfgang
The Longest Day

Buttons, Red
The Longest Day
The Poseidon Adventure

Bux, Ishaq
The Rocky Horror Picture Show

Byington, Spring
The Charge of the Light Brigade
Moby Dick

Byrne, Eddie
Star Wars

Byrne, Gabriel
Excalibur

Byrne, Michael
A Bridge Too Far
Indiana Jones and the Last Cru-
    sade

C

Caan, James
A Bridge Too Far
The Godfather

Cabot, Bruce
King Kong

Cabot, Sebastian
Ivanhoe

Caesar, Sid
A Guide for the Married Man

Cagney, James
White Heat
Yankee Doodle Dandy

Cagney, Jeanne
Yankee Doodle Dandy

Caine, Michael
Battle of Britain
A Bridge Too Far
The Man Who Would Be King

Caine, Shakira
The Man Who Would Be King

Cairney, John
A Night to Remember

Calcutt, Stephen
The Rocky Horror Picture Show

Calhern, Louis
Duck Soup
Julius Caesar
The Last Days of Pompeii

Call, R.D.
Waterworld

Callan, Michael
The Victors

Callaway, Cheryl Lynn
The Bridges at Toko-Ri

Calleia, Joseph
The Alamo

Calnan, Matilda
Star!

Calvey, Mahiri
Braveheart

Campanini, Pippo
1900

Campbell, Adrienne
Close Encounters of the Third
  Kind

Campbell, Nell
The Rocky Horror Picture Show

Campbell, Rob
Unforgiven

Candido, Candy
Peter Pan

Cannon, Pomeroy
The Four Horsemen of the Apocalypse

Cantinflas
Around the World in 80 Days

Canutt, Yakima
Stagecoach

Capell, Peter
Paths of Glory

Cardenas, Elsa
Giant

Cardinal, Tantoo
Dances With Wolves
Legends of the Fall

Cardinale, Claudia
Fitzcarraldo
Once Upon a Time in the West

Carey, Harry
Red River

Carey, Jr., Harry
Red River

Carey, Timothy
Paths of Glory

Carlisle, Harry
Reds

Carmichael, Hoagy
The Best Years of Our Lives

Carney, Art
A Guide for the Married Man

Carol, Martine
Around the World in 80 Days

Carr, Charmian
The Sound of Music

Carradine, David
The Long Riders

Carradine, John
Around the World in 80 Days
Cheyenne Autumn

The Court Jester
The Grapes of Wrath
Stagecoach
The Ten Commandments

Carradine, Keith
The Long Riders
Nashville

Carradine, Robert
The Long Riders

Carrier, Corey
Nixon

Carroll, Edwina
2001: A Space Odyssey

Carroll, Larry
Rocky

Carson, Bob
The Greatest Show on Earth

Carteny, Marilu
Once Upon a Time in the West

Carter, Michael
Return of the Jedi

Cartwright, Angela
The Sound of Music

Cartwright, Fabian
Henry V

Cartwright, Veronica
Alien
The Birds
The Right Stuff

Casaravilla, Carlos
55 Days at Peking

Casey, Eli
Lost Horizon

Casey, Sue
Paint Your Wagon

Casini, Stefania
1900

Cassel, Jean-Pierre
Those Magnificent Men in Their
  Flying Machines, or How I
  Flew from London to Paris
  in 25 Hours and 11 Minutes

Cassell, Wally
White Heat

Cassidy, Joanna
Blade Runner

Cassidy, Ted
Butch Cassidy and the Sundance Kid

Castellano, Richard
The Godfather

Castelnuovo, Nino
The English Patient

Castle, John
Antony and Cleopatra

Catlett, Walter
Pinocchio

Cauldwell, Brendan
Far and Away

Cavanaugh, Christine
Babe

Cavicchia, Sylvio
Napoleon

Cawdron, Robert
The Private Life of Sherlock
  Holmes

Cazale, John
The Deer Hunter
The Godfather
The Godfather, Part II

Ceasar, Sid
It's a Mad Mad Mad Mad World

Cecil, Hugh
The Rocky Horror Picture Show

Chakatouny, Acho
Napoleon

Chakiris, George
West Side Story

Chakrabandhu, M.R.B.
The Bridge on the River Kwai

Chamberlain, Kenneth
Reds

Chamberlain, Richard
The Three Musketeers
The Towering Inferno

Chamberlin, Howland
The Best Years of Our Lives

Chandler, Lane
Samson and Delilah

Chaney, Jr., Lon
High Noon

Chaplin, Geraldine
Doctor Zhivago
Nashville
The Three Musketeers

Chapman, Graham
Monty Python and the Holy Grail

Charleson, Ian
Gandhi

Chase, Barrie
It's a Mad Mad Mad Mad World

Chase, Duane
The Sound of Music

Chasing His Horse, Nathan Lee
Dances With Wolves

Chaykin, Maury
Dances With Wolves

Chen, Joan
The Last Emperor

Chereau, Patrice
The Last of the Mohicans

Cherkasov, Nikolai
Alexander Nevsky
Ivan the Terrible, Part I and II

Cheung, Leslie
Farewell My Concubine

Chiaki, Minoru
Seven Samurai

Chianese, Dominic
The Godfather, Part II

Chiba, Ichiro
Seven Samurai

Chow, Michael
55 Days at Peking

Christian, Susanne
Paths of Glory

Christie, Audrey
Carousel

Christie, Julie
Doctor Zhivago
Far From the Madding Crowd
Hamlet

Christy, James V.
Raging Bull

Chun, Li
Farewell My Concubine

Churchill, Berton
Stagecoach

Ciafalio, Carl
Far and Away

Ciannelli, Edward
Gunga Din

Claire, Imogen
The Rocky Horror Picture Show

Clark, Bridgetta
The Four Horsemen of the Apocalypse

Clark, Davison
The Scarlet Empress

Clark, Fred
White Heat

Clark, Ken
South Pacific

Clarke, Warren
Antony and Cleopatra

Clarke-Smith, D.A.
Quo Vadis?

Clary, Robert
The Hindenburg

Claux, Moire
The Road Warrior

Clay, Nicholas
Excalibur

Cleese, John
Monty Python and the Holy Grail

Clemente, Steve
King Kong

Cless, Buck
South Pacific

Cleveland, Carol
Monty Python and the Holy Grail

Clift, Montgomery
From Here to Eternity
Red River

Clifton, Elmer
The Birth of a Nation

Clive, E.E.
The Charge of the Light Brigade

Clute, Chester
Yankee Doodle Dandy

Cobb, Lee J.
Exodus
High Noon

Coburn, Brian
Love and Death

Coburn, Charles
Around the World in 80 Days

Coburn, James
The Great Escape
The Magnificent Seven

Coby, Fred
White Heat

Cochran, Steve
The Best Years of Our Lives
White Heat

Colasanto, Nicholas
Raging Bull

Colbert, Claudette
Cleopatra

Cole, George
Cleopatra

Colley, Kenneth
The Empire Strikes Back
Return of the Jedi

Collier Jr., William
Cimarron

Collin, John
Star!

Collins, G. Pat
White Heat

Collins, Jack
The Towering Inferno

Collins, Paul
Peter Pan

Collins, Phil
Hook

Collins, Ray
The Best Years of Our Lives

Citizen Kane
The Magnificent Ambersons

Collins, Rufus
The Rocky Horror Picture Show

Collins, Stephen
Star Trek: The Motion Picture

Colman, Ronald
Around the World in 80 Days
Lost Horizon

Colon, Miriam
Scarface

Coltrane, Robbie
Henry V

Comingore, Dorothy
Citizen Kane

Comont, Mathilde
The Thief of Bagdad

Conklin, Chester
Greed

Connally, Merrill
Close Encounters of the Third Kind

Connery, Sean
A Bridge Too Far
Indiana Jones and the Last Crusade
The Longest Day
The Man Who Would Be King
The Wind and the Lion

Connor, Edric
Moby Dick

Connors, Chuck
The Big Country

Connors, Mike
The Ten Commandments

Conrad, William
The Conqueror

Conried, Hans
Peter Pan

Conroy, Frank
The Last Days of Pompeii

Considine, Tim
Patton

Conversi, Luciano
The Bible

Conway, Tom
Peter Pan

Cooley, Isabelle
Cleopatra

Cooley, Jack
The Wind and the Lion

Coombs, Carol
It's a Wonderful Life

Cooper, Bobby
The Magnificent Ambersons

Daily, Elizabeth
Pee-Wee's Big Adventure

Dall, John
Spartacus

Daly, James
Planet of the Apes

Damia, Maryse
Napoleon

Damon, Matt
Saving Private Ryan

Dan, Li
Farewell My Concubine

Dance, Louis
Napoleon

Dane, Karl
The Big Parade

Daniell, Henry
The Sea Hawk

Daniels, Anthony
The Empire Strikes Back
Return of the Jedi
Star Wars

Daniels, William
Reds

Danilova, A.
Alexander Nevsky

Danning, Sybil
The Three Musketeers

Dano, Royal
The Right Stuff

Danson, Ted
Saving Private Ryan

Dantine, Helmut
Alexander the Great

Darien, Frank
The Grapes of Wrath

Darren, James
The Guns of Navarone

Darrieux, Danielle
Alexander the Great

Darro, Frankie
Pinocchio

Darwell, Jane
The Grapes of Wrath

Dasburg, Andrew
Reds

Davenport, Harry
The Hunchback of Notre Dame

Davenport, Nigel
A Man For All Seasons

David, Keith
Platoon

David, Thayer
Little Big Man
Rocky

Davidson, John
The Last Days of Pompeii

Davidtz, Embeth
Schindler's List

Davies, Jeremy
Saving Private Ryan

Davies, Rita
Monty Python and the Holy Grail

Davis, Gary Lee
Far and Away

Davis, Harry
America America

Davis, Tess
Reds

Davis, William
Samson and Delilah

Dawkins, Paul
Far From the Madding Crowd

Day, Josette
Beauty and the Beast

Day, W. Percy
Napoleon

Day-Lewis, Daniel
The Last of the Mohicans

de Ansorena, Robert
Napoleon

De Brulier, Nigel
The Four Horsemen of the
  Apocalypse

de Camp, Rosemary
Yankee Doodle Dandy

de Carlo, Yvonne
The Ten Commandments

de Corsia, Ted
The Conqueror

De Grasse, Sam
The Birth of a Nation
Intolerance

de Havilland, Olivia
The Adventures of Robin Hood
The Charge of the Light Brigade
Gone With The Wind

de Hoyos, Jorge Martinez
The Magnificent Seven

de Leza, Marisa
Alexander the Great

De Mille, Katherine
The Crusades

De Niro, Robert
The Deer Hunter
The Godfather, Part II
The Mission
1900
Once Upon a Time in America
Raging Bull

De Sepia, Francesca
The Godfather, Part II

De Wolff, Francis
Ivanhoe
Moby Dick

De Young, Cliff
Glory

Deacon, Richard
The Birds
Carousel

Dean, James
Giant

Dearing, Olive
Samson and Delilah

Deary, Tony
The Road Warrior

Deering, Olive
The Ten Commandments

Dehner, John
Carousel
The Right Stuff

Dekker, Albert
Beau Geste
The Wild Bunch

del Rio, Delores
Cheyenne Autumn

del Rio, Teresa
Alexander the Great

Delalande, Anatole
Cyrano de Bergerac

Delgado, Roger
Antony and Cleopatra

Demarest, William
It's a Mad Mad Mad Mad World

Demick, Irina
The Longest Day
Those Magnificent Men in Their
  Flying Machines, or How I
  Flew from London to Paris
  in 25 Hours and 11 Minutes

Dench, Judi
Hamlet
Henry V

Dennis, John
From Here to Eternity

Denny, Reginald
Around the World in 80 Days

Depardieu, Gerard
1900
Cyrano de Bergerac
Hamlet

Depp, Johnny
Platoon

Derek, John
Exodus
The Ten Commandments

Dern, Laura
Jurassic Park

Deschanel, Mary Jo
The Right Stuff

Desmond, Paul
Legends of the Fall

Devine, Andy
Around the World in 80 Days
High Noon
It's a Mad Mad Mad Mad World
Stagecoach

Devlin, J.G.
Far and Away

Dexter, Alan
Paint Your Wagon

Dexter, Brad
The Magnificent Seven

Di, Tong
Farewell My Concubine

Diamond, Selma
It's a Mad Mad Mad Mad World

DiCaprio, Leonardo
Titanic

Diehl, John
Nixon

Dierkes, John
The Alamo
Red River

Dierkop, Charles
Butch Cassidy and the Sundance Kid

Diesel, Vin
Saving Private Ryan

Dietrich, Marlene
Around the World in 80 Days
The Scarlet Empress

Dieudonne, Albert
Napoleon

Dieudonne, Yvette
Napoleon

Digges, Dudley
Moby Dick

Dillaway, Don
The Magnificent Ambersons

Dillon, Kevin
Platoon

Dillon, Melinda
Close Encounters of the Third
Kind

Dimech, John
Lawrence of Arabia

Dinsdale, Reece
Hamlet

Dix, Richard
Cimarron

Dixon, Donna
Nixon

Dixon, Jill
A Night to Remember

Dixon, MacIntyre
Reds

Dobkin, Lawrence
Patton

Dodd, Ken
Hamlet

Dodds, Philip
Close Encounters of the Third
Kind

Donahue, Troy
The Godfather, Part II

Donald, James
The Bridge on the River Kwai
The Great Escape

Donat, Peter
The Hindenburg

Donlevy, Brian
Beau Geste

Doody, Alison
Indiana Jones and the Last Crusade

Doohan, James
Star Trek Generations
Star Trek: The Motion Picture

Doqui, Robert
Nashville

Dorey, Reubin
The Story of Adele H.

Dorn, Michael
Star Trek Generations

Dornacker, Jane
The Right Stuff

Doucette, John
Patton

Douglas, Kirk
Paths of Glory
Spartacus

Douglas, Robert
Ivanhoe

Douglas, Sarah
Superman

Dourif, Brad
Heaven's Gate

Dover, Nancy
Cimarron

Dow, Bill
Legends of the Fall

Dowklee, Kannikar
The Bridge on the River Kwai

Downer, David
The Road Warrior

Downs, Jane
A Night to Remember

Drayton, Noel
The Court Jester

Dresser, Louise
The Scarlet Empress

Dreyfuss, Justin
Close Encounters of the Third
Kind

Dreyfuss, Richard
Close Encounters of the Third
Kind
Jaws

Driscoll, Bobby
Peter Pan

Dru, Joanne
Red River

Du Count, George
Gunga Din

Du Crow, Tote
The Thief of Bagdad

Duffel, Bee
Monty Python and the Holy Grail

Dullea, Keir
2001: A Space Odyssey

Dumbrille, Douglass
Julius Caesar
The Lives of a Bengal Lancer
The Ten Commandments

Dumont, Margaret
Duck Soup

Dun, Dennis
The Last Emperor

Dunaway, Faye
Little Big Man
The Three Musketeers
The Towering Inferno

Dunham, Joanna
The Greatest Story Ever Told

Dunn, Geoffrey
Quo Vadis?

Dunn, Kevin
Nixon

Dunne, Irene
Cimarron

Durant, Will
Reds

Durante, Jimmy
It's a Mad Mad Mad Mad World

Durden, Richard
Batman

Durkin, Grace
Cleopatra

Durkin, Patrick
Raiders of the Lost Ark

Guilfoyle, Paul
White Heat

Guinness, Alec
The Bridge on the River Kwai
Doctor Zhivago
The Empire Strikes Back
Lawrence of Arabia
Return of the Jedi
Star Wars

Gunner, Robert
Planet of the Apes

Gunton, Bob
Glory

Guve, Bertil
Fanny and Alexander

Gwyllim, Jack
Lawrence of Arabia
A Man For All Seasons

H

Hackett, Buddy
It's a Mad Mad Mad Mad World

Hackman, Gene
A Bridge Too Far
The Poseidon Adventure
Reds
Superman
Unforgiven
Young Frankenstein

Hageb, Fijad
Ishtar

Hagerty, Julie
Airplane!

Hagman, Larry
Nixon
Superman

Hagney, Frank
It's a Wonderful Life

Hairston, Jester
The Alamo

Hale, Alan
The Adventures of Robin Hood
The Crusades
The Four Horsemen of the Apoc-
alypse
The Last Days of Pompeii
The Sea Hawk

Hale, Creighton
Orphans of the Storm

Hale, Richard
Julius Caesar

Haley, Jack
The Wizard of Oz

Hall, Albert
Apocalypse Now

Hall, Jerry
Batman

Hall, Juanita
South Pacific

Hall, Michael
The Best Years of Our Lives

Hall, Porter
Once Upon a Time in the West

Hallam, John
Antony and Cleopatra

Halton, Charles
The Best Years of Our Lives
It's a Wonderful Life

Hamill, Mark
The Empire Strikes Back
Return of the Jedi
Star Wars

Hamilton, George
The Victors

Hamilton, Margaret
The Wizard of Oz

Hamilton, Murray
Jaws

Hamilton, Suzanna
Out of Africa

Hammond, Nicholas
The Sound of Music

Hammond, Raushan
Hook

Hampden, Walter
The Hunchback of Notre Dame

Han, Lei
Farewell My Concubine

Han, Maggie
The Last Emperor

Handl, Irene
The Private Life of Sherlock
Holmes

Hanks, Tom
Saving Private Ryan

Hannah, Daryl
Blade Runner

Hannen, Nicholas
Quo Vadis?

Hanrahan, Bill
Raging Bull

Hansard, Paul
The Private Life of Sherlock
Holmes

Harada, Mieko
Ran

Harding, Vincent
Far From the Madding Crowd

Hardwick, Paul
Romeo and Juliet

Hardwicke, Cedric
Around the World in 80 Days
The Hunchback of Notre Dame
The Ten Commandments

Hardy, Gene
The Bridges at Toko-Ri

Hardy, Sam
King Kong

Hare, Lumsden
The Crusades
Gunga Din
The Lives of a Bengal Lancer

Harlan, Kenneth
The Poseidon Adventure

Harlowe, Peter
Gandhi

Harper, Jessica
Love and Death

Harper, Kate
Batman

Harper, Paul
The Wild Bunch

Harper, Robert
Once Upon a Time in America

Harper, Tess
Ishtar

Harris, Barbara
Nashville

Harris, Ed
Nixon
The Right Stuff

Harris, Heath
Gallipoli

Harris, Jared
Far and Away

Harris, Leon
Contact

Harris, Richard
The Bible
The Guns of Navarone
Unforgiven

Harris, Robert H.
America America

Harris, Rosemary
Hamlet

Harris, Rossie
Airplane!

Harrison, Linda
Planet of the Apes

Harrison, Rex
Cleopatra

Harrison, Simon
The Wind and the Lion

Harron, Robert
The Birth of a Nation

Intolerance

Hartman, Phil
Pee-Wee's Big Adventure

Hartmann, Sadakichi
The Thief of Bagdad

Harvey, Laurence
The Alamo

Harvey, Paul
Once Upon a Time in the West

Hasson, Jamiel
Gunga Din

Hastings, Bob
The Poseidon Adventure

Hathwell, Carl
The Story of Adele H.

Hatosy, Shawn Wayne
The Postman

Hattagidi, Rohini
Gandhi

Hauer, Rutger
Blade Runner

Hausner, Jerry
Paths of Glory

Havers, Nigel
Empire of the Sun

Hawkins, Jack
The Bridge on the River Kwai
Lawrence of Arabia

Hawkins, Ronnie
Heaven's Gate

Haworth, Jill
Exodus

Hayakawa, Sessue
The Bridge on the River Kwai

Hayden, James
Once Upon a Time in America

Hayden, Sterling
Dr. Strangelove, or: How I
    Learned to Stop Worrying
    and Love the Bomb
The Godfather
1900

Haydn, Richard
The Sound of Music
Young Frankenstein

Hayes, Frank
Greed

Hayes, George "Gabby"
Once Upon a Time in the West

Hayman, David
Rob Roy

Hays, Robert
Airplane!

Hayward, David
Nashville

Hayward, Susan
Beau Geste
The Conqueror

Healy, Ted
The Poseidon Adventure

Heathcote, Thomas
A Man For All Seasons

Hedaya, Dan
Nixon

Hedenbratt, Sonya
Fanny and Alexander

Hedren, Tippi
The Birds

Heflin, Van
The Greatest Story Ever Told

Hellman, Irving
Pee-Wee's Big Adventure

Helm, Levon
The Right Stuff

Helmond, Katherine
The Hindenburg

Helpmann, Robert
55 Days at Peking
Henry V

Hemsley, Estelle
America America

Henabery, Joseph
The Birth of a Nation

Henderson, Shirley
Rob Roy

Henin, Georges
Napoleon

Henkel, Anna
1900

Henley, Drewe
Star Wars

Henn, Carrie
Aliens

Henriksen, Lance
Aliens
Close Encounters of the Third
    Kind
The Right Stuff

Henry, Jean
Napoleon

Hepburn, Katharine
Long Day's Journey into Night

Herbert, Emmanuel
Reds

Herbert, Holmes
The Adventures of Robin Hood
The Charge of the Light Brigade

Herbert, Percy
The Bridge on the River Kwai

Herbert, Sidney
Orphans of the Storm

Heriat, Philippe
Napoleon

Herman, Jimmy
Dances With Wolves

Hern, Pepe
The Magnificent Seven

Herrmann, Edward
Nixon
Reds

Hershey, Barbara
The Right Stuff

Hersholt, Jean
The Four Horsemen of the Apoc-
    alypse
Greed

Herzinger, Charles
Once Upon a Time in the West

Heston, Charlton
Antony and Cleopatra
The Big Country
55 Days at Peking
The Greatest Show on Earth
The Greatest Story Ever Told
Hamlet
Planet of the Apes
The Ten Commandments
The Three Musketeers

Heston, Fraser
The Ten Commandments

Hey, Virginia
The Road Warrior

Heylan, Syd
The Road Warrior

Heywood, John
The Lighthorsemen

Heywood, Pat
Romeo and Juliet

Hickey, William
Little Big Man

Hidalgo, Maria Lujan
Evita

Hidari, Bokuzen
Seven Samurai

Higgins, Anthony
Raiders of the Lost Ark

Hill, Benny
Those Magnificent Men in Their
    Flying Machines, or How I
    Flew from London to Paris
    in 25 Hours and 11 Minutes

Hill, Bernard
Titanic

Hill, Ramsay
The Crusades

Hiller, Colette
Aliens

Hiller, Wendy
A Man For All Seasons

Hillie, Verna
Duck Soup

Hillman, Ty
The Horse Whisperer

Hinds, Ciaran
Excalibur

Hinds, Samuel S.
It's a Wonderful Life

Hingle, Pat
Batman

Hinwood, Peter
The Rocky Horror Picture Show

Hittscher, Paul
Fitzcarraldo

Hobbes, Halliwell
The Sea Hawk

Hoenig, Heinz
Das Boot

Hoffman, Dustin
Hook
Ishtar
Little Big Man

Hoffman, Gaby
Field of Dreams

Hohl, Arthur
Cleopatra

Holbrook, Walter
The Charge of the Light Brigade

Holden, Fay
Samson and Delilah

Holden, William
The Bridge on the River Kwai
The Bridges at Toko-Ri
The Towering Inferno
The Wild Bunch

Holliman, Earl
The Bridges at Toko-Ri
Giant

Hollis, John
The Empire Strikes Back

Holloway, Stanley
The Private Life of Sherlock
    Holmes

Holloway, Sterling
It's a Mad Mad Mad Mad World

Holm, Ian
Alien
Henry V

Holman, Harry
It's a Wonderful Life

Holmes, Maynard
The Magnificent Ambersons

Holmes, Stuart
The Four Horsemen of the Apoc-
    alypse

Holst, Svea
Fanny and Alexander

Holt, David
The Last Days of Pompeii

Holt, Jack
The Poseidon Adventure

Holt, Patrick
Ivanhoe

Holt, Tim
The Magnificent Ambersons
Stagecoach

Holton, Mark
Pee-Wee's Big Adventure

Homma, Fumiko
Seven Samurai

Hong, James
Blade Runner

Hootkins, William
Batman
Raiders of the Lost Ark

Hope, Bob
The Greatest Show on Earth

Hope, William
Aliens

Hopkins, Anthony
A Bridge Too Far
Legends of the Fall
Nixon

Hopkins, Bo
The Wild Bunch

Hopkins, Harold
Gallipoli

Hopper, Dennis
Apocalypse Now
Giant
Waterworld

Hordern, Michael
Alexander the Great
Cleopatra

Horne, Geoffrey
The Bridge on the River Kwai

Horton, Edward Everett
It's a Mad Mad Mad Mad World
Lost Horizon

Horton, Helen
Alien

Hoskins, Bob
Hook
Nixon

Howard, Clint
Far and Away

Howard, John
Lost Horizon

Howard, Leslie
Gone With The Wind

Howard, Rance
Far and Away

Howard, Trevor
Around the World in 80 Days
Battle of Britain
Gandhi
Ryan's Daughter
Superman

Howell, Tom
E. T. The Extra-Terrestrial

Hoyt, John
Cleopatra
The Conqueror

Hsieh, Warren
South Pacific

Hubbell, Ann
Star!

Huber, Harold
The Poseidon Adventure

Hudson, Rock
Giant

Hughes, Robin
Star!

Hulce, Tom
The Hunchback of Notre Dame

Humphrey, Harry
The Magnificent Ambersons

Hunt, Linda
Dune

Hunter, Ian
The Adventures of Robin Hood

Hunter, Jeffrey
A Guide for the Married Man
The Longest Day

Hunter, Kenneth
The Adventures of Robin Hood

Hunter, Kim
Planet of the Apes

Huntley, G.P.
Beau Geste
The Charge of the Light Brigade

Huppert, Isabelle
Heaven's Gate

Hurst, Brandon
The Thief of Bagdad

Hurst, Ryan
The Postman

Hurt, John
Alien
Contact
Heaven's Gate
A Man For All Seasons

Kemmerling, Warren J.
Close Encounters of the Third
  Kind

Kempson, Rachel
Out of Africa

Kennedy, Arthur
Cheyenne Autumn
Lawrence of Arabia

Kennedy, Edgar
Duck Soup
The Poseidon Adventure

Kennedy, George
Shenandoah

Kennedy, Jihmi
Glory

Keogh, Des
Ryan's Daughter

Keogh, Jimmy
Far and Away

Kerensky, Oleg
Reds

Kerr, Bill
Gallipoli
The Lighthorsemen

Kerr, Deborah
From Here to Eternity
Julius Caesar
The King and I
Quo Vadis?

Kerr, John
South Pacific

Keyes, Evelyn
Around the World in 80 Days
Gone With The Wind

Khambatta, Persis
Star Trek: The Motion Picture

Kidder, Margot
Superman

Kidman, Nicole
Far and Away

Kim, Jacqui
Star Trek Generations

Kimbrough, Charles
The Hunchback of Notre Dame

Kimura, Ko
Seven Samurai

King, Larry
Contact

King, Leslie
Orphans of the Storm

King, Morgana
The Godfather

King, Wright
Planet of the Apes

Kinghorne, Sally
Monty Python and the Holy Grail

Kingsbury, Craig
Jaws

Kingsley, Ben
Gandhi
Schindler's List

Kinnear, Roy
The Three Musketeers

Kinnell, Murray
The Last Days of Pompeii

Kinney, Terry
The Last of the Mohicans

Kinskey, Leonid
Duck Soup

Kinski, Klaus
Aguirre, the Wrath of God
Doctor Zhivago
Fitzcarraldo

Kirby, Bruno
The Godfather, Part II

Kitchen, Michael
Out of Africa

Klaus, Henry
The Four Horsemen of the Apocalypse

Kline, Kevin
The Hunchback of Notre Dame

Knight, Esmond
Henry V

Knight, Fuzzy
Once Upon a Time in the West

Knight, Wayne
Jurassic Park

Knotts, Don
It's a Mad Mad Mad Mad World

Knowles, Patric
The Adventures of Robin Hood
The Charge of the Light Brigade

Knox, Mickey
White Heat

Kodama, Kenji
Ran

Kodo, Kuninori
Seven Samurai

Koenig, Walter
Star Trek Generations
Star Trek: The Motion Picture

Kohlmar, Lee
Orphans of the Storm

Kohut, Walter
A Bridge Too Far

Kolker, Henry
The Last Days of Pompeii

Kopache, Thomas
Star Trek Generations

Korsmo, Charlie
Hook

Kosinski, Jerzy
Reds

Koslo, Paul
Heaven's Gate

Kosugi, Yoshio
Seven Samurai

Kotto, Yaphet
Alien

Koubitzky, Alexandre
Napoleon

Kraisman, Gabriel
Evita

Kramer, Jeffrey
Jaws

Krape, Evelyn
Babe

Krauss, Henry
Napoleon

Kretschmann, Thomas
Queen Margot

Krimer, Harry
Napoleon

Kristofferson, Kris
Heaven's Gate

Kroll, Abe
Ishtar

Kroll, Hanna
Ishtar

Kruger, Otto
High Noon

Kulle, Jarl
Fanny and Alexander

Kumagai, Jiro
Seven Samurai

Kuss, Richard
The Deer Hunter

L

La Rocque, Rod
The Hunchback of Notre Dame

La Verne, Lucille
Orphans of the Storm

Labow, Hilary
The Rocky Horror Picture Show

Lacey, Catherine
The Private Life of Sherlock
  Holmes

Lacey, Ronald
Raiders of the Lost Ark

Ladd, Alan
Citizen Kane

Laffan, Patricia
Quo Vadis?

Lagutin, I.
Alexander Nevsky

Lahr, Bert
The Wizard of Oz

Lamarr, Hedy
Samson and Delilah

Lamb, Peadar
Far and Away

Lambert, Paul
Planet of the Apes

Lamour, Dorothy
The Greatest Show on Earth

Lampin, Georges
Napoleon

Lancaster, Burt
Field of Dreams
From Here to Eternity
1900

Landau, Martin
The Greatest Story Ever Told

Landis, Jeanette
Star!

Landis, Monte
Pee-Wee's Big Adventure

Lane, Charles
It's a Mad Mad Mad Mad World

Langdon, Lillian
Intolerance

Langdon, Sue Ane
A Guide for the Married Man

Lange, Jessica
Rob Roy

Lansbury, Angela
The Court Jester
The Greatest Story Ever Told
Samson and Delilah

Lapotaire, Jane
Antony and Cleopatra

Larbi, Doghmi
The Man Who Would Be King

Laretei, Kabi
Fanny and Alexander

Larkin, James
Henry V

Larking, John
The Lighthorsemen

LaSardo, Robert
Waterworld

Latimore, Frank
Patton

Laughlin, Tom
South Pacific

Laughton, Charles
The Hunchback of Notre Dame
Moby Dick
Spartacus

Laurie, John
Henry V

Lavarre, Louis
Cyrano de Bergerac

Lawford, Peter
Exodus
The Longest Day

Lawlor, Sean
Braveheart

Lawrence, Barbara
The King and I

Lawrence, Lynley
Star!

Lawrence, W.E.
Intolerance

Lazareff, Serge
The Lighthorsemen

Mesurier, John Le
Those Magnificent Men in Their
    Flying Machines, or How I
    Flew from London to Paris
    in 25 Hours and 11 Minutes

Leachman, Cloris
Butch Cassidy and the Sun-
    dance Kid
Young Frankenstein

Leah, Petra
The Rocky Horror Picture Show

Ledebur, Frederick
Alexander the Great
Moby Dick

Leder, Erwin
Das Boot

Ledger, Peggy
The Rocky Horror Picture Show

Lee, Candace
South Pacific

Lee, Christopher
The Private Life of Sherlock
    Holmes
The Three Musketeers

Lee, Duke
Stagecoach

Lee, Etta
The Thief of Bagdad

Lee, Jennie
The Birth of a Nation

Lee, Mark
Gallipoli

Lee, Ronreaco
Glory

Leggatt, Alison
Far From the Madding Crowd

Leiber, Fritz
The Hunchback of Notre Dame

Leigh, Vivien
Gone With The Wind

Leitch, Donovan
Glory

LeMassena, William
Carousel

Lemmon, Jack
The Great Race
Hamlet

Lenard, Mark
Star Trek: The Motion Picture

Lennie, Angus
The Great Escape

Leno, Jay
Contact

Leonard, David
The Robe

Leonard, Sheldon
It's a Wonderful Life

Leone, Sergio
Once Upon a Time in America

Leslie, Joan
Yankee Doodle Dandy

Lester, Mark
Oliver!

Letizia, Jodi
Rocky

Leursse, Jean-Pierre
The Story of Adele H.

Leventon, Annabel
The Rocky Horror Picture Show

Leverington, Shelby
The Long Riders

Levine, Isaac Don
Reds

Levy, Shmulik
Schindler's List

Lewgoy, Jose
Fitzcarraldo

Lewis, Diana
Rocky

Lewis, Garrett
Star!

Lewis, Geoffrey
Heaven's Gate
The Wind and the Lion

Lewis, Mitchell
The Wizard of Oz

Lewis, Ralph
The Birth of a Nation
Intolerance

Lewis, Sheldon
Orphans of the Storm

Lewis, Sylvia
The Conqueror

Lewis, Vera
Intolerance
King Kong

Leyton, John
The Great Escape

Li, Gong
Farewell My Concubine

Lieven, Albert
The Guns of Navarone

Ligon, Tom
Paint Your Wagon

Lillie, Beatrice
Around the World in 80 Days

Linn, Bambi
The King and I

Linn, Rex
The Postman

Liotta, Ray
Field of Dreams

Lipton, Peggy
The Postman

Lisi, Virna
Queen Margot

Lister, Francis
Moby Dick

Little, Michele
White Heat

Littman, Julian
Evita

Livanov, Boris
October

Livingston, Jock
Star!

Livingston, Paul
Babe

Lo Bianco, Tony
Nixon

Lockhart, Gene
Carousel

Lockwood, Gary
2001: A Space Odyssey

Lodge, John
The Scarlet Empress

Loggia, Robert
The Greatest Story Ever Told
Scarface

Loline, Nicolas
Napoleon

Lom, Herbert
Spartacus

Lombard, Karina
Legends of the Fall

London, Damian
Star!

Lone, John
The Last Emperor

Loo, Richard
The Conqueror

Lorre, Peter
Around the World in 80 Days

Losee, Frank
Orphans of the Storm

Louise, Madame
The Story of Adele H.

Love, Bessie
Reds

Love, Montagu
The Adventures of Robin Hood
The Crusades
Gunga Din
The Sea Hawk

Lovell, Dyson
Romeo and Juliet

Lovell, Roderick
Ivanhoe

Low, Chuck
The Mission

Lowe, Rob
Contact

Loy, Myrna
The Best Years of Our Lives

Lucantoni, Alberto
The Bible

Luckey, Susan
Carousel

Luckham, Cyril
A Man For All Seasons

Ludwig, Salem
America America

Luft, Krysztof
Schindler's List

Lukas, Paul
55 Days at Peking

Luke, Keye
Around the World in 80 Days

Lundigan, William
The Sea Hawk

Lunghi, Cherie
Excalibur
The Mission

Luske, Tommy
Peter Pan

Lutter III, Alfred
Love and Death

Lynley, Carol
The Poseidon Adventure

Lyovshin, Alexander
The Battleship Potemkin

M

MacDonald, Ian
High Noon
White Heat

MacDonald, Jeanette
The Poseidon Adventure

MacGinnis, Niall
Alexander the Great
Henry V

Mack, Hughie
Greed

MacLachlan, Kyle
Dune

MacLaine, Shirley
Around the World in 80 Days

MacLaren, Ian
Cleopatra

MacNaughton, Robert
E. T. The Extra-Terrestrial

Macola, Beatrice
Schindler's List

Macollum, Barry
Beau Geste

Macquarrie, George
Duck Soup

MacRae, Gordon
Carousel
The King and I

Macready, George
The Great Race
Julius Caesar
Paths of Glory
Tora! Tora! Tora!

Madden, Peter
The Private Life of Sherlock
    Holmes

Madigan, Amy
Field of Dreams

Madonna
Evita

Maggio, Pupella
The Bible

Mahashi, Tatsuya
Tora! Tora! Tora!

Mahon, Kevin
Raging Bull

Maim, Mona
Fanny and Alexander

Majorino, Tina
Waterworld

Malden, Karl
Cheyenne Autumn
Patton

Malet, Arthur
Hook

Malikyan, Kevork
Indiana Jones and the Last Crusade

Malkovich, John
Empire of the Sun

Malmsjo, Jan
Fanny and Alexander

Maloney, Michael
Hamlet
Henry V

Mamakos, Peter
The Conqueror

Mamo
Moby Dick

Mancini, Claudio
Once Upon a Time in the West

Manes, Gina
Napoleon

Mann, Danny
Babe

Mann, Paul
America America

Manning, Irene
Yankee Doodle Dandy

Mansfield, Jayne
A Guide for the Married Man

Marais, Jean
Beauty and the Beast

Marceau, Sophie
Braveheart

March, Elspeth
Quo Vadis?

March, Fredric
Alexander the Great
The Best Years of Our Lives
The Bridges at Toko-Ri

March, Hal
A Guide for the Married Man

Margo,
Lost Horizon

Margolyes, Miriam
Babe

Margulies, David
Ishtar

Marie, Francois
Cyrano de Bergerac

Marion-Crawford, Howard
Lawrence of Arabia

Marion, Madeleine
Cyrano de Bergerac

Marley, J. Peverell
The Greatest Show on Earth

Marley, John
America America
The Godfather

Marriott, Sylvia
The Story of Adele H.

Mars, Kenneth
Butch Cassidy and the Sundance Kid
Young Frankenstein

Marsh, Jean
Cleopatra

Marsh, Linda
America America

Marsh, Mae
The Birth of a Nation
Intolerance

Marshal, Alan
The Hunchback of Notre Dame

Marshall, Bob
Nixon

Marshall, Brenda
The Sea Hawk

Marshall, E.G.
Nixon
Tora! Tora! Tora!

Marshall, Zena
Those Magnificent Men in Their Flying Machines, or How I Flew from London to Paris in 25 Hours and 11 Minutes

Marstini, Rosita
The Big Parade

Martel, K.C.
E.T. The Extra-Terrestrial

Martin, Damon
Pee-Wee's Big Adventure

Martin, Gilbert
Rob Roy

Martin, Lewis
The Court Jester

Martin, Pamela Sue
The Poseidon Adventure

Martin, Roger
The Story of Adele H.

Martin, Ross
The Great Race

Martin, Strother
Butch Cassidy and the Sundance Kid
The Wild Bunch

Martini, Max
Saving Private Ryan

Martino, Al
The Godfather

Marvin, Lee
Paint Your Wagon

Marx, Chico
Duck Soup

Marx, Groucho
Duck Soup

Marx, Harpo
Duck Soup

Marx, Zeppo
Duck Soup

Mason, James
Julius Caesar

Mason, Louis
Stagecoach

Massey, Daniel
Star!

Masson, Vicki
Rob Roy

Masterson, Mary Stuart
The Postman

Mastrantonio, Mary Elizabeth
Scarface

Masur, Richard
Heaven's Gate

Matheson, Karen
Rob Roy

Matheson, Murray
Star!

Mathews, Sheila
The Towering Inferno

Matsui, Norio
Ran

Matthau, Walter
A Guide for the Married Man

Matthews, Al
Aliens

Matthews, Lester
Star!

Mature, Victor
The Robe
Samson and Delilah

Maureen, Mollie
The Private Life of Sherlock Holmes

Maxudian, Max
Napoleon

Maxwell, Edwin
Cleopatra
Duck Soup

Maxwell, Paul
A Bridge Too Far
Indiana Jones and the Last Crusade

Maxwell, Roberta
The Postman

May, Jack
The Man Who Would Be King

May, Jodhi
The Last of the Mohicans

May, Martin
Das Boot

Mayer, Arthur
Reds

Mayhew, Peter
The Empire Strikes Back
Return of the Jedi
Star Wars

Mayo, Virginia
The Best Years of Our Lives
White Heat

Mazer, Bill
Raging Bull

Mazurki, Mike
Around the World in 80 Days
It's a Mad Mad Mad Mad World
Samson and Delilah

Mazurki, Mike
Cheyenne Autumn

Mazzello, Joseph
Jurassic Park

McAnally, Ray
The Mission

McArthur, Brian
Rob Roy

McCallum, David
The Great Escape
A Night to Remember

McCambridge, Mercedes
Giant

McCardie, Brian
Rob Roy

McClure, Doug
Shenandoah
South Pacific

McClure, Marc
Superman

McConaughey, Matthew
Contact

McCormack, Catherine
Braveheart

McCowen, Alec
Henry V

A Night to Remember

McCrindle, Alex
Star Wars

McDaniel, Hattie
Gone With The Wind

McDevitt, Ruth
The Birds

McDiarmid, Ian
Return of the Jedi

McDonald, Francis J.
Samson and Delilah

McDonald, Jack
Greed

McDonnell, Mary
Dances With Wolves

McDowall, Roddy
Cleopatra
The Greatest Story Ever Told
The Longest Day
Planet of the Apes
The Poseidon Adventure

McDowell, Claire
The Big Parade

McDowell, Malcolm
Star Trek Generations

McElhinney, Ian
Hamlet

McEnery, John
Romeo and Juliet

McEwan, Geraldine
Henry V

McFadden, Gates
Star Trek Generations

McFadyen, Angus
Braveheart

McFadyen, Myra
Rob Roy

McGinley, John C.
Platoon

McGinley, Sean
Braveheart

McGlynn, Sr., Frank
Once Upon a Time in the West

McGoohan, Patrick
Braveheart

McGovern, Barry
Far and Away

McGovern, Elizabeth
Once Upon a Time in America

McGraw, Charles
The Birds
The Bridges at Toko-Ri
It's a Mad Mad Mad Mad World
Spartacus

McGuire, Bruce
Batman

McGuire, Dorothy
The Greatest Story Ever Told

McGuire, Tucker
A Night to Remember

McIntire, Tim
Shenandoah

McIntyre, Leila
Once Upon a Time in the West

McKenna, Siobhan
Doctor Zhivago

McKenzie, Tim
Gallipoli
The Lighthorsemen

McKern, Leo
A Man For All Seasons
Ryan's Daughter

McLaglen, Victor
Around the World in 80 Days
Gunga Din

McLarty, Ron
The Postman

McMillan, Kenneth
Dune

McMullan, James
Shenandoah

McNamara, J. Patrick
Close Encounters of the Third Kind

McQueen, Butterfly
Gone With The Wind

McQueen, Steve
The Great Escape
The Magnificent Seven
The Towering Inferno

McShane, Ian
Battle of Britain

McWade, Robert
Cimarron

Meaney, Colm
Far and Away
The Last of the Mohicans

Means, Russell
The Last of the Mohicans

Meatloaf
The Rocky Horror Picture Show

Meek, Donald
Stagecoach

Meeker, Ralph
Paths of Glory

Mello, Jay
Jaws

Memmoli, George
Rocky

Morier-Genoud, Phillippe
Cyrano de Bergerac

Morley, Robert
Around the World in 80 Days
Those Magnificent Men in Their
    Flying Machines, or How I
    Flew from London to Paris
    in 25 Hours and 11 Minutes

Morris, Wayne
Paths of Glory

Morrow, Jeff
The Robe

Morse, Robert
A Guide for the Married Man

Moschin, Gastone
The Godfather, Part II

Moses, Albert
The Man Who Would Be King

Moses, Mark
Platoon

Motiva
Moby Dick

Mount, Peggy
Oliver!

Mowbray, Alan
The King and I

Moya, Alejandro
The Mission

Moya, Bercelio
The Mission

Mucci, David
Unforgiven

Mudie, Leonard
Cleopatra

Mulholland, Mark
Far and Away

Mullavy, Greg
The Hindenburg

Mulligan, Richard
Little Big Man

Munch, Richard
Patton

Mundin, Herbert
The Adventures of Robin Hood
Moby Dick

Munson, Ona
Gone With The Wind

Murphy, Gerard
Once Upon a Time in America
Waterworld

Murphy, Maurice
The Crusades

Murphy, Michael
Nashville

Murphy, Wesley
Far and Away

Murrow, Edward R.
Around the World in 80 Days

Murtagh, John
Rob Roy

Myrtil, Odette
Yankee Doodle Dandy

N

Nail, Jimmy
Evita

Naish, J. Carrol
Beau Geste
The Charge of the Light Brigade
The Lives of a Bengal Lancer

Nakadai, Tatsuya
Ran
Yojimbo

Nambu, K.
The Thief of Bagdad

Napier, Alan
The Court Jester
Julius Caesar

Nascimento, Milton
Fitzcarraldo

Nathan, Adele
Reds

Natwick, Mildred
The Court Jester

Nazvanov, Mikhail
Ivan the Terrible, Part I and II

Nearing, Scott
Reds

Neeson, Liam
Excalibur
The Mission
Rob Roy
Schindler's List

Nehring, Harry
Schindler's List

Neidorf, David
Empire of the Sun
Platoon

Neil, Hildegard
Antony and Cleopatra

Neill, Noel
Superman

Neill, Sam
The Horse Whisperer
Jurassic Park

Nelson, Gene
The King and I

Nelson, Sandy
Braveheart

Nero, Franco
The Bible

Newman, Paul
Butch Cassidy and the Sun-
    dance Kid
Exodus
The Towering Inferno

Newson, Jeremy
The Rocky Horror Picture Show

Newton, Robert
Around the World in 80 Days
Henry V

Nezu, Jinpachi
Ran

Nicholls, Anthony
A Man For All Seasons

Nichols, Allan
Nashville

Nichols, Nichelle
Star Trek: The Motion Picture

Nichols, Robert
Giant

Nicholson, Jack
Batman
Reds

Nielsen, Leslie
Airplane!
The Poseidon Adventure

Nikandrov, Vasili
October

Nilsson, Kjell
The Road Warrior

Nimoy, Leonard
Star Trek: The Motion Picture

Nishimura, Ko
Yojimbo

Niven, David
Around the World in 80 Days
The Charge of the Light Brigade
55 Days at Peking
The Guns of Navarone

Nixon, Marni
The Sound of Music

Noble, Robert
The Adventures of Robin Hood

Nolan, Jeanette
The Horse Whisperer

Nomura, Takeshi
Ran

North, Alan
Glory

North, John Ringling
The Greatest Show on Earth

Saving Private Ryan

Preston, Joshua
Nixon

Preston, Michael
The Road Warrior

Preston, Robert
Beau Geste

Price, Vincent
The Ten Commandments

Prochnow, Juergen
Das Boot
Dune
The English Patient

Prosky, Robert
Far and Away

Provine, Dorothy
The Great Race
It's a Mad Mad Mad Mad World

Prowse, David
The Empire Strikes Back
Return of the Jedi
Star Wars

Pryce, Jonathan
Evita

Pudovkin, Vsevolod
Ivan the Terrible, Part I and II

Purcell, Noel
Moby Dick

Puri, Amrish
Gandhi

Purvis, Jack
The Empire Strikes Back
Star Wars

Pyke, Hy
Blade Runner

Pyle, Denver
The Alamo
The Great Race
Shenandoah

Q

Qi, Lu
Farewell My Concubine

Quaid, Dennis
The Long Riders
The Right Stuff

Quaid, Randy
The Long Riders

Qualen, John
Cheyenne Autumn
The Grapes of Wrath
Red River

Quayle, Anthony
The Guns of Navarone

Lawrence of Arabia

Quillan, Eddie
The Grapes of Wrath
Moby Dick

Quinn, Aidan
Legends of the Fall
The Mission

Quinn, Anthony
The Guns of Navarone
Lawrence of Arabia

Quinn, Francesco
Platoon

Quinn, Patricia
The Rocky Horror Picture Show

R

Raft, George
Around the World in 80 Days

Raftis, Louis
Raging Bull

Rain, Douglas
2001: A Space Odyssey

Raines, Christina
Nashville

Rainey, Ford
White Heat

Rains, Claude
The Adventures of Robin Hood
The Greatest Story Ever Told
Lawrence of Arabia
The Sea Hawk

Ralph, Jessie
The Poseidon Adventure

Ramsay, Melanie
Hamlet

Ramsen, Bert
Nashville

Ransome, Prunella
Far From the Madding Crowd

Rapp, Larry
Once Upon a Time in America

Rassam, Julien
Queen Margot

Rathbone, Basil
The Adventures of Robin Hood
The Court Jester
The Last Days of Pompeii

Ratoff, Gregory
Exodus

Ratzenburger, John
A Bridge Too Far

Rauch, Siegfried
Patton

Ravenscroft, Christopher
Henry V

Rawlinson, Brian
Far From the Madding Crowd

Rebello, Chris
Jaws

Redeker, Quinn K.
The Deer Hunter

Redford, Robert
A Bridge Too Far
Butch Cassidy and the Sun-
    dance Kid
The Horse Whisperer
Out of Africa

Redgrave, Corin
A Man For All Seasons

Redgrave, Michael
Battle of Britain

Reed, Donna
From Here to Eternity
It's a Wonderful Life

Reed, Oliver
Oliver!
The Three Musketeers

Reed, Pamela
The Long Riders
The Right Stuff

Reed, Rex
Superman

Reed, Robert
Star!

Reed, Tracy
Dr. Strangelove, or: How I
    Learned to Stop Worrying
    and Love the Bomb

Reeve, Christopher
Superman

Reeves, George
From Here to Eternity
Samson and Delilah

Regas, George
The Charge of the Light Brigade

Reicher, Frank
King Kong

Reid, Beryl
Star!

Reid, Wallace
The Birth of a Nation

Reimbold, Bill
Raiders of the Lost Ark

Reiner, Carl
A Guide for the Married Man
It's a Mad Mad Mad Mad World

Reiser, Paul
Aliens

Remar, James
The Long Riders

Rennie, Michael
The Robe

Repnikova
The Battleship Potemkin

Repo-Martell, Liisa
Unforgiven

Repulles, Alejandro
Aguirre, the Wrath of God

Reubens, Paul
Pee-Wee's Big Adventure

Revill, Clive
The Private Life of Sherlock
    Holmes

Rey, Fernando
Antony and Cleopatra

Rhodes, Donnelly
Butch Cassidy and the Sun-
    dance Kid

Rhys-Davies, John
Indiana Jones and the Last Cru-
    sade
Raiders of the Lost Ark

Ribisi, Giovanni
The Postman
Saving Private Ryan

Ricciardi, William
The Poseidon Adventure

Rice, Justin M.
The Last of the Mohicans

Richard, Emily
Empire of the Sun

Richards, Ariana
Jurassic Park

Richardson, Miranda
Empire of the Sun

Richardson, Ralph
Battle of Britain
Doctor Zhivago
Exodus
Long Day's Journey into Night

Richter, Daniel
2001: A Space Odyssey

Richter, Ralph
Das Boot

Riehle, Richard
Glory

Rietty, Robert
The Bible

Rimmer, Shane
Dr. Strangelove, or: How I
    Learned to Stop Worrying
    and Love the Bomb
Out of Africa

Rimoux, Alain
Cyrano de Bergerac

Rivas, Carlos
The King and I

Rivera, Cecilia
Aguirre, the Wrath of God

Rivera, Geraldo
Contact

Rizzo, Giacomo
1900

Roach, Bert
The Poseidon Adventure

Robards, Jason
Long Day's Journey into Night
Once Upon a Time in the West
Tora! Tora! Tora!

Roberts, Julia
Hook

Robertson, Andrew
Far From the Madding Crowd

Robinson, Bruce
Romeo and Juliet
The Story of Adele H.

Robinson, Charles
Shenandoah

Robinson, Edward G.
Cheyenne Autumn
The Ten Commandments

Robinson, James
Braveheart

Robinson, Jay
The Robe

Robson, Flora
55 Days at Peking
The Sea Hawk
Those Magnificent Men in Their
    Flying Machines, or How I
    Flew from London to Paris
    in 25 Hours and 11 Minutes

Roby, George
Henry V

Rocket, Charles
Dances With Wolves

Rockland, Jeffrey
Doctor Zhivago

Roddy, Drew
The Magnificent Ambersons

Roeves, Maurice
The Last of the Mohicans

Rogers, Dinah Ann
Star!

Rojo, Gustavo
Alexander the Great

Rojo, Helena
Aguirre, the Wrath of God

Rojo, Ruben
Alexander the Great

Roland, Edward
Aguirre, the Wrath of God

Roland, Gilbert
Around the World in 80 Days
Cheyenne Autumn
The Sea Hawk

Rolla, Philippe
Napoleon

Rolston, Mark
Aliens

Romero, Cesar
Around the World in 80 Days

Rondell, Ronald R.
Beau Geste

Rooney, Mickey
The Bridges at Toko-Ri
It's a Mad Mad Mad Mad World

Rose, Christine
Ishtar

Rose, William L.
Fitzcarraldo

Roskilly, Charles
Batman

Ross, Katharine
Butch Cassidy and the Sun-
    dance Kid
Shenandoah

Ross, Ricco
Aliens

Ross, Shirley
The Poseidon Adventure

Rossi-Drago, Eleonora
The Bible

Rossiter, Leonard
2001: A Space Odyssey
Oliver!

Rostom, Hichem
The English Patient

Roth, Tim
Rob Roy

Roudenko, Wladmir
Napoleon

Rounsevile, Robert
Carousel

Rourke, Mickey
Heaven's Gate

Rozakis, Gregory
America America

Rozsa, Miklos
The Private Life of Sherlock
    Holmes

Rub, Christian
Pinocchio

Rubinek, Saul
Nixon
Unforgiven

Ruck, Alan
Star Trek Generations

Ruddock, John
Quo Vadis?

Rudley, Herbert
The Court Jester

Rudolph, Claude-Oliver
Das Boot

Rudolph, Mary
Nixon

Ruick, Barbara
Carousel

Ruspoli, Esmeralda
Romeo and Juliet

Russek, Jorge
The Wild Bunch

Russell, Byron
Moby Dick

Russell, Dora
Reds

Russell, Harold
The Best Years of Our Lives

Russo, Giaani
The Godfather

Russo, James
The Postman

Rutherford, Ann
Gone With The Wind

Ryan, Joseph R.
Field of Dreams

Ryan, Robert
The Longest Day
The Wild Bunch

Ryan, Tim
From Here to Eternity

Ryder, Amy
Once Upon a Time in America

Ryriev, Erik
Ivan the Terrible, Part I and II

Ryu, Daisuke
Ran

Sadoff, Fred
The Poseidon Adventure

Sagalle, Jonathan
Schindler's List

Sagnier, Ludivine
Cyrano de Bergerac

Sainpolis, John
The Four Horsemen of the
    Apocalypse

Saint, Eva Marie
Exodus

St. Clair, Elizabeth
Star!

St. Helier, Ivy
Henry V

St. John, Antoine
The Wind and the Lion

St. John, Betta
The Robe

St. Johns, Adela Rogers
Reds

Sakakida, Keiji
Seven Samurai

Sakall, S.Z.
Yankee Doodle Dandy

Sakamoto, Ryuichi
The Last Emperor

Salazar, Angel
Scarface

Saldana, Theresa
Raging Bull

Salinger, Diane
Pee-Wee's Big Adventure

Sallis, Zoe
The Bible

Sambrell, Aldo
Antony and Cleopatra

Sanborn, Helen
The Charge of the Light Brigade

Sanchez, Jaime
The Wild Bunch

Sanda, Dominique
1900

Sanders, George
Ivanhoe
Samson and Delilah

Sanders, Jay O.
Glory

Sanderson, William
Blade Runner

Sandland, Barbara
Star!

Sandoval, Miguel
Jurassic Park

Sands, Tommy
The Longest Day

Sanford, Erskine
The Best Years of Our Lives
Citizen Kane
The Magnificent Ambersons

Santana, Arnaldo
Scarface

Santaniello, Enzo
Once Upon a Time in the West

Santos, Joe
The Postman

Sarandon, Susan
The Rocky Horror Picture Show

Sarkar, Sam
Legends of the Fall

Saunders, Terry
The King and I

Savage, John
The Deer Hunter

Savalas, Telly
The Greatest Story Ever Told

Sawalha, Nadim
The Wind and the Lion

Sawamura, Ikio
Yojimbo

Sayle, Alexei
Indiana Jones and the Last Cru-
    sade

Sazanka, Kyu
Yojimbo

Scala, Gia
The Guns of Navarone

Scardino, Jack
The Deer Hunter

Scheider, Roy
Jaws

Schell, Maximillian
A Bridge Too Far

Schiaffino, Rosanna
The Victors

Schildkraut, Joseph
Cleopatra
The Crusades
Orphans of the Storm

Schilling, Gus
Citizen Kane
The Magnificent Ambersons

Schneider, Romy
The Victors

Schollin, Christina
Fanny and Alexander

Schwartz, Austin
The Horse Whisperer

Schwartz, Dustin
The Horse Whisperer

Schweig, Eric
The Last of the Mohicans

Schwiers, Ellen
1900

Scofield, Paul
Henry V
A Man For All Seasons

Scorsese, Charles
Raging Bull

Scorsese, Martin
Raging Bull

Scott, Amber
Hook

Scott, Cynthia
Aliens

Scott, George C.
The Bible
Dr. Strangelove, or: How I
   Learned to Stop Worrying
   and Love the Bomb
The Hindenburg
Patton

Scott, Martha
The Ten Commandments

Scott, Timothy
Butch Cassidy and the Sundance Kid

Scott Thomas, Kristin
The English Patient
The Horse Whisperer

Scourby, Alexander
Giant

Seberg, Jean
Paint Your Wagon

Secombe, Harry
Oliver!

Seda, Job
Out of Africa

Sedgwick, Charles
The Charge of the Light Brigade

Segal, George
The Longest Day

Segui, Pierre
The Deer Hunter

Seldes, George
Reds

Sellars, Elizabeth
55 Days at Peking

Sellers, Peter
Dr. Strangelove, or: How I
   Learned to Stop Worrying
   and Love the Bomb

Semmelrogge, Martin
Das Boot

Senda, Koreya
Tora! Tora! Tora!

Serato, Massimo
55 Days at Peking

Serna, Pepe
Scarface

Servilla, Carmen
Antony and Cleopatra

Seth, Roshan
Gandhi

Sevareid, Eric
The Right Stuff

Sewell, Rufus
Hamlet

Seweryn, Andrzej
Schindler's List

Seymour, Anne
Field of Dreams

Seymour, Ralph
Empire of the Sun

Shamsi, Mohammad
The Man Who Would Be King

Shannon, Harry
Citizen Kane

Shannon, Richard
The Bridges at Toko-Ri

Sharif, Omar
Doctor Zhivago
Lawrence of Arabia

Sharif, Tarek
Doctor Zhivago

Shatner, William
Star Trek Generations
Star Trek: The Motion Picture

Shaughnessy, Mickey
From Here to Eternity

Shaw, Bernard
Contact

Shaw, Brinsley
The Four Horsemen of the
   Apocalypse

Shaw, Robert
Battle of Britain
Jaws
A Man For All Seasons

Shawn, Dick
It's a Mad Mad Mad Mad World

Shea, Eric
The Poseidon Adventure

Shea, Gloria
The Last Days of Pompeii

Shean, Al
The Poseidon Adventure

Shearer, Harry
The Right Stuff

Sheen, Charlie
Platoon

Sheen, Martin
Apocalypse Now
Gandhi

Sheldon, Douglas
Ryan's Daughter

Shelton, Marley
Nixon

Shemayne, Steve
Little Big Man

Shenar, Paul
Scarface

Shepard, Sam
The Right Stuff

Shepherd, Simon
Henry V

Shepley, Michael
Henry V

Sherf, Howard
Field of Dreams

Sheybal, Vladek
The Wind and the Lion

Shields, Art
Reds

Shimada, Shoga
Tora! Tora! Tora!

Shimura, Takashi
Seven Samurai
Yojimbo

Shire, Talia
The Godfather
The Godfather, Part II
Rocky

Siegmann, George
The Birth of a Nation

Silvani, Aldo
Rocky

Silvers, Phil
A Guide for the Married Man
It's a Mad Mad Mad Mad World

Sim, Gerald
Ryan's Daughter

Simmons, Floyd
South Pacific

Simmons, James
Henry V

Simmons, Jean
The Big Country
The Robe
Spartacus

Simms, Stephen
Henry V

Simon, S.S.
Greed

Simpson, O.J.
The Towering Inferno

Simpson, Russell
The Grapes of Wrath
The Poseidon Adventure

Warner, H.B.
It's a Wonderful Life
Lost Horizon
The Ten Commandments

Warren, Percy
Moby Dick

Warrender, Harold
Ivanhoe

Warrick, Ruth
Citizen Kane

Warwick, Richard
Romeo and Juliet

Warwick, Virginia
The Four Horsemen of the Apocalypse

Washburn, Bryant
Stagecoach

Washburn, Deric
The Deer Hunter

Washington, Denzel
Glory

Waters, Nick
The Lighthorsemen

Waterston, Sam
Heaven's Gate
Nixon

Watford, Gwen
Cleopatra

Wayne, John
The Alamo
The Conqueror
The Greatest Story Ever Told
The Longest Day
Red River
Stagecoach

Wayne, Patrick
The Alamo
Cheyenne Autumn
Red River
Shenandoah

Weathers, Carl
Rocky

Weaver, Doodles
The Birds

Weaver, Sigourney
Alien
Aliens

Weaving, Hugo
Babe

Webb, Daniel
Henry V

Weber, Jacques
Cyrano de Bergerac

Webster, Byron
The Poseidon Adventure

Weinstone, Will
Reds

Weir, Andrew
Braveheart

Weisser, Norbert
Schindler's List

Welch, Raquel
The Three Musketeers

Weld, Tuesday
Once Upon a Time in America

Welles, Gwen
Nashville

Welles, Orson
Citizen Kane
A Man For All Seasons
Moby Dick

Wells, Marie
The Scarlet Empress

Wells, Vernon
The Road Warrior

Welsh, Kenneth
Legends of the Fall

Wenli, Jiang
Farewell My Concubine

Wennemann, Klaus
Das Boot

West, Rebecca
Reds

Westerfield, James
The Magnificent Ambersons

Westerman, Floyd "Red Crow"
Dances With Wolves

Weston, Jack
Ishtar

Whalen, Sean
Waterworld

Whaley, Frank
Field of Dreams

Whately, Kevin
The English Patient

Whitaker, Forrest
Platoon

White, Dean
The Best Years of Our Lives

White, Jesse
It's a Mad Mad Mad Mad World

White, M.
The Story of Adele H.

White, Sheila
Oliver!

Whitehead, O.Z.
The Grapes of Wrath

Whiteley, Arkie
The Road Warrior

Whiting, Leonard
Romeo and Juliet

Whitman, Stuart
The Longest Day
Those Magnificent Men in Their
    Flying Machines, or How I
    Flew from London to Paris
    in 25 Hours and 11 Minutes

Whitmore, James
The King and I
Planet of the Apes
Tora! Tora! Tora!

Whitmore, Jr., James
The Long Riders

Whitney, Grace Lee
Star Trek: The Motion Picture

Whorf, Richard
Yankee Doodle Dandy

Wickes, Mary
The Hunchback of Notre Dame

Widmark, Richard
The Alamo
Cheyenne Autumn

Wiest, Dianne
The Horse Whisperer

Wilcoxon, Henry
Cleopatra
The Crusades
The Greatest Show on Earth
Samson and Delilah
The Ten Commandments

Wild, Jack
Oliver!

Wilde, Cornel
The Greatest Show on Earth

Wilder, Gene
Young Frankenstein

Wilke, Robert
High Noon

Willey, Leonard
The Adventures of Robin Hood

William, Warren
Cleopatra

Williams, Billy Dee
Batman
The Empire Strikes Back
Return of the Jedi

Williams, Emlyn
Ivanhoe

Williams, Harcourt
Henry V

Williams, Lucita
Reds

Williams, Olivia
The Postman

Williams, Peter
The Bridge on the River Kwai

Williams, Ralph
The Story of Adele H.

Williams, Robin
Hamlet
Hook

Williams, Treat
Once Upon a Time in America

Williamson, Nicol
Excalibur

Willman, Noel
Doctor Zhivago

Wills, Chill
The Alamo
Giant

Wilson, Brian Anthony
The Postman

Wilson, Dorothy
The Last Days of Pompeii

Wilson, Eleanor D.
Reds

Wilson, Elizabeth
The Birds

Wilson, Scott
The Right Stuff

Winling, Jean-Marie
Cyrano de Bergerac

Winslet, Kate
Hamlet
Titanic

Winters, David
West Side Story

Winters, Jonathan
It's a Mad Mad Mad Mad World

Winters, Shelley
The Greatest Story Ever Told
The Poseidon Adventure

Wisden, Robert
Legends of the Fall

Withers, Jane
Giant
The Hunchback of Notre Dame

Wolfe, Ian
Julius Caesar
Reds

Wolff, Frank
America America
Once Upon a Time in the West

Wolfheim, Louis
Orphans of the Storm

Wong, Anna May
The Thief of Bagdad

Wong, B.D.
Jurassic Park

Wong, Kimi
The Rocky Horror Picture Show

Wong, Victor
The Last Emperor

Wood, John
The Last Days of Pompeii

Wood, Natalie
The Great Race
West Side Story

Wood, Peggy
The Sound of Music

Woods, Harry M.
Beau Geste

Woods, James
Contact
Nixon
Once Upon a Time in America

Wooland, Norman
Ivanhoe
Quo Vadis?

Wooley, Sheb
Giant
High Noon

Woolf, Henry
The Rocky Horror Picture Show

Woolvett, Jaimz
Unforgiven

Worden, Hank
Red River

Workman, Jennie
The King and I

Worsley, Julia
Evita

Worthington, William
Duck Soup

Wray, Fay
King Kong

Wright, Amy
The Deer Hunter

Wright, Max
Reds

Wright, Teresa
The Best Years of Our Lives

Wu, David
Farewell My Concubine

Wu, Tao
The Last Emperor

Wu, Vivian
The Last Emperor

Wuhl, Robert
Batman

Wyatt, Jane
Lost Horizon

Wycherly, Margaret
White Heat

Wymark, Patrick
Battle of Britain

Wyngarde, Peter
Alexander the Great

Wynn, Ed
The Greatest Story Ever Told

Wynn, Keenan
Dr. Strangelove, or: How I
    Learned to Stop Worrying
    and Love the Bomb
The Great Race
Nashville
Once Upon a Time in the West

Y

Yamada, Isuzu
Yojimbo

Yamamura, So
Tora! Tora! Tora!

Yang, Fei
Farewell My Concubine

Yeager, Chuck
The Right Stuff

Yershov, V.
Alexander Nevsky

Ying, Ruocheng
The Last Emperor

Yip, William
The King and I

York, Michael
Romeo and Juliet
The Three Musketeers

York, Susannah
Battle of Britain
A Man For All Seasons

You, Ge
Farewell My Concubine

Young, Burt
Once Upon a Time in America
Rocky

Young, Gig
The Hindenburg

Young, Jack
Yankee Doodle Dandy

Young, John
Monty Python and the Holy Grail

Young, Loretta
The Crusades

Young, Ric
The Last Emperor

Young, Richard
Indiana Jones and the Last Cru-
    sade

Young, Sean
Blade Runner
Dune

Young, Stephen
Patton

Yowlachie, Chief
Red River

Yui, Masayuki
Ran

Yuill, Jimmy
Henry V

Yulin, Harris
Scarface

Yunupingu, Charles
Gallipoli

Z

Zane, Billy
Titanic

Zappa, William
The Road Warrior

Zeismer, Jerry
Apocalypse Now

Zharov, Mikhail
Ivan the Terrible, Part I and II

Zoppe, Alberto
The Greatest Show on Earth

Zucco, George
The Hunchback of Notre Dame

Zycon, Mark
Monty Python and the Holy Grail

Director Index

A

Abrahams, Jim
Airplane!

Alexandrov, Grigori
October

Allen, Irwin
The Towering Inferno

Allen, Woody
Love and Death

Altman, Robert
Nashville

Anderson, Michael
Around the World in 80 Days

Annakin, Ken
The Longest Day
Those Magnificent Men in Their
    Flying Machines, or How I
    Flew from London to Paris
    in 25 Hours and 11 Minutes

Attenborough, Richard
A Bridge Too Far
Gandhi

Avildsen, John G.
Rocky

B

Baker, Roy
A Night to Remember

Beatty, Warren
Reds

Bergman, Ingmar
Fanny and Alexander

Bertolucci, Bernardo
1900
The Last Emperor

Boorman, John
Excalibur

Branagh, Kenneth
Hamlet
Henry V

Brooks, Mel
Young Frankenstein

Burton, Tim
Batman
Pee-Wee's Big Adventure

C

Cameron, James
Aliens
Titanic

Capra, Frank
It's a Wonderful Life
Lost Horizon

Carson, David
Star Trek Generations

Caton-Jones, Michael
Rob Roy

Chereau, Patrice
Queen Margot

Cimino, Michael
The Deer Hunter
Heaven's Gate

Cocteau, Jean
Beauty and the Beast

Cooper, Merian C.
King Kong
The Last Days of Pompeii

Coppola, Francis Ford
Apocalypse Now
The Godfather
The Godfather, Part II

Costner, Kevin
Dances With Wolves
The Postman

Curtiz, Michael
The Adventures of Robin Hood
The Charge of the Light Brigade
The Sea Hawk
Yankee Doodle Dandy

D

De Mille, Cecil B.
Cleopatra
The Crusades

The Greatest Show on Earth
Once Upon a Time in the West
Samson and Delilah
The Ten Commandments

De Palma, Brian
Scarface

Dieterle, William
The Hunchback of Notre Dame

Donner, Richard
Superman

E

Eastwood, Clint
Unforgiven

Edwards, Blake
The Great Race

Eisenstein, Sergei
Alexander Nevsky
The Battleship Potemkin
Ivan the Terrible, Part I and II
October

F

Fleischer, Richard
Tora! Tora! Tora!

Fleming, Victor
Gone With The Wind
The Wizard of Oz

Ford, John
Cheyenne Autumn
The Grapes of Wrath
High Noon
Red River
Stagecoach

Foreman, Carl
The Victors

Frank, Melvin
The Court Jester

Fukasaku, Kinji
Tora! Tora! Tora!

The "Director Index" lists all
directors credited in the main
review section, alphabetically by
last names. Make sure you also
check back to the "Cast Index" to
see if your favorite director may
have also done an acting cameo
in a film.

G

Gance, Able
Napoleon

Geronimi, Clyde
Peter Pan

Gibson, Mel
Braveheart

Gilliam, Terry
Monty Python and the Holy Grail

Griffith, D.W.
The Birth of a Nation
Intolerance
Orphans of the Storm

Guillermin, John
The Towering Inferno

H

Hamilton, Guy
Battle of Britain

Hand, David
Snow White and the Seven
  Dwarfs

Hathaway, Henry
High Noon
The Lives of a Bengal Lancer

Hawks, Howard
Red River

Herzog, Werner
Aguirre, the Wrath of God
Fitzcarraldo

Heston, Charlton
Antony and Cleopatra

Hill, George Roy
Butch Cassidy and the Sundance Kid

Hill, Walter
The Long Riders

Hitchcock, Alfred
The Birds

Howard, Ron
Far and Away
White Heat

Huston, John
The Bible
The Man Who Would Be King
Moby Dick

I

Ingram, Rex
The Four Horsemen of the Apocalypse

J

Jackson, Wilfred
Peter Pan

Joffe, Roland
The Mission

Jones, Terry
Monty Python and the Holy Grail

K

Kaige, Chen
Farewell My Concubine

Kaufman, Philip
The Right Stuff

Kazan, Elia
America America

Keighley, William
The Adventures of Robin Hood

Kelly, Gene
A Guide for the Married Man

Kershner, Irvin
The Empire Strikes Back

King, Henry
Carousel

Koster, Henry
The Robe

Kramer, Stanley
It's a Mad Mad Mad Mad World

Kubrick, Stanley
2001: A Space Odyssey
Dr. Strangelove, or: How I
  Learned to Stop Worrying
  and Love the Bomb
Paths of Glory
Spartacus

Kurosawa, Akira
Ran
Seven Samurai
Yojimbo

L

Lang, Walter
The King and I

Lean, David
The Bridge on the River Kwai
Doctor Zhivago
Lawrence of Arabia
Ryan's Daughter

Leone, Sergio
Once Upon a Time in America
Once Upon a Time in the West

LeRoy, Mervyn
Quo Vadis?

Lester, Richard
The Three Musketeers

Lloyd, Frank
Moby Dick

Logan, Joshua
Paint Your Wagon
South Pacific

Lucas, George
Star Wars

Lumet, Sidney
Long Day's Journey into Night

Luske, Hamilton
Peter Pan
Pinocchio

Lynch, David
Dune

M

Mankiewicz, Joseph L.
Cleopatra
Julius Caesar

Mann, Michael
The Last of the Mohicans

Marquand, Richard
Return of the Jedi

Marshall, George
High Noon

Marton, Andrew
The Longest Day

Masuda, Toshio
Tora! Tora! Tora!

May, Elaine
Ishtar

McCarey, Leo
Duck Soup

McLaglen, Andrew V.
Shenandoah

Milius, John
The Wind and the Lion

Miller, George
The Road Warrior

Minghella, Anthony
The English Patient

N

Neame, Ronald
The Poseidon Adventure

Noonan, Chris
Babe

Zinnemann, Fred
From Here to Eternity
High Noon
The King and I
A Man For All Seasons

Zucker, David
Airplane!

Zucker, Jerry
Airplane!

Zwick, Edward
Glory
Legends of the Fall

Writer Index

A

Abdullah, Achmed
The Lives of a Bengal Lancer

Abrahams, Jim
Airplane!

Alexandrov, Grigori
October

Allen, Woody
Love and Death

Ambler, Eric
A Night to Remember

Annakin, Ken
Those Magnificent Men in Their
    Flying Machines, or How I
    Flew from London to Paris
    in 25 Hours and 11 Minutes

Arcalli, Franco
1900

Argento, Dario
Once Upon a Time in the West

B

Baker, Melville
The Last Days of Pompeii

Balderston, John L.
The Lives of a Bengal Lancer

Banta, Milt
Peter Pan

Barrett, James Lee
The Greatest Story Ever Told
Shenandoah

Bart, Lionel
Oliver!

Bartlett, Sy
The Big Country

Beatty, Warren
Reds

Beck, Reginald
Henry V

Behn, Harry
The Big Parade

Behrman, S.N.
Quo Vadis?

Benchley, Peter
Jaws

Benton, Robert
Superman

Benvenuti, Leonardo
Once Upon a Time in America

Bergman, Ingmar
Fanny and Alexander

Bertolucci, Bernardo
1900
The Last Emperor
Once Upon a Time in the West

Bertolucci, Giuseppe
1900

Blake, Michael
Dances With Wolves

Blank, Dorothy Ann
Snow White and the Seven
    Dwarfs

Boam, Jeffrey
Indiana Jones and the Last Cru-
    sade

Bolt, Robert
Doctor Zhivago
Lawrence of Arabia
A Man For All Seasons
The Mission
Ryan's Daughter

Boorman, John
Excalibur

Brackett, Leigh
The Empire Strikes Back

Bradbury, Ray
Moby Dick

Braga, Brannon
Star Trek Generations

Branagh, Kenneth
Hamlet
Henry V

Briley, John
Gandhi

Brooks, Mel
Young Frankenstein

Brusati, Franco
Romeo and Juliet

Bryden, Bill
The Long Riders

Buchman, Sidney
Cleopatra
Lost Horizon

Buckner, Robert
Yankee Doodle Dandy

Burgess, Anthony
Cyrano de Bergerac

Burnett, W.R.
The Great Escape

C

Cameron, James
Aliens
Titanic

Capra, Frank
It's a Wonderful Life

Carriere, Jean-Claude
Cyrano de Bergerac

Carson, Robert
Beau Geste

Castle, Nick
Hook

Cavett, Frank
The Greatest Show on Earth

Chapman, Graham
Monty Python and the Holy Grail

Chase, Borden
Red River

Chayefsky, Paddy
Paint Your Wagon

Chereau, Patrice
Queen Margot

Cimino, Michael
The Deer Hunter
Heaven's Gate

Clarke, Arthur C.
2001: A Space Odyssey

Clavell, James
The Great Escape

The "Writer Index" provides a
complete listing of writers cited
within the reviews. The listings
are alphabetical by last name,
and the films are listed
chronologically from most recent
to the oldest. Some actors and
directors will show up here as
they tend to do a lot of writing
themselves.

Cleese, John
Monty Python and the Holy Grail

Coctaeu, Jean
Beauty and the Beast

Coppola, Francis Ford
Apocalypse Now
The Godfather
The Godfather, Part II
Patton

Cormack, Bartlett
Cleopatra

Cottrell, William
Peter Pan
Pinocchio

Creedon, Richard
Snow White and the Seven
    Dwarfs

Creelman, James Ashmore
The Last Days of Pompeii

Crichton, Michael
Jurassic Park

Crowe, Christopher
The Last of the Mohicans

D

D'Amico, Maestro
Romeo and Juliet

Davies, Jack
Those Magnificent Men in Their
    Flying Machines, or How I
    Flew from London to Paris
    in 25 Hours and 11 Minutes

Davies, Valentine
The Bridges at Toko-Ri

Dawson, Jan
The Story of Adele H.

De Bernardi, Peiero
Once Upon a Time in America

de Maris, Merrill
Snow White and the Seven
    Dwarfs

Deal, Borden
The Scarlet Empress

Dent, Alan
Henry V

Diamond, I.A.L.
The Private Life of Sherlock
    Holmes

Dolman, Bob
Far and Away

Donati, Sergio
Once Upon a Time in the West

Druyan, Ann
Contact

Dunne, Phillip
The Robe

E

Eisenstein, Sergei
Alexander Nevsky
The Battleship Potemkin
Ivan the Terrible, Part I and II
October

Englander, Otto
Pinocchio
Snow White and the Seven
    Dwarfs

Estabrook, Howard
Cimarron

F

Fairbanks, Douglas
The Thief of Bagdad

Fairchild, William
Star!

Fancher, Hampton
Blade Runner

Farrow, John
Around the World in 80 Days

Foreman, Carl
The Bridge on the River Kwai
The Guns of Navarone
High Noon
The Victors

Forrester, Larry
Tora! Tora! Tora!

Frank, Bruno
The Hunchback of Notre Dame

Frank, Frederick M.
Samson and Delilah
The Greatest Show on Earth
The Ten Commandments

Frank, Melvin
The Court Jester

Fraser, George MacDonald
The Three Musketeers

Fry, Christopher
The Bible

Furthman, Jules
Moby Dick

G

Gance, Abel
Napoleon

Gariss, Jack
The Ten Commandments

Gary, Romain
The Longest Day

George, Peter
Dr. Strangelove, or: How I
    Learned to Stop Worrying
    and Love the Bomb

Gidding, Nelson
The Hindenburg

Giler, David
Aliens

Gilliam, Terry
Monty Python and the Holy Grail

Goff, Ivan
White Heat

Goldenberg, Michael
Contact

Goldman, William
A Bridge Too Far
Butch Cassidy and the Sun-
    dance Kid

Goodrich, Frances
It's a Wonderful Life

Gordon, Bernard
55 Days at Peking

Gottlieb, Carl
Jaws

Grant, James Edward
The Alamo

Greatorex, Wilfred
Battle of Britain

Green, Walon
The Wild Bunch

Griffith, D.W.
The Birth of a Nation
Intolerance
Orphans of the Storm

Griffiths, Trevor
Reds

Gruault, Jean
The Story of Adele H.

Guille, Francis Vernor
The Story of Adele H.

Guiol, Fred
Giant
Gunga Din

Guthrie, Jr., A.B.
Red River

H

Hackett, Albert
It's a Wonderful Life

Hamm, Sam
Batman

Hammerstein, Oscar
South Pacific

Hannant, Brian
The Road Warrior

Harris, Vernon
Oliver!

Hart, Jim V.
Hook

Hartman, Phil
Pee-Wee's Big Adventure

Hashimoto, Shinobu
Seven Samurai

Hayes, Terry
Mad Max 2

Helgeland, Brian
The Postman

Herzog, Werner
Aguirre, the Wrath of God
Fitzcarraldo

Heston, Charlton
Antony and Cleopatra

Hibler, Winston
Peter Pan

Hill, Gladys
The Man Who Would Be King

Hill, Walter
Aliens

Hoch, Winton
Red River

Howard, Ron
Far and Away

Howard, Sidney
Gone With The Wind

Hunter, Evan
The Birds

Hurd, Earl
Snow White and the Seven
    Dwarfs

Huston, John
The Man Who Would Be King
Moby Dick

I

Ide, Masato
Ran

Idle, Eric
Monty Python and the Holy Grail

Ingster, Boris
The Last Days of Pompeii

J

Jabotinsky, Vladimir
Samson and Delilah

Jacoby, Michael
The Charge of the Light Brigade

Jarre, Kevin
Glory

Jennings, Talbot
Moby Dick

Johnson, Nunnally
The Grapes of Wrath

Jones, Grover
The Lives of a Bengal Lancer

Jones, Ian
The Lighthorsemen

Jones, James
The Longest Day

Jones, Terry
Monty Python and the Holy Grail

Joseph, Edmund
Yankee Doodle Dandy

K

Kalmar, Bert
Duck Soup

Kasdan, Lawrence
The Empire Strikes Back
Raiders of the Lost Ark
Return of the Jedi

Kaufman, Philip
Raiders of the Lost Ark
The Right Stuff

Kaus, Gina
The Robe

Kazan, Elia
America America

Keach, James
The Long Riders

Keach, Stacy
The Long Riders

Kenneway, James
Battle of Britain

Kikushima, Ryuzo
Tora! Tora! Tora!
Yojimbo

Knox, Mickey
Once Upon a Time in the West

Koch, Howard
The Sea Hawk

Koepp, David
Jurassic Park

Kubrick, Stanley
2001: A Space Odyssey
Dr. Strangelove, or: How I
    Learned to Stop Worrying
    and Love the Bomb
Paths of Glory

Kurosawa, Akira
Ran
Seven Samurai
Yojimbo

L

LaGravenese, Richard
The Horse Whisperer

Lamb, Harold
The Crusades
Once Upon a Time in the West
Samson and Delilah

Landon, Margaret
The King and I

Langley, Noel
Ivanhoe
The Wizard of Oz

Lasky, Jr., Jesse L.
Samson and Delilah
The Ten Commandments

Laurents, Arthur
West Side Story

Lawrence, Vincent
Cleopatra

Lee, Lillian
Farewell My Concubine

Lehman, Ernest
The King and I
The Sound of Music
West Side Story

Leigh, Rowland
The Charge of the Light Brigade

Leone, Sergio
Once Upon a Time in the West

Lerner, Alan Jay
Paint Your Wagon

Leudtke, Kurt
Out of Africa

Levien, Sonya
The Hunchback of Notre Dame
The King and I
Quo Vadis?

Levinson, Richard
The Hindenburg

Link, William
The Hindenburg

Livingston, Harold
Star Trek: The Motion Picture

Loewe, Frederick
Paint Your Wagon

Logan, Joshua
South Pacific

Loos, Anita
The Poseidon Adventure

Lucas, George
The Empire Strikes Back
Raiders of the Lost Ark
Return of the Jedi
Star Wars

Ludwig, William
The King and I

Lynch, David
Dune

Lyndon, Barre
The Greatest Show on Earth

M

MacDougall, Ranald
Cleopatra

MacKenzie, Aeneas
The Ten Commandments

Macpherson, Jeannie
Once Upon a Time in the West

Mahin, John Lee
Quo Vadis?

Mankiewicz, Herman J.
Citizen Kane

Mankiewicz, Joseph L.
Cleopatra
Julius Caesar

Mann, Michael
The Last of the Mohicans

Marno, Malia S.
Hook

Martin, Mardik
Raging Bull

Mathis, June
The Four Horsemen of the
    Apocalypse
Greed

Mathison, Melissa
E.T. The Extra-Terrestrial

Maxwell, Ronald F.
Gallipoli

May, Elaine
Ishtar

Mayes, Wendell
The Poseidon Adventure

McNutt, William Slavens
The Lives of a Bengal Lancer

Mecchi, Irene
The Hunchback of Notre Dame

Medioli, Enrico
Once Upon a Time in America

Milius, John
Apocalypse Now
The Wind and the Lion

Millard, Oscar
The Conqueror

Miller, George
Babe
The Road Warrior

Miller, Seton I.
The Adventures of Robin Hood
The Sea Hawk

Minghella, Anthony
The English Patient

Moffat, Ivan
Giant

Moore, Ronald D.
Star Trek Generations

Murphy, Tab
The Hunchback of Notre Dame

N

Newman, David
Superman

Newman, Leslie
Superman

Nichols, Dudley
The Crusades
Stagecoach

Noonan, Chris
Babe

North, Edmund H.
Patton

Nugent, Frank S.
Red River

O

O'Bannon, Dan
Alien

O'Brien, Richard
The Rocky Horror Picture Show

Oguni, Hideo
Ran
Seven Samurai
Tora! Tora! Tora!

Olivier, Laurence
Henry V

Osborn, Paul
The Scarlet Empress
South Pacific

P

Palin, Michael
Monty Python and the Holy Grail

Pallenberg, Rospo
Excalibur

Panama, Norman
The Court Jester

Parker, Alan
Evita

Pavlenko, P.
Alexander Nevsky

Peckinpah, Sam
The Wild Bunch

Peet, Bill
Peter Pan

Peoples, David Webb
Blade Runner
Unforgiven

Peploe, Mark
The Last Emperor

Perelman, S.J.
Around the World in 80 Days

Perrin, Nat
Duck Soup

Petersen, Wolfgang
Das Boot

Poe, James
Around the World in 80 Days

Pursall, David
The Longest Day

Puzo, Mario
The Godfather
The Godfather, Part II
Superman

R

Rader, Peter
Waterworld

Raine, Norman Reilly
The Adventures of Robin Hood

Raphael, Frederic
Far From the Madding Crowd

Rappeneau, Jean-Paul
Cyrano de Bergerac

Reubens, Paul
Pee-Wee's Big Adventure

The Magnificent Ambersons

White, Noni
The Hunchback of Notre Dame

Wilder, Billy
The Private Life of Sherlock
    Holmes

Wilder, Gene
Young Frankenstein

Wilkinson, Christopher
Nixon

Williamson, David
Gallipoli

Willingham, Calder
Little Big Man
Paths of Glory

Wilson, Carey
Moby Dick

Wilson, Michael
The Bridge on the River Kwai

Lawrence of Arabia
Planet of the Apes

Wittliff, Bill
Legends of the Fall

Woods, Jr., Frank E.
The Birth of a Nation

Woods, Lotta
The Thief of Bagdad

Woolf, Edgar Allan
The Wizard of Oz

Wyler, Robert
The Big Country

Y

Yordan, Phillip
55 Days at Peking

Young, Waldemar
Cleopatra
The Crusades
The Lives of a Bengal Lancer
Once Upon a Time in the West

Z

Zaillian, Steven
Schindler's List

Zeffirelli, Franco
Romeo and Juliet

Zucker, David
Airplane!

Zucker, Jerry
Airplane!

Cinematographer Index

The "Cinematographer Index" provides a complete listing of cinematographers, or directors of photography, as they are also known, cited within the reviews. The listings are alphabetical by last name, and the films are listed chronologically, from most recent to the oldest.

Furuya, Osamu
Tora! Tora! Tora!

G

Gaudio, Tony
The Adventures of Robin Hood

Glennon, Bert
The Scarlet Empress
Stagecoach

Green, Jack N.
Unforgiven

Griggs, Loyal
The Bridges at Toko-Ri
The Greatest Story Ever Told
Red River
The Ten Commandments

Guffey, Burnett
From Here to Eternity

H

Hall, Conrad L.
Butch Cassidy and the Sundance Kid

Haller, Ernest
Gone With The Wind

Harlan, Russell
The Great Race
Red River

Hickox, Sid
White Heat

Hilyard, Jack
The Bridge on the River Kwai
55 Dyas at Peking

Himeda, Sinsaku
Tora! Tora! Tora!

Hirschfeld, Gerald
Young Frankenstein

Howe, James Wong
Yankee Doodle Dandy

Hume, Alan
Return of the Jedi

J

June, Ray
The Court Jester

K

Kaminski, Janusz
Saving Private Ryan
Schindler's List

Kaufman, Boris
Long Day's Journey into Night

Keley, W. Wallace
The Ten Commandments

Kemper, Victor J.
Pee-Wee's Big Adventure

Khondji, Darius
Evita

Kline, Richard H.
Star Trek: The Motion Picture

Koenekamp, Fred J.
Patton
The Towering Inferno

Krasker, Robert
Alexander the Great
Henry V

Krause, George
Paths of Glory

Kruger, Jules
Napoleon

L

Lang, Charles
The Lives of a Bengal Lancer
The Magnificent Seven

LaShelle, Joseph
The Conqueror

Laszlo, Ernest
It's a Mad Mad Mad Mad World
Star!

Leavitt, Sam
Exodus

Lesnie, Andrew
Babe

Levent, Pierre
The Longest Day

Lhomme, Pierre
Cyrano de Bergerac

Linden, Edward
King Kong

Lindenlaub, Karl Walter
Rob Roy

Lindley, John
Field of Dreams

Lindon, Lionel
Around the World in 80 Days

Lohmann, Paul
Nashville

M

MacDonald, Joseph
A Guide for the Married Man

MacMillan, Kenneth
Henry V

Marley, J. Peverell
The Ten Commandments

Marsh, Oliver T.
The Poseidon Adventure

Mauch, Thomas
Aguirre, the Wrath of God
Fitzcarraldo

McCord, Ted
The Sound of Music

Mellor, William C.
Giant
The Greatest Story Ever Told

Menges, Chris
The Mission

Metty, Russell
Spartacus

Milner, Victor
Cleopatra
The Crusades
Once Upon a Time in the West

Miyagawa, Kazuo
Yojimbo

Moore, Ted
A Man For All Seasons

Morris, Oswald
The Guns of Navarone
The Man Who Would Be King
Moby Dick
Oliver!

Moskvin, Andrei
Ivan the Terrible, Part I and II

N

Nakai, Asakazu
Ran
Seven Samurai

Nilsen, Vladimir
October

Nykvist, Sven
Fanny and Alexander

P

Pacheco, Rafael
Antony and Cleopatra

Persin, Henri
The Longest Day

Planer, Franx
The Big Country

Polito, Sol
The Adventures of Robin Hood
The Charge of the Light Brigade
The Sea Hawk

Popov, Vladimir
The Battleship Potemkin
October

Pratt, Roger
Batman

R

Rennahan, Ray
Gone With The Wind

Reynolds, Ben F.
Greed

Richardson, Robert
The Horse Whisperer
Nixon
Platoon

Robinson, George
Once Upon a Time in the West

Roeg, Nicolas
Far From the Madding Crowd

Rosson, Harold
The Wizard of Oz

Rotunno, Giuseppe
The Bible

Rousselot, Philippe
Queen Margot

Ruttenberg, Joseph
Julius Caesar

S

Saito, Takao
Ran

Salomon, Mikael
Far and Away

Sartov, Hendrik
Orphans of the Storm

Satoh, Masamichi
Tora! Tora! Tora!

Schoedsack, Ernest B.
Greed

Seale, John
The English Patient

Seitz, John F.
The Four Horsemen of the
    Apocalypse

Semler, Dean
The Lighthorsemen
The Road Warrior
Waterworld

Shamroy, Leon
Cleopatra
The King and I
Planet of the Apes
The Robe
South Pacific

Sharp, Henry
Duck Soup

Skall, William V.
Quo Vadis?

Slocombe, Douglas
Indiana Jones and the Last Cru-
    sade
Raiders of the Lost Ark

Sparkuhl, Theodor
Beau Geste

Spinotti, Dante
The Last of the Mohicans

Stine, Clifford
Spartacus

Stine, Harold E.
The Poseidon Adventure

Storaro, Vittorio
1900
Apocalypse Now
Ishtar
The Last Emperor
Reds

Stout, Archie
Beau Geste

Stradling, Harry
Little Big Man

Surtees, Robert
The Hindenburg
The King and I
Quo Vadis?

Suschitzky, Peter
The Empire Strikes Back
The Rocky Horror Picture Show

T

Taylor, Gilbert
Dr. Strangelove, or: How I
    Learned to Stop Worrying
    and Love the Bomb
Star Wars

Taylor, J.O.
King Kong

Taylor, Ronnie
Gandhi

Thomson, Alex
Excalibur
Hamlet

Tisse, Edouard
Alexander Nevsky
The Battleship Potemkin
Ivan the Terrible, Part I and II
October

Toland, Gregg
The Best Years of Our Lives
Citizen Kane
The Grapes of Wrath

Toll, John
Braveheart
Legends of the Fall

U

Ueda, Masaharu
Ran

Unsworth, Geoffrey
2001: A Space Odyssey
A Bridge Too Far
A Night to Remember
Superman

V

Vacano, Jost
Das Boot

Van Oostrum, Kees
Gallipoli

Vanlint, Derek
Alien

W

Waite, Ric
The Long Riders

Walker, Joseph
It's a Wonderful Life
Lost Horizon

Walker, Vernon L.
King Kong

Warren, John F.
The Ten Commandments

Watkin, David
Out of Africa
The Three Musketeers

Waxman, Harry
A Bridge Too Far

Composer Index

A

Addison, John
A Bridge Too Far

Allaman, Eric
The Battleship Potemkin

Alwyn, William
A Night to Remember

Anka, Paul
The Longest Day

Antheil, George
Once Upon a Time in the West

Arlen, Harold
The Wizard of Oz

Arnold, Malcolm
Battle of Britain
The Bridge on the River Kwai

Auric, Georges
Beauty and the Beast

Axt, William
The Big Parade

B

Bacharach, Burt
Butch Cassidy and the Sun-
    dance Kid

Bajawa
Ishtar

Barry, John
Dances With Wolves
Out of Africa

Bart, Lionel
Oliver!

Baskin, Richard
Nashville

Bell, Daniel
Fanny and Alexander

Bennett, Richard Rodney
Far From the Madding Crowd

Bennett, Robert Russell
The King and I

Bernstein, Elmer
Airplane!
The Great Escape
The Magnificent Seven
The Ten Commandments

Bernstein, Leonard
West Side Story

Black, Karen
Nashville

Blackton, Jay
The King and I

Blakley, Ronee
Nashville

Bregovic, Goran
Queen Margot

Breil, Joseph Carl
The Birth of a Nation
Intolerance

Britten, Benjamin
Fanny and Alexander

Burwell, Carter
Rob Roy

Byrne, David
The Last Emperor

C

Cahn, Sammy
The Court Jester
Peter Pan

Carbonara, Gerard
Stagecoach

Carradine, Keith
Nashville

Churchill, Frank
Peter Pan
Snow White and the Seven
    Dwarfs

Cohan, George M.
Yankee Doodle Dandy

Conti, Bill
The Right Stuff
Rocky

Cooder, Ry
The Long Riders

Coppola, Carmine
Apocalypse Now
The Godfather, Part II
Napoleon

D

Darby, Ken
High Noon
The King and I
South Pacific

Davis, Carl
The Four Horsemen of the
    Apocalypse
Napoleon

Delerue, Georges
A Man For All Seasons
Platoon

Deutsch, Adolph
The King and I

DeWolfe
Monty Python and the Holy Grail

Doldinger, Klaus
Das Boot

Doyle, Patrick
Hamlet
Henry V

Duning, George
From Here to Eternity

E

Edelman, Randy
Gallipoli
The Last of the Mohicans

Elfman, Danny
Batman
Pee-Wee's Big Adventure

Eno, Brian
Dune

The "Composer Index" provides a complete listing of composers, arrangers, lyricists, or bands that have provided an original music score for a film. The names are alphabetical by last name, and the films are listed chronologically from most recent to the oldest.

F

Fenton, George
Gandhi

Fielding, Jerry
The Wild Bunch

Fine, Sylvia
The Court Jester

Fried, Gerald
Paths of Glory

Friedhofer, Hugo
The Best Years of Our Lives

G

Gold, Ernest
Exodus
It's a Mad Mad Mad Mad World

Goldsmith, Jerry
Alien
Patton
Planet of the Apes
Star Trek: The Motion Picture
Tora! Tora! Tora!
The Wind and the Lion

Goodwin, Ron
Battle of Britain
Those Magnificent Men in Their
    Flying Machines, or How I
    Flew from London to Paris
    in 25 Hours and 11 Minutes

Green, Johnny
Oliver!

H

Hadjidakis, Manos
America America

Hageman, Richard
Stagecoach

Hammond, John
Little Big Man

Harline, Leigh
Pinocchio
Snow White and the Seven
    Dwarfs

Harling, W. Franke
Stagecoach

Hartley, Richard
The Rocky Horror Picture Show

Hayasaka, Fumio
Seven Samurai

Hayton, Lennie
Star!

Helmerson, Frans
Fanny and Alexander

Herrmann, Bernard
The Birds
Citizen Kane
The Magnificent Ambersons

Hey, Jerry
Return of the Jedi

Hirschhorn, Joel
The Poseidon Adventure

Honegger, Arthur
Napoleon

Horner, James
Aliens
Braveheart
Field of Dreams
Glory
Legends of the Fall
Titanic
White Heat

Howard, James Newton
The Postman
Waterworld

I

Innes, Neil
Monty Python and the Holy Grail

J

Jacobs, Marianne
Fanny and Alexander

Jarre, Maurice
Doctor Zhivago
Lawrence of Arabia
The Longest Day
The Man Who Would Be King
Ryan's Daughter

Jaubert, Maurice
The Story of Adele H.

Jiping, Zhao
Farewell My Concubine

Johnson, Laurie
Dr. Strangelove, or: How I
    Learned to Stop Worrying
    and Love the Bomb

Jones, Trevor
Excalibur
The Last of the Mohicans

K

Kalmar, Bert
Duck Soup

Kaplan, Sol
The Victors

Kasha, Al
The Poseidon Adventure

Kopp, Rudolph G.
Cleopatra
The Crusades

Korngold, Erich Wolfgang
The Adventures of Robin Hood
The Sea Hawk

L

Legrand, Michel
The Three Musketeers

Leipold, John
Stagecoach

Loewe, Frederick
Paint Your Wagon

M

Mancini, Henry
The Great Race

Mansfield, David
Heaven's Gate

May, Brian
Gallipoli
The Road Warrior

Mayuzumi, Toshiro
The Bible

McCarthy, Dennis
Star Trek Generations

Meisel, Edmund
The Battleship Potemkin
October

Mendoza, David
The Big Parade

Menken, Alan
The Hunchback of Notre Dame

Millo, Mario
The Lighthorsemen

Moroder, Giorgio
Scarface

Moross, Jerome
The Big Country

Morricone, Ennio
1900
The Mission

Once Upon a Time in America
Once Upon a Time in the West

Morris, John
Young Frankenstein

Murray, Lyn
The Bridges at Toko-Ri

Myers, Stanley
The Deer Hunter

N

Nascimbene, Mario
Alexander the Great

Newman, Alfred
Beau Geste
The Grapes of Wrath
The Greatest Story Ever Told
Gunga Din
The Hunchback of Notre Dame
The King and I
The Robe
South Pacific

Newman, Thomas
The Horse Whisperer

Niehaus, Lennie
Unforgiven

North, Alex
Cheyenne Autumn
Cleopatra
Spartacus

O

O'Brien, Richard
The Rocky Horror Picture Show

P

Peters, William F.
Orphans of the Storm

Petit, Jean-Claude
Cyrano de Bergerac

Previn, Andre
Long Day's Journey into Night
Paint Your Wagon

Prince
Batman

Prokofiev, Sergei
Alexander Nevsky
Ivan the Terrible, Part I and II
Love and Death

R

Riddle, Nelson
Paint Your Wagon

Robertson, Robbie
Raging Bull

Roder, Milan
The Lives of a Bengal Lancer

Rodgers, Richard
Carousel
The King and I
The Sound of Music
South Pacific

Roemheld, Heinz
Yankee Doodle Dandy

Rota, Nino
The Godfather
The Godfather, Part II
Romeo and Juliet

Rozsa, Miklos
Ivanhoe
Julius Caesar
The Private Life of Sherlock
    Holmes
Quo Vadis?

Ruby, Harry
Duck Soup

S

Sakamoto, Ryuichi
The Last Emperor

Sato, Masaru
Yojimbo

Schoen, Vic
The Court Jester

Scott, John
Antony and Cleopatra

Shankar, Ravi
Gandhi

Shire, David
The Hindenburg

Shostakovich, Dimitri
October

Shuken, Leo
Stagecoach

Silvestri, Alan
Contact

Skinner, Frank
Shenandoah

Smith, Paul
Pinocchio
Snow White and the Seven
    Dwarfs

Sondheim, Stephen
Reds

Stainton, Philip
Moby Dick

Steiner, Max
The Charge of the Light Brigade
Cimarron
Gone With The Wind
King Kong
The Last Days of Pompeii
White Heat

Stothart, Herbert
Moby Dick

Su, Cong
The Last Emperor

T

Takemitsu, Toru
Ran

Tiomkin, Dimitri
The Alamo
55 Days at Peking
Giant
The Guns of Navarone
High Noon
It's a Wonderful Life
Lost Horizon
Red River

Toto
Dune

V

Vangelis
Blade Runner

von Sternberg, Josef
The Scarlet Empress

Vuh, Popol
Aguirre, the Wrath of God
Fitzcarraldo

W

Walton, William
Battle of Britain
Henry V

Ward, Edward
The Poseidon Adventure

Webb, Roy
The Last Days of Pompeii

Webber, Andrew Lloyd
Evita

Webster, Paul Francis
55 Days at Peking

Westlake, Nigel
Babe

Williams, John
Close Encounters of the Third
    Kind
E. T. The Extra-Terrestrial
Empire of the Sun
The Empire Strikes Back
Far and Away
A Guide for the Married Man
Hook

Indiana Jones and the Last Cru-
    sade
Jaws
Jurassic Park
Nixon
The Poseidon Adventure
Raiders of the Lost Ark
Return of the Jedi
Saving Private Ryan
Schindler's List
Star Wars
Superman
The Towering Inferno

Yared, Gabriel
The English Patient

Young, Victor
Around the World in 80 Days
The Conqueror
The Greatest Show on Earth
Red River
Samson and Delilah

Alternative Titles Index

The "Alternative Titles Index" lists variant and/or translated titles of films in the review section. The films are listed alphabetically.

A

Aguirre, der Zorn Gottes
See Aguirre, the Wrath of God

B

Babe, the Gallant Pig
See Babe

Bawang Bie Ji
See Farewell My Concubine

Bible...In The Beginning, The
See The Bible

Boat, The
See Das Boot

Bodyguard, The
See Yojimbo

Bronenosets Potyomkin
See The Battleship Potemkin

C

Clansman, The
See The Birth of a Nation

E

Eighth Wonder of the World, The
See King Kong

F

Fanny Och Alexander
See Fanny and Alexander

Flying High
See Airplane!

Frankenstein Jr.
See Young Frankenstein

L

L'Historie d'Adele H
See The Story of Adele H.

La belle et la bete
See Beauty and the Beast

La Bibbia
See The Bible

La Reine Margot
See Queen Margot

Los Tres Mosqueteros
See The Three Musketeers

M

Mad Max 2
See The Road Warrior

Magnificent Seven, The
See Seven Samurai

Monkey Planet
See Planet of the Apes

N

Napoleon vu par Abel Gance
See Napoleon

Nineteen Hundred
See 1900

Novecento
See 1900

O

October 1917
See October

Oktiabr
See October

Oktyabr
See October

P

Patton: A Salute to a Rebel
See Patton

Patton: Lust for Glory
See Patton

Potemkin
See The Battleship Potemkin

S

Shichinin No Samurai
See Seven Samurai

Shoeless Joe
See Field of Dreams

T

Ten Days that Shook the World
See October

Those Magnificent Men in Their Flying Machines
See Those Magnificent Men in Their Flying Machines, or How I Flew from London to Paris in 25 Hours and 11 Minutes

Those Were the Happy Times
See Star!

W

William Shakespeare's Julius Caesar
See Julius Caesar

William Shakespeare's Hamlet
See Hamlet

Y

Yojimbo the Bodyguard
See Yojimbo

Yojinbo
See Yojimbo